W9-ADQ-996

THE AMERICANS

BY

HUGO MÜNSTERBERG
PROFESSOR OF PSYCHOLOGY
AT HARVARD UNIVERSITY

TRANSLATED BY
EDWIN B. HOLT, PH.D.
INSTRUCTOR AT HARVARD UNIVERSITY

NEW YORK
McCLURE, PHILLIPS & CO.
MCMVII

Published November, 1904, N

Fourth Impression

THE AMERICANS

PREFACE

PREFACE

IN the Preface to my "American Traits," in which I defended German ideals and criticised some American tendencies, I said, some years ago: "It has been often questioned whether I am right in fighting merely against American shortcomings from a German point of view, and in trying to destroy prejudices on this side of the water; whether it is not, in a still higher degree, my duty to attempt the same for the other side; — for German prejudices concerning the United States are certainly not less severe, and the points in which Germany might learn from American culture not less numerous. The question is fair, and I shall soon put before the German public a book on American life — a book which deals in a detailed way with the political, economic, intellectual, and social aspects of American culture. Its purpose is to interpret systematically the democratic ideals of America."

Here is the book; it fulfils the promise, and it might appear that no further explanation is needed. And yet, in sending a book into the world, I have never felt more strongly the need of prefatory excuses — excuses not for writing the book, but for agreeing to its translation into English.

To outline American life for readers beyond the sea is one thing; to appear before an American audience and to tell them solemnly that there is a Republican and a Democratic party, and that there are troubles between capital and labour, is quite another thing. To inform my German countrymen about America may be to fill a long-felt want; but, as a German, to inform the Americans on matters which they knew before they were born seems, indeed, worse than superfluous.

When I was urged, on so many sides, to bring my "Americans" before the Americans, it was, therefore, clear to me from the outset that I ought not to do it myself under any circumstances. If I had translated the book myself, it would have become simply an English book, written in English by the author; and yet its only possible right to existence must lie in its reflected character, in its having been written for others, in its coming back to the New World from the Old. My friend, Dr. Holt, who has been for years my assistant in the Harvard Psychological Laboratory, has assisted, therefore, in this social psychological experiment, and translated the book from the German edition.

I have been still more influenced by another consideration. If the book were chiefly a record of facts, it would be folly for a foreigner to present it to the citizens; but the aim of the book is a quite different one. To make a real scientific study of the facts, I should have felt utterly incompetent; indeed, it may be doubted whether any one could hope to master the material of the various fields: a division of labour would then become necessary. The historian, the politician, the economist, the jurist, the engineer, and many others would have to co-operate in a scholarly investigation of American events; and I have no right to any of these titles. I am merely a psychologist, and have not set out to discover new material. The only aim of the book is to study the American man and his inner tendencies; and, perhaps, a truer name for my book would have been "The Philosophy of Americanism." For such a task the outsider may be, after all, not quite unsuited, since the characteristic forces make themselves more easily felt by him than by those who have breathed the atmosphere from their childhood. I am, therefore, anxious to insist that the accent of the book lies on the four chapters, "Spirit of Self-Direction," "Spirit of Self-Realization," "Spirit of Self-Perfection," and "Spirit of Self-Assertion"; while those chapters on the economic and political problems are the least important of the book, as they are meant merely by way of illustration. The lasting forces and tendencies of American life are my topics, and not the problems of the day. For this reason the book is translated as it appeared six months ago in Germany, and the events and statistical figures of the last few months have not been added; the Philosophy of Americanism is independent of the happenings of yesterday. The only changes in the translation are abbreviations; for instance, the industrial tables, which every American can get easily from the government reports, are abridged; and, above all, the chapters which deal with the German-Americans are left out, as better remaining an esoteric discussion for the Germans.

The purpose of finding the deeper impulses in American life necessarily demands a certain ignoring of the shortcomings of the hour. If we aim to work out and to make clear the essentials of the American mission in the world, we cannot take the attitude of the reformer, whose attention belongs, first of all, to the blunders and frailties of the hour; they are to us less important by-products. The grumbler in public life sees in such a view of the American, of course, merely a fancy picture of an imaginary creature; he is not aware that every portrayal involves abstraction, and that a study in Americanism means, indeed, a study of the Americans as the best of them are, and as the others should wish to be.

But the optimism of my book has still another source. Its outspoken purpose has been to awaken a better understanding of Americans in the German nation. Whoever fights against prejudices can serve the truth merely in emphasizing the neglected good sides, and in somewhat retouching in the picture the exaggerated shadows. But just here arises my strong reluctance. The optimism and the style of a defender were sincere, and necessary to the book when it addressed itself to the Germans; is it necessary, is it, indeed, sincere, to place such a eulogy of Americanism before the Americans? I know too well that, besides the self-direction, self-realization, self-perfection, and self-assertion there is, more vivid still, the spirit of self-satisfaction, whose story I have forgotten to include in this volume. Have I the right to cater to this spirit?

But is it not best that the moods of criticism and optimism alternate? The critical eagerness of the reformer which attacks the faults and follies of the day is most necessary; but it turns into discouraging pessimism if it is not supplemented by a profession of faith in the lasting principles and deeper tendencies. The rôle of the critic I have played, perhaps, more often and more vehemently than is the foreigner's right. My book on "American Traits" has been its sharpest expression. Does that not give me, after all, a moral right to supplement the warning cry by a joyful word on the high aims of true Americanism? My duty is only to emphasize that I am myself fully aware of the strong one-sidedness, and that this new book is not in the least meant to retract the criticisms of my "American Traits." The two books are meant to be like the two pictures of a stereoscope, which must be seen both together to get the full plastic effect of reality. It is certainly important to remind the nation frequently that there are political corruption and pedagogical blundering in the world; but sometimes it is also worth while to say that Americanism is something noble and inspiring, even for the outsiders, with whom naturally other impulses are stronger — in fact, to make clear that this Americanism is a consistent system of tendencies is ultimately, perhaps, only another way of attaining the reformer's end.

Only one word more — a word of thanks. I said the aim of the book was to bring the facts of American life under the point of view of general principles, but not to embody an original research in American history and institutions. I have had thus to accept the facts ready-made, as the best American authors present them; and I am thus their debtor everywhere. Since the book is popular in its style, I have no foot-notes and scholarly quotations, and so cannot enumerate the thousand American sources from which I have taken my material. And I am not speaking here merely of the great standard books and specialistic writings, but even the daily and weekly papers, and especially the leading monthly magazines, have helped to fill my note-books. My thanks are due to all these silent helpers, and I am glad to share with them the welcome which, in competent quarters, the German edition of the book has found.

HUGO MÜNSTERBERG

CAMBRIDGE, MASS.,
October 25, 1904

CONTENTS

I. POLITICAL LIFE

II. ECONOMIC LIFE

III. INTELLECTUAL LIFE

IV. SOCIAL LIFE

PART ONE

POLITICAL LIFE

CHAPTER ONE

The Spirit of Self-Direction

WHOSOEVER wishes to describe the political life of the American people can accomplish this end from a number of starting points. Perhaps he would begin most naturally with the Articles of the Constitution and expound the document which has given to the American body-politic its remarkable and permanent form; or he might ramble through history and trace out from petty colonies the rise of a great world-power; or he might make his way through that multitude of events which to-day arouse the keenest public interest, the party strifes and presidential elections, the burdens and amenities of city and state, the transactions of the courts and of Congress. Yet all this would be but a superficial delineation. Whoever wishes to understand the secret of that baffling turmoil, the inner mechanism and motive behind all the politically effective forces, must set out from only one point. He must appreciate the yearning of the American heart after self-direction. Everything else is to be understood from this.

In his social life the American is very ready to conform to the will of another. With an inborn good-nature, and often too willingly, perhaps, he lends himself to social situations which are otherwise inconvenient. Thus his guest, for instance, is apt to feel like a master in his house, so completely is his own will subordinated to that of the guest. But, on the other hand, in the sphere of public life, the individual, or a more or less restricted group of individuals, feels that it must guide its own activities to the last detail if these are to have for it any value or significance whatsoever. He will allow no alien motive to be substituted — neither the self-renunciation of fidelity or gratitude, nor the æsthetic self-forgetfulness of hero-worship, nor even the recognition that a material advantage would accrue or some desirable end be more readily achieved if the control and responsibility were to be vested in some one else. This self-direction is neither arbitrary nor perverse; least of all does it indicate a love of ease or aversion to toil. In Russia, as a well-known American once said, serfdom could be wiped out by a stroke of the Czar's pen, and millions of Russians would be freed from slavery with no loss of life or property. "We Americans had to offer up a half-million lives and many millions' worth of property in order to free our slaves. And yet nothing else was to be thought of. We had to overcome that evil by our own initiative, and by our own exertions reach our goal. And just because we are Americans and not Russians no power on earth could have relieved us of our responsibility."

When in any people the desire of self-direction dominates all other motives, the form of government of that people is necessarily republican. But it does not conversely follow that every republic is grounded in this spirit of self-direction. Hence it is that the republic of the United States is so entirely different from all other republics, since in no other people is the craving for self-determination so completely the informing force. The republics of Middle and South America, or of France, have sprung from an entirely different political spirit; while those newer republics, which in fundamental intention are perhaps more similar, as for instance Switzerland, are still not comparable because of their diminutive size. The French republic is founded on rationalism. The philosophy of the eighteenth century, with its destructive criticism of the existing order, furnished the doctrines, and from that seed of knowledge there grew and still are growing the practical ideals of France. But the political life of the United States sprang not from reasoned motives but from ideals; it is not the result of insight but of will; it has not a logical but a moral foundation. And while in France the principles embodied in the constitution are derived from theory, the somewhat doubtful doctrines enunciated in the Declaration of Independence are merely a corollary to that system of moral ideals which is indissolubly combined with the American character.

It is not here to be questioned whether this character is purely the cause and not also the effect of the American system; but so much is sure, that the system of political relations which has sprung from these ethical ideals constitutes the actual body-politic of America. Such is the America which receives the immigrant and so thoroughly transforms him that the demand for self-determination becomes the profoundest passion of his soul. Such is the America toward which he feels a proud and earnest patriotism. For the soil on which his kingdom has been reared he knows but scanty sentiment or love; indeed, the early progress of America was always an extension of the frontier, an unremitting pushing forth over new domain. The American may be linked by personal ties to a particular plot of land, but his national patriotism is independent of the soil. It is also independent of the people. A nation which in every decade has assimilated millions of aliens, and whose historic past everywhere leads back to strange peoples, cannot with its racial variegation inspire a profound feeling of indissoluble unity. And yet that feeling is present here as it is perhaps in no European country. American patriotism is directed neither to soil nor citizen, but to a system of ideas respecting society which is compacted by the desire for self-direction. And to be an American means to be a partizan of this system. Neither race nor tradition, nor yet the actual past binds him to his countryman, but rather the future which together they are building. It is a community of purpose, and it is more effective than any tradition, because it pervades the whole man. Participation in a common task holds the people together, a task with no definite and tangible end nor yet any special victory or triumph to look forward to, but rather a task which is fulfilled at each moment, which has its meaning not in any result but in the doing, its accomplishment not in any event which may befall, but only in the rightness of the motive. To be an American means to co-operate in perpetuating the spirit of self-direction throughout the body-politic; and whosoever does not feel this duty and actively respond to it, although perhaps a naturalized citizen of the land, remains an alien forever.

If the new-comer is readily assimilated in such a society, commonly, yet it must not be overlooked that those who come from across the seas are not selected at random. Those who are strong of will are the ones who seek out new spheres of activity. Just those whose satisfaction in life has been stunted by a petty and oppressive environment have always cherished a longing for the New World. That conflict which every one must wage in his own bosom before he can finally tear himself away from home, has schooled the emigrant for the spirit of his new home; and only those who have been impelled by the desire for self-direction have had the strength to break the ties with their own past. Thus it is that those of Germanic extraction adapt themselves so much more quickly and thoroughly to the political spirit of America than those of Romanic blood. The Latin peoples are much more the victims of suggestion. Being more excitable, they are more imitative, and therefore as individuals less stable. The Frenchman, Italian, or Spaniard is often a sympathetic member of the social life of the country, but in its political life he introduces a certain false note; his republicanism is not the American republicanism. As a moral ideal he has little or no concern with the doctrine of self-direction.

The American political system, therefore, by no means represents an ideal of universal significance; it is the expression of a certain character, the necessary way of living for that distinct type of man which an historically traceable process of selection has brought together. And this way of living reacts in its turn to strengthen the fundamental type. Other nations, in whom other temperamental factors no less significant or potent or admirable are the fundamental traits, must find the solution of their political problems in other directions. No gain would accrue to them from any mere imitation, since it would tend to nothing but the crippling and estranging of the native genius of their people.

The cultivated American of to-day feels this instinctively. Among the masses, to be sure, the old theme is still sometimes broached of the world-wide supremacy of American ideals: and a part of the necessary paraphernalia of popular assemblages will naturally consist in a reaffirmation that the duty of America is to extend its political system into every quarter of the globe; other nations will thus be rated according to their ripeness for this system, and the history of the world appear one long and happy education of the human race up to the plane of American conceptions. But this tendency is inevitable and not to be despised. It must more nearly concern the American than the citizen of other states to propagate his ideals, since here everything depends on each individual co-operating with all his might, and this co-operation must succeed best when it is impelled by an uncritical and blindly devoted faith. And such a faith arouses, too, a zealous missionary spirit, which wants to carry this inspired state-craft unto all political heathen. But the foreigner is apt to overestimate these sentiments. The cultivated American is well aware that the various political institutions of other nations are not to be gauged simply as good or bad, and that the American system would be as impossible for Germany as the German system for America.

Those days are indeed remote when philosophy tried to discover one intrinsically best form of government. It is true that in the conflicts of diverse nations the old opposition of realistic and idealistic, of democratic and aristocratic social forces is repeated over and over. But new problems are always coming up. The ancient opposition is neutralized, and the problem finds its practical solution in that the opposing forces deploy their skirmish lines in other territory. The political ideas which led to the French Revolution had been outlived by the middle of the nineteenth century. A compromise had been effected. The whole stress of the conflict had transferred itself to social problems, and no one earnestly discussed any more whether republic or monarchy was the better form of government. The intellectual make-up of a people and its history must decide what shall be the outward form of its political institutions. And it is to-day tacitly admitted that there are light and shade on either side.

The darker side of democracy, indeed, as of every system which is founded on complete individualism, can be hidden from no one; nor would any one be so foolish, even though he loved and admired America, as to deny that weaknesses and dangers, and evils both secret and public, do there abound. Those who base their judgments less on knowledge of democratic forces than on obvious and somewhat sentimental social prejudices are apt to look for the dangers in the wrong direction. A German naturally thinks of mob-rule, harangues of the demagogue, and every form of lawlessness and violence. But true democracy does not allow of such things. A people that allows itself to turn into a mob and to be guided by irresponsible leaders, is not capable of directing itself. Self-direction demands the education of the nation. And nowhere else in the world is the mere demagogue so powerless, and nowhere does the populace observe more exemplary order and self-discipline.

The essential weakness of such a democracy is rather the importance it assigns to the average man with his petty opinions, which are sometimes right and sometimes wrong, his total lack of comprehension for all that is great and exceptional, his self-satisfied dilettanteism and his complacency before the accredited and trite in thought. This is far less true of a republic like the French, with its genius for scepticism, a republic nourished in æsthetic traditions and founded on the ruins of an empire. The intellectual conditions are there quite different. But in an ethical democracy, where self-direction is a serious issue, domination by the average intelligence is inevitable; and those who are truly great are the ones who find no scope for their powers. Those who appear great are merely men who are exploiting to the utmost the tendencies of the day. There are no great distinctions or premiums for truly high achievements which do not immediately concern the average man, and therefore the best energies of the nation are not spurred on to their keenest activity. All ambition is directed necessarily toward such achievements as the common man can understand and compete for — athletic virtuosity and wealth. Therefore the spirit of sport and of money-getting concerns the people more nearly than art or science, and even in politics the domination of the majority easily crowds from the arena those whose qualifications do not appeal to its mediocre taste. And by as much as mature and capable minds withdraw from political life, by so much are the well-intentioned masses more easily led astray by sharp and self-interested politicians and politics made to cater to mean instincts. In short, the danger is not from any wild lawlessness, but from a crass philistinism. The seditious demagogue who appeals to passion is less dangerous than the sly political wire-puller who exploits the indolence and indifference of the people; and evil intent is less to be feared than dilettanteism and the intellectual limitations of the general public.

But, on the other hand, it is also certain that when it comes to a critical comparison between the weaknesses and theoretical dangers of democracy and aristocracy, the American is at no loss to serve up a handsome list of shortcomings to the other side. He has observed and, perhaps overestimating, he detests the spirit of caste, the existence of those restrictions which wrongfully hamper one individual and as undeservedly advantage another. Again, the American hates bureaucracy and he hates militarism. The idea of highest authority being vested in a man for any other reason than that of his individual qualifications goes against all his convictions; and his moral feeling knows no more detestable breed of man than the incompetent aspirant who is servile with his superiors and brutal to his inferiors. It is typically un-American. And if, in contrast to this, one tries to do justice to the proved advantages of monarchy, of aristocracy and the spirit of caste, to justify the ruler who stands above the strife of parties, and to defend that system of symbols by which the sentiment of the past is perpetuated in a people, and the protection which is instituted for all the more ideal undertakings which surpass the comprehension of the masses, or if one urges the value of that high efficiency which can arise only from compact political organization — then the American citizen swells with contempt. What does he care for all that if he loses the inestimable and infinite advantage which lies in the fact that in his state every individual takes an active hand, assumes responsibility, and fights for his own ideals? What outward brilliancy of achievement would compensate him for that moral value of co-operation, intiative, self-discipline, and responsibility, which the poorest and meanest citizen enjoys? It may be that an enlightened and well-meaning monarch sees to it that the least peasant can sit down to his chicken of a Sunday; but God raised up the United States as an example to all nations, that it shall be the privilege of every man to feel himself responsible for his town, county, state, and country, and even for all mankind, and by his own free initiative to work to better them. The strife of parties would better be, than that a single man should be dead to the welfare of his country; and it is good riddance to aristocracy and plenty, if a single man is to be prevented from emulating freely the highest that he knows or anywise detained from his utmost accomplishment.

All such speculative estimates of different constitutional forms lead to no result unless they take into account the facts of history. Every side has its good and evil. And all such discussions are the less productive in that superiorities of constitution, although soundly argued, may or may not in any given country be fully made use of, while on the other hand defects of constitution are very often obviated. Indeed, to take an example from present tendencies in America, nothing is more characteristic than the aristocratic by-currents through which so many dangers of democracy are avoided. Officially, of course, a republic must remain a democracy, otherwise it mines its own foundations, and yet we shall see that American social and political life have developed by no means along parallel lines but rather stand out often in sharp contrast. The same is true of Germany. Official Germany is aristocratic and monarchic through and through, and no one would wish it other; but the intimate life of Germany becomes every day more democratic, and thus the natural weaknesses of an aristocracy are checked by irresistible social counter-tendencies. It may have been the growing wealth of Germany which raised the plane of life of the middle classes; or the industrial advance which loaned greater importance to manufacturer and merchant, and took some social gloss from the office-holding class; it may have been the colonial expansion which broadened the horizon and upset a stagnant equilibrium of stale opinion; or, again, the renewed efforts of those who felt cramped and oppressed, the labourers, and, above all, the women; it does not matter how it arose — a wave of progress is sweeping over that country, and a political aristocracy is being infused with new, democratic blood.

Now in America, as will often appear later, the days are over in which all aristocratic tendencies were strictly held back. The influence of intellectual leaders is increasing, art, science, and the ideals of the upper classes are continually pushing to the front, and even social lines and stratifications are beginning more and more to be felt. The soul of the people is agitated by imperialistic and military sentiments, and whereas in former times it was bent on freeing the slaves it now discovers "the white man's burden" to lie in the subjugation of inferior races. The restrictions to immigration are constantly being increased. Now of course all this does not a whit prejudice the formal political democracy of the land; it is simply a quiet, aristocratic complement to the inner workings of the constitution.

The presence, and even the bare possibility, here, of such by-currents, brings out more clearly how hopeless the theoretical estimation of any isolated form of statehood is, if it neglects the factors introduced by the actual life of the people. The American democracy is not an abstractly superior system of which a European can approve only by becoming himself a republican and condemning, incidentally, his own form of government: it is rather, merely, the necessary form of government for the types of men and the conditions which are found here. And any educated American of to-day fully realizes this. No theoretical hair-splitting will solve the problem as to what is best for one or another country; for that true historical insight is needed. And even when the histories of two peoples are so utterly dissimilar as are those of America and Germany, it by no means follows, as the social by-currents just mentioned show, that the real spirit of the peoples must be unlike. Democratic America, with its unofficial aristocratic leanings, has, in fact, a surprising kinship to monarchical Germany, with its inner workings of a true democracy. The two peoples are growing into strong resemblance, although their respective constitutions flourish and take deeper root.

The beginnings of American history showed unmistakably and imperatively that the government of the American people must be, in the words of Lincoln, "a government of the people, by the people, and for the people." No one dreamed when the Constitution of the United States was framed, some hundred and seventeen years ago, that this democratic instrument would ever be called on to bind together a mighty nation extending from Maine to California. And, indeed, such a territorial expansion would undoubtedly have stretched and burst the unifying bonds of this Constitution, if the distance between Boston and San Francisco had not meanwhile become practically shorter than the road from Boston to Washington was in those early days. But that this Constitution could so adapt itself to the undreamt broadening of conditions, that it could continue to be the mainstay of a people that was indefinitely extending itself by exchange and purchase, conquest and treaty, and that in no crisis has an individual or party succeeded in any tampering with the rights of the people; all this shows convincingly that the American form of state was not arbitrarily hit on, but that it was the outcome of an historical development.

* * * * * * * * * *

The spirit of this commonwealth was not first conceived in the year 1787. It was strong and ripe long before the delegates from the Thirteen States assembled under Washington's leadership in Independence Hall at Philadelphia. The history of the English colonists to the Atlantic coast shows from the very first what weight they attached to the duties and rights of the individual, and foretells as well the inevitable result, their unloosing from the mother country and final declaration of their independence.

We may consider the different lines of development which began early in the seventeenth century, after the feeble attempts at colonization from England, France and Spain in the latter half of the sixteenth century had miscarried and left socially no traces. French settlements flourished as early as 1605, chiefly however in Nova Scotia and other parts of Canada, and in 1609 settlements of Dutch, whose colony on the Hudson River, the present New York, soon passed over into English hands. The development of the Spanish colonies on the Gulf of Mexico went on outside the territory of these young United States; and so the story of the meagre years of America is comprised in the history of the English colonies alone.

These colonies began diversely but came to resemble one another more and more as time went on. There can be no greater contrast than between the pioneer life of stout-willed men, who have left their native soil in order to live in undisturbed enjoyment of their Puritan faith, seeking to found their little communities on simple forms of self-government, and on the other hand the occupation of a rich trading company under royal charter, or the inauguration of a colony of the crown. But these differences could not be preserved. The tiny independent communities, as they grew in consideration, felt the need of some protecting power and therefore they looked once more to England; while, on the other hand, the more powerful, chartered colonies tended to loose themselves from the mother country, feeling, as they soon did, that their interests could not be well administered from across a broad ocean. In spite of the protecting arm of England, they felt it to be a condition of their sound growth that they should manage their domestic affairs for themselves. Thus it happened that all the colonies alike were externally dependent on England, while internally they were independent and were being schooled in citizenship.

The desire for self-government as a factor in the transformations which went on can very easily be traced; but it would be harder to say how far utilitarian and how far moral factors entered in. Virginia took the first step. Its first settlement of 1606 was completely subject to the king, who granted homesteads but no political rights to the colonists. It was a lifeless undertaking until 1609, when its political status was changed. The administration of the colony was entrusted to those who were interested in its material success. It became a great business undertaking which had everything in its favour. At the head was a London company, which for a nominal sum had been allowed to purchase a strip of land having four hundred miles of seacoast and extending inland indefinitely. This land contained inestimable natural resources, but needed labour to exploit them. The company then offered to grant homes on very favourable terms to settlers, receiving in return either cash or labour; and these inducements, together with the economic pressure felt by the lower classes at home, brought about a rapid growth of the colony. Now since this colony was organized like a military despotism, whose ruler, however, was no less than three thousand miles away, the interests of the company had to be represented by officials delegated to live in the colony. The interests of these officials were of course never those of the colonists, and presently, moreover, unscrupulous officials commenced to misuse their power; so that as a result, while the colony flourished, the company was on the brink of failure. The only way out of this difficulty was to concede something to the colonists themselves, and harmonize their interests with those of the company by granting them the free direction of their own affairs. It was arranged that every village or small city should be a political unit and as such should send two delegates to a convention which sat to deliberate all matters of common concern. This body met for the first time in 1619; and in a short time it happened, as was to be expected, that the local government felt itself to be stronger than the mercantile company back in London. Disputes arose, and before five years the company had ceased to exist, and Virginia became a royal province. But the fact remained that in the year 1619 for the first time a deliberative body representing the people had met on American soil. The first step toward freedom had been taken. And with subtle irony fate decreed that in this same year of grace a Dutch ship should land the first cargo of African negroes in the same colony, as slaves.

That other form of political development, which started in the voluntary compact of men who owned no other allegiance, was first exemplified in the covenant of those hundred and two Puritans who landed from the Mayflower at Plymouth, in the year 1620, having forsaken England in order to enjoy religious freedom in the New World. A storm forced them to land on Cape Cod, where they remained and amid the severest hardships built up their little colony, which, as no other, has been a perpetual spring of moral force. Even to-day the best men of the land derive their strength from the moral courage and earnestness of life of the Pilgrims. Before they landed they signed a compact, in which they declared that they had made this voyage "for ye glory of God and advancement of ye Christian faith, and honour of our King and countrie," and that now in the sight of God they would "combine . . . togeather into a civil body politik for our better ordering and preservation and furtherance of ye end aforesaid, and by vertue hearof to enacte, constitute and frame such just and equal lawes, ordinances, actes, constitutions and offices from time to time, as shall be thought most meete and convenient for ye generall good of ye colonie."

The executive was a governor and his assistants, elected annually from the people: while the power to make laws remained with the body of male communicants of the church. And so it remained for eighteen years, until the growth of the colony made it hard for all church-members to meet together, so that a simple system of popular representation by election had to be introduced. This colony united later with a flourishing trading settlement, which centred about Salem; and these together formed the Massachusetts Bay Colony, which in 1640 numbered already twenty thousand souls.

The covenant which was drawn up on board the Mayflower is to be accounted the first voluntary federation of independent Americans for the purposes of orderly government. The first written constitution was drawn up in the colony of Connecticut, a colony which repeated essentially the successful experiments of New Plymouth, and which consisted of agricultural settlements and small posts for trading with the Indians situated at Windsor and Hartford and other places along the Connecticut Valley. Led by common interests, they adopted in 1638 a formal constitution.

There was still a third important type of colonial government, which was at first thoroughly aristocratic and English, and nevertheless became quickly Americanized. It was the custom of the King to grant to distinguished men, under provision of a small tribute, almost monarchical rights over large tracts of land. The first such man was Lord Baltimore, who received in 1632 a title to the domain of Maryland, on the Chesapeake Bay. He enjoyed the most complete princely prerogatives, and pledged to the crown in return about a fifth part of the gold and silver mined in his province. In 1664 Charles the Second gave to his brother, the Duke of York, a large territory, which was soon broken up, and which included what are now known as the States of Vermont, New Jersey, and Delaware. The great provinces of Georgia and Carolina — now North and South Carolina — were awarded by the same King to one of his admirals, Sir William Penn, for certain services. Penn died, and his son, who found himself in need of the sixteen thousand pounds which his father had loaned to the King, gratified that monarch by accepting in their stead a stretch of coast lands extending between the fortieth and forty-third degrees of latitude.

In this way extensive districts were turned over to the caprice of a few noblemen; but immediately the spirit of self-direction took everywhere root, and a social-political enthusiasm proceeded to shape the land according to new ideals. Carolina took counsel of the philosopher, Locke, in carrying out her experiment. Maryland, which was immediately prospered with two hundred men of property and rank, chiefly of Roman Catholic faith, started out with a general popular assembly, and soon went over to the representative system. And Penn's constructive handiwork, the Quaker State of Pennsylvania, was intended from the first to be "a consecrated experiment." Penn himself explained that he should take care so to arrange the politics of his colony that neither he himself nor his successors should have an opportunity to do wrong. Penn's enthusiasm awoke response from the continent: he himself founded the "city of brotherly love," Philadelphia; and Franz Daniel Pastorius brought over his colony of Mennonites, the first German settlers, who took up their abode at Germantown.

Thus it was that the spirit of self-reliant and self-assertive independence took root in the most various soils. But that which led the colonies to unite was not their common sentiments and ambitions, but it was their common enemies. In spite of the similarity of their positions there was no lack of sharp contrasts. And perhaps the most striking of these was the opposition between the southern colonies, with their languid climate, where the planters left all the work to slaves, and the middle and northern provinces, where the citizens found in work the inspiration of their lives. The foes which bound together these diverse elements were the Indians, the French, the Spanish, and lastly their parent race, the English.

The Indian had been lord of the land until he was driven back by the colonists to remoter hunting territory. The more warlike tribes tried repeatedly to wipe out the white intruder, and constantly menaced the isolated settlements, which were by no means a match for them. Soon after the first serious conflict in 1636, the Pequot war, Rhode Island, which was a small colony of scattered settlements, made overtures toward a protective alliance with her stronger neighbours. In this she was successful, and together with Massachusetts, Plymouth, New Haven, and Connecticut, formed the United Colonies of New England. This union was of little practical importance except as a first lesson to the colonies to avoid petty jealousies and to consider a closer mutual alliance as a possibility which would by no means impair the freedom and independence of the uniting parties.

The wars with the French colonies had more serious consequences. The French, who were the natural enemies of all English settlements, had originally planted colonies only in the far north, in Quebec in 1608. But during those decades in which the English wayfarers were making homes for themselves along the Atlantic coast, the French were migrating down from the north through the valley of the Saint Lawrence and along the Great Lakes to the Mississippi River. Then they pressed on down this stream to its mouth and laid title to the tremendous tracts which it drains, in the name of the French crown. This country they called after King Louis XIV, Louisiana. They had not come as colonists, but solely with an eye to gain, hoping to exploit these untouched resources in behalf of the Canadian fur traffic; and close on the heels of the trader came the Catholic priest. Thus the territory that flanked the English colonies to inland fell into French hands, whereas the land-grants of the English crown so read that only the Pacific Ocean should be the western boundary. A collision was therefore inevitable, although indeed mountains and virgin forests separated the coastland settlements from the inland regions of the Mississippi where the French had planted and fortified their trading posts.

When, in 1689, war broke out in Europe between England and France, a fierce struggle began between their representatives in the New World. But it was not now as it had been in the Indian war, where only a couple of colonies were involved. All the colonies along the coast were threatened by a common enemy. A congress of delegates convened at New York in April of 1690, in which for the first time all the colonies were invited to take part. Three long wars followed. The greatest advantage on the French side was that from the first they had been on good terms with the Indians, whose aid they were now able to enlist. But the French were numerically weak, and received but little assistance from their mother country. When in 1766 the last great war broke out the English colonies had a population of a million and a quarter, while the French had only a tenth as many. Chiefly and finally, the English colonists were actual settlers, hardened and matured through carrying the responsibilities of their young state, and fighting for hearth and home; the French were either traders or soldiers. The principle of free government was destined on this continent to triumph. Washington, then a young man, led the fight; the English Secretary of State, William Pitt, did everything in his power to aid; and the victory was complete. By the treaty of 1763 all French possessions east of the Mississippi were given to England, with the exception of New Orleans, which, together with the French possessions west of the Mississippi, went to Spain. Spain meanwhile ceded Florida to England. Thus the entire continent was divided between England and Spain.

But the Seven Years War had not merely altered the map of America; it had been an instructive lesson to the colonists. They had learned that their fortunes were one; that their own generals and soldiers were not inferior to any which England could send over; and lastly, they had come to see that England looked at the affairs of the colonies strictly from the point of view of her own gain. Herewith was opened up a new prospect for the future: the French no longer threatened and everything this side of the Mississippi stood open to them and promised huge resources. What need had they to depend further on the English throne? The spirit of self-direction could now consistently come forward and dictate the last move.

It is true that the colonists were still faithful English subjects, and in spite of their independent ambitions they took it for granted that England would always direct their foreign policy, would have the right to veto such laws as they passed, and that the English governors would always be recognized as official authorities. But now the English Parliament planned certain taxations that were the occasion of serious dispute. The Thirteen Colonies, which in the meantime had grown to be a population of two million, had by their considerable war expenditures shown to the debt-encumbered Britons the thriving condition of colonial trade. And the latter were soon ready with a plan to lay a part of the public taxation on the Americans. It was not in itself unfair to demand of the colonies some contribution to the public treasury, since many of the expenditures were distinctly for their benefit; and yet it must have seemed extraordinary to these men who had been forced from childhood to shift for themselves, and who believed the doctrine of self-government to be incontrovertible. They objected to paying taxes to a Parliament in which they had no representation; and the phrase, "no taxation without representation," became the motto of the hour.

The Stamp Tax, which prescribed the use of revenue stamps on all American documents and newspapers, was received with consternation, and societies called the Sons of Freedom were formed throughout the land to agitate against this innovation. The Stamp Tax Congress, which met in New York in 1765, repudiated the law in outspoken terms. Nor did it halt with a mere expression of opinion; the spirit of self-direction was not to be molested with impunity. Close on the resolve not to observe the law, came the further agreement to buy no English merchandise. England had to waive the Stamp Tax, but endless mutterings and recriminations followed which increased the bitterness. Both sides were ripe for war when, in 1770, England issued a proclamation laying a tax on all tea imported to the colonies. The citizens of Boston became enraged and pitched an English ship-load of tea into the harbour. Thereupon England, equally aroused, proceeded to punish Boston by passing measures designed to ruin the commerce of Boston and indeed all Massachusetts. The Thirteen Colonies took sides with Massachusetts and a storm became imminent. The first battle was fought on the 19th of April, 1775; and on July 4th, 1776, the Thirteen Colonies declared their independence of England. Henceforth there were to be no colonies but in their place thirteen free states.

The Declaration of Independence was composed by Jefferson, a Virginian, and is a remarkable document. The spirit that informs it is found in the following lines: "We hold these truths to be self-evident, that all men are created equal; that they are endowed by their Creator with certain unalienable rights; that among these are life, liberty, and the pursuit of happiness. That to secure these rights, governments are instituted among men, deriving their just powers from the consent of the governed . . ." The sins of the English king and people against America are enumerated at length, and in solemn language the United States of America are declared independent of the English people, who are henceforth to be as "the rest of mankind, enemies in war, in peace friends." This Declaration was signed by delegates from the states in Independence Hall, in Philadelphia, where hung the famous bell, with its inscription, "Proclaim liberty throughout all the land, unto all the inhabitants thereof."

The spirit of self-direction had triumphed; but the dangers were by no means wholly passed. England sent over no more governors, and had indeed been repulsed; but she had as yet no intention of giving in. The war dragged on for five long years, and the outcome was uncertain until in 1781 Cornwallis was brought to surrender. Then England knew that she had lost the contest. The king desired still to prolong the war, but the people were tired of it and, the ministry having finally to yield, peace was declared in April of the year 1783. This was no assurance of an harmonious future, however. That solidarity which the colonies had felt in the face of a common enemy now gave way to petty jealousies and oppositions, and the inner weakness of the new Union was revealed. In itself the Union had no legal authority over the several states, and while during the war the affairs of the country had fallen into disorder, yet the Union had no power to conduct foreign diplomacy or even to collect customs.

It was rather in their zeal for self-direction that at first considerable portions of the population seemed disinclined to enlarge the authority of the central organization. Self-direction begins with the individual or some group of individuals. The true self-direction of society as a whole was not to be allowed to encroach on the rights of the individual, and this was the danger feared. Each state, with its separate interests and powers, would not give up its autonomy in favour of an impersonal central power which might easily come to tyrannize over the single state in much the same way as the hated English throne had done. And yet the best men of the country were brought at length more and more to the opposite view; a strong central authority, in which the states as a whole should become a larger self-directing unit, carrying out and ensuring the self-direction of the component members, was seen to be a necessity. Another congress of representatives from all the states was convened in Independence Hall, at Philadelphia, and this body of uncommonly able men sat for months deliberating ways by which the opposing factions of federalism and anti-federalism could be brought together in a satisfactory alliance. It was obvious that compromises would have to be made. So, for instance, it was conceded that the smallest state, like the largest, should be represented in the senate by two delegates: and the single state enjoyed many other rights not usual in a federation. But, on the other hand, it was equally certain that the chief executive must be a single man with a firm will, and that this office must be refilled at frequent intervals by a popular election. A few had tentatively suggested making Washington king, but he stood firm against any such plan. The republican form of government was in this instance no shrewdly devised system which was adopted for the sake of nicely spun theoretical advantages — it was the necessity of the time and place, the natural culmination of a whole movement. It was as absolutely necessary as the consolidation of the German states, eighty years later, under an imperial crown. The congress eventually submitted a constitutional project to the several state legislatures, for their summary approval or rejection. Whereon the anti-federalistic factions made a final effort, but were outvoted, and the Constitution was adopted. In 1789 George Washington was elected the first president of the United States.

It would take a lively partisan to assert, as one sometimes does, that this Constitution is the greatest achievement of human intellect, and yet the severest critics have acknowledged that a genius for statesmanship is displayed in its text. Penned in an age which was given over to bombastic declamation, this document lays down the fundamental lines of the new government with great clearness and simplicity. "We, the people of the United States," it begins, "in order to form a more perfect union, establish justice, insure domestic tranquillity, provide for the common defence, promote the general welfare, and secure the blessings of liberty to ourselves and our posterity, do ordain and establish this Constitution for the United States of America." This is the entire introduction. The contents come under seven articles. The first article provides for the making of laws, this power to be vested in a Congress consisting of a Senate and House of Representatives; for the business and daily routine of this Congress, as well as its powers and obligations. The second article provides for the executive power, to be vested in the person of the President, who is elected every fourth year; the third article provides for a judiciary; the fourth defines the mutual relations of separate states; and the last three articles concern the adoption of the Constitution and the conditions under which it may be amended.

The need of amendments and extensions to this Constitution was foreseen and provided for. How profoundly the original document comprehended and expressed the genius of the American people may be seen from the fact that during a century which saw an unexampled growth of the country and an undreamed-of transformation of its foreign policy, not a single great principle of the Constitution was modified. After seventy-seven years one important paragraph was added, prohibiting slavery; and this change was made at a tremendous cost of blood. Otherwise the few amendments have been insignificant and concerned matters of expediency or else, and more specially, further formulations of what, according to American conceptions, are the rights of the individual. Although the original Constitution did not contain a formal proclamation of religious freedom, freedom of speech, of the press, and of public assemblage, this was not because those who signed the document did not believe in these things, but because they had not aimed to make of the Constitution of the Union either a treatise on ethics or yet a book of law. But as early as 1789 the states insisted that all the rights of the individual, as endorsed by the national ideals, should be incorporated in the articles of this document. In the year 1870 one more tardy straggler was added to the list of human rights, the last amendment; the right of the citizens to vote was not to be abridged on account of race, colour, or previous condition of servitude.

Of the other amendments, the tenth had been tacitly assumed from the first year of the Republic; this was that "The powers not delegated to the United States by the Constitution, nor prohibited by it to the States, are reserved to the States respectively, or to the people." This principle also was surely in no way at variance with the spirit of the original document. It was, indeed, the lever that ensured the great efficacy of the Constitution, so that by its provisions the centrifugal forces were never disturbed by centripetal ones; an equilibrium was effected between the tendencies that made for unity and those that made against it, in such a way that the highest efficiency was ensured to the whole while the fullest encouragement was given to the enterprise and initiative of the parts. In no direction, probably, would an improvement have been possible. More authority concentrated at the head would have impeded general activity, and less would have lost the advantages of concerted action; in neither case would material growth or the reconciliation of conflicting opinions have been possible. Constant compensation of old forces and the quickening of new ones were the secret of this documented power, and yet it was only the complete expression of the spirit of self-direction, which demands unremittingly that the nation as a whole shall conduct itself without encroaching on the freedom of the individual, and that the individual shall be free to go his own ways without interfering with the unfettered policy of the nation.

Under the auspices of this Constitution the country waxed and throve. As early as 1803 its land area was doubled by the accession of Louisiana, which had been ceded by Spain to France, and was now purchased from Napoleon for fifteen million dollars — an event of such far-reaching importance that the people of St. Louis have not inappropriately invited the nations of the earth to participate in a Louisiana Purchase Exposition. In 1845 Texas was taken into the Union, it having broken away from Mexico just previously and constituted itself an independent state. The large region on the Pacific slope known as Oregon came in 1846 to the United States by treaty with England, and when finally, in 1847, after the war with Mexico, New Mexico and California became the spoils of the victor and in 1867 Russia relinquished Alaska, the domain of the country was found to have grown from its original size of 324,000 square miles to one of 3,600,000. The thirteen states had become forty-five, since the newly acquired lands had to be divided. But all this growth brought no alteration in the Constitution, whose spirit of self-direction, rather, had led to this magnificent development, had fortified and secured the country, and inspired it with energy and contentment. The population also has grown under this benevolent Constitution. Millions have flocked hither to seek and to find prosperity on this new and inexhaustible soil. The area has increased ten-fold, but the population twenty-fold; and the new-comers have been disciplined in the school of self-direction and educated to the spirit of American citizenship.

* * * * * * * * * * *

There is a certain kind of character which must be developed in this school. It is true, of course, that there is no one model which just fits every one, the native-born Yankee as well as the European immigrant, the farmer as well as the resident in cities. The Irish-American is not the German-American, nor is the New Englander like the Virginian, nor the son of the East like his brother in the West. The infinite shadings of personal character, temperament, and capacity which nature has produced, have, of course, not been lost. And, nevertheless, just as the human race in America has begun to differentiate into a species which is anthropologically distinct, and this partly under the influence of the climate since the species has several characters in common with the aboriginal Indian, so also in the moral atmosphere of this body-politic a distinct type of human character is undoubtedly being evolved; and one may note with perpetual surprise how little the other great divisions of social life, as of rich and poor, cultivated and ignorant, native-born and immigrant, manual labourer and brain-worker — how little these differentiate the American citizen in his political capacity. Of course only the political life is in question here; that new groupings and divisions are being continually formed in the economic, intellectual, and social life need not concern us for the present. In the individual it may not be easy to follow the threads through the tissue of his psychic motions, but in the abstract and schematic picture of the type it is by no means impossible to trace them out.

What is it, then, which the American has gotten from his training? Many and apparently unrelated lessons are taught in the school of self-direction, and perhaps none of them are without their dangers. For it is here not a matter of theoretical knowledge, which may be remembered or forgotten and may be well or ill selected, but which in itself involves no scale of excellence and, therefore, has no need to be tempered or restrained. Theoretical knowledge cannot be overdone or exaggerated into untruth. But the practical conduct which is here in question is different; it involves an ideal, and in such a way that a man may not only misapprehend or forget what is the best course of action, but also he may err in following it, he may give it undue place and so neglect opposing motives which in their place are no less requisite. In short, conduct, unlike knowledge, demands a fine tact and unflagging discernment for the fitness of things. In this sense it cannot be denied that the teaching of American democracy is itself the source of serious errors, and that the typical American citizen is by no means free from the failings of his virtues. His fundamental traits may be briefly sketched, and from the excellencies which he strives for many of his defects can be understood.

There is, firstly, a group of closely related impulses, which springs from the American's unbounded belief in his own strength, a trait which in the last analysis must be, of course, the foundation-stone of any doctrine of self-direction. He will not wait for others to look out for him, counsel him, or take cognizance of his interests, but relies wholly on his own judgment and his own strength, and believes no goal too high for his exertions to attain. Every true

American will have found in himself some trace of this spirit. Each day of his life has suggested it to him, and all the institutions of his country have reinforced the teaching. Its most immediate result is such a strength of initiative as no other people on earth possesses, an optimism, a self-reliance and feeling of security which contribute more than half to his success. Faint heart is not in the American's dictionary. Individual, corporation, or country may be undecided, and dispute whether a certain end is desirable or whether a certain means is best to a given end, but no one ever doubts or goes into his work with misgivings lest his strength be not enough to traverse the road and reach the goal. And such an attitude encourages every man to exert himself to the utmost. The spirit of self-direction is here closely allied with that self-initiative which is the mainspring of the economic life of America. But the initiative and optimistic resolution shown in the political arena astonish the stranger more than the same traits displayed in the economic field. It is shown in the readiness for argument, in which every one can express himself accurately and effectively; in the indefatigable demand that every public office shall be open to the humblest incumbent, and in the cool assurance with which thousands and thousands of persons, without any technical knowledge or professional training, assume the most exacting political offices, and become postmasters, mayors, ministers and ambassadors, without even pausing before their grave responsibilities. But most of all, American initiative is shown in the structure of all her institutions, great or small, which minimizes transitions and degrees between higher and lower, and so facilitates the steady advance of the individual. Each and all must have the chance to unfold and there must be no obstacles to hinder the right ambition from its utmost realization. Every impulse must be utilized; and however far toward the periphery a man may be born he must have the right of pressing forward to the centre. The strength of this nation lies at the periphery, and the American government would never have advanced so unerringly from success to success if every village stable-lad and city messenger-boy had not known with pride that it depends only on himself if he is not to become President of the United States.

But the transition is easy and not well marked from such strength to a deplorable weakness. The spirit of initiative and optimism is in danger of becoming inexcusable arrogance as to one's abilities and sad underestimation of the value of professional training. Dilettanteism is generally well-meaning, often successful, and sometimes wholly admirable; but it is always dangerous. When brawny young factory-hands sit on a school committee, sturdy tradesmen assume direction of a municipal postal service, bankers become speakers in legislature, and journalists shift over to be cabinet ministers, the general citizen may sometimes find cold comfort in knowing that the public service is not roped off from private life, nor like to become effete through stale traditions. It is very evident that America is to-day making a great effort to ward off the evils of amateurish incompetence and give more prominence to the man of special training. And yet it cannot be denied that very noticeably in the intellectual make-up of the American his free initiative and easy optimism are combined with a readiness to overestimate his own powers and with a bias for dilettanteism.

Another psychological outcome of this individualism seems inevitable. When every member of a nation feels called on to pass judgment on all subjects for himself, it will come about that public opinion reaches an uncommonly high mean level, but it will also happen that the greatest intellects are not recognized as being above this mean. The genius, who in his day is always incomprehensible to the masses, goes to waste; and the man who sees beyond the vulgar horizon fights an uphill battle. The glittering successes are for the man whose doings impress the multitude, and this fact is necessarily reflected in the mind of the aspirant, who unconsciously shapes his ambitions to the taste of the many rather than of the best. Wherever the spirit of initiative possesses all alike, a truly great individual is of course insufferable; any great advance must be a collective movement, and the best energies of the country must be futilely expended in budging the masses. It is no accident that America has still produced no great world genius. And this is the other side of the vaunted and truthful assertion, that whenever in a New England town a question is brought to an open debate, the number of those who will take a lively, earnest, orderly, and intelligent part in the discussion is perhaps greater in proportion to the total number of inhabitants than in any place in Europe.

This leads us to a second consequence of the desire for self-direction. It stimulates not only initiative and self-reliance, but also the consciousness of duty. If a man earnestly believes that the subject must also be potentate, he will not try to put off his responsibilities on any one else but will forthwith set himself to work, and prescribe as well his own due restrictions. If a neighbourhood or club, town, city, or state, or yet the whole federation sees before it some duty, the American will not be found waiting for a higher authority to stir him up, for he is himself that authority; his vote it is which determines all who are to figure in the affair. Wherefore he is constrained by the whole system to an earnest and untiring co-operation in everything. This is not the superficial politics of the ale-house, with its irresponsible bandying of yeas and nays. When Secretary of the Navy under McKinley, Mr. Long said that when the cabinet at Washington was in conference, every member was of course better posted on the matter than the average citizen; but that nevertheless a dozen villagers, say in northern Maine, would read their New York and Boston papers and talk over the affairs with as much intelligence and as good a comprehension of the points at issue as would appear at any cabinet debates. This was by no means meant as a reflection on his colleagues of the cabinet, but as a frank recognition of an aspect of American life which invariably surprises the foreigner. One needs only to recall the discussion which preceded the last presidential election, and more especially the one preceding that; the silver question was the great issue, and evening after evening hundreds of thousands listened to technical arguments in finance such as no European orator could hope to lay before a popular assembly. Huge audiences followed with rapt attention for hours lectures on the most difficult points of international monetary standards. And this intellectual seriousness springs from the feeling of personal responsibility which is everywhere present. The European is always astonished at the exemplary demeanour of an American crowd; how on public occasions great multitudes of men and women regulate their movements without any noticeable interference by the police, how the great transportation companies operate with almost no surveillance of the public, trusting each person to do his part, and how in general the whole social structure is based on mutual confidence to a degree which is nowhere the case in Europe. The feeling that the ruler and the ruled are one pervades all activities, and its consequences are felt far beyond the political realm. Especially in the social sphere it makes for self-respect among the lower classes; they adapt themselves readily to discipline, for at the same time they feel themselves to be the masters; and the dignity of their position is the best security for their good behaviour.

But here, too, excellence has its defects. Where every one is so intensely aware of an identity between political authority and political subject, it is hard for the feeling of respect for any person whatsoever to find root. The feeling of equality will crop out where nature designed none, as for instance between youth and mature years. A certain lack of respect appears in the family and goes unpunished because superficially it corresponds to the political system of the land. Parents even make it a principle to implore and persuade their children, holding it to be a mistake to compel or punish them; and they believe that the schools should be conducted in the same spirit. And thus young men and women grow up without experiencing the advantages of outer constraint or discipline.

Hitherto we have considered only those intellectual factors derived from the spirit of self-direction which bear on the will of the individual, his rights and duties; but these factors are closely bound up with the others which concern the rights and privileges of one's neighbour. We may sketch these briefly. Deeply as he feels his own rights, the American is not less conscious of those of his neighbour. He does not forget that his neighbour may not be molested and must have every opportunity for development and the pursuit of his ambitions, and this without scrutiny or supervision. He recognizes the other's equal voice and influence in public affairs, his equally sincere sense of duty and fidelity to it. This altruism expresses itself variously in practical life. Firstly, in a complete subordination to the majority. In America the dissenting minority displays remarkable discipline, and if the majority has formally taken action, one hears no grumbling or quibbling from the discontented, whether among boys at play or men who have everything at stake. The outvoiced minority is self-controlled and good-natured and ready at once to take part in the work which the majority has laid out; and herein lies one of the clearest results of the American system and one of the superior traits of American character.

Closely related to this is another trait which lends to American life much of its intrinsic worth — the unconditional insistence in any competition on equal rights for both sides. The demand for "fair play" dominates the whole American people, and shapes public opinion in all matters whether large or small. And with this, finally, goes the belief in the self-respect and integrity of one's neighbour. The American cannot understand how Europeans so often reinforce their statements with explicit mention of their honour which is at stake, as if the hearer is likely to feel a doubt about it; and even American children are often apt to wonder at young people abroad who quarrel at play and at once suspect one another of some unfairness. The American system does not wait for years of discretion to come before exerting its influence; it makes itself felt in the nursery, where already the word of one child is never doubted by his playmates.

Here too, however, the brightest light will cast a shadow. Every intelligent American is somewhat sadly aware that the vote of a majority is no solution of a problem, and he realizes oftener than he will admit that faith in the majority is pure nonsense if theoretical principles are at issue. This is a system which compels him always where a genius is required to substitute a committee, and to abide by the majority vote. The very theory of unlimited opportunity has its obvious dangers arising, here as everywhere, from extremes of feeling and so exaggeration of the principle. The recognition of another's rights leads naturally to a sympathy for the weaker, which is as often as not unjustified, and easily runs over into sentimentalism, not to say an actual hysteria of solicitude. And this is in fact a phase of public opinion which stands in striking contrast to the exuberant health of the nation. What is even worse, the ever-sensitive desire not to interfere in another's rights leads to the shutting of one's eyes and letting the other do what he likes, even if it is unjust. And in this way a situation is created which encourages the unscrupulous and rewards rascality.

For a long time the blackest spot on American life, specially in the opinion of German critics, has been the corruption in municipal and other politics. We need not now review the facts. It is enough to point out that a comparison with conditions in Germany, say, is entirely misleading if it is supposed to yield conclusions as to the moral character of the American people. Unscrupulous persons who are keen for plunder, are to be found everywhere; merely the conditions under which the German public service has developed and now maintains itself make it almost impossible for a reprobate of that sort to force his entrance. And if a German official were discovered in dishonest practices it would be, in fact, discrediting to the people. In America the situation is almost reversed. The conditions on which, according to the American system, the lesser officials secure their positions, specially in municipal governments, and the many chances of enriching oneself unlawfully and yet without liability to arrest, while the regular remuneration and above all the social dignity of the positions are relatively small, drive away the better elements of the population and draw on the inferior. The charge against the Americans, then, should not be that they make dishonest officials, but that they permit a system which allows dishonest persons to become officials. This is truly a serious reproach, yet it is not a charge of contemptible dishonesty but of inexcusable complacency; and this springs from the national weakness of leniency toward one's neighbour, a trait which comes near to being a fundamental democratic virtue. It cannot be denied, moreover, that the whole nation is earnestly and successfully working to overcome this difficulty.

The denunciations of the daily papers, however, must not be taken as an indication of this, for the uncurbed American press makes the merest unfounded suspicion an occasion for sensational accusations. Any one who has compared in recent years the records of unquestionably impartial judicial processes with the charges which had previously been made in the papers, must be very sceptical as to the hue and cry of corruption. Even municipal politics are much better than they are painted. The easiest way of overcoming every evil would be to remove the public service from popular and party influences, but this is, of course, not feasible since it would endanger the most cherished prerogatives of individualism. Besides, the American is comforted about his situation because he knows that just this direct efficiency of the people's will is the surest means of thoroughly uprooting the evil as soon as it becomes really threatening. He may be patient or indifferent too long, but if he is once aroused he finds in his system a strong and ready instrument for suddenly overturning an administration and putting another in its stead. Moreover, if corruption becomes too unblushing an "educational campaign" is always in order. James Bryce, who is of all Europeans the one most thoroughly acquainted with American party politics, gives his opinion, that the great mass of civil officials in the United States is no more corrupt than that of England or Germany. An American would add, however, that they excel their European rivals in a better disposition and greater readiness to be of service.

But the situation is complicated by still another tendency which makes the fight for clean and disinterested politics difficult. The spirit of self-direction involves a political philosophy which is based on the individual; and the whole commonwealth has no other meaning than an adding up of the rights of separate individuals, so that every proposal must benefit some individual or other if it is to commend itself for adoption. Now since the state is a collection of numberless individuals and the law merely a pledge between them all, the honour of the state and the majesty of the law do not attach to a well organized and peculiarly exalted collective will, which stands above the individual. Such a thing would seem to an individualist a hollow abstraction, for state and law consist only in the rights and responsibilities of such as he. From this more or less explicitly formulated conception of political life there accrue to society both advantages and dangers. The advantages are obvious: the Mephistophelian saying, "Vernunft wird Unsinn, Wohltat Plage," becomes unthinkable, since the body-politic is continually tested and held in check by the lively interests of individuals. Any obvious injustice can be righted, for above the common weal stands the great army of individuals by whom and for whom both state and law were made.

But the disadvantages follow as well. If state and law are only a mutual restraint agreed on between individuals, the feeling of restraint becomes lively in proportion as the particular individuals in question can be pointed to, but vanishingly weak when, in a more intangible way, the abstract totality requires allegiance. So one finds the finest feeling for justice in cases of obligation to an individual, as in contracts, for instance, and the minimum sense of right where the duty is toward the state. There is no country of Europe where the sense of individual right so pervades all classes of the inhabitants, a fact which stands in no wise contradictory to the other prevalent tendency of esteeming too lightly one's righteous obligations to city or state. Men who, in the interests of their corporations, try to influence in irregular ways the professional politicians in the legislatures, observe nevertheless in private life the most rigid principles of right; and many a one who could safely be trusted by the widows and orphans of his city with every cent which they own, would still be very apt to make a false declaration of his taxable property.

There is a parallel case in the sphere of criminal law. Possibly even more than the abuses of American municipal politics, the crimes of lynch courts have brought down the condemnation of the civilized world. Corruption and "lynch justice" are usually thought of as the two blemishes on the nation, and it is from them that the casual observer in Europe gets a very unfavourable impression of the American conception of justice. We have already tried to rectify this estimate in so far as it includes corruption, and as regards lynching it is perhaps even more in error. Lynch violence is of course not to be excused. Crime is crime; and the social psychologist is interested only in deciding what rubric to put it under. Now the entire development of lynch action shows that it is not the wanton violence of men who have no sense of right, but rather the frenzied fulfillment of that which we have termed the individualistic conception of justice. The typical case of lynching is found, of course, in Southern States with a considerable negro population. A negro will have attempted violence on a white woman, whereon all the white men of the neighbourhood, assuming that through the influence of his fellow negroes the criminal would not be duly convicted, or else feeling that the regular legal penalty would not suffice to deter others from the same crime, violently seize the culprit from out the jurisdiction of the law, and after a summary popular trial hang him. But these are not men who are merely seeking a victim to their brutal instinct for murder. It is reported that after the deed, when the horrid crime has been horribly expiated, the participants will quietly and almost solemnly shake one another by the hand and disperse peacefully to their homes, as if they had fulfilled a sacred obligation of citizenship. These are men imbued with the individualistic notion of society, confident that law is not a thing whose validity extends beyond themselves, but something which they have freely framed and adopted, and which they both may and must annul or disregard as soon as the conditions which made it necessary are altered. It is a matter of course that such presumption is abhorred and condemned in the more highly civilized states of the Union, also by the better classes in the Southern States; and a lyncher is legally a murderer. His deed, however, is not to be referred psychologically to a deficient sense of justice. That which is the foundation of this sense, resentment at an infringement of the individual's rights and belief in the connection between sin and expiation, are all too vividly realized in his soul.

We have dwelt on these two offshoots of the individualistic idea of law because they have been used constantly to distort the true picture of American character. Rightly understood, psychologically, these phenomena are seen to be black and ugly incidents, which have little to do with the national consciousness of right and honour; they are the regrettable accompaniments of an extreme individualism, which in its turn, to be sure, grows naturally out of the doctrine of self-direction. Every American knows that it is one of the most sacred duties of the land to fight against these abuses, and yet the foreigner should not be deceived into thinking, because so and so many negroes are informally disposed of each year, and the politicians of Philadelphia or Chicago continue to stuff their pockets with spoils in ways which are legally unpunishable, that the American is not thoroughly informed with a respect for law. He has not taken his instruction in the system of self-direction in vain. And the German who estimates the tone of political life in America by the corruption and lynch violence narrated in the daily papers, is like the American who makes up his opinion of the German army, as he sometimes does, from the harangues of social democrats on the abuses of military officers, or from sensational disclosures of small garrisons on the frontier.

One more trait must be mentioned, finally, which is characteristic of every individualistic community, and which, having been impressed on the individual by the American system, has now reacted and contributed much to the working out of this system. The American possesses an astonishing gift for rapid organization. His highest talents are primarily along this line, and in the same way every individual has an instinct for stationing himself at the right place in any organization. This is true both high and low, and can be observed on every occasion, whether in the concerted action of labouring men, in a street accident, or in any sort of popular demonstration. For instance, one has only to notice how quickly and naturally the public forms in orderly procession before a ticket-office. This sure instinct for organization, which is such an admirable complement to the spirit of initiative, gives to the American workman his superiority over the European, for it is lamentably lacking in the latter, and can be replaced only by the strictest discipline. But this instinct finds its fullest expression in the political sphere. It is this which creates parties, guarantees the efficiency of legislatures, preserves the discipline of the state, and is in general the most striking manifestation of the spirit of self-direction. But we have seen that none of the merits of this system are quite without their drawbacks, and this gift for organization has also its dangers. The political parties which it fosters may become political "machines," and the party leader a "boss" — but here we are already in the midst of those political institutions with which we must deal more in detail.

CHAPTER TWO

Political Parties

THE Presidency is the highest peak in the diversified range of political institutions, and may well be the first to occupy our attention. But this chief executive office may be looked at in several relations: firstly, it is one of the three divisions of the Government, which are the executive, the legislative, and the judicial. And these might well be considered in this order. But, on the other hand, the President stands at the head of the federation of states; and the structural beauty of the American political edifice consists in the repetition of the whole in each part and of the part in every smaller part, and so on down. The top governmental stratum of the federation is repeated on a smaller scale at the head of each of the forty-five states, and again, still smaller, over every city. The governor of a state has in narrower limits the functions of the President, and so, within still narrower, has the mayor of a city. We might, then, consider the highest office, and after that its smaller counterparts in the order of their importance.

But neither of these methods of treatment would bring out the most important connection. It is possible to understand the President apart from the miniature presidents of the separate states, or apart from the Supreme Court, or even Congress, but it is not possible to understand the President without taking account of the political parties. It is the party which selects its candidate, elects him to office, and expects from him in return party support and party politics. The same is true, moreover, of elections to Congress and to the state legislatures. For here again the party is the background to which everything is naturally referred, and any description of the President, or Congress, or the courts, which, like the original Constitution, makes no mention of the parties, appears to us to-day as lacking in plastic reality, in historical perspective. We shall, therefore, attempt no such artificial analysis, but rather describe together the constitutional government and the inofficial party formations. They imply and explain each other. Then on this background of party activities we can view more comprehensively the President, Congress, the Supreme Court, and the entire politics of the federation and the states.

We must not forget, however, that in separating any of these factors from the rest, we deal at once with highly artificial abstractions, so that this description will have continually to neglect many facts and cut the threads that cross its path. The history of the American Presidency shows at all times its close connection with other institutions. A treaty or even a nomination by the President requires the ratification of the Senate before it is valid; and on the other side, the President can veto any bill of Congress. Even the Supreme Court and the President can hardly be considered apart, as was seen, for instance, in the time of Cleveland, when his fiscal policy took final shape in an income tax which the Supreme Court declared unconstitutional, and therefore unlawful; or again when the colonial policy of McKinley was upheld and validated by a decision of the same court. Again, the party politics of state and town are no less intimately related to the federal government and the Presidency. Here, too, the leadings are in both directions; local politics condition the national, and these in turn dominate the local. Cleveland was a man who had never played a part in national politics until he became the executive head of the nation. As Mayor of Buffalo he had been so conspicuous throughout the State of New York as to be elected Governor of that state, and then in the state politics so won the confidence of his party as to be nominated and elected to the highest national office. McKinley, on the other hand, although he, too, had been the Governor of a state, nevertheless gained the confidence of his party during his long term of service in Congress.

Similarly it may be said that local politics are the natural path which leads to any national position, whether that of senator or representative. And inversely the great federal problems play an often decisive rôle in the politics of the states with which they strictly have no connection. Federal party lines divide legislatures from the largest to the smallest, and even figure in the municipal elections. Unreasonable as it may seem, it is a fact that the great national questions, such as expansion, free trade, and the gold standard, divide the voters of a small village into opposing groups when they have to elect merely some one to the police or street-cleaning department. It is, therefore, never a question of a mechanical co-ordination and independence of parts, but of an organic interdependence, and every least district of the Union is thoroughly *en rapport* with the central government and doings of the national parties.

There are political parties in every country, but none like the American parties. The English system presents the nearest analogy, with its two great parties, but the similarity is merely superficial and extends to no essential points. Even in the comparison between America and Germany it is not the greater number of the German parties that makes the real difference. For the German his party is in the narrower sense a group of legislators, or, more broadly, these legislators together with the general body of their constituents. The party has in a way concrete reality only in the act of voting and the representation in parliament of certain principles. Of course, even in Germany there exists some organization between the multitude of voters and the small group which they return to the Reichstag. Party directors, who are for the most part the representatives themselves, central committees and local directors, local clubs and assemblies are all necessary to stir up the voters and to attend to various formalities of the election; but no one has dreamt of a horde of professional politicians who are not legislators, of party leaders who are more powerful than the representative to be elected, or of parties which are stronger than either the parliament or the people. The American party is first of all a closely knit organization with extensive machinery and rigid discipline; to be represented in Congress or legislature is only one of its many objects.

This situation is, however, no accident. One may easily understand the incomparable machinery and irresistible might of the parties, if one but realizes a few of the essential factors in American party life. First, of course, comes the tremendous extent of the field in which the citizens' ballots have the decision. If it were as it is in the German elections to the imperial diet, the American party organization would never have become what it is. But besides the elections to Congress, the state legislatures and local assemblies, there is the direct choice to be made for President, vice-president, governor, the principal state officials and deputies, judges of the appellate court, mayor and city officials, and many others. The entire responsibility falls on the voters, since the doctrine of self-direction ordains that only citizens of the state shall vote for state officials, and of the city for city officers. The governor, unlike an "Oberpräsident," is not appointed by the Government, nor a mayor by any authority outside his city. The voter is nowhere to be politically disburdened of responsibility. But, with the direct suffrage, his sphere of action is only begun. Almost every one of the men he elects has in turn to make further appointments and choices. The members of a state legislature elect senators to Congress, and both governor and mayor name many officials, but most of all, the President has to give out offices from ambassadors and ministers down to village postmasters and light-house keepers, in all of which there is ample chance to put the adherents of one's party in influential positions. Thus the functions of the American voter are incomparably more important and far-reaching than those of the German voter.

But even with this, the political duties of the American citizen in connection with his party are not exhausted. The spirit of self-direction demands the carrying out of a principle which is unknown to the German politician. The choice and nomination of a candidate for election must be made by the same voting public; it must be carried on by the same parliamentary methods, and decided strictly by a majority vote. There are in theory no committees or head officials to relieve the voting public of responsibility, by themselves benignly apportioning the various offices among the candidates. A party may propose but one candidate for each office, whereas there will often be several men within the party who wish to be candidates for the same office, as for instance, that of mayor, city counsellor, or treasurer. In every case the members of a party have to select the official nominee of their party by casting ballots, and thus it may happen that the contest between groups within the party may be livelier than the ultimate battle between the parties.

Now on a large scale such transactions can be no longer carried on directly. All the citizens of the state cannot come together to nominate the party candidate for governor. For this purpose, therefore, electors have to be chosen, every one by a strict majority vote, and these meet to fix finally on the candidates of the party. And when it comes to the President of the whole country, the voting public elects a congress of electors, and these in turn choose other electors, and this twice-sifted body of delegates meets in national convention to name the candidate whom the party will support in the final, popular elections. Through such a strict programme for nominations the duties of the voters towards their party are just doubled, and it becomes an art considerably beyond the ability of the average citizen to move through this regressive chain of elections without losing his way. It requires, in short, an established and well articulated organization to arrange and conduct the popular convocations, to deliberate carefully on the candidates to be proposed for nomination, and to carry the infinitely complicated and yet unavoidable operations through to their conclusion.

Finally, another factor enters in, which is once more quite foreign to the political life of Germany. Every American election is strictly local, in the sense that the candidate is invariably chosen from among the voters. In Germany, when a provincial city is about to send a representative to the Reichstag, the party in power accounts it a specially favourable circumstance if the candidates are not men of that very city, to suffer the proverbial dishonour of prophets in their own country, and prefers to see on the ballot the names of great party leaders from some other part of the empire. And when Berlin, for example, selects a mayor, the city is glad to call him from Breslau or Königsberg. This is inconceivable to the American. It is a corollary to the doctrine of self-determination that whenever a political district, whether village or city, selects a representative, the citizens shall not only nominate and elect their candidate, but that they shall also choose him from their own midst. But this makes it at once necessary for the party to have its organized branches in every nook and corner of the country. A single central organization graciously to provide candidates for the whole land is not to be thought of. The party organization must be everywhere efficient, and quick to select and weigh for the purposes of the party such material as is at hand. It is obvious that this is a very intricate and exacting task, and that if the organization were sentimental, loose, or undisciplined, it would go to pieces by reason of the personal and other opposing interests which exist within it. And if it were less widely branched or less machine-like in its intricate workings, it would not be able to do its daily work, pick candidates for posts of responsibility, nominate electors, and elect its nominees; and eventually it would sink out of sight. The American political party is thus an essentially complete and independent organization.

Two evils are necessarily occasioned by this invulnerable organization of party activities, both of which are peculiar and of such undoubtedly bad consequences as to strike the most superficial observer, and specially the foreigner; and yet both of which on closer view are seen to be much less serious than one might have supposed at first. After a party has grown up and become well organized in its purpose of representing these or those political principles and of defending and propagating them, it may at length cease to be only the means to an end, and become an end unto itself. There is the danger that it will come to look on its duties as being nothing else than to keep itself in power, even by denying or opposing the principles with which it has grown up. Moreover, such an organization exacts a colossal amount of labour which must be rewarded in some form or other; and so it will find it expedient, quite apart from the political ideals of the party, to exert its influence in the patronage of state and other offices. The result is that the rewards and honours conferred necessarily draw men into the service of the party who care less for its ideals than for the emoluments they are to derive. And thus two evils spring up together; firstly, the parties lose their principles, and, secondly, take into their service professional politicians who have no principles to lose. We must consider both matters more in detail, the party ideals and the politicians.

America has two great parties, the Republican, which is just now in power, and the Democratic. Other parties, as, for instance, the Populist, are small, and while they may for a while secure a meagre representation in Congress, they are too insignificant to have any chance of success in the presidential elections: although, to be sure, this does not prevent various groups of over-enthusiastic persons from seizing the politically unfitting and impracticable occasion to set up their own presidential candidate as a sort of figure-head. Any political amateur, who finds no place in the official parties, may gather a few friends under his banner and start a new, independent party; but the bubble bursts in a few days. And even if it is a person like Admiral Dewey, whose party banner is the flag under which he has sent an enemy's fleet to the bottom, he will succeed only in being amusing. The regular, organized parties are the only ones which seriously count in politics. It sometimes happens, however, that a few months before the elections a small band of politically or industrially influential men will meet to consider the project of a third party, while their real aim is to create a little organization whose voting power will be coveted by both of the great parties. In this way the founders plan to force one or both of these to make concessions to the principles of their little group, since the most important feature is that Republicans and Democrats are so nearly equally balanced that only a slight force is needed to turn the scales to either side. In recent elections McKinley and Cleveland have each been elected twice to the Presidency, and no one can say whether the next presidential majority will be Republican or Democrat. On Cleveland's second election the Democrats had 5,556,918, and the Republicans 5,176,108 votes, while the Populists made a showing of one million votes. But four years later the tables were turned, and McKinley won on 7,106,199 votes, while Bryan lost on 6,502,685. It is clear, therefore, that neither of the parties has to fear that a third party will elect its candidate; nor can either rest on old laurels, for any remission of effort is a certain victory for the other side. A third party is dangerous only in so far as it is likely to split up one of the two parties and so weaken it in an otherwise almost equal competition.

What, now, are the principles and aims of the Republican and Democratic parties? Their names are not significant, since neither do the Republicans wish to do away with American democracy, nor do the Democrats have any designs on the republican form of government. At the opening of the nineteenth century the present Democrats were called "Democratic-Republicans," and this long abandoned name could just as well be given to all surviving parties. Neither aristocracy nor monarchy nor anarchy nor plutocracy has ever so far appeared on a party programme, and however hotly the battle may be waged between Republicans and Democrats, it is forever certain that both opponents are at once Democrats and Republicans. Wherein, then, do they differ?

The true party politician of America does not philosophize overmuch about the parties; it is enough for him that one party has taken or is likely to take this, and the other party that position on the living questions, and beyond this his interest is absorbed by special problems. He is reluctant enough when it comes to taking up the nicer question of deducing logically from the general principles of a party what attitude it ought to take on this or that special issue. The nearest he would come to this would be conversely to point out that the attitude of his opponents directly refutes their party's most sacred doctrines. Those who philosophize are mostly outsiders, either sojourners in the country, or indigenous critics who are considerably more alive to the unavoidable evils of party politics than to the merits. From such opponents of parties as well as from foreigners, one hears again and again that the parties do not really stand for any general principles at the present time, that their separate existence has lost whatever political significance it may have had, and that to-day they are merely two organizations preserving a semblance of individuality and taking such attitude toward the issues of the day as is likely to secure the largest number of votes, in order to distribute among their members the fruits of victory. The present parties, say these critics, were formed in that struggle of intellectual forces which took place during the third quarter of the last century; it was the dispute over slavery which led to the Civil War. The Republican party was the party of the Northern States in their anti-slavery zeal; the Democratic was the party of the slave-holding Southern States; and the opposition had political significance as long as the effects of the war lasted, and it was necessary to work for the conciliation and renewed participation of the defeated Confederacy. But all this is long past. Harrison, Cleveland, Blaine, Bryan, McKinley, and Roosevelt became the standard-bearers of their respective parties long after the wounds of the war had healed. And it is no outcome from the original, distinguishing principles of the parties, if the slave-holding party takes the side of free-trade, silver currency and anti-imperialism, while the anti-slavery elements stay together in behalf of the gold standard, protection, and expansion.

It looks, rather, as if the doctrines had migrated each to the other's habitat. The party which was against slavery was supporting the rights of the individual; how comes it, then, to be bitterly opposing the freedom of trade? And how do the friends of slavery happen to champion the cause of free-trade, or, more remarkably, to oppose so passionately to-day the oppression of the people of the Philippines? And what have these questions to do with the monetary standard? It looks as if the organization had become a body without a soul. Each party tries to keep the dignity of its historic traditions and at every new juncture bobs and ducks before the interests and prejudices of its habitual clientèle, while it seeks to outwit the opposite party by popular agitation against persistent wrongs and abuses or by new campaign catch-words and other devices. But there is no further thought of consistently standing by any fundamental principles. This hap-hazard propping up of the party programme is evinced by the fact that either party is divided on almost every question, and the preference of the majority becomes the policy of the party only through the strict discipline and suppression of the minority. The Republicans won in their campaign for imperialism, and yet no anti-imperialist raised his voice more loudly than the Republican Senator Hoar. The Democrats acclaimed the silver schemes of Bryan, but the Gold Democrats numbered on their side really all the best men of the party. Again, on other important issues both parties will adopt the same platform as soon as they see that the masses are bound to vote that way. Thus neither party will openly come out for trusts, but both parties boast of deprecating them; and both profess likewise to uphold civil-service reform. This is so much the case that it has often been observed that within a wide range the programmes of the two parties in no way conflict. One party extols that which the other has never opposed, and the semblance of a difference is kept up only by such insistent vociferation of the policy as implies some sly and powerful gainsayer. And then with the same histrionic rage comes the other party and pounces on some scandal which the first had never thought of sanctioning. In short, there are no parties to-day but the powerful election organizations which have no other end in view than to come into power at whatever cost. It should seem better wholly to give up the out-lived issues, and to have only independent candidates who, without regard to party pressure, would be grouped according to their attitude on the chief problems of the day.

And yet, after the worst has thus been said, we find ourselves still far removed from the facts. Each separate charge may be true, but the whole be false and misleading: even although many a party adherent admits the justness of the characterization, and declares that the party must decide every case "on its merits," and that to hold to principles is inexpedient in politics. For the principles exist, nevertheless, and have existed, and they dominate mightily the great to and fro of party movements. Just as there have always been persons who pretend to deduce the entire history of Europe from petty court intrigues and jealousies of the ante-room or the boudoir, so there will always be wise-heads in America to see through party doings, and deduce everything from the speculative manipulations of a couple of banking houses or the private schemes of a sugar magnate or a silver king. Such explanations never go begging for a credulous public, since mankind has a deep-rooted craving to see lowness put on exhibition. No man is a hero, it is said, in the eyes of his valet. Nations, too, have their valets; and with them, too, the fact is not that there are no heroes, but that a valet can see only with the eyes of a valet.

It is true that the party lines of to-day have developed from the conflicting motives of the Civil War. But the fundamental error which prevents all insight into the deeper connections, lies in supposing that the anti-slavery party was first inspired by the individual fate of the negro, or in general the freedom of the individual. We must recall some of the facts of history. The question of slavery did not make its first appearance in the year 1860, when the Republican party became important. The contrast between the plantation owners of the South, to whom slave labour was apparently indispensable, and the industry and trade of the North, which had no need of slaves, had existed from the beginning of the century and was in itself no reason for the formation of political parties. It was mainly an economic question which, together with many other factors, led to a far-reaching opposition between the New England States and the South, an opposition which was strengthened, to be sure, by the moral scruples of the Puritanical North. But the earlier parties were not marked off by degrees of latitude, and furthermore the Southerner was by no means lacking in personal sympathy for the negro. The question first came into politics indirectly. It was in those years when the Union was pushing out into the West, taking in new territories and then making them into states by act of Congress, according to the provisions of the Constitution. In 1819 the question came up of admitting Missouri to the Union, and now for the first time Congress faced the problem as to whether slavery should be allowed in a new state. The South wished it and the North opposed it. Congress finally decided that Missouri should be a slave state, but that in the future slavery should be forbidden north of a certain geographical line. Thus slavery came to be recognized as a question within the jurisdiction of the federal Congress. Wherewith, if Congress should vote against slavery by a sufficient majority, it could forbid the practice in all the Southern states. And this would mean their ruin.

It came thus to be for the interest of the Southern states, which at that time had a majority, to see to it that for every free state admitted to the Union there should be at least one new slave state; this in order to hold their majority in Congress. Now it happened at that time that the territories which, by reason of their population, would have next to be admitted, lay all north of the appointed boundary and would, therefore, be free states. Therefore the slave-holders promulgated the theory that Congress had exceeded its jurisdiction and interfered with the rights of the individual states. The matter was brought before the Supreme Court, and in 1857 a verdict was given which upheld the new theory. Thus Congress, that is, the Union as a whole, could not forbid slavery in any place, but must leave the matter for each state to decide. Herewith an important political issue was created, and a part of the country stood out for the rights of the Union, a part for those of the individual states. The group of men who at that time foresaw that the whole Union was threatened, if so far-reaching rights were to be conceded to the states, was the Republican party. It rose up defiantly for the might and right of the federation, and would not permit one of the most important social and economic questions to be taken out of the hands of the central government and left to local choice. It was, of course, not a matter of chance that slavery became the occasion of dispute, but the real question at issue was the jurisdiction of the Federal Government. The federal party won, under the leadership of Abraham Lincoln. His election was the signal for the slave states to secede, South Carolina being the first. In February, 1861, these states formed a Confederation, and the Union was formally cleft. In his inaugural speech of the following March, Lincoln firmly declared that the Union must be preserved at all cost. The Civil War began in April, and after fearful fighting the secessionists were returned to the Union, all slaves were freed, and the Southern states were reconstructed after the ideas of the Republican party. The opposing party, the Democratic, was the party of decentralization. Its programme was the freedom of the individual state but not the servitude of the individual man.

When one understands in this way the difference between the two parties, one sees that the Republicans were not for freedom nor the Democrats for slavery, but the Republicans were for a more complete subordination of the states to the federation and the Democrats were for the converse. This is a very different point of view, and from it very much which seems incompatible with the attitude of the two parties toward the question of slavery may now be seen as a necessary historical consequence.

If we cast a glance at foregoing decades, we see that ever since the early days of the republic there has been hardly a time when these two forces, the centralizing and the decentralizing, have not been in play. It has lain deep in the nature of Teutonic peoples to pull apart from one another, while at the same time the struggle for existence has forced them to strong and well unified organization, so that scarcely a single Teutonic people has been spared that same opposition of social forces which is found in America. The origin of the Constitution itself can be understood only with reference to these antagonistic tendencies. The country wanted to be free of the miserable uncertainty, the internal discord and outward weakness which followed the Declaration of Independence; it wanted the strength of unity. And yet every single state guarded jealously its own rights, suspected every other state, and wished to be ensured against any encroachment of the federal power. And so the Constitution was drawn up with special precautions ensuring the equilibrium of power. At once, in Washington's cabinet, both tendencies were distinctly and notably represented. There sat the distinguished Hamilton, the minister of finance and framer of the Constitution, who was a tireless champion of the federal spirit, and beside him sat Jefferson, the minister of state, who would have preferred to have the federation transact nothing but foreign affairs and who believed in general the less the legislation the better for the people. The adherents of Hamilton's policy formed the federalist party, while Jefferson's supporters were called the Democratic Republicans. The names have changed and the special issues have altered with the progress of events; indeed, apparently the centralist party has gone twice out of existence, yet it was actually this party of which Lincoln became the leader. Jefferson's party, on the other hand, in spite of its change of name, has never as an organization ceased to exist. The Democrats who, in 1860, wished to submit the question of slavery to the individual states, were the immediate heirs of the anti-federalists who had elected their first president in 1800.

Now if the centralizing and decentralizing character of the two parties is borne in mind, their further development down to the present day can be understood. This development seems disconnected and contradictory only when the slavery question is thought to be the main feature and the Republicans are accounted the champions of freedom and the Democrats of slavery. Even Bryce, who has furnished by far the best account of the American party system, underestimates somewhat the inner continuity of the parties. Even he believes that the chief mission of the Republican party has been to do away with slavery and to reconstruct the Southern states, and that since this end was accomplished as far back as in the seventies, new parties ought naturally to have been formed by this time. Although the old organizations have in fact persisted, a certain vagueness and lack of vitality can be detected, he says, in both parties. According to that conception, however, it would be incomprehensible why those who formerly went forth to put an end to slavery now advance to bring the Filipinos into subjection, and to detain the poor man from purchasing his necessities where they are the cheapest.

As we have seen, the Democrats were the party which was true to the Jeffersonian principles, and in opposition to the supporters of congressional authority defended the rights and free play of the individual states. And the Republicans were those who wished to exalt beyond any other the authority of the Federal Government. This is the key to everything which has since come to pass. At the last presidential elections there were three great party issues — the tariff, the currency, and the question of expansion. In deciding on all three of these points, the parties have conformed to their old principles. Free-trade versus protective tariff was not a new bone of contention. Jefferson's party had urged free-trade with all the nations of the earth at the very beginning of the century, and, of course, a decentralizing party which likes as little supervision and paternalism as possible, will always concede to the individual his right to buy what he requires where it will cost the least. The Democrats did not oppose a tariff for revenue, to help defray the public expenses, but they objected on principle to that further tariff which was laid on goods in order to keep the prices of them high and so to protect home industries. The centralists, that is, the whigs or the Republicans, on the contrary, by their supreme confidence in the one national government, had early been led to expect from it a certain protection of the national market and some regulation of the economic struggle for existence. And protective tariff was one of the main planks in their platform early in the century.

It is clear, once more, that the anti-centralists had a direct and natural interest in the small man, his economic weaknesses and burdens; every member of society must have equal right and opportunity to work out his career. It does not contradict this that the Democrats believed in slavery. In the Southern states the negro had come in the course of generations to be looked on as property, as a possession to be held and utilized in a special way, and any feeling of personal responsibility was of a patriarchal and not a political nature. The peculiarly democratic element in the position taken was the demand that the slavery question be left with the separate states to decide. As soon as fellow citizens were concerned, the anti-centralist party held true to its principles of looking out for the members on the periphery of society. In this way the party favoured the progressive income tax, and has always espoused any cause which would assist the working-man against the superior force of protected capital, or the farmer against the machinations of the stock market.

The exaggerated notions as to the silver standard of currency originated outside of the Democratic party, and have intrinsically nothing to do with democracy. But as soon as a considerable part of the people from one cause or another began really to believe that nothing but a silver currency could relieve the condition of the artisans and farmers, it became logically necessary for the party which opposed centralization to adopt and foster this panacea, however senseless it might seem to the more thoughtful elements within the party. And it was no less necessary for the party which upholds federal authority to oppose unconditionally anything which would endanger the coinage and credit of the country. The gold standard is specifically a Republican doctrine only when it is understood to repudiate and oppose all risky experimenting with bi-metallism.

In the new imperialistic movement, on the other hand, it was the Democrats who were put on the defensive. Any one who leans toward individualism must instinctively lean away from militarism, which makes for strength at the centre; from aggressive movements to annex new lands, whereby the owners are deprived of their natural rights to manage their own affairs, and from any meddling with international politics, for this involves necessarily increased discretionary powers for the central government. It is not that the Democrats care less for the greatness of their fatherland, but they despise that jingo patriotism which abandons the traditions of the country by bringing foreign peoples into subjection. It is left for the centralists to meet the new situation squarely, undertake new responsibilities, and convince the nation that it is strong and mature enough now to play a decisive rôle in the politics of the world. And thus the two great parties are by no manner of means two rudderless derelicts carried hither and thither by the currents ever since the Civil War, but, rather, great three-deckers following without swerve their appointed courses.

The parties have sometimes been distinguished as conservative and liberal, but this is rather a reminiscence of conditions in Europe. Both of the parties are really conservative, as results from both the American character and the nature of the party organization. Even in the most radical Democratic gathering the great appeal is never made in behalf of some advantageous or brilliant innovation but on the grounds of adherence to the old, reliable, and well-nigh sacred party principles. If either party is at present departing from the traditions of the past, it is the Republican party, which has always figured as the more conservative of the two. Yet such a distinction is partly true, since the centralists in conformity to their principles must specially maintain the Federal authority and precedent, while the Democratic party is more naturally inclined to give ear to discontented spirits, clever innovators, and fantastic reformers, lest some decentralizing energy should be suppressed. So the Republican party gains a fundamental and cheerful complacence with the prevailing order of things, while the Democratic party, even when it is in power, can never come quite to rest. The contrast is not that between rich and poor; the Democratic party has its quota of millionaires, and the Republican has, for instance, in its negro clientage many of the poorest in the land. But the Republican party is filled with self-satisfaction and the consciousness of power and success, while the Democrats are forever measuring the actual according to an ideal which can never be realized. Like all centralists, the Republicans are essentially opportunists and matter-of-fact politicians; and the Democrats, like all anticentralists, are idealists and enthusiasts. It has been well said that a Democratic committee is conducted like a debating club, but a Republican like a meeting of the stockholders in a corporation.

These facts clearly hint at a certain personal factor which influences the citizen's allegiance to one or other of the parties. In meeting a man on a journey one has very soon the impression, though one may often be mistaken, as to what party he belongs to, although he may not have spoken a word about politics. But more distinctive than the personal bias are the groupings by classes and regions which have come about during the course of time. In the North and West the Republicans have the majority among the educated classes, but in the South the educated people are Democrats, particularly since the negro population there holds to the old abolition party, so that the whites are the more ready to be on the other side. The lower classes are moved by the most diverse motives; the farmer is inclined to be Republican and the artisan of the cities Democratic; Protestants are more often Republicans and Catholics Democrats, a partition which began with the early identification of the Puritan clergy of

New England with the Republican party. This resulted in an affiliation of Catholicism and Democracy which has had very important consequences, particularly in municipal politics; the Irish, who are invariably Catholics, vote with the Democratic party. The Germans and Swedes, specially in the West, are mostly Republicans. In these ways the most complicated combinations have come about, particularly in the Middle West, where many of the larger states are always uncertain at election time. In the elections of the State of New York, the Democrats and Republicans have been alternately successful. Very often the capital city votes differently from the rural districts, as in Massachusetts, which is a stalwart Republican state, although Boston, owing to the Irish population, is Democratic.

* * * * * * * * * * *

These considerations as to the groupings of the party adherents bring us directly to our second question — who are the party politicians? We have aimed to refute the assertion that the parties are without their principles, but there is the further assertion that the politicians are without principles. In asking whether politics are really in the hands of unscrupulous men, one should first ascertain whether there are any honourable motives which would lead a man to devote himself thereto. And it appears that nowhere else are there such powerful inducements for a conscientious man to go into politics. First of all there is the best possible motive, the wish to see one's country governed according to one's own ideas of justice and progress, and the desire to work in this way for the honour, security, and welfare of the nation. Any one who has witnessed the American presidential elections once or twice will be convinced that the overwhelming majority of voters casts its votes in a truly ethical spirit, although, of course, the moral feeling is now more, now less, profound. At times when technical matters are chiefly the order of the day, or at best matters of expediency, enthusiasm for a party victory has to be kept up in other ways; but when it comes to questions of the national solidarity and honour, or of justice and freedom, then really high ethical enthusiasm holds place before all other political motives. In fact, the keen party spirit of the American is rather in danger of making him feel a virtuous indignation against the opposing party, even in regard to purely technical issues, as if it had fallen into mere frivolity or been criminally irresponsible. And in this way the American is never at a loss for a moral stream of some sort to keep the political mill-wheel turning.

After patriotic enthusiasm come the economic and social motives which even the most high-flown idealist would not designate as corrupt. It is not only just, but it is actually the ideal of politics that every portion of the population, every class and calling, as well as every geographical section, should see its peculiar interests brought up for political debate. It is possible for an equilibrium of all existing forces to be reached only when all elements alike are aware of their chance to assert themselves. Nothing could be gained if agriculture were to become political sponsor for the industrial interests, or if industry were to assume the care and protection of agriculture. A due and proper emphasis by the respective interests of their own needs will always be an honourable and, for the public welfare, useful incentive to political efficiency. It is not to be doubted that in this way American politics have always induced millions of citizens to the liveliest participation. As we have seen, free-trade and protective tariff grew out of the chief demands of the two parties; but this does not prevent the same party opposition from standing in a way for the diverse and partly contradictory interests of Northern industry and Southern plantation life. Hence the parties are immediately interested in trade and commerce. In a similar way the interests of the West have been bound up in bi-metallism schemes, while the commercial integrity of the East depends on a gold currency. Legislation affecting trusts and banks and the policy of expansion touch some of the deepest economic problems, and summon all those concerned to come forward and play their part. The same holds true of social interests. The negro, struggling against legislation aimed directly at himself, seeks social protection through the Republican party, while the Irish, Swedes, and Russians also look for political recognition to advance their social interests.

Now these moral, social, and economic motives interest the citizen of every land in politics; but there are other considerations here in play, which, although no less honourable, figure less importantly in Germany for example. First of all stands loyalty to the traditions of one's party. The son joins the party of his father, and is true to it for life. In this way many are held in the party net who otherwise might not agree to its general tenets. In a country where there are many parties with only slight shades of difference, where, say, the national-liberals are only a step removed from the independents or the independent-conservatives, each new election period offers the voter a free choice between parties. But where there are only two camps a party loyalty is developed which leaves very much less to personal inclination, and makes possible a firm party discipline. Then the citizen may come to say of his party as of his fatherland, "It may be right or wrong, it is still my party." A man like Hoar may use all the force of his rhetoric to condemn imperialism and to stigmatize it as a crime, and he may leave no stone unturned to bring his own Republican party to abandon the imperialistic policy, and yet, if his recommendations are officially outvoiced, he will not falter in supporting the regular candidates of his party, imperialists though they be, as against the anti-imperialist Democratic candidates. The typical American will rather wait for his own party to take up and correct the evils which he most deplores than go over to the other party which may be already working for the same reforms.

To be sure, there are Americans who account this point of view narrow or even culpable, and who reserve the right of judging the programmes of both parties afresh each time and of casting their lot on the side which they find to be right. The example of Carl Schurz will be readily recalled, who in 1896 delivered notable speeches in favour of McKinley against Bryan, but came out in 1900 for Bryan as against McKinley. He was a Republican on the first occasion, because at that time the question of currency was in the foreground, and he thought it paramount to preserve the gold standard, while in the next election he went over to the Democrats because the question of expansion had come to the fore, and he preferred the short-sighted silver policy to the unrighteous programme of war and subjugation. The number of such independent politicians is not small, and among them are many of the finest characters in the land. Behind them comes the considerable class of voters who may be won over to either party by momentary considerations of business prosperity, by any popular agitation for the sake of being with the crowd, by personal sympathies or antipathies, or merely through discontent with the prevailing régime. If there were not an appreciable part of the people to oscillate in this way between the parties, the elections would fall out the same way from year to year, the result could always be told beforehand, and neither party would have any incentive to active effort; in short, political life would stagnate. Thus the citizens who owe no party allegiance but take sides according to the merits of the case are very efficient practically: in a way they represent the conscience of the country, and yet three-fourths of the population would look on their political creed with suspicion, or, indeed, contempt. They would insist that the American system needs great parties, and that parties cannot be practically effective if there is no discipline in their organization — that is, if the minority of their membership is not ready to submit cheerfully to the will of the majority. If any man wishes to make reforms, he should first set about to reform his party. Whereas, if on every difference of opinion he goes over to the enemy's camp, he simply destroys all respect for the weight of a majority, and therewith undermines all democracy. It is as if a party, which found itself defeated at the polls, should start a revolution; whereas it is the pride of the American people to accept without protest the government which the majority has chosen. And so party allegiance is taken as the mark of political maturity, and the men who hold themselves superior to their parties are influential at the polls, but in the party camps they see their arguments held in light esteem. They are mistrusted by the popular mind.

In addition to all this the American happens to be a born politician. On the one hand the mere technique of politics fascinates him; every boy is acquainted with parliamentary forms, and to frame amendments or file demurrers appeals vastly to his fancy. It is an hereditary trait. On the other hand, he finds in the party the most diversified social environment which he may hope to meet. Aside from his church, the farmer or artisan finds his sole social inspiration in his party, where the political assemblies and contact with men of like opinions with himself make him feel vividly that he is a free and equal participant in the mighty game. Moreover, local interests cannot be separated from those of the state, nor these from the affairs of the whole country; for the party lines are drawn even in the smallest community, and dominate public discussions whether great or small, so that even those who feel no interest in national questions but are concerned only with local reforms, perhaps the school system or the police board, find themselves, nevertheless, drawn into the machinery of the great national parties.

Yet another motive induces the American to enter politics, a motive which is neither good nor bad. Party politics have for many an aspect of sport, as can be easily understood from the Anglo-Saxon delight in competition and the nearly equal strength of the two parties. All the marks of sport can be seen in the daily calculations and the ridiculous wagers which are made, and in the prevalent desire to be on the side of the winner. Not otherwise can the parades, torch-light processions, and other demonstrations be explained, which are supposed to inspire the indifferent or wavering with the conviction that this party and not the other will come out victorious.

The American, it is seen, has ample inducements to engage in the activities of party, from the noblest patriotic enthusiasm down to the mere excitement over a sport. And it is doubtless these various motives which sustain the parties in their activity and supply such an inexhaustible sum of energy to the nation's politics. By them the masses are kept busily turning the political wheels and so provided with a political schooling such as they get in no other country.

But we have seen that to enlist in the service of a political party means more than to discuss and vote conscientiously, to work on committees, or to contribute to the party treasury. Every detail of elections, local or national, in every part of the country, has to be planned and worked out by the party organization; and particularly in the matter of nomination of candidates by the members of the party, the work of arranging and agitating one scheme or another has become a veritable science, demanding far more than merely amateur ability. It must not be forgotten that in questions of a majority the American complacent good humour is put aside. The party caucuses are managed on such business-like methods that even in the most stormy debates the minutest points of expediency are kept well in mind. If the several interests are not represented with all that expertness with which an attorney at court would plead the cause of a client, their case is as good as lost. The managers have to study and know the least details, be acquainted with personal and local conditions, with the attitude of the press, of the officials, and of the other party leaders. Those members of the organization who conduct the large federal sections and so deal with more than local affairs, have to be at once lawyers, financiers, generals, and diplomats. Shrewd combinations have to be devised in which city, state, and national questions are nicely interwoven and matters of personal tact and abstract right made to play into each other; and these arrangements must be carried out with an energy and discretion that will require the undivided attention of any man who hopes to succeed at the business. Thus the American conditions demand in the way of organization and agitation such an outlay of strength as could not be expected of the citizens of any country, except in times of war, unless in addition to patriotic motives some more concrete inducements should be offered. And thus there are certain advantages and rewards accruing to the men who devote themselves to this indispensable work.

The first of these inducements is, presumably, honour. The personal distinctions which may be gotten in politics cannot easily be estimated after German standards. There are both credits and debits which the German does not suspect. To the former belongs the important fact that all offices up to the very highest can be reached only by the way of party politics. The positions of president, ambassadors, governors, senators, ministers, and so forth are all provided with salaries, but such inadequate ones as compared with the scale of living which is expected of the incumbents that no one would even accept any of these positions for the sake of the remuneration. In most cases an actual financial sacrifice has to be made, since the holding of office is not an assured career, but rather a brief interruption of one's private business. It is to be remembered, moreover, that a civil office carries no pension. And thus it frequently happens that a man ends his political career because he has spent all of his money, or because he feels it a duty to secure his financial position. Reed, who was in a way the most important Republican leader, gave up his position as speaker of the House of Representatives and broke off all political entanglements in order to become partner in a law firm. In the same way Harrison, on retiring from the presidency, resumed his practice of law, and Day resigned the secretaryship of state because his financial resources were not adequate. An ambassador hardly expects his salary to be more than a fraction of his expenditures. Now this circumstance need excite no pity, since there is an abundance of rich men in America, and the Senate has been nicknamed the Millionaire's Club; but it should serve to show that honour, prestige, and influence are the real incentives to a political career, and not the "almighty dollar," as certain detractors would have one believe. There are persons, to be sure, who have gotten money in politics, but they are few and insignificant beside those who have been in politics because they had money. The political career in America thus offers greater social rewards than in Germany, where the holding of office is divorced from politics, where the government is an hereditary monarchy and strongly influenced by an hereditary aristocracy, and where even the merest mayor or city councilman must have his appointment confirmed by the government.

Since the social premiums of the political life are so many and so important it may seem astonishing that this career does not attract all the best strength of the nation, and even embarrass the parties with an overplus of great men. The reasons why it does not are as follows: Firstly, distinctions due merely to office or position have not in a democratic country the same exclusive value which they have with an aristocratic nation. The feeling of social equality is much stronger, and all consideration and regard are paid to a man's personal qualities rather than to his station. A land which knows no nobility, titles, or orders is unschooled in these artificial distinctions, and while there is some social differentiation it is incomparably less. One looks for one's neighbour to be a gentleman, and is not concerned to find out what he does during office hours. The reputation and influence which are earned in political life are much more potent than any honour deriving from position. But here is found a second retarding factor: the structure of American politics does not conduce to fame. In Germany the party leaders are constantly in the public eye; they deliver important speeches in the Reichstag or the Landtag, and their oratorical achievements are read in every home. In America the debates of Congress are very little read, and those of the state legislatures almost not at all; the work of government is done in committees. The speeches of the

Senate are the most likely to become known, and yet no one becomes famous in America through his parliamentary utterances, and public sentiment is seldom influenced by oratorical performances at Washington.

In the third place, every American party officer must have served in the ranks and worked his way up. It is not every man's business to spend his time with the disagreeable minutiæ of the local party organization; and even if he does not dislike the work, he may well object to the society with which he is thrown in these lower political strata. A fourth and perhaps the principal item comes in here. In its lowest departments politics can be made to yield a pecuniary return, and for this reason attracts undesirable and perhaps unscrupulous elements whose mere co-operation is enough to disgust better men and to give the purely political career a lower status in public opinion than might be expected in such a thoroughly political community.

This question of the pecuniary income from political sources is even by the Americans themselves seldom fairly treated. There are three possible sources of income. Firstly, the representatives of the people are directly remunerated; secondly, the politician may obtain a salaried federal, state, or municipal office; and, thirdly, he may misuse his influence or his office unlawfully to enrich himself. It is a regrettable fact that the first source of revenue attracts a goodly number into politics. It is not the case with Congress, but many a man sits in the state legislatures who is there only for the salary, while in reality the monetary allowance was never meant as an inducement but as a compensation, since otherwise many would be deterred altogether from politics. But the stipend is small and attracts no one who has capacity enough to earn more in a regular profession. It attracts, however, all kinds of forlorn and ill-starred individuals, who then scramble into local politics and do their best to bring the calling into disrepute. And yet, after all, these are so small a fraction of the politicians as to be entirely negligible. There would be much worse evils if the salaries were to be abolished. There are others who make money in criminal ways, and of course they have ample opportunity for deception, theft, and corruption in both town and country. Their case is not open to any difference of opinion. It is easy for a member of the school committee to get hold of the land on which the next school-house is to be built, and to sell it at a profit; or for a mayor to approve a street-car line which is directly for the advantage of his private associates; or for a captain of police to accept hush money from unlawful gambling houses. Everybody knows that this sort of thing is possible, and that the perpetrators can with difficulty be convicted, yet they occasionally are and then get the punishment which they deserve. But this is no more a part of the political system than the false entries of an absconding cashier are a part of banking. And even if every unproved suspicion of dishonesty were shown to be well founded, the men who so abuse their positions would be as much the exceptions as are those who enter politics for the sake of the salary. We shall return later to these excrescences.

Of the three sources of income from politics, only one remains to be considered — the non-legislative but salaried offices with which the politician may be rewarded for his pains. This is the first and surest means by which the party keeps its great and indispensable army of retainers contentedly at work. And here the familiar evils enter in which are so often held up for discussion in Germany. An American reformer, in criticizing the condition of the parties, is very apt not to distinguish between the giving out of offices to professional politicians as rewards and the later corrupt using of these offices by their incumbents. And as soon as the politician receives an income from the public treasury, the reformer will cry "stop thief." The so-called "spoils system," by which the federal offices in the patronage of the President are distributed to those who have worked hardest in the interests of the victorious party, will occupy our attention when we come to the political problems of the day. We shall have then to mention the advantages and disadvantages of civil service reform. But it must be said right here that, however commendable this reform movement may be in many respects, and in none more than in the increased efficiency which it has effected in the public service, nevertheless the spoils system cannot be called dishonourable, and no one should characterize professional politicians as abominable reprobates because they are willing to accept civil positions as rewards from the party for which they have laboured.

It is a usage which has nothing to do with the corrupt exploitation of office, and the German who derives from it the favourite prejudice against the political life of the United States must not suppose that he has thereby justified the German conception of office. Quite on the contrary, no one ever expects the German government to bestow offices, titles, or orders on members of the political opposition, to confirm, for instance, an independent for the position of Landrat or a social democrat for city councillor, while co-operation in the plans of the government never goes unrewarded. Above all, a German never looks on his official salary as a sort of present taken from the public treasury, but as the ordinary equivalent of the work which he does, while the American has a curious conception of the matter quite foreign to the German, which is the ground for his contempt of the "spoils system." To illustrate by a short example: a state attorney who had been elected to the same office time after time, was asked to renew his candidacy at the coming elections. But he declined to do so, and explained that he had been supported for twenty years out of the public funds, and that it was therefore high time for him to earn his own living by the ordinary practice of law. A German cannot understand this conception, traditional though it is in America, but he can easily see that the man who shares such views as to public salaries will naturally consider it an act of plunder when the party in power distributes the best public posts to its own followers.

The case would be somewhat different if the politicians who step into offices were essentially incapable or indolent, though this is aside from the principle in question. Germans have recently become used to seeing a general or a merchant become minister. In America it is a matter of course that a capable man is qualified, with the aid of technically trained subordinates, for any office. And no one denies that politicians make industrious office-holders. And yet the same remarkable charge is always made, that the holder of an office receives a gift from the public chest.

These considerations are not meant as an argument against civil service reform, which is supported by the best men of both parties, although they are not exactly the most zealous party "heelers." But the superficial assertion must be refuted, that the spoils system shows lack of morality in party politics. No unprejudiced observer would find anything improper in the attitude of those who endure the thankless and arduous labours imposed by the party for the sake of a profitable position in the government service. It would be equally just to reproach the German official with lack of character because he rises to a high position in the service of the government. If this were the true idea, Grover Cleveland, who has done more than any other president for the cause of civil service reform, could be said actually to have favored the spoils system. In an admirable essay on the independence of the executive, he says:—

"I have no sympathy with the intolerant people who, without the least appreciation of the meaning of party work and service, superciliously affect to despise all those who apply for office as they would those guilty of a flagrant misdemeanor. It will indeed be a happy day when the ascendancy of party principles and the attainment of wholesome administration will be universally regarded as sufficient rewards of individual and legitimate party service. . . . In the meantime why should we indiscriminately hate those who seek office? They may not have entirely emancipated themselves from the belief that the offices should pass with party victory, but in all other respects they are in many instances as honest, as capable, and as intelligent as any of us."

There are such strong arguments for separating public office from the service of party, that every reformer is amply justified if on his native soil he stigmatizes the present usage as corrupt. But the representation that all professional politicians are despicable scamps because they work for their party in the hope of being preferred for public office, is unjust and misleading when it is spread abroad in other countries. Abuses there are, to be sure, and the situation is such as to attract swarms of worthless persons. It is true, moreover, that even in the higher strata of professional politics there is usually less of broad-minded statesmanship than of ingenious compromise and clever exploitation of the opposing party's weaknesses and of popular whims and prejudices. Petty methods are often more successful than enlightened ones, and cunning men have better chances than those who are more high-minded. In the lower strata, moreover, where it is important to cajole the voting masses into the party fold, it may be inevitable that men undertake and are rewarded for very questionable services. Nevertheless the association of party and office is not intrinsically improper.

In the same category of unjust reproaches, finally, belongs the talk over the money paid into the party treasury. It is, of course, true that the elections both great and small eat up vast sums of money; the mountains of election pamphlets, the special trains for candidates who journey from place to place in order to harangue the people at every rural railway station, from the platform of the coach — Roosevelt is said at the last election in this way to have addressed three million persons — the banquet-halls and bands of music, and the thousand other requisites of the contest are not to be had for nothing. It is taken as a matter of course that the supporters of the party are taxed, and of course just those will be apt to contribute who look for further material benefit in case of victory; it is also expected that, of course, the larger industries will help the propaganda of the high-tariff party, that the silver mine owners will generously support bi-metallism, and that the beer brewers will furnish funds when it is a question between them and the Prohibitionists. But in the endeavour to hurt the opposing party some persons make such contributions a ground of despicable slander. Any one who considers the matter really without prejudice will see not only that the American party politics are a necessary institution, but also that they are infinitely cleaner and better than the European newspaper reader will ever be inclined to believe.

CHAPTER THREE

The President

THE President of the United States is elected by the people every four years. He may be re-elected and, so far as the Constitution provides, he may hold the first position in the land for life, by terms always of four years at a time. A certain unwritten law, however, forbids his holding office for more than two terms. George Washington was elected for two terms, and after him Thomas Jefferson, James Madison, James Monroe, Andrew Jackson, Abraham Lincoln, Ulysses Grant, Grover Cleveland, and William McKinley; that is, nine out of twenty presidents have received this distinction. No president has served a third term of office, because since Washington declined to be nominated for a third time the conservative sense of the Americans has cherished the doctrine that no man should stand at the helm of the nation longer than eight years.

At the present day it is urged from many sides that the provisions of the Constitution ought to be changed. It is said that the frequently recurring presidential elections, with the popular excitement which they involve during the months immediately preceding, are an appreciable disturbance to economic life and that the possibility of being re-elected is too apt to make the President in the first term of office govern his actions with an eye to his second election. It is proposed, therefore, that every President shall be elected for six years and that re-election shall be forbidden by the Constitution. Experience of the past, however, hardly speaks for such a plan. The inclination shown by the President to yield to popular clamours or the instances of his party has been very different with different presidents, but on the whole it has not been noticeably greater in the first than in the second term of office. More especially, the disadvantages which come from the excitement over elections are certainly made up for by the moral advantage which the act of election brings to the people. The presidential election is a period of considerable reflection and examination of the country's condition, and everybody is worked up to considerable interest; and the more changeable the times are so much the more rapidly new problems come up. Therefore there should be no thought of putting the decisive public elections, with their month-long discussions, at further intervals apart.

The most important duties and prerogatives of the President involve foreign as well as domestic affairs, and of the latter the most important concern the administration; a less important, although by no means an insignificant, part of his duties relates to legislation. The President is commander-in-chief of the army and of the navy, and with the approval of a majority of the Senate he appoints ambassadors, consuls, judges of the Supreme Court, and all the higher federal officials. Subject to the ratification of two-thirds of the Senate, he concludes treaties with foreign powers and regulates diplomatic relations. He has, moreover, the right to send back inside of ten days, with his veto, any bill which Congress has passed, and in this case the bill can become law only by being once more voted on by Congress and receiving in both houses a two-third's majority. The President has the power to convene both houses in special sessions, and is expected to send messages to both houses when they meet, in which he describes the political situation of the country and recommends new measures. In addition to this he has the right of pardon and the right to afford protection to individual states against civil violence, if they cannot themselves quell the disturbance.

Such are the principal features of the presidential office, and it is clear that here as everywhere in American civil law the spirit of precaution has tried from the outset to limit the possibilities of abuse. Although he is commander-in-chief of the army, the President has not the right to declare war, this right being given to Congress. The President negotiates with foreign representatives and signs all treaties, but these are not valid until the Senate has approved them with a two-thirds vote. He nominates government officials, but once again only with the sanction of the Senate. The President convenes Congress and recommends matters for its legislative consideration, but the President cannot, like the German Government, lay bills before Congress for its ratification. While the President sends his message to Congress his ministers have not, as in Germany, a seat in parliament, and cannot, therefore, in the debates actively support the President's policy.

The President is authorized to veto any bill that is passed through Congress, but his veto is not final since the bill can still become a law if Congress is sufficiently of one accord to override his veto. Therefore a whimsical or arbitrary president would find small scope for his vagaries so long as he keeps within his powers, while if he exceeds them he can be impeached, like a king under old English law. The House of Representatives can at any time file complaint against the President if he is suspected of treason or corruption or any other crime. In such case the Senate, under the chairmanship of a judge of the Supreme bench, constitutes a court of trial which is empowered to depose the President from office. Up to the present time but one president, Andrew Johnson, has been impeached, and he was acquitted. The seditionary ambition of a man who should try to gain complete control, to overthrow the Constitution, and at the head of the army, or of the populace, or, as might be more likely, of the millionaires, to institute a monarchy, would have no chance of success. Neither a Napoleon nor a Boulanger would be possible in America.

In spite of these provisions, it is to be observed that tremendous power is in the hands of this one man. Thousands and thousands of officials appointed by his predecessor can be removed by a stroke of his pen, and none can take their places except those whom he nominates. And he can put a barrier before any law such as Congress could only in exceptional cases ride over. Cleveland, for instance, who to be sure made the freest use of his authority in this respect, vetoed more than three hundred bills, and only twice did Congress succeed in setting aside his veto. The President may negotiate with foreign powers up to the point where a loyal and patriotic Congress has hardly any choice but to acquiesce. The President can virtually force Congress to a declaration of war, and if insurrection breaks out in any state he can at his pleasure employ the federal troops on behalf of one or the other faction, and when war has once been declared the presidential authority grows hourly in importance. The army and navy stand under his direction, and since the Constitution makes him responsible for the maintenance of law and order in the country he becomes virtually dictator in case of an insurrection. Bryce says very justly that Abraham Lincoln exercised more power than any man in England since Oliver Cromwell, and the anti-imperialistic papers of America always assert that in their Philippine policy McKinley and Roosevelt have taken on themselves more authority than any European monarch, excepting the Czar, could acquire.

In two respects the President is more important as compared with the representatives of the people, even in times of peace, than the king of England or the President of France. Firstly, his cabinet is entirely independent of the voice of parliament, and it has often been the case that while a majority in Congress sharply opposed the party policy of the President, this has not influenced the composition of his cabinet. The cabinet ministers are the representatives of the presidential policy, and they do not even take part in the doings of Congress.

Secondly, the President is not less but rather more than Congress a representative of the people. A monarch who takes up a position against the parliament thereby antagonizes the people. The President of France is elected by the people, but only through their parliamentary representatives; the chambers elect him, and therefore he is not an independent authority. The President of the United States, on the other hand, is in his own person a symbol of the collective will of the people, as opposed to the different members of Congress, which is of diverse composition and chosen on more local issues. There is moral authority, therefore, vested in the President. He is the true will of the people and his veto is their conscience. It is almost astonishing that a Republican democracy should have put such tremendous power into the hands of a single man. It is the more striking inasmuch as the Declaration of Independence related at length the sins of the English monarch. But we must bear in mind that the framers of the Constitution had to make a new and dangerous experiment, wherein they were much more afraid of that so far unknown and incalculable factor, the rule of the people, than the power of that single person whose administrative possibilities they had, in the colonial days, been able to observe in the governors of the several states. These had been diminutive but, on the whole, encouraging examples. Before all else the great and incomparable George Washington, the popular, dashing, and yet cautious aristocrat, had presided at the deliberations in which the Constitution was discussed, and had himself stood tangibly before the popular mind as the very ideal of a president.

Thus the President stands with tremendous powers at the helm of the nation. Who has sought him out for this position from the hundreds of thousands, whose hot ambition has led them to dream of such a distinction, and who has finally established him in this highest elective office on the face of the earth? The Constitution makes no other provision for the selection of a candidate than that he shall have been born in the land, that he shall be at least thirty-five years old, and shall have resided at least fourteen years in this his native country. On the other hand, the Constitutional provisions for his election are highly complicated, much more so indeed than the circumstances really call for. In fact, while the electoral procedures still comply with the wording of the original Constitution, actual conditions have so changed since the establishment of the Union that the prescribed machinery is not only partly unnecessary, but in some cases even works in opposition to what had been originally intended, and inconsistently with itself. The law requires, merely to mention the main point, that every state shall elect by popular vote a certain number of men who are called electors, and that a majority of the electors shall choose the President. For each state the number of electors is the same as that of the representatives which it sends to both houses of Congress together; it depends, therefore, on the number of inhabitants. Out of the 447 electors, 36 come from the State of New York, 32 from Pennsylvania, 24 from Illinois, 23 from Ohio, 15 from Massachusetts, but only 4 from Colorado, Florida, or New Hampshire; and only 3 from Delaware, Idaho, North Dakota, Utah, and several others. In case the vote of the electors should give no absolute majority to any candidate, the House of Representatives has to elect the President from among the three candidates who have received the greatest number of electoral votes.

The intention of the men who framed the Constitution in making these roundabout electoral provisions is clear enough; the election was not meant to be made directly by the people. When in the first discussions of the Constitution it was suggested that the President be elected directly by the people, some of the framers called the scheme chimerical and others called it impracticable. Indeed, some even doubted whether the people would be competent to choose the electors since, it was said, they would know too little about the persons and so would be liable to grave errors. This mistrust went so far, it is said, that leaving the election of the highest executives directly to the people seemed as unnatural as asking a blind man to match colors. The first plan which was at all approved by the Assembly was that Congress should elect the President; and not until later did it adopt the system of electors. It was hoped that for the electoral college the people would select the best, most experienced, and most cautious men of the country, and that these men should be left quite free to choose the highest executive as carefully and conscientiously as possible: and so it really happened when the electors met for the first time and fixed unanimously on George Washington.

But the situation is somewhat changed to-day: for a hundred years it has been the case that the electors have inevitably been deprived of all free choice. They are as passive as a printed ballot. They are no longer elected in order to come to a decision as to the best President, but merely to vote for this or that special candidate as designated, and for a hundred years not a single elector has disappointed this expectation. Thus the election of the President is practically accomplished on the day in November when the electors are voted for. McKinley defeated Bryan for the Presidency on the ninth of November, 1900, although no elector had officially voted for either one or the other; nor would he have a chance to vote until the first day of January, when he was mechanically to deposit his ballot.

The indirect election prescribed by the Constitution has therefore become to all intents and purposes a direct one, and the whole machinery of electors is really superfluous. It may, indeed, be said to have become contradictory in itself.

Since the original intention to make an electoral college of the best citizens has been frustrated by the popular spirit of self-determination, the electoral apparatus can have to-day no other significance than to give expression to the voice of the majority.

But now just this it is in the power of the electoral system completely to suppress. Let us suppose that only two candidates are in question. If the election were simply a direct one, of course that candidate would win who received the most votes; but with electors this is not the case, because the number of electors who are pledged to vote for these two candidates need not at all correspond to the number of ballots cast on the two sides. If in the State of New York, for instance, three-fifths of the population are for the first candidate and two-fifths for the second, the three-fifths majority determines the whole list of 36 electors for the first candidate, and not an elector would be chosen for the other. Now it can very well happen that a candidate in those states in which he secures all the electors will have small majorities, that is, his opponent will have large minorities, while his opponent in the states which vote for him will have large majorities; and in this way the majority of electors will be pledged for that candidate who has received actually the smaller number of votes. It is a fact that both Hayes in 1877 and Harrison in 1889 were constitutionally elected for the Presidency by a minority of votes.

While in form the voters choose only the electors from their state, nevertheless these ballots thus actually count for a certain candidate. At the last election 292 electors voted for McKinley, and 155 for Bryan, while for the McKinley electors 832,280 more votes were cast than for the Bryan electors. We have already seen how it is that the best man will no longer, as in Washington's time, be unequivocally elected by the people, and why, although a unanimous choice of President has not taken place since Washington's time, nevertheless no more than two candidates are ever practically in question. It was for this that we have discussed the parties first. The parties are the factor which makes it impossible for a President to be elected without a contest, and which, as early as 1797, when the successor of Washington had to be nominated, divided the people in two sections, the supporters of Jefferson and of Adams. At the same time, however, the parties prevent the division from going further, and bring it about that this population of millions of people compactly organizes itself for Presidential elections in only two groups, so that although never less than two, still never more than two candidates really step into the arena.

For both great parties alike, with their central and local committees, with their professional politicians, with their leaders and their followers, whether engaging in politics out of interest or in hope of gain, as an ideal or as sport — for all alike comes the great day when the President is to be elected. For years previous the party leaders will have combined and dissolved and speculated and intrigued, and for years the friends of the possible candidates have spoken loudly in the newspapers, since here, of course, not only the election but also the nomination of the candidate depends on the people. Although the election is in November, the national conventions for nominating the party candidates come generally in July. Each state sends its delegation, numbering twice as many as the members of Congress from that state, and each delegation is once more duly elected by a convention of representatives chosen by the actual voters out of their party lists. In these national conventions the great battles of the country are fought, that is, within the party, and here the general trend of national politics is determined. It is the great trial moment for the party and the party heroes. At the last election McKinley and Bryan were the opposing candidates, and it is interesting to trace in their elections by the respective conventions two great types of party decision.

McKinley had grown slowly in public favour; he was the accomplished politician, the interesting leader of Congress, the sympathetic man who had no enemies. When the Republican convention met at Chicago, in 1888, he was a member of the delegation from Ohio and was pledged to do his utmost for the nomination of John Sherman. The ballots were cast five different times and every time no one candidate was found to have a majority. On the sixth trial one vote was cast for McKinley, and the announcement of this vote created an uproar. A sudden shifting of the opinions took place amid great acclamation, and the delegations all went over to him. He jumped up on a stool and called loudly through the hall that he should be offended by any man who voted for him since he himself had been pledged to vote for Sherman. Finally a compromise was found in Benjamin Harrison. At the convention in Minneapolis four years later McKinley was chairman, and once more the temptation came to him. The opponents of Harrison wished to oppose his re-election by uniting on the Ohio statesman, and again it was McKinley himself who turned the vote this time in favour of Harrison. His own time came finally in 1896. In the national convention at St. Louis 661 votes were cast in the first ballot for McKinley, while 84 were cast for Thomas Reed, 61 for Quay, 58 for Morton, and 35 for Allison. And when, in 1900, the national convention met in Philadelphia, 926 votes were straightway cast for McKinley, and none opposing. His was the steady, sure, and deserved rise from step to step through tireless exertions for his party and his country.

Bryan was a young and unknown lawyer, who had sat for a couple of years in the House of Representatives like any other delegate, and had warmly upheld bi-metallism. At the Democratic national convention at Chicago in 1896 almost nobody knew him. But it was a curious crisis in the Democratic party. It had been victorious four years previous in its campaign for Cleveland against Harrison, but the party as such had enjoyed no particular satisfaction. The self-willed and determined Cleveland, who had systematically opposed Congress tooth and nail, had fallen out with his party and nowhere on the horizon had appeared a new leader. And after a true statesman like Cleveland had come to grief, the petty politicians, who had neither ideas nor a programme, came to their own. Every one was looking for a strong personality when Bryan stepped forth to ingratiate himself and his silver programme in the affections of his party. His arguments were not new, but his catch-words were well studied, and here at last stood a fascinating personality with a forceful temperament which was all aglow, and with a voice that sounded like the tones of an organ. And when he cried out, "You must not nail humanity to a cross of gold," it was as if an omen had appeared. He became at once the Democratic candidate for the Presidency, and six months later six and one-half million votes were cast for him against the seven million for McKinley. Nor did the silver intoxication succumb to its first defeat. When the Democrats met again in 1900, all the endeavours of those who had adhered to a gold currency were seen to be futile. Once again the silver-tongued Nebraskan was carried about in triumph, and not until its second defeat did the Democratic party wake up. Bryanism is now a dead issue, and before the next Presidential election the programme of the Democratic party will be entirely reconstructed.

Thus the presidents of the nation grow organically out of the party structure, and the parties find in turn their highest duty and their reward in electing their President. The people organized in a party and the chief executive which that party elects belong necessarily together. They are the base and the summit. Nothing but death can overthrow the decision of the people; death did overthrow, indeed, the last decision after a few months, in September, 1901, when the cowardly assassination accomplished by a Polish anarchist brought the administration of McKinley to an end. As the Constitution provides, the man whom the people had elected to the relatively insignificant office of Vice-President became master in the White House.

The Vice-Presidency is from the point of view of political logic the least satisfactory place in American politics. Very early in the history of the United States the filling of this office occasioned many difficulties, and at that time the provisions of the Constitution referring to it were completely worked over. The Constitution had originally said that the man who had the second largest number of votes for the Presidency should become Vice-President. This was conceived in the spirit of the time when the two-party system did not exist and when it was expected that the electors should not be restricted by the voting public in their choice of the best man. As soon, however, as the opposition between the two parties came into being, the necessary result of such provision was that the presidential candidate of the defeated party should become Vice-President, and therefore that President and Vice-President should always represent diametrically opposed tendencies. A change in the Constitution did away with this political impossibility. Each elector was instructed to deposit separate ballots for President and Vice-President, and that candidate became Vice-President who received the largest number of votes for that office, both offices being thus invariably filled by candidates of the same party.

In spite of this the position has developed rather unsatisfactorily for an obvious reason. The Constitution condemns the Vice-President, so long as the President holds office, to an ornamental inactivity. It is his duty to preside at sessions of the Senate, a task which he for the most part performs silently, and which has not nearly the political significance enjoyed by the Speaker of the House of Representatives. On the other hand, men still in the prime of life are almost always elected to the Presidency; the possibility is therefore almost always lost sight of that the President can die before the expiration of his four years' term of office. The result has been that less distinguished men, who have, nevertheless, served their parties, are usually chosen for this insignificant and passive rôle. The office is designed to be an honour and a consolation to them, and sometimes for one reason or another their candidacy is supposed otherwise to strengthen the outlook of the party. It is not accident that while in the several states the Lieutenant-Governor is very often the next man to be elected Governor, it has never so far happened that a Vice-President has been elected to the Presidency.

Now in the unexpected event of the President's death a man stands at the helm whom no one really wants to see there; and it has five times happened that the chief executive of the nation has died in office, and four times, indeed, only a few months after being installed, so that the Vice-President has had to guide the destinies of the country for almost four years. When Tyler succeeded to the place of Harrison in 1841, there arose at once unfavourable disputes with the Whig party, which had elected him. When, after the murder of Lincoln in 1865, Johnson took the reins, it was his own Republican party which regretted having elected this impetuous man to the Vice-Presidency; and when, in 1881, after the assassination of Garfield, his successor, Arthur, undertook the office, and filled it indeed by no means badly, considerable consternation was felt throughout the country when people saw that so ordinary a professional politician was to succeed Garfield, on whom the country had pinned its faith.

On the death of McKinley a Vice-President succeeded him toward whom, in one respect at least, the feeling was very different. If ever a man was born to become President that man was Theodore Roosevelt. Nevertheless, he had not been elected in expectation of becoming President, and at first the whole country felt once more that it was a case which had lain outside of all reasonable calculations. Roosevelt's friends had asked him to make a sacrifice and to accept a thankless office because they knew that his name on the ballot of the Republican party — for his Rough Rider reputation during the war was still fresh — would be pretty sure to bring about the election of McKinley. The opponents also of this strong and energetic young man, against his stoutest protestations, upheld his candidacy with every means in their power. Firstly because they wanted to get rid of him as Governor of the State of New York, where he made life too hard for the regular politicians, and secondly because they relied on the tradition that holding the Vice-Presidency would invalidate him as a Presidential candidate in 1904. Neither friends nor enemies had thought of such a possibility as McKinley's death. Roosevelt's friends had rightly judged; the hero of San Juan did bring victory to his party. His enemies, on the other hand, had entirely missed their mark not only on the outcome, but from the very beginning. Odell became Governor of New York, and quite unexpectedly he stood out even more stoutly against the political corruptionists. And, on the other hand, Roosevelt's impulsive nature quickly found ways to break the traditional silence of the Vice-President and to keep himself before the eyes of the world. There is no doubt that in spite of all traditions his incumbency would have been a preparation for the presidential candidacy. But when, through the crime committed at Buffalo, everything came out so differently from that which the politicians expected, it seemed to the admirers of Roosevelt almost like the tragic hand of fate; he had done his best to attain on his own account the Presidency, and now it came to him almost as the gift of chance. Only the next election may be expected to do him full justice.

The successive moments in his rapid rise are generally known. Roosevelt was born in New York in 1858, his father being a prosperous merchant and well-known philanthropist, and a descendant of an old Knickerbocker family. The son was prepared for college and went to Harvard, where he made a special study of history and political economy. After that he travelled in Europe, and when he was still only twenty-four years old, he plunged into politics. He soon obtained a Republican seat in the state legislature of New York, and there commenced his tireless fight for reform in municipal and state administration. In 1889 President Harrison appointed him Commissioner of the Civil Service, but he resigned this position in 1895 in order to become Chief of Police in New York. Only two years later he was once more called from municipal to national duties. He was appointed Assistant Secretary of the Navy. All this time his administrative duties did not interrupt his literary, historical, and scientific work. He had begun his career as an author with his studies in the history of the navy and his admirable biographies of American statesmen. When he was thirty years old he wrote the first part of his great work, "The Winning of the West," and often between the publication of his scientific works he published lesser books, describing his adventures as huntsman in the primeval wilderness, and later on volumes in which his social and political essays were collected.

Then the Spanish War arose and the Assistant Secretary could not bear to sit at his desk while others were moving to the field of battle. He gathered about him a volunteer regiment of cavalry, in which the dare-devil cow-punchers of the prairie rode side by side with the adventurous scions of the most distinguished families in Boston and New York. Roosevelt's friend, Wood, of the regular army, became Colonel in this soon-famous regiment, and Roosevelt himself Lieutenant-Colonel. A few days after they had successfully stormed the hill at San Juan, Wood became General and Roosevelt Colonel.

His native State of New York received him on his home-coming with general rejoicing, and he found himself a few months later Governor of the State. At Albany he showed tremendous energy, put through popular reforms, and fought against the encroachments of the industrial corporations. It had been his personal wish to be Governor for a second year, but this was denied him by the admirable doings of his Eastern enemies and Western admirers at the national convention of June, 1900, held in Pennsylvania, where he was forced to become candidate for the position of Vice-President. On the 14th of September, 1901, in Buffalo, he took the Presidential oath of office.

At that time a quiet anxiety for the future was mingled with the honest sorrow which the whole land felt for the death of McKinley. A nation which had been sunning itself in peace suddenly found itself under the leadership of an impulsive colonel of cavalry, who carried in his hand the banner of war. The nation was in the midst of an economic development which needed before everything else to have a mature and careful leader who was honoured and trusted by all classes, and who would be able to effect some work of reconciliation between them; when suddenly there stood in the place of a most conservative statesman an impetuous young man who was not intimately connected with industrial life, who had for a long time made himself unpopular with party politicians, and whom even his admirers in the land seemed hardly to trust on account of his hasty and determined impetuosity. Roosevelt had been envisaged by the masses, through the cinematograph of the press, in campaign hat and khaki uniform, just in the attitude of taking San Juan hill. Nearly everybody forgot that he had for a long time quietly carried on the exacting labours of Police Commissioner in the largest city of the country; and forgot how, from his first year of study at Harvard on, every day had been given to preparing himself for public service and for acquiring a thorough understanding of all the political, social, and economic problems which the country had to face; they forgot also that he had wielded the sword for only a few months, but the pen of the historian for about two decades. Roosevelt's first public utterance was a pledge to continue unchanged the peaceful policy of his predecessor and always to consider the national prosperity and honour. Still, people felt that no successor would be able to command that experience, maturity, and party influence which McKinley had had.

There have been differences of opinion, and, as was to be expected, complaints and criticisms have come from the midst of his own party. Yet any one who looks at his whole administration will see that in those first years Roosevelt won a more difficult and brilliant victory than he had won over the Spanish troops.

He had three virtues which especially overcame all small criticism. The people felt, in the first place, that a moral force was here at work which was more powerful than any mere political address or diplomatic subtlety. An immediate ethical force was here felt which owned to ideas above any party, and set inner ideals above merely outward success. Roosevelt's second virtue was courage. A certain purely ethical ideal exalted above all petty expediencies was for him not only the nucleus of his own creed, but was also his spring of action; and he took no account of personal dangers. Here was the key-note of all his speeches — it is not enough to approve of what is right, it is equally necessary to act for it fearlessly and unequivocally. Then he went on to his work, and if, indeed, in complicated political situations the President has had at times to clinch some points by aid of compromise, nevertheless the nation has felt with growing confidence that at no serious moment has he wavered a hair's breadth from the straight line of his convictions, and that he has had the courage to disregard everything but what he held to be right. And, thirdly, Roosevelt had the virtue of being sincere.

McKinley also had purposed to do right, but he had hardly an occasion for displaying great courage since so incomparably discreet a politician as he was could avoid every conflict with his associates, and he was ever the leader on highways which the popular humour had indicated. Thus the masses never felt that he was at bottom lacking in courage or that he always put off responsibility on others. The masses did, however, instinctively feel that McKinley's astute and kindly words were not always sincere; his words were often there to conceal something which was locked up behind his Napoleonic forehead. And now there succeeded him an enthusiast who brimmed over with plain expressions of what he felt, and whose words were so convincingly candid and so without reservation that every one had the feeling of being in the personal confidence of the President.

There was a good deal more besides his moral earnestness, his courage, and his frank honesty which contributed to Roosevelt's entire success. His lack of prejudice won the lower classes, and his aristocratic breeding and education won the upper, while the middle classes were enthusiastic over his sportsmanship. No President had been more unprejudiced or more truly democratic. He met the poor miner on the same footing as he met the mine owner; he invited the negro to the White House; he sat down and broke bread with the cow-boys; and when he travelled he first shook the sooty hand of the locomotive engineer before he greeted the gentlemen who had gathered about in their silk hats. And, nevertheless, he was in many years the first real aristocrat to become President. The changes in the White House itself were typical. This venerable Presidential dwelling had been, up to Roosevelt's time, in its inner arrangements a dreary combination of bare offices, somewhat crudely decorated private dwelling, and cheerless reception-halls. To-day it is a very proper palace, containing many fine works of art, and office-seekers no longer have access to the inner rooms. His predecessors, the Clevelands and Harrisons and McKinleys, had been, in fact, very respectable philistines. They had come from the middle classes of the country, which are in thought and feeling very different from that upper class which, up to a short time ago, had bothered itself less about practical politics than about general culture, literature, art, criticism, and broadly conceived industrial operations, combined with social high-life. This class, however, had begun at length to feel that it ought not to disdain to notice political abuses, to walk around the sea of troubles; but had begun to take up arms and by opposing end them. Aristocracy had too long believed in political mercenaries.

Roosevelt was the first to lift himself from these circles and become a great leader. Not alone the nobility of his character but also of his culture and traditions was shown in his entire habit of mind. Never in his speeches or writings has he cited that socially equalizing Declaration of Independence, and while his speeches at banquets and small gatherings of scholarly men have been incomparably more fascinating than his strenuous utterances to the voters, which he has made on his public tours, it has been often less the originality of his thoughts and still less the peculiarly taking quality of his delivery, than the evidences of ripe culture, which seem to pervade his political thought. Thus the smaller the circle to which he speaks the greater is his advantage; and in speaking with him personally on serious problems one feels that distinction of thought, breadth of historical outlook, and confidence in self have united in him to create a personality after the grand manner.

The impression which Roosevelt has made on his own country has not been more profound than his influence on the galaxy of nations. At the very hour when the United States by their economic and territorial expansion stepped into the circle of world powers, they had at their head a personality who, for the first time in decades, had been able to make a great, characteristic, and, most of all, a dramatic impression on the peoples of Europe. And if this hour was to be made the most of it was not enough that this leader should by his impulsiveness and self-will, by his picturesque gestures and effective utterance, chain the attention of the masses and excite all newspaper readers, but he must also win the sympathies of the keener and finer minds, and excite some sympathetic response in the heads of monarchies. A second Lincoln would never have been able to do this, and just this was what the moment demanded. The nation's world-wide position in politics needed some comparable expansion in the social sphere. Other peoples were to welcome their new comrades not only in the official bureau but also in the reception-room, and this young President had always at his command a graceful word, a tactful expedient, and a distinguished and hospitable address. He was, in short, quite the right man.

Any new person taking hold so firmly has to disturb a good many things; busied with so much, he must overturn a good deal which would prefer to be left as it was. The honest man has his goodly share of enemies. And it is not to be denied that Roosevelt has the failings of his virtues, and these have borne their consequences. Many national dangers, which are always to be feared from officials of Roosevelt's type, are largely obviated by the democratic customs of the country. He lives amid a people not afraid to tell him the whole truth, and every criticism reaches his ear. And there is another thing not less important: democracy forces every man into that line of activity for which the nation has elected him. A somewhat overactive mind like Roosevelt's has opinions on many problems, and his exceptional political position easily betrays one at first into laying exceptional weight on one's own opinions about every subject. But here the traditions of the country have been decisive; it knows no President for general enlightenment, but only a political leader whose private opinions outside politics are of no special importance. In this as in other respects Roosevelt has profited by experience. There is no doubt that when he came to the White House he underestimated the power of Senators and party leaders. The invisible obstructions, which were somehow hidden behind the scenes, have no doubt given him many painful lessons. In his endeavour to realize so many heartfelt convictions, he has often met with arbitrary opposition made simply to let the new leader feel that obstructions can be put in his way unless he takes account of all sorts of factors. But these warnings have really done him no harm, for Roosevelt was not the man to be brought by them into that party subserviency which had satisfied McKinley. They merely held him back from that reckless independence which is so foreign to the American party spirit, and which in the later years of Cleveland's administration had worked so badly. Indeed, one might say that the outcome has been an ideal synthesis of Cleveland's consistency and McKinley's power of adaptation.

For the fanatics of party Roosevelt has been, of course, too independent, while to the opponents of party he has seemed too yielding. Both of these criticisms have been made, in many different connections, since everywhere he has stood on a watch tower above the fighting lines of any party. When in the struggles between capital and labour he seriously took into account the just grievances of the working-man he was denounced as a socialist. And when he did not at once stretch out his hand to demolish all corporations he was called a servant of the stock exchange. When he appointed officials in the South without reference to their party allegiance, the Republicans bellowed loudly; and when he did not sanction the Southern outrages against the negro the Democrats became furious. When everything is considered, however, he has observed the maxim of President Hayes, "He best serves his party who serves his country best."

In this there has been another factor at work. Roosevelt may not have had McKinley's broad experience in legislative matters, nor have known the reefs and bars in the Congressional sea, but for the executive office, for the administration of civil service and the army and navy, for the solution of federal, civil, and municipal problems his years of study and travel have been an ideal preparation. Behind his practical training he has had the clear eye of the historian. The United States had their proverbial good luck when the Mephistos of the Republican party prevailed on the formidable Governor of New York to undertake the thankless office of Vice-President. If this nomination had gone as the better politicians wished it to go, the death of McKinley would have placed a typical politician at the helm instead of the best President which the country has had for many years.

* * * * * * * * * * *

The President is closely associated with the Cabinet, and he is entirely free in his choice of advisers. There is no question here of the influence of majorities on the composition of the ministry, as there is in England or France. In this way Cleveland, in his second term, had already announced by his choice of cabinet ministers that he should go his own ways regardless of the wire-pullers of the party. He gave the Secretaryship of War to his former private secretary; the position of Postmaster-General to his former partner in law; the Secretaryship of Justice to a jurist who had never taken any interest in politics. His Secretary of the Interior was a personal friend, and the Secretary of Foreign Affairs a man who shortly before had left the ranks of the Republican party to become a Cleveland Democrat. The Secretaryships of Commerce and the Treasury were the sole cabinet positions which were given to well-known party leaders. The very opposite was to have been expected from a man of McKinley's disposition. Even when he became the chief executive of the country he remained the devoted servant of his party, and just as his success was owing in large part to his sympathetic relations with all the important factions in Congress, so the success of his Cabinet was due to his having chosen none but men who had enjoyed for a long time the confidence of the party.

Roosevelt did at the outset an act of political piety when he left the Cabinet, for the time being, unchanged. It was at the same time a capital move toward reassuring public opinion, which had stood in fear of all sorts of surprises, owing to his impetuous temperament. Slowly, however, characteristic readjustments were made and a new cabinet office was created under his administration, the Secretaryship of Commerce and Labour. This was entrusted to Cortelyou, who had been the private secretary of two presidents, and who, through his tact, discretion, and industry, had contributed not a little to their practical success.

The highest minister in order of rank is the Secretary of State, who is the Minister for Foreign Affairs, and who, in the case that both the President and Vice-President are unable to complete their term of office, assumes the Presidency. He is responsible for the diplomatic and consular representation of the United States and he alone negotiates with representatives of foreign powers at Washington; moreover, it is through him that the President treats with the separate states of the Union. He publishes the laws passed by Congress and adds his signature to all of the President's official papers. He is, next to the President, so thoroughly the presiding spirit of the administration that it is hardly a mistake to compare him to the Chancellor of the German Empire. It happens at the moment that the present incumbent makes this comparison still more apt, since John Hay, the present Secretary of Foreign Affairs, resembles Count von Bülow in several ways. Both have been in former years closely affiliated to the national heroes of the century, both have gotten their training in various diplomatic positions, both are resourceful, accommodating, and brilliant statesmen, and both have a thoroughly modern temperament, intellectual independence bred of a broad view of the world, both are apt of speech and have fine literary feeling. Hay was the secretary of President Lincoln until Lincoln's death, and has been secretary of the embassies in France, Austria, and Spain, has taken distinguished place in party politics, has been Assistant Secretary of State, Ambassador to England, and in 1898 was placed at the head of foreign affairs. His "Ballads," "Castilian Days," and "Life of Lincoln," call to mind his literary reputation.

How far foreign affairs are really conducted by the President and how far by the Secretary of State is, of course, hard to say, but, at any rate, the representatives of foreign powers treat officially only with the Secretary, who has his regular days for diplomatic consultation, so that the relations of foreign representatives to the President, after their first official introduction, remain virtually social. Yet all important measures are undertaken only with the approval of the President, and on critical questions of international politics the whole cabinet deliberates together. Hay's personal influence came clearly before the public eye especially in his negotiations regarding the Central American canal, and in his handling of the Russian and Asiatic problems. Particularly after the Chinese imbroglio he came to be generally reputed the most astute and successful statesman of the day. It will probably not be far wrong to ascribe such tendencies in American politics as are friendly toward England chiefly to his influence. On the other hand, he is supposed to feel no special leanings toward Germany.

The Secretary of the Treasury is next in rank. He administers the Federal finances to all intents and purposes like a large banker, or, rather, like a bank president who should have Congress for his board of directors. Since customs and international revenues are levied by the Federal Government, and not by the several states, and since the expenditures for the army and navy, for the postal service, and for the Federal Government itself, the national debt and the mints come under Federal administration, financing operations are involved which are so extensive as to have a deciding influence on the banking system of the entire country.

The third official in rank is the Secretary of War, while the Secretary of the Navy holds only the sixth place, with the Attorney-General and the Postmaster-General in between. The General Staff of the Secretary of War, which was organized in 1903, is composed of officers of high rank, although the Secretary himself is a civilian. In the case of the army, as well as of the navy, the functions of the secretary are decidedly more important than those, say, of a Prussian Minister. They concern not only administration, but also, in case of war, are of decisive weight on the movements of all the forces, since the President as commander-in-chief has to act through these ministers. Elihu Root was for almost five years Secretary of War; and on his retirement in January, 1904, Roosevelt declared: "Root is the greatest man who has appeared in our times in the public life of any country, either in the New World or the Old."

The position of Attorney-General is less comparable with a corresponding office in the German state. This minister of the President has no influence on the appointment of judges or the administration of the courts. The official representative of justice in the Cabinet is really an exalted lawyer, who is at the same time the President's legal adviser. So far as appointments to office go, the Secretary of the Post Office Department has practically no influence regarding those who are under him, since the tremendous number of postal officials of any considerable importance have to be confirmed in their appointments by the Senate, so that the appointing power has virtually gone over to that body. On the other hand, the whole postal service is under his direction; but it is here not to be forgotten that the American railroads and, what the German may think more extraordinary, the telegraph lines, are not government property.

The Secretary of the Interior is merely a name for a great many unrelated administrative functions. In the long list of duties which fall to this office comes education, although this seemingly most important responsibility is really rather slight, since all educational matters fall to the separate states and the Federal Government has nothing to do but to give out statistics and information, to collect material, and to offer advice. The national Bureau of Education is not empowered to institute any practical changes. A much more important function, practically, of the Secretary of the Interior is the Pension Bureau, since the United States pay yearly about $138,000,000 in pensions. Other divisions are the Patent Office, which grants every year about 30,000 patents, the Railroad Bureau, the Indian Bureau, and the Geological Survey. The Secretary of Agriculture has not only certain duties connected with agriculture, but is also in charge of the Weather Bureau, and of zoölogical, botanical, and chemical institutes, and especially of the large number of scientific departments which indirectly serve the cause of agriculture. Last in rank comes the recently created Secretary of Commerce and Labour, who has charge of the Corporation Bureau, the Labour Bureau, the Census Bureau, and the Bureaus of Statistics, Immigration, and Fisheries.

There are some 240,000 positions under the direction of these ministers; and all of these, from ambassadors to letter-carriers, are in the national service and under the appointment of the President, and are entirely independent of the government of the separate states in which the offices are held.

CHAPTER FOUR

Congress

THERE is an avenue which leads from the White House in a direct line to the Capitol, the dominating architectural feature of Washington. On walking up the broad terraces one comes first to the great central hall, over which rises the dome; to the right one passes through the Hall of Fame and comes finally to the uncomfortably large parliamentary chamber, in which 386 Representatives sit together as the direct delegates of the people. Going from the central hall to the left one passes by the apartments of the Supreme Court, and comes finally to the attractive room in which the ninety state delegates hold their sessions. The room on the right is called the "House," on the left the Senate; both together make up Congress, the law-giving body of the nation. When the thirteen states which first formed the Union in the year 1778 adopted the Articles of Federation, it was intended that Congress should be a single body, in which each state, although it might be represented by a varying number of members, should nevertheless have the right to only one vote. Nine years later, however, the final Constitution of the United States replaced this one simple system by dividing Congress into Senate and House of Representatives, doing this simply by analogy with the traditions of the state governments. Pennsylvania was the only state which had but one legislative chamber, while the others had taken over from England the system of double representation and had carried out the English tradition, although probably nothing was further from their intention than to divide their legislators into lords and commoners.

For the United States the dual division inevitably seemed the shortest way to balance off conflicting requirements. On the one side every state, even the smallest, should have the same prerogatives and equal influence: on the other side, every citizen must count as much as every other, so that the number of inhabitants must be duly represented. It was necessary, therefore, to create one chamber in which all States should have the same number of Representatives, and another in which every delegate should represent an equal number of voters. Furthermore, on the one hand a firm and conservative tradition was to be built up, while on the other the changing voice of the people was to be reflected. It was, therefore, necessary to remove one chamber from popular election and leave it to the appointment of the separate state legislatures. It was also necessary to put the age for candidacy for this chamber high, and to make the term of office rather long, and finally to contrive that at any one time only a fraction of the numbers should be replaced, so that a majority of the members could carry on their work undisturbed. The other chamber, however, was to be completely replaced by frequent direct popular elections. Thus originated the two divisions of Congress which so contrast in every respect. A comparison with European double legislative systems is very natural, and yet the Senate is neither a Bundestag, nor a Herrenhaus, nor a House of Lords; and the House of Representatives is fundamentally different from the Reichstag. One who wishes to understand the American system must put aside his recollections of European institutions, since nothing except emphasis on the difference between the American and European legislatures will make clear the traditions of Washington.

As has been said, the Senators are representatives of the several states; every state sends two. The State of New York, with its seven million inhabitants, has no more representatives in the Senate than the State of Wyoming, which has less than one hundred thousand inhabitants. Every Senator is elected for six years by the law-giving body of the individual state. Every second year a third of the Senators retire, so that the Senate as a whole has existed uninterruptedly since the foundation of the Union. Curiously enough, however, the Senators vote independently, and thus it often happens that the two Senators from one State cast opposite votes. A candidate for the Senate has to be thirty years old.

The members of the House are elected every two years and by

direct popular vote. The number of delegates is here not prescribed by the Constitution. It is constantly modified on the basis of the ten-year census, since every state is entitled to a number of delegates proportionate to its population. While there were slaves, who could not vote, the slave states nevertheless objected to the diminution in the number of their representatives, due to the fact that the negro was not considered an inhabitant, and it was constitutionally provided to compute the number of Representatives on the basis that every slave was equivalent to three-fifths of a man. To-day neither colour nor race constitutionally affects the right to vote. On the other hand, the nation as such does not concern itself to consider who is allowed to vote, but leaves this completely to the different states, and requires only that for the national elections in every state the same provisions are observed which are made for the elections to the state legislature. Moreover, it is left to every state in what wise it shall choose the allotted number of Representatives at Washington. Thus, for instance, in those four Western States in which women are allowed to vote for members of the legislature, women have also the right to vote for Congressmen.

The first House of Representatives had 65 members, while the House of 1902 had 357, and the political centre of gravity of the country has so shifted that the states which originally made up Congress send now only 137 of the members. The number of delegates has recently been increased to 386. The age of candidacy is 25, and while a Senator must have lived in the country for nine years, only seven years are required of a Representative.

The differences in the conditions of election are enough to bring it about that the personal make-up of the two Houses, as had been originally intended, give very different impressions. The dignity of being Senator is granted to but few, and to these for a long time, and as it is bestowed by that somewhat small circle of the legislators of the state, is naturally accounted the highest political honour; it is thus desired by the most successful leaders of public life and the most respected men of the several states. The ideal condition is, to be sure, somewhat frustrated, since in reality the members of a state legislature are generally pledged, when they themselves are elected, to support this or that particular candidate for the Senate. Thus the general body of voters exerts its influence after all pretty directly; and, moreover, this distinction depends not a little, in the West and especially in the thinly populated states, on the possession of great wealth. Since, however, in these cases such wealth has generally been won by exceptional energy and keen insight, even in this way men come to Washington who are a good deal above the average voter, and who represent the most significant forces in American popular life earnestly, worthily, and intelligently.

In the last Senate the average age of ninety Senators was sixty years, and seventeen were more than seventy years old. Sixty-one of them were jurists, eighteen were business men, three were farmers, and two had been journalists. As to the jurists, they are not men who are still active as attorneys or judges. Generally men are in question who went over early from the legal profession into politics, and who have lived almost entirely in politics. Indeed, not a few of these lawyers who have become legislators have been for some years in commercial life at the head of great industrial or railroad corporations, so that the majority of jurists is no indication whatsoever of any legal petrifaction. All sides of American life are represented, and only such professions as that of the university scholar or that of the preacher are virtually excluded because circumstances make it necessary for the Senator to spend six winters in Washington. It will be seen that politics must have become a life profession with most of these men, since many are elected four and five times to the Senate. Among the best known Senators, Allison, Hoar, Cockrell, Platt, Morgan, Teller, and several others have been there for more than twenty-five years. Of course the conservative traditions of the Senate are better preserved by such numerous re-elections than by any possible external provision.

It is also characteristic of the composition of the Senate that, with a single exception, no Senator was born on the European continent. Nelson, the Senator from Minnesota, came from Norway when he was a boy. Thus in this conservative circle there is little real representation of the millions who have immigrated to this country. In the autobiographies of the Senators, two relate that, although they were born in America, they are of German descent; these are Wellington, the Senator from Maryland, and

Dietrich, the Senator from Nebraska. The Senators are notoriously well-to-do, and have been called the "Millionaires' Club"; and yet one is not to suppose that these men have the wealth of the great industrial magnates. Senator Clarke, of Montana, whose property is estimated at one hundred million dollars, is the single one who, according to American standards, could be called rich. Most of the others have merely a few modest millions, and for many the expensive years of residence in Washington are a decided sacrifice. And, most of all, it is certain that the Senators who are materially the least well-off are among the most respected and influential. The most highly educated member of the Senate would probably be the young delegate from Massachusetts, the historian Lodge, who is the President's most intimate friend; but the most worthy and dignified member has been the late Senator from Massachusetts, the impressive orator, Hoar.

It is a matter of course that the social level of the House of Representatives lies considerably lower. Here it is intended that the people shall be represented with all their diverse interests and ambitions. The two-thirds majority of lawyers is found, however, even here; of the 357 members of the last House, 236 had been trained in law, 63 were business men, and 17 were farmers. The House is again like the Senate, since, in spite of the fact that the membership is elected entirely anew, it remains in good part made up of the same people. The fifty-eighth Congress contained 250 members who had already sat in the fifty-seventh. About one-tenth of the Representatives have been in the House ten years. The general physiognomy is, however, very different from that of the Senate. It is more youthful, less serene and distinguished, and more suggestive of ordinary business. The average age is forty-eight years, while there are some men under thirty. The total impression, in spite of several exceptions, suggests that these men come from the social middle class. However, it is from just this class that the notably clear-cut personalities of America have come; and the number of powerful and striking countenances to be seen in the House is greater than that in the German Reichstag. The Representatives, like Senators, have a salary of $5,000 and their travelling expenses.

What is now the actual work of these two chambers in Congress, and how do they carry it on? The work cannot be wholly separated from its manner of performance. Perhaps the essentials of this peculiar task and method could be brought together as follows: on the basis of committee reports, Congress decides whether or not to accept bills which have been proposed by its members. This is indeed the main part of the story. Congress thus passes on proposed bills; its function is purely legislative, and involves nothing of an executive nature. On the other hand, these bills have to be proposed by members of Congress; they cannot be received from the President or from members of his Cabinet. Thus the Executive has no influence in the law-giving body. The method of transacting business, finally, consists of laying the emphasis on the deliberations in committees, and it is there that the fate of each bill is virtually settled. The committee determines whether the proposed measure shall come before the whole House; and both House and Senate have finally to decide about accepting the measure. Each of these points requires further comment.

So far as the separation of the legislative and executive functions of the government is concerned, it is certainly exaggeration to say that it is complete, as has often been said. There is, to be sure, a somewhat sharper distinction than is made in Germany, where the propositions of the Executive form the basis of legislative activity; and yet even in the United States the ultimate fate of every measure is dependent on the attitude taken by the President. We have seen that a bill which is sent by Congress to the President can be returned with his veto, and in that case becomes a law only when on a new vote in both Houses it receives a two-thirds majority. A law which obtains only a small majority in either one of the Houses can thus easily be put aside by the Executive.

On the other hand, Congress has a very important participation in executive functions, more particularly through the Senate, inasmuch as all appointments of federal officers and the ratification of all treaties require the approval of the Senate. International politics, therefore, make it necessary for the President to keep closely in touch with at least the Senate, and in the matter of appointments the right of the Senators to disapprove is so important that for a large number of local positions the selection has been actually left entirely to the Senators of the respective states. The Constitution gives to Congress even a jurisdictional function, in the case that any higher federal officers abuse their office. When there is a suspicion of this, the House of Representatives brings its charges and the Senate conducts the trial. The last time that this great machinery was in operation was in 1876, when the Secretary of War, Belknap, was charged and acquitted; thus suspicion has not fallen on any of the higher officials for twenty-eight years.

The separation of the Legislative from the Executive is most conspicuously seen in the fact that no member of the Cabinet has a seat in Congress. At the beginning of the Congressional session the President sends his message, in which he is privileged politically to pour out his entire heart. Yet he may only state his hopes and desires, and may not propose definite bills. The Cabinet ministers, however, are responsible solely to the President, and in no wise to Congress, where they have no right to discuss measures either favourably or unfavourably. They do not come into contact with Congress. This is in extreme contrast with the situation in England, where the ministers are leaders of the Parliamentary party. The American sees in this a strong point of his political system, and even such a man as the former ambassador to Germany, Andrew D. White, who admired so much of what he saw there, considers the ministerial benches in the German and French representative chambers a mistake. It occasions, he says, a constant and vexatious disagreement between the delegates of the people and the ministers, which disturbs the order and effectiveness of parliamentary transactions. The legislative work should be transacted apart, and the popular representatives ought to have only one another to take care of.

We must not, however, understand that there are practically no relations existing between Congress and the ministry. A considerable part of the bills, which have to be discussed, consist, of course, in appropriations for public expenditures, so far as these come out of the federal rather than the state treasuries. Such appropriations included at the last time $139,000,000 for pensions, $138,000,000 for the post office, $91,000,000 for the army, $78,000,000 for the navy, $26,000,000 for rivers and harbours, and so on; making in all $800,000,000 for the annual appropriations, besides $253,000,000 for special contracts. Thus the total sum of appropriations in one session of Congress amounted to over $1,000,000,000, in America called a billion. This authorized appropriation has to be made on the basis of proposals, submitted by the members of Congress; but it is a matter of course that every single figure of such propositions has to come originally from the bureau of the army or navy, or whatever department is concerned, if it is to serve as the basis of discussion. Thus while the Executive presents to Congress no proposals for the budget, it hands over to the members of Congress so empowered the whole material; and this is, after all, not very different from the European practice. However, the voice of the Executive is indeed not heard when the budget is under debate. The members of Congress who are to receive the ministerial propositions through mediation of the Treasury, must belong to the House; for one of the few advantages which the House of Representatives has over the Senate is that it has to initiate all bills of appropriation. This is a remnant of the fundamental idea that all public expenditures should be made only at the instance of the taxpayers themselves, wherefore the directly elected members of the House are more fitted for this than are the Senators, who are indirectly elected. This single advantage is less than it looks to be, since the Senate may amend at will all bills of appropriation that it receives from the House.

Thus every measure which is ever to become law must be proposed by members of Congress. One can see that this privilege of proposing bills is utilized to the utmost, from the simple fact that during every session some fifteen thousand bills are brought out. We may here consider in detail the way in which the House transacts its affairs. It is clear that if more than three hundred voluble politicians are set to the task of deliberating in a few months on fifteen thousand laws, including all proposed appropriations, that a perfect babel of argument will arise which can lead to no really fruitful result, unless sound traditions, strict rules and discipline, and autocratic leadership hold this chaotic body within bounds. The American instinct for organization introduced indeed long ago a compact orderliness. Here belongs first of all that above-mentioned committee system, which in the House is completed by the unique institution of the Speaker. But one thing we must constantly bear in mind: the whole background of Congressional doings is the two-party system. If the House or the Senate were to break out in the prismatic variegation of the German parliamentary parties, no speaker and no system of committees would be able to keep the elements in hand. It is, after all, the party in majority which guarantees order, moulds the committees into effective machines, and lends to the Speaker his extraordinary influence.

The essential feature of the whole apparatus lies in the fact that a bill cannot come up before the House until it has been deliberated in committee. The chairman of the committee then presents it personally at some meeting. The presiding officer, the so-called Speaker, exerts in this connection a threefold influence; firstly, he appoints the members of all the committees, of which, for instance, there were in the last Congress sixty-three. The most important, and, therefore, the largest, of these committees are those on appropriations, agriculture, banking, coinage, foreign and Indian affairs, interstate and foreign commerce, pensions, the post office, the navy, railroads, rivers and harbours, patents, and finance. Both the majority and minority parties are represented in every committee, and its chairman has almost unlimited control in its transaction of business. All members of the more important committees are experienced men, who have been well schooled in the traditions of the House.

The Speaker is allowed further to decide as to what committee each bill shall be referred. In many cases, of course, there is no choice; but it not seldom happens that there are several possibilities, and the decision between them often determines the fate of the bill. In the third place, the Speaker, as chairman of the Committee on Rules, decides what reports, of those which have been so far prepared by the committees, shall come up for discussion at each meeting of the House. As soon as the committee has agreed on recommendations, its report is put on the calendar; but whether it then comes up for debate in the House depends on a good many factors. In the first place, of course, many of the proposed matters take naturally first rank, as for instance, the appropriations. The chairman of the Committee on Appropriations is given the floor whenever he asks for it; thus there are express trains on this Congressional railroad which have the right-of-way before suburban trains, and then, too, there are special trains which take preference before everything else. But aside from such committee reports as are especially privileged, a very considerable opportunity of selection exists among those which remain.

It is here that the really unlimited influence of the Speaker comes in. He is in no way required to give the floor to the committees which ask for it first. If the chairman of the committee is not called on by the Speaker for his report, he is said to be not "noticed" and he is helpless. Of course, whether he is noticed or not depends on the most exact prearrangement. If now a bill is finally reported to the House, it is still not allowed an endless debate, for the Speaker is once more empowered to appoint a particular time when the debate must end, and thereby he is able to come around any efforts at obstruction. If, however, the minority wishes to make itself heard by raising the point of no quorum, then not only those who are voting, but all those who are present in the House, are counted, and if these are not enough the delinquents can be hunted out and forced to come in. But in most cases there is little or no debate, and the resolutions of the committee are accepted by the House without a word. In certain of the most important cases, as in matters of appropriation or taxation, the House constitutes itself a so-called committee of the whole. Then the matter is seriously discussed under a special chairman, as at the session of an ordinary committee. Even here it is not the custom to make long speeches, and the members are often contented with a short sketch of their arguments, and ask permission to have the rest published in the Congressional Report. The speeches which thus have never been delivered are printed and distributed in innumerable copies through the district from which that speaker comes and elsewhere as well.

Thus if an ordinary Representative proposes a measure, which perhaps expresses the local wishes of his district, such a bill goes first to the Secretary and from him to the Speaker. He refers it to a special committee, and at the same time every Representative receives printed copies of it. The committee decides whether the bill is worth considering. If it has the good fortune to be deliberated by the committee it is often so amended by the members that little remains of its original substance. If it then has the further good fortune to be accepted by the committee, it comes on the House calendar, and waits until the Committee on Rules puts it on the order of the day. If it then has the exceptional good fortune of being read to the House it has a fairly good chance of being accepted.

But of course its pilgrimage is not ended here. It passes next to the Senate, and goes through much the same treatment once more; first a committee, then the quorum. If it does not there come up before the quorum, it is lost in spite of everything; but if it does finally come up, after all hindrances, it may be amended once more by the Senate. If this happens, as is likely, its consideration is begun all over again. A composite committee from both Houses considers all amendments, and if it cannot come to an agreement the measures are doomed. If the committee does agree, the close of the session of Congress may intervene and prevent its last hearing in the House, and in the next Congress the whole process is repeated. But if a measure has passed through all these dangers and been approved by both Houses, the President then has the opportunity to put his veto on it.

Thus it comes about that hardly a tenth part of the bills which are introduced each year ever become laws, and that they are sifted out and amended surely and speedily. Indeed, it can hardly be doubted that a large part of the fifteen thousand bills are introduced out of personal consideration for constituents, or even out of less worthy motives, with no expectation that they will possibly be accepted. Moreover, the popular tribunal, the House, spares itself too great pains, because it knows that the Senate will certainly amend all its provisions; and the Senate indulges itself in voting unnecessary favours to constituents because it relies on their negation by the House.

The Senate works on fundamentally the same plan. When a Senator brings his proposition, it goes likewise to the appropriate committee, then is read before a quorum, and is passed on to the other chamber. Nevertheless, there is a considerable difference in procedure; the House behaves like a restless popular gathering, while the Senate resembles a conference of diplomats. The House is a gigantic room, in which even the best orators can hardly make themselves heard, and where hundreds are writing or reading newspapers without paying any attention to the man who speaks. But the Senate is a parliamentary chamber, where a somewhat undue formality prevails. A strict discipline has to be observed in the House in order to preserve its organization, while the Senate needs no outward discipline because the small circle of elderly gentlemen transacts its business with perfect decorum.

Thus the Senate tolerates no Speaker over it, no president with discretionary powers. In the Senate both parties have the right to appoint the members of the committees. The Chairman of the Senate must also not fail to notice any one who asks for the floor; whoever wishes to speak has every chance, and this freedom implies of course that the debates shall not be arbitrarily terminated by the Chairman. A debate can be closed only by unanimous consent. The influence of the Chairman of the Senate is, therefore, only a shadow beside that of the Speaker, and since the Chairman is not elected by the Senate itself, but is chosen directly by the people in the person of the Vice-President of the United States, it may happen that this Chairman belongs to the party in minority, and that he has practically no influence at all. Conformably with the extreme formality and courtesy of the Senate, majorities are counted on the basis of the votes actually cast, and not, as in the House, on the basis of members actually present. For both Houses alike it is possible for those who intend to be absent to be paired off beforehand, so that if one absentee has announced himself for, and another against, a certain bill, they can both be counted as having voted.

It is clear what the consequences of this unlimited exchange of Senatorial courtesy must be; the concessions in outward form must lead immediately to compromises and tacit understandings. If a debate can be closed only by unanimous agreement, it is possible for a single opposing politician to obstruct the law-making machinery. A handful of opponents can take the stand for weeks and block the entire Senate. Such obstructionist policy has to be prevented at any cost, and therefore on all sides and in every least particular friendly sympathy must be preserved. Of course, the opposition between the two parties cannot be obviated; so much the more, then, it is necessary for each man to be bound by personal ties to every other, and to feel sure of having a free hand in his own special interests so long at least as he accords the same right to others in theirs. Thus, merely from the necessity of preserving mutual good feeling, it too often happens that the other members close their eyes when some willing Senator caters to local greed or to the special wishes of ambitious persons or corporations, by proposing a Congressional bill.

This "Senatorial courtesy" is most marked in the matter of the appointment of officials, where matters go smoothly only because it has been agreed that no proposals shall be made without the approval of the Senators of the state concerned. Every Senator knows that if to-day one local delegate is outvoted, the rebellion may to-morrow be directed against another; and thus many a doubtful appointment, given as hush money or as a reward for mean political services, is approved with inward displeasure by courteous colleagues merely in order to save the principle of individual omnipotence. There is no doubt that in this way the individual Senator comes to have much more power than does a single Representative. The latter is really the member of a party, with no special opportunities for satisfying his individual wishes; while the Senator may have his personal points of view, and is really an independent factor.

If to-day the Senate, contrary to the expectation of former times, really plays a much more important röle before the public than the House, this is probably not because more important functions are given to the Senate, but because it is composed of persons of whom every one has peculiar significance in the political situation, while the House is nothing but a mass-meeting with a few leaders. This increased importance before the public eye works back again on the Senator's opinion of himself, and the necessary result is a steady increase in the Senate's aspirations and the constant growth of its rights. Perhaps the most characteristic exhibition of this has been the gradual evolution of the part taken by the Senate in the matter of foreign treaties. The Constitution requires the ratification of the Senate, and the original construction was that the Administration should present a treaty all made out, which the Senate had to accept or reject as it stood. But soon the Senate arrogated to itself the right to amend treaties, and then it came about that the Senate would never accept a treaty without injecting a few drops of its own diplomatic wisdom. It might be that these would be merely a change of wording, but just enough to let the President feel the Senatorial power. The result has been that the treaties that are now presented to the Senate are called nothing but proposals.

Looking behind the scenes one discovers that at bottom, even in the Senate, only a few have real influence. The more recently appointed Senators earn their spurs in unimportant committees, and even if they get into more important ones they are constrained by tradition to fall in line behind the more experienced members. In the House there is half a dozen, and in the Senate perhaps a dozen men who shape the politics of the country. Here, as in all practical matters, the American is ready to submit to an oligarchical system so long as he knows that the few in question derive their power from the free vote of the many. In fact nothing but oligarchy is able to satisfy the profoundly conservative feeling of the American. Behind the scenes one soon discovers also that the Senatorial courtesy, which neutralizes the party fanaticism and encourages compromises to spring up like mushrooms, still leaves room for plenty of fighting; and even intrigue thrives better on this unctuous courtesy than in the coarser soil of the lower house. The sanctified older Senators, such as Allison, Frye, Platt, Aldrich, and Hale, know where to place their levers so as to dislodge all opposition. Perhaps McKinley's friend, Hanna, who was the grand virtuoso in Republican party technique, knew how always to overcome such political intrigue; but even Roosevelt's friend, Lodge, has sometimes found that the arbitrarily shaped traditions of the seniors weigh more than the most convincing arguments of the younger men.

The moral level of Congress is, in the judgment of its best critics, rather high. The fate of every one of the thousands of bills is settled virtually in a small committee, and thus, time after time, the weal and woe of entire industries or groups of interests depend on one or two votes in the committee. The possible openings for corruption are thus much greater in Congress than in any other parliament, since no other has carried the committee system to such a point. In former times political scoundrels went around in great numbers through the hotels in Washington and even in the corridors of the Capitol trying to influence votes with every device of bribery. To be sure, it is difficult to prove that there are no such hidden sins to-day; but it is the conviction of those who are best able to judge that nothing of the sort any longer exists. To be sure, there are still lobbyists in Washington, who as a matter of business are trying to work either for or against impending bills, but direct bribery is no longer in question. On the slightest suspicion the House itself proceeds to an investigation and appoints a committee, which has the right of collecting sworn testimony; and time after time these suspicions have been found to be unjust.

A different verdict, however, would have to be passed if only that delegate were to be called morally upright who surveys every question from the point of view of the welfare of the entire nation; for then indeed the purity of Congress will be by no means free from doubt. Few Americans, however, would recognize such a political standard. When great national questions come up for discussion Congress has always shown itself equal to the occasion, and when the national honour is at stake, as it was during the Spanish War, party lines no longer exist; but when the daily drift of work has to be put through it is the duty of every man to uphold as obstinately as possible the interests of his constituency. Especially the political interests of his party then become predominant, and, seen from a higher point of view, there are no doubt many sins committed in this direction. Many a measure is given its quietus by one party, not because of any real inexpediency, but simply in order to embarrass the other party, to tie up the Administration, and thus to weaken the hopes of that party at the next election. In recent years such party tactics on both sides have prevailed time after time. Most frequently it is the present minority, under its leader, Senator Gorman, which has resorted to this policy and held out against the most reasonable propositions of the Republicans, simply because these measures would have increased the Republican respect before the nation.

On the other hand, party lines are all the time being broken through by these or those local interests, and any one observing the distribution of votes cast in the House will see clearly how, oftentimes, the parties mingle while the issue lies perhaps between two different geographical sections. When oleomargarine is the order of the day the representatives of the farming districts are lined up against those from industrial sections. If it is a question of getting Congress to approve the great irrigation measures, whole troops of Democrats hasten to forget that, according to their fundamental principles, such an undertaking belongs to the state, and not to the federal, government; the representatives from all the Democratic states which are to be benefited by such irrigation, fall into sweet accord with the Republicans. Thus the party divisions are all the time being forgotten for the moment, and it looks as if this weakening of party bonds were on the increase. By supporting his party principles each Congressman assists toward the next victory of his party, but by working for the interests of his locality he is surer of his own renomination. The requirement that a candidate must reside in the district that elects him naturally strengthens his consideration for the selfish claims of his constituency. Thus it is only at notable moments that the popular representative stands above all parties; he generally stands pat with his own party, and if the voters begin to nod he may take his stand somewhat below the parties.

Yet, on looking at Congress as a whole, one has the impression that it accomplishes a tremendous amount of work, and in a more sober, business-like, and efficient way than does any other parliament in the world. There is less talking against time; in fact, there is less talking of any kind, and because the Administration is not represented at all there is less fighting. The transactions as a whole are therefore somewhat less exciting; a single Congressman has less opportunity to become personally famous. Yet no American would desire to introduce a ministerial bench at the Capitol, or to have the next Congress adopt Austrian, French, German, or English methods.

CHAPTER FIVE

Justice

GOING from the hall beneath the central dome of the Capitol toward the Senate, in the left wing one passes by an extraordinary room, in which there is generally a crowd of people. The nine judges of the federal court, the Supreme Court of the United States, are sitting there in their black gowns, between Greek columns. The President and his Cabinet, the Senate, and the House of Representatives fill the American with a pride which is tempered by some critical judgment on this or that feature, or perhaps by a lively party dissatisfaction. But every American who is competent to judge looks on the Supreme Court with unqualified admiration. He knows very well that no force in the country has done more for the peace, prosperity, and dignity of the United States. In the constitutional make-up of the Federal Government, the Supreme Court is the third division, and co-ordinate with the Legislative and the Executive departments.

The jurisprudence of a nation forms a totality; and therefore it will not do to discuss the work of the nine men sitting at the Capitol, without throwing at least a hasty glance at the administration of justice throughout this enormous country. There is hardly anything more confusing to a European; and while the Englishman finds many features which are reminiscent of English law, the German stands helpless before the complicated situation. It is, most of all, the extreme diversity of methods which disquiets him. It will be quite impossible to give here even a superficial picture of the machinery of justice. A few hints must suffice at this point, while we shall consider many features in other connections, especially in discussing social problems.

The jurisprudence adopted by the United States comes from three sources. The average American, on being asked what the law of his country is, would say that it is "common law." If we except the State of Louisiana, which by a peculiarity has the Napoleonic Code, this reply suffices for a rough idea. But if a German, having in mind perhaps the two German law books, the penal and the civil codes, both of which he can put so easily into his pocket, were to ask after some formulation of the common law, he would be shown a couple of huge bookcases with several hundred stout volumes. Common law is not a law book, nor is it a system of abstract formulations, nor yet a codification of the prevailing ideas of justice. It is, in fact, the sum total of judicial decisions. The establishment of common law signifies that every new case as it comes up is decided in conformity with previous decisions. The earlier decision may be a bad one, and very much offend one's sense of justice; but if no superior authority has annulled it, it becomes historic law and determines the future course of things. American law came originally from the English. The early English colonists brought with them across the ocean the ideas of the English judges, and the states which have sprung up lately have taken their law from the thirteen original states. If to-day, in Boston or San Francisco, any one finds a piece of jewelry on the street and another snatches it from him, he can have the thief arrested, although the object found is not his property. The judge will decide that he has a right to the object which he has found until the original owner appears, and the judge will so decide because in the year 1722 a London chimney-sweep found a valuable ornament, out of which a jeweler later stole a precious stone; and the English judge decided in favour of the chimney-sweep.

The disadvantages of such a system are obvious. Instead of a single book of law embodying the will of the nation, the decisions handed down by single insignificant judges in different parts of the world, decisions which originated under wholly other states of civilization and from other traditions, still have final authority. Again and again the judge has to adapt himself to old decisions, against which his sense of right morally rebels. Yet the deep, ethical motive behind this legal system is certainly plainly evident. The Anglo-Saxon would say that a national code cannot be constructed arbitrarily and artificially. Its only source is in the careful, responsible decisions given down by the accredited representatives of the public will in actual disputes which have arisen. There is no right or wrong, he would say, until two persons disagree and make a settlement necessary, and the judge who decides the case creates the right with the help of his own conscience; but as soon as he has given his decision, and it is set aside by no higher authority, the principle of the decision becomes justice for all times. Every day sees new formulations of justice, because new conflicts between human wills are always arising and require new settlements; but up to the moment when a decision is made there exist only two conflicting desires existing in the matter, but nothing which could be called justice.

Although it seems at first sight as if a legal system, which is composed of previous decisions, would soon become antiquated and petrified, the Anglo-Saxon would say with firm conviction that just such justice is the only one which can be living, because it springs not out of rationalistic preconceptions, but from actual experience. The Anglo-Saxon jurisprudence is full of historical reality and of picturesque individuality. It has grown as organically as language, and is, in the estimation of the Anglo-Saxon, as much superior to a mere code as the ordinary speech of a people, in spite of all its historical inconsistencies, is superior to an artificially constructed speech like Volapük. And he would find many other points of superiority. He would say, for instance, that this is the only system which gives to every man on the judge's bench the serious sense of his responsibility; for the judge knows that in every case which he decides, he settles not only the fortunes of James and John there present, but he influences for all times the conception of justice of the entire nation. He feels especially that the binding force of previous decisions reassures the public sense of right, and lends a continuity which could never be afforded by the theoretical formulations of an abstract code.

Another factor must be taken into account. A judicial decision which is forgotten as quickly as the voice of the judge who speaks it, can never have so considerable an influence on the public mind as one which itself creates law. In one sense, to be sure, the German judge creates law too; the penal code sets wide limits to the punishment of a criminal, and within these limits the judge assigns a certain penalty. He does in a sense create the right for this particular case; but the characteristic difference is, that in the

German Empire no subsequent decision is in the least affected by such preceding decision. The German judge finds justice prescribed for him and he is its servant, while the American makes it and is its master. This gives to the judicial utterance an historical weight and enduring significance, which contribute vastly toward keeping judicial doings in the focus of the public consciousness.

The same is brought about in still another way. Since the decision of the judge is largely dependent on previous cases, the fate of the parties contending may depend on whether they are able to point to previous decisions which are favourable to their side. The layman cannot do this, and it falls to the counsel. In this wise a sphere of action is open to the American lawyer which is incomparably greater than that of any German Anwalt. The former has to concern himself not only with the case in hand, but he has to connect this concrete instance with the whole historic past. Thus the profession of the lawyer comes to have an inner importance which is unknown to the European, and which in many cases necessarily exceeds the importance of the judge, since he is bound to comply with the decisions adduced by the counsels for both sides. The judges are selected from the ranks of lawyers, and are, therefore, brought up in the idea that law is composed of former decisions, and that the decisions of the bench are admirable only so far as they are consistent enough with the earlier ones to force the conviction and respect of the lawyers. Thus barristers and judges are entirely at one, and are together entrusted with the public sense of right, as it has developed itself historically, and as it is day by day added to and perpetuated, so that it shall be a never-failing source of quickening to the conscience of the masses.

In the masses of the people, on the other hand, the natural tendencies are favourable anyhow for developing a lively sense of justice. It is a necessity devolving naturally on the individualistic view of things. The protection of individual rights and the inviolability of the individual person, with all that belongs to it, are the individualist's most vital concern. Many outward features of American life may seem, indeed, to contradict this, but any one who looks more deeply will see that everywhere the desire for justice is the essential trait of both the individual and the nation; and the public consciousness would rather endure the crassest absurdities and misunderstandings in public affairs than the least conscious violation in the administration of justice. Again and again important trials go to pieces on small technical errors, from which the severe sense of justice of the American is not able to free itself. The public is always willing to endure any hardship rather than to tolerate any maladministration of justice.

On the finest square in Boston stands a large and magnificent hotel, erected by rich capitalists The building laws provide that structures facing that square shall not exceed a height of ninety feet; but in violation of the law certain cornices and balustrades were added to this building above the ninety-foot line, in order to give an artistic finish to the structure, and still to turn practically every inch allowed by law to account for rentals, which are high in so palatial a building. Every one agreed that this ornamental finish was highly decorative and satisfactory in the æsthetic sense, but that it must, nevertheless, be taken down, because it violated the law by some seven feet. The cornice and balustrades have, therefore, been demolished at great expense, and a handsome structure has been made absolutely hideous — a veritable monstrosity. The best square in the city is disfigured, but every Bostonian looks on this building with gratification. Beautiful architectural detail may indeed have been sacrificed; but the public conscience has won, and it is on this that the nation rests.

It is merely incidental that very much, and indeed much too much, of that which the Germans account matters of justice, is relegated by the American point of view to other tribunals; some, for instance, are held to be political questions, and thus it often appears to the foreigner as if there had been a violation of justice where really there has been only some political abuse. But matters of that sort loom up whenever any nation tries to form an opinion about another. In Germany, indeed, the American seems to see many violations of justice, where the German would find only an historically established social or political abuse.

As we have said, American justice is based on the decisions handed down in earlier cases. But this is, after all, only one of the three sources of law. That form of law-making is also here recognized which in Europe is the only form; the law-making by the majority of the people's representatives. We have seen how

Congress passes every year hundreds of laws. Many of these are indeed special measures, with no universal application; not a few, however, are of very broad application and involve an unlimited number of possible instances. And just as the Congress of the United States, so also can the legislature of each state prescribe general regulations, applicable within the state. Such laws made by the legislature are technically called statutes. These are engrossed in the statute-books of the state, and supersede all opposed decisions which may then exist. The federal judge, like the judge in a special state, is therefore bound to earlier decisions only so far as these are not expressly annulled by statutes.

Here we find one of the main reasons for the extraordinary complexities of the American law; forty-five legislatures are making laws for their several states, and in this way they of course give expression to the diversity of local needs and the varying grades of culture. At the same time, the principle of law, based on earlier decisions, is always combined with the principle of the statute-book. In the cases, both of the laws of Congress and those of the separate states, the judges who first come to apply the statutes in practice, are privileged to make their own interpretation; and here, too, the interpretation handed down in the judge's decision is valid for all future cases.

In both the federal and state courts a legal action may be carried from the lower to the higher courts, and the decision of the highest tribunal becomes definitely law. The forty-five-fold diversity refers thus not merely to the statutes of the separate states, but also to the interpretations of those statutes which have been given by the upper courts of those states.

The third source of law is the only one that prescribes absolute uniformity for all parts of the country. This is the Constitution of the United States. The Constitution must not be conceived as the creation of Congress; Congress was created by the Constitution. Therefore every provision of the Constitution is a higher law than any bill which Congress can pass, just as the law made by Congress is higher than the decision of any judge. No Congress can modify a clause of the Constitution. The assent of the entire people is necessary for such a revision. Congress can, however, propose an amendment to the Constitution, and a two-thirds majority in the Senate and the House suffice to bring the proposed change before the nation, to be voted on. It has then to be passed on by the forty-five state legislatures, and will become a law with the approval of three-quarters of the states.

At first glance it seems as if this were a judicial machinery which would be far too complicated to work smoothly; it seems as if sources of friction had been arbitrarily devised, and as if continual collisions between the authorities of the several systems would be inevitable. This is true in two instances especially; firstly, the judicial machinery, which carries out the federal laws, sometimes collides with that of the separate states. Then, secondly, the complicated system of Constitutional provisions, devised a hundred years since, may interfere with the progressive measures of Congress or the separate states; and this must be a source of much uncertainty in law. These are the actual difficulties of a legal sort. Everything else, as for instance the enormous diversity of the laws in the separate states, is of course very inconvenient, but gives rise to no conflicts of principle.

Neither of these two difficulties finds its counterpart in Germany. In no Prussian city is there a German tribunal side by side with the Prussian, no imperial judge beside the local judge; nor can one conceive of a conflict in the German Empire between the creators of the legal code and the law-givers who frame the provisions of the Constitution. This doubleness of the judicial officials is in every part of the Union, however, characteristic of the American system and necessary to it. The wonderful equilibrium between centripetal and centrifugal forces which characterizes the whole American scheme of things makes it impossible from the outset for either the whole Federation to become the sole administrator of justice, or for such administration, on the basis of federal law, to be left entirely to the separate states. As a matter of course, a clear separation of jurisdiction has been necessary. The Constitution provides for this in a way clearly made necessary by the conditions under which the Federation was formed. Justice in the army and navy, commercial policies, and political relations with other countries; weights and measures, coinage, provisions, interstate commerce, and the postal system, the laws of patents and copyrights, of bankruptcy, and of naturalization, the laws of river and harbour, cases of treason, and much else are left to the Federation as a whole. While all these matters fall naturally within the scope of federal law, there are, on the other hand, obvious reasons whereby certain classes of persons should be under the jurisdiction of the federal courts. These are, firstly, diplomatic ministers and consuls; secondly, either actual or legal parties when they belong in different states; thirdly, and most important, the states themselves. Wherever a state is party to an action, the Supreme Federal Court must hear the case and give the decision. On the other hand, the Constitution declares expressly that, wherever jurisdiction is not explicitly conferred on the federal courts, it pertains to the individual states; therefore, much the larger part of criminal law belongs to the states, and so the laws of marriage and inheritance, of contract, property ownership, and much else.

For the administration of cases within its jurisdiction, the Federation has divided the whole country into twenty-seven districts, whose boundaries coincide partly with state lines, and of which each has a district court. Groups of such districts form a circuit, of which each has a circuit court, which sits on the more important cases, especially civil cases involving large interests. And, finally, there is a court of appeals. These districts and circuits are now coincident with the regions lying in the jurisdiction of the several states. In their method of procedure the federal and the state courts resemble each other, especially in the general conduct of criminal cases, which is everywhere the same, because the Constitution itself has fixed the main features. Both state and federal courts are alike bound by the extraordinarily rigid rules framed by the Constitution in order to protect the innocent man against the severity of the law.

No criminal can be condemned except by a jury which has been sworn to perform its duty, and before he comes before this jury a provisional jury has to make the accusation against him. Thus one sworn jury must be convinced of the justice of the suspicion before a second jury can give its verdict. A person cannot be brought up for trial twice for the same crime; no one can be compelled to testify against himself; every one has the right to be brought before a jury in the district where the crime was committed, to hear all the testimony against him, to have counsel for his own defence, and to avail himself of the strong arm of the law in bringing to court such witnesses as would speak in his favour;

cruel or excessive penalties may not be fixed, nor a man's freedom or property interfered with except after due process of law. The Constitution provides this, and a good deal else, and thus makes the conduct of trials uniform. In other respects, however, there are not a few differences which are not so obvious in the courts. Among these is the circumstance that federal judges are appointed for life, while the judges of the separate states are elected for short periods of from four to seven years.

The relations between constitutional laws and legislative laws seem even more complicated. Here, too, in a way, the same province is covered by a two-fold system of laws. The fixed letter of the Constitution and the living decisions by a majority in Congress or in a state legislature, stand in opposition to each other. It is established that no legislature can ride over the Constitution; and if the interpretation of a court brings out a contradiction between the two systems, a conflict arises which in principle makes justice uncertain. If we now ask how it is possible that all such conflicts have disappeared without the least prejudice to the national sense of justice, how in spite of all these possibilities of friction no disturbance is seen, or how in a land which has been overrun with serious political conflicts, a jurisprudence so lacking in uniformity has always been the north star of the nation — the reply will be that the Supreme Court has done all this. The upper federal court has been the great reconciling factor in the history of the United States, and has left behind it a succession of honourable memorials. Its most distinguished chief justice has been John Marshall, who presided over it from 1801 to 1835. He was America's greatest jurist, and contributed more than any one else toward impressing the spirit of the Constitution on the country.

The German reader who hears of the Supreme Court sitting at the Capitol, must not turn back in his mind to the Imperial Court at Leipzig. The Supreme Court is by no means the sole court of highest instance, for the suits in single states which properly fall within the jurisdiction of a state can go no higher than the highest court of appeal of that state. The Supreme Court in Washington is the court of last instance for federal cases; but in order to disburden the judges in Washington, there are large classes of civil cases pertaining to the federal courts, which can be carried no higher than the federal court of appeals of a given circuit.

Much more important than the cases in which the Supreme Court is really the court of highest instance for federal suits, are those others in which it is at once the court of first and last instance; these are the processes which the Constitution assigns immediately to the Supreme Court. They are chiefly suits in which a single state, or in which the United States is itself a party, for the Supreme Bench alone can settle disagreements between states and decide whether the federal or state laws conflict with the Constitution. In this sense the Supreme Court is higher than both President and Congress. If it decides that a treaty which the Executive has concluded, or a law which has been passed by the Legislative, violates the Constitution, then the doings of both Congress and the President are annulled. There is only one way by which a decision of the Supreme Court can be set aside—namely, by the vote of a three-fourths majority of all the states; that is, by an amendment of the Constitution. There are some instances of this in the history of the United States; but virtually the decision of the nine judges of the Supreme Court is the highest law of the land.

The Supreme Court has annulled Congressional measures twenty-one times and state statutes more than two hundred times, because these were at variance with the Constitution. Many of these have been cases of the greatest political importance, long and bitterly fought out in the legislatures, and followed with excitement by the public. The whole country has often been divided in its opinion on a legal question, and even the decision itself of the nine judges has sometimes been handed down with only a small majority. Nevertheless, for many years the country has every time submitted to the oracle of the Supreme Court, and considered the whole issue definitely closed.

One is not to suppose that the Supreme Court occupies itself with handing down legal verdicts in the abstract and in a way declaring its veto whenever Congress or some legislature infringes the Constitution. Such a thing is out of the question, since theoretically the Supreme Court, although the equal is not the superior of Congress; most of all, it is a court and not a legislature. The question of law does not come up then before this tribunal until there is a concrete case which has to be decided, and the Supreme Court has always declined to hand down a theoretical interpretation in advance of an actual suit. As early as the eighteenth century, Washington was unable to elicit from the Supreme Court any reply to a hypothetical question. Even when the actual case has come up, the Supreme Court does not say that a certain law is invalid, but decides strictly on the one case before it, and announces on what principle of the law it has based its decision. If there is a disagreement between two laws, the decision of the Court simply lays the practical emphasis on one rather than on the other. It is true that in this way nothing but one single case is decided; but here the principle of common law comes in — one decision establishes a point of law, and the Supreme Court and all lower courts likewise must in future hand down verdicts conformable thereto. The legislative law so superseded is thus practically annulled and made non-existent. In the Supreme Court one sees again that the security of national justice rests on the binding force of former decisions.

It will be enough to point out two decisions which have been given in recent years and which have interested the whole country. In the year 1894 Congress passed a new tax law; one clause of this law taxed every income which was larger than a certain amount. It was taxation of the wealthy. So far as income was obtained by actal labour the tax was undoubtedly valid. But New York barristers doubted the constitutionality of this tax in so far as it was laid on the interest from securities or on rents; because the Constitution expressly says that direct taxation for the country must be levied by the separate states, and in such a way that the whole sum to be raised shall be apportioned among the different states according to their population. The counsels of the wealthy New Yorkers said this provision ought to apply here. The difference would be for every rich man in thickly populated states a very considerable one. If the tax was to be apportioned according to population, the poor states must also bear their share. While it came to be levied on the individuals the largest part of the burden would fall to the millionaires, who are grouped in a few states. The Supreme Court would say nothing so long as the discussion was theoretical. Finally, a case was tested; when the lawyers were prepared, a certain citizen refused to pay the income tax and let the matter go to court. The first barristers in the country were divided on the question, as was also the Supreme

Court. The majority decided in favour of the citizen who refused to pay the tax, because in its opinion the tax was a direct one, and therefore the constitutional provision relating to direct taxation was in force. By this one decision the income tax was set aside, and instead of ten thousand new suits being brought, of which the outcome was already clear, the excess taxes were everywhere paid back. At bottom this was the victory, over both President and Congress, of a single eminent barrister, who is to-day the ambassador to England.

A still more important decision, because it involved the whole political future of the United States, was that on the island possessions. By the treaty with Spain, Porto Rico had become a possession of the United States, and was therefore subject to United States law; but Congress proceeded to lay a tariff on certain wares which were imported from the island. There were two possible views. On the one hand, the Constitution prescribes that there shall be no customs duties of any sort between the states which belong to the Union; and since Porto Rico is a part of the Union the rest of the states may not levy a tariff on imports from the island. On the other hand, the Constitution empowers Congress to regulate at its discretion the affairs of such territory as belongs to the United States, but has not yet been granted the equal rights of states; thus the other provision of the Constitution would not immediately apply to this island. The question had never before been decided, because the Indian territories, the Mexican accessions, and Alaska had never been treated as Porto Rico now was. Congress had previously taken for granted that the Constitution was in force for these territories, but now the imperialistic tendencies of politics had created a new situation, and one which had to be settled.

Here too, of course, the Supreme Court did not try to settle the theoretical question which was stirring the whole country; but presently came the action of Downes *vs.* Bidwell, a simple suit in which a New York commercial house was the complainant, and the New York Customs the defendant. In case the provisions of the Constitution were to hold for the entire domain of the United States, the tariff which Congress had enacted was unconstitutional, but if the Constitution was to hold only for the states, while Congress was sovereign over all other possessions, the tariff was constitutional. The Supreme Court decided for this latter interpretation by five votes against four, and the commercial house paid its tax. Therewith the principle was decided for all time, and if to-morrow the United States should get hold of Asia and Africa, it is assured from the outset that the new domain would not be under the Constitution, but under the authority of Congress — simply because Downes lost his case against Customs Inspector Bidwell, and had to pay six hundred dollars in duty on oranges.

This last case shows clearly that the decisions by no means always support the Constitution against legislative bodies; and statistics show that although in two hundred cases the verdict has been against the legislatures, it has been more often decided in their favour. The entire history of the Supreme Court shows that in a conservative spirit it has always done full justice to both the centralizing and particularizing tendencies. It has shown this conciliatory attitude especially by the firm authority with which it has decided the hazardous disputes over boundaries and other differences, between the several states, so that such disputes really come up no longer. For a century the Supreme Court has been a shining example of a federal tribunal.

Such complete domination of the national life could not have been attained by the Supreme Bench if it had not remained well above all the doings of the political parties, and that it does so may seem surprising when one considers the conditions under which the judges are appointed. The President selects the new judge whenever, by death or retirement, a vacancy occurs among the nine judges; and the Senate confirms the selection. Party factors, therefore, determine the appointment, and in point of fact Democratic Presidents have always appointed judges belonging to their own party, and Republicans have done the same. The result is that both parties are represented in the Supreme Court. That in political questions, such as the case of Porto Rico, which we have mentioned, party conceptions figure somewhat in the decision of the judges is undoubted. Yet they figure only in the sense that allegiance to one or the other party involves certain fundamental convictions, and these necessarily come into play in the judicial verdict. On the other hand, there is never the least suspicion that the judges harbour political schemes or seek in their decision to favour either political party. This results from the fact that it is a matter of honour with both parties to place really the most distinguished jurists in these highest judicial offices — jurists who will be for all time an honour to the administration which appointed them. They are almost exclusively men who have never taken part in technical politics, but who have been either distinguished judges elsewhere or else leading barristers, and who, from the day of their appointment on, will be only judges. Their position is counted among the most honourable which there is, and it would almost never happen that a jurist would decline his appointment, although the position, like all American official positions, is inadequately rewarded; the salary is ten thousand dollars, while any great lawyer is able to earn many times that sum. At the present moment there sits on the Supreme Bench a group of men, every one of whom represents the highest kind of American spirit. The bustle and confusion, which prevail in the two wings of the Capitol, does not invade the hall where the nine judges hold their sessions. These men are, in the American public mind, the very symbol of conscience.

We shall have occasion to consider later on the administration of justice by the nation, under various points of view. While in many respects this will appear less conscientious and more especially less deliberate, it will, nevertheless, recall not a few admirable features of the Supreme Court.

CHAPTER SIX

City and State

THE Constitution, the President and his Cabinet, the Senate, the House of Representatives, and the Supreme Court, in short all of those institutions which we have so far sketched, belong to the United States together. The European who pictures to himself the life of an American will inevitably come to think that these are the factors which most influence the life of the political individual. But such is not the case; the American citizen in daily life is first of all a member of his special state. The organization of the Union is more prominent on the surface than that of the single state, but this latter is more often felt by the inhabitants.

The quality of an American state can be more easily communicated to a German than to an Englishman, Frenchman, or Russian. The resident of Bavaria or Saxony knows already how a man may have a two-fold patriotism, allegiance to the state and also to the empire; so that he can recognize the duties as well as the privileges which are grouped around two centres. The essentials of the American state, however, are not described by the comparison with a state in the German Empire, which is relatively of too little importance; for in comparison with the Union the American state has more independence and sovereignty than the German. We have observed before that it has its own laws and its own court of last appeal; but these are only two of the many indications of its practical and theoretical independence. The significant organic importance of the state shows itself not less clearly if one thinks of the cities subordinate to it, rather than of the Federation which is superior to it. While the German state is more dependent on the Federation than is the American, the German city is more independent of the state than is any city in the United

States. The political existence of the American city is entirely dependent on the legislature of its state. The Federation on the one hand and the cities on the other, alike depend for their administrative existence on the separate states.

It is not merely an historical relic of that time when the thirteen states united, but hesitated to give up their individual rights to the Federation; a time when there were only six cities of more than eight thousand inhabitants. Nothing has changed in this respect, and it is not only the Democratic party to-day which jealously guards state rights; the state all too often tyrannizes still over the large cities within its borders. There are some indications, indeed, that the state rights are getting even more emphasis than formerly — perhaps as a reaction against the fact that, in spite of all constitutional precautions, those states which have close commercial relations tend practically to merge more and more with one another.

On observing the extraordinary tenacity with which the federal laws and the local patriotism of the individual cling to the independence of each one of the forty-five states, one is inclined to suppose that it is a question of extremely profound differences in the customs, ideals, temperaments, and interests of the different states. But such is not at all the case. The states are, of course, very unlike, especially in size; Texas and Rhode Island, for instance, would compare about as Prussia and Reuss. There are even greater differences in the density of population; and the general cast of physiognomy varies in different regions of the country. The Southerner shows the character bred by plantation life; the citizen of the North-east evinces the culture bred of higher intellectual interests; while the citizens of the West attest the differences between their agricultural and mining districts. Yet the divisions here are not states, but larger regions comprising groups of states, and it sometimes happens that more striking contrasts are found within a certain state than would be found between neighbouring states. The state lines were after all often laid down on paper with a ruler, while nature has seldom made sharp lines of demarcation, and the different racial elements of the population are fairly well mixed. For the last century the pioneers of the nation have carried it steadily westward, so that in many states the number of those born in the state is much less than of those who have migrated to it; and of course the obstinate assertion of the prerogatives of such a state does not arise from any cherished local traditions to which the inhabitants are accustomed. The special complexion of any provincial district, moreover, is assailed from all sides and to a large extent obliterated, in these days of the telegraph and of extraordinarily rapid commercial intercourse and industrial organization.

The uniformity of fashions, the wide-spread distribution of newspapers and magazines, the great political parties, and the intense national patriotism all work towards the one end — that from Maine to California the American is very much the same sort of man, and feels himself, in contrast with a foreigner, to be merely an American. And yet in spite of all this each single state holds obstinately to its separate rights. It is the same principle which we have seen at work in the American individual. The more the individuals or the states resemble one another the more they seem determined to preserve their autonomy; the more similar the substance, the sharper must be the distinctions in form.

The inner similarity of the different states is shown by the fact that, while each one has its own statute-book and an upper court which jealously guards its special constitution, nevertheless all of the forty-five state constitutions are framed very much alike. The Constitution of the United States would by no means require this, since it prescribes merely that every state constitution shall be republican in form; and yet not a single state has taken advantage of its great freedom. The constitutions of the older states were modelled partly on the institutions of the English fatherland, partly on those of colonial days; and when many of these features were finally embodied in the Federal Constitution, they were reflected back once more in the constitutions of the states which later came to be. The new states have simply borrowed the general structure of the older states and of the Federation, without much statesmanlike imagination; although here and there is some adaptation to special circumstances. There are indeed some odd differences at superficial points, and inasmuch as, in contrast to the Federal Constitution, the state constitutions have frequently been reshaped by the people, a reactionary tendency or some radical and hasty innovation has here and there been incorporated.

The principles, however, are everywhere the same. Each state has framed a reduced copy of the Federal Constitution, and one finds a still more diminutive representation of the same thing in the American city charter. Yet we must not forget here that, although theoretically and constitutionally the state is greater than the city, yet in fact the city of New York has a population eighty times as large as the State of Nevada, with its bare 40,000 inhabitants; or, again, that the budget of the State of Massachusetts is hardly a quarter as large as that of Boston, its capital city.

Thus, like the Union, both city and state have a charter and an executive, a dual legislature, and a judiciary, all of which reproduce on a small scale all the special features of the federal organization. The city charter is different from that of the state, in that it is not drawn up by the inhabitants of the city, but, as we have said, has to be granted by the state legislature. The head of the state executive, the governor, is in a way a small president, who is elected directly by the people, generally for a two years' term of office. In the city government the mayor corresponds to him, and is likewise elected by the citizens; and in the larger cities for the same period. A staff of executive officers is provided for both the mayor and the governor.

Under the city government are ranged the heads of departments, who are generally chosen by the mayor himself; New York, for instance, has eighteen such divisions — the departments of finance, taxation, law, police, health, fire, buildings, streets, water-supply, bridges, education, charities, penal institutions, park-ways, public buildings, etc. The most important officials under the state government are always the state secretary, the state attorney-general, and the treasurer. Close to the governor stands the lieutenant-governor, who, after the pattern of the federal government, is president of the upper legislative chamber. The governor is empowered to convene the legislature, to approve or to veto all state measures, to pardon criminals, to appoint many of the lower officials, although generally his appointment must be confirmed by the upper legislative body, and he is invariably in sole command of the state militia. The legislature of the state is always, and that of the cities generally, divided into two chambers. Here again the membership in the upper chamber is smaller than that of the lower and more difficult to obtain. Often the state legislature does not meet in the largest city, but makes for itself a sort of political oasis, a diminutive Washington. The term of office in the legislature is almost always two years, and everywhere the same committee system is followed as at the Capitol in Washington. Only a member of the legislative body can propose bills, and such propositions are referred at once to a special committee, where they are discussed and perhaps buried. They can come to the house only through the hands of this committee. The freedom given to the state legislature is somewhat less than that given by the Constitution to Congress. While all the parliamentary methods are strikingly and often very naïvely copied after those in use at Washington, the state constitutions were careful from the outset that certain matters should not be subject to legislative egotism. On the other hand the state legislature hands down many of its rights to inferior bodies, such as district, county, and city administrations; but in all these cases in which there is a real transfer of powers, it is characteristic that these really pertain to the state as such, and can, therefore, be withdrawn by the state legislatures from the smaller districts at any time.

The entire administration of the state falls to the state legislature; that is, the measures for public instruction, taxation, public works, and the public debt, penal institutions, the supervision of railroads, corporations, factories, and commerce. In addition to this there are the civil and criminal statutes, with the exception of those few cases which the Constitution reserves for federal legislation; and, finally, there is the granting of franchises and monopolies to public and industrial corporations. Of course, within this authority there is nothing which concerns the relation of one state to other states or to foreign powers, nor anything of customs revenues or other such matters as are enacted uniformly for all parts of the country by the federal government. The state has, however, the right to fix the conditions under which an immigrant may become a naturalized citizen; and a foreigner becomes an American citizen by being naturalized under the law of any one of the forty-five states. All this gives an exceedingly large field of action to state legislatures, and it is astonishing how little dissimilar are the provisions which the different states have enacted.

The city governments are very diverse in size, but in all the larger cities consist of two houses. The German reader must not suppose that these work together like the German magistrate and the municipal representative assembly. Since in America the legislative and executive are always sharply sundered, the heads of departments under the executive — that is, the German Stadträte — have no place in the law-making body. The dual legislative is, therefore, in a way an upper and lower municipal representative assembly, elected in different ways and having similar differences in function as the two chambers of Congress. Here too, for instance, bills of appropriation have to originate in the lower house. Oddly enough, the city legislative is generally not entrusted with education, but this is administered by a separate municipal board, elected directly by the people. One who becomes acquainted with the intellectual composition of the average city father, will find this separation of educational matters not at all surprising, and very beneficent and reasonable.

In general, one may say that the mayor is more influential in the city government than that body which represents the citizens; this in contrast to the situation in the state government, where the governor is relatively less influential than the legislature. The chief function of the governor is really a negative one, that of affixing his veto from time to time on an utterly impossible law. The mayor, on the other hand, can shape things and leave the stamp of his personality on his city. In the state, as in the city, it often happens that the head of the executive and a majority of the legislative belong to opposite parties, and this not because the party issues are forgotten in the local elections, but because the methods of election are different.

The division of public affairs into city and state issues leaves, of course, room for still a third group, namely, the affairs of communities which are still smaller than cities. These, too, derive their authority entirely from the state legislature, but all states leave considerable independence to the smaller political units. In local village government the historic differences of the various regions show out more clearly than in either state or city government. The large cities are to all intents and purposes cast in the same mould everywhere; their like needs have developed like forms of life; and the coming together of great numbers of people have everywhere created the same economic situation. But the scattered population gets its social and economic articulation in the

North, South, and West, in quite different ways; and this difference, at an early time when the problems of a large city were so far not known, led to different types of village organizations, which have been historically preserved.

When the English colonies were growing up, the differences in this connection between the New England states and Virginia were extreme. The colonies on the northern shores, with their bays and harbours, their hilly country and large forests, could not spread their population out over large tracts of land, and were concentrated within limited regions; and this tendency was further emphasized by Puritan traditions, which required the population to take active part in church services. There naturally was developed a local form of government for small districts, which corresponded to old English traditions. The citizens gathered from all parts of every district to discuss their common affairs and to decide what taxes should be raised, what streets built, and, most of all, what should be done for their churches and schools, and for the poor. In Virginia, on the other hand, where very large plantations were laid out, there could be no such small communities; the population was more scattered, and affairs of general interest had necessarily to be entrusted to special representatives, who were in part elected by small parishes and in part appointed by the governor. The political unit here was not the town, but the county.

The difference in these two types is the more worthy of consideration because it explains how the North and South have been able to contribute such different and yet such equally valuable factors to all the great events of American history. New England and Virginia were the two centres of influence in Revolutionary times and when the Union was being completed, but their influences were wholly different. New England served the country by effecting an extraordinarily thorough education of its masses. by giving them a long schooling in local self-government; each individual was obliged to meditate on public affairs. Virginia, however, gave to the country its brilliant leaders; the masses remained backward, but the county representatives practised and trained themselves to the rôle of leading statesmen. Between these two extremes lay the Middle Atlantic States, where a mixed form of town and county representation had necessarily developed from the social conditions; and these three types, the Northern, Southern, and mixed, worked slowly back during the nineteenth century from the coast toward the West. Settlers in the new states carried with them their familiar forms of local government, so that to-day these three forms may still be found through the country. To-day the chief functions of town governments are public instruction, care for the poor, and the building of roads. Religious life is, of course, here as in the city, state, and Union, wholly separated from the political organization. The police systems of these local governments in town and village are wholly rudimentary. While the police system is perhaps the most difficult chapter in American city government, the country districts have always done very well with almost none. This reflects the moral vigour of the American rural population. The people sleep everywhere with their front doors open, and everywhere presuppose the willing assistance of their neighbours. It was not until great populations commenced to gather in cities, that those social evils arose, of which the police system, which was created to obviate them, is itself not the least.

Any one overlooking this interplay of public forces sees that in town and city, state and Union, it is not a question of forcing administrative energies into a prescribed sphere of action. They expand everywhere as they will, both from the smaller to the larger sphere and from the larger to the smaller. Therefore, the Union naturally desires to take on itself those functions of state legislation in which a lack of uniformity would be dangerous; as, for instance, the divorce laws, the discrepancies in which between different states are so great that the necessity of more uniform divorce regulations is ever becoming more keenly felt. At present it is a fact that a man who is divorced under the laws of Dakota and marries again can be punished in New York for bigamy. A similar situation exists in regard to certain trade regulations, where there are unfortunate discrepancies. Many opponents of the trusts want even an amendment to the Constitution which will bring them under federal law, and prevent these huge industrial concerns from incorporating under the too lax laws of certain states.

Still easier is it for the states to interfere in the city governments. If the Union wishes to make new regulations for the state, the Federal Constitution has to be amended; while if the state wants to hold a tighter rein on city government it can do so directly, for, as we have seen, the cities derive all their powers from the state legislature. There is, indeed, considerable tendency now to restrict the privileges of cities, and much of this is sound, especially where the state authority is against open municipal corruption. The general tendency is increasing to give the state considerable rights of supervision over matters of local hygiene, industrial conditions, penal and benevolent institutions. The advantages of uniformity which accrue from state supervision are emphasized by many persons, and still more the advantage derived from handing over hygienic, technical, and pedagogical questions to the well-paid state experts, instead of leaving them to the inexperience of small districts and towns. There is no doubt that on these lines the functions of the state are being extended slowly but steadily.

Then again the cities and towns in their turn are tending to absorb once more such forces as are subordinate to them, and thus to increase the municipal functions. The fundamental principles which have dominated the economic life in the United States and brought it to a healthful development, leave the greatest possible play for private initiative; thus not very long ago it was a matter of course that the water supply, the street lighting, the steam and electric railways should be wholly in the hands of private companies. A change is coming into these affairs, for it is clearly seen that industries of this sort are essentially different from ordinary business undertakings, not only because they make use of public roads, but also because such plants necessarily gain monopolies which find it easy to levy tribute upon the public. In recent years, therefore, city governments have little by little taken over the water supplies, and tend somewhat to limit the sphere of other private undertakings of this sort — as, for instance, that of street-lighting. At the same time there is an unmistakable tendency for city and town to undertake certain tasks which are not economically necessary, and which have been left hitherto to private initiative. Cities are building bath-houses and laundries, playgrounds and gymnasiums, and more especially public libraries and museums, providing concerts and other kinds of amusements and bureaus for the registration of those needing employment; in short, are everywhere taking up newly arisen duties and performing them at public expense.

There is, on the other hand, a strong counter-current to these tendencies of the large units to perform the duties of the small — the strong those of the weak, the city those of the individual, the state those of the city, and the Union those of the state. The opposition begins already in the smallest circle of all, where one sees a strong anti-centralizing tendency. The county or city is not entitled, it is said, to expend the taxpayers' money for luxuries or for purposes other than those of general utility. It should be generous philanthropists or private organizations that build museums and libraries, bath-houses and gymnasiums, but not the city, which gets its money from the pockets of the working classes. Although optimists have proposed it, there will certainly be for a long time yet no subsidized municipal theatres; and it is noticeable that the liberal offers of Carnegie to erect public libraries are being more and more declined by various town councils, because Carnegie's plan of foundation calls for a considerable augmentation from the public funds. And wherever it is a question of indispensable services, such as tramways and street-lighting, the majority generally says that it is cheaper every time to pay a small profit to a private company than to undertake a large business at the public expense. From the American point of view private companies are often too economical, while public enterprises are invariably shamelessly wasteful.

The city pays too dear and borrows at too high a rate; in short, regulates its transactions without that wholesome pressure exerted by stockholders who are looking for dividends. Worst of all, the undertakings which are carried on by municipalities are often simply handed over to political corruption. Instead of trained experts, political wire-pullers of the party in office are employed in all the best-paid positions, and even where no money is consciously wasted, a gradual laxness creeps in little by little, which makes the service worse than it would ever be in a private company, which stands all the time in fear of competition. For this reason the American is absolutely against entrusting railroads and telegraph lines to the hands of the state. When a large telegraph company did not adequately serve the needs of the public, another concern spread its network of wires through the whole country;

and since then the Western Union and Postal Telegraph have been in competition, and the public has been admirably served. But what relief would there have been if the state had had a monopoly of the telegraph lines, with politicians in charge who would have been indifferent to public demands? The wish to be economical, to keep business out of politics, and to keep competition open, all work together, so that the extension of municipal functions, although ardently wished on many sides, goes on very slowly; and it is justly pointed out that whenever private corporations in any way abuse their privileges the community at large has certainly plenty of means for supervising them, and of giving them franchises under such conditions as shall amply protect public interests. When a private company wishes to use public streets for its car-tracks, gas or water pipes, or electric wires, the community can easily enough grant the permission for a limited length of time, reserving perhaps the right to purchase or requiring a substantial payment for the franchise and a portion of the profits, and can leave the rest to public watchfulness and to the regular publication of the company's reports. It is not to be doubted that the tendencies in this direction are to-day very marked.

Just as private initiative is trying not to be swallowed up by the community, so the community is trying to save itself from the state. So far as the village, town, or county is concerned, nobody denies that state experts could afford a better public service than the inexperienced local boards, and, nevertheless, it is felt that every place knows best after all just what is adapted to its own needs. The closest adaptation to local desires, as, say, in questions of public schools and roads, has been always a fundamental American principle. This principle started originally from the peculiar conditions which existed in the several colonies and from the needs of the pioneers; but it has led to such a steady progress in the country's development that no American would care to give it up, even if here and there certain advantages could be had by introducing greater uniformities. There is a still more urgent motive; it is only this opportunity of regulating the affairs of the small district which gives to every community, even every neighbourhood, the necessary schooling for the public duties of the American citizen. If he is deprived of the right to take care of his own district, that spirit of self-determination and independence cannot develop, on which the success of the American experiment in democracy entirely depends. Political pedagogy requires that the state shall respect the individuality of the small community so far as this is in any way possible.

The relation between the city and the state is somewhat different; no one would ask the parliamentarians of the state legislature to hold off in order that the population of the large city may have the opportunity to keep their political interests alive and to preserve their spirit of self-determination. This spirit is at home in the streets of the great city; it is not only wide-awake there, but it is clamorous and almost too urgent. When, now, the municipalities in their struggle against the dictation of the state, meet with the sympathies of intelligent people, this is owing to the simple fact that the city, in which all cultured interests are gathered generally, has in all matters a higher point of view than the representatives of the entire state, in which the more primitive rural population predominates. When, for instance, the provincial members which the State of New York has elected meet in Albany, and with their rural majority make regulations for governing the three million citizens of New York City, regulations which are perhaps paternally well meant, but which sometimes show a petty distrust and disapproval of that great and wicked place, the result is often grotesque. The state laws, however, favour this sort of dictation.

The state constitutions still show in this respect the condition of things at a time in which the city as such had hardly come into recognition. The nineteenth century began in America with six cities of over eight thousand inhabitants, and ended with 545. Moreover, in 1800 those six places contained less than four per cent. of the population, while in 1900 the 545 cities contained more than thirty-three per cent. thereof. Since only a twenty-fifth part of the nation lived in cities, the greater power of the scattered provincial population seemed natural; but when now a third of the nation prefers city life, and especially the more intelligent, more educated, and wealthy third, the limitations to independent municipal rights become an obstacle to culture.

Finally, the states themselves are opposing on good grounds every assumption of rights by the Federation — the same good grounds, indeed, which the community has for opposing the state, and many others besides. It is felt that historically it has been the initiative of individuals rather than of the central government which has helped the nation to make its tremendous strides forward, and that this initiative should not only be rewarded with privileges, but should also be stimulated by duties. The more nearly one state is like another, so much the more energetically does it forbid the others to interfere in its affairs; and the more it is like the Union the more earnestly it seeks not to let its distinct individuality be swallowed up. Besides the moral effort toward state individuality, there is a powerful state egotism at work in many states which makes for the same end. Back of everything, finally, there is the fear of the purely political dangers which are involved in an exaggerated centralization. We have seen in this a fundamental sentiment of the Democratic party.

Thus at every step in the political organization centrifugal and centripetal forces stand opposite each other in the Federal Union, in the state, in the county, and in the city. And public opinion is busy discussing the arguments on both sides. Every day sees movements in one or the other direction, and there is never any let up. In all these discussions it is a question of conflicting principles, which in themselves seem just. There is, however, another contrast — that between principle and lack of principle. In the Union, the state, and the city, centralists and anti-centralists meet on questions of law; but in each one of these places there are groups of people working against the law and trying in every way to get around it. In these discussions there is a true and false, but in the conflicts there is a right and wrong; and here argumentation is not needed, but sheer resistance. If one does not purposely close one's eyes, one cannot doubt that the public life of America holds certain abuses, which are against the spirit of the Constitution and which too often come near to being criminal. One can ask, to be sure, if that lack of conscience does not have place in every form of state in one way or another, and if the necessity of developing a sound public spirit to fight against abuse may itself not be an important factor in helping on the spirit of self-determination to victory.

Any one who should write the history of disorganizing forces in American public life will have the least to say about federal politics, a good deal more about those of the state, and most of all about those of the city. Certain types of temptation are repeated at every stage. There is, for instance, the legislative committee, which is found alike in Congress, in the state legislatures, and in the city councils. Bills are virtually decided at first by two or three persons who exert their influence behind the closed doors of the committee room; and naturally enough corrupt influences can much more easily make their way there than in the discussions of the whole house. If a municipal committee has a bill under discussion, the acceptance of which means hundreds of thousands of dollars saved or lost to the street railway company, then certainly, although the president and directors of the company will not themselves take any unlawful action, yet in some way some less scrupulous agent will step in who will single out a bar-keeper or hungry advocate or fourth-class politician in the committee, who might be amenable to certain gilded arguments. And if this agent finds no such person he will find some one else who does not care for money, but who would like very well to see his brother-in-law given a good position in the railway company, or perhaps to see the track extended past his own house.

Of course the same thing happens when a measure is brought before the state legislature, and the vote of some obscure provincial attorney on the committee means millions of dollars to the banking firm, the trust, the mining company, or the industrial community as a whole. Here the lobby gets in its work. The different states are, of course, very different in this respect; the cruder forms of bribery would not avail in Massachusetts and would be very dangerous; but they feel differently about such things in Montana. As we have already said, Congress is free of such taints.

Another source of temptation, which likewise exists for all American law-giving bodies, arises from the fact that all measures must be proposed by the members of such body. Thus local needs are taken care of by the activity of the popular representatives, and, therefore, the number of bills proposed becomes very large. Just as during the last session of Congress, 17,000 measures were proposed in the lower house, hundreds of thousands of bills are brought before the state legislatures and city councils. There is never a lack of reasons for bringing up superfluous bills. And since the system of secret committees makes it difficult for the individual representative to appear before the whole house and to make a speech, it follows that the introduction of a few bills is almost the only way in which the politician can show his constituency that he was not elected to the legislature in vain, and that he is actually representing the interests of his supporters. A milder form of this abuse consists of handing in bills which are framed by reason of personal friendships or hatreds; and the same thing appears in uglier form when it is not a question of personal favour, but of services bought and paid for, not of personal hatred, but of a systematic conspiracy to extort money from those who need legislation. The milder form of wrongdoing, in which it is only a question of personal favours, can be found everywhere, even in the Capitol at Washington, and the much-boasted Senatorial courtesy lends a sort of sanction to the abuse.

This evil is strengthened, as it perhaps originated, by the tacit recognition of the principle that every legislator represents, first of all, his local district. It is not expected of a senator that he shall look at every question from the point of view of the general welfare, but rather that he shall take first of all the point of view of his state. It has indeed been urged that the senator is nothing but an ambassador sent to represent his state before the federal government. If this is so, it follows at once that no state delegate ought to have any control over the interests of another state, and so the wishes of any senator should be final in all matters pertaining to his own state. From this it is only a small step to the existing order of things, in which every senator is seconded on his own proposals by his colleagues, if he will second them on theirs. In this way each delegate has the chance to place the law-giving machinery at the service of those who will in any way advance his political popularity among his constituents, and help him during his next candidacy. And then, too, a good deal is done merely for appearances; bills are entered, printed, and circulated in the local papers to tickle the spirits of constituents, while the proposer himself has not supposed for a moment that his proposition will pass the committee. Things go in the state legislatures in quite the same way. Each member is first of all the representative of his own district, and he claims a certain right of not being interfered with in matters which concern that district. In this way he is accorded great freedom to grant all sorts of legislative favours which will bring him sufficient returns, or to carry through legal intrigues to the injury of his political opponents. And here in the state legislature, as in the city council, where the same principles are in use, there is the best possible chance of selling one's friendly services at their market value. If a railroad company sees a bill for public safety proposed which is technically senseless and exaggerated, which will impede traffic in the state, and involve ruinous expenditures, it will naturally be tempted not to sit idle in the hope that a majority of the committee will set the bill aside; for that course would be hazardous. It may be that all sorts of prejudices will work together toward reporting the bill favourably. If the company wants to be secure, it will rather try such arguments as only capitalists have at their command. And it has here two ways open: either to "convince" the committee or else to make arrangements with the man who proposed the bill, so that he shall recall it. If the possibility of such doings once exists in politics, there is no means of preventing dishonourable persons from making money in such ways; not only do they yield to temptation after they have been elected, but also they seek their elections solely in order to exploit just such opportunities.

Here we meet that factor which distinguishes the state legislature, particularly of those states whose traditions are less firmly grounded, and still more the city councils, so completely from the federal chambers in Washington. The chance to misuse office is alike in all three places, but men who have entered the political arena with honourable motives very seldom yield to criminal temptation. The usual abuses are committed almost wholly by men who have sought their political office solely for the sake of criminal opportunities; and this class of pseudo-politicians can bring itself into the city council very easily, in the state legislature without much difficulty, but almost never into Congress. If it were attractive or distinguished or interesting to be in the state legislature, or on the board of aldermen, there would be a plenty of worthy applicants for the position, and all doubtful persons would find the door closed; but the actual case is quite different.

To be a member of Congress, to sit in the House of Representatives or perhaps in the Senate, is something which the very best men may well desire. The position is conspicuous and picturesque, and against the background of high political life the individual feels himself entrusted with an important rôle. And although many may hesitate to transfer their homes to the federal capital, nevertheless the country has never had difficulty in finding sufficient Representatives who are imbued with the spirit of the Constitution. On the other hand, to serve as popular representative in the state legislature means for the better sort of man, unless he is a professional politician, a considerable sacrifice. The legislature generally meets in a remote part of the state, at every session requires many months of busy work on some committee, and most of this work is nothing but disputing and compromising over the thousand petty bills, in which no really broad political considerations enter. It is a dreary, dispiriting work, which can attract only three kinds of men: firstly, those who are looking forward to a political career in the service of the party machine and undergo a term in the state legislature only as preparation for some more important office; secondly, those who are glad of the small and meagre salary of a representative; and finally, those whose modest ambition is satisfied if they are delegated by their fellow-citizens in any sort of representative capacity. Therefore the general level of personality in the state legislature is low. Men who have important positions will seldom consent to go, and when influential persons do enter state politics it is actually with a certain spirit of renunciation, and not so much to take part in the business of the legislature as to reform the legislature itself. Since this is the case, it is not surprising that the most unwholesome elements flock thither, extortioners and corrupt persons who count on it, that in regard to dishonourable transactions, the other side will have the same interest in preserving silence as themselves.

We must also not forget that the American principle of strictly local representation works in another way to keep down the level of the smaller legislative bodies. If the Representative of a certain locality must have his residence there, the number of possible candidates is very much restricted. This is even more true of the city government, where the principle of local representation requires that every part of the city, even the poorest and most squalid, shall elect none but men who reside in it. To be sure, there is a good deal in this that is right; but it necessarily brings a sort of people together in public committee with whom it is not exactly a pleasure for most men to work. The questions which have to be talked over here are still more trivial, and more than that, the motives which attract corrupt persons are somewhat more tangible here; since in the rapid growth of the great city the awarding of monopolies and contracts creates a sort of spoilsman's paradise. As the better elements hold aloof from this city government, by so much more do corrupt persons have freer play.

The relation of the city to both the state and Federation is even more unfavourable when one comes to consider not the legislative, but the executive, department. Whereas in Washington, for example, a single man stands at the head of every department in the administration, and is entirely responsible for the running of things, there has frequently been in the city administrations, up to a short time ago, a committee which is so responsible — this in agreement with the old American idea that a majority can decide best. Where, however, a single man was entrusted with administrative powers, he was selected generally by the mayor and the city council together, and they seldom called a real expert to such a position. In any case, since the administration depends wholly on party politics, and the upper staff changes with each new party victory, there is no such chance for a life career here as would tempt competent men to offer their services.

In this part of the government, moreover, there is more danger from the administration by committees than anywhere else. The responsibility of a majority cannot be fixed anywhere; and where the mayor and aldermen work together in the selection of officials, neither of the two parties is quite responsible for the outcome — which is naturally not to be compared with the closely guarded election of officials under German conditions. For in Germany the selection of the head of a city department will lie between a few similarly trained specialists, while the administration of a New York or a Chicago department, as, say, that of the police or of street-cleaning, is thought to presuppose no special preparation, and therefore the number of possible candidates is unlimited. It is not surprising that such irresponsible committees are not above corruption, and that many a man who has received a well-paid administrative position in return for his services to the party, proceeds to make his hay while the sun shines. It is true that there are many departments where no such temptation comes in question. It is, for example, universally believed that the fire departments of all American cities are admirably managed. The situation is most doubtful in the case of the police departments, which, of course, are subject to the greatest temptations; and here, too, there can be the worst abuses in some ways along with the highest efficiency in others. The service for public protection in a large city may be admirably organized and crime strenuously followed up, and nevertheless the police force may be full of corruption. Thieves and murderers are punctiliously suppressed, while at the same time the police are extorting a handsome income from bar-rooms which evade the Sunday laws, from public-houses which exist in violation of city statutes, and from unlawful places of amusement.

To be sure, we must again and again emphasize two things. In the first place, it is probable that nine-tenths of the charges are exaggerated and slanderous. The punishments are so considerable, the means of investigation so active, and the public watchfulness so keen, both on account of the party hostility and by virtue of a sensational press, that it would be hardly comprehensible psychologically, if political crime in the lowest strata of city or state were to be really anything but the exception. The many almost fanatically conducted investigations produce from their mountains of transactions only the smallest mice, and the state attorney is seldom able to make out a case of actual bribery. In this matter the Anglo-Americans are pleased to point out that wherever investigations have ended in making out a case which could really be punished, the person has been generally an Irishman or some other European immigrant. In any case, the collection of immigrants from Europe in the large cities contributes importantly to the unhappy condition of city politics.

In the second place, we must urge once more that the mere distribution of well-paid municipal positions to party politicians is not necessarily in itself an abuse. When, for instance, in a large city, a Republican is succeeded by a Democratic mayor, he can generally bestow a dozen well-paid and a hundred or two more modest commissions to men who have helped in the party victory. But he will be careful not to pick out those who are wholly unworthy, since that would not only compromise himself, but would damage his party and prevent its being again victorious. If he succeeds, on the other hand, in finding men who will serve the city industriously, intelligently, and ably in proportion to their pay, it is ridiculous to call the promise of such offices by way of party reward in any sense a plundering of the city, or to make it seem that the giving of positions to colleagues of one's party is another sort of corruption.

The evils of public life and the possibility of criminal practices are not confined to legislative and executive bodies. The judiciary also has its darker side. One must believe fanatically in the people in order not to see what judicial monstrosities occasionally come out of the emphasis which is given to the jury system. The law requires that the twelve men chosen from the people to the jury must come to a unanimous decision; they are shut in a room together and discuss and discuss until all twelve finally decide for guilty or not guilty. If they are not unanimous, no verdict is given, and the whole trial has to begin over again. A single obstinate juryman, who clings to his particular ideas, is able, therefore, to outweigh the decision of the other eleven. And it is to be remembered that every criminal case is tried before a jury. The case is still worse if all twelve agree, but agree only in their prejudices. Especially in the South, but also in the West sometimes, juries return decisions which simply insult the intelligence of the country. It is true that the unfairness is generally in the direction of declaring the defendant not guilty.

The law's delay is also exceedingly regrettable, as well as the extreme emphasis on technicalities, in consequence of which no one dares, even in the interests of justice, to ignore the slightest inaccuracy of form — a fact whose good side too, of course, no one should overlook. It is most of all regrettable that the choice of judges depends to so large an extent on politics, and that so many judicial appointments are made by popular elections and for a limited term. The trouble here is not so much that a faithful party member is often rewarded with a judicial position, since for the matter of that there are equally good barristers to be chosen from either party for vacant positions on the bench; the real evil is that during his term of office the judge cannot help having an eye to his reëlection or promotion to some higher position. This brings politics into his labours truly, and it too often happens that a ready compliance with party dictates springs up in the lower judicial positions. Only the federal and the superior state courts are entirely free from this.

In a similar way, politics sometimes play a part in the doings of the state attorney. He is subordinate to the state or federal executive, that is, to a party element which has contracted obligations of various sorts, and it may so happen that the state attorney will avoid interfering here and there in matters where a justice higher than party demands interference. Especially in the quarrels between capital and labour, one hears repeatedly that the state attorney is too lenient toward large capitalists. Then there are other evils in judicial matters arising from the unequal scientific preparation of jurists; the failing here is in the judicial logic and pregnancy of the decision.

Finally, one source which is a veritable fountain of sin against the commonwealth is the power of the party machine. We have traced out minutely how the public life of the United States demands two parties, how each of these may hope for victory only if it is compactly organized, and how such organizations need an army of more or less professional politicians. They may be in the legislature or out of it; it is their position in the party machine which gives them their tremendous powers — powers which do not derive from constitutional principles nor from law, but which are in a way intangible, and therefore the more liable to abuse.

Richard Croker has never been mayor of New York, and yet he was for a long time dictator of that city, no matter what Democratic mayor was in office, and remained dictator even from his country place in England. He ruled the municipal Democratic party machine, and therefore all the mayors and officials were merely pawns in his hands. Millions of dollars floated his way from a thousand invisible sources, all of which were somehow connected with municipal transactions; and his conscience was as elastic as his pocket-book. That is what his enemies say, while his friends allege him to be a man of honour; and nothing has really been proved against him. But at least one thing is incontestable, that the system of the party machine and the party boss makes such undemonstrable corruption possible. Almost every state legislature is in the clutches of such party mandarins, and even men who are above the suspicion of venality misuse the tempting power which is centred in their hands in the service of their personal advantage and reputation, of their sympathies and antipathies, and transform their Democratic leadership into autocracy and terrorism. In the higher sense, however, every victory which they win for their party is like the victory of Pyrrhus, for their selfish absolutism injures the party more than any advantage which it wins at the polls benefits it. Their omnipotence is, moreover, only apparent, for in reality there is a power in the land which is stronger than they, and stronger than Presidents or legislatures, and which takes care that all the dangers and evils, sins and abuses that spring up are finally thrown off without really hindering the steady course of progress. This power is public opinion.

CHAPTER SEVEN

Public Opinion

WE have spoken of the President and Congress, of the organization of court and state, and, above all, of the parties, in order to show the various forms in which the genius of the American nation has expressed itself. It may seem almost superfluous to recognize public opinion as a separate factor in political affairs. It is admitted that public opinion is potent in æsthetic, literary, moral, and social problems, with all of which parties and constitutions have nothing to do. But it might be supposed that when a people has surrounded itself with a network of electoral machinery, supports hundreds of thousands of representatives and officials, has perfected parties with their armies of politicians and legislatures which every year discuss and pass on thousands of laws — it might be supposed that in regard to political questions public opinion would have found its complete expression along official channels, and in a sense would have exhausted itself. Yet this is not the case. The entire political routine, with its paraphernalia, forms a closed system, which is distinct in many ways from the actual public opinion of the country.

It is indeed no easy matter to find under what conditions the will of a people can most directly express itself in the official machinery of politics. Many Germans, for instance, entertain the notion that no government is truly democratic except the cabinet be in all matters dependent on a majority in parliament; and they are astonished to learn that in democratic America Congress has no influence on the election of the highest officials; that the President, in fact, may surround himself with a cabinet quite antagonistic to the political complexion of Congress. But no American believes that politics would represent public opinion any better if this independence of the Executive and his cabinet were to be modified, say in conformity with the English or French idea. The reasons for a discrepancy between public opinion and official politics lie anyhow not in the special forms prescribed by the Constitution, but in the means by which the forms prescribed by the Constitution are practically filled by the nation. In the English Constitution, for instance, there is nothing about a cabinet; and yet the cabinet is the actual centre of English politics. American politics might keep to the letter of the Constitution, and still be the truest reflection of public opinion. That they are not such a reflection is due to the strong position of the parties. The rivalry of these encourages keen competition, in which the success of the party has now become an end in itself quite aside from the principles involved. Personal advantages to be derived from the party have become prominent in the minds of its supporters; and even where the motives are unselfish, the tactics of the party are more important than its ideals. But tactics are impossible without discipline, and a party which hopes to be victorious in defending its own interests or in opposing others' will be no mere debating club, but a relentlessly strict and practical organization. Wherewith the control must fall to a very few party leaders, who owe their positions to professional politicians — that is, to men who for the most part stand considerably below the level of the best Americans.

The immense number of votes cast in the Presidential elections is apt to hide the facts. Millions vote for one candidate and millions for the other, without knowing perhaps that a few months before the national convention some ten or twelve party leaders, sitting at a quiet little luncheon, may have had the power to fix on the presidential candidate. And these wise foreordainings are even less conspicuous in the case of governors, senators, or representatives. Everywhere the masses believe that they alone decide, and so they do between the nominees of one party and of the other, or sometimes between several candidates within the party; but they are not aware that a more important choice is made behind the scenes before these candidates make their appearance.

As with the incumbents, so it is with the platform. The party leaders practically decide what questions shall be made the political issues; and this is the most important function of all. We have seen that dissenting groups can hardly hope on ordinary occasions to make a break in the firm party organization, and though they may vigorously discuss questions which have not been approved by the party leaders, they will, nevertheless, arrive at no practical results. It therefore happens very often that voters are called on to decide issues which seem to them indifferent, or to choose between two evils, and can expect nothing from either candidate in the matters which they think most vital. They go to the polls merely out of consideration for their party. Thus, in reality, the people do not decide the issues on which they are to vote, nor on the candidates whom they elect, nor yet on the party leaders who do decide these things. Nor can the people, if discontented with the party in power, recall that party during its term of office. In Germany the government can dissolve parliament if new issues arise; in England the Cabinet resigns if it fails to carry a measure; but in America the party with a congressional majority has nothing to fear during its appointed term. In short, the political life of America is dominated by those forces which rule the parties, and only in so far as the nation is filled with the party spirit, is the official political hierarchy an expression of the nation's will.

Now it is not in the nature of public opinion to nerve itself up to clear and definite issues. Unless worked on by party demagogues, it never formulates itself in a mere yes or no, but surveys the situation impartially, seeing advantages and disadvantages on both sides, and passes a conservative judgment. The man who thinks only of parties will often agree to a compromise which is unjust to both parties and in general unworthy of them; but the man who takes his stand above the parties knows that many problems are not fathomed with a yea or nay; he does not see two opposite sides between which an artificial compromise is to be found, but he appreciates the given situation in its organic unity and historical perspective. Historical understanding of the past and moral seriousness for the future guarantee his right judgment. He sees the practical opposition of interests, which is always more complex than the two-horned dilemma that the parties advertise, in a true light, and testimony of experts instead of politicians suggests to him the rational solution of the problem. The actual course of action to be followed may coincide with the plan of one or the other party, or may be a compromise between them, and yet it will be a distinct policy. In such decisions there lives ever the spirit of immediate reality; no artificial dichotomy nor any political tactics are involved, and the natural moral feeling of a healthy nation is then sufficient for every issue. Nowhere is this naïve moral sense more potent among the masses than in America; will then these unpartisan convictions have no weight in political life? Will they not rather strive to have an independent effect on the destinies of the nation? The centre and real expression of these politics for essentials is the system of public opinion.

We have seen that every American legislature has two parts, an upper and a lower house, which have different ways of procedure and different prerogatives. One might similarly say that the parties with all their paraphernalia are merely the lower house of the nation, while Public Opinion is the upper house; and only the two houses together constitute the entire national political life. The nation is represented in each branch, but in different senses. In a way the parties express quantitatively the will of the nation, and public opinion does it qualitatively. Whenever a quantitative expression is wanted, the issues must be sharply contrasted in order to separate clearly the adherents of each; all fine shades and distinctions have to be sacrificed to an artificial clearness of definition, much as is done in mechanics, when any motion is schematically represented, as the diagonal in a parallelogram of two other forces. As a quantity any yea or nay is as good as any other, and the intensity of any party movement is due to the accumulation of small increments. The great advantage of this lower house is, as of every lower house, that its deliberations can be brought to an end and its debates concluded. Every political election is such a provisional result.

It is very different in the upper house. Public opinion accepts no abstract schematizations, but considers the reality in all its complication, and in its debates no weight is given to any show of hands or other demonstration of mere numbers. Crass contrasts do not exist here, but only subtle shadings; men are not grouped as friends and foe, but they are seen to differ merely in their breadth of outlook, their knowledge, their energy, and in their singleness of heart. The end in view is not to rush politics, but to reform politics and in all matters to shape public events to national ideals. Here one vote is not like another, but a single word wisely and conscientiously spoken is heard above the babel of thousands. And here the best men of the nation have to show themselves, not with programmes nor harangues, but with a quiet force which shapes and unites public opinion and eventually carries all parties before it.

Public opinion may be responsible now for a presidential veto on a bill of Congress, now for the sudden eclipse of a party leader, or the dropping of a list of candidates, or again it may divide a party in the legislature. Public opinion forces the parties, in spite of themselves, to make mere party advantage secondary to a maturer statesmanship.

Germans will not readily appreciate this double expression of the popular will; they would find it more natural if party life and public opinion were one. For in Germany the conditions are quite different. In the first place there are a dozen parties, which express the finer shades of public opinion more adequately than the two parties can in America. And this division into many small parties prevents the development of any real party organization such as would be needed by a party assuming entire responsibility for the affairs of the nation. The nearest approach to two great parties is the opposition between all the "bürgerliche" parties on the one hand and the social democrats on the other. But the development of really responsible parties is hardly to be expected, since the German party is allowed only a small degree of initiative. The representatives of the people have the right to accept or reject or to suggest improvements in the proposals of the government; but with the government rest the initiative and the responsibility. The government stands above the parties, and is not elected by the people nor immediately dependent on them. It originates most of the legislative and executive movements, and therewith represents exactly that moral unity of the nation which is above all parties, and which is represented in America by public opinion; while in America the government is the creature of the parties.

One should not draw the conclusion that the public opinion of America is the quintessence of pure goodness. Public opinion in the United States would be no true indication of the forces at work in the nation if it did not represent all the essentials of the typical American. In order to find this typical man, it would be misleading simply to take the average of the millions; one leaves out of account the great herd of colourless characters, and selects the man who harmoniously combines in himself, without exaggeration, the most striking peculiarities of his countrymen. He is not easy to find, since eccentricity is frequent; one man is grotesquely patriotic, another moral to intolerance, another insipidly complacent, and another too optimistic to be earnest or too acquisitive to be just.

And yet if one goes about much in American society, one finds oneself now and then, not only in New York or Boston or Washington, but quite as well in some small city of the West, in a little circle of congenial men who are talking eagerly, perhaps over their cigars after dinner; and one has the feeling that the typical American is there. His conversation is not learned nor his rhetoric high-flown; but one has the feeling that he is alive and worth listening to, that he sees things in sharp perspective, is sincerely moral, and has something of his own to say. Party politics do not interest him specially, although as citizen he goes to a few meetings, contributes to the party funds, and votes on election day if the weather permits. But he speaks of politics generally with a half-smile, and laughs outright at the thought of himself running for the legislature. He sees the evil about him, but is confident that everything will come around all right; the nation is young, strong, and possessed of boundless resources for the future. Of course he understands the prejudices of the masses, and knows that mere slap and dash will not take the place of real application in solving the problems which confront the nation; he knows, too, that technical proficiency, wealth, and luxury alone do not constitute true culture. And herewith his best energies are enlisted; he contributes generously to libraries and universities, and very likely devotes much of his time to the city schools. But he is frank to confess, as well, that he has a weakness for good-fellowship and superficiality, preferring operetta to tragedy every time. He is not niggardly in anything; to be so is too unæsthetic. At first one is astonished by his insouciance and the optimism with which he makes the best of everything. One feels at once his good nature and readiness to help, and finds him almost preternaturally ready to be just to his opponents and overlook small failings. He envelops everything with his irrespressible sense of humour, and is always reminded of a good story, which he recounts so drolly and felicitously that one is ready to believe that he never could be angry. But this all changes the instant the talk turns from amusing stupidities or little weaknesses and goes over to indecency or corruption or any baseness of character. Then the typical American is quite changed; his genuine nobility of soul comes out and he gives his unvarnished opinion, not blusteringly, but with self-controlled indignation. One feels that here is the real secret of his character; and one is surprised to see how little he cares for political parties or social classes. He will fiercely condemn the delinquencies of his own party or the unfair dealings of his own social set. It now appears how honestly religious he is, and how far the inner meaning of his life lies beyond the merely material.

Such a good fellow it is, with all his greater and lesser traits, who may at any time voice undiluted public opinion. Thousands who are better, wiser, more learned, or less the spendthrift and high-liver, and the millions of inferior natures, will show one trait or another of the national character in higher relief. And yet the type is well marked; it is always optimistic and confident in the future of America, indifferent to party tactics, but enthusiastically patriotic. It is anxious to be not merely prosperous but just and enlightened as well; it is almost hilariously full of life, and yet benevolent and friendly; conservative although sensitive, without respect for conventions and yet religious, sanguine but thoughtful, scrupulously just to an opponent but unrelenting toward any mean intent. Probably the most characteristic traits of public opinion are a patient oversight of mistakes and weaknesses, but relentless contempt and indignation for meanness and lack of honour. This is in both respects the very reverse of the party spirit, which is too apt to hinge its most boasted reforms on trivial evils, and pass over the greatest sins in silence.

One element of public opinion should be suggested in even the briefest sketch — its never-failing humour. It is the antiseptic of American politics, although it would be better, to be sure, if political doings could be aseptic from the outset. But probably dirty ambition and selfishness are harder to keep down in a democracy than anywhere else. The humour of public opinion stands in striking contrast, moreover, to party life; as one cannot fail to discover on looking closely. Party tactics demand that the masses have hammered into them the notion that the sacred honour of the nation lies with their party, but that on the other side there lies hopeless ruin. The man who urges this dogma must keep a very solemn face, for if he were to bring it out with a twinkle in his eye, he would destroy the force of his suggestion. The voter, too, is serious in his duties as a citizen, and demands of the candidates this extremely practical mien and solemn party arrogance. But when the same citizen talks the matter over with his friends, he is no longer a stickler for party, but a voicer of public opinion, and he sees at once the humour of the situation. He punctures the party bubbles with well-aimed ridicule. So it happens that the population is more ruled by humour here than anywhere else, while the party leaders stand up, at least before the public, in the most solemn guise. Just as in some American states the men drink wine at home, but at official banquets call for mineral water; so out of the political harness one may commit excesses of humour, but in it one must be strictly temperate. This is, of course, the reverse of the well-known English method, where the masses are rather dull, while the leaders are famous wits and cynics. America would never allow this. When one meets leading politicians or members of the Cabinet in a social way, one is often amazed at their ready wit, and feels that these men have decidedly the capacity to shine as do their English colleagues. But that would wreck the party service. The people are sovereign; public opinion has, therefore, the right to ironical humour, and can smilingly look down on the parties from a superior height; while those who play the party game of government have still to keep demure and sober. In England it is the Cabinet, in America public opinion, which assumes the gentle rôle of wit. Hardly could the contrast between aristocracy and democracy be more clearly exemplified.

If some one should ask who makes public opinion, he might well be referred at first to that class which at present does not enjoy the suffrage, and presumably will not for some time to come — the women. The American woman cares little enough for party politics, and this is not so much because she has no rights. If she had the interest she probably would have the rights. But while the best people have no wish to see the women mix in with the routine of party machinery, this is not at all in order that they may not concern themselves with the public problems of the day. On the contrary, women exert a marked influence on public opinion; and here, as might be expected, it is not the organized crusades, like the temperance movement, which count, but rather their less noisy demonstrations, their influence in the home and their general rightness of feeling. Every reform movement which appeals to moral motives is advanced by the public influence of women, and many a bad piece of jobbery is defeated by their instrumentality.

If the boundaries between the sexes are forgotten in the matter of public opinion, so even more are those between the various classes. Public opinion is not weakened by any class antipathies. To be sure, every profession and occupation has its peculiar interests, and in different quarters the public opinion takes on somewhat different hues; the agricultural states have other problems than the industrial; the South others than the North; and the mining districts still others of their own. But these are really not differences of public opinion, but different sectors of the one great circle. In spite of the diverse elements and the prejudices which go to make up public opinion, it is everywhere remarkably self-consistent. This is because it is the voice of insight, conscience, and brotherly feeling, as against that of carelessness, self-interest, and exclusiveness. The particular interests of capital and labour, of university and primary school, of city and country, have not their special representatives at the court of public opinion. And least in evidence of all, of course, are the officials and professional politicians. These men are busy in strictly party affairs, and have no time to dabble in the clear stream of public opinion. At best, a few distinguished senators or governors, together with the President and an occasional member of the Cabinet, come to have an immediate influence on public opinion.

The springs of public opinion flow from the educated and substantial members of the commonwealth, and are often tinged at first with a very personal colouring; but the streamlets gather and flow far from their sources and every vestige of the personal is lost. Ideas go from man to man, and those which are typically American find as ready lodgment with the banker, the manufacturer, or the scholar as with the artisan or the farm-hand. Any man who appeals to the conscience, morality, patriotism, or brotherly feeling of the American, or to his love of progress and order, appeals to no special parties or classes, but to the one public opinion, the community of high-minded citizens to the extent of their disinterestedness.

Yet even such a public opinion requires some organization and support. Bold as the statement may sound, the American newspaper is the main ally of public opinion, serving that opinion more loyally than it serves either official politics or the party spirit. The literary significance of the newspaper we shall consider in another connection, but here only its public influence. An American philosophizing on the newspapers takes it as a matter of course that they serve the ends of party politics; and it is true enough that party life as it is would not be possible without the highly disseminated influence of the newspaper. A German coming to the country is apt to deny it even this useful function. He is acquainted in Europe with those newspapers which commence on the first page with serious leading articles, and relegate the items of the day to a back page along with the advertisements. But here he finds newspapers which have on the first pages not a word of editorial comment and hardly even a serious piece of politics — nothing, in fact, but an unspeakable muddle of undigested news items; and as his eye rests involuntarily on the front page, with its screaming headlines in huge type, he will find nothing but crimes, sensational casualties, and other horrors. He will not before have realized that the devouring hunger of the American populace for the daily news, has brought into existence sheets of large circulation adapted to the vulgar instincts of the millions, the giant headlines of which warn off the educated reader from as far as he can see them; that paper is not for him. But a foreigner does not realize the injustice of estimating the political influence of the press from a glance at these monstrosities, which could not thrive abroad, not so much because the masses are better and more enlightened as because they care less about reading. Moreover, he will come slowly to realize that what he missed from the front page is somewhere in the middle of the paper; that the street-selling makes it necessary to make the most of sensations on the outside, and to put the better things where they are better protected. And so he learns that the American newspaper does express opinions, although its looks belie it.

The better sort of American newspaper is neither a party publication nor yet merely a news-sheet, but the conscious exponent of public opinion. Its columns contain a tiresome amount of party information, it is true; but a part of this is directly in the interests of an intelligent public opinion, since every citizen needs to be instructed in all the phases of party life, of political and congressional doings, and in regard to the candidates who are up for office. It is to be admitted, moreover, that some of the better newspapers, although not the very best, are unreservedly committed to the leaders of some party — in short, are party organs. In the same way several newspapers are under the domination of certain industrial interests and cater to the wishes of a group of capitalists. But any such policy has to be managed with the utmost discretion, for the American newspaper reader is far too experienced to buy a sheet day after day which he sees to be falsified; and he has enough others to resort to, since the competition is always keen, and even middle-sized cities have three or four large daily papers.

It is perhaps fortunate that any such extreme one-sidedness is not to the commercial advantage of the newspapers, for in America they are preëminently business enterprises. Their financial success depends in the first place on advertisements, and only secondarily on their sales in the streets. The advertising firm does not care whether the editorials and news items are Republican or Democratic, but it cares very much about the number of copies which are circulated; and this depends on the meritorious features which the paper has over competing sheets. Newspapers like the German, which count on only a small circle of readers, and these assured, at least for the time being, by subscriptions, can far more readily treat their readers cavalierly and constrain their attention for a while to a certain party point of view. In an American city the daily sales are much greater than the subscriptions, and the sheets which get the most trade are those which habitually treat matters from all sides, and voice opinions which fall in with every point of view. Of course, this circumstance cannot prevent every paper from having its special political friends and foes, its special hobbies, its own style, and, above all, its peculiar material interests. But, on the whole, the American newspaper is extraordinarily non-partisan on public questions, notwithstanding the statements in many German books to the contrary; and the ordinary reader might peruse a given paper for weeks, except just on the eve of an election, without really knowing whether it was Republican or Democratic. Now one party and now the other is brought up for criticism, and even when the sheet is distinctly in favour of a certain side, it will print extracts from the leading articles of opposing journals, and so well depict the entire situation that the reader can form an opinion for himself.

While the newspapers are in this way largely emancipated from the yoke of parties, they are the exponents of a general set of tendencies which, in opposition to party politics, we have called public opinion. In other words, the papers stand above the parties with their crudely schematic programmes and issues, and aspire to measure men and things according to their true worth. Though ostensibly of one party, a journal will treat men of its own side to biting sarcasm, and magnanimously extol certain of its opponents. The better political instincts, progress and reform, are appealed to; and if doubtful innovations are often brought in and praised as reforms, this is not because the newspaper is the organ of a party, but rather of public sentiment, as it really is or is supposed to be. The newspaper reflects in its own way all the peculiarities of public opinion — its light-heartedness and its often nervous restlessness, its conservative and prudent traits, its optimism, and its ethical earnestness; above all, its humour and drastic ridicule. It is well known that the American newspaper has brought the art of political caricature to perfection. The satirical cartoon of the daily paper is of course much more effective than that of the regular comic papers. And these pictures, although directed at a political opponent, are generally conceived in a broader spirit than that of any party. The cap and bells are everywhere in evidence, and there is nothing dry or pedantic. From the dexterous and incisive leading article to the briefest jottings, one notes the same good humour and playful satire which are so characteristic of public opinion. This general humorous turn makes it possible to give an individual flavour to the most ordinary pieces of daily news, so that they have a bearing considerably broader than the bare facts of the case, and may conceivably add their mite to public opinion. And herewith a special newspaper style has come in, a combination of a photographically accurate report and the whimsical feuilleton. Thus it happens that the best papers editorially persuade where they cannot dictate to their readers, and so, apart from party politics, nourish public opinion and create sentiment for or against persons, and legislative and other measures, while ostensibly they are merely giving the news of the last twelve hours.

There is another distinctly American invention — the interview. Doubtless it was first designed to whet the reader's curiosity with the piquant suggestion of something personal or even indiscreet. In Europe, where this form of reporting is decidedly rudimentary, it usually evinces neither tact nor taste; whereas in America it is really a literary form, and so familiar now as to excite no remark. It has come to be peculiarly the vehicle of public opinion, as opposed to party politics. The person interviewed is supposed to give his personal opinions, and it is his authority as a human personality which attracts the reader. A similar function is served by the carefully selected letters to the editor, which take up a considerable space in the most serious sheets.

The outer form of the newspaper is a matter really of the technical ability of the American, rather than of his political tastes; and it is to be observed at once that the general appearance, and above all, the whole system of getting and printing news rapidly, is astonishing. Every one has heard of the intrepid and fertile reporters, and how on important occasions they leave no stone unturned to obtain the latest intelligence for their papers. But the persistence of these men is less worthy of note than the regular system by which the daily news is gathered and transmitted to every paper in the land. With an infallible scent, a pack of reporters follows in the trail of the least event which may have significance for the general public. A good deal of gossip and scandal is intermingled, to be sure, and much that is trivial served up to the readers; but granted for once, that millions in the lower classes, as members of the American democracy, wish, and ought to wish, to carry home every night a newspaper as big as a book, then, of course, such a hunger for fresh printed matter can be satisfied only by mental pabulum adapted to the vulgar mind. The New York *Evening Post* will have nothing of this sort; it appeals more to bank directors and professors; but shop-hands prefer the *World*. It is the same as with the theatres; if the ordinary citizen is prosperous enough to indulge frequently in an evening at the theatre, then, of course, melodrama and farce will become the regular thing, since the common man must always either laugh or cry.

The lightning news service is, of course, somewhat superficial and frequently in error, not to say that it is served up often with the minimum of taste; but the readers gladly take the risk of mistakes for the sake of the greater advantage it is to public opinion to have a searchlight which penetrates every highway and byway, showing up every sign of change in the social or political situation, and every intimation of danger.

And if reporters are accused of being indiscreet, one must first inquire whether the fault does not really lie with some one or other who, while pretending to shrink from publicity, really wants to see his name in the paper. Any one familiar with the newspapers of the country knows that he is perfectly safe in telling any editor, and even any reporter, whatever he likes if he adds the caution that he does not wish it given out. It will not be printed. The American journalist is usually a gentleman, and can be relied on to be discreet. The principal journalists and editors of the leading newspapers are among the ablest men of the country, and they often go over to important political positions and become even ministers and ambassadors.

The powerful influence of the American newspapers is outwardly displayed in the sumptuous buildings which they occupy. While in Europe the newspapers are published generally in very modest quarters, where the editors have to sit in dingy rooms, the buildings of the American newspapers compare favourably with the best commercial edifices; and the whole business is conducted on an elaborate scale. Scarcely less astonishing are their achievements in the way of illustration. While the most select papers decline on principle to appeal to the taste for sensation, many large papers have yielded to the demand, and have brought the technique of illustration nearly to perfection. A few hours after any event they will have printed a hundred thousand copies of the paper with pictures taken on the spot, and reproduced in a manner of which any European weekly might well be proud.

Taken all in all, the American press very worthily represents the energy, prosperity, and greatness of the American nation; and at the same time with its superficial haste, its vulgarity and excitability, with its lively patriotism and irrepressible humour, it clearly evinces the influence of democracy. The better the paper the more prominent are the critical and reflective features; while the wider the circulation, the more noticeable are the obtrusive self-satisfaction and provincialism, and the characteristic disdain of things European. Going from the East to the West, one finds a fairly steady downward gradation in excellence, although some samples of New York journalism can vie for crude sensationalism with the most disgusting papers of the Wild West. And yet the best papers reach a standard which in many respects is higher than that of the best journals of the Old World. A paper like the *Boston Transcript* will hardly find its counterpart in the German newspaper world; and much good can be said of the *Sun*, *Tribune*, *Times*, and *Post* in New York, the *Star* in Washington, the *Public Ledger* in Philadelphia, the *Sun* in Baltimore, the *Eagle* in Brooklyn, the *Tribune* in Chicago, the *Herald* in Boston, the *Evening Wisconsin* in Milwaukee, and many others which might be named. Even small cities like Springfield, Massachusetts, produce such large and admirable papers as the *Springfield Republican*. And to be just, one must admit that the bad papers could be condensed into tolerably good ones by a liberal use of the blue pencil. For their mistakes lie not so much in their not having good contributions as in their inclusion of crude and sensational material by way of spice. Very often the front page of a paper will be overrun with the most offensive scandals, caricatures, and criminal sensations, while the ninth and tenth pages will offer editorials and other articles of decided merit. The newspapers which care only for a large circulation will have something for everybody; and they are not far out of the way in calculating that the educated reader who looks first at the editorials and political dispatches, will have enough that is unregenerate in his soul to make him relish a sideward glance at the latest sensational reports. The newspaper is content on the whole not to bore its readers, and to hold a close rein on public opinion rather than on party politics.

With all this, it is not to be denied that there are lower motives which degrade journalism. One of the chief temptations lies in the amalgamation of newspaper politics and party activities. The editor who, in the interests of public opinion, scans all the parties with a critical eye and professes to be impartial, is for this very reason the more tempted to misuse his position for private gain. He may diligently support one party in the name of impartiality and fairness, while in reality he counts on a remunerative office if that party is successful; and from this point the steps are few to the moral state of those who attack a certain party or an industrial enterprise in order to discover the error of their position on receipt of a sufficient compensation. The energy with which some newspapers stand up for certain financial interests casts grave doubt on their personal independence; and yet direct bribery plays an exceedingly small rôle, and the government or a foreign country is never the corrupting influence. Very much more important are the vanity and selfishness of newspaper proprietors, who for one reason or another choose to lead the public astray. But such perversities are less dangerous than one might think, for the American newspaper reader reads too much and is politically too discerning to take these newspapers at their face value. The mood induced by one paper is corrected by another; and while the journalist is tickled at his own shrewdness in writing only what his readers will like, the reader slyly preserves his self-respect and belief in his own critical ability, by hunting out everything with which he does not agree and reading that carefully. If the journal is above the party, the reader is above the journal, and thus it is that the newspapers are the most influential support of public opinion.

In this, however, they do not enjoy a monopoly; beside them are the weekly and monthly papers. Here again we shall consider their literary merits in another connection, but their greatest significance lies in their influence on public opinion. The political efforts of the weekly papers are mostly indirect; they deal primarily with practical interests, religious and social problems, and literary matters; but the serious discussions are carried on as it were against a political background which lends its peculiar hue to the whole action. The monthly magazines are somewhat more ambitious, and consider politics more directly. In their pages, not merely professional politicians, but the very ablest men of the nation, are accustomed to treat of the needs and duties of city and state; and these discussions are almost never from a one-sided point of view. A magazine like the *North American Review* usually asks representatives of both parties to present their opinions on the same question; and a similar breadth of view is adopted by the *Atlantic Monthly*, the *Review of Reviews*, and other leading monthlies, whose great circulation and influence are hardly to be compared with similar magazines of Europe. The point of view common to all is that of a very critical public opinion, well above party politics and devoted to national reform and everything which makes for progress and enlightenment. Much the same can be said of those magazines which combine politics with literature and illustrations, such as the *Century*, *Harper's*, *Scribner's*, *McClure's*, and many others. When *McClure's Magazine*, for example, presents to its half-million readers month after month an illustrated history of the Standard Oil Trust, every page of which is an attack on secret evasions of the law, it is not serving the interests of any party, but is reading public opinion a lesson.

The spoken word vies with the printed. The capacity of Americans, and especially of the women, to listen to lectures is well-nigh abnormal. And in this way social and political propagandas find a ready hearing, although a purely party speech would not be effective outside of a party convention. The wit and pathos of the speaker generally reach a level considerably above mere matters of expediency, and appeal to public opinion from a broadly historical point of view. The dinner speaker is also a power, since he is not constrained, as in Germany, to sandwich his eloquence in between the fish and game or to make every speech wind craftily around and debouch with the inevitable "dreimal Hoch." He is quite at liberty to follow either his whims or his convictions, and herein has come to be a recognized spring of public opinion.

Finally, somewhat the same influence is exerted by the countless clubs and associations, and the various local and national societies which are organized for specific ends. Every American of the better sort belongs to any number of such bodies, and although concerning two-thirds of them he knows no more than that he pays his dues, there is left a third for which he sincerely labours. There is much in these organizations which is one-sided, egotistical, and trivial, and yet in the most of them there is something which is sound and right. There is not one at least which fails to strengthen the conviction that every citizen is called to be the bearer of public opinion. Just as the parties complain that the voters neglect the routine duties of the organization, so to be sure do the strenuous reformers of the country complain that the ranks behind them informally break step. But the main thing is that behind them there is a host, and that public opinion is to-day as thoroughly organized as the official parties, and that it sees each day more clearly that its qualitative effect on the national life is at least equally important with the quantitative efficacy of the parties.

Every important question is treated by both organizations, public opinion, and the parties. At the approach of a great election the parties create such a stir and bustle that for a couple of months the voice of public opinion seems hushed. Party tactics rule the day. But on the other hand, public opinion has its own festivals, and above all, works on tirelessly and uninterruptedly, except for the short pause just before elections. Public opinion reacts equally on both parties, forces them to pass laws that the politicians do not relish, and to repeal others that the politicians would gladly keep; and, ignoring these men, it brings the public conscience to bear on the issues to be pressed, the candidates to be nominated, and the leaders to be chosen.

CHAPTER EIGHT

Problems of Population

WE have surveyed public opinion and party politics as two distinct factors in the American national consciousness, as two factors which are seldom in complete agreement, and which are very often in sharp opposition, but which finally have to work together like an upper and lower legislative chamber in order to solve the problems of the day. We have not the space to speak minutely of all these problems themselves with which the American is at the present moment occupied; since the politics of the day lie outside of our purpose. This purpose has been to study that which is perennial in the American spirit, the mental forces which are at work, and the forms in which these work themselves out. But the single questions on which these forces operate, questions which are to-day and to-morrow are not, must be left to the daily literature. It is our task, however, to indicate briefly in what directions the most important of these problems lie. Every one of them would require the broadest sort of handling if it were to be in the least adequately presented.

So many problems which in European countries occupy the foreground, and which weigh particularly on the German mind, are quite foreign to the American. Firstly, the church problem as a political one is unknown to him. The separation of church and state is so complete, and the results of this separation are viewed on all sides with so much satisfaction, that there is nowhere the least desire to introduce a change. It is precisely in strictly religious circles that the entire independence of the church is regarded as the prime requisite for the growth of ecclesiastical influence. Even the relations between the church and party politics are distinctly remote, and the semi-political movements once directed against the Catholic Church are already being somewhat forgotten.

There is no Jesuit question, and the single religious order which has precipitated a real political storm has been the sect of Mormons, which ecclesiastically sanctions an institution that the monogamous laws of the nation forbid. Even here the trouble has been dispelled by the submission of the Mormon Church.

As a matter of course, America has also never known a real conflict between the executive and the people. The government being always elected at short intervals by the people and the head of the state with his Cabinet having no part in legislation, while his executive doings merely carry out the wishes of the dominant political party, of course no conflicts can arise. To be sure, there can be here and there small points of friction between the legislative and executive, and the President can, during his four years of office, slowly drift away from the party which elected him, and thus bring about some estrangement; but even this would only be an estrangement from the professional politicians of his party. For experience has shown that the President, and on a smaller scale the governor of a state, is successful in breaking with his party only when he follows the wishes of public opinion instead of listening to the dictates of his party politicians. But in that case the people are on his side. One might rather say that the conflicts between government and people, which in Europe are practically disputes between the government and the popular representatives of political parties, repeat themselves in America in the sharp contrast between public opinion on the one hand and the united legislative and executive on the other; since the government is itself of one piece with the popular representation. Public opinion, indeed, preserves its ancient sovereignty as against the whole system of elections and majorities.

There is another vexation spared to the American people; it has no Alsace-Lorraine, no Danish or Polish districts; that is, it has no elements of population which seek to break away from the national political unity, and by their opposition to bring about administrative difficulties. To be sure, the country faces difficult problems of population, but there is no group of citizens struggling to secede; and in the same way the American has nothing in the way of emigration problems. Perhaps one may also say finally that social democracy, especially of the international variety, has taken such tenuous root that it can hardly be called a problem, from the German point of view. For although there is a labour question, this is not the same as social democracy. The labour movements, as part of the great economic upheaval, are certainly one of the main difficulties to be overcome by the New World; but the social democratic solution, with its chiefly political significance, is essentially unknown to the American. All this we shall have to consider in other connections. Although this and that which worry the European appear hardly at all in American thought, there is, on the other hand, a great sea of problems which have mercifully been spared to the European. It is due to the transitional quality of our time that on this sea of problems the most tempestuous are those of an economic character. The fierce conflicts of recent Presidential elections have been waged especially over the question of currency, and it is not until now that the silver programme may be looked on as at least provisionally forgotten. These conflicts were immediately preceded by others which concerned protection and free-trade, and the outlook is clear that these two parties will again meet each other in battle array.

Meanwhile the formation of large trusts has loomed up rapidly as a problem, and in this one sees the real influence of public opinion as against that of party politics, since both parties would doubtless have preferred to leave the trusts alone. At the same time the great strikes, especially that of the Pennsylvania coal districts, have brought the conflicts between capital and labour so clearly to the national consciousness that the public attention is strained on this point. Others say that the most serious economic problem of the United States is the irrigation of the parched deserts of the West, where whole tracts of land, larger than Germany, cannot be cultivated for lack of water; while American engineers, however, now think it entirely possible with a sufficient outlay of money to irrigate this region artificially. Still others regard the tax issue as of prime importance; and the circle of those who believe in single-tax reform is steadily growing. Every one agrees also that the status of national banks needs to be extensively modified; that the reckless devastation of forests must be stopped; and that the commercial relations between the states must be regulated by new laws. Some are hoping for new canals, others for the subvention of American ships. In short, the public mind is so filled with important economic questions that others which are merely political stand in the background; and, of course, political questions so tremendous as was once that of independence from England and the establishment of the Federation, or later, the slave question and the secession of the South, have not come up through four happy decades.

Besides the economic problems there are many social problems which appear in those quarters where public opinion is best organized, and spread from there more and more throughout political life; such are the question of woman's suffrage, and the half economic and half social problem of the extremes between poor and rich, extremes which were unknown to the New World in the early days of America and even until very recent times. The unspeakable misery in the slums of New York and Chicago, in which the lowest immigrants from Eastern Europe have herded themselves together and form a nucleus for all the worst reprobates of the country, is an outcome of recent years and appeals loudly to the conscience of the nation. On the other side, the fatuous extravagance of millionaires threatens to poison the national sense of thrift and economy.

Among these social problems there belongs specially the earnest desire of the best citizens to develop American art and science at a pace comparable with the extraordinary material progress of the country. Doubtless the admirable results which have here been obtained, came from the extraordinary earnestness with which public opinion has discussed these problems. The great development of universities, the increase in the number of libraries and scientific institutions, the creation of museums, the observance of beauty in public buildings, and a hundred other things would never have come about if public opinion had let things go their own way; here public opinion has consciously done its duty as a governing power. Somewhat nearer the periphery of public thought there are various other social propagandas, as that for the relief of the poor and for improving penal institutions; the temperance movement is flourishing, and the more so in proportion as it gives up its fanatical eccentricities. Also the fight against what the American newspaper reader calls the "social evil," attracts more and more serious attention.

Besides all these, there is a considerable number of purely political problems; first among these are the problems of population, and notably the questions of immigration and of the negro; then come internal problems of government, such as civil service and municipal reforms, which especially engage the public eye; finally, the problems of external politics, in which the watchwords of imperialism and the Monroe Doctrine can be heard shouted out above all others. At least we must briefly take our bearings, and see why these problems exist, although the treatment cannot be exhaustive.

The first issue in the problem of population is, as we have said, that which concerns immigration; and this is just now rather up before public opinion since the last fiscal year which was closed with the beginning of July, 1903, showed the largest immigration ever reached, it being one-tenth greater than the previous record, which was for the year ending in 1882. The facts are as follows: The total immigration to the United States has been twenty million persons. The number of those who now live in the United States, but were born in foreign countries, is more than ten millions; and if we were to add to these those who, although born here, are of foreign parentage, the number comes up to twenty-six millions. Last year 857,000 immigrants came into the country. Out of the ten millions of the foreign-born population, 2,669,000 have come from Germany, and 1,619,000 from Ireland.

The fluctuations in immigration seem to depend chiefly on the amount of prosperity in the United States, and, secondly, on the economic and political conditions which prevail from year to year in Europe. Up to 1810 the annual immigration is estimated to have been about 6,000; then it was almost wholly interrupted for several years, owing to the political tension between the United States and England; as soon as peace was assured the immigration increased in 1817 to 20,000; and in the year 1840 to 84,000. The hundred thousand mark was passed in 1842, and from then on the figure rose steadily, until in 1854 it amounted to 427,000. Then the number fell off rapidly. It was a time of business depression in the United States, and, moreover, the slavery agitation was already threatening a civil war. The immigration was least in 1861, when it had sunk to 91,000. Two years later it began to rise again, and in 1873 was almost half a million. And again there followed a few years of business depression, with its correspondingly lessened immigration. But the moment economic conditions improved, immigration set in faster than ever before, and in

1882 was more than three-quarters of a million. Since 1883 the average number of persons coming in has been 450,000, the variation from year to year being considerable. The business reverses of 1893 cut the number down to one-half, but since 1897 it has steadily risen again.

Such bare figures do not show that which is most essential from the point of view of public opinion, since the quality of the immigration, depending as it does on the social condition of the countries from which it comes, is the main circumstance. In the decade between 1860 and 1870, 2,064,000 European wanderers came to the American shores; of these 787,000 were Germans, 568,000 English, 435,000 Irish, 109,000 Scandinavians, 38,000 Scotch, and 35,000 French. Now for the decade between 1890 and 1900 the total number was 3,844,000; of these Germany contributed 543,000, Ireland 403,000, Norway and Sweden 325,000, England 282,000, Scotland 60,000, and France 36,000. On the other hand, we find for the first time three countries represented which had never before sent any large number of immigrants; Italy, Russia, and Austria-Hungary. In the decade ending 1870 there were only 11,000 Italians, 7,000 Austrians, and 4,000 Russians, while in the decade ending in the year 1900 the Russian immigrants, who are mostly Poles and Jews, numbered 588,000, the Austrian and Hungarian 597,000, and the Italian no less than 655,000; and the proportion of these three kinds of immigrants is steadily increasing. In the year 1903 Germany sent only 40,000, Ireland 35,000, and England 26,000; while Russia sent 136,000, Austria-Hungary 206,000, and Italy 230,000. Herein lies the problem.

A few further figures may help to make the situation clearer. For instance, it is interesting to know what proportion of the total emigration from Europe came to America. In round numbers we may say that since 1870 Europe has lost 20,000,000 souls by emigration, and that some 14,000,000 of these, that is, more than two-thirds, have ultimately made their homes in the United States of America. Of the German emigrants some 85 or 90 per cent. have gone to the United States; of the Scandinavian as many as 97 per cent.; while of the English and Italian only 66 and 45 per cent. respectively. It is worth noting, moreover, that in spite of the extraordinary increase in immigration, the percentage of foreign-born population has not increased; that is, the increase of native-born inhabitants has kept up with the immigration. In 1850 there were a few more than two million foreign-born inhabitants, in 1860 more than four millions, in 1870 there were five and a half millions, in 1880 six and a half millions, in 1890 nine and a quarter millions, and in 1900 ten and one-third millions. In 1850 these foreigners amounted, it is true, to only 11 per cent. of the population; but in 1860 they had already become 15 per cent. of the whole, and diminished in 1870 to 14.4 per cent., in 1880 to 13.3 per cent.; in 1890 they were 14.8 per cent., and in 1900 13.6 per cent.

The State of New York has the largest number of foreigners, and in the last fifty years the percentage of foreigners has risen steadily from 21 per cent. to 26 per cent. Pennsylvania stands second in this respect, and Illinois third. On the other hand, the small states have the largest percentage of foreign population. North Dakota has 35 per cent. and Rhode Island 31 per cent. The Southern states have fewest foreigners of any. These figures are, of course, greatly changed if we add to them the persons who were not themselves born in other countries, but of whom one or both parents were foreigners. In this way the foreign population in the so-called North Atlantic States is 51 per cent., and is 34 per cent. throughout the country. If a foreigner is so defined, the cities of New York and Chicago are both 77 per cent. foreign.

These figures are enough by way of mere statistics. The thing which arouses anxiety is not the increasing number of immigrants, but the quality of them, which grows continually worse. Just fifty years ago the so-called Know-Nothings made the anti-foreign sentiment the chief plank of their programme, but the "pure" American propaganda of the Know-Nothings was forgotten in the excitement which waged over slavery; and the anti-foreign issue has never since that time been so brutally stated. There has always been much objection to the undeniable evils involved in this immigration, and the continual cry for closer supervision and restriction of immigration has given rise to several new legal measures. Partly, this movement has been the expression of industrial jealousy, as when, for instance, Congress in 1885, in an access of protectionist fury, forbade the immigration of "contract labour," that is, forbade any one to land who had already arranged to fill a certain position. This measure was meant to protect the workmen from disagreeable competition. But right here the believers in free industry object energetically. It is just the contract labour from the Old World which brings new industries and a new development of old industries into the country, and such a quickening of industry augments the demand for labour to the decided advantage of native workmen. The law still stands in writing, but in practice it appears to be extensively corrected, since it is very easily evaded.

The more important measures, however, have arisen less from industrial than from social and moral grounds. Statistics have been carefully worked up again and again in order to show that the poor-houses and prisons contain a much larger percentage of foreigners than their proportionate numbers in the community warrant. In itself this will be very easy to understand, owing to the unfavourable conditions under which the foreigner must find himself, particularly if he does not speak English, in his struggle for existence in a new land. But most striking has been the manner in which the magic of statistics has shown its ability to prove anything it will; for other statistics have shown that if certain kinds of crime are considered, the foreign-born Americans are the best children the nation has. The question of illiteracy has been discussed in similar fashion. The percentage of immigrants who can neither read nor write has seemed alarmingly high to those accustomed to the high cultivation of the northeastern states, but gratifyingly small to those familiar with the negro population in the South. One unanimous opinion has been reached; it is that the country is bound to keep out such elements from its borders as are going to be a public burden. At first idiots and insane persons, criminals, and paupers made up this undesirable class, but the definition of those who are not admitted to the country has been slowly broadened. And since the immigration laws require the steamship companies to carry back at their own expense all immigrants who are not allowed to land, the selection is actually made in the European ports of embarkation. In this wise the old charge that the agents of European packet companies encouraged the lowest and worst individuals of the Old World to expend their last farthing for a ticket to the New World, has gradually died out. Nevertheless, in the last year, 5,812 persons were sent back for lack of visible means of support, 51 because of criminal record, and 1773 by reason of infectious diseases.

The fact remains, however, that the social mires of every large city teem with foreigners, and that among these masses the worst evils of municipal corruption find favourable soil, that all the sporadic outbreaks of anarchy are traceable to these foreigners, and that the army of the unemployed is mostly recruited from their number. These opinions were greatly strengthened when that change in the racial make-up set in which we have followed by statistics, and which a census of the poorer districts in the large cities quickly proves: Italians, Russian Jews, Galicians, and Roumanians everywhere. The unprejudiced American asks with some concern whether, if this stream of immigration is continued, it will not undermine the virility of the American people. The American nation will continue to fulfil its mission so long as it is inspired with a spirit of independence and self-determination; and this instinct derives from the desire of freedom possessed by all the Germanic races. In this way the German, Swedish, and Norwegian newcomers have adapted themselves at once to the Anglo-Saxon body politic, while the French have remained intrinsically strangers. Their number, however, has been very small. But what is to happen if the non-Germanic millions of Italians, Russians, and Turks are to pour in unhindered? It is feared that they will drag down the high and independent spirit of the nation to their low and unworthy ideals. Already many citizens wish to require of the immigrants a knowledge of the English language, or to make a certain property qualification by way of precaution against unhappy consequences, or perhaps to close entirely for awhile the portals of the nation, or, at least, to make the conditions of naturalization considerably harder in order that the Eastern European, who has never had a thought of political freedom, shall not too quickly receive a suffrage in the freest democracy of the world. And those most entitled to an opinion unconditionally demand at the least the exclusion of all illiterates.

Against all this there stand the convictions of certain rather broader circles of people who point with pride at that great American grist-mill, the public school, which is supposed to take the foreign youth into its hopper, grind him up quickly and surely, and turn him out into good American material. It is, in fact, astonishing to look at the classes in the New York schools down on the East Side, where there is not a child of American parentage, and yet not one who will admit that he is Italian, Russian, or Armenian. All these small people declare themselves passionately to be "American," with American patriotism and American pride; and day by day shows that in its whole system of public institutions the nation possesses a similar school for the foreign-born adult. Grey-haired men and adolescent youths, who in their native countries would never have emerged from their dull and cringing existence, hardly touch the pavement of Broadway before they find themselves readers of the newspaper, frequenters of the political meetings, and in a small way independent business men; and they may, a few years later, be conducting enterprises on a large scale. They wake up suddenly, and although in this transformation every race lends its own colour to the spirit of self-determination, nevertheless the universal trait, the typical American trait, can appear in every race of man, if only the conditions are favourable.

In the same direction it is urged once more that America needs the labour of these people. If Southern and Eastern Europe had not given us their cheaper grades of workmen, we should not have been able to build our roads or our railroads, nor many other things which we have needed. In former decades this humble rôle fell to the Germans, the Scandinavians, and the Irish, and the opposition against their admission was as lively as it now is against the immigrants from the south and east of Europe; while the development of the country has shown that they have been an economic blessing; and the same thing, it is said, will be true of the Russians and Poles. There are still huge territories at our disposal which are virtually unpopulated, untold millions can still employ their strength to the profit of the whole nation, and it would be madness to keep out the willing and peaceable workers. Moreover, has it not been the proud boast of America that her holy mission was to be a land of freedom for every oppressed individual, an asylum for every one who was persecuted? In the times then of her most brilliant prosperity is she to be untrue to her noble rôle of protectress, and leave no hope to those who have been deprived of their human rights by Russian or Turkish despots, by Italian or Hungarian extortionists, to disappoint their belief that at least in the New World even the most humble man has his rights and will be received at his true value? Thus the opinions differ, and public opinion at large has come as yet to no decision.

A curious feature in the immigration problem is the Chinese question, which has occasioned frequent discussion on the Pacific coast. The Chinaman does not come here to enjoy the blessings of American civilization, but merely in order to earn a competence in a short time so that he can return to his Asiatic home and be forever provided for. He does not bring his family with him, nor attempt in any way to adapt himself; he keeps his own costume, stays apart from his white neighbours, and lives, as for instance in the Chinese Quarter of San Francisco, on such meagre nourishment and in such squalid dwellings that he can save up wealth from such earnings as an American workman could hardly live on. A tour through the Chinese sleeping-rooms in California is in fact one of the most depressing impressions which the traveller on American soil can possibly experience. The individuals lie on large couches, built over one another in tiers, going quite up to the ceiling; and in twenty-four hours three sets of sleepers will have occupied the beds. Under such conditions the number of newcomers steadily increased because large commercial firms imported more and more coolie labour. Between 1870 and 1880 more than 122,000 had come into the country. Then Congress began to oppose this immigration, and since 1879 has experimented with various laws, until now the Chinese workman is almost wholly excluded. According to the last census there were only 81,000 Chinese in the whole United States.

More attractive than the yellow immigrants to these shores are the red-skinned aborigines of the land, the Indians, whom the Europeans found when they landed. The world is too much inclined, however, to consider the fate of the Indian in a false light, just because his manner of life captures the fancy and his picturesque barbarity has often attracted the poet. The American himself is rather inclined to see in his treatment of the Indian a grave charge against his own nation, and to find himself guilty of the brutal extermination of a native race. To arrive at such an opinion he assumes that in former centuries great tribes of Indians scoured the tremendous hunting-grounds of the land. But science has done away with this fanciful picture, and we know to-day that these millions of natives never existed. There are to-day about 270,000 Redskins, and it is very doubtful whether the number was ever much greater. It is true, of course, that between Central America and the Arctic Sea, hundreds of different Indian languages were spoken, and many of these languages have twenty or thirty different dialects. But the sole community in which such a dialect developed would include only a few hundred persons, and broad tracts of land would lie between the neighbouring communities. They used to live in villages, and wandered over the country only at certain seasons of the year in order to hunt, fish, and collect fruits.

As soon as the European colonies established themselves in the country the Indians used to take part in their wars, and on such occasions were supplied by the colonists with arms and employed as auxiliary forces. But the delights of these new methods of warfare, which they learned quickly, broke up their own peaceful life. The new weapons were employed for war between the Indian races, and eventually were turned by the Indians against the white settlers themselves. But, after all, the peaceful contact of Indians and whites was more productive of results. Only the French and Spanish permitted a mixture of the races, and in Canada especially to-day there is a mixed race of French and Indians; while in Mexico a large part of the inhabitants is Spanish and Indian. The truly American population sought above all else peaceably to disseminate its own culture; some Indian races became agricultural and devoted themselves to certain industrial pursuits.

Since the time when the United States gained actual possession of a larger part of the continent, a systematic Indian policy has been pursued, although administered largely, it must be admitted, in the American interests, and yet with considerable consideration of the natural inclinations of these hunting peoples. In various states, territories were set apart for them, which were certainly more than adequate to afford their sustenance; schools were built, and even institutions of higher learning; and through solemn treaties with their chiefs important rights were assigned to different races. To be sure, the main idea has always been to persuade the Indians to take up agricultural pursuits; to live merely by hunting flesh and eating wild fruits seemed hardly the thing at a time when millions of people were flocking westward out of Europe. Therefore, with every new treaty, the Indian reservations have been made smaller and smaller. The Indians, who would have preferred always to keep up their wild hunting life, felt, and still feel, that this has been unjust, and certainly many of their racial peculiarities have made it difficult to adapt American legal traditions fairly to their needs. The Indians had no idea of the private ownership of the soil; they considered everything as belonging to their tribe, and least of all had they any notion of the inheritance of property in the American sense. The Indian children belonged to the mother's family and the mother never belonged to the tribe of the father.

Although all these sources of friction have led the Indian to feel unjustly treated, it is still true that there has been scarcely any actually destructive oppression. The very races which have been influenced most by American culture have developed favourably. Last year the Indian mortality was 4,728, and the number of births 4,742; the Indians are, therefore, not dying out. The largest community is in the so-called Indian Territory and consists of 86,000 people, while there are 42,000 in Arizona. The several Indian reservations together embrace 117,420 square miles.

* * * * * * * * * * *

The Indian question is the least serious problem of all those which concern population in America; by far the most difficult is the negro question. The Indian lives within certain reservations, but the negro lives everywhere side by side with the American. So also the Indian troubles are narrowly confined to a small reservation in the great field of American problems, but the negro question is met everywhere in American thought, and in connection with every American interest. There could hardly be a greater contrast than that between the Indian and the negro; the former is proud, self-contained, selfish and revengeful, passionate and courageous, keen and inventive. The negro, on the other hand, is subservient, yielding, almost childishly good natured, lazy and sensual, without energy or ambition, outwardly apt to learn, but without any spirit of invention or intellectual independence. And still one ought not to speak of these millions of people as if they were of one type. On the Gulf of Mexico there are regions where the black population lives almost wholly sunk in the superstitions of its African home; while in Harvard University a young negro student has written creditable essays on Kant and Hegel. And between these opposite poles exists a population of about nine millions.

The negro population of America does not increase quite so rapidly as the white, and yet in forty years it has increased twofold. In the year 1860, before the slaves were freed, there were 4,441,000 blacks; in 1870, 4,880,000; in 1880, 6,580,000; in 1890, 7,470,000; in 1900, 8,803,000. In view of this considerable increase of the negro, it is not to be expected that the problem will lose anything of its urgency by the more rapid growth of the white population. And at the same time the physical contrast between the races is in no wise decreasing, because there is no mixing of the white and black races to-day, as there very frequently was before the war. It will not be long before the coloured population will be twice the entire population which Canada to-day has. These people are distributed geographically, so that much the largest part lives in those states which before the war practised slavery. To be sure, an appreciable part has wandered into the northern states, and the poorer quarters of the large cities are well infiltrated with blacks. Four-fifths, however, still remain in the South, owing probably to climatic conditions; the negro race thrives better in a warm climate. But it belongs there economically also, and has nearly every reason for staying there in future.

Nevertheless, the negro question is by no means a problem for the South alone; the North has its interests, and it becomes clearer all the time that the solution of the problem will depend in large part on the co-operation of the North. In the first place it was the North which set the negro free, and which, therefore, is partly responsible for what he is to-day; and it must lie with the North to decide whether the great dangers which to-day threaten can in any way be obviated. Europe has so far considered only one feature of the negro question — that of slavery. All Europe read "Uncle Tom's Cabin," and thought the difficulty solved as soon as the negro was freed from his chains and the poorest negro came into his human right of freedom. Europe was not aware that in this wise still greater problems were created, and that greater springs of misery and misfortune for the negro there took their origin. Nor does Europe realize that opposition between whites and blacks has never been in the history of America so sharp and bitter and full of hatred as it is to-day. Just in the last few years the hatred has grown on both sides, so that no friend of the country can look into the future without misgivings. "Das eben ist die Frucht der bösen Tat."

Yet where did the sin begin? Shall the blame fall on the English Parliament, which countenanced and even encouraged the trade in human bodies, or shall it fall on the Southern States, which kept the slaves in ignorance, and even threatened to punish any one who should instruct them? Or shall it fall on the Northern States, which were chiefly responsible for immediately granting to the freedmen, for the sake of party politics, all prerogatives of fellow-citizenship? Or shall the fault be put on the negro himself, who saw in his freedom from slavery an open door to idleness and worthlessness?

For generations the white man has regarded the black man as merchandise, has forcibly dragged him from his African jungles to make him work in ignorance and oppression on the cotton, rice, and tobacco fields of a white master. Then all at once he was made free and became an equal citizen in a country which, in its abilities, its feelings, its laws, and its Constitution, had the culture of two thousand years behind it. How has this emancipation worked on these millions? The first decade was a period of unrest and of almost frightened awakening to the consciousness of physical freedom, in the midst of all the after-effects of the fearful war. The negro was terrified by Southern secret societies which were planning vengeance, and confused by the dogmas of unscrupulous politicians who canvassed the states which had been so savagely shaken by the war, in order to gather up whatever might be found; and he was confused by a thousand other contradictions in public sentiment. Nowhere was there a secure refuge. Then followed the time in which the negroes hoped to employ their political power to advantage; the negroes were to be prospered by their ballot. But they found this to be a hopeless mistake. Then they believed a better way was to be found in the public schools and books. But the negro was again turned back; he needed not knowledge but the power to do, not books but a trade. So his rallying-cry has shifted. The blacks have never lost heart, and in a certain sense it must in justice be added the whites have never lacked good-will. And yet, after forty years of freedom, the results are highly discouraging.

On the outside there is much that speaks of almost brilliant success. The negroes have to-day in the United States 450 newspapers and four magazines; 350 books have been written by negroes; half of all the negro children are regularly taught in schools; there are 30,000 black teachers, school-houses worth more than $10,000,000, forty-one seminaries for teachers, and churches worth over $25,000,000. There are ten thousand black musicians and hundreds of lawyers. The negroes own four large banks, 130,000 farms, and 150,000 homes, and they pay taxes on $650,000,000 worth of real and personal property. The four past decades have therefore brought some progress to the freedman. And yet, in studying the situation, one is obliged to say that these figures are somewhat deceptive. The majority of negroes are still in such a state of poverty and misery, of illiteracy and mental backwardness, that the negroes who can be at all compared with the middle class of Americans are vanishingly few. Even the teachers and the doctors and pastors seem only very little to differ from the proletariat; and although there is many a negro of means, it is still a question whether he is able to enjoy his property, whether the dollar in his hand is the same as in the hand of a white man.

A part of the black population has certainly made real progress, but a larger part is humanly more degraded than before the slaves were freed; and if one looks at it merely as a utilitarian, considering only the amount of pleasure which the negroes enjoy, one cannot doubt that the general mass of negroes was happier under slavery. Their temperament is crueller to them than any plantation master could have been. The negro — we must have no illusions on that point — has partly gone backward. The capacity for hard work which he acquired in four generations of slavery, he has in large part lost again during forty years of freedom; although, indeed, the tremendous cotton harvests from the Southern States are gathered almost wholly by negro labour. It must be left to anthropology to find out whether the negro race is actually capable of such complete development as the Caucasian race has come to after thousands of years of steady labour and progress. The student of social politics need not go into such speculations; he faces the fact that the African negro has not had the thousands of years of such training, and therefore, although he might be theoretically capable of the highest culture, yet practically he is still unprepared for the higher duties of civilization. Under the severe discipline of slavery he overcame his lazy instincts and learned how to work both in the field and in the shop, according as the needs of his master required, and became in this way a useful member of society; but he was relieved of all other cares. His owner provided him with house and nourishment, cared for him in illness, and protected him like any other valuable piece of property.

All this was suddenly changed on the great day when freedom was declared; no one compelled the negro to work then; he was free to follow his instinct to do nothing; no one punished him when he gave himself over to sensuality and indolence. But on the other side nobody now took care of him; in becoming his own master he remained his own slave. He was suddenly pushed into the struggle for existence, and the less he was forced to learn the less he was ready for the fight. There thus grew up an increasing mass of poverty-stricken negroes, among whom immorality and crime could thrive; and oftentimes the heavy weight of this mass has dragged down with it those who would have been better. Worst of all, it has strengthened the aversion of the whites a hundred-fold, and the best members of the negro race have had to suffer for the laziness, the sensuality, and the dishonesty of the great masses.

The real tragedy is not in the lives of the most miserable, but in the lives of those who wish to rise, who feel the mistakes of their fellow-negroes and the injustice of their white opponents, who desire to assimilate everything high and good in the culture about them, and yet who know that they do not, strictly speaking, belong to such a culture. The negroes of the lower type are sunk in their indifference; they while away the hours in coarse enjoyments, and are perfectly content with a few watermelons while they dance and sing. The onlooker is disheartened, but they themselves laugh like children. The better negroes, on the other hand, feel all the hardship and carry the weight of the problem on their souls. They go through life fully conscious of an insoluble contradiction in their existence; they feel that it is denied them to participate immediately in life, and that they must always see themselves with the eyes of others, and lead in a way a double existence. As one of them has recently said, they are always conscious of being a problem.

They themselves have not chosen their lot, they did not come of their own accord from Africa, nor gladly take on the yoke of slavery; nor were they by their own efforts saved from slavery. They have been passive at every turn of fortune. Now they wish to commence to do their best and to give their best, and they have to do this in an environment for which they are wholly unprepared and which is wholly beyond them in its culture They have not themselves worked out this civilization; they belong historically in another system, and remain here at best mere imitators. And the better they succeed in being like their neighbours, the more they become unlike what they ought naturally to develop into.

This feeling of disparateness leads directly to the feeling of embitterment. In the general masses, however, it is the feeling of incompetence to support the struggle for existence successfully which turns necessarily into a bitter hatred of the whites. And the more the lack of discipline and the laziness of the black cause the whites to hold him in check, so much the more brightly burns this hatred. But all students of the South believe that this hatred has come about wholly since the negro was declared free. The slave was faithful and devoted to his master, who took care of him; he hated work, but did not hate the white man, and took his state of slavery as a matter of course, much as one takes one's inability to fly. A patriarchal condition prevailed in the South before the war, in spite of the representations made by political visionaries. Indeed, it is sometimes difficult not to doubt whether it was necessary to do away with slavery so suddenly and forcibly; whether a good deal of self-respect would not have been saved on both sides, and endless hatred, embitterment, and misery spared, if the Northern States had left the negro question to itself, to be solved in time through organic rather than mechanical means. Perhaps slavery would then have gone gradually over into some form of patriarchal relation.

It is too late to philosophize on this point; doctrinarianism has shaped the situation otherwise. The arms of the Civil War have decided in favour of the North. It is dismal, but it must be said that the actual events of the ensuing years of peace have decided rather in favour of the view of the South. To comprehend this fully, it is not enough to ask merely, as we have done so far, how the negro now feels; but more specially to ask what the American now thinks.

What is to-day the relation between the white man and the negro? There is a difference here between the North and the South, and yet one thing is true for both: the American feels that the cleft between the white and black races is greater now than ever before. So far as the North is concerned, the political view of the problem has probably changed very little. Specially the New England States, whose exalted ethical motives were beyond all doubt — as perhaps is not so certain of the Middle States — still sympathize to-day with the negro as a proper claimant of human rights. But unfortunately one may believe in the negro in the abstract, and yet shrink from contact with him in the concrete. The personal dislike of the black man, one might even call it an æsthetic antipathy, is really more general and wide-spread in the North than in the South. South of Washington one can scarcely be shaved except by a negro, while north of Philadelphia a white man would quite decline to patronize a coloured barber. A Southerner is even not averse to having a black nurse in the house, while in the Northern States that would never be thought of. Whenever the principle is to be upheld, the negro is made welcome in the North. He is granted here and there a small public office; he delivers orations, and is admitted to public organizations; he marches in the parades of war veterans, and a few negroes attend the universities. And still there is no real social intercourse between the races. In no club or private house and on no private occasions does one meet a negro. And here the European should bear specially in mind that negroes are not seldom men and women whose faces are perhaps as white as any Yankee's, and who often have only the faintest taint of African blood.

At the very best the Northerner plays philanthropist toward the negro, takes care of his schools and churches, helps him to help himself, and to carve out his economic freedom. But even here the feeling has been growing more and more in recent years that the situation is somehow fundamentally false, and that the North has acted hastily and imprudently in accepting the emancipated negro on terms of so complete equality. The feeling of dissatisfaction is growing in the North, and it is not an accident that the negro population of the North grows so slowly, although the negro is always ready to wander, and would crowd in great numbers to the North if he might hope to better his fortunes there. The negro feels, however, intensely that he is still less a match for the energetic Northerner in the industrial competition than for the white man of the South, and that it is often easier to endure the hatred of the Southerner than the coldly theoretical sufferance of the Northerner when joined, as it is, with a personal distaste so pronounced.

In the South it is quite different. There could hardly be an æsthetic aversion for the race, when for generations blacks and whites have lived together, when all the servants of the home have been coloured, and the children have grown up on the plantations with their little black playmates. There has been a good deal in the easy good-nature of the negro which the Southern white man has always found sympathetic, and he responded in former times to the disinterested faithfulness of the slaves with a real attachment. And although this may have been such fondness as one feels for a faithful dog or an intelligent horse, there was in it, nevertheless, no trace of that physical repulsion felt by the Northerner. The same is fundamentally true to-day, and the rhetorical emphasis of the physical antipathy toward the black which one finds in Southern speeches is certainly in part hypocritical. It is true that even to-day the poorest white man would think himself too good to marry the most admirable coloured woman; but the reason of this would lie in social principles, and not, as politicians would like to make it appear, in any instinctive racial aversion, since so long as the negroes were in slavery the whites had no aversion to such personal contamination.

The great opposition which now exists is twofold: it is on the one hand political and on the other social. The political situation of the South has been indeed dominated in the last forty years by the negro question. There have been four distinct periods of development; the first goes from the end of the Civil War to 1875. It was the time when the negro had first received the suffrage and become a political factor, the most dreary time which the South ever knew. It was economically ruined, was overrun with a disgusting army of unscrupulous politicians, who wanted nothing but to pervert the ignorant coloured voters for the lowest political ends. The victorious party in the North sent its menials down to organize the coloured quarry, and by mere numbers to outdo all independent activities of the white population.

One can easily understand why a Southern historian should say that the Southern States look back without bitterness on the years of the war, when brave men met brave men on the field of battle; but that they are furious when they remember the years which followed, when the victors, partly out of mistaken philanthropy, partly out of thoughtlessness and indifference, and partly out of evil intent, hastened to put the reins of government into the hands of a race which was hardly out of African barbarism; and thus utterly disheartened the men and women who had built up the splendid culture of the Old South. Perhaps there was no phase of American history, he says, so filled with poetry and romantic charm as the life of the South in the last ten years before the war; and certainly no period has been so full of mistakes, uncertainties, and crime as the decade immediately following. A reaction had to come, and it came in the twenty years between 1875 and 1895. The South betook itself to devious methods at the ballot-box. It was recognized that falsification of election returns was an evil, but it was thought to be a worse evil for the country to be handed over to the low domination of illiterate negroes. The political power of the negro has been broken in this way. Again and again the same method was resorted to, until finally the public opinion of the South approved of it, and those who juggled with the ballot-box were not pursued by the arm of the law, because the general opinion was with them.

There has been another and more important fact. Slowly all party opposition between the whites vanished, and the race question became the sole political issue. To be sure, there have been free-traders and protectionists in the South, and representatives of all other party principles; but all genuine party life flagged and all less important distinctions vanished at the ballot-box when the whites rallied against the blacks, and since the negroes voted invariably with the Republican party, which had set them free, the entire white population of the South has become Democratic. By this political consolidation, the power of the negro has been further restricted.

People have gradually become convinced, however, that political life stagnates when large states have only the one fixed idea, as if hypnotized by the race issue. The need has been felt anew of participating once more in all the great problems which interest the nation and which create the parties. The South looks back longingly on the time when it used to furnish the most brilliant statesmen of the nation. The South has become also aware that so soon as public opinion allows a systematic corruption of the ballot-box, then every kind of selfishness and corruption has an easy chance to creep in.

Let once the election returns be falsified in order to wipe out a negro majority, and they may be falsified the next time in favour of some commercial conspiracy. An abyss opens up which is truly bottomless. So a third period has arrived. In place of nullifying the negro suffrage by illegal means, the South has been thinking out legal measures for limiting it. The Constitution prescribes merely that no one shall be deprived of his vote by reason of his colour, but it has been left to the several states to determine what the other conditions shall be which govern the right to vote. Thus any state is free to place a certain property condition, or to require a certain degree of education from every man who votes; but all such conditions must apply to all inhabitants of the state alike; thus, for instance, in four states, and only in those four, do women enjoy the suffrage. Now the Southern States have commenced to make extensive use of this state privilege. They are not allowed to exclude the negro as a negro since the Northern States have added the Fifteenth Amendment of the Constitution, and there would be no hope of altering this. But so long as the educational status of the negro is so far behind that of the white man, the number of those who cannot read is still so large that a heavy blow is struck at negro political domination when a state decides to restrict the suffrage to those who can read and understand the Constitution. It is clear that at the same time the test of this which necessarily has to be made leaves the coveted free-play to the white man's discretion.

The last few years have witnessed a great advance of this new movement. The political power of the negro is less than ever, and the former illegal measures to circumvent it are no longer needed. It cannot be denied that in two ways this works directly in the interests of civilization. On the one hand, it incites the negro population to take measures for the education of its children, since by going to school the negro can comply with the conditions of suffrage. On the other hand, it frees Southern politics from the oppressive race question, and allows real party problems to become once more active issues among the whites. The political contrast is, therefore, to-day somewhat lessened, although both parties regard it rather as a mere cessation of hostilities; since it is by no means certain that Northern political forces at Washington will not once more undo this infringement on the negroes' rights, and whether once more, in case of a real party division between the Southern whites, the negroes will not have the deciding vote. If the doctrinarianism of the North should actually prevail and be able to set aside these examinations in reading and in intelligence which have been aimed against the negro, on the ground that they are contrary to the Constitution, it would indeed frustrate a great movement toward political peace. When the abolitionists at the end of the Civil War granted the suffrage to the negroes, they were at least able to adduce one very good excuse; they claimed that the Southern States would continue in some new form to hold the negro in subjection if he was not protected by either a military guard or by his right to vote, and since the army was to be disbanded the right to vote was given him. To-day there is no such danger; the legal exclusion of the Southern negro from the ballot-box must be accounted an advance.

The social question, however, is even more important to-day than the political one, and it is one which grows day by day. We have said already that the Southerner has no instinctive aversion to the negro race, and his desire for racial purity is not an instinct but a theory, of which the fathers of the present white man knew nothing. To be sure, the situation cannot be simply formulated, but it probably comes nearest to the truth to say that the white man's hatred is the inherited instinct of the slave-holder. In all his sentiments the Southerner is dominated by the once natural feeling that the negro is his helpless subject. The white man is not cruel in this; he wants to protect the negro and to be kind, but he can allow him no will of his own. He has accustomed himself to the slavish obedience of the negro, as the opium-eater is accustomed to his opium. And to give up the paralyzing drug is intolerable to his nervous system.

The everywhere repeated cry that the purity of the race is in danger, if social equality is established, is only a pretext; it is in truth the social equality itself which calls forth the hysterical excitement. No white man, for instance, in the South would go into the dining-room of a hotel in which a single negro woman should be sitting; but this is not because a mere proximity would be disagreeable, as it would actually be to the Northerner, but because he could not endure such appearance of equality. So soon as a little white child sits beside the negro woman, so that she is seen to be a servant and her socially inferior station is made plain, then her presence is no longer felt to be at all disagreeable.

In his fight against social equality with the negro, the Southerner resorts to more and more violent means; and while he works himself up to an increasing pitch of excitement by the energy of his opposition, the resulting social humiliation increases the embitterment of the negro. That no white hotel, restaurant, theatre, or sleeping-car is open to the black is a matter of course; this is virtually true also in the North. But it has contributed very much to renewed disaffection, that also the ordinary railroad trains and street cars begin to make a similar distinction.

The South is putting a premium on every kind of harsh social affront to the black man, and relentlessly punishes the slightest social recognition. When the president of a negro college was the guest of a Northern hotel and the chamber-maid refused to put his room to rights and was therefore dismissed, the South got together, by a popular subscription, a large purse for this heroine. It is only from this point of view that one can understand the great excitement which swept through the South when President Roosevelt had the courage to invite to his table Booker T. Washington, the most distinguished negro of the country. Professor Basset, the historian, has declared, amid the fierce resentment of the South, that, with the exception of General Lee, Booker Washington is the greatest man who has been born in the South for a hundred years. But who inquires after the merits of a single man when the principle of social inequality is at stake? If the President had worked for several months from early to late at his desk with Booker T. Washington, the fact would have passed unnoticed. But it is simply unpardonable that he invited him to the luncheon table, and even very thoughtful men have shaken their heads in the opinion that this affront to the social superiority of the white man will very sadly sharpen the mutual antagonism.

We must not overlook in this connection the various minor circumstances which have strengthened the lingering feeling of the slave-owner. First of all, there is the unrestrained sensuality of the negro, which has led him time after time to attempt criminal aggressions on white women, and so contributed infinitely to the misery of his situation. It is a gross exaggeration when the Southern demagogue reiterates again and again that no man in the South can feel that his wife, his sister, or daughter is secure from the bestiality of the blacks; and yet it cannot be denied that such crimes are shockingly frequent, and they are the more significant, since the continual fear of this danger seriously threatens the growth of farming life with its lonely farm-houses. Here the barbarities of lynch law have come in, and the rapid growth of racial hatred may be seen in the increased number of lynchings during recent years. But every lynching reacts to inoculate hatred and cruel ferocity in the public organism, and so the bestial instincts and the lawless punishments work together to debase the masses in the Southern States.

It is not only a question of the immorality of the negro and the lynch courts of the white man, but in other ways the negro shows himself inclined to crime, and the white man to all sorts of lawless acts against him. The negroes are disproportionately represented in Southern prisons, although this comes partly from the fact that the black man is punished for the slightest misdemeanour, while the white man is readily let off. In fact, it is difficult in the South to find a jury to convict a white man of any crime done against a negro. This application of a two-fold standard of justice leads quickly to a general arbitrariness which fits only too well with the natural instincts of the slave-holder. Arbitrary privileges in place of equal rights have always been the essential point in his existence, and so it happens that even where no negroes are in question Southern juries hand down verdicts which scandalize the whole country. Indeed, there is no doubt that secret attempts have even been made, in all sorts of devious forms, to re-establish the state of slavery. For some small misdemeanour negroes are condemned to pay a very heavy fine, and to furnish this they have to let themselves out to some sort of contract labour under white masters, which amounts to the same thing as slavery. Here again the whole country is horrified when the facts come to be known. But no means have yet been thought of for lessening the bitter hatred which exists, and so long as the sharp social contrast remains there will continue to be evasions and violations of the law, to give vent to the hatred and bitter feeling.

What now may one look for, that shall put an end to these unhappy doings? The Africans have had their Zionists, who wish to lead them back to their native forests in Africa, and many people have recently fancied that the problem would be solved by forcible deportation to the Philippines. These dreams are useless; nine million people cannot be dumped on the other side of the ocean, cannot be torn from their homes. Least of all could they be brought to combine with the entirely different population of the Philippines. More than that, the South itself would fight tooth and nail against losing so many labourers; it would be industrially ruined, and would be more grievously torn up than it was after the Civil War, if in fact some magic ship could carry every black to the negro republic of Liberia, on the African coast. For the same reason it is impracticable to bring together all negroes in one or two Southern States and leave them to work out their own salvation. In the first place, no state would be willing to draw this black lot, while the white population of the other Southern States would suffer fully as much. The student of social politics, finally, cannot doubt for a moment that the negro progresses only when he is in constant contact with white men, and degenerates with fearful speed when he is left to himself.

Among those negroes who have been called to be the leaders of their people, and who form an independent opinion of the situation, one finds two very different tendencies. One of these is to reform from the top down, the other from the bottom up. The energies of Dubois are typical of the first tendency, Booker Washington's of the second. Dubois, and many of the most educated and advanced negroes with him, believe in the special mission of the negro race. The negro does not want to be, and ought not to be, a second order of American, but the United States are destined by Providence to develop two great and diverse but co-operating peoples, the Americans and the negroes. It is therefore the work of the African not simply to imitate the white man's culture, but to develop independently a special culture suited to his own national traits. They feel instinctively that a few great men of special physiognomy, two or three geniuses coming from their race, will do more for the honour of their people and for the belief in its possibilities, than the slow elevation of the great mass. They lay strong emphasis on the fact that in his music, religion, and humour the negro has developed strongly individual traits, and that the people who forty years ago were in slavery have developed in a generation under unfavourable circumstances a number of shining orators, politicians, and writers. Thus they feel a most natural ambition to make a way for the best and strongest, to elevate them, and to incite them to their highest achievements. The ideal is thus, in the work of the most gifted leaders to present to the world a new negro culture, by which the right of independent existence for the black race in America may be secured.

Booker Washington and his friends wish to go a quieter road; and he has with him the sympathies of the best white people in the country. They look for salvation not from a few brilliantly exceptional negroes, but from the slow and steady enlightenment of the masses; and their real leaders are to be not those who accomplish great things as individuals, but rather they who best serve in the slow work of uplifting their people. These men see clearly that there are to-day no indications of really great accomplishments and independent feats in the way of culture, and that such things are hardly to be looked for in the immediate future. At the very best it is a question of an unusual talent for imitating an alien culture.

If, then, one can hardly speak of brilliant genius in the upper strata — and it is to be admitted that Booker Washington himself is not a really great, independent, and commanding personality — it would be on the other hand much more distorted to estimate the negro from his lowest strata, from the lazy and criminal individuals. The great mass of negroes is uneducated and possesses no manual training for an occupation; but it is honest, healthy, and fit social material, which only needs to be trained in order to become valuable to the whole community. First of all, the negro ought to learn what he has once learned as a slave — a manual trade; he should perfect himself in work of the hands or in some honest agricultural occupation, not seek to create a new civilization, but more modestly to identify his race with the destinies of the white nation by real, honest, thoughtful, true, and industrious labour. Brilliant writers they do not need so much as good carpenters and school-teachers; nor notable individual escapades in the tourney-field of culture so much as a general dissemination of technical training. They need schools for manual training and institutes for the development of technical teachers.

Booker Washington's own institution in Tuskegee has set the most admirable example, and the most thoughtful men in the North and South alike are very ready to help along all his plans. They hope and believe that so soon as the masses of coloured people have begun to show themselves somewhat more useful to the industry of the country as hand-workers, expert labourers, and farmers, that then the mutual embitterment will gradually die out and the fight for social equality slowly vanish. For on this point the more thoughtful men do not deceive themselves; social equality is nothing but a phrase when it is applied to the relation of millions of people to other millions. Among the whites themselves no one ever thinks of any real social equality; the owner of a plantation no more invites his white workmen in to eat with him than he would invite a coloured man. And when the Southern white replies scornfully to any one who challenges his prejudices, with the convincing question, "Would you let your sister marry a nigger?" he is forgetting, of course, that he himself would not let his sister marry nine-tenths of the white men of his community. Social equality can be predicated only of small groups, and in all exactness only of individuals.

Thus it might be said that peace is advanced to-day chiefly by the increasing exertions for the technical industrial education of the black workman. But it is not to be forgotten that the negro himself, and with him many philanthropists of the North, comprehends the whole situation very differently from the Southern supporters of the movement. These latter are contented with recent tendencies, because the negro's vote is curtailed in the political sphere, and because he comes to be classed socially with the day-labourer and artisan. The negro, however, looks on this as a temporary stage in his development, and hopes in good time to outgrow it. He is glad that the election returns are no longer falsified on his account, and that legal means have been resorted to. But of course he hopes that he will soon grow beyond these conditions, and be finally favoured once more with the suffrage, just as any white man is.

It is much the same in the social sphere. He may be satisfied for the present that the advantages of manual training and farm labour are brought to the fore, but this must only be to lead his race up step by step until it has developed from a mere working class to entire social equality. That which the negro approves for the moment is what any white man in the Southern States would fix as a permanent condition. And so it appears that even in this wise no real solution of the problem has been reached, although a cessation of hostilities has been declared. But all these efforts on the part of leaders and philanthropists, these deliberations of the best whites and blacks in both the North and South, are still far from carrying weight with the general public; and thus, although the beginnings toward improvement are good, it remains that on the outside the situation looks to-day darker than ever before.

Whoever frees himself from theoretical doctrines will hardly doubt that the leading whites of the Southern States have to-day once more the better insight, since they know the negro better than the Northerners do. They demand that this limitation of the negro in his political rights and in his daily occupation shall be permanent, and that thus an organic situation shall come about in which the negro, although far removed from an undeserved slavery, shall be equally far from the complete enjoyment of that civilization which his own race has not worked out. That is, he is to be politically, economically, and socially dependent. If this had happened at the outset, the mutual hatred which now exists would never have been so fierce; and if the African succeeds materially he will hardly notice the difference, while the white man will feel with satisfaction that his superiority has been vindicated. The condition of the island of Jamaica is a good instance in point. Its inhabitants are strikingly superior to the debased negroes of the Republic of Hayti.

But it is not to be forgotten that history has repeatedly shown how impossible it is for a people numbering millions, with limited rights, to dwell in the midst of an entirely free race. Oppression and injustice constantly arise from the limitation of rights, and thence grow retaliation and crime. And the hour in which the American people narrow down the rights of ten million blacks may be the starting-point for fearful struggles. The fact remains that the real solution of the question is nowhere in sight. The negro question is the only really dark cloud on the horizon of the American nation.

CHAPTER NINE

Internal Political Problems

THE problems of population, especially those concerning the immigration and the negro, have taken considerable of our attention. We shall be able to survey problems of internal politics more quickly, since we have already met most of them in considering the American form of government. The insane programme of those who desire no government at all, that is, anarchy, is one of the American's political problems only when the deed of some foreign assassin gives him a sudden fright. Then all sorts of propositions are on foot to weed out anarchism stem and root; but after a little time they subside. One sees how difficult it is to draw the lines, and the idea of suppressing free political speech is too much against the fundamental principles of the American democracy. But the fundamental principles of anarchism, or rather its fundamental confusions, have so little hope of influencing the conservative ideas of the Americans, that there need be no fear of anarchism creeping into the national mind. In so far as there is any such problem in America, it is connected solely with the question of immigration. Up to the present time, the government has been content to forbid acknowledged anarchists to land; but this involves such an un-American intermeddling with private convictions that the regulation will hardly be tolerated much longer. The true American, in any case, believes in state ordinances and loves his governmental machinery.

This apparatus itself of government has many details which offer problems, indeed, and are much discussed. Some of its elements have been added recently by President Roosevelt; the most important of them is the newly created Department of Commerce and Labour. This new division of the government, with over ten thousand officials, embraces also the Bureau of Corporations, which is designed to collect statistics regarding trusts and the overcoming of their influence; but the struggle promises to be a two-sided one. To the present administration belongs also the creation of a general staff for the Army, and on this head there seems to be a unanimous opinion that the Army is distinctly benefited by the measure. In some other directions, moreover, the make-up of the Army has become more similar to European models; new schools of war have been founded and the plan of holding great manœuvres introduced. The weakness of the military system is that preferments go according to seniority. It is clear to all that a merely mechanical advancement of officers is not advantageous to the military service; and yet everybody is afraid, if the uniform principle is given up and personal preferment is introduced, that all sorts of regrettable political and social influences will be brought to bear in the matter. Many persons see a difficult problem here; the young officer has almost no incentive to-day to special exertions.

The government has more and various plans with regard to the Navy. There, too, it seems as if a general staff similar to that of the Army is indispensable. The steady growth of the Navy itself is assured, since every one recognizes that America could not carry out its present policy without a strong fleet. The fleet, which dates virtually from 1882, won the hearts of the imperialistic public by its victories at Manila and Santiago; and its growth is nowhere seriously opposed. Likewise, the Navy is introducing more large manœuvres. The real difficulty lies in lack of men; it becomes more and more difficult to get officers and sailors; and even in the question of manning a ship, the inevitable negro question plays a part.

There are many open questions also in regard to the diplomatic and consular service. The United States maintains an uncommonly large number of consuls, whose enterprise is nowhere contested, but whose preparation, tact, and personal integrity often leave a good deal to be desired. Their remuneration through fees contributes a good deal toward creating unwholesome conditions. The personnel of the diplomatic service is perhaps still more unequal than that of the consular. Since early times the United States has had the discernment to send some of its most distinguished men to fill important ambassadorial positions. At a time when the international relations of the country were still insignificant, such a position was often given to distinguished authors and poets, who represented their country at a foreign court in an intellectual and cultivated way, and contributed much to its esteem. This can happen no longer, and yet America has had again and again the good fortune to send to diplomatic positions men of uncommon caliber; scholars like Andrew D. White, statesmen like John Hay, and brilliant jurists like Choate. The danger still subsists, however, that men who are merely rich, and who have done small services to Senators, expect in return a diplomatic appointment, for the sake of the social glory. There is a growing desire to make the diplomatic service a regular career, in which a man progresses step by step.

As to the postal service, the foremost problem is now that of free delivery in rural districts. The tremendous extent of the country and the thinness of its population had at first made it a matter of course that the farmer should fetch his own mail from the nearest village. The rural letter-carrier was unknown, as he is still unknown in small towns; every man in the village goes to the post-office to get his newspapers and letters. But like every country at the present time, the United States is trying to check the continual afflux of population into the cities. It is obvious that specially with the intellectual make-up of the American, every effort must be made to make rural life less monotonous and tiresome, and that it is necessary most of all to establish ready communication between the remote farm-houses and the rest of the world. The more frequently and easily the farming people receive their letters and magazines, so much the less do they feel tempted to leave the soil. For this reason the very expensive rural delivery has spread rapidly. In the last year nine thousand new appointments were made in this service. Another important problem connected with the Post-Office is the fact that it does not pay for itself, because it carries printed matter at unprofitably low rates, and in this way has stimulated to an extraordinary degree the sending of catalogues and advertising matter. One can see how far this goes from the fact that a short time ago a factory for medicine sent out so many copies of a booklet advertising its specific through the so-called "testimonials," that a railway train with eight large freight cars was necessary to carry them to the nearest post-office. Part of the difficulty comes from the private ownership of the railroads, whose contracts with the government for carrying the mails involve certainly no loss to the stockholders.

In similar wise, all of the great departments of government have their problems, large or small, and the most important of these must be dealt with when we come to speak of the economic situation. But there is one problem that is common to all branches of the government; it is the most important one which concerns internal affairs, and although it is discussed somewhat less actively to-day than in former years, it continues none the less in some new form or other to worry the parties, the government, and more especially public opinion. It is the question of civil-service reform.

We have touched on this question before when we spoke of the struggles between parties, and of the motives which bring the individual into the party service. Some things remain to be said by way of completely elucidating one of the most important problems of American public life. To commence with, if we abstract from the civil service in city and state — although the question is much the same there — that is, if we take into account only the federal service — we find over a hundred thousand official appointments: and the question is — Shall these appointments, with their assured salaries, be distributed to adherents of the party in power, chiefly with reference to their services to the party, or shall these positions be removed from all touch with the parties and given to the best and ablest applicants? It is clear that the problem could easily be so exhibited that the appointment of the best and most capable applicant, without reference to his party, should seem to be absolutely and unequivocally necessary, and as if any other opinion could proceed only from the desire to work corruption. The situation is not quite so simple, however.

In the first place, every one is aware that the highest administrative positions are invariably places of confidence, where it is very necessary that the incumbent shall be one in thought and purpose with the Executive; and this is more than ever necessary in a democracy composed of two parties. If the majority of the people elects a certain President in order to carry out the convictions of one party in opposition to the other, the will of the people would be frustrated if the upper members of the governmental staffs were not to be imbued with the same party ideas. A Republican President could not work together with a Democratic Secretary of State without sacrificing the efficiency of his administration, and struggling along on such compromises as would ultimately make meaningless the existence of two organized parties. A Republican Secretary of State must have, however, if he is to be spared a good deal of friction, an assistant secretary of state with whom he is politically in harmony; and so it goes on down.

But if we begin at the bottom and work up, the situation looks different. The book-keeper to the ministry, the small postal clerk, or the messenger boy in the treasury, has no opportunity to realize his personal convictions. He has merely his regular task to perform, and is not immediately concerned whether the policy of state is Republican or Democratic, imperialistic or anti-imperialistic. We have then to ask — Where lie the boundaries between those higher positions in which the private convictions of the incumbents ought properly to be with the administration, and those lower positions where party questions are in no way involved?

Opinions vary very widely as to where this boundary lies. Some put it rather low, and insist that the American by his whole political training is so thoroughly a creature of the party, that true harmony in state offices can be had only if the whole service from top to bottom is peopled with adherents of the ruling party; and this opinion, although it may be refuted on good grounds, is neither absurd nor dishonest. The population of Germany is divided to-day into a civil and a social-democratic party, and it appears to the dominant civil party by no means unnatural to exclude the social-democrats so far as possible from participation in the public service.

It is quite possible, moreover, for each party to furnish competent incumbents for all the leading positions; and so long as capable men can be found who will acquit themselves well in office, there is of course no reason for charging the party with greed or spoils-gathering, as if the public funds were a pure gift, and it were unworthy to accept an official appointment given in recognition of services to the party. We have already emphasized how extremely German conceptions differ from American on this point, and how the customary reiteration in Germany of the unfavourable comments made by certain American reform enthusiasts, leads to much misunderstanding. It is well-known that Germany has, for instance, for the university professors a system of state appointment, which rests wholly on personal recommendation; this in sharp contrast to England, where the candidates for every vacant chair must compete, and where no one can be called who does not compete; or with France, where the positions are awarded on the basis of an examination.

The considerations which we have stated are not at all to be taken as an argument against civil-service reform, but only as an indication that the problem is complicated and has its pros and cons. In fact, the grounds for the widest possible extension of a civil-service independent of party are many and urgent. In the first place, the service itself demands it. The appointments by party are really appointments on the basis of recommendations and wishes of political leaders. The Senators, for instance, from a certain state advise the President as to who should be appointed for postmasters in the most important post-offices; and the smaller positions are similarly filled on the recommendation of less influential politicians.

Therefore, it is only to a limited extent that there is any real estimation of the capacity and fitness of the proposed incumbent. Public opinion is always watchful, however, and the politician is generally afraid to press an appointment which he knows would be disapproved by public opinion, or which would later be seen to be absurd, would damage his own political credit, and perhaps even wreck his political future.

It is equally true that the political parties have become expert in sifting human material and finding just the right people for the places; and that, moreover, the American with his extraordinary capacity for adaptation and organization easily finds himself at home in any position and fills it creditably. And yet it remains, that in this way the best intentioned appointer works in the dark, and that a technical examination would more accurately select the fittest man from among the various candidates.

Most of all, by this method of appointment on the ground of political influence, where the petitions of the incumbent's local friends, commendatory letters from well-known men, and the thousand devices of the wire-puller play an important part, the feeling of individual responsibility is always largely lost. The head of the department must rely on local representatives, and these politicians again know that they do not themselves actually make the appointments; and the candidate is put into office with no exertion on his own part — almost passively.

It is not to be denied that in this way many an unworthy man has come to office. The very lowest political services have been rewarded with the best positions. Political candidates have had to promise before their election to make certain appointments to office which had nothing at all to do with the fitness of the appointee; and such appointee, when actually instated, has not only neglected his office, but sometimes criminally misused it for embezzlement and fraudulent contracts, for government deals in which he has had some personal advantage, or for the smuggling in of friends and relatives to inferior positions. Politicians have too often sought to exact all sorts of devious personal and political services from those whom they have previously recommended for office in order to hush them up. Through the intrigues of such men all sorts of unnecessary positions have been created, in order to provide for political friends from the public treasury; and the contest for these personal nominations has consumed untold time and strength in the legislative chambers. No one can fail to see that such sores will develop over and over in the political organism so long as the principle is recognized of making official appointments on the basis of party allegiance. While criminal misuse of such a practice is the exception, and the honourable endeavour to pick out the best candidates and their honest performance of duty are the rule, nevertheless every thoughtful friend of the country's welfare must wish to make all such exceptions impossible.

There is another unfavourable effect which such a system must have, within the party itself. A man who is put into office by politicians, unless he is a strong man, will labour in the interests of his benefactors, will carry party politics into places where they do not belong, and be ready to let the party rob him of a certain portion of his salary as a contribution to the party treasury, as has been customary for a long time. In this way salaries have been increased in order that a considerable portion might redound to the party treasury, and thus the means be won for bringing the party victoriously through the next elections; and in this way the official has been able to assure himself as good an office, or perhaps a better one, in the future. The same thing happens once more in city politics where the funds levied on city officials have made a considerable share of the party's assets. There has been good reason, therefore, why public opinion has for a long time demanded, and with increasing energy, an entire change in such a state of things; and aside from the positions of actual confidence, in which in fact only men of a certain political faith could be of any service, it has demanded that public offices be put on a non-partisan basis and given out with a view solely to the efficiency of the appointee.

Such a problem hardly existed during the first forty years of American constitutional government; officials were appointed in a business-like way. A man in office stayed there as long as he did his duties well, and the advent of a new party in the higher positions had very little influence on the lower ones. It was deemed tyranny to dismiss a competent official in order to put a party adherent in his position. The statistics show that at that time not more than forty-two changes on the average were made on such political grounds every year. The opposite practice first arose in the cities, and especially in New York, whence it spread to the state, where in 1818 a whole regiment of party followers was established in the government offices of the state by Van Buren. And under President Jackson the principle finally became adopted in the federal government. About the year 1830, it became an unwritten law that official positions should be the spoils of victory at the elections and go to the favoured party. People were aware that there was no better way of getting party adherents to be industrious than to promise them positions if they would help the party to gain its victory. The reaction commenced at about the middle of the last century, closely following on a similar movement in England.

As the power of the English Parliament grew, popular representatives had demanded their share in the distributing of offices, and an obnoxious trading in salaries had become prevalent. When at last the abuses became too frequent, just before the middle of the last century, England instituted official examinations in order to weed out the obviously unfit candidates. It was not really a true competition, since the candidate was still appointed to office by the politicians. But the examination made sure of a minimal amount of proper training.

The American Congress followed this example during the fifties. Certain groups of minor positions were made, for which appointment could be had only after an examination. England now went further on the same course, and America followed her lead. On both sides of the ocean the insignificant examination of the candidate who had backing, became a general examination for all who wished to apply; so that the position came to be given to the best candidate. The Civil-Service Commission was instituted by President Grant, and for thirty years its beneficent influence has steadily grown, and it has made great inroads on the old system. The regular politicians who could not endure being deprived of the positions which they wished to pledge to their campaign supporters have naturally tried time after time to stem the current, and with some success. In 1875 Congress discontinued the salaries which had been paid the Commissioners; then competitive examinations were given up, and in their stead single examinations instituted for candidates who had been recommended by political influence.

But here, if anywhere, public opinion has been stronger than party spirit. Under President Hayes, and then under Garfield and Arthur, the competitive system was partly reinstated, and while the number of positions which were open only to those who had successfully passed the public examinations increased, at the same time the reprehensible taxation of officials for party ends was finally stopped. This did not prevent a certain smaller number of positions from retaining their partisan complexion; and the opinions and party creed of these incumbents continued to be important, so that whenever one party succeeded another, a certain amount of change was still necessary. So there remain two great divisions of the public service — the political offices which the President fills by appointment in co-operation with the Senate, and the so-called "classified" offices which are given out on the basis of public examinations. Public opinion and the sincere supporters of civil-service reform, among whom is President Roosevelt himself, are working all the time for an increase in the number of classified positions and a corresponding decrease in the political group.

The open opponents of this movement, of whom there are many in both parties, are hard at work in the opposite direction, and are too often supported by the faint-hearted friends of the reform, who recognize its theoretical advantages, but have some practical benefit to derive by pursuing the methods which they decry. There is no doubt that again in the last ten years some steps have been taken backward, and on various pretexts many important positions have been withdrawn from the classified service and restored to Senatorial patronage.

The actual situation is as follows. There are 114,000 non-classified positions, with a total salary of $45,000,000, and 121,000 classified positions which bring a salary of $85,000,000. Among the former, where no competition exists, over 77,000 are post-masterships; then there are consular, diplomatic, and other high positions, and a large number of places for labourers. In the classified service, there are 17,000 positions for officials who live in Washington, 5,000 of which are in the treasury. The committees on the commission have about 400 different kinds of examinations to give. Last year 47,075 persons were examined for admission to the civil service; 21,000 of these for the government service, 3,000 for the customs, and 21,000 for the postal service. There were about 1,000 examinations more for advancements in office and exchange from one part of the service to another, and 439 persons were examined for service in the Philippines. Out of all these applicants 33,739 passed the examinations, and of these 11,764 obtained positions which are theirs for life, independent of any change which may take place at the White House. It is a matter of course that the security which these positions give of life-long employment is the highest incentive to faithful service and conscientious and industrious labour.

The difference between the two services was again clearly brought out in the last great scandal, which greatly stirred up the federal administration. The Post-Office Department had closed a number of contracts for certain utensils from which certain officials, or at least their relatives, made considerable profits. Everything had been most discreetly hidden, and it took an investigation of several months to uncover the crookedness. But when everything had come out, it appeared that the officials who were seriously involved all belonged to the unclassified service, while the classified service of the Post-Office was found to be an admirable example of conscientious and faithful office-holding. Certain it is that such criminal misuse, even among the confidential positions, is a rare exception; it is no less sure that the temptations are much greater there. A man who holds office, not because he is peculiarly fitted for it, but because he has been generally useful in politics, knowing as he does that the next time the parties change places his term of office will be up, will always be too ready to use his position for the party rather than for the country, and finally for himself and his pocket-book rather than for his party.

Now, if civil-service reform is to spread or even to take no steps backward, public opinion must be armed for continual battle against party politicians. But it is an insult to the country when, as too often happens, some one tries to make it appear that the opponents of reform are consciously corrupt. The difficulty of the problem lies just in the fact that most honourable motives may be uppermost on both sides; and one has to recognize this, although one may be convinced that the reformer has the better arguments on his side. The filling of positions by party adherents, as a reward for their services, puts an extraordinary amount of willing labour at the service of the party. And undoubtedly the party system is necessary in America, and demands for its existence just such a tremendous amount of work. The non-classified positions are to the American party politicians exactly what the orders and titles which he can award are to the European monarch; and the dyed-in-the-wool party leader would in all honesty be glad to throw overboard the whole "humbug" of civil-service reform, since he would rather see his party victorious — that is, his party principles acknowledged in high federal places — than see his country served as economically, faithfully, and ably as possible. In fact, the regular party politician has come to look on the frequent shake-up among office-holders as an ideal condition. Just as no President can be elected more than twice, he conceives it to be unsound and un-American to leave an official too long in any one position.

The full significance of the problem comes out when one realizes that the same is true once more in the separate state, and again in every municipality. The states and cities have their classified service, appointment to which is independent of party allegiance, as of governor or mayor, and in addition to this confidential positions for which the governor and legislature or the mayor and city council are responsible. Municipal service has attracted an increasing amount of public attention in recent years, owing to the extremely great abuses which it can harbour.

Fraudulent contracts, the grant of handsome monopolies to street railway, gas, electric-light, telephone, and pier companies, the purchase of land and material for public buildings, and the laying out of new streets — all these things, owing to the extraordinarily rapid growth of municipalities, afford such rich opportunities for theft, and this can be so easily hidden from the state attorney, that frightfully large numbers of unscrupulous people have been attracted into public life. And the more that purely municipal politics call for a kind of party service which is very little edifying or interesting to a gentleman in frock and silk hat, so much the more other kinds of men force their way into politics in large cities and get control of the popular vote, not in order to support certain principles, but to secure for themselves positions from the winning party, of which the salary is worth something and the dishonest perquisites may be "worth" a great deal more. Even here again the service to the city is not necessarily bad, and certainly not so bad as the scandal-mongering press of the opposite party generally represents it. Most of the office-holders are decent people, who are contented with the moderate salary and modest social honour of their positions. Nevertheless, a good deal that is impure does creep in, and the service would be more efficient if it could be made independent of the party machine. Public opinion is sure of this.

Each party is naturally convinced that the greatest blame belongs with the other, and in strict logic one can no more accuse one party of corruption than the other. The Republican party in a certain sense whets the general instinct for greed more than the Democratic, so that its opponents like to call it "the mother of corruption." It is a part of the Republican confession of faith, in consequence of its centralizing spirit, that the state cannot leave everything to free competition, but must itself exert a regulating influence; thus the Republican does not believe in free-trade, and he thinks it quite right for an industry or any economic enterprise which is going badly, or which fancies that it is not prospering enough, or which for any reason at all would like to make more money, to apply to the state for protection, and to be favoured at the expense of the rest of the community. The principle of complete equality is here lost, and the spirit of preference, of favours for the few against the many, and of the employment of public credit for the advantage of the avaricious, is virtually recognized. And when this spirit has once spread and gone through all party life, there is no way of preventing a situation in which every one applies to the public funds for his own enrichment, and the strongest industries secure monopolies and influence the legislatures in their favour by every means which the party has at its disposal.

The Democrats, on the other hand, desire equal rights for all, and free competition between all economic enterprises; they approve of all centrifugal and individualistic tendencies. And yet if the state does not exert some regulative influence, the less moral elements of society will misuse their freedom, and they will be freer in the end than the citizens who scrupulously and strictly govern themselves. And the spirit of unrestraint and immorality will be ever more in evidence. The Democratic party will be forced to make concessions to this idea if it desires to retain its domination over the masses, and any one who first begins to make concessions to individual crookedness is necessarily inoculated. Thus it happens that in the Republican party there is a tendency to introduce corruption from above, and in the Democratic party from below.

If in a large town, say, the Republican party is dominant, the chief public enemies will be the industrial corporations, with their tremendous means and their watered securities; but if the Democratic party is uppermost, the worst enemies will be the liquor dealers, procurers, and gamblers. Correspondingly, in the former case, the honour of the city council which closes huge contracts with stock companies will succumb, while in the latter it will be the conscience of the policeman on the corner who pockets a little consideration when the bar-keeper wants to keep open beyond the legal hour. And since the temptation to take small bribes are ten thousand times more frequent than the chances for graft on a large scale, the total damage to public morals is about the same in both cases. But we must repeat once more that these delinquencies are after all the exception rather than the rule, and happily are for the most part expiated behind the bars of a penitentiary.

Most of all, it must be insisted that public opinion is all the time following up these excrescences on party life, and that public opinion presses forward year by year at an absolutely sure pace, and purifies the public atmosphere. All these evil conditions are easy to change. When Franklin came to England he was alarmed to see what fearful corruptions prevailed in English official life; such a thing was unknown at that time in America. Now England has long ago wiped out the blot, and America, which fell into its political mire a half-century later, will soon be out again and free; just as it has got rid of other nuisances. Every year brings some advance, and the student of American conditions should not let himself be deceived by appearances.

On the surface, for instance, the last mayoralty election in New York City would seem to indicate a downward tendency. New York two years previously had turned out the scandalous Tammany Hall gang with Van Wyck and his brutal extortionist, Chief of Police Devery, by a non-partisan alliance of all decent people in the city. New York had elected by a handsome majority Seth Low, the President of Columbia University, to be its mayor, and thereby had instated the principle that the best municipal government must use only business methods and be independent of political parties. Seth Low was supported by distinguished reformers in both parties, and was brilliantly successful in placing the entire city government on a distinctly higher level. The public schools, the general hygiene, the highways, and the police force were all thoroughly cleansed of impure elements and reformed without regard to party, on the purest and most business-like principle.

And then came the day for another election. Once more the independent voters, including the best men in both parties, the intellectual leaders and the socially dominant forces of the city, were banded together again to save their city of three million inhabitants from party politics, and to insure by their co-operation a continuance of the honest, business-like administration. They made Seth Low their candidate again; he was opposed by McClellan, the candidate of Tammany Hall, the party which loudly declares that "To the victors belong the spoils," and that the thousands of municipal offices are to be the prey of party adherents. This was the candidate of the party which admitted that all the hopes of the worst proletariat, of prostitution and vagabondage, depended on its success; the candidate of a party which declared that it would everywhere rekindle the "red light," that it would not enforce the unpopular temperance laws, and that it would leave the city "wide open." On the day of election 251,000 votes were cast for Mayor Low, but 313,000 for Colonel McClellan.

Now, does this really indicate that the majority of the city of New York consists of gamblers, extortioners, and criminals? One who read the Republican campaign literature issued before the election might suppose so. After reading on every street corner and fence and on giant banners the campaign cry, "Vote for Low and keep the grafters out," one might think that 300,000 pick-pockets had united to force out a clean administration and to place corruption on the throne. But on looking more closely at the situation one must see that no such thing was in question. Seth Low had furnished a clean administration, yet not a perfect one, and his mistakes had so seriously disaffected many citizens that they would rather endure the corruption of Tammany Hall than the brusqueness and various aggravations which threatened from his side.

Of these grievances, a typical one was the limitation of German instruction in the public schools. From the pedagogical point of view, this was not wholly wrong; and leading educationists, even German ones, had recommended the step. But at the same time the great German population was bitterly offended, and the whole discussions of the school board had angered the German citizens enough to cool off considerably their enthusiasm for reform. Then on top of this, Low's administration had rigorously enforced certain laws of Sunday observance which the German part of the population cordially hated. Here, too, Mayor Low was undoubtedly right; he was enforcing the law; but when two years previously he had wished to win over the German vote, he had promised more than he could fulfill. But, most of all, Seth Low was socially an aristocrat, who had no common feeling with the masses; and whenever he spoke in popular assemblies he displayed no magnetism. Every one felt too keenly that he looked down on them from his exalted social height.

Against him were the Tammany people, of whom at least one thing must be said: they know the people and their needs. They have grown up among the people. In contrast to many a Republican upstart who, according to the European fashion, is servile to his superiors and harsh with his inferiors, these Tammany men are harsh to their superiors — that is, they shake the nerves of the more refined — but are servile before the masses and comply with every wish. And most of all, they are really the friends of the populace, sincerely true and helpful to it. Moreover, just these great masses have more to suffer under a good administration than under the corrupt government which lets every one do as he likes. These people do not notice that the strict, hygienic administration reduced the death-rate and the list of casualties, and improved the public schools; but they notice when for such improvements they have to pay a cent more in taxation, or have to put safer staircases or fire-escapes on their houses, or to abandon tottering structures, or if they are not allowed to beg without a permit, or are forbidden to throw refuse in the streets. In short, these people notice a slight expense or an insignificant prohibition, and do not see that in the end they are greatly benefited. And so, when the day of reckoning comes, when the election campaigns are fought, in which distinguished reformers deliver scholarly addresses on the advantages of a non-partisan administration while the candidates of the people excite them with promises that they shall be free from all these oppressive burdens — it is no wonder that Seth Low is not returned to the City Hall, and that McClellan, who by the way is a highly educated and cultured politician, is entrusted with the city government.

Such an outcome is not a triumph for vice and dishonour. In two years the reformers will probably conquer again, since every administration makes its enemies and so excites opposition. But there can be no doubt that even on this occasion public opinion, with its desire to reform, has triumphed, although the official friends of reform were outdone; such a man as the former Chief of Police, Devery, will be impossible in the future. Public opinion sees to it that when the two parties stand in opposition the fight is fought each successive time on a higher level. And Tammany of to-day as compared with the Tammany of years gone by is the best evidence for the victory of public opinion and the reformers.

CHAPTER TEN

External Political Problems

THE attitude of America in international affairs can hardly be referred to any one special trait of mind. If one were to seek a simple formula, one would have to recognize in it a certain antithesis of mood; an opposition which one encounters in the American people under the most varied circumstances, and which perhaps depends on the fact that it is a people which has developed an entirely new culture, although on the basis of the high culture of the Old World. When we come to speak of American intellectual life we shall have again to consider this extraordinary combination of traits. The people are youthful and yet mature; they are fresher and more spontaneous than those of other mature nations, and wiser and more mature than those of other youthful nations; and thus it is that in the attitude of the Americans toward foreign affairs the love of peace and the delight in war combine to make a contrast which has rarely been seen. Doubtless there is an apparent contradiction here, but this contradiction is the historical mark of the national American temperament; and it is not to be supposed that the contradiction is solved by ascribing these diverse opinions to diverse elements in the population, by saying, for instance, that one group of citizens is more warlike, another more peaceable; that perhaps the love of hostile interference springs from the easily excited masses, while the love of peace is to be sought in their more thoughtful leaders, or that perhaps, on the other hand, the masses are peaceably industrious while their leaders draw them into war.

Such is not at all the case. There is not any such contrast between the masses and the classes; personal differences of opinion there are and some individuals are more volatile than others, but the craze for expansion in its newest form finds strong supporters and violent opponents in all parties and occupations. The most characteristic feature is, that just those who show the love for war most energetically are none the less concerned, and most earnestly so, for the advance of peace. President Roosevelt is the most striking example of the profound combination of these opposing tendencies in one human breast.

Every movement toward peace, in fact every international attempt toward doing away with the horrors of war, has found in the New World the most jealous and enthusiastic supporters; whenever two nations have come to blows the sympathies of the Americans have always been on the side of the weaker nation, no matter which seemed to be the side of justice. And the mere circumstance that two nations have gone to war puts the stronger power in a bad light in the eyes of America.

The nation has grown strong by peaceful industry; its greatest strength has lain in trade and the arts, its best population has come across the ocean in order to escape the military burdens of Europe; and the policy of the founders of the Republic, now become a tradition, was always to hold aloof from any dealings with the quarrelsome continent of Europe. During the short time of its existence, the United States has settled forty-nine international disputes in a peaceable court of arbitration, and oftentimes these have been in extemely important matters; and America has been a party in over half of the disputes which have been settled before a court of arbitration in recent times. America was an important participant in the founding of the Peace Tribunal at The Hague. When negotiations for that tribunal threatened to be frustrated by the opposing nations of Europe, the American government sent its representatives to the very centre of the opposition, and won a victory for the side of peace.

It is almost a matter of course that it is the munificent gift of an American which has erected a palace at The Hague for this international Peace Tribunal. While the European nations are groaning under the burden of their standing armies, and are weakened by wars over religious matters or the succession of dynasties, happy America knows nothing of this; her pride is the freedom of her citizens, her battles are fought out at the ballot-box. The disputes between sects and royal houses are unknown in the New World; its only neighbours are two oceans on the east and west, and on the north and south good friends. No end of progress remains to be made, but everything works together under the protection of the American Constitution to produce a splendid home in the New World for peace. America is the one world power which makes for peace; and it will only depend on the future growth of this nation, which has been ordained to become such an example, whether the idea of peace will finally prevail throughout the world over the immoral settlement of disputes by mere force of arms.

All this is not merely the programme of a party or of a group of people, but the confession of faith of every American. The American finds no problem here, since none would dispute the contention. It has all impressed itself so fully on the consciousness of the American people that it gives to the whole nation a feeling of moral superiority. Nor is this merely the pathos uttered in moral orations; it is the conviction with which every child grows up and with which every farmer goes to his plough, every artisan and merchant to his machine and desk, and the President to his executive chamber. And this conviction is so admirable that it has always been contagious, and all Europe has become quite accustomed to considering the Republic across the water a the firmest partisan of peace. The Republic has in fact been this, is now, and always will be so; while the riddle is — how it can be such a friend of peace when it was conceived in war, has settled its most serious problems by war, has gone to war again and again, has almost played with declarations of war, is at war today, and presumably will be at war many times again.

The Spanish war has shown clearly to European onlookers the other side of the shield, and many have at once concluded that the boasted American love of peace has been from the first a grand hypocrisy, that at least under McKinley's administration an entirely new spirit had suddenly seized the New World. But McKinley's predecessor, Cleveland, in the disputes arising between England and Venezuela, had waved the sabre until it hissed so loudly that it was not at all due to the American love of peace but rather to England's preoccupation in the Transvaal which prevented the President's message and the national love of interference from stirring up a war. And it is now several years since the successor of McKinley moved into the White House, yet

McKinley's war is still going on; for although a war has never been officially declared in the Philippines, war seems the only correct name for the condition which there prevails.

This Philippine question is a real political problem. That America is to serve the interests of peace is certain; every one is agreed on that; and the great majority of the people was also enthusiastically in favour of ending the Spanish misrule in Cuba. But the same is not true of the war in the Philippines, and becomes less true every day. The enthusiasts have subsided, the masses have become indifferent, while the politicians carry on the discussion; and since it is a question of motives which cannot be put aside for the present, and which at any time may so excite the nation as to become the centre of political discussion, it is well worth while to look more fully into these points.

The imperialists say that the events in the Pacific Ocean have followed exactly the traditions of the land; that expansion has always been a fundamental instinct of the nation; that its whole development shows that from the day when the Union was founded it commenced to increase its territory. The tremendous expansion gained by the purchase of Louisiana was followed by the annexation of Florida, and still later by that of the great tract called Texas. In the war with Mexico the region between Texas and California was acquired. Alaska was next gathered in. The narrow strip originally occupied by the Thirteen States became a huge country within a century, and thus the nation simply remains true to its traditions in stretching out over the ocean and carrying the Stars and Stripes toward Asia.

To this the anti-imperialists reply, on the contrary, that the United States is repudiating an honourable history and trampling down that which has been sacred for centuries. For if there has been any underlying principle at all to guide the United States in moments of perplexity, it has been a firm faith in the rights of people to govern themselves. The United States has never exchanged or acquired a foot of land without the consent of those who dwelt thereon. Where such lands have held nothing but the scattered dwellings of isolated colonists there existed no national consent to be consulted, and where there were no people no national self-government could come in question; neither Louisiana, California, nor Alaska was settled by a real nation, and Texas had of itself decided to become independent of Mexico. But the Philippines are inhabited by ten million people, with striking national traits and an organized will; and the United States, for the first time in history, now misuses its strength by oppressing another nation and forcing its own will on a prostrate people.

Now the imperialists reply they do not mean at all to dispute the right of self-government, a principle on which the greatness of our nation is founded. But it is a narrow and absurd conception of self-government which regards every people, however backward and unruly, capable thereof, and divinely privileged to misrule itself. The right of self-government must be deserved; it is the highest possession of civilized nations, and they have earned it by labour and self-discipline. The Americans derive their right to govern themselves from the toil of thirty generations. The Filipinos have still to be educated up to such a plane. To this the anti-imperialists enquire, Is that to be called education which subdues, like rebels, a people desirous of freedom? Are you helping those people by sending soldiers to assert your sovereignty?

And the imperialists reply again that we have sufficiently shown, in the case of Cuba, how seriously we take our moral obligations toward weaker peoples. When we had done away by force of arms with all Spanish domination in America, and had Cuba quite in our power, all Europe was convinced that we should never relax our hold, and that the war would result simply in a mere annexation of the rich island; in short, that we should pursue a typical European policy. But we have shown the world that America does not send her sons to battle merely for aggrandizement, but only in a moral cause; just as we demanded of the conquered Spaniards no indemnity, so we have made a general sacrifice for Cuba. We have laboured tirelessly for the hygiene and the education of the island, have strengthened its trade and awakened to new life the country which had been desolated by Spanish misrule, and, having finished the work, we have restored to Cuba her freedom and her right of self-government; and we recognize that we owe a similar duty to the Philippines. We have not sought to obtain those islands. At the outset of the war no American foresaw that the island kingdom in the tropics, ten thousand miles away, would fall into our hands; but when the chain of events brought it about, we could not escape the call of duty. Were we to leave the discontented Philippine population once more to the cruelty of their Spanish masters, or were we to displace the Spaniards and then leave the wild race of the islands to their own anarchy, and thus invoke such internal hostilities as would again wipe out all the beginnings which had been made toward culture? Was it not rather our duty to protect those who turned to us, against the vengeance of their enemies, and before all else to establish order and quietude? The anti-imperialists retort — the quietude of a grave-yard. If America's policy had been truly unselfish, it should have made every preparation for dealing with the Philippines as it had dealt with Cuba; instead of fighting with the Filipinos we should at once have co-operated with Aguinaldo and sent over a civil instead of a military regiment. Nor is the world deceived into supposing that our boasted civil rule in the Philippines is anything more than a name, used in order somewhat to pacify the sentimentalists of the New England States; while in reality our rule is a military one, and the small success of a few well-meaning civil officials merely distracts the world's attention from the constant outbreaks of war. We have not worked from the point of view of the Philippines, but from that of the United States.

The imperialists answer that it is no disgrace to have been patriotic to our Fatherland; the national honour requires us, indeed, to remain for the present in the Philippines, and not to take down the flag which we have hoisted so triumphantly. We should not flee before a few disaffected races living in those islands. Then the other side replies, you have not protected the honour of your nation, but you have worked its disgrace. The honour of America has been the moral status of its army; it was America's boast that its army had never lost the respect of an enemy, and that it had held strictly aloof from every unnecessary cruelty. But America has learned a different lesson in the Philippines, and such a one as all thoughtful persons have foreseen; for when a nation accustomed to a temperate climate goes to the tropics to war with wild races which have grown up in cruelty and the love of revenge, it necessarily forgets its moral standards, and gives free rein to the lowest and worst that is in it. The American forces have learned there, to their disgrace, to conquer by deception and trickery; to be cruel and revengeful, and so return torture for torture.

Then the imperialists say that this is not a question of the army which was landed in the tropical islands, but of the whole American people, which undertook new duties and responsibilities for the islands, and wished to try, not only its military, but also its political, economic, and social powers along new lines. A people also must grow and have its higher aspirations. The youthful period of the American nation is over; manhood has arrived, when new and dangerous responsibilities have to be assumed. To this the anti-imperialists reply, that a nation is surely not growing morally when it gives up the principles which have always been its sole moral strength. If it gives up believing in the freedom of every nation and carries on a war of subjugation, it has renounced all moral development, and instead of growing it begins internally to decay. But this, the imperialists say, is absurd — since, outwardly, at least, we are steadily growing; our reputation before other nations is increasing with our military development; we have become a powerful factor in the powers of the world, and our Philippine policy shows that our navy can conquer even in remote parts of the earth, and that in the future America will be a power to reckon with everywhere. But, on the contrary, say the others, our nation held a strong position so long as, in accordance with the Monroe Doctrine, it was able to keep any European power from getting a foothold on the American continents, and so long as we made the right of self-government a fundamental principle of our international politics. But the instant we adopted a policy of conquest and assumed the right to subjugate inferior peoples because our armies were the stronger, the Monroe Doctrine became at once and for the first time an empty phrase, if not a piece of arrogance. We are no better than the next nation; we have no right to prevent others from acting like ourselves, and we have sacrificed our strong position, and shall be led from war to war, and the fortunes of war are always uncertain.

The imperialists reply somewhat more temperately: — Ah, but the new islands will contribute very much to our trade. Their possession means the beginning of a commercial policy which will put the whole Pacific Ocean at the disposal of the American merchant. Who can foresee what tremendous developments may come from availing ourselves of regions lying so advantageously? When Congress in 1803 started to buy the great Province of Louisiana from France, there were also narrow-minded protests. At that time, too, anti-imperialists and fanatics became excited, and said that it was money thrown away; the land would never be populated. While to-day, a hundred years later, the world prepares to celebrate the anniversary of the purchase of Louisiana by a magnificent exposition at St. Louis — a transaction which has meant for the country a tremendous gain in wealth and culture. America is destined to be the mistress of the Pacific Ocean, and as soon as the canal is built across the isthmus the economic importance of the Philippines will appear more clearly every day. The anti-imperialists deny this. The financial statement of the entire war with Spain to the present moment shows that $600,000,000 have been wasted and ten thousand young men sacrificed without any advantage being so much as in sight. Whereto the imperialists reply: — There are other advantages. War is a training. The best thing which the nation can win is not riches, but strength; and in the very prosperity of America the weakening effect of luxury is greatly to be feared. The nerves of the nation are steeled in the school of war, and its muscles hardened. But the other side says that our civilization requires thousands of heroic deeds of the most diverse kinds, more than it needs those of the field of battle; and that the American doctrine of peace is much better adapted to strengthen the moral courage of the nation and to stimulate it than the modern training of war, which, in the end, is only a question of expenditure and science. What we chiefly need is serious and moral republican virtue. The incitements toward acquisition and the spirit of war, on the other hand, destroy the spirit of our democracy, and breed un-American, autocratic ambitions. War strengthens the blind faith of the leaders in their own dictatorial superiority, and so annihilates the feeling of independence and responsibility in the individual; and this is just the way for the nation to lose its moral and political integrity. The true patriotism which our youth ought to learn is not found in noisy jingoism, but in the silent fidelity to the Declaration of Independence of our fathers.

Thus the opinions are waged against one another, and so they will continue to be. We must emphasize merely again and again that that majority which to-day is on the side of the imperialists believes at the same time enthusiastically in the international movement for peace, and quite disinterestedly favours, as far as possible, the idea of the peace tribunal. Most of all, the treatment of Cuba certifies to the honourable and peaceful tendencies of the dominant party. That which was done under Wood's administration for the hygiene of a country which had always been stricken with yellow fever, for the school and judicial systems of that unfortunate people, is remarkable; and the readiness with which the new republic was afterward recognized, and with which, finally, by special treaties extensive tariff reductions were made to a people really dependent on trade with America, makes one of the most honourable pages in American history. And all this happened through the initiative of these same men whose Philippine policy has been styled in the Senate Napoleonic. Thus the fact remains that there is an almost inexplicable mixture in the American nature of justice and covetiveness, conscience and indifference, love of peace and love of war.

The latest phase in expansion has been toward the south. America has assumed control of Panama. Constitutionally, the case is somewhat different here. Panama belonged to the Republic of Colombia, and when the government of Colombia, which conducts itself for the most part like the king and his advisers in a comic opera, tried to extort more money than was thought just from Washington before it would sign the treaty giving the United States a right to build a canal through Panama, and at first pretended to decline the treaty altogether, a revolution broke out in the part of the country which was chiefly affected. Panama declared itself an independent state, and the United States recognized its claim to independence, and concluded the canal treaty, not with Colombia, but with the upstart government of Panama. This was really part and parcel of the general imperialistic movement. We need not ask whether the American government encouraged Panama to secede; it certainly did nothing of the sort officially, although it is perfectly certain that the handful of people in Panama would not have had the slightest chance of escaping unpunished by Colombia if it had not been for American protection; indeed, it seemed to feel sure beforehand that the United States would keep Colombia at bay. And in fact, the baby republic was recognized with all the speed of telegraph and cable, and the treaty was signed before Panama had become quite aware of its own independence; while at the same time Colombia's endeavour to bring the rebellious district into line was suppressed with all the authority of her mighty neighbour.

It is not to be denied that this transaction called into play new principles of international politics; nor can it be excused on the ground that new governments have been quickly recognized before. Never before had the United States declared a rebellion successful so long as the old government still stood, and the new one was able to hold out only by virtue of the interference of the United States itself. It is to be admitted that this was an imperialistic innovation, as was the subjugation of the Filipinos. But we should not be so narrow as to condemn a principle because it is new. All past history makes the expansion of American influence necessary; the same forces which make a state great continue to work through its later history. America must keep on in its extension, and if the methods by which the present nations grow are necessarily different from those by which the little Union was able to stretch out into uninhabited regions a hundred years ago, then, of course, the expansion of the twentieth century must take on other forms than it had in the nineteenth. But expansion itself cannot stop, nor can it be altered by mere citations from the Declaration of Independence, or pointings to the petty traditions of provincial days. The fight which the anti-imperialists are waging is thoroughly justified in so far as it is a fight against certain outgrowths of such expansion which have appeared in the Philippines, and most of all when it is against the loss to the Republic, through expansion, of its moral principles and of its finer and deeper feelings through the intoxication of power. But the fight is hopeless if it is waged against expansion itself. The course of the United States is marked out.

* * * * * * * * * * *

It requires no special gift of prophecy to point out that the next expansion will be toward the north. Just as the relations in Panama were fairly obvious a half year before the catastrophe came, the suspicion cannot be now put by that at a time not far hence the Stars and Stripes will wave in the northwestern part of Canada, and that there too the United States will be unwilling to lower its flag.

A newspaper is published in Boston which announces every day, at the top of the page, in bold type, that it is the first duty of the United States to annex Canada. On the other hand, one hears the opinion that nothing could be worse for the United States than to receive this immense, thinly populated territory even as a gift. There are the same differences of opinion on the other side of the boundary; some say that the Canadians are glad to be free from the problems which face the United States, from its municipal politics, its boss rule in political parties, and from the negro and Philippine questions, and that Canadian fidelity to the English Crown is not to be doubted for a moment. While others admit quite openly that to be annexed to the United States is the only natural thing that can happen to Canada. The immediate future will probably see some sort of compromise. It is wholly unlikely that the eastern part of Canada, in view of all its traditions, will prove untrue to its mother country; whereas the western part of Canada is under somewhat different economic conditions; it has so different a history, and is to-day so much more closely related to the United States than to England that the political separation will hardly continue very long. The thousands who have gone from the United States across the Canadian frontier in order to settle the unpeopled Northwest will, in the not distant future, give rise to some occasion in which economic and political logic will decree a transfer of the allegiance of Western Canada, with the exception of a narrow strip of land along the Pacific Coast. The area of the United States would then include a new region of about 250 million acres of wheat lands, of which to-day hardly two millions are in cultivation.

The Canadian problem, of course, arose neither to-day nor yesterday. The first permanent colony in Canada was a French colony, begun in the year 1604. Frenchmen founded Quebec in the year 1608, and French settlements developed along the St.

Lawrence River. In the year 1759 General Wolfe conquered Quebec for the English, and in the following year the whole of Canada fell into their power. English and Scotch immigrants settled more and more numerously in Upper Canada. The country was divided in 1791 in two provinces, which were later called Ontario and Quebec; and in 1867, by an act of the British Parliament, Ontario, Quebec, New Brunswick, and Nova Scotia were made into one country. A short time thereafter the government of the new country bought the possessions of the Hudson Bay Company, and soon afterward the large western region called Manitoba was organized as a distinct province. In 1871 British Columbia was taken in, and in the eighties this extensive western land was divided into four provinces. During this time there were all sorts of interruptions, wars with the Indians, and disputes over boundaries; but there has never been open warfare between Canada and the United States. The many controversies that have arisen have been settled by treaty, and a court of arbitration met even recently in London to settle a dispute about boundaries which for many years had occasioned much feeling. It was a question whether the boundary of the Northwest should lie so as to leave to Canada a way to the coast without crossing United States territory. The boundaries were defined by the treaties as lying a certain distance from the coast; was this coast meant to be mainland, or was it coastline marked out by the off-lying groups of islands? This was a question of great economic importance for a part of Canada. The court decided in favour of the United States, but the decision does not belong on one of the most honourable pages of American history. It had been agreed that both England and the United States should appoint distinguished jurists to the court of arbitration; and this the English did, while the United States sent prejudiced politicians. This has created some embitterment in Canada, and the mood is not to-day entirely friendly, although this will doubtless give way in view of the great economic development which works toward union with the United States.

Such a union would be hindered very much more by the friendly relations existing between the United States and England. At the time when the family quarrel between mother and daughter countries had made an open breach, it seemed almost certain that America would take the first good opportunity of robbing England of her Canadian possessions. Even before the early colonies decided on revolution, they tried to draw the northern provinces into their train. And when the new Union was formed, it seemed a most natural thing for all English speaking inhabitants of the American Continent to participate therein. It was no friendliness toward England that diverted the expansion of the young country toward the south rather than toward the north. It was rather the influence of the Southern States of the Federation which encouraged the expansion toward the south, because in that way their adjacent territory was increased, and therewith the number of the slave states represented in Congress; and the institution of slavery was thereby better protected from Northern interference. England was the hereditary foe of the country for an entire century, and every school boy learned from his history book to hate England and to desire revenge. But this has been wholly changed in recent years by the sympathy which John Bull showed during the Spanish war, and by his far-seeing magnanimity shown on a hundred occasions. There are already preparations making for a special court of arbitration to sit on all Anglo-American disputes, and the mood of the American people is certainly inclined to avoid everything that would unnecessarily offend England. American politicians would thus hesitate very long before attempting so bold a step as the annexation of Canada; and thus it is that the Canadian problem gets into the programme of neither party. Another consideration which perhaps makes a difference is that no party is quite sure which side would be the gainer; whether among the millions of people in the Canadian West there would be found to be more Republicans or Democrats. Therefore, Canada is not now an issue between the parties. Nevertheless, the problem grows more and more important in public opinion, and however much Congress may be concerned to avoid a war with England, and determined never deliberately to bring about any disloyalty in Canada, we may be certain that once the American farmers and gold miners in Northwestern Canada have set the pro-American ball rolling, then the general mood will speedily change and the friendly resolutions toward England which will be proposed by Senators will sound very feeble.

The most natural desire, which seems to be wide-spread, is for reciprocity with Canada. Both countries are aware that they are each other's best purchasers, and yet they put difficulties in the way of importing each other's products. American industry has already invested more than $100,000,000 for branch factories in Canada, in order to avoid duties; and the industry of New England would doubtless be much benefited if Canadian coal might be delivered duty-free along the Atlantic coast; nevertheless, the chief disadvantages in the present arrangements fall to Canada. A treaty was concluded in 1854 which guaranteed free entrance to the markets of the United States for all Canadian natural products, and during the twelve years in which the treaty was in force, Canadian exports increased fourfold. Then the American protective tariff was restored; and while, for example, the agricultural products which Canada sold to the United States in 1866 amounted to more than $25,000,000, they had decreased by the beginning of the twentieth century to $7,367,000; and all Canadian exports to the United States, with the exception of coin and precious metals, in spite of the tremendous growth of both countries, had increased at the same time only 5 per cent. Canada, on the other hand, contented herself with modest duties, so that the commerce of the United States with Canada has increased from $28,000,000 in the year 1866 to $117,000,000 in the year 1900. The necessary result of this policy of exclusion on the part of the United States has necessarily been closer economic relations between Canada and England. The Canadian exports to Great Britain have increased steadily, and the bold plans of those who are to-day agitating a tariff union for all Great Britian would, of course, specially benefit Canadian commerce.

But the United States knows this, and does not fail to think on the future. The agitation for new commercial treaties with Canada does not spring from the supporters of free-trade, but from some most conservative protectionists, and may be ascribed even to McKinley and Dingley; and this agitation is steadily growing. On the other hand, Canada is by no means unanimously enthusiastic for the universal British reciprocity alliance. The industrial sections of Eastern Canada see things with different eyes from the agrarians of Western Canada, and opinions are just as diverse as they are in England. The economic needs of the

East and West are so fundamentally different, and since the West so greatly needs reciprocity, it is coming more and more to look for a solution of this problem by seeking, through a union of the West with the United States, all that which England cannot offer. The government of Canada, which comprises remarkably effective and intelligent men, is aiming to nip the incipient disaffection of the West in the bud, by means of its railroad policy. Railroad lines connect to-day the western portion of Canada much more closely with the eastern portion than with the northern parts of the United States.

The economic possibilities of Western Canada are enormous, and would suffice for a population of a hundred million. The supply of lumber exceeds that of the United States. Its gold regions are more extensive, its coal and iron supplies are inexhaustible, its nickel mines the richest in the world; it has twice the supply of fish of the United States, and its arable lands could feed the population of the United States and Europe together. Everything depends on making the most of these possibilities, and the Canadian of the West looks with natural envy on the huge progress which the entirely similar regions of the United States are making, and is moved to reflect how different things would be with him if only the boundary lines could be altered.

More than anything else, however, the Westerner feels that a spirit of enterprise, industrial energy, and independent force is needed to exploit these enormous natural resources, such as the inhabitants of a dependent colony can never have. Even when a colony like Canada possesses a certain independence in the administration of its own affairs, it is still only the appearance and not the fact of self-government. One sees clearly how colourless and dull the intellectual life of Canada is, and how in comparison with the very different life of England on the one hand, and of the United States on the other, the colonial spirit saps and undermines the spirit of initiative. The people do not suffer under such a rule; they do not feel the political lack of fresh air, but they take on a subdued and listless way of life, trying to adapt themselves to an alien political scheme, and not having the courage to speak out boldly. This depression is evinced in all their doings; and this is not the spirit which will develop the resources of Western Canada. But this infinite, new country attracts to its pioneer labours fresh energies which are found south of the Canadian line and across the ocean. The Scotch, Germans, Swedes, and especially Americans emigrate thither in great numbers. The farmers in the western United States are to-day very glad to sell their small holdings, in order to purchase broad tracts of new, fresh ground in Canada, where there is still no lack of room. They will be the leaders in this new development of the West. And while they bring with them their love of work and enterprise, they are of course without sympathy with Canadian traditions; nor do they feel any patriotism toward the country: their firmest convictions point toward such political freedom as the United States offers. Whether the tariff schemes of England will be able to win back some advantages for Canada, only the future can say. It is more likely that inasmuch as the Philippine agitation has extended the influence of the United States into the tropics, the climatic equilibrium will be restored by another extension into the Canadian Northwest.

* * * * * * * * * * *

The relations of the United States to Cuba and to the Philippines, to Panama and to Canada, have been regulated by the immediate needs of the country without bringing into special prominence any general principles. Economic interest and general ethics have so far sufficed, and only here and there has mention been made of the fundamental doctrines contained in the Declaration of Independence. The case of South America is quite different; the policy of the United States toward South America is dictated to-day neither by economic interests nor moral principles; in fact, it is a mockery of morals and a great prejudice to American industry. The sole source of this policy is an abstract political doctrine, which a long time ago was both economically and morally necessary, but is to-day entirely without value; this is the Monroe Doctrine. The observance of this famous doctrine is one of the most interesting instances of the survival of an outlived political principle, and the blind way in which this prejudice is still favoured by the masses, so that even the leading politicians would not dare, at the present time, to defend the real interests of the country by opposing this doctrine, shows clearly how democracy favours rule of thumb, and how the American people is in its thought conservative to the last degree. The Monroe Doctrine has done the United States good service, and redounded to both its profit and its honour. And so no one ventures to disturb it, although it has long ceased to bring anything except disadvantage. Some of the best people know this; but where the people rule it is as true as where a monarch rules, that the misfortune of rulers is not to wish to hear the truth.

The blind folly of the Americans in holding tenaciously to the antiquated Monroe Doctrine is surpassed only by the madness of those Europeans who wish to take up arms against that doctrine. All the declarations of the Old World to the effect that the Monroe Doctrine is an unheard of piece of arrogance, and that the Americans have no right to assert themselves in such a way, and that it is high time forcibly to call their right in question, are historically short-sighted as well as dangerous. They are unhistorical, because there really was a time when this doctrine was necessary to the existence of the United States, and when, therefore, the country had a right to assert such doctrine; and now that it has been silently respected for a hundred years, any protest against it comes too late. Opposition to the doctrine from the side of Europe would be foolish, because no European country has any really vital reason for calling it in question, and there would be a very lively war indeed if Europe were to try to overstep the Monroe Doctrine as long as the great mass of the American people still hold it sacred. The Monroe Doctrine must and will succumb, but it will only be through the convictions of the Americans, never because some European nation threatens to batter down the wall. The logic of events is, after all, stronger than the mere inertia of inherited doctrines. The hour seems near when the error and folly of the Monroe Doctrine are about to be felt in wider circles than ever before. The opposite side is already ably supported in addresses and essays. Soon the opposition will reach the newspapers, which are to-day, of course, still unanimous on the popular side; and whenever a wholesome movement commences among the American people it generally spreads with irresistible speed. We have seen how rapidly the imperialistic idea took hold on the masses, and the repudiation of the theory of Monroe will follow quite as rapidly; since the nation cannot, for the sake of a mere whim, permanently forget its best interests. It is only a question of overcoming the inertia of long custom.

The spirit of the Monroe Doctrine was abroad long before the time of Monroe. It was agreed, from the earliest days of the federal government, that the new nation should keep itself clear of all political entanglement with Europe, that it would not mix in with the destinies of European peoples, and that it would expect of those peoples that they should not spread the boundaries of their possessions over to the American continents. When President Washington, in 1796, took his farewell of the nation, he recommended an extension of commercial relations with Europe, but entire aloofness from their political affairs. "The nations of Europe," he said, "have important problems which do not concern us as a free people. The causes of their frequent mis understandings lie far outside of our province, and the circumstance that America is geographically remote will facilitate our political isolation, and the nations who go to war will hardly challenge our young nation, since it is clear that they will have nothing to gain by it."

This feeling, that America was to have nothing to do with European politics, and that the European nations should on no condition be allowed to extend their sphere of action on to the American continents, grew steadily. This national conviction rested primarily on two motives: firstly, America wanted to be sure of its national identity. It felt instinctively that, if it were to become involved in European conflicts, the European powers might interfere in the destinies of the smaller and growing nation, and that the danger of such interference would increase tremendously if the great nations of Europe were to gain a foothold in the neighbourhood of the young republic on this side of the ocean. In the second place, this nation felt that it had a moral mission to perform. The countries of Europe were groaning under oppression, whereas this nation had thrown off the English yoke, and proposed to keep the new continent free from such misrule. In order to make it the theatre for an experiment of modern democracy, no absolute monarchs were to set foot in this new world; the self-government of the people was to remain unquestioned, and every republic was to be free to work out its own salvation.

Thus the desire for self-protection and a moral interest in the fight against absolutism have prescribed a course of holding aloof from European affairs, and of demanding that Europe should not reach out toward the American continents. This has become a cardinal principle in American politics. The opportunity soon came to express this principle very visibly in international politics. The Holy Alliance between Austria, Russia, and Prussia was believed by America, ever since 1822, to have been arranged in order to regain for Spain the Spanish colonies in South America. England wished to ally itself with the United States; but they, with excellent tact, steered their course alone. In 1822 the United States recognized the independence of the Central American republics; and in 1823, President Monroe, in his message to Congress, which was probably penned by John Quincy Adams, who was then Secretary of State, set down this policy in black and white. Monroe had previously asked ex-President Jefferson for his opinion, and Jefferson had written that our first and fundamental maxim should be, never to involve ourselves in European disputes; and our second, never to permit Europe to meddle in cis-Atlantic affairs, North and South America having their own interests, which are fundamentally different from those of Europe. Now the message of President Monroe contained the following declarations: "That we should consider any attempt on their part [of the allied powers] to extend their system to any portion of this hemisphere as dangerous to our peace and safety," and "that we could not view any interposition for the purpose of oppressing [governments on this side of the water whose independence we had acknowledged], or controlling in any manner their destiny by any European power, in any other light than as a manifestation of an unfriendly disposition toward the United States."

Thus the famous Monroe Doctrine was announced to the world, and became an international factor sufficiently potent even to prevent Napoleon from realizing his plans regarding Mexico, and in more recent times to protect Venezuela from the consequences of her misdeeds. And although, at just that time of the Venezuelan dispute, the old Monroe Doctrine was in so far modified that the Presidential message conceded to European powers their right to press their claims by force of arms, so long as they claimed no permanent right of occupation, nevertheless the discussions ended with the extreme demand that foreign powers should be content with the promise of a South American state to pay its debts, and should receive no security; nor did the United States give security for the payment, either. After eighty years the doctrine is still asserted as it has been from the first, although the situation is in all respects very different. A few brief instances of these changes must suffice us.

In the first place, the two fundamental motives which gave rise to the doctrine, and in which all important documents are so clearly enunciated from the time of Washington to that of Monroe, have long since ceased to exist. The contrast between Europe as the land of tyranny and America as a democratic free soil, no longer holds; nor can the notion be bolstered up any longer, even for political ends. In the first place all countries of Western Europe now enjoy popular representation, while the Latin republics of South America, with the exception of Chili and the Argentine Republic, are the most absurd travesties of freedom and democracy. Conditions in Venezuela and Colombia are now pretty well known. It has been shown, for instance, that about one-tenth of the population consists of highly cultivated Spaniards, who take no part in politics, and suffer under a shameless administrative misrule; that some eight-tenths more are a harmless and ignorant proletariat of partly Spanish and partly Indian descent — people who likewise have no political interest, and who are afraid of the men in power — while the remaining tenth, which is of mixed Spanish, Indian, and negro blood, holds in its hands the so-called republican government, and keeps itself in power with every device of extortion and deception, and from time to time splits up into parties which throw the whole country into an uproar, merely for the personal advantages of the party leaders.

Even in America there is no longer a political back-woodsman who supposes that a republic like what the founders of the United States had in mind, can ever be made out of such material; and when, in spite of this, as in the negro question, some one gets up at the decisive moment of every discussion and tries to conjure with the Declaration of Independence, even such an appeal now often misses its effect. Since the Americans have gone into the Philippines they can no longer hold it an axiom that every government must be justified by the assent of the governed. People have learned to understand that the right of self-government must be earned, and is deserved only as the reward of hard work; that nations which have not yet grown to be orderly and peaceable need education like children who are not yet of age and do not know what is good for them. To say that the pitiable citizen of a corrupt South American republic is freer than the citizen of England, France, or Germany would be ridiculous; to protect the anarchy of these countries against the introduction of some European political system is at the present time not a moral obligation, surely, which the American Republic need feel itself called on to perform. The democratic idea, as realized in American life, has become much more influential on the governments of Europe than on those of South America, notwithstanding their lofty constitutions, which are filled with the most high-flown moral and philosophical utterances, but are obeyed by no one.

Now the other motive which supported the Monroe Doctrine, namely, the security of the United States and of their peaceful isolation, has to-day not the slightest validity; on the contrary, it is the superstitious faith in this doctrine which might conceivably endanger the peace of the country. Of course, this is only in so far as the doctrine applies to South America, not to Central America. It would indeed be impossible for the United States to allow, say Cuba, in passing from Spanish hands, to come into possession of another European nation; in fact, no part of Central America could become the seat of new European colonies without soon becoming a seat of war. The construction of the canal across the isthmus confirms and insures the moral and political leadership of the United States in Central America and the Antilles. But the situation is quite different in South America. The Americans are too apt to forget that Europe is much nearer to the United States than, for instance, the Argentine Republic, and that if one wants to go from New York to the Argentine Republic, the quickest way to go is by way of Europe. And the United States have really very little industrial intercourse or sympathy with the Latin republics. A European power adjoins the United States from the Atlantic to the Pacific Ocean; and the fact that England, at one time their greatest enemy, abuts along this whole border has never threatened the peace of the United States; but it is supposed to be an instant calamity if Italy or England or Holland gets hold of a piece of land far away in South America, in payment of debts or to ensure the safety of misused colonists.

So long as the United States were small and weak, this exaggerated fear of unknown developments was intelligible; but now that the country is large and strong, and the supposed contrast between the Old and New Worlds no longer exists, since the United States are much more nearly like the countries of Europe than like the South American republics, any argument for the Monroe Doctrine on the ground of misgivings or fear comes to be downright hysterical. In the present age of ocean cables, geographical distances disappear. The American deals with the Philippines as if they were before his door, although they are much farther from Washington than any South American country is from Europe. Occasions for dispute with European countries may, on the other hand, come up at any time without the slightest reference to South America, since the United States have now become an international power; it requires merely an objectionable refusal to admit imports, some diplomatic mishap, or some unfairness in a matter of tariff.

If, on the other hand, the European countries were to have colonies in South America, as they have in Africa, no more occasions for complaint or dissatisfaction would accrue to the United States than from the similar colonies in Africa. No Russian or French or Italian colony in South America would ever in the world give rise to a difficulty with the United States through any real opposition of interests, and could only do so because a doctrine forbidding such colonies, which had been adopted under quite different circumstances, was still bolstered up and defended. If the Monroe Doctrine were to-day to be applied no farther than Central America, and South America were to be exempted, the possibilities of a conflict with European powers would be considerably decreased. That which was meant originally to guarantee peace, has, under the now wholly altered conditions, become the greatest menace of war.

But the main point is not that the motives which first led to the Monroe Doctrine are to-day invalid; the highest interests of the United States demand that this moribund doctrine be definitely given up. In the first place, it was never doubted that the exclusion of the Old World countries from the new American continents was only the conclusion of a premise, to the effect that the Americans themselves proposed to confine their political interests to their own continent. That was a wise policy in the times of Washington and Monroe; and whether or not it would have been wise in the time of McKinley, it was in any case at that time thrown over. The Americans have united with the European forces to do battle in China; they have extended their own dominion toward Asia; they have sent men-of-war to Europe on political missions; in short, the Americans have for years been extending their political influence around the world, and Secretary Hay has for a long time played an influential part in the European concert of powers. The United States have too often defended their Monroe claim on the ground of their own aloofness from these powers to feel justified in urging the claim when they no longer do keep aloof.

There is another and more important consideration. The real interest of the United States with regard to South America is solely that that land shall develop as far as possible, that its enormous treasures shall be exploited, and that out of a prosperous commercial continent important trade advantages shall accrue to the United States. This is possible only by the establishment of order there — the instant termination of anarchy. As long as the Monroe Doctrine is so unnecessarily held to, the miserable and impolitic stagnation of that ravaged country can never be bettered, since all the consequences of that doctrine work just in the opposite direction. It is sufficiently clear that progress will not be made until fresh, healthy, enterprising forces come in from outside; but now so soon as an Englishman or German or other European undertakes to earn his livelihood there, he is at once exposed to the shameless extortion and other chicanery of the so-called governments. And when European capital wishes to help the development of these countries, it is given absolutely no protection against their wretched politics. And all this is merely because the chartered rascals in power know that they can kill and steal with impunity, so long as the sacred Monroe Doctrine is there, like an enchanted wall, between them and the mother countries of their victims; they know only too well that no evil can come to them, since the statesmen at Washington are bound down to a prejudice, and required scrupulously to protect every hair on their precious heads. All this prevents any infusion of good blood from coming into these countries, and so abandons the land entirely to the indolence of its inhabitants. The conditions would be economically sounder, in almost every part of South America, if more immigrants came in, and more especially if those that came could take a larger part in the governments.

It would be somewhat different if the United States were to admit, as a consequence of the Monroe Doctrine, its own responsibility for the public administration of these countries, for their debts and for whatever crimes they commit; in other words, if the United States were virtually to annex South America. There is no thought of this; the United States have recently, in the Venezuela matter, clearly declined all responsibility. If, while declining the responsibility, the United States persist in affirming the Monroe Doctrine, they are to be charged inevitably with helping on anarchy, artificially holding back the progress of one of the richest and least developed portions of the earth, and thereby hurting their own commercial outlook more than any European protective tariff could possibly do. The greater part Europe takes in South America, so much the more will trade and commerce prosper; and in this pioneer labour, as history has shown, the patient German is the best advance-agent. Almost all the commercial relations between the United States and the South American republics are meditated by European, and especially German, business houses. The trade of the United States with South America is to-day astonishingly small, but when finally the Monroe barrier falls away it will develop enormously.

In all this America has not, from its previous policy, derived even the modest advantage of endearing itself to the inhabitants of these South American republics. Quite on the contrary, the Monroe Doctrine sounds like the ring of a sword in the South American ear. The American of the south is too vividly reminded that, although the province of the United States is after all only a finite portion of the New World, the nation has, nevertheless, set itself up as the master of both continents; and the natural consequence is, that all the small and weak countries join forces against the one great country and brood continually over their mistrust. The attempts of the United States to win the sympathies of the rest of America have brought no very great results — since, in the States, sympathy has been tempered with contempt, and in South America with fear. In short, the unprejudiced American must come back every time to the *ceterum censeo* that the Monroe Doctrine must finally be given up.

One point, however, must always be emphasized — that all the motives speaking against the doctrine will be efficient only so far as they appeal to the soul of the American people, and overthrow there the economically suicidal Monroe Doctrine. On the other hand, Europe would gain nothing by trying to tear in pieces the sacred parchment; no possible European interest in South America would compare in importance with the loss of friendship of the United States. And so long as the overwhelming majority of Americans holds to its delusions, the hostility would be a very bitter one. Indeed, there would be no surer way of stopping the gradual abandonment of the doctrine than for Europe to attempt to dispute its validity.

The process of dissolution must take place in America; but the natural interest and needs of the country so demand this development that it may be confidently expected. A new time has come: the provinciality of the Monroe Doctrine no longer does for America as a world power, and events follow their logical development; the time will not be long before the land of the Stars and Stripes will have extended across Western Canada to Alaska, and have annexed the whole of Central America; while the Latin republics of South America, on the other hand, will have been sprinkled in with English, Italian, French, and German colonies; and most of all, those republics themselves, by the lapse of the Monroe Doctrine, will have been won over to law and order, progress and economic health. The United States are too sound and too idealistic to continue to oppose the demands of progress for the sake of a mere fetish.

Thus the dominion of this world power will grow. The influence of the Army, and even more of the Navy, will help in this growth; even if the dreams of Captain Hobson are not realized. To be sure, the dangers will also grow apace; with a great navy comes the desire to use it. Nevertheless, one must not overlook the fact that international politics are much less a subject of public thought and discussion in America than in Europe. For the American thinks firstly of internal politics, and secondly of internal politics, and lastly of internal politics; and only at some distant day does he plan to meditate on foreign affairs. Unless the focus of public attention is distinctly transferred, the idea of expansion will meet with sufficient resistance to check its undue growth.

There is specially a thoroughgoing distrust of militarism, and an instinctive fear that it works against democracy and favours despotism; and there is, indeed, no doubt that the increasingly important relations between this country and foreign powers put more authority into the hands of the Presidential and Senatorial oligarchy than the general public likes to see. Every slightest concealment on the part of the President or his Cabinet goes against the feelings of the nation, and this state of feeling will hardly alter; it comes from the depths of the American character. On the other hand, it is combined with a positive belief in the moral mission of the United States, which are destined to gain their world-wide influence, not by might, but by the force of exemplary attainment, of complete freedom, admirable organization, and hard work. Any one who observes the profound sources of this belief will be convinced that any different feelings in the public soul, any greed of power, and any imperialistic instincts, are only a passing intoxication. In its profoundest being, America is a power for peace and for ethical ideals.

PART TWO

ECONOMIC LIFE

CHAPTER ELEVEN

The Spirit of Self-Initiative

"THE spirit aids! from anxious scruples freed, I write, 'In the beginning was the deed!'" Others might write: In the beginning was the inexhaustible wealth of the soil; and still others, if their memory is short, might be tempted to say: In the beginning were the trusts! One who wishes to understand the almost fabulous economic development of the United States must, indeed, not simply consider its ore deposits and gold mines, its coal and oil fields, its wheat lands and cotton districts, its great forests and the supplies of water. The South Americans live no less in a country prospered by nature, and so also do the Chinese. South Africa offers entirely similar conditions to those of the North American continent, and yet its development has been a very different one; and, finally, a consideration of the peculiar forms of American industrial organization, as, for instance, the trusts, reveals merely symptoms and not the real causes which have been at work.

The colossal industrial successes, along with the great evils and dangers which have come with them, must be understood from the make-up of the American character. Just as we have traced the political life of America back to a powerful instinct for self-determination, the free self-guidance of the individual, so we shall here find that it is the instinct for free self-initiative which has set in motion this tremendous economic fly-wheel. The pressure to be up and doing has opened the earth, tilled the fields, created industries, and developed such technical skill as to-day may even dream of dominating the world.

But to grant that the essentials of such movements are not to be found in casual external circumstances, but must lie in the mental make-up of the nation, might lead in this case to ascribing the chief influence to quite a different mental trait. The average European, permeated as he is with Old World culture, is, in fact, convinced that this intense economic activity is the simple result of unbounded greed. The search for gold and the pursuit of the dollar, we often hear, have destroyed in the American soul every finer ambition; and since the American has no higher desire for culture, he is free to chase his mammon with undisguised and shameless greed. The barbarity of his soul, it is said, gives him a considerable economic advantage over others who have some heart as well as a pocket-book, and whose feelings incline to the humane.

Whether such a contemptuous allegation is a useful weapon in the economic struggle, is not here in question. One who desires to understand the historical development of events in the New World is bound to see in all such talk nothing but distortion, and to realize that Europe could face its own economic future with less apprehension if it would estimate the powers of its great competitor more temperately and justly, and would ask itself honestly if it could not learn a thing or two here and there.

Merely to ape American doings would, in the end, avail nothing; that which proceeds from intellectual and temperamental traits can be effectively adopted by others only if they can acquire the same traits. It is useless to organize similar factories or trusts without imitating in every respect the men who first so organized themselves. Whether this last is necessary, he alone can say who has understood his neighbours at their best, and has not been contented to make a merely thoughtless and uncharitable judgment. A magnificent economic life such as that of America can never spring from impure ethical motives, and the person is very naïve who supposes that a great business was ever built up by mere impudence, deception, and advertising. Every merchant knows that even advertisements benefit only a solid business, and that they run a bad one into the ground. And it is still more naïve to suppose that the economic strength of America has been built up through underhanded competition without respect to law or justice, and impelled by nothing but a barbarous and purely material ambition. One might better believe that the twenty-story office buildings on lower Broadway are supported merely by the flagstones in the street; in point of fact, no mere passer-by who does not actually see the foundations of such colossal structures can have an idea of how deep down under the soil these foundations go in order to find bed-rock. Just so the colossal fabric of American industry is able to tower so high only because it has its foundation on the hard rock of honest conviction.

In the first place, we might look into the American's greed for gold. A German observes immediately that the American does not prize his possessions much unless he has worked for them himself; of this there are innumerable proofs, in spite of the opposite appearances on the surface. One of the most interesting of these is the absence of the bridal dower. In Germany or France, the man looks on a wealthy marriage as one of the most reliable means of getting an income; there are whole professions which depend on a man's eking out his entirely inadequate salary from property which he inherits or gets by marriage; and the eager search for a handsome dowry — in fact, the general commercial character of marriage in reputable European society everywhere — always surprises Americans. They know nothing of such a thing at home. Even when the parents of the bride are prosperous, it is unusual for a young couple to live beyond the means of the husband. Everywhere one sees the daughters of wealthy families stepping into the modest homes of their husbands, and these husbands would feel it to be a disgrace to depend on their prosperous fathers-in-law. An actual dowry received from the bride's parents during their lifetime is virtually unknown. Another instance of American contempt for unearned wealth, which especially contrasts with European customs, is the disapproval which the American always has for lotteries. If he were really bent on getting money, he would find the dower and the lottery a ready means; whereas, in fact, the lottery is not only in all its forms forbidden by law, but public opinion wholly disapproves of games of chance. The President of Harvard University, in a public address given a short time since, in which he spoke before a large audience of the change in moral attitude, was able to give a striking illustration of the transformation in the fact that two generations ago the city of Boston conducted a lottery, in order to raise money for rebuilding a university structure which had been destroyed by fire. He showed vividly how such a transaction would be entirely unthinkable to-day, and how all American feelings would revolt at raising money for so good a cause as an educational institution by so immoral a means as a public lottery. The entire audience received this as a matter of course, apparently without a suspicion as to how many cathedrals are being built in Europe to-day from tickets at half a dollar. It was amusing to observe how Carnegie's friend, Schwab, who had been the greatly admired manager of the steel works, fell in public esteem when news came from the Riviera that he was to be seen at the gaming-tables of Monaco. The true American despises any one who gets money without working for it. Money is not the thing which is considered, but the manner of getting it. This is what the American cares for, and he prizes the gold he gets primarily as an indication of his ability.

At first sight it looks as if this disinclination to gambling were not to be taken seriously. It would signify nothing that the police discover here and there a company of gamblers who have barricaded the door; but a European might say that there is another sort of speculative fever which is very prevalent. Even Americans on the stock exchange often say, with a smile: We are a gambling nation; and from the point of view of the broker it would be so. He sees how all classes of people invest in speculative securities, and how the public interests itself in shares which are subject to the greatest fluctuations; how the cab-driver and the hotel waiter pore nervously over the quotations, and how new mining stocks and industrial shares are greedily bought by school teachers and commercial clerks. The broker sees in this the people's desire for gambling, because he is himself thoroughly aware of the great risks which are taken, and knows that the investors can see only a few of the factors which determine prices.

But in the public mind all this buying and selling looks very different. The small man, investing a few dollars in such doubtful certificates, never thinks of himself as a gambler; he thinks that he understands the market; he is not trusting to luck, but follows the quotations day by day for a long time, and asks his friends for "tips," until he is convinced that his own discretion and cunning will give him an advantage. If he were to think of his gain as matter of chance, as the broker thinks it is, he would not only not invest his money, but would be no longer attracted by the transactions. And whenever he loses, he still goes on, believing that he will be able the next time to figure out the turn of the market more accurately.

The same is true of the wagers which the Anglo-Saxon is always making, because he loves excitement. For him a wager is not a true wager when it is merely a question of chance. Both sides make calculations, and have their special considerations which they believe will determine the outcome, and the winner feels his gain to be earned by his shrewdness. An ordinary game of chance does not attract the American — a fact which may be seen even in the grotesque game of poker. In a certain sense, the American's aversion to tipping servants reveals, perhaps, the same trait. The social inferiority which he feels to be implied in the acceptance of a fee, goes against the self-respect of the individual; but there is the additional disinclination here to receiving money which is not strictly earned.

There are positive traits corresponding to these negative ones; and especially among them may be noticed the use to which money is put after it is gotten. If the American were really miserly, he would not distribute his property with such a free hand. Getting money excites him, but keeping it is less interesting, and one sees not seldom the richest men taking elaborate precautions that only a small part of their money shall fall to their children, because they think that the possession of money which is not self-earned is not a blessing. From these motives one may understand at once the magnificent generosity shown toward public enterprises.

Public munificence cannot well be gauged by statistics, and especially not in America. Most of the gifts are made quietly, and of course the small gifts which are never heard about outweigh the larger ones; and, nevertheless, one can have a fair idea of American generosity by considering only the large gifts made for public ends. If we consider only the gifts of money which are greater than one thousand dollars, and which go to public institutions, we have in the year 1903 the pretty sum of $76,935,000. There can be no doubt that all the gifts under one thousand dollars would make an equal sum.

Of these public benefactions, $40,700,000 went to educational institutions. In that year, for instance, Harvard University received in all $5,000,000, Columbia University $3,000,000, and Chicage University over $10,000,000; Yale received $600,000, and the negro institute in Tuskegee the same amount; Johns Hopkins and the University of Pennsylvania received about half of a million each. Hospitals and similar institutions were remembered with $21,726,000; $7,583,000 were given to public libraries, $3,996,000 for religious purposes, and $2,927,000 to museums and art collections. Any one who lives in America knows that this readiness to give is general, from the Carnegies and Rockefellers down to the working-men, and that it is easy to obtain money from private purses for any good undertaking.

One sees clearly, again, that the real attraction which the American feels for money-making does not lie in the having but only in the getting, from the perfect equanimity, positively amazing to the European, with which he bears his losses. To be sure, his irrepressible optimism stands him in good stead; he never loses hope, but is confident that what he has lost will soon be made up. But this would be no comfort to him if he did not care much less for the possession than for the getting of it. The American chases after money with all his might, exactly as on the tennis-court he tries to hit the ball, and it is the game he likes and not the prize. If he loses he does not feel as if he had lost a part of himself, but only as if he had lost the last set in a tournament. When, a short time ago, there was a terrific crash in the New York stock market and hundreds of millions were lost, a leading Parisian paper said: "If such a financial crisis had happened here in France, we should have had panics, catastrophies, a slump in *rentes*, suicides, street riots, a ministerial crisis, all in one day: while America is perfectly quiet, and the victims of the battle are sitting down to collect their wits. France and the United States are obviously two entirely different worlds in their civilization and in their way of thinking."

As to the estimation of money and its acquirement, France and the United States are indeed as far apart as possible, while Germany stands in between. The Frenchman prizes money as such; if he can get it without labour, by inheritance or dowry, or by gambling, so much the better. If he loses it he loses a part of himself, and when he has earned enough to be sure of a livelihood, he retires from money-making pursuits as soon as possible. It is well known that the ambition of the average Frenchman is to be a *rentier*. The American has exactly the opposite idea. Not only does he endure loss with indifference and despise gain which is not earned, but he would not for any price give up the occupation of making money. Whether he has much or little, he keeps patiently at work; and, as no scholar or artist would ever think of saying that he had done enough work, and would from now on become a scientific or literary *rentier* and live on his reputation, so no American, as long as he keeps his health, thinks of giving up his regular business.

The profession of living from the income of investments is virtually unknown among men, and the young men who take up no money-making profession because they "don't need to," are able to retain the social respect of their fellows only by undertaking some sort of work for the commonwealth. A man who does not work at anything, no matter how rich he is, can neither get nor keep a social status.

This also indicates, then, that the American does not want his money merely as a means for material comfort. Of course, wealthy Americans are becoming more and more accustomed to provide every thinkable luxury for their wives and daughters. Nowhere is so much expended for dresses, jewelry, equipages and service, for country houses and yachts, works of art and private libraries; and many men have to keep pretty steadily at work year in and year out in order to meet their heavy expenditures. And the same thing is repeated all down the social scale. According to European standards, even the working-man lives luxuriously. But, in spite of this, no person who has really come into the country will deny that material pleasures are less sought after for themselves in the New World than in the Old. It always strikes the European as remarkable how very industrious American society is, and how relatively little bent on pleasure. It has often been said that the American has not yet learned how to enjoy life; that he knows very well how to make money, but not how to enjoy it. And that is quite true; except that it leaves out of account the main point—which is, that the American takes the keenest delight in the employment of all his faculties in his work, and in the exercise of his own initiative. This gives him more pleasure than the spending of money could bring him.

It is, therefore, fundamentally false to stigmatize the American as a materialist, and to deny his idealism. A people is supposed to be thoroughly materialistic when its sphere of interests comprises problems relating only to the world of matter, and fancies itself to be highly idealistic when it is mainly concerned with intangible objects. But this is a pure confusion of ideas. In philosophy, indeed, the distinction between materialistic and idealistic systems of thought is to be referred to the importance ascribed to material and to immaterial objects. Materialism is, then, that pseudo-philosophical theory which supposes that all reality derives from the existence of material objects; and it is an idealistic system which regards the existence of matter as dependent on the reality of thought. But it is mere play on words to call nations realistic or idealistic on the strength of these metaphysical conceptions, instead of using the words in their social and ethical significations. For in the ethical world a materialistic position would be one in which the aim of life was enjoyment, while that point of view would be idealistic which found its motive not in the pleasant consequences of the deed, but in the value of the deed itself.

If we hold fast to the meaning of materialism and idealism in this ethical sense, we shall see clearly that it is entirely indifferent whether the people who have these diametrically opposed views of life are themselves busy with tangible or with intangible things. The man who looks at life materialistically acts, not for the act itself, but for the comfortable consequences which that act may have; and these consequences may satisfy the selfish pleasure as well if they are immaterial as if they are material objects. It is indifferent whether he works for the satisfaction of the appetites, for the hoarding up of treasures, or for the gratification to be found in politics, science, and art. He is still a materialist so long as he has not devotion, so long as he uses art only as a means to pleasure, science only as a source of fame, politics as a source of power; and, in general, so long as the labour that he does is only the means to an end. But the man who is an idealist in life acts because he believes in the value of the deed. It makes no difference to him whether he is working on material or intellectual concerns; whether he speaks or rhymes, paints, governs, or judges; or whether he builds bridges and railroad tracks, drains swamps and irrigates deserts, delves into the earth, or harnesses the forces of nature. In this sense the culture of the Old World threatens at a thousand points to become crassly materialistic, and not least of all just where it most loudly boasts of intellectual wealth and looks down with contempt on everything which is material. And in this sense the culture of the New World is growing to the very purest idealism, and by no means least where it is busy with problems of the natural world of matter, and where it is heaping up economic wealth.

This is the main point: The economic life means to the American a realizing of efforts which are in themselves precious. It is not the means to an end, but is its own end. If two blades of grass grow where one grew before, or two railroad tracks where there was but one; if production, exchange, and commerce increase and undertaking thrives, then life is created, and this is, in itself, a precious thing. The European of the Continent esteems the industrial life as honest, but not as noble; economic activities seem to him good for supporting himself and his family, but his duty is merely to supply economic needs which are now existing.

The merchant in Europe does not feel himself to be a free creator like the artist or scholar: he is no discoverer, no maker; and the mental energy which he expends he feels to be spent in serving an inferior purpose, which he serves only because he has to live. That creating economic values can itself be the very highest sort of accomplishment, and in itself alone desirable, whether or not it is useful for the person who creates, and that it is great in itself to spread and increase the life of the national economic organization, has been, indeed, felt by many great merchants in the history of Europe, and many a Hanseatic leader realizes it to-day. But the whole body of people in Europe does not know this, while America is thoroughly filled with the idea. Just as Hutten once cried: "Jahrhundert, es ist eine Lust, in dir zu leben: die Wissenschaften und die Kûnste blûhen," so the American might exclaim: It is a pleasure to live in our day and generation; industry and commerce now do thrive. Every individual feels himself exalted by being a part of such a mighty whole, and the general intellectual effects of this temper show themselves in the entire national life.

A nation can never do its best in any direction unless it believes thoroughly in the intrinsic value of its work; whatever is done merely through necessity is never of great national significance, and second-rate men never achieve the highest things. If the first minds of a nation look down with contempt on economic life, if there is no real belief in the ideal value of industry, and if creative minds hold aloof from it, that nation will necessarily be outdone by others in the economic field. But where the ablest strength engages with idealistic enthusiasm in the service of the national economic problems, the nation rewards what the people do as done in the name of civilization, and the love of fame and work together spur them on more than the material gain which they will get. Indeed, this gain is itself only their measure of success in the service of civilization.

The American merchant works for money in exactly the sense that a great painter works for money; the high price which is paid for his picture is a very welcome indication of the general appreciation of his art: but he would never get this appreciation if he were working for the money instead of his artistic ideals. Economically to open up this gigantic country, to bring the fields and forests, rivers and mountains into the service of economic progress, to incite the millions of inhabitants to have new needs and to satisfy these by their own resourcefulness, to increase the wealth of the nation, and finally economically to rule the world and within the nation itself to raise the economic power of the individual to undreamt-of importance, has been the work which has fascinated the American. And every individual has felt his co-operation to be ennobled by his firm belief in the value of such an aim for the culture of the world.

To find one's self in the service of this work of progress attracts even the small boy. As a German boy commences early to write verses or draw little sketches, in America the young farmer lad or city urchin tries to come somehow into this national, industrial activity; and whether he sells newspapers on the street or milks the cow on a neighbour's farm, he is proud of the few cents which he brings home — not because it is money, but because he has earned it, and the coins are the only possible proof that his activities have contributed to the economic life of his country. It is this alone which spurs him on and fills him with ambition; and if the young newspaper boy becomes a great railroad president, or the farmer's lad a wealthy factory owner, and both, although worth their millions, still work on from morning till night consumed by the thought of adding to the economic life of their nation, and to this end undertake all sorts of new enterprises, the labour itself has been, from beginning to end, its own reward. The content of such a man's life is the work of economic progress.

Men who have so felt have made the nation great, and no American would admit that a man who gave his life to government or to law, to art or science, would be able to make his life at all more significant or valuable for the ends of culture. This is not materialism. Thus it happens that the most favoured youths, the socially most competent talents, go into economic life, and the sons of the best families, after their course at the university, step enthusiastically into the business house. One can see merely from ordinary conversation how thoroughly the value of economic usefulness is impressed on the people. They speak in America of industrial movements with as much general interest as one would find manifested in Europe over politics, science, or art. Men who do not themselves anticipate buying or selling securities in the stock market, nevertheless discuss the rise and fall of various industrial and railroad shares as they would discuss Congressional debates; and any new industrial undertaking in a given city fills the citizens with pride, as may be gathered from their chance conversations.

The central point of this whole activity is, therefore, not greed, nor the thought of money, but the spirit of self-initiative. It is not surprising that this has gone through such a lively development. Just as the spirit of self-determination was the product of Colonial days, so the spirit of self-initiative is the necessary outcome of pioneer life. The men who came over to the New World expected to battle with the natural elements; and even where nature had lavished her treasures, these had still to be conquered; the forests must be felled and the marshes drained. Indeed, the very spot to which the economic world comes to-day to celebrate the hundredth anniversary of the Louisiana Purchase, the city of St. Louis, which has to-day 8,000 factories, it must not be forgotten was three generations ago a wilderness.

From the days when the first pioneers journeyed inland from the coast, to the time, over two hundred years later, when the railroad tracks were carried over the Rocky Mountains from the Atlantic to the Pacific Ocean, the history of the nation has been of a long struggle with nature and of hard-earned conquests; and for many years this fight was carried on by men who toiled single-handed, as it were — by thousands of pioneers working all at once, but far apart. The man who could not hold out under protracted labour was lost; but the difficulty of the task spurred on the energies of the strong and developed the spirit of self-initiative to the utmost. It was fortunate that the men who came over to undertake this work had been in a way selected for it: for only those who had resolution had ventured to leave their native hearth-stones. Only the most energetic risked the voyage across the ocean in those times, and this desire to be up and doing found complete satisfaction in the New World; for, as Emerson said: "America is another name for opportunity."

The heritage of the pioneer days cannot vanish, even under the present changed conditions. This desire to realize one's self by being economically busied is indeed augmented to-day by many other considerations. Both the political and the social life of the democracy demand equality, and therefore exclude all social classes, and titles, and all honourary political distinctions. Now, such uniformity would, of course, be unendurable in a society which had no real distinctions, and therefore inevitably such distinguishing factors as are not excluded come to be more and more important. A distinction between classes on the basis of property can be met in monarchial countries by a distinction in title and family, and so made at least very much less important than in democratic nations. And thus it necessarily comes about that, where an official differentiation is objected to on principle, wealth is sought as a means to such discrimination. In the United States, however, wealth has this great significance only because it is felt to measure the individual's successful initiative; and the simple equation between prosperity and real work is more generally recognized by the popular mind than the actual conditions justify. Thus it happens also that the

American sets his standard of life high. He wishes in this way to express the fact that he has passed life's examination well, that he has been enterprising, and has won the respect of those around him. This desire for a high standard of living which springs from the intense economic enthusiasm works back thereon, and greatly stimulates it once more.

One of the first consequences of this spirit of initiative is, that every sort of true labour is naturally respected, and never involves any disesteem. In fact, one sees continually in this country men who go from one kind of labour to another which, according to European ideals, would be thought less honourable. The American is especially willing to take up a secondary occupation besides his regular calling in order to increase his income, and this leads, sometimes, to striking contrasts. Of course there are some limits to this, and social etiquette is not wholly without influence, although the American will seldom admit it. No one is surprised if a preacher gives up the ministry in order to become an editor or official in an industrial organization; but every one is astonished if he becomes agent for an insurance company; amazed if he goes to selling a patent medicine, and would be positively scandalized if he were to buy a beer-saloon.

It is much the same with avocations. If the student in the university tutors other students, it is quite right; if, during the university vacation, he becomes bell-boy in a summer hotel, or during the school year attends to furnaces in order to continue his studies, people are sorry that he has to do this, but still account him perfectly respectable; but if, on the other hand, he turns barber or artist's model, he is lost, because being a model is passive — it is not doing anything; and cutting hair is a menial service, not compatible with the dignity of the student. And thus it is that the social feeling in the New World practically corrects the theoretical maxims as to the equal dignity of every kind of labour, although, indeed, such maxims are very much more generally recognized than in the Old World. And everywhere the deciding principle of differentiation is the matter of self-initiative.

The broadly manifest social equality of the country, of which we shall have to speak more minutely in another connection, would be actually impossible if this belief in the equivalence of all kinds of work did not rule the national mind. Whether the work brings much or little, or requires much or little preparation, is thought to be unimportant in determining a man's status; but it is important that his life involves initiative, or that he not merely passively exists.

A people which places industrial initiative so high must be industrious; and, in fact, there is no profounder impression to be had than that the whole population is busily at work, and that all pleasures and everything which presupposes an idle moment are there merely to refresh people and prepare them for more work. In order to be permanently industrious, a man has to learn best how to utilize his powers; and just in this respect the American nation has gone ahead of every other people. Firstly, it is sober. A man who takes liquor in the early part of the day cannot accomplish the greatest amount of work. When the American is working he does not touch alcohol until the end of the day, and this is as true of the millionaire and bank president as of the labourer or conductor. On the other hand, the American workman knows that only a well-nourished body can do the most work, and what the workman saves by not buying beer and brandy he puts into roast beef. It has often been observed, and especially remarked on by German observers, that in spite of his extraordinary tension, the American never overdoes. The working-man in the factory, for example, seldom perspires at his work. This comes from a knowledge of how to work so as in the end to get out of one's self the greatest possible amount.

Very much the same may be said of the admirable way in which the Americans make the most of their time. Superficial observers have often supposed the American to be always in a hurry, whereas the opposite is the case. The man who has to hurry has badly disposed of his time, and, therefore, has not the necessary amount to finish any one piece of work. The American is never in a hurry, but he so disposes his precious time that nothing shall be lost. He will not wait nor be a moment idle; one thing follows closely after another, and with admirable precision; each task is finished in its turn; appointments are made and kept on the minute; and the result is, that not only no unseemly haste is necessary, but also there is time for everything. It is astonishing how well-known men in political, economic, or intellectual life, who are loaded with a thousand responsibilities and an apparently unreasonable amount of work, have, by dint of the wonderful disposition of their own time and that of their assistants, really enough for everything and even to spare.

Among the many things for which the American has time, by reason of his economical management of it, are even some which seem unnecessary for a busy man. He expends, for example, an extraordinary large fraction of his time in attending to his costume and person, in sport, and in reading newspapers, so that the notion which is current in Europe that the American is not only always in a hurry, but has time for nothing outside of his work, is entirely wrong.

This saving of strength by the proper disposal of time corresponds to a general practicality in every sort of work. Business is carried on in a business-like way. The banker, whose residence is filled with sumptuous treasures of art, allows nothing unpractical to come into his office for the sake of adornment. A certain strict application to duty is the feeling one gets from every work-room; and while the foreigner feels a certain barrenness about it, the American feels that anything different shows a lack of earnestness and practical good sense. The extreme punctuality with which the American handles his correspondence is typical of him. Statistics show that no other country in the world sends so many letters for every inhabitant, and every business letter is replied to on the same day with matter-of-fact conciseness. It is like a tremendous apparatus that accomplishes the greatest labour with the least friction, by means of the precise adaptation of part to part.

A nation which is after self-initiative must inspire the spirit of initiative in every single co-operator. Nothing is more characteristic of this economic body than the intensity with which each workman — taking the word in its broadest sense — thinks and acts for himself. In this respect, too, outsiders often misunderstand the situation. One hears often from travellers in America that the country must be dwarfing to the intelligence of its workmen, because it uses so much machinery that the individual workman comes to see only a small part of what is being done in the factory and, so to say, works the same identical lever for life. He operates always a certain small part of some other part of the whole. Nothing could be less exact, and a person who comes to such a conclusion is not aware that even the smallest duties are extremely complex, and that, therefore, specialization does not at all introduce an undesirable uniformity in labour. It is specialization on the one hand which guarantees the highest mastery, and on the other lets the workman see even more the complexity of what is going on, and inspires him to get a full comprehension of the thing in hand and perhaps to suggest a few improvements.

Any man who is at all concerned with the entire field of operations, or who is moving constantly from one special process to another, can never come to that fully absorbed state of the attention which takes cognizance of the slightest detail. Only the man who has concentrated himself and specialized, learns to note fine details; and it is only in this way that he becomes so much a master in his special department that any one else who attempts to direct him succeeds merely in interfering and spoiling the output. In short, such a workman is face to face with intricate natural processes, and is learning straight from nature. It is in the matter of industrial technique exactly as in science. A person not acquainted with science finds it endlessly monotonous, and cannot understand how a person should spend his whole life studying beetles or deciphering Assyrian inscriptions. But a man who knows the method of science realizes that the narrower a field of study becomes, the more full of variety and unexpected beauties it is found to be. The triumph of technical specialization in America lies just in this. If a single man works at some special part of some special detail of an industrial process, he more and more comes to find in his narrow province an amazing intricacy which the casual observer looking on cannot even suspect; and only the man who sees this complexity is able to discover new processes and improvements on the old. So it is that the specialized workman is he who constantly contributes to perfect technique, proposes modifications, and in general exercises all the intelligence he has, in order to bring himself on in his profession. Just as we have seen how the spirit of self-determination which resides at the periphery of the body politic has been the peculiar strength of American political life, so this free initiative in the periphery, this economic resourcefulness of the narrow specialists, is the peculiar strength of all American industry.

The spirit of self-initiative does not know pettiness. Any one who goes into economic life merely for the sake of what he can get out of it, thinks it clever to gain small, unfair profits; but whosoever views his industry in a purely idealistic spirit, and really has some inner promptings, is filled with an interest in the whole play — sees an economic gain in anything which profits both capital and labour, and only there, and so has a large outlook even within his narrow province. The Americans constantly complain of the economic smallness of Europe, and even the well-informed leaders of American industry freely assert that the actual advance in American economic culture does not lie in the natural resources of the country, but rather in the broad, free initiative of the American people. The continental Europeans, it is said, frustrate their own economic endeavours by being penny-wise and observant of detail in the wrong place, and by lacking the courage to launch big undertakings. There is no doubt that it was the lavishness of nature which firstly set American initiative at work on a broad scale. The boundless prairies and towering mountains which the pioneers saw before them inspired them to undertake great things, and to overlook small hindrances, and in laying out their first plans to overlook small details. American captains of industry often say that they purposely pay no attention to a good many European methods, because they find such pedantic endeavour to economize and to achieve minute perfections to be wasteful of time and unprofitable.

The same spirit is found, as well, in fields other than the industrial. When the American travels he prefers to pay out round sums rather than to haggle over the price of things, even although he pays considerably more thereby than he otherwise would. And nothing makes him more angry than to find that instead of stating a high price at the outset, the person with whom he is dealing ekes out his profit by small additional charges. This large point of view involves such a contempt of petty detail as to astonish Europeans. Machines costing hundreds of thousands of dollars, which were new yesterday, are discarded to-day, because some improvement has been discovered; and the best is everywhere found none too good to be used in this magnificent industrial system. If the outlay is to correspond to the result, there must be no parsimony.

A similar trait is revealed in the way in which every man behaves toward his neighbour. It is only the petty man who is envious, and envy is a word which is not found in the American vocabulary. If one's own advantage is not the goal, but general economic progress, then the success of another man is almost as great a pleasure as one's own success. It is for the American an æsthetic delight to observe, and in spirit to co-operate with economic progress all along the line; and the more others accomplish the more each one realizes the magnificence of the whole industrial life. Men try to excel one another, as they have to do wherever there is free competition; and such rivalry is the best and surest condition for economic progress. Americans use every means in their power to succeed, but if another man comes out ahead they neither grumble nor indulge in envy, but rather gather their strength for a new effort. Even this economic struggle is carried on in the spirit of sport. The fight itself is the pleasure. The chess-player who is checkmated in an exciting game is not sorry that he played, and does not envy the winner.

This conviction, that one neither envies nor is envied, whereby all competitive struggle comes to be pervaded with a certain spirit of co-operation, ennobles all industrial activities, and the immediate effect is a feeling of mutual confidence. The degree to which Americans trust one another is by no means realized on the European Continent. A man relies on the self-respect of his commercial associates in a way which seems to the European mind almost fatuous, and yet herein lies just the strength and security of the economic life of this country.

It is interesting, in a recently published harangue against the Standard Oil Company, to read what a high-handed, Napoleonic policy Rockefeller has pursued, and then, in the midst of the fierce accusations, to find it stated that agreements involving millions of dollars and the economic fate of thousands of people were made merely orally. All his confederates took the word of Rockefeller to be as good as his written contract, and such mutual confidence is everywhere a matter of course, whether it is a millionaire who agrees to pay out a fortune or a street urchin who goes off to change five cents. Just as public, so also commercial, affairs get on with very few precautions, and every man takes his neighbour's check as the equivalent of money. The whole economic life reveals everywhere the profoundest confidence; and undoubtedly this circumstance has contributed, more than almost anything else, to the successful growth of large organizations in America.

The spirit of self-initiative goes out in another direction. It makes the American optimistic, and so sure of success that no turn of fortune can discourage him. And such an optimism is necessary to the man who undertakes great enterprises. It was an undertaking to cross the ocean, and another to press on from the coast to the interior; it was an undertaking to bring nature to terms, to conjure up civilization in a wild country, and to overcome enemies on all hands; and yet everything has seemed to succeed. With the expansion of the country has grown the individual's love of expansion, his delight in undertaking new enterprises, not merely to hold his own, but to go on and to stake his honour and fortune and entire personality in the hope of realizing something as yet hardly dreamed of. Any Yankee is intoxicated with the idea of succeeding in a new enterprise; he plans such things at his desk in school, and the more venturesome they are the more he is fascinated.

Nothing is more characteristic of this adventurous spirit than the way in which American railroads have been projected. In other countries railroads are built to connect towns which already exist. In America the railroad has created new towns; the engineer and capitalist have not laid their tracks merely where the land was already tilled, but in every place where they could foresee that a population could support itself. At first came the railroad, and then the men to support it. The freight car came first, and then the soil was exploited and made to supply the freight. Western communities have almost all grown up around the railway stations. To be sure, every railway company has done this in its own interest, but the whole undertaking has been immediately productive of new civilization.

Any person who optimistically believes that a problem has only to be discovered in order to be solved, will be sure to develop that intellectual quality which has always characterized the American:

the spirit of invention. There is no other country in the world where so much is invented. This is shown not merely in the fact that an enormous number of patents is granted every year, but also where there is nothing to patent, the Yankee exercises his ingenuity every day. From the simplest tool up to the most complicated machine, American invention has improved and perfected, and made the theoretically correct practically serviceable as well. To be sure, the cost of human labour in a thinly settled country has had a great influence on this development; but a special talent also has lain in this direction — a real genius for solving practical problems. Every one knows how much the American has contributed to the perfection of the telegraph, telephone, incandescent light, phonograph and sewing-machine, to watch-making machinery, to the steamboat and locomotive, the printing-press and typewriter, to machinery for mining and engineering, and to all sorts of agricultural and manufacturing devices. Invention and enterprise are seen working together in the fact that every new machine, with all its improvements, goes at once to every part of the country. Every farmer in the farthest West wants the latest agricultural machinery; every artisan adopts the newest improvements; in every office the newest and most approved telegraphic and telephonic appliances are used; in short, every man appropriates the very latest devices to further his own success. Of course, in this way the commercial value of every improvement is greatly increased, and this encourages the inventor to still further productiveness. It so happens that larger sums of money are lavished in perfect good faith in order to solve certain problems than any European could imagine. If an inventor can convince a company that his principle is sound, the company is ready to advance millions of dollars for new experiments until the machine is perfected.

The extraordinarily wide adoption of every invention does not mean that most inventions are made by such men as Edison and Bell and their colleagues. Every factory workman is quite as much concerned to improve the tools which his nation uses, and every artisan at his bench is busy thinking out this or that little change in a process or method; and many of them, after their work, frequent the public libraries in order to work through technical books and the Patent Reports. It is no wonder that an

American manufacturer, on hearing that a new machine had been discovered in Europe, conservatively declared that he did not know what the machine was, but knew for sure that America would improve on it.

Only one consequence of the spirit of self-initiative remains to be spoken of — the absolute demand for open competition. In order to exercise initiative, a man must have absolutely free play; and if he believes in the intrinsic value of economic culture, he will be convinced that free play for the development of industrial power is abstractly and entirely right. This does not wholly exclude an artificial protection of certain economic institutions which are weak — as, for instance, the protection of certain industries by means of a high tariff — so long as in every line all men are free to compete with one another. Monopoly is the only thing — because it strangles competition — which offends the instinct of the American; and in this respect American law goes further than a European would expect. One might suppose that, believing as they do in free initiative, Americans would claim the right of making such industrial combinations as they liked. When several parallel railroads, which traverse several states and compete severely with one another, finally make a common agreement to maintain prices, they seem at first sight to be exercising a natural privilege. The traffic which suffers no longer by competition is handled at a less expense by this consolidation, and so the companies themselves and the travelling public are both benefited. But the law of the United States takes a different point of view. The average American is suspicious of a monopoly, even when it is owned by the state or city; he is convinced from the beginning that the service will in some way or other be inferior to what it would be under free competition; and most of all, he dislikes to see any industrial province hedged in so that competitors are no longer free to come in. The reason why the trusts have angered and excited the American to an often exaggerated degree is, that they approach perilously near to being monopolies.

This spirit of self-initiative under free competition exists, of course, not alone in individuals. Towns, cities, counties, and states evince collectively just the same attitude; the same optimism and spirit of invention and initiative, and the same pioneer courage, inspire the collective will of city and state. Especially in the West, various cities and communities do things in a sportsman-like way. It is as if one city or state were playing foot-ball against another, and exerting every effort to win: and here once more there is no petty jealousy. It was from such an optimistic spirit of enterprise, certainly, that the city of St. Louis resolved to invite all the world to its exposition, and that the State of Missouri gave its enthusiastic approval and support to its capital city. The sums to be laid out on such bold undertakings are put at a generous figure, and no one asks anxiously whether he is ready or able to undertake such a thing, but he is fascinated by the thought that such an industrial festival around the cascades of Forest Park, near the City of St. Louis, will stimulate the whole industrial life of the Mississippi Valley. One already sees that Missouri is disposed to become a Pennsylvania of the West, and to develop her rich resources into a great industry.

We must not suppose, in all this, that such a spirit of initiative involves no risk, or that no disadvantages follow into the bargain. It may be easily predicted that, just by reason of the energy which is so intrinsic to it, self-initiative will sometime overstep the bounds of peace and harmony. Initiative will become recklessness, carelessness of nature, carelessness of one's neighbour, and, finally, carelessness of one's self.

A reckless treatment of nature has, in fact, characterized the American pioneer from the first. The wealth of nature has seemed so inexhaustible, that the pioneers found it natural to draw on their principal instead of living on their income. Everywhere they used only the best which they found; they cut down the finest forests first, and sawed up only the best parts of the best logs. The rest was wasted. The farmers tilled only the best soil, and nature was dismantled and depleted in a way which a European, who is accustomed to precaution, finds positively sinful. And the time is now passed when this can go on safely. Good, arable land can nowhere be had for nothing to-day; the cutting down of huge forests has already had a bad effect on the rainfall and water supply, and many efforts are now being made to atone for the sins of the past by protecting and replanting. Intensive methods are being introduced in agriculture; but the work of thoughtful minds meets with a good deal of resistance in the recklessness of the masses, who, so far as nature is in question, think very little of their children's children, but are greedy for instant profits.

The man, moreover, who ardently desires to play an important part in industry is easily tempted to be indifferent of his fellows. We have shown that an American is not jealous or distrustful of them, that he gives and expects frankness, and that he respects their rights. But when he once begins to play, he wants to win at any cost; and then, so long as he observes the rules of the game, he considers nothing else; he has no pity, and will never let his undertaking be interfered with by sentimental reasons. There is no doubt at all that the largest American industrial enterprises have ruined many promising lives; no doubt that the very men who give freely to public ends have driven their chariots over many industrial corpses. The American, who is so incomparably good-natured, amiable, obliging, and high-minded, admits himself that he is sharp in trade, and that the American industrial spirit requires a sort of military discipline and must be brutal. If the captain of industry were anxiously considerate of persons' feelings, he would never have achieved industrial success any more than a compassionate and tearful army would win a victory.

But the American is harder on himself than on any one else. We have shown how, in his work, he conserves his powers and utilizes them economically; but he sets no bounds to the intellectual strain, the intensity of his nervous activities, and only too often he ruins his health in the too great strain which brings his success. The bodies of thousands have fertilized the soil for this great industrial tree — men who have exhausted their power in their exaggerated commercial ambitions. The real secret of American success is that, more than any other country in the world, she works with the young men and uses them up. Young men are in all the important positions where high intellectual tension is required.

In other directions, too, the valuable spirit of self-initiative shows great weaknesses and dangers. The confidence which the American gives his neighbour in business often comes to be inexcusable carelessness. In reading the exposures made of the Ship-Building Trust, one sees how, without a dishonest intent, crimes can actually be committed merely through thoughtless confidence. One sees that each one of the great capitalists here involved relied on the other, while no one really investigated for himself.

There is another evil arising from the same intense activity, although, to be sure, it is more a matter of the past than of the future. This is the vulgar display of wealth. When economic usefulness is the main ambition, and the only measure of success is the money which is won, it is natural that under more or less primitive social conditions every one should wish to attest his merits by displaying wealth. Large diamonds have then much the same function as titles and orders; they are the symbols of successful endeavour. In its vulgar form all such display is now virtually relegated to undeveloped sections of the country. In the parts where culture is older, where wealth is in its second or third generation, every one knows that his property is more useful in the bank than on his person.

In spite of this, the nation expends an unduly large part of its profits in personal adornment, in luxuries of the toilet, in horses and carriages and expensive residences. The American is bound to have the best, and feels himself lowered if he has to take the second best. The most expensive seats in an auditorium are always the best filled, and the opera is thinly attended only when it is given at reduced prices. It is just in the most expensive hotels that one has to engage a room beforehand. Everywhere that expenditure can be observed by others, the American would rather renounce a pleasure entirely than enjoy it in a modest way. He wants to appear everywhere as a prosperous and substantial person, and therefore has a decided tendency to live beyond his means. Extravagance is, therefore, a great national trait. Everything, whether large or small, is done with a free hand. In the kitchen of the ordinary man much is thrown away which the European carefully saves for his nourishment; and in the kitchens of the government officials a hundred thousand cooks are at work, as if there were every day a banquet. Even when the American economizes he is fundamentally extravagant. His favourite way of saving is by buying a life insurance policy; but when one sees how many millions of dollars such companies spend in advertising and otherwise competing with one another, and what prodigious amounts they take in, one cannot doubt that they also are a means of saving for wealthy men, who, after after all, do not know what real economy is.

If the whole outward life is pervaded by this pioneer spirit of self-initiative, there is another factor which is not to be overlooked; it is the neglect of the æsthetic. Any one who loves beauty desires to see his ideal realized at the present moment, and the present itself becomes for him expressive of the past, while the man whose only desire is to be active as an economic factor looks only into the future. The bare present is almost valueless, since it is that which has to be overcome; it is the material which the enterprising spirit has to shape creatively into something else. The pioneer cannot be interested in the present as a survivor of the past; it shows to him only that which is to do, and admonishes his soul to prepare for new achievement. On Italian soil one's eye is offended by every false note in the general harmony. The present, in which the past still lives, fills one's consciousness, and the repose of æsthetic contemplation is the chief emotion. But a man who rushes from one undertaking to another seeks no unity or harmony in the present; his retina is not sensitive to ugliness, because his eye is forever peering into the future; and if the present were to be complete and finished, the enterprising spirit would regret such perfection and account it a loss — a restriction of his freedom, an end to his creation. It would mean mere pleasure and not action. In this sense the American expresses his pure idealism in speaking of the "glory of the imperfect."

The Italian is not to be disparaged for being unlike the American and for letting his eye rest on pleasing contours without asking what new undertakings could be devised to make reality express his own spirit of initiative. One must also not blame the American if he does not scrutinize his vistas with the eye of a Florentine, if he is not offended by the ugly remains of his nation's past, the scaffolding of civilization, or if he looks at them with pride, noting how restlessly his countrymen have stuck to their work in order to shape a future from the past. In fact, one can hardly take a step in the New World without everywhere coming on some crying contrast between mighty growth and the oppressive remains of outgrown or abortive activities. As one comes down the monumental steps of the Metropolitan Museum, in which priceless treasures of art are collected, one sees in front of one a wretched, tumbled-down hut where sundry refreshments are sold, on a dirty building-lot with a broken fence. It looks as if it had been brought from the annual county fair of some remote district into this wealthiest street of the world.

Of course such a thing is strikingly offensive, but it disturbs only a person who is not looking with the eye of the American, who can therefore not understand the true ethical meaning of American culture, its earnest looking forward into the future. If the incomplete past no longer met the American's eye in all its poverty and ugliness and smallness, he would have lost the main-spring of his life. That which is complete does not interest him, while that which he can still work on wholly fascinates and absorbs him. It is true here, as in every department of American life, that superficial polish would be only an imitation of success; friction and that which is æsthetically disorganized, but for this very reason ethically valuable, give to his life its significance and to his industry its incomparable progress.

CHAPTER TWELVE

The Economic Rise

INTROITE, nam et hic dii sunt—here, too, the gods are on their throne. The exploiting of the country, the opening of the mines, the building of factories and railroads, trade and barter, are not in question here as the mere means of livelihood, but as a spontaneous and creative labour, which is undertaken specifically in the interests of progress. In this confession of faith we have found the significance of American industrial life, in the spirit of self-initiative its greatest strength. Only such men as desire to take part in the economic era of creation, to meet their neighbours openly and trustingly and to rely on their spoken word, in short, to believe in the intrinsic worth of industry—only such men can weave the wonderful fabric of New World industry. A race of men carrying on commerce merely in order to live, feeling no idealism impelling them to industry, would never, even in this richly-endowed America, have produced such tangible results or gained such power.

Nevertheless, the country itself must not be forgotten by reason of its inhabitants. It was the original inducement to the inhabitants to turn so industriously to the spade and plough. Where the spade has dug, it has brought up silver and gold, coal and iron; and where the plough has turned, it has evoked a mammoth growth of wheat and corn. Seas and rivers, bays and mountains have produced a happy configuration of the land and pointed out the routes for traffic; oil-wells have flown freely, and the water-power is inexhaustible; the supply of fish and fowl, the harvests of tropical fruits and of cotton have been sufficient to supply the world. And all this was commenced by nature, before the first American set his foot on the continent.

And while it was the lavish hand of nature which first brought prosperity to the inhabitants, this prosperity became, in its turn, a new stimulus to the economic exploitation of further natural resources. It provided the capital for new undertakings; it also helped on the extraordinary growth of economic demand, it made the farmer and the artisan the best patrons of thriving industries, and made the economic circulatory system pulsate with increasing strength through the national organization.

There are, besides the purely economic conditions, certain political and administrative ones. American history has developed in a free atmosphere such as cannot be had in countries with ancient traditions, and which, even in the New World, at least in the eastern part of it, is disappearing day by day. Of course, such elbow-room has not been an unqualified blessing. It has been attended by evils and has made sacrifices necessary. But these have always touched the individual. The community has gained by the freedom of economic conditions. For instance, railroads, such as were built through the whole West during the pioneer years of America, would not be permitted for a moment by a German government. Such flimsy bridges, such rough-and-ready road-beds, such inadequate precautions on crossings were everywhere a serious menace; but those who were injured were soon forgotten, while the economic blessings of the new railroads which transported hundreds of thousands of people into uninhabited regions, and left them to gather the treasure of the soil, continued. They could never have been built if people had waited until they were able to construct by approved methods. After the great pioneer railroads had accomplished their mission, the time came when they were replaced by better structures. And they have been built over many times, until to-day the traffic is sufficiently safe. It still belongs, in a way, to the confession of faith of this religion of self-initiative that each man shall be free to risk not only his property, but also his own life, for the sake of enterprise. No board of commissioners may interfere to tell an American not to skirt a precipice.

Such instances of complete freedom, where life and limb are unsafe, disappear day by day. Guide-posts are put at every railroad crossing, and civil authorities take more and more interest in safety appliances for factories and in the security of city buildings; in fact, hygienic regulations in some Eastern cities to-day go even further than they go in Germany. Nevertheless, in such matters as involve not dangers, but merely traditions or preferences, a large amount of democratic freedom can still be had in the New World. Over the broad prairies there are no signs lawfully warning persons to turn to the right and not to walk on the grass. The American himself not only regards this country as the land of "unlimited possibilities," but more specially he regards the European Continent as the country of impossible limitations. Bureaucracy is to his mind the worst enemy of industrial life, because it everywhere provides the most trivial obstacles to that spirit of adventure and daring which seeks to press on into the future; and in the end it is sure to bring all enterprise to a standstill. It is important for this freedom that the whole economic legislation is regulated, first of all, not by the Union, but by the several states, and that thus every variety of industrial life going on in any state shall be so well represented that every attempt to bring up artificial restraints shall be nipped in the bud.

To this negative factor is to be added a positive one. Every one knows that the mighty growth of the American industry and of its whole commercial life would not have been possible without the carefully adapted protective tariff of recent years. The Dingley and the McKinley tariff laws have not, of course, produced that great advance, but they have powerfully aided it. And at the same time enormous sums have been derived therefrom and expended by the government in improving the water-ways and harbours. The government has spent vast sums in helping agriculture, and done much to irrigate the arid portions of the country. Economic problems in general receive great consideration in Washington and in every state capital. Besides such general political activities, there are more special ones. The nation's agriculture, for instance, is tremendously assisted by scientific researches, which are carried on by the Department of Agriculture. The army of American consuls is incomparably alert in seeking out favourable openings for American trade with other nations, and the consular reports are distributed promptly and free of charge from Washington to all parts of the country.

The political attitude of the nation works in still another way to favour general prosperity. The country has a unified organization which favours all economic enterprises. Although seventeen times as large as Germany, the country is nevertheless one splendid unit without internal customs barriers, under one law, and free from sectional distrusts. For, wherever commercial intercourse goes on between different states, the common federal law is in force.

Perhaps even more important than the national unity is the democratic equality throughout the population. However diverse these eighty million people may be, they form a homogeneous purchasing public. Every new style or fashion spreads like wild-fire from New York to San Francisco, and in spite of their differences, the day-labourer and the millionaire both have a certain similarity of tastes and requirements, so that the industrial producer and the distributor find it easy to make and keep in stock all articles which are called for. Instead of the freakish and fanciful demand which makes the European industrial life so difficult, everybody in America wants the same pattern as his neighbour, perhaps a little finer and better, but still the same general thing. And this brings it about that producers can manufacture in large quantities, and wholesale production and the ease of placing wares on the market encourage again the uniformity of taste and requirement, and help on the popular tendency toward mutual imitation throughout the country.

But now, instead of recounting the conditions which have helped to make the story, we must narrate the story itself. The German can listen to it with pleasure, since it is about one of Germany's best patrons — a nation which always buys from Germany in proportion to its own prosperity, and one whose adversity would bring misfortune to Germany. The story can be most quickly told in figures, as is the favourite American way; for, if the American has a special mania, it is to heap up all sorts of statistics.

We shall best study the statistical variations through long intervals of time, in order not to be led astray by temporary fluctuations. When, a few years ago, an industrial and financial relapse had set in in Germany, and England was suffering from the war in the Transvaal, while America was undertaking a gigantic work of organization which promised to have marvellous results, the United States suddenly appeared as the economic mistress of the world, to the astonishment and apprehension of all other countries. Soon after that German trade and industry began to revive and England recovered itself, while in America industrial extravagance and financial inflation were bringing about their necessary evil consequences. Then the public opinion of other countries swung at once to the other extreme, as if America's success had been entirely spurious. People suddenly turned about and believed that the time of American prosperity was over, rejoiced with ghoulish glee over the weakness of the enemy, despised his foolhardiness, and gossiped about his industrial leaders. But it was only in other countries that men like Schwab, the president of the Steel Trust, had been looked on as a Napoleon of industry; and when he was not able to retain his position, European papers were as pleased as if a Napoleonic army had been wiped out. Such insignificant events of the day are able to distort the judgment of great movements; picturesque mishaps strike the attention, and are taken to indicate great movements.

The actual advance in economic life of the United States was not such a sudden thing as it seemed to nervous Europe, nor was there any reverse such as Europe delighted to record. To be sure, America has passed through several great crises; but her history is nevertheless one of steady, even and healthy development in economic organization. The American himself is inclined to believe that severe crises are not to be feared any more; but however that may be, the long-predicted downfall has not come to-day, and is not even in sight. The general progress persists, and the decline in stock-market securities, which has been here and there abroad the signal for alarm, is itself a part of the sound development. When one looks at the whole rise one realizes that the young nation's development has been great and powerful, and such as was never before known in the history of civilization. Figures will show this better than adjectives. What now do the United States produce? The wheat of the country amounted, in the year 1850, to only 100 million bushels; in 1870 to 235 millions; 522 millions in 1900; 637 in 1903. The corn harvest was 592 millions in 1850; 1,094 in 1870; 2,105 in 1900; 2,244 in 1903. There were 52 million pounds of wool in 1850; 162 in 1870; 288 in 1900; 316 in 1902. But cotton is "king." In 1850 the cotton harvest amounted to 2.3 million bales; 3.1 millions in 1870; 9.4 in 1900 and 10.7 in 1903; 110,000 tons of sugar were produced in 1850 and last year 310,000 tons. The dreaded American petroleum was not flowing in 1850. It appears in the statistical tables of 1859 in the modest quantity of 8,400 gallons; in 1870 there were 220 million gallons; in 1900, 2,661 million, and in 1903 there were 3,707 million gallons. The coal output of the country began in 1820 with 365 tons and amounted in 1850 to 3 million tons; in 1870 to 33 million; in 1900 to 240 million; in 1902 to 269 million tons. In the middle of the last century 563,000 tons of iron ore were mined; 1.6 million tons in 1870; 13.7 in 1900, and 18 million in 1903. The manufacture of steel began in 1867 with 19,000 tons and in 1870 amounted to 68,000 tons, to 10.1 million tons in 1900; 14.9 millions in 1902. Of copper, 650 tons were mined in 1850; 12,000 tons in 1870; 270,000 tons in 1900; and 294,000 tons in 1902. The silver production in the middle of the century was estimated at $50,000; in 1870 at $16,000,000, and in 1900 at $74,000,000; in the last three years it has gone back to $71,000,000. The highest point was reached in 1892, with $82,000,000. On the other hand, the production of gold has grown steadily in the last twenty years, although it had reached its first high point back in the fifties. In the year 1853, $65,000,000 worth of gold was produced. The amount decreased slowly but steadily to $30,000,000 in the year 1883, and has since risen almost steadily until in 1903 it amounted to $74,000,000. The total output of minerals was valued at $218,000,000 in 1870, and $1,063,000,000 in 1900.

This steady growth of natural products is repeated in the agricultural and industrial spheres. The number of farms was given at 1.4 million in the middle of the last century, with the total value of $3,967,000,000; in 1870 there were 2.6 million farms valued at $8,944,000,000; and in 1900 there were 5.7 million, valued at $20,514,000,000. In 1870, 5.9 million people engaged in agriculture; 10.4 million in 1900. The total value of agricultural products amounted, in 1870, to $1,958,000,000, and in 1900 to $3,764,000,000. All domestic animals — cattle, horses, mules, sheep and pigs — amounted in 1850 to $544,000,000;

in 1870 to $1,822,000,000; in 1900 to $2,228,000,000, and in 1903 to $3,102,000,000.

The greatest growth, however, is shown in industry. In 1850 there were 123,000 industrial plants with 957,000 employees, paying wages of $236,000,000, and with an output worth $1,019,000,000. In 1870 there were 252,000 factories, with 2 million workmen, paying $775,000,000 in wages, and with an output worth $4,232,000,000; in 1890 there were 3,550,000 factories, 4.7 million workmen, a salary list of $2,283,000,000, and a product worth $9,372,000,000. In 1900 there were 512,000 factories, with 5.7 million workmen, a pay-roll of $273,500,000, and an output worth $13,039,000,000. Statistics here cannot be brought up to the present time, since a careful industrial census is made only every ten years; but this glance over the half century shows at once that there has been a very steady increase, and that it is no mushroom growth due to the recently enacted protective tariffs.

The economic rise of the nation is well reflected in its foreign commerce. If we disregard the imports and exports of precious metals, the international commerce of the United States shows a total import in the year 1903 of $1,025,719,237, and a total export of $1,420,141,679. We must analyze these two figures in several ways, and compare them with similar figures in the past. In one way they show a decrease, since in the year 1903 the exports exceeded the imports by over 394 millions, but in the preceding year by 477 millions. This unfavourable change is not from any decrease in exports, but from a remarkable increase in imports; in fact, the exports were 38 millions more than during the previous year, while the imports were 122 millions more.

Thus, in the year 1903, the total foreign trade of the United States exceeded that of all previous years, and reached the astonishing figure of $2,445,000,000. Although before the year 1900 the total trade was less than two billions, it reached the sum of one billion as early as the year 1872; exports and imports together amounted in 1830 to 134 millions; in 1850 to 317 millions; in 1860 to 687 millions; in 1870 to 828 millions; in 1880 to 1,503 millions; in 1890 to 1,647 millions, and in 1900 to 2,244 millions. During this period the balance of trade shifted frequently. In 1800, for instance, there was an import balance of 21 millions, and similarly in the decades ending in 1810, 1820, and 1830. In the decade which ended in 1840 there was an average export balance of 29 millions. The tables turned in the next decade ending in the year 1850, when there was an average import balance of 29 millions; in the decade ending 1860, of 20 millions, and in the following decade, of 43 millions. But then the exports suddenly increased, and have exceeded the imports for the last twenty-five years. In 1880 the imports were 667 millions, and the exports 835 millions; in 1890 the imports were 789 millions, and the exports 857 millions; in 1900 the imports were 849 millions, and the exports 1,394 millions; in 1901 the imports were 823, and the exports 1,487; in 1902 the imports were 903, and the exports 1,381; and in 1903, as given above, the imports were 1,025, and the exports 1,420 millions.

Let us now look at the American imports more closely. Letting all our figures represent million dollars, we learn that during the last year imports of bread-stuffs and live animals were 212; of raw materials 383; of half-finished products 97; of manufactured products 169, and of articles of luxury in general 145. The food products imported, which comprise to-day 21 per cent. of all imports, comprised 31 per cent. in 1880; and at that time the necessary manufactured articles were also a larger proportion of the whole, being then 20 per cent. against 16 per cent. to-day. On the other hand, raw materials, which were then 25 per cent., are to-day 38 per cent., and articles of luxury have increased from 10 to 14 per cent. of the total imports. Of the half-manufactured products imported, the most important were the chemicals, valued at 38 millions; then come wooden wares worth 11, oil worth 10, iron worth 8, skins and leather worth 5 millions. Of raw materials the most valuable were skins and furs, which amounted last year to 58 millions; raw silk was next, with 50; vegetable fibres, such as hemp, 34; rubber 32, iron and steel 30. This last figure is an exceptional one, and is due to the fact that during the year the American steel industries were taxed to their utmost by consumers' demands. In the year 1902 the iron and steel imports were only 9, and in 1901 only 3 millions. The imports of raw chemicals amounted to 23 millions, and tin the same; wool 21, copper 20; wood 11, and cotton 11.

The exports, arranged according to the sources of production, amounted, last year, to 873 million dollars' worth of agricultural products, 407 of factory products, 57 of products of the forest, 39 of mines, and 7 from fisheries. Of the remainder, 6 millions were from other domestic sources, and 27 had come from other countries. The agricultural exports reached their highest point in 1901, when they amounted to 943, and also the export of manufactured articles is now 3.4 less than in 1901 and 26 less than in 1900. But the statistics of manufactures show sufficiently that there has been no decrease in output, but merely that the home consumption has increased. Apart from these accidental fluctuations of the past three years, the exports have steadily increased. In 1800 the agricultural exports were 25 millions; the industrial 2; in 1850 the former were 108, the latter 17; in 1880 they were 685 and 102 respectively, and in 1900 they were 835 and 433.

If we look at the foreign trade with regard to the countries traded with, we shall find Europe first in both exports and imports. In the year 1903 the imports from Europe to the United States were 547, the exports to Europe 1029; the imports from Canada and Mexico were 189, and the exports thereto 215. From South America the imports were 107, the exports 41; from Asia the imports were 147, the exports 58; from Australia they were 21 and 37, and from Africa 12 and 38.

The trade balances with individual countries in Europe were as follows: England bought from the United States 523 million dollars' worth, and sold the value of 180; then comes Germany, which bought 174 and sold 111; France bought only 70 and sold 87; Austria bought 6 and sold 10; Russia bought 7 and sold the same amount. After England and Germany the best purchaser was Canada, which imported from the United States 123 and exported thereto 54. Germany imports more from the United States than from any other country. Germany imports very much less from Russia, and still less from Austria and Great Britain. Among the countries to which Germany exports her wares the United States has third place, England and Austria having the first and second. America imports from Germany firstly drugs and dye-stuffs, then manufactured cotton, silk, and iron goods, books, pictures, and works of art, clay ware, china, lithographs, toys, etc. No other class amounts to more than 10 million marks.

There is a steady increase in almost every class, and the total imports from Germany were 17 per cent. larger last year than during the year previous; 71 per cent. more than in 1898; 138 per cent. more than in 1880; 198 per cent. more than in 1875, and 343 per cent. more than in 1870.

The principal export of the United States to Germany is cotton. Ten years ago the amount exported was 34 million dollars' worth; in 1901, it was 76; in the following year only 70, but in the year 1903, 84, the amount exported in that year being 957,000,000 pounds. The exports of wheat to Germany amounted in 1896 to only 0.608 million dollars; in the following year to 1.9; in the next year to 3.1; in 1899 to 7.6; and in 1902 to 14.9; but in 1903 to only 11.1. The exports of corn fluctuate still more widely. In the year 1901 Germany bought 17 millions, in 1903 only 6.6. The exportation of petroleum reached its largest figure in 1900, with 8 millions, and in 1893 was 6.3.

Enough of these dry figures. They would look still more striking if compared with the statistics of other countries. More wheat grows in the United States than in any other country, and more corn than in all the other countries put together; more cattle and hogs are slaughtered than in any other country, and three-fourths of the world's cotton harvest is grown in the United States. No other country mines so much coal, petroleum, iron, copper, and lead, or produces so much leather or charcoal. In short, the most important articles entering into manufactures are more plentiful than in any other country of the world. But even on looking over these figures of international trade, one does not get so adequate an impression of the immense economic activity as by actually seeing the wheels of this great machine in motion. One must see the power stations at Niagara, the steel works of Pittsburg, the slaughter-houses of Chicago, the textile factories of New England, the printing-presses of New York, the watch factories of Massachusetts and Illinois, the grain-elevators of Buffalo, the mills of Minneapolis, the locomotive and ship works near Philadelphia, and the water front of New York City, in order to understand the tremendous forces which are constantly at work.

A single factory turns out 1,500 locomotives every year. A Chicago factory which makes harvesting machinery covers 140 acres, employs 24,000 men, and has made two million machines which are now in use. It has fifty ships to bring its wood and iron, and every day loads a hundred freight cars with its finished products. And enterprise on this large scale is found not merely in staple articles, but in more trivial wares. It is a familiar fact that in Germany the large department stores make very slow progress against small shops, while in America the great shops meet at once with popular favour. Their huge advertisements in newspapers and magazines vie with their shop windows in attracting trade. It is nothing uncommon for the manufacturer of a breakfast food or some chemical preparation to spend over a million dollars a year for humorous advertisements. In the *Ladies' Home Journal* one insertion on the advertising pages costs six dollars per line, and the lines are short. A short time ago a soap concern leased the back outside cover of a magazine for a period of time and paid $150,000 therefor.

More impressive, however, than anything that the traveller is able to see to-day is the comparison with what existed yesterday. Our figures have very well shown that the speed of development has been rapid everywhere and sometimes almost explosive. A typical example of this is found in agricultural machinery. The manner of tilling the ground was wholly revolutionized in 1870, when the first ploughing-machine was offered for sale to the American farmer. Since then improvements have been made continually, until to-day every farmer rides on his machines; and the steam-plough, which sows and harrows at the same time, has reduced the amount of time spent on these processes to one-fifteenth of what it formerly was, and the cost of every sheaf of wheat to one-quarter. The machines of to-day sow and fertilize at the same time, and place the seeds at just the desired depth beneath the surface. There are other machines which take the corn from the cob, at the same time cutting up the cobs, and turn out a bushel of corn in a minute, for which a good labourer used to take two hours.

The threshing-flail was abandoned long ago, and the combined mowing and threshing machine is perhaps the most clever invention of all. It cuts the kernels from the stalk, threshes and winnows them, and packs them in bags; and all this as quickly as the horses are able to travel down the field. The machines which separate the cotton from the cotton seed are the only thing that makes it possible to gather a harvest of ten million bales. In former times it took a person about ten hours to remove the seeds from a pound and a half of cotton. The machine cleans 7,000 pounds in the same time.

In just the same way the inventive genius of the American has everywhere increased the output of his factories. His chief aim is to save labour, and hence to devise automatic processes wherever they are possible, so that turning a crank or touching a lever shall accomplish as much as hard work once accomplished. This continual process of invention and improvement, and the fertile resourcefulness of every workman and capitalist, their readiness to introduce every improvement without delay and without regard to expense, have contributed more to the enormous economic progress than all the protective tariff or even than the natural resources of the soil itself.

Extreme jingoes see in this huge growth only the beginning of something yet to come, and in their dreams imagine a day when America shall rule the markets of the world. But no one should be deceived by such ideas. The thoughtful American knows very well that, for instance, the great increase of his export trade has by no means overcome all obstacles. He knows that American wages are high, and that prosperity makes them more so, because the American workman is better able than the European to demand his share of all profits. Also the thoughtful American does not expect to gain the European market by "dumping" his wares. In the apprehension of dull times he may snatch an expedient for getting rid of accumulations which the home market will not take off his hands. In ordinary times industry will not do this, because it knows the demoralizing effect produced on the home country when it is known that the manufacturer is selling more cheaply abroad than at home. The American is afraid of demoralizing the domestic market more than anything else; since, owing to the strong tendency toward industrial imitation, any economic depression spreads rapidly, and can easily cause a general collapse of prices. Even the elaborate pains taken to replace human labour in the American labour-saving machines are often quite made up for by the thoughtless waste of by-products and by the general high-handedness of conducting business.

While America has a tremendous advantage in the fact that coal can be readily brought to the industrial centres, and that the products can be delivered cheaply throughout the country, it stands under the disadvantage that most of its exports are shipped in foreign bottoms, so that the freight charges go to foreigners; for the American merchant-marine is wholly inadequate to the needs of American trade. If America is strong by reason of protective tariff, England intends, perhaps, to remind her daughter country that the American game can be played by two. Protection is no monopoly. While the natural wealth of this country is inexhaustible, the American knows that the largest profits will go to the country which manufactures them; and while the American is energetic and intelligent in getting a foothold in foreign markets, he finds that other nations also have some counterbalancing virtues which he neither has nor can get. First of these is the patience to study foreign requirements, and then the ways of guarding against wastefulness. He has one incomparable advantage, as we have seen — his economic idealism, his belief in the intrinsic value of economic progress, his striving to be economically creative in order to satisfy the restlessness which is in him. The economic drawback of this point of view is not far to seek. The spirit of individual initiative awakens in the workman the demand for equal rights, and intensifies the fight between capital and labour more than in any other country, and puts such chains on industry as are spared to America's competitors in the markets of the world. In short, the thoughtful American knows very well that the markets of the world are to be won for his products only one by one, and that he will meet competitors who are his equals; that there will be difficulties on difficulties, and that the home market from time to time will make heavy imports necessary. He knows that he cannot hope simply to overthrow the industry of all Europe, nor to make the industrial captains of the New World dictators of the earth.

That which he does expect, however, is sure to happen; namely, that the progress of America will be in the future as steady as it has been in the past. The harvests of all the states will not always prosper, nor speculators be always contented with their profits, but the business life of the nation as a whole, unless all signs fail, need fear no setbacks or serious panics.

The United States have gone through six severe crises — in 1814, 1819, 1837, 1857, 1873, and 1893. There is much to indicate that the trite idea of the rhythmical recurrence of crises will be given up henceforth. And although just now, after years of great expansion, contraction is setting in, still the times are not to be compared with preceding crises, and particularly not with the bitter days of 1893. Let us examine what happened in that year. The unhappy experiences of the early nineties resulted naturally from an abnormal expansion of credit. Five or six years of prosperity had gone before, and therewith every industry which contributed to personal gratification was stimulated to excess. An unreasonable craze for building went over the country, and real estate rose constantly. But the country had not developed economically in other directions to a corresponding degree. Too many superfluous undertakings had been started, and houses and lands were everywhere heavily mortgaged. As early as 1890 things began to tremble, and three years later the final crash came. More than 15,000 bankruptcies followed one another during that year, of which the total obligations were $350,000,000; and in the three following years matters were hardly any better. Everything was paralyzed. The farmer was in debt, the artisan out of employment, the miner had to be fed by charity, and since the purchasing power of millions of people was destroyed, there was no one to support industry and trade. It was a veritable economic collapse, with all the symptoms of danger; but the organism recovered without the aid of a physician, by its own healthy reaction, and in such wise that a relapse will hardly take place in the future.

The catastrophe prepared for the return to strength by destroying many business concerns which were not fit to survive, and leaving only the strongest in the field. But this result is, of course, not a lasting one, because in prosperous years all sorts of poor businesses start up again; good years stimulate superfluous production. The permanent result was the lesson which industry learned, in prudence and economy. There is very much in this direction still to be learned, yet the last crisis accomplished a great deal. For instance, in the stock-yards a single company had formerly thrown away annually portions of the animals which would have yielded six million pounds of lime, 30 million pounds of fat, and 105 million pounds of fertilizer, and a few years later the total dividends of that company were paid by the by-products which had been thrown away a short time before. The same thing has happened in the mines and oil-wells, in the fields and in the forests.

Owing to the special gift which the American has for invention, this period brought out a great number of devices looking toward economy. In iron factories and coal mines, and in a thousand places where industry was busy, expenses were cut down and profits were increased, more labour-saving devices were invented, and all sorts of processes were accomplished by ingenious machines. American industry derived advantages from this period in which the nation had to be economical, which it will never outlive.

Although such great economy helps out in bad times, it does not in itself revive trade. It is difficult to say where and how the revival set in, since the most diverse factors must have been at work. But the formation of the great trusts was not a cause of such revival, but merely a symptom of it. The real commencement seems to have been the great harvest which the country enjoyed in the fall of 1897. When wheat was scarce in Russia and India, and therefore throughout the world, America reaped the largest harvest in years, and despite the enormous quantity the European demand carried prices up from week to week. The farmer who in 1894 had received forty-nine cents for each bushel of wheat, now received eighty-one cents, and at the same time had his bins full. Of course there could be only one result. The farmers who had been economizing and almost impoverished for several years became very prosperous, and called for all sorts of things which they had had to go without — better wagons and farming implements, better clothing, and better food. In a country where agriculture is so important, this means prosperity for all industries.

The shops in every village were busy once more, and the large industries again started up one by one. The effect on the railroads was still more important. The good times had stimulated the building of many competing lines of railroad, which were very good for the country, but less profitable to their owners. The lean years just passed had brought great demoralization to these lines. One railroad after another had gone into a receiver's hands, and the service was crippled. Every possible cent was saved and coaches and road-beds were sparingly renewed. Now came an enormous freight demand to carry the great harvest to market, and to serve the newly revived industries. The railroads rapidly recovered; their service was restored. The railroads brought prosperity once more to the iron and steel industries; new rails and ties were absolutely necessary, and the steel industry started forward and set everything else in motion with it. Artisans became prosperous again and further stimulated the industries which they patronized; coal was wanted everywhere, and so the mines awakened to new life.

Then the Spanish War was begun and brought to the nation an unexpected amount of self-confidence, which quickened once more its industrial activity. Such were the internal conditions which made for growth, and the external conditions were equally favourable. In 1898 America harvested 675 million bushels of wheat, and the enormous quantity of 11 million bales of cotton. By chance, moreover, the production of gold increased to $64,000,000; and this, with the enormous sums which foreign countries paid for American grain, considerably increased the money in circulation. This was the time for the stock market to enjoy a similar boom. During the crisis it had nervously withheld from activity and looked with distrust on the West and South, which were now being prospered by great harvests. Everything had formerly been mortgaged in those regions, and from the despair of the Western farmer the ill-advised silver schemes had arisen to fill the eastern part of the country with anxiety. But now the election of McKinley had assured the safety of the currency; the silver issue was laid low; the debts of the Western farmer had been paid within a few years by magnificent crops, and the Western States had come into a healthy state of prosperity. Now the stock markets could pluck up courage. In the stock market of New York in the year 1894 only 49,000,000 shares were bought and sold. In 1897 the market began to recover, and 77,000,000 shares were exchanged; in 1898 there were 112,000,000, and in 1899, 175,000,000 shares.

In the winter of 1898-99 the formation of trusts commenced in good earnest, and this was a glad day for the stock markets.

Large amounts of capital which had been only cautiously offered now sought investment, and since the market quotations could rise more quickly than industries could grow, it was a favourable time for reorganizing industry and making great combinations with a capital proportioned to the happy industrial outlook. In the State of New Jersey alone, a state which specially invited all such organizations by means of its very lenient laws of incorporation, hundreds of such combinations were incorporated with a total nominal capital of over $4,000,000,000. To be sure, in just this connection there was very soon a recoil. In December of 1899, a great many of these watered-stock issues collapsed, although the industries themselves went on unharmed. But this activity of the stock market, in spite of its fluctuating quotations, was of benefit to industrial life.

Meanwhile wealth in town and country increased, owing to the general activity of all factors. In a few years the number of savings-banks accounts was doubled, and railroads had only the one complaint — that they could not get enough cars to carry all the wheat, corn, wood, iron, cattle, coal, cotton, and manufactures offered for transportation. In two years the number of money-orders sent through the post-offices increased by 7 millions, and the number of letters and packages by 361 millions. Now, too, came a time of magnificent philanthropy; private endowments for education and art increased in one year more than $50,000,000.

Along with all this came an increase in foreign trade; here, too, bad times had prepared the way. When the home market was prostrate, industry had sought with great energy to get a footing in foreign markets; and by low prices, assiduous study of foreign demands, and good workmanship, it had slowly conquered one field after another, so that when good times came there was a splendid foundation built for a foreign commerce. America sold bicycles and agricultural machinery, boots, cotton cloth, paper, and watches, and eventually rails, bridges, and locomotives in quantities which would never have been thought of before the panic. And the country became at the same time more than ever independent of European industry. In 1890 America bought $357,000,000 of foreign manufactures and sold of her own only $151,000,000. In 1899 its purchases were $100,000,000 less and its exports nearly $200,000,000 more.

And at the same time, owing to the tremendous crops, the total export of native products reached the sum of $1,233,000,000, and therewith the United States had for the first time reached the highest place among the exporting countries of the world — a position which had formerly belonged to Great Britain. The trade balance of the United States, even in the first year of prosperity, 1898, brought $615,000,000 into the country. The year in which the American Navy, by a rapid succession of victories, demonstrated that the nation was politically a world power, brought the assurance that it was no less a world power commercially. Already the Russian trans-Siberian Railway was using American rails, American companies were building bridges in India, American cotton goods driving out British competition in China, and the movement was still going on. One large harvest followed another.

The wheat harvest in 1901 reached the unprecedented figure of 736 million bushels, and in 1902 of 987 millions. In the same year there were 670 million bushels of barley, and as many as 2,523 million bushels of corn. A corn harvest is almost always profitable, because it keeps and can easily be stored until the right time comes to sell it; and then, too, the farmers are always ready to use it for feed, which further helps its price. Corn has done more than any other harvest to bring wealth into the West. The cotton crop stayed at its ten-million mark, and nearly 70 million barrels of petroleum flowed every year. The demands made on the railroads increased month by month, until finally last year there were weeks in which no freight could be received, because the freight yards were full of unloaded cars. And at the head of everything moved the iron and steel industries. The larger the harvests the more lively was the industry of the country, and the more busy the factories and railroads became the more the iron industry prospered. The manufacture of iron and steel increased steadily, and in 1898 amounted to 11.9 million meter-tons of pig-iron, and 9 million of steel; in 1900, to 14 of pig-iron and 10 of steel; in 1902, to 18 and 15: while the production of the entire earth was only 44 and 36 respectively.

But in spite of this tremendous growth, the prices also rose. Railroads which in the spring had made contracts for new rails were able a few months later to sell their old rails at prices which were 25 per cent. higher than the former price of new rails, because meanwhile the price of steel had risen enormously. If it is true that the iron industry can be taken as an index of national prosperity, there is no doubt at all that prosperity was here. No city in the country experienced such a growth in its banking as Pittsburg, where the banking transactions in 1899 amounted to $1,500,000,000.

This tempestuous expansion in every direction, which lasted from 1897 to 1903, is no longer going on. A counter-movement has set in again. So many factors are at work that it is hard to say where the reaction commenced, although undoubtedly the great coal strikes were the first important indication. The feverish building activity of the country is very largely over, and this decrease has considerably affected the steel industry. Perhaps the refusal of bankers further to countenance the financial operations of the railroads has been an even more important matter. During the years of prosperity the railroads had obtained credit so easily that the scale of expenditure on most railroads had become too lavish, and in particular large sums had been spent in converting railroad shares into bonds. Now the financial world began to react and refused to furnish any more funds, whereon the railroads, which were among the best patrons of the steel industry, had to retrench. And this depressed the state of business, and the otherwise somewhat diminished industry cut down the freight traffic. Other industries had to suffer when the building and iron industries declined. The purchasing power of the working-man has decreased somewhat, and general industry is a trifle dull. This has affected stock quotations, and nervousness in financial circles has been increased by the mishaps and miscalculations of well-known operators. This has worked back in various directions, and so it is natural that pessimists at home and the dear friends of the country abroad have predicted a panic.

But it will not come. The situation has been too largely corrected, and the country has learned a lasting lesson from previous years. When a collapse came in the early nineties, after a time of prosperity and over-expenditure in every sort of undertaking, the national situation was in every way different. There was a great deal of real weakness, and there were many unnecessary and unconservative business ventures on foot. All this is different to-day. The credit which the railroads at that time had overdrawn on had been used to lay thousands of miles of tracks where as yet there was no population. During the recent years of prosperity, on the contrary, the railroads have been extended relatively little, and the expenditures have been mainly for improved equipment and service. The railroads have been made more efficient and substantial, their indebtedness is less, and the considerable contraction of business cannot do them serious harm. Indeed, many persons believe that the great strain which the boom of the last few years has put on the railroads has been a decided disadvantage to them. The excessive traffic has disturbed regular business, increased the danger from accidents, and considerably raised the charges for maintenance. In general, the railroads would prefer a normal to an abnormal traffic demand.

The same is true of industry. Such tremendous pressure as the last few years have brought cannot be borne without loss. The factories were obliged to hire working-men much below the average grade of intelligence, and the slight decline of industrial demand has made it possible to dismiss the inferior men and to keep only the more efficient. Industry itself is to-day like the railroads, thoroughly sound and prosperous, and the small fluctuations in profits are not nearly so great as the declines in market quotations.

Financial operations and labour are largely independent of each other. The output can be undisturbed when the value of shares is being wiped out in the market. American stocks do not represent the actual value of the industrial plants which have been combined to form a trust, but represent in part certain advantages which it is calculated will accrue from the consolidation of business — economies of administration and obviation of competition. The real economic life will not be damaged if such shares, which for the most part have remained in the strong-boxes of the very rich, decline from their fictitious values. Such fluctuations have always happened, and may happen in the very height of prosperity, without doing any harm to industry itself. Thus, for instance, in 1898 an enormous over-speculation commenced in copper shares. Their price was artificially raised and raised, and in the summer of 1899 this house built of share certificates collapsed, and great was the fall thereof; but the price of copper itself was uninfluenced. A pound of copper in the year 1897 brought only the average price of 11 cents; in 1899 its average price was 17 cents, although the copper securities were going down steadily. Not only is industry itself on a sound basis, and the improvements which it introduced in the last panic are not only still in force, but also certain needs have now been met at home which formerly were met only by foreign countries; and at the same time commerce has been so energetically carried into other countries, that there is now a readier outlet than ever in case the domestic purchasing power should again be suspended.

But there are still more important factors. The first of these is the recent and complete independence of this country from European capital. Since year after year the exports of the United States to Europe have exceeded the imports by hundreds of millions of dollars, the debt which Europe so contracted has been paid for the most part by returning the industrial and other bonds which Europe owned against America. It was this which had greatly contributed to the crisis in the early nineties; Europe withdrew her capital. In 1892 the United States paid back $500,000,000 of European capital, and to-day very little is left to pay. In 1893 the United States exported $108,000,000 in gold, but imported only $22,000,000. In the year 1898 the imports of gold to the United States were $105,000,000 more than the exports. Last year the balance was still in favour of the United States; and it would be impossible to-day, in case of any stringency in the money market of the country, for the withdrawal of European capital to precipitate a panic.

Another factor is that the political situation is now certain, as it was not at the time of the last panic. The silver schemes of the West then filled the country with apprehension, whereas to-day there are no such political fears. However the Presidential election may turn out, there will be no dangerous experiments tried with the currency; and even if both parties should mildly oppose the trusts, the nation nevertheless knows that just the formation of these trusts has contributed to the steadiness and security of economic prosperity, that it has done away with unnecessary competition, has brought about an orderly and uniform production, and that although the purchasers of watered stocks may have been bitten, the purchasers of the finished products have suffered little inconvenience.

Then there are two other factors whose significance for economic solidity cannot be overestimated. The first of these is the increasing independence of the agricultural West, and the second is the industrial revival of the South. The financial condition of the New York Stock Exchange to-day no more represents the industrial life of the whole nation, as it did ten years ago. The West, which before the panic of 1893 was up to its ears in debts owned by the East, is now, by reason of six tremendous harvests, prosperous and independent, and its purchasing power and business enterprise are no longer affected by the fluctuations of Wall Street. Even if the shares of all New Jersey corporations should collapse, the nation could continue to buy and sell, produce, manufacture, and transport, because the Western agricultural states would suffer no relapse of prosperity. They have paid off their mortgages and laid money by; the farmer has bought his daughter a parlour organ, sent his sons to college, and bent all his energies to making his West into an economic paradise. Migration has once more set in from the Eastern to the Western States, while during the poor years it had almost stopped; and Western economic influence is asserting itself more and more in the political field.

The same is more or less true of the South. In former times, whenever a cotton harvest brought prosperity, the South still did not take the trouble to utilize its ample resources outside of the plantations. It did not try to mine its coal and iron deposits, nor exploit its forests, nor grow wheat and corn, nor manufacture cotton into cloth, nor the cottonseed into oil. It left all this to the North. But during hard times the South has learned its lesson, and at the time of the last great revival the whole South developed an almost undreamed-of economic activity. The exploitation of forests and coal and iron deposits made great strides, and the factories turned out articles to the value of $2,000,000,000. Cotton is still the staple article of the South, but the bales no longer have to be sent to the North to be made into cloth. As early as 1899 there were 5 million spindles in operation, and the manufacture of cotton has made the South more independent than any number of bales produced for export could have made it.

This economic independence of one another of large sections of the country, and at the same time of European capital, combined with the large increase of commerce with the whole world, the improvement in economic appliances, and a surprising growth in technical science and technical instruction, has created a national economic situation which is so different from that which prevailed in the beginning of the nineties, that there is no analogy to justify the pessimist in predicting another such panic. It had to come at that time. Industrial forces had suffered a serious disaster and had to go back to camp in order to recuperate. Since then they have been striding forward, swerving a little now and then, it may be, to avoid some obstacle, but they are still marching on as they have marched for seven years with firm and steady step, and keeping time with the world-power tune which the national government is playing.

CHAPTER THIRTEEN

The Economic Problems

WE have aimed to speak of the American as he appears in the economic world — of the American in his actual economic life and strife — rather than merely of his inanimate manufactures. That is, we have wished specially to show what forces have been at work in his soul to keep him thus busied with progress. And although we have gone somewhat further, in order to trace the economic uplift of the last decades, nevertheless we have chiefly aimed merely to show the workings of his mind and heart — not the economic history of the American, but the American as little by little he builds that history, has been the point of interest.

Seen from this point of view, everything which stands in the foreground of the actual conflict becomes of secondary interest. The problems leading to party grievances which are solved now one way, now another, and which specially concern different portions of society, different occupations or geographical sections, contribute very little to reveal the traits that are common to all sections, and that must, therefore, belong to the typical American character. If we have given less thought to the political problems of the day than to the great enduring principles of democracy, we need still less concern ourselves with the disputes of the moment in the economic field. The problems of protection, of industrial organization, of bimetallism, and of labour unions are not problems for which a solution can be attempted here.

And nevertheless, we must not pass by all the various considerations which bear on these questions. We might neglect them as problems of American economy; and purely technical matters, like bank reform or irrigation, we shall indeed not discuss. But as problems which profoundly perplex the national mind, exercise its best powers, and develop its Americanism, silver, trusts, tariff, and labour unions require minuter consideration. The life and endeavour of the Americans are not described if their passionate interest in such economic difficulties is not taken into account; not, once more, as problems which objectively influence the developing nation, but as problems which agitate the spirit of the American. An exhaustive treatment is, of course, out of the question, if for no other reason than that it would distort our perspective of things. Had we only the objective side of the problems to consider, we might, perhaps, doubt even whether there were any problems; whether they were not rather simple events, bringing in their train certain obvious consequences, whether deplorable or desirable. These economic problems are, indeed, not in the least problematical. The silver question will not be brought up again; the trusts will not be dissolved; the protective tariff will not be taken off and labour unions will not be gotten rid of. These are all natural processes, rather than problems; but the fact that these events work diversely on men's feelings, are greeted here with delight and there with consternation, and are accompanied by a general chorus of joy and pain, gives the impression that they are problems. This impression seizes the American himself so profoundly that his own reaction comes to be an objective factor of importance in making history. It is not to be doubted that the course of these much-discussed economic movements is considerably influenced by prejudices, sentiments, and hobbies.

The Silver Question

Perhaps the power of mere ideas — of those which are clear, and, even more, those which are confused — is shown in none of these problems more strongly than in the silver question. If any problem has been really solved, it is this one; and still no one can say that it has dropped out of the American mind, although, for strategic reasons, politicians ignore it. The sparks of the fire still glow under the ashes of two Presidential campaigns. The silver schemes have too strongly fixed public attention to be so quickly forgotten, and any day may see them revive again. Just here the possibility of prejudices which would not profit by experience has been remarkably large, since the question of currency involves such complicated conceptions that fallacious arguments are difficult to refute. And such a situation is just the one where the battle of opinions can be waged the hottest: the silver question has, in fact, more excited the nation than any other economic problem of the last ten years. And there can be no doubt that many valid arguments have been urged on the wrong side, and some untenable theses on the right side.

The starting-point of the discussion lay in the law of 1873, which, for the first time in the United States, excluded silver coin from the official currency. There had already been differences of opinion before the passage of this law. The friends of silver say that in 1792 the United States permitted the coinage of both silver and gold without limit, and that silver was the actual monetary standard. And, although by accidents of production the relative value of the precious metals, which had been 15 to 1, later became 16 to 1, nevertheless the two metals continued to be regarded equally important until the surreptitious crime of 1873. It was a secret crime, they say, because the law was debated and published at a time when the nation could have no clear idea of what it meant. The Civil War had driven gold coin out of the country, every one was using paper, and no one stopped to ask whether this paper would be redeemed in gold or silver, and no one was accustomed to seeing gold coins in circulation. General Grant, who was President at that time, signed the bill without any suspicion that it was anything more than a technical measure, much less that it was a criminal hold-up of the nation on the part of the rich. And great was the disaster; for the law demonetized silver, brought a stringency of gold, lowered prices tremendously, depressed the condition of the nation, and brought the farmers to poverty, so it was said.

The opponents of bimetallism recognize no truth in this story. They say that in the first third of the nineteenth century the silver dollar was counted equal to the gold dollar, at the ratio of 15 ounces to 1 ounce of metal; but since this ratio did not continue to correspond with the market price, and the gold of the country went to Europe, because it there brought a better value, the official ratio was changed as early as 1834 to 16 to 1. This rate put a small premium on gold, and virtually established a gold standard for American currency. The owners of silver mines no longer had silver coined in the country, because they could get more money for their silver bars abroad; and so, as a matter of fact, during the next decade only 8 million silver dollars were coined, and this denomination virtually went out of circulation. Only the fractional silver currency could be kept in the country, and that only by resorting to the trick of making the coins proportionately lighter than the legal weight of the silver dollar.

The currency became, therefore, to all intents and purposes, a gold one, and nobody was discontented with it, because silver was then less mined. From 1851 to 1855, for instance, the average silver production of the United States was only $375,000, while that of gold was $62,000,000. Then came the lean years of the Rebellion. The government borrowed from the banks, in the autumn of 1861, $100,000,000 in gold, and in the following year issued $150,000,000 of unsecured greenbacks. Thereupon the natural laws of exchange drove all sound currency out of the country, and $150,000,000 more greenbacks were soon issued. The premium on gold went higher and higher, and reached its highest point in 1864, when the price was 185 per cent. of the normal value. After the war confidence was restored, the paper dollar rose from 43 to 80 cents; but the quantity of paper in circulation was so tremendous that metallic money was never seen, and not until the early seventies did conditions become solid enough for the treasury to take steps to redeem the greenbacks.

But this was just the time when all the civilized nations were adopting the gold standard — a time in which the production of gold had become incredibly large. The two decades between 1850 and 1870 had brought five times as much gold bullion into the world as the preceding two decades, and the leading financiers of all countries were agreed that it was high time to make gold the universal standard of exchange. The general movement was begun in the conference of 1867 held in Paris. Germany led in adopting the gold standard; the United States followed in 1873. The gold dollar, which since the middle of the century had been the actual standard of American currency, became now the official standard, and silver coinage was discontinued. There was nothing of secrecy or premeditated injustice, for the debates lasted through several sessions of Congress.

If, nevertheless, the so-called crime remained unnoticed, and so many Senators failed to know what they were doing, this was not because the transactions went on in secret, nor because the use of paper money had made every one forget the problems of metallic currency, but rather because no one felt at that time that he would be injured by the new measure, although the attention of everybody had been called to the discussions. The owners of silver mines themselves had no interest in having their mineral made into coin, and no one was disturbed to see silver go out of circulation. All the trouble and all the hue and cry about a secret plot did not commence until several years later, when, for entirely independent reasons, circumstances had considerably changed. The step had been taken, however, and the principle has not been repudiated. The unlimited coinage of silver has not been permitted by the United States since 1873.

Nevertheless, silver was destined soon again to become regular currency. Hard times followed the year 1873, prices fell and the value of silver fell with them, and bimetallic coinage had been discontinued. Bimetallists connected these facts, and said that the price of silver fell because the commercial world had stopped coining it. For this reason the only other coined metal, which was gold, became dear, which meant, of course, that prices became cheap, and that the farmer got a low price for his harvests. And thus the population was driven into a sort of panic.

A ready expedient was suggested: it was to coin silver once more, since that would carry off the surplus and raise the price; while on the other hand, the increased amount of coin in circulation would bring prices up and restore the prosperity of the farmers and artisans. This is the main argument which was first heard in 1876, and was cried abroad with increasing loudness until twenty years later it was not merely preached, but shouted by frenzied masses, and still in 1900, misled the Democratic party. But the desire for an increased medium of circulation is by no means the same as the demand for silver coinage. After the Civil War the public had demanded more greenbacks just as clamorously as it now demanded silver. It was also convinced that nothing but currency was needed to make high values, no matter what the value of the currency itself.

So far as these main facts are concerned, which have been so unjustly brought into connection, there can be no doubt that the depreciation of silver was brought about only in very small part by the coinage laws. To be sure, the cessation of silver coinage by several large commercial powers had its effect on the value of silver; but India, China, and other countries remained ready to absorb large amounts of silver for coinage; and in fact the consumption of silver increased steadily for a long time. The real point was that the production of silver increased tremendously at just the time when the production of gold was falling off. From 1851 to 1875, $127,000,000 worth of gold on an average was mined annually, but from 1876 to 1890 the average was only $108,000,000; while, on the other hand, the average production of silver in those first twenty-five years was only $51,000,000, but in the following fifteen years came up to $116,000,000. The output of gold therefore decreased 15 per cent., while that of silver increased 127 per cent. Of course, then silver depreciated. Now the future was soon to show that increased coinage of silver would not raise its price. Above all, it was an arbitrary misconstruction to ascribe bad times to the lack of circulating medium. Later times have shown that, under the complicated credit system of the country, prices do not depend on the amount of legal tender in circulation in the industrial world. The speed of circulation is a factor of equal importance with the amount of it; and, most important of all, is the total credit, which has no relation to the amount of metallic currency. When more money was coined it remained for the time being unused, and could not be put in circulation until the industrial situation recovered from its depression.

Thus the bad times of the seventies were virtually independent of coinage legislation: but public agitation had set in, and as early as 1878 met with considerable success. In that year the so-called Bland Bill was passed, over the veto of President Hayes, which required the treasury of the United States to purchase and coin silver bars to the value of not less than 2 million, and not more than four million, dollars every month. This measure satisfied neither the one side nor the other. The silverites wanted unlimited coinage of silver; for, if a limit was put, the standard was still gold, even though the price of silver should be somewhat helped. The other side saw simply that the currency of the country would be flooded with depreciated metal, and one which was really an unofficial and illegal circulating medium. It was known that the silver, after being coined into dollars, would be worth more than its market value, and it was already predicted that all the actual gold of the country would be taken abroad and replaced by silver. The "gold bugs" also saw that this legislation would artificially stimulate the mining of silver if there should actually be any increase in its price.

The new law was thus a bad compromise between two parties, although to many it seemed like a safe middle way between two dangers. Some recognized in the unlimited coinage of silver the dangers of a depreciated currency, but believed that the adoption of the gold standard would be no less dangerous, because gold was too scarce to satisfy the needs of the commercial world. It was said that free silver would poison the social organism and free gold would strangle it, and that limited silver coinage, along with unlimited gold coinage, would therefore be the only safe thing.

But it soon appeared that such legal provisions would have no effect in restoring the value of the white metal. Although the government facilitated in every way the circulation of the new silver coins, they nevertheless came back to the treasury. No matter how many silver dollars were distributed as wages, they found their way at once to the retail shops, then to the banks, and then to Washington. It appeared that the nation could not keep more than sixty or seventy million dollars' worth in circulation, while there were already more than $400,000,000 lying idle in Washington. The banks boycotted silver at first; but the more important fact was that the price of silver did not rise, but kept on falling. It was the amount produced and naturally consumed, and not the amount coined, which regulated the price of silver. In the year 1889 the relative values of silver and gold were as 22 to 1; and the true value of the silver dollar coined under the Bland Bill was only seventy-two cents. Congress now proposed to take a more serious measure looking toward a higher price for silver.

In July, 1890, a law was passed whereby the treasury was obliged to buy four and one-half million ounces of silver every month at the market price, and against this to issue treasury certificates to the corresponding amount, which should be redeemable either in gold or silver; since, as that law declared, the United States asserted the equal status of the two metals. The law did not prescribe the number of silver certificates which were to be issued, since the weight of silver to be purchased was fixed and the value of it depended on the market. Only a few months afterward it became clear that even this energetic stroke would not much help the price of silver. The silver and gold dollars would have been really equal to each other if an ounce of silver had brought a market price of $1.29. In August, 1890, silver came up to $1.21 an ounce, and fell the next year to $1.00, and in 1892 to $0.85. But while the price of silver was falling, gold was rapidly leaving the country.

In April, 1893, the gold reserve of the treasury fell for the first time below the traditional hundred millions. It was a time of severe economic depression. The silverites still believed that the rise of silver had not commenced because its purchase was restricted to monthly installments, and they clamoured for unlimited purchases of silver. But the nation opposed this policy energetically. President Cleveland called an extra session of Congress, and after a bitter fight in the Senate, the law providing for the purchases of silver and issue of silver certificates was repealed, in November of 1893. The Democratic party had split on this measure, and then arose the two divisions, the Gold Democrats who followed Cleveland, and the Silver Democrats who found a leader a year later in Bryan, and dictated the policy of the Democratic party for the following decade.

Looking on American economic history from the early seventies to the middle nineties without prejudice, one cannot doubt not only that the entire legislation relative to coinage has had scarcely any influence on the price of gold and silver — since the price of silver has fallen steadily in spite of the enormous amounts purchased — but also that the general industrial situation, the movement of prices, and the volume of business have been very little affected by these financial measures.

The strongest influence which they have had has been a moral one. Business became active and foreign commerce revived as soon as the confidence in the American currency was restored.

This result, of course, contradicted the expectations and wishes of the apostles of silver. International confidence declined in proportion as a legal tender standing for a depreciated metal was forced into circulation. It was not the amount of silver, but the fear of other countries as to what that amount might become, which most injured American commerce. And the great achievement of Cleveland's Administration was to reassure the world of our solidity.

Otherwise the economic fluctuations depended on events which were very little related to the actual amount of gold on hand. If, in certain years, the amount of circulation increased, it was the result rather than the cause of industrial activity; and when, in other years, a speculative movement collapsed, less money was used afterward, but the shortage of money did not cause the collapse. Then, too, harvests were sometimes good and at other times bad, and foreign commerce changed in dependence on quite external events in Europe. There were, moreover, certain technical improvements in agricultural and industrial processes which rapidly lowered prices and which took effect at independent times and seasons.

The year 1893 was a time in which a great many factors worked in one direction. The overbuilding of railways and a too great expansion of iron industries had been followed by a terrible reaction; a surplus of commodities on all the markets of the world caused prices to fall, and the international distrust of silver legislation in the United States made the situation worse. European capital, on which all undertakings then depended, was hurriedly withdrawn; thousands of businesses failed, and small men fell into debt. The actual panic did not last long, and Cleveland's successful move of 1893 restored the international confidence. But the situation of the general public was not so readily improved. This was the psychological moment in which the silver question, which had hitherto interested relatively restricted circles, so suddenly came to excite the entire nation that in 1896 the main issue of the Presidential campaign was silver or gold currency. The silver craze spread most rapidly among the farmers, who had suffered more from overproduction than had the manufacturers. The manufacturer sold his wares more cheaply, but in greater quantities, because he improved his methods, and, moreover, he bought his raw materials more cheaply. But the fall in the prices of wheat and corn and other agricultural products which affected the farmer was only in small part due to more intensive cultivation, but rather to the greater area of land which had been planted. The farmer in one state was not benefited by the fact that great areas in some other state were now for the first time laid down to wheat and corn. As prices fell he produced no more, and thus agriculture suffered more severely than industry. While the farmer was able to get for two sheaves of wheat only as much as he used to get for one, he thought, of course, that his patrons had too little money, and was readily convinced that if more money could only be coined, he would get good prices again.

There was another argument in addition to this, which could still even more easily be imposed on the ignorant, and not only on the farmer, but on all classes that were in debt. Silver was cheaper than gold, and if debts were paid in it the creditor lost and the debtor won. It was at this time that the conflict of interests between the great capitalists and the labouring masses began to arouse political excitement. Distrust found its way into a good part of the population, and finally a hatred of capitalists and monopolies, and of the stock market most of all.

This hatred vented itself in a mad clamour for silver. If Congress would authorize an unlimited silver coinage at the ratio of 16 to 1, while the market ratio was down to 33 to 1 — so that the silver dollar would be worth hardly fifty cents, and so that the farmer could sell his wheat or maize for a dollar when it was really worth but half a dollar — then at last the robbers on the stock exchange would be well come up with. In reality, these two arguments contradicted each other, for the farmer would be benefited by more silver money only if the market value of silver could be brought up to that of gold; while he would be favoured in the payment of debts only if gold could be brought down to the value of silver. But once let there be any sort of distress, and any ghost of relief haunting the general mind, then logic is totally forgotten. A new faith arises, the power of which lies in suggestion. The call for free-silver coinage at the old ratio of 16 to 1 fascinated the agricultural masses as well as the lower classes in cities, just as the idea of a future state of socialism fascinates German working-men to-day.

And just as one cannot understand the German people without taking into account their socialistic delusions, so one cannot understand the American masses to-day without tracing out the course of the silver propaganda. It was the organizing power of a watchword which gave the delusion such significance, and which, for perhaps the first time, gave voice to the aversion which the masses felt toward the wealthy classes; and so, like the socialistic movement in Germany, it took effect in far wider circles than the points over which the discussion started would have justified.

But the masses could hardly be stirred up to such a powerful agitation merely on the basis of the specious arguments spread about by ignorant fanatics, or even with the substantial support of the indebted farmer. In the middle nineties the literature of the silver question swelled enormously. A mere appeal to the passions of those who hated capital would not have been enough, and even the argument that the amount of money in a country alone regulates prices could have been refuted once for all. A financial and an intellectual impetus were both necessary to the agitation, and both were to be had. Distinguished political economists saw clearly certain unfairnesses and evils in a simple gold standard, and urged many an argument for bimetallism which the masses did not wholly follow, but which provided material for general discussion. And financial aid for the silver side flowed freely from the pockets of those who owned silver mines. Of course, there was no doubt that these mine-owners would be tremendously prospered by any radical legislation for silver. In the days of the Bland Bill even the poorest silver mines were in active operation, whereas now everything was quiet. The discussions which ostensibly urged the right of the poor man against the rich said nothing at all of the deep schemes of the silver-mine owners. These men did not urge their claims openly, but they paid their money and played the game shrewdly.

We have already fully compared the political traits of the two parties; and it will be understood at once that the contest for silver, as a movement for the rights of the poor man against those of the capitalist, would have to be officially waged by the Democratic party, while the Republican party would, of course, take the other side. The nation fought out the great battle in two heated Presidential campaigns; and in 1896 as well as in 1900, the contest was decided in favour of the gold currency. The currency legislation of the Republican Congresses has held to a conservative course. In March, of 1900, the treasury was instructed, on demand, to redeem all United States notes in gold, so that all the money in circulation came to have absolutely the same value. The old silver certificates, of which to-day $450,000,000 are in circulation, can at any time be exchanged for gold coin, and the Secretary of the Treasury was entirely right in showing in his last annual report that it was this wise provision alone which obviated a panic at the time when stock market quotations dropped so suddenly in the year 1903. Thus the finances of the country are definitely on a gold basis.

But, as we have said, we are not interested in the material aspects of the currency situation, and still less shall we undertake a profound discussion of bimetallism, as scientific circles are to-day considering it. The significance of a limited double standard, especially in view of the commerce with the East, and of the effect it will have in quieting the international struggle to get the yellow metal, is much discussed by thoughtful persons. The United States have sent a special commission to visit other countries in order to persuade them that some international agreement as to the monetary recognition of silver is desirable.

All this does not interest us. We care for the silver question only as a social movement. No other problem has so profoundly moved the nation; even the questions of expansion and imperialism have so far aroused less general interest. It is only too likely that if hard times return once more, the old craze will be revived in one form or another. The silver intoxication is not over to-day, and the western part of the country is merely for the moment too busy bringing its tremendous crops to harvest, and carrying its gold back home, to think of anything else.

The Tariff Question

The silver question, which was of such great significance yesterday, was very complicated, and only very few who discussed it knew all the difficulties which it involved. This is not true of the tariff question, which may at any time become the main political issue. As the problem of protective tariff is generally discussed, it involves only the simplest ideas.

The dispute has come from a conflict of principle and motive, but not from any difference of opinion as to the effect of protective measures. Here and there it has been maintained, as it has in other countries, that the foreigner pays the tariff; and this argument has, indeed, occasioned keen and complicated discussions. But, for the most part, no academic questions are involved, rather conditions merely which are obvious to all, but toward which people feel very differently, according to their occupation, geographical position, and political convictions. The struggle is not to be conceived as one between protective tariff and free trade, but rather as between more or less protective tariff — since, in spite of variations, the United States have, from the very outset, enacted a tariff greater than the needs of the public treasury, with the idea of protecting domestic labour from foreign competition.

Indeed, it can be said that the policy of protection belongs even to the prehistory of the United States, and that it has contributed measurably to building up the Union. While America was an English colony, England took care to suppress American industries; agriculture and trade were to constitute the business of the colonists. The War for Independence altered the situation, and native industries began to develop, and they had made a brave start in many states before the war was ended. But as soon as the ties with England had been broken, the separate states manifested diverse interests, and interfered in their trade with one another by enacting customs regulations. It looked as if a tariff war on American soil would be the first fruits of freedom from the common oppressor. There was no central power to represent common interests, to fix uniform revenues for the general good, and uniform protection for the industry of the country. And when one state after another was persuaded to give up its individual rights to the Federation, one of the main considerations was the annulment of such interstate customs, which were hindering economic development, and the establishment of a uniform protection for industry. The tariff law of 1789 contained, first of all, such provisions as ensured the necessary public revenue, tariff on goods in whose manufacture the

Americans did not compete; and then other tariffs which were meant to protect American industries.

So, at the outset, the principle of protective tariff was made an official policy by the United States; and since, through the highly diversified history of more than eleven decades, the nation has still held instinctively to this policy, we can hardly doubt that the external and internal conditions under which the country has stood have been favourable to such a policy. The tremendous natural resources, especially of iron, copper, lumber, fur, cotton, wool, and other raw materials, and the inexhaustible supply of energy in the coal-fields, oil-wells, and water-falls, have afforded the material conditions without which an industrial independence would have been impossible. The optimistic American has found himself in this land of plenty with his energy, his inventive genius, and his spirit of self-determination. It was predestined that the nation should not only till the fields, produce raw materials, and engage in trade, but that it should set stoutly to work to develop its own industries. Therefore, it seemed natural to pass laws to help these along, although the non-industrial portions of the country, and all classes which were not engaged in industry, were for a time inconvenienced by higher prices.

Once launched, the country drifted further and further in the direction of protective duties. In 1804 a tariff was enacted on iron and on glassware, with unquestionably protective intent. It is true that, in general, the principal increases in the beginning of the century were planned to accelerate the national income. The War of 1812 especially caused all tariffs to be doubled. But this war stirred up patriotism and a general belief in the abilities of the nation. Native industries were now supported by patriotic enthusiasm, so that in 1816 the duties on cotton and woollen goods and on manufactured iron were increased for the sake of protection. And the movement went on. New tariff clauses were enacted, and new friends won over, often in their own selfish interests, until the early thirties. The reaction started in the South, which profited least from the high tariff. Compromises were introduced, and many of the heaviest duties were taken off. By the early forties, when the movement lapsed, duties had been reduced by about 20 per cent.

At this time the divided opinions in favour of raising or lowering duties commenced to play an important part in politics. Protective tariff and tariff reduction were the watchwords of the two parties. In 1842 the Protectionist party got the reins of government, and at once put heavy duties on iron, paper, glass, and cotton and woollen goods. Four years later, tariffs were somewhat reduced, owing to Democratic influences; but the principle of protection was still asserted, as is shown by the fact that tea and coffee, which were not grown in the country, were not taxed, while industrial manufactured articles were taxed on the average 30 per cent. The Democrats continued to assert their influence, and won a victory here and there. Wool was admitted free in 1857. Then came bad times. After a severe commercial crisis, imports decreased and therewith the customs revenues. The demand for high tariff then increased, and the Republicans got control of Congress, and enacted in the year 1861 the Morrill Tariff, which, although strongly protective, was even more strongly a Republican party measure. It aimed to discriminate in protecting the industries of those states which the Republican party desired to win over. Then came the Civil War, the enormous expense of which required all customs and taxes to be greatly increased.

The war tariff of 1864 was enacted for the sake of revenue, but its effect was decidedly protective. And when the war was over, and tariffs might have been reduced so far as revenue went, industries were so accustomed to the artificial protection that no one was willing to take off duties. Some customs, even such as those on woollen and copper, were considerably increased in the next few years, while those on coffee and tea were again entirely removed.

In general, it was a time of uncertain fluctuations in the tariff until the year 1883, when the whole matter was thoroughly revised. In certain directions, the customs were lowered; in others, increased. Specially the higher grades of manufactured articles were put under a higher tariff, while the cheaper articles used by the general public were taxed more lightly. A short time after this, President Cleveland, as leader of the Free-Trade Democrats, came out with a famous message against protection. The unexpected result was, that after the tariff question had thus once more been brought to the front, the Republicans gained a complete victory for their side, and enacted a tariff more extreme than any which had gone before, and which protected not only existing industries, but also such as it was hoped might spring up. Even sugar was now put on the free list, because it had been taxed merely for revenue, and not for protection. While, on the other hand, almost all manufactured articles which were made in the country were highly protected. This was specially the case with velvet, silk, woollen, and metal goods. This was the well-known McKinley Tariff.

The Democrats won the next election, although not on the issue of industrial legislation, and as soon as they came into power they upset the high tariffs. Their Wilson Tariff Bill of 1894, the result of long controversies, showed little internal consistency. Too many compromises had been found necessary with these or those influential industries in order to pass the bill at all. Yet, on the whole, customs were considerably lowered, and for the first time in a long while raw materials, such as wool, were put on the free list. But Democratic rule did not last long. McKinley was victorious in 1896, and in the following year the Dingley Tariff was passed in accordance with Republican ideas of protection, and it is still in force.

The total revenues derived from this source in the year 1902 were $251,000,000, and in 1903 were $280,000,000. Let us analyze the first amount. Its relative importance in the total revenue may be seen from the fact that the internal duties on liquor, tobacco, etc., amounted to $271,000,000, and that the postal budget for the year was $121,000,000. The customs duties of $251,000,000 are officially divided into five classes. The first is live animals and breadstuffs, with sugar at the head bringing in $52,000,000. The sugar duty had not existed ten years before, but the Wilson Tariff of 1894 could not have been enacted if the beet-sugar Senators from Louisiana had not been tossed a bone. In 1895 the revenue on sugar amounted to $15,000,000, and in 1901 to $62,000,000. After sugar, in this year of 1903, came fruits and nuts with 5, vegetables with 3, meat, fish, and rice with only 1 million dollars each. The second class comprises raw materials. Wool yielded 10.9, skins 2.6, coal 1 million dollars, and every other class still less. In the third class are the semi-manufactured products, with chemicals yielding 5.4, tin plate 2.9, wooden-ware 1.8, silk 1.1, and fur 1 million dollars. The fourth class comprises finished products. Linen goods yielded 14, woollen goods 13, cotton goods 10, metallic wares 6, porcelain 5.6, leather goods 3.1, and wooden and paper wares each 1 million dollars. Articles of luxury make the last class, with tobacco bringing 18.7, silk goods 16, laces 13, alcoholic drinks 10, jewelry 2.4, feathers 1.4, and toys 1.3 million dollars. The total imports for the year were $903,000,000, of which $396,000,000 entered free of duty; but of these last only 10 per cent. were half or wholly finished products, 90 per cent. being food or raw materials. The duty was collected from imports worth $507,000,000, and 64 per cent. came from manufactured articles. Thus the Dingley Tariff was a complete victory for protection.

No one now asks to have the duties raised, but the Democratic party is trying all the time to have them lowered, so that the question is really whether they shall be lower or remain where they are. Of course, the Republicans have a capital argument which looks unanswerable — success. The history of American protection, they say, is the history of American industrial progress. The years during which native industry has been protected from foreign competition by means of heavy duties have been the times of great development, and years of depression, disaster, and panic have regularly followed whenever free-traders have removed duties. The tariff has never been higher than under the McKinley and the Dingley bills, and never has the economic advance been more rapid or forceful. What is the use, they say, of representing to the working-man that he could buy a suit so much cheaper if the tax on woollen goods were removed? For if it were, and free-trade were to be generally adopted, he would go about without employment, his wife and children would be turned out into the street, and he would be unable to buy even the cheapest suit. Whereas to-day, he is well able to pay the price which is asked. The wealth of fancy with which this sort of argument is constantly varied, and tricked out with word and phrase suited to every taste, is almost overpowering. But the alternative between the high wage which can afford to pay for the expensive suit, and the lower wage which cannot afford to pay for the cheap suit, becomes still more cogent since the fanatical protectionist is able to prove that under a high tariff wages have in fact risen, while the price of the suit has not. Yet the extreme free-trader can prove, with equal certainty, that under free-trade the suit would actually be much cheaper, while wages would in the end be even higher.

It cannot be doubted that a number of industries are to-day very prosperous which could not have gotten even a foot-hold except by a century of protection. And no Democrat denies this. But he doubts whether the hot-house forcing of such industries has benefited the country, and he believes that the artificial perpetuation of great industrial combinations, which have been able, by means of a protective tariff, to put an artificially high price on the food and other necessary articles used by the masses, has worked infinitely more harm than good.

It is undoubtedly true that many industries have not only been protected, but have actually been created. The tin plate industry is, perhaps, the best example of this. The United States used to obtain the tin plates needed in industry from Wales, and at unreasonably high prices. Twice the Americans tried to introduce the industry at home, but were at once undersold by the English and "frozen out." Then the McKinley Tariff put a duty on tin plate of 70 per cent. ad valorem, and the American industry was able to make headway. In 1891, 1,036 million pounds of tin plate were imported, and none was produced at home; two years later only 628 million pounds were imported, and 100 million pounds manufactured at home; and ten years later only 117 million pounds came over the sea, while 894 million pounds were produced in this country. It has been much the same in the manufacture of watches. The United States imported all their watches a few years ago. They were then taxed 10 per cent. for revenue, being accounted articles of luxury, and could not be profitably made inside the country. But when Congress taxed them 25 per cent., the industry grew up. It produced at first watches after European models; but American ingenuity soon came to be extended to this field, improved machinery for the manufacture of watches was devised, and now a tremendous industry provides every American schoolboy with a watch which is better and cheaper than the corresponding European article. Even the silk industry may well be considered the foster child of protection.

The free-traders reply, that all this may have been very well for a period of transition from an agricultural to an industrial state; but that the great change has now been completed, and the burdensome duties which keep our prices high might perfectly well be dropped, since our industries are now strong enough to compete with foreign industries.

But just at this point the Republican comes out less optimistically than before. He says that American industry has indeed developed with fabulous speed, and that the industrial exports of the country, which now amount to 30 per cent. of the total, are a great showing, but this is a symptom which ought not to be overrated. When prices throughout the rest of the world fell, and England was paralyzed for the moment, although the domestic demand had not yet reached its height, conditions combined so favourably, it is true, as to cause the export trade in American manufactured articles to increase rapidly. But this may not be permanent. Industry is still not able to fill all the demands of the home market; on the contrary, at the very time when American iron and steel industries seemed likely to conquer foreign markets, it was found that some sudden increase in domestic requirements necessitated large importations. While the iron and steel exports decreased by $25,000,000 between 1900 and 1903, the imports during the same time increased $31,000,000, and iron and steel include mostly unfinished products.

Thus even the strongest and most powerful industries greatly need protection still against foreign competition. It is, Thomas Reed has said, entirely mistaken to look on protection as a sort of medicine, to be left off as soon as possible. It is not medicine, but nourishment. The high tariff has not only nursed infant industries, but it is to feed them through life. For it is not a happy expedient, but a system which is justified by its results, and of which the final import is that the American market is for the American people. Protection is a wall behind which the American people can carry on their industrial life, and so arrange it that wages shall be not only absolutely but relatively greater than wages in Europe.

At a time when everything looked so prosperous as in the last few years of industrial activity, it is difficult to contest the powerful argument which the Republicans make in appealing to success.

Every one is afraid that a change in tariff might turn back this tide. And if there have been reverses in the last few years it has been pointed out that speculators and corporation magnates have been the chief sufferers, and they are the ones who, least of all, would wish the tariffs removed.

It has been an unfavourable time, therefore, for the free-traders, and their really powerful party has been rather faint-hearted in its fight against the Dingley Tariff. Its satisfaction with the Wilson Tariff was not unmixed, and although it could truthfully say that the law as actually passed was not a Democratic measure since it received six hundred and forty amendments in the Senate, nevertheless it realizes that the legislative measures of the last Democratic régime pleased nobody thoroughly and contributed a good deal to the subsequent Republican victory.

Nevertheless, the Democrats feel that the Republican arguments are fallacious. It is not the protective tariff, they say, which has brought about American prosperity, but the natural wealth of the country, together with the energy and intelligence of its inhabitants. The high level of education, the free government, the pioneer ardour of the people, and the blessings of quick and rapid railway connections have made America great and prosperous. If, indeed, any legal expedients have been decisive in producing this happy result, these have been the free-trade measures, since the Republicans quite overlook the fact that the main factor making for our success has been the absolute free-trade prevailing between the forty-five states. What would have become of American industries if the states had enacted tariffs against one another, as the country does against the rest of the world, and as the countries of Europe do against one another? The entire freedom of trade from Maine to California, and from Canada to Mexico, that is, the total absence of all legislative hindrances and the possibility of free exchange of natural products and manufactures without payment of duties, has made American industry what it is; and it is the same idea which the Democrats cherish for the whole world. They desire to get for America the advantages from free-trade which England has derived.

All the well-known free-trade arguments — moral, political, and economic — are then urged; and it is shown, again and again, that every nation will succeed best in the long run by carrying on only such industries as it is able to in free competition with the world. It is true, admittedly, that if our tariff were removed a number of manufactures would have to be discontinued, and that the labourers would for a time be without work, as happens whenever a new machine is discovered, or whenever means of transportation are facilitated. The immediate effect is to take labour from the workman. But in a short time adaptation takes place, and in the end the new conditions automatically provide a much greater number of workmen with profitable employment than before. America would lose a part of the home market if she adopted free-trade, but would be able to open as many more doors to foreign countries as recompense. Her total production would in the end be greater, and all articles of consumption would be cheaper, so that the workmen could buy the same wares with a less amount of labour, and the adjustment of the American scale of wages would better enable the Americans to compete with the labour of other countries.

But no doubt the times do not favour such logic. The Americans are too ready to believe the statement of Harrison, that the man who buys a cheaper coat is the cheaper man. And quite too easily the protectionists reply to all arguments against excluding foreign goods with the opposite showing that, in spite of the high tariff, the imports from abroad are steadily increasing. Under the Dingley Tariff, in the year 1903, not only the raw materials, but also the half and wholly manufactured articles, and articles of luxury, imported increased to a degree which had never been reached in the years of the Wilson Tariff. The raw materials imported under a Democratic tariff reached their high point in 1897, with $207,000,000; when the Dingley Tariff was adopted the figure decreased to $188,000,000, but then rose rapidly and amounted in 1902 to $328,000,000, and in 1903 to $383,000,000. Finished products declined at first from $165,000,000 to $94,000,000, but increased in 1903 to $169,000,000. Articles of luxury sank from $92,000,000 to $74,000,000, but then mounted steadily until in the year 1903 they were at the unprecedented figure of $145,000,000.

In spite of this, the Democratic outlook is improving; not because people incline to free-trade, but because they feel that the tariff must be revised, that certain duties must be decreased, and others, so far as reciprocity can be arranged with other countries, abolished. Everybody sees that the international trade balance of last year shows a movement which cannot keep on. America cannot, in the long run, sell where she does not buy. She will not find it profitable to become the creditor of other nations, and will feel it to be a wiser policy to close commercial treaties with other nations to the advantage of both sides. Reciprocity is not a theory of the Democratic party merely, but is the sub-conscious wish of the entire nation, as may be concluded from the fact that McKinley's last great speech voiced this new desire.

He had, more than any one else, a fine scent for coming political tendencies; and his greatness always consisted in voicing to-day what the people would be coming to want by to-morrow. On the fifth of September, 1901, at the Buffalo Exposition, he made a memorable speech, in which he said: "We must not repose in fancied security that we can forever sell everything and buy little or nothing. If such a thing were possible, it would not be best for us or for those with whom we deal. We should take from our customers such of their products as we can use without harm to our industries and labour. Reciprocity is the natural outgrowth of our wonderful industrial development under the domestic policy now firmly established. What we produce beyond our domestic consumption must have a vent abroad. The excess must be relieved through a foreign outlet, and we should sell anywhere we can and buy wherever the buying will enlarge our sales and productions, and thereby make a greater demand for home labour. The period of exclusiveness is past. The expansion of our trade and commerce is the pressing problem. Commercial wars are unprofitable. A policy of good will and friendly trade relations will prevent reprisals. Reciprocity treaties are in harmony with the spirit of the times. Measures of retaliation are not.

"If perchance some of our tariffs are no longer needed for revenue or to encourage and protect our industries at home, why should they not be employed to extend and promote our markets abroad?"

This was the same McKinley whose name had been the apprehension of Europe, and who in fact more than any one else was morally responsible for the high-tariff movement in the United States. The unique position which his service of protection had won him in the party, would perhaps have enabled this one man to lead the Republican party down from its high tariff to reciprocity. But McKinley has unhappily passed away, and no one is here to take his place.

His successor has not had, in the first place, a great interest in questions of commerce. He has necessarily lacked, moreover, such strong authority within his party as would enable him to bring opposing interests into line on such a new policy. The young President was too much suspected of looking askance on great industrial companies. If he had placed himself at the head of the Republicans who were hoping to reduce the tariff, he would have been branded as a free-trader, and would not have been credited with that really warm feeling for protected American industries which in the case of McKinley was taken as a matter of course. More than that, the opponents deterred him, and would have deterred any one else who might have come in McKinley's footsteps, or perhaps even McKinley himself, with the ghost of bad times which are to come whenever a certain feeling of insecurity is spreading through the commercial world.

Everybody felt that, if the question of tariff should be opened up, unforeseen disputes might ensue. On questions of tariff every industry wields a lever in its own favour, and the Wilson Tariff had sufficiently shown how long and how tragico-comic can be the course from the law proposed to the law accomplished. It was felt everywhere that if the country should be brought into unrest by the fact that no industry could know for some years what its future was to be or where Congress might chance to take off protection, that all industry would be greatly injured. There could be no new undertakings for years, and whatever the ultimate result might be, the mere feeling of uncertainty would make a crisis sufficient to turn the tide of prosperity. And American reciprocity was after all only a matter of philanthropy; for the experience with Canada and Hawaii, it was said, only showed that reciprocity meant benevolence on the part of America.

If America is to be philanthropical, there is enough to do in other ways; but if America is to preserve her commercial interests and her prosperous industries, it is absolutely necessary not to stir up trouble and push the country once more into tariff disturbances and expose industry to doubts and misgivings. And this ghost has made its impression. McKinley's words have aroused only a faint echo in the party. The need, however, which he instinctively felt remains, and public opinion knows it. It is only a question as to when public opinion will be stronger than party opinion.

There is another thing which gives the anti-protectionists a better chance. Democrats say that high tariff has favoured the trusts. This may be true or false, and statistics speak for both views. But here is a watchword for the party which makes a deep impression, for the trusts are popularly hated. This, too, may be right or wrong, and may be still more easily argued for both sides, but the fact remains, and the seductive idea that abolishing high tariff will deal a fatal blow to the hated, extortionate, and tyrannical trusts gets more hold on the masses day by day. In vain the protectionists say that there is not a real monopoly in the whole country; that every instance of extortionate price calls out competition at once, and injures the trust which charges such price; that protection benefits the small and poor companies as much as the large, and that an attempt to injure the large companies by free-trade enactments would kill all small companies on the instant. And, besides, politics ought not to be run in the spirit of hatred. But the embitterment exists, and arguments avail little. It is incontestable that, of all the motives which are to-day felt to work against protection, the one most effective with the masses is their hatred of the trusts. Herewith we are led from the tariff question to this other problem — the trusts.

The Trust Question

"*Von der Parteien Hass und Gunst verwirrt*"— to be hated and to be favoured by the parties is the fate of the trusts. But the odd thing is that they are not hated by one party and favoured by the other; but both parties alike openly profess their hatred and yet show their favour by refraining after all from any action. And this inconsistency is not due to any intentional deception.

To be sure, a good deal of it is political policy. The evils and dangers of many trust formations are so obvious that no party would like to praise them openly, and no party will dispense with the cheap and easy notoriety of declaring itself for open competition and against all monopolies. On the other hand, the power of the trusts is so great that neither party dares to break with them, and each has its special favourites, which could not be offended without prejudicing its campaign funds. Nevertheless, the deeper reason does not lie in the matter of expediency, but rather in the fact that no relief has been proposed which promises to be satisfactory. Some want to treat the evil superficially, as a quack doctor tries to allay secondary symptoms; and others want, as President Roosevelt has said, to end the disease by killing the patient. The fact that this inventive nation has still not solved its great economic problem, is probably because the trusts have grown necessarily from the organic conditions of American life, and would continue to exist in spite of all legislative hindrances which might be proposed against them.

When Queen Elizabeth, in violation of the spirit of Anglo-Saxon law, distributed in the course of a year nearly fifty industrial monopolies, and caused the price of some commodities to be doubled, the House of Commons protested in 1601, and the Queen solemnly declared that she would revoke all privileges which endangered industrial freedom; and from that time on, monopolies were done away with. The American people are their own sovereign, and the effect of monopolies is now about the same as it was in England three hundred years ago. But the New World sovereign cannot issue a proclamation revoking the monopolies which it has granted, or at least it knows that the monopolies, if taken from one, would be snatched by another. It is true that the present form of trusts could be made illegal for the future, but some other form would appear, to compass the same ends; and if certain economic departments should be liberated by a free-trade legislation, the same forces would gather at other points. We must consider the essence of the matter rather than its outward form.

The essence is certainly not, as the opponents of trusts like to represent, that a few persons are enriched at the expense of many; that the masses are plundered to heap up wealth for a small clique. The essence of the movement does not lie in the distribution of wealth, but in the distribution of power. The significance of the movement is that in recent times the control of economic agencies has had to become more strongly concentrated. It is a mere attendant circumstance that in the formation of the trusts large financiers have pocketed disproportionately large profits, and that the leading trust magnates are the richest men of the country. The significance of their position lies in the confidence which is put in them. But the actual economic endeavour has been for the organized control of larger and larger undertakings. It has been very natural for the necessary consolidation of smaller parts into new and larger units to be accomplished by men who are themselves rich enough to retain a controlling share in the whole business; but this is a secondary factor, and the same result could have been had if mere agents had been appointed by the owners to all the great positions of confidence.

Almost the same movement has gone on in other economic spheres than the industrial. Railroad companies are all the time being consolidated into large companies, controlled by fewer and fewer men, until finally a very few, like Morgan, Vanderbilt, Rockefeller, Harriman, Gould, Hill, and Cassatt, virtually control the whole railroad system. But this economic movement in the railroad world would not really stop if the state were to take over all the railroads, and a single badly paid secretary of railroads should be substituted for the group of millionaires. The main point is that the savings of the whole country are invested in these undertakings, and are looking for the largest possible returns, and get these only when leadership and control are strongly centralized.

The very obvious opulence of the leaders naturally excites popular criticism, but it has been often shown that the wealth of these rich people has not increased relatively to the average prosperity of other classes, and the corporations themselves make it possible to distribute the profits saved by concentration throughout the population. The famous United States Steel Company had last year 69,000 stockholders, and the shares of American railroads are owned by more than a million people. For instance, the Pennsylvania Railroad alone has 34,000 stock and bond holders, who intrust the control to a very few capitalists. In fact, the whole railway system belonging to a million people is controlled by about a dozen men; and the Steel Company with its 69,000 owners is managed by twenty-four directors, who in turn are guided by the two presidents of the administration and finance committees. The chief point is thus not the concentration of ownership, but the concentration of power.

This same movement toward concentration has taken place in the banking business; and here the point is certainly, not that one man or a few men own a main share in the banks, but only that a few men are put in charge of a group of financial institutions for the sake of organized management. In this way the public is more uniformly and systematically served, and the banks are more secure, by reason of their mutual co-operation.

Among the directors of the Bank of Commerce there are, for instance, directors of two life-insurance companies which have a capital of $750,000,000, and of eight trust companies; and the directors of these trust companies are at the same time directors of other banks, so that they all make a complete chain of financial institutions. And they stand more or less under the influence of Morgan. There is, likewise, another system of banks, of which the chief is the National City Bank, which is dominated by Rockefeller; and these personal connections between banks are continued to the industrial enterprises, and then on to the railroad companies. For instance, the Rockefeller influence dominates not only banks and trust companies whose capital is more than $400,000,000, the famous Standard Oil Company with a capital of $100,000,000, the Lackawanna Steel Company worth $60,000,000, and the gas companies of New York worth $147,000,000, but also the St. Paul Railroad, which is capitalized at $230,000,000, the Missouri, Kansas and Texas at $148,000,000, and the Missouri Pacific at $212,000,000.

It is certainly true that such tremendous influence under present conditions can be gotten only by men who actually own a huge capital. And yet the essential economic feature is always the consolidation of control, which is found necessary in every province of industry, and which entirely overtops the question of ownership. It has been estimated that the twenty-four directors of the United States Steel Company exert a controlling influence in two hundred other corporations; that back of them are the largest banks in the whole country, about half the railroads, the largest coal, oil, and electric companies, and the leading telegraph, express, and life-insurance companies, etc. They control corporations with a capital of nine billions of dollars: and such consolidation is not to be undone by any artificial devices of legislation.

If economic life, by reason of the dimensions which it has assumed in the last decades, requires this welding together of interests in every department, then the formation of syndicates and trusts is only a phase in the necessary development; and to prevent the formation of trusts would affect the form, and not the essence of the movement. Indeed, the form has already changed a number of times. The earliest trusts were so organized that a number of stock companies united as such and intrusted their business to a new company, which was the "trust." That system was successfully abolished; the trust itself seemed unassailable, but the state could revoke the charters of the subsidiary companies, because by the law of most states these latter might continue only so long as they carried on the functions named in their charters; that is, so long as they carried on the transaction of their affairs themselves. A stock company has not the right, possessed by an individual, to intrust its property to another. And if the stock companies which came together into a trust were dissolved, the trust did not exist. In this way the State of New York proceeded against the Sugar Trust, Ohio against the Standard Oil Company, and Illinois against the Chicago Gas Company.

But the course of events has shown that nothing was gained by this. Although it was recognized that corporations could not legally combine to form a trust, nevertheless the stockholders controlling the stock of separate companies could join as individuals and contribute their personal holdings to a new company which was virtually a trust; and in this form the trusts which had been demolished were at once reorganized. Moreover, of course any number of stock companies can simply dissolve and merge into one large company, or they may keep their individuality but make important trade agreements with one another, and so indirectly fulfil the purposes of a trust. In short, the ways of bringing assenting industrial enterprises under one management and so of virtually making a given industry into a monopoly, are manifold.

To promote the development of trusts, there was nothing necessary but success at the outset. If the first trusts were successful, the device would be imitated so long as there was any prospect of profit. It really happened that this imitation went on finally as a sort of mania, where no special saving of profits could be predicted; one trust followed another, and the year 1903 saw 233 purely industrial trusts incorporated, of which 31 had a capital of over $50,000,000 each, and of which the total capitalization was over nine billions.

At first sight it might look as if this movement would be really sympathetic to the American people in general. The love of size generated in the nation by the lavishness of nature must welcome this consolidation of interest, and the strong spirit of self-initiative claiming the right of individuals to unite and work together must surely favour all sorts of co-operation. As a fact now an opposite tendency operates, which after all springs from the same spirit of self-initiative. The freely acting individual must not be prevented by a stronger force from using the strength he has. Everything which excludes free competition and makes the individual economically helpless seems immoral to the American. That is old Anglo-Saxon law.

The common law of England has at all times condemned agreements which tend toward monopoly, and this view dominates the American mind with a force quite surprising to the European who has become accustomed at least to monopolies owned by the state. The laws of almost all the separate states declare agreements tending toward a monopoly to be illegal; and federal legislation, in its anti-trust measures of 1887 and 1890, has seconded this idea without doing more than formulating the national idea of justice. The law of the country forbids, for instance, all agreements looking to the restriction of trade between different states of the country or with foreign nations. Senator Foraker, in February, 1904, called down public displeasure by proposing a law which permitted such agreements restricting commerce so long as the restriction was reasonable. It was feared at once that the courts would think themselves justified in excusing every sort of restraint and monopolistic hindrance. And yet there is no doubt that the interpretation of what should constitute "restriction" to commerce was quite as arbitrary a matter as the interpretation of what should be "reasonable." Indeed, the economic consolidation of competing organizations by no means necessarily cuts off the beneficent effects of competition. When, for instance, the Northern Securities Company united several parallel railway lines, it asserted justly that the several roads under their separate corps of officials would still compete for public favour. Yet the public and the court objected to the consolidation. The one real hindrance to the propagation of trusts lies in this general dread of every artificial check to free competition.

Many circumstances which have favoured the formation of trusts are obvious. In the first place, the trust can carry on business more cheaply than the component companies individually. The general administration is simplified by doing away with parallel positions, and all expenses incident to business competition are saved. Then, too, it can make larger profits since when competition stops, the fixing of prices lies quite with itself. This is of course not true, in so far as other countries are able to compete; but here comes in the function of the protective tariff, which permits the trust to raise its prices until they equal those of foreign markets plus the tariff.

The good times which America has enjoyed for some years have also favoured the development of trusts. When the harvests are good and the factories all busy, high prices are readily paid. The trusts can do even better than single companies by shutting down unprofitable plants and adapting the various remaining plants for mutual co-operation. Then, too, their great resources enable them to procure the best business intelligence. In addition to all this came a series of favourable external circumstances. First was the rapid growth of American capital which was seeking investment. In the seventies, the best railroad companies had to pay a rate of 7 per cent. in order to attract investors; now they pay 3½ per cent. Capital lies idle in great quantities and accumulates faster than it can find investment. This has necessarily put a premium on the organization of new trusts. Then, too, there was the well-known uniformity of the market, so characteristic of America. The desire to imitate on the one side, and patience and good nature on the other, give to this tremendous region of consumption extending from the Atlantic to the Pacific Ocean a uniformity of demand which greatly favours manufacture on a gigantic scale. This is in sharp contrast with the diversity of requirements in Europe.

It has been, doubtless, also important that the American feels relatively little attached to his special business. Just as he loves his Fatherland really as a conception, as an ideal system, but feels less bound to the special piece of soil where he was born and will leave his own farm if he is a farmer and go westward in search of better land, so the American passionately loves business as a method, without being over attached to his own particular firm. If the opening is favourable, he gives up his business readily to embark on another, just as he gives up an old-fashioned machine in favour of an improved one.

Just this quality of mind is so different from the German that here would be probably the greatest hindrance to the organization of trusts in Germany. The German feels himself to have grown up in his special business, which he may have inherited from his father, just as the peasant has grown up on his farm, and he does not care to become the mere employee of a large trust. Another contributory mental trait has been the friendly confidence which the American business man puts in his neighbour. The name is here appropriate; the trusts in fact repose to a high degree on mutual trust, and trusts like the American could not develop wherever there should be mutual distrust or jealousy in the business world. Finally, the laws themselves have been favourable, in so far as they have favoured the issue of preferred stock in a way very convenient to trusts, but one which would not have been approved in Europe. And, moreover, the trusts have made considerable use of the diversity existing between the laws of different states.

There have been retarding factors, too. We have mentioned the most important of all — the legal discountenance of all business agreements tending to create a monopoly or to restrain trade. There have been others, however. One purpose of the trusts is to put prices up and so to make the necessities of life dearer. It is the people who pay the prices — the same people who elect Congress and determine the tariffs and the laws; so that every trust works in the knowledge that putting up prices tends immediately to work back on business by calling forth tariff revision and anti-trust laws.

One source of great profit to the trusts has been the possibility of restricting output. This method promised gain where natural products were in question, such as oil, tobacco, and sugar, of which the quantity is limited, and further for all technical patents. Where, however, there is no such limitation the most powerful corporation will not be able to avoid competition, and if it tries to buy up competing factories to stop such competition, still more are built at once, solely with the purpose of extorting a high ransom from the trusts; and this game is ruinous. In other departments again consolidation of business means very little economy; Morgan's marine trust is said not to have succeeded for this reason. In short, not all industries are susceptible of being organized as trusts, and the dazzling profits of certain favoured trusts too easily misled those who were in pursuit of fortune into forgetting the difference between different businesses. Trusts were formed where they could not be profitable. Perhaps the real founders themselves did not overlook the difference; but they counted on the great hungry public to overlook it, until at least most of the shares should have been disposed of.

As a fact, however, the reluctance of the great investing public has been a decidedly restraining factor too. The securities spoiled before the public had absorbed them; everywhere the complaint went up of undigested securities. The public came early to suspect that the promoters were making their profits not out of the legitimate economies to be saved by the trusts, but by enormously overcapitalizing them and taking large blocks of stock for themselves.

There was still another unfavourable influence on public opinion. The main profits of a protected trust lie in its being able to sell more dearly than it could if exposed to foreign competition. But now if the consolidated industry itself proposes to sell to other countries, it must of course step down to the prevailing level of prices. It must therefore sell more cheaply abroad than at home. But this is soon found out, and creates a very unfavourable impression. The American is willing to pay high prices, as far as that goes; but when he has to pay a price double what the same factory charges for the same goods when delivered in Europe, he finds the thing wholly unnatural, and will protest at the next election. Thus there have been plenty of factors to counteract the favourable conditions, and the history of trusts has certainly not been for their promoters a simple tale of easy profits.

Now, if we do not ask what has favoured or hindered the trusts, nor how they have benefited or jeopardized their founders, but rather look about to see what their effect on the nation has been and will be, some good features appear at once. However much money may have been lost, or rather, however fictitious values may have been wiped out in the market, the great enterprises are after all increasing the productive capacity of the nation and its industrial strength in the fight with other peoples. They give a broad scope to business, and bring about relations and mutual adaptations which would never have developed in the chaotic struggling of small concerns. They produce at the same time by the concentration of control an inner solidarity which allows one part to function for another in case there are hindrances or disasters to any part of the great organism, and this is undoubtedly a tremendous factor for the general good. A mischance which, under former conditions, would have been disastrous can be survived now under this system of mutual interdependence: thus it can hardly be doubted that the combined action of the banks in the year 1903 prevented a panic; since, when stocks began to fall, the banks were able to co-operate as they would not have been able previously to their close affiliation.

Furthermore, economic wealth can now be created more advantageously for the nation. The saving of funds which were formerly spent in direct competition is a true economy, and the trusts have asserted again and again that as a matter of fact they do not put up prices, but that they make sufficient profits in saving what had formerly been wasted in business hostilities. Certainly the trusts make it possible to isolate useless or superannuated plants, without causing a heavy loss to the owners, and thus the national industry is even more freely adaptable to changing circumstances than before; and this advantage accrues to the entire country. The spirit of enterprise is remarkably encouraged and the highest premiums are put on individual achievement. Almost all the men who hold responsible positions in the mammoth works of the Steel Trust have worked up, like Carnegie himself, from the bottom of the ladder, and made their millions simply by working better than their fellows.

On the other hand, the trusts have their drawbacks. One of the most regrettable to the American mind is their moral effect. The American distrusts such extreme concentration of power and capital; it looks toward aristocracy, oligarchy, and tyranny. At the same time the masses are demoralized, and in very many cases individual initiative is strangled. There are, as it were, nothing but officials obeying orders; no men acting wholly on their own responsibility. Work ceases to be a pleasure, because everything goes by clock-work; the trust supersedes the independent merchant and manufacturer just as the machine has superseded the independent artisan.

The trusts have other demoralizing effects. Their resources are so tremendous as in the end to do away with all opposition. The independent man who hopes to oppose the great rival, can too easily be put in a position in which he is made to choose between beggary and the repudiation of all his principles. Everybody knows the shameless history of the Standard Oil Company, which has strangled not merely weak proprietors, but, much more, has strangled strong consciences. Then, too, the whole system of over-capitalization is immoral. Large trusts can hardly be formed except by purchasing the subsidiary companies at fancy prices, and issuing stock which in large part represents the premium paid to the promoters. Indeed, this whole system of community of interests which puts thousands of corporations into the hands of a few men who everywhere play into one another's hands, must bring it about that these men will soon grow careless and overlook one another's irregularities in a way which will threaten sober business traditions. The whole country was shocked on hearing the revelations of the Shipbuilding Trust, and seeing with what criminal carelessness the organization went on in a little group of friends, and how the methods of poker-playing were applied to transactions of great moment. The fundamental objection, however, is always that it is immoral to kill competition by agreements which create a monopoly.

Now, what can be done to obviate these evils? Apparently the first thing would be a revision of the tariff; and yet even their opponents must agree that there is only an indirect relation between the protective tariff and the trusts. It is true that the high tariffs have helped to create those industries which have now come together in trusts, and if the industries were to be wiped out, of course there would be nothing left of consolidations. But it is surely not true that the trusts are the immediate effect of the tariff, and the more a revised tariff were to let in foreign competition so much the more would the national industries need to form themselves into trusts for the sake of the benefits of consolidated management. All the business advantages and all the moral evils of trusts would still remain, even though the dividends were to sink. And the trusts would not be carried off the field unless American industry itself should utterly succumb to the foreign enemy.

Most of all, however, it seems clear that any policy prejudicial to the conditions of production and distribution would first of all, and most sadly, hit the competitors of the trusts. There is no absolute monopoly in any American industry. Indeed, even the Sugar Refining Company has a few outside competitors, and there is a legion of independent producers outside of the Steel Trust who are themselves in part organized in groups, and in many industries the trusts do not comprise even half of the manufacturers. Now, if the high tariff wall should be torn down so that a flood of cheap foreign manufactures could come in, it is certain that the first sufferers would be the small independent companies, which would be drowned out, while the mighty trusts would swim for a long time. Indeed, the destruction of such home competition would greatly benefit the trusts. Some of the strongest of these would hardly be reached at all by a reduction of the tariff — as, for instance, the strongest of them, the Petroleum Trust, which does not enjoy any protection. And it is also to be asked if trusts do not prosper in free-trade England? So soon as the water is squeezed out of their stocks, as has in good part lately happened, the trusts would still have a great advantage after protective duties should be abolished. And at the same time the necessary depression of wages which would result from that movement would endanger the whole industrial fabric. Moreover, the social and moral evils of the trusts would persist. Therefore the Republican party, which is just now in power, will take no part in solving the trust question by reducing the tariff.

Those Republicans who oppose the trusts are much more inclined to proceed to federal legislation. President Roosevelt has, in a number of speeches which are among the most significant contributions to the whole discussion, pointed to this way again and again. The situation is complicated and has shifted from time to time. The real difficulty lies in the double system of legislative power which we have already explicitly described. We have seen that all legislative power which is not expressly conferred on the Union belongs to the several states; specially has each state the right to regulate the commercial companies to which it has given charters. But if the company is such a one as operates between several states — as, for instance, one which transports goods from one state to another — it is regulated by federal law. Now, as long ago as the year 1890, in the so-called Sherman Act, Congress passed draconic regulations against interstate trusts. The law threatens with fine and imprisonment any party to a contract which restricts interstate commerce. It can be said of this law that it entirely did away with the trusts in their original form, in which the various companies themselves composed the trust. At the same time the federal officials were strongly seconded by the judicial doings of the separate states, as we have already seen. But the effect has only been to drive industry into new forms, and forms which are not amenable to federal regulations, but fall under the jurisdiction of the separate states. Corporations were formed which have their home in a certain state, but which by the tremendous capital of their members have been able to acquire factories distributed all through the country. Indeed, they are not real trusts any more, and the name is kept up only because the new corporations have descended from trusts and accomplish the same purpose.

Of course, this change would have been of no advantage for the several companies if the stern spirit shown by Congress in this legislation had been manifested once more by the separate states, that is, if each separate state had forbidden what the Union had forbidden; but so long as a single state in the whole forty-five permitted greater freedom to business than the others, of course all new companies would be careful to seek out that state and settle there. And, what was more important, would there pay taxes — a fact which tended to persuade every state to enact convenient trust laws.

Now, it is not a question between one state and forty-four

others, but rather between the diversities of all the forty-five. Almost every state has its peculiar provisions, and if its laws are favourable to the trusts this is because, as each state says, if it were to stand on high moral grounds it would only hurt itself by driving away profitable trusts, and would not benefit the whole country, because the trusts would simply fly away and roost in some other state. More especially the industrially backward Western States would be always ready to entertain the trusts and pass most hospitable laws, for the sake of the revenue which they could thereby get for their local purposes. And so it is quite hopeless to expect the trusts to be uprooted by the legislation of the separate states. If all forty-five states were to pass laws such as govern stock companies in Massachusetts, there would be no need of further legislation; and it is also no accident, of course, that there are very few trusts in the State of New York. All the great trusts whose directors reside in the metropolis have their official home across the river in the State of New Jersey, which has made great concessions to the companies.

If these companies are to be reached by law, the surest way seems to be by taking a radical step and removing the supervision of large stock companies from the single states, and transferring it to the federal government; this is the way which President Roosevelt has repeatedly recommended. In our political section we have explicitly shown that such a change cannot be introduced by an act of Congress, but only by an amendment to the Constitution, which cannot be made by Congress, since it is in itself a product of the Constitution. Congress would be able only to take the initiative, and two-thirds of both houses would have to support the proposition to change the Constitution; and this change would have to be ratified by three-fourths of the state legislatures themselves. Now, it would be difficult to get a two-thirds majority in both houses on any question hostile to trusts; but it is quite out of the question to induce the three-fourths of the states to cripple their own rights in so important a matter as the regulation of stock companies; particularly as in economic matters local power is necessary to local optimism, and the weaker states would never consent to give up such rights, since they would be forced to see industrial laws framed according to the requirements of the more highly developed states. Was the President, then, in his speeches, like Don Quixote, tilting against the windmills; or was he proposing, as some of his opponents said, quite impracticable solutions in order to divert attention from such a handy solution as that of tariff reduction? And was he declaiming loudly against the trusts before the public in order really to help on the friends of capital?

Perhaps another point of view may be found. It may be that President Roosevelt proposed a constitutional amendment in order to arouse discussion along certain lines, and in order specially to have the chance of demonstrating that federal control of those overgrown business enterprises is necessary, and that their control by the several states is dangerous. It looks indeed as if such discussion would have been highly superfluous if not insincere, if it were true that the sole way of helping the situation were the quite impossible constitutional amendment.

But such is not the case; there is another way of reaching the same end without meeting the difficulties involved in changing the Constitution. Of course, the President was not free to discuss this means, nor even to mention it. This way is, we think, for the Supreme Court to reverse its former decision, and to modify its definition of interstate commerce in closer accord with the latest developments of the trusts. We have seen that there are drastic laws relating to interstate commerce which have overthrown all the earlier trusts; but a corporation claiming home in New Jersey, although owning factories in different states and dependent on the co-operation of several states for its output, is to-day treated by the Supreme Court as a corporation pertaining to one state. If, now, the Supreme Court were to decide that such a corporation transacts interstate commerce, then all the severity of the existing federal laws would apply to such corporations, and everything which could be accomplished by an amendment to the Constitution would be effected by that one decision. Of course, the President could not suggest this, since the Supreme Court is coordinate with the Executive; yet if public attention should be awakened by such a discussion, even the judges of the Supreme Court might consider the matter in a new light.

To be sure, this would at the same time require the Supreme Court somewhat to modify its previous interpretation of the Anti-Trust Law itself, and not merely its application; since otherwise, if the trusts come under federal jurisdiction, the law might wipe out the new trusts, as it did the old, instead merely of regulating them. In view of the recently published memoirs of Senator Hoar, there can be no doubt that the Supreme Court has interpreted the law forbidding the restraint of trade more strictly than was originally intended in the bill which Hoar himself drew up. Congress meant to refer to agreements in restraint of trade in a narrow, technical sense, while the court has interpreted this law as if it were to apply to every agreement which merely regulates production or sale in any place. But this unnecessarily severe construction of the law by the unexpected verdict of the court can of course be set aside by a further Congressional measure, and therefore offers no difficulty.

The Administration might proceed in still another way. A good deal has been said of greater publicity in public affairs, and in the last few years energetic measures have already been taken at the instance of the President. Many of the evils of trusts lie in their concealment of the conditions under which they have been organized; and the new Department of Commerce is empowered to take official testimony concerning all such matters, and to demand this under oath. Whether this will be an ultimate gain is doubted by many, since those acquainted with the matter say that the secrets of modern book-keeping make it impossible to inspect the general condition of a large industrial concern when its promoters desire to conceal the truth. While if one were to go back of the books and lay bare every individual fact to the public eye, the corporations would be considerably injured in their legitimate business. And in any case, this new effort at publicity has so far no judicial sanction. One large trust has already refused to give the information desired because its counsel holds the Congressional law to be unconstitutional, and this matter will have to be settled by the Supreme Court.

The most thoughtful minds are coming slowly to the opinion that neither tariff provisions nor legislation is necessary, but that the matter will eventually regulate itself. The great collapse of market values has opened the eyes of many people, and the fall in the price of commodities manufactured by trusts works in much the same direction. People see, more and more, that most of the evils are merely such troubles as all infant organisms pass through. The railroads of the country were also at first enormously overcapitalized, but the trouble has cured itself in the course of time. The surpluses have been spent on improvements, and railroad shares to-day represent actual values. Such a change has in fact already set in among the trusts. Paternal regulation by the government, which prescribes how industry shall go on, is always essentially distasteful to Americans. Exact regulative measures which shall be just cannot be framed beforehand by any government. Even Adam Smith believed, for instance, that the form of organization known as a stock company was suitable for only a few kinds of business. The American prefers to submit all such questions to the actual business test. All experimental undertakings are sifted by natural selection, and the undesirable and unnecessary ones fall through. It is true that many lose their property in such experiments, but that is only a wholesome warning against thoughtless undertakings and against hasty belief that the methods profitable in one field must be profitable in every other. It is true that here and there a man will make large profits rather too easily, but Roosevelt has well said that it is better that a few people become too rich than that none prosper.

The development of affairs shows most of all that prices can be inflated for a short time, but that they slowly come back to a reasonable figure so long as there are no real monopolies. The experience of the last ten years teaches, moreover, that the most important factor which works against the trusts is the desire for independence on the part of capitalists, who do not for a long time willingly subordinate themselves to any corporation, but are always tempted to break away and start once more an independent concern.

And comparing the situation in 1904 with that of 1900, one sees that in spite of the seeming growth of the trust idea, the trusts themselves have become more solid by the squeezing out of fictitious valuations; they are more modest, content themselves with less profits, and they are much less dangerous because of the competition which has grown up around them. The trusts which originally ruled some whole industry through the country are to-day satisfied if they control two-thirds of it. A single fundamental thought remains firm, that the development of industry demands a centralized control. This idea works itself out more and more, and would remain in spite of any artificial obstruction which might be put before it. But the opposite tendencies are too deeply rooted in human nature, in Anglo-Saxon law, and in the American's desire for self-initiative, to let this centralization go to dangerous limits.

But those who will not believe that the trusts, with their enormous capitals, can be adequately restrained in this way, may easily content themselves with that factor which, as the last few years have shown, speaks more energetically than could Congress itself — this is organized labour. The question of capital in American economy is regulated finally by the question of labour.

The Labour Question

As the negro question is the most important problem of internal politics, so the labour question is the most important in American economic life; and one who has watched the great strikes of recent years, the tremendous losses due to the conflicts between capital and labour, may well believe that, like the negro question, this is a problem which is far from being solved. Yet this may not be the case. With the negro pessimism is justified, because the difficulties are not only unsolved, but seem unsolvable. The labour question, however, has reached a point in which a real organic solution is no longer impossible. Of course, prophecies are dangerous; and yet it looks as if, in spite of hard words, the United States have come to a condition in which labourers and capitalists are pretty well satisfied, and more so perhaps than in any other large industrial nation. It might be more exact to say that the Americans are nearer the ideal condition for the American capitalist and the American labourer, since the same question in other countries may need to be solved on wholly different lines.

In fact, the American problem cannot be looked into without carefully scrutinizing how far the factors are peculiar to this nation. Merely because certain general factors are common to the whole industrial world, such as capital, machinery, land values, labour, markets, and profits, the social politician is inclined to leave out of account the specific form which the problem takes on in each country. The differences are chiefly of temperament, of opinions, and of mode of life.

It is, indeed, a psychological factor which makes the American labour question very different from the German problem. This fact is neglected, time after time, in the discussions of German theorists and business men. It is, for instance, almost invariably affirmed in Germany that the American government has done almost nothing toward insuring the labourer against illness, accident, or old age, and that therefore America is in this respect far inferior to Germany. It can easily be foreseen, they say, that American manufacturers will be considerably impeded in the world's market as soon as the progress of civilization forces them to yield this to the working-man.

The fact is that such an opprobrium betrays a lack of understanding of American character. The satisfaction felt in Germany with the laws for working-men's insurance is fully justified; for they are doubtless excellent under German conditions, but they might not seem so satisfactory to the average American nor to the average American labourer. He looks on it as an interesting economic experiment, admirable for the ill-paid German working-man, but wholly undesirable for the American. The accusation that the American government fails in its duty by not providing for those who have served the community, is the more unjust, since America expends on the average $140,000,000 in pensions for invalid veterans and their widows, and is equally generous wherever public opinion sees good cause for generosity.

It cannot be doubted that the American labourer is a different sort of creature from the Continental labourer; his material surroundings are different, and his way of life, his dwelling, clothes and food, his intellectual nourishment and his pleasures, would seem to the European workmen like luxuries. The number of industrial labourers in the year 1880 was 2.7 million, and they earned $947,000,000; in 1890 it was 4.2 million earning $1,891,000,000; and in 1900 there were 5.3 million labourers earning $2,320,000,000; therefore, at the time of the last census, the average annual wage was $437. This average figure, however, includes men, women, and children. The average pay of grown men alone amounts to $500. This figure gives to the German no clear idea of the relative prosperity of the working-man without some idea of the relation between German and American prices.

One reads often that everything is twice as expensive in America as in Germany, while some say that the American dollar is worth only as much as the German mark — that is, that the American prices are four times the German; and still others say that American prices are not a bit higher than German. The large German-American steamships buy all their provisions of meat in New York rather than in Hamburg or Bremen, because the American prices are less. If one consults, on the other hand, a doctor or lawyer in New York, or employs a barber or any one else for his personal services, he will find it a fact that the American price is four times as high as the German. The same may be said of articles of luxury; for bouquets and theatre tickets the dollar is equal to the mark. It is the same with household service in a large town; an ordinary cook receives five dollars per week, and the pay of better ones increases as the square of their abilities. Thus we see at once that an actual comparison of prices between the United States and Europe cannot be made. A dollar buys five marks' worth of roast beef and one mark's worth of roses.

In general, it can be said that the American is better off as regards all articles which can be made in large quantities, and worse off in articles of luxury and matters of personal service. The ready-made suit of clothes is no dearer in America than in Germany and probably better for the price, while the custom-made suit of a first-class tailor costs about four times what it would cost in Germany. All in all, we might say that an American who lives in great style and spends $50,000 a year can get no greater material comforts than the man in Germany who spends a third as much — that is, 70,000 marks. On the other hand, the man who keeps house with servants, but without luxuries, spending, say, $5,000 a year, lives about like a man in Germany who spends 10,000 marks — that is, about half as much. But any one who, like the average labourer, spends $500 in America, unquestionably gets quite as much as he would get with the equal amount of 2,100 marks in Germany.

But the more skilled artisan gets $900 on the average — that is, about three times as much as the German skilled workman; so that, compared with the wages of higher-paid classes, the workingmen are paid relatively much more than in Europe. The average labourer lives on the same plane as the German master artisan; and if he is dissatisfied with the furnishings of his home it is not because he needs more chairs and tables, but because he has a fancy for a new carpet or a new bath-tub. In this connection we are speaking always of course of the real American, not the recent immigrants from Southern and Eastern Europe, who are herded together in the worst parts of large cities, and who sell their labour at the lowest rate. The native American labourer and the better class of German and Irish immigrants are well clothed and fed and read the newspapers, and only a small part of their wages goes for liquor.

More important than the economic prosperity of the American working-man, though not wholly independent of it, is the social self-respect which he enjoys. The American working-man feels himself to be quite the equal of any other citizen, and this not merely in the legal sense. This results chiefly from the intense political life of the country and the democratic form of government, which knows no social prerogatives. It results also from the absence of social caste. There is a considerable class feeling, but no artificial lines which hinder any man from working up into any position. The most modest labourer knows that he may, if he is able, work up to a distinguished position in the social structure of the nation.

And the most important thing of all is probably the high value put on industry as such. We have spoken of this in depicting the spirit of self-initiative. In fact, the back-ground of national conceptions as to the worth of labour must be the chief factor in determining the social condition of the working-man. When a nation comes to that way of thinking which makes intellectual activities the whole of its culture, while economic life merely serves the function of securing the outward comforts of the nation as it stretches on toward its goal of culture, then the industrial classes must content themselves with an inferior position, and those who do bodily labour, with the least possible amount of personal consideration. But when a nation, on the other hand, believes in the intrinsic worth of industrial culture, then the labour by which a man lives becomes a measure of his moral worth, and even intellectual effort finds its immediate ethical justification only in ministering to the complex social life; that is, only so far as it is industry.

Such now is the conception of the American. Whether a

person makes laws, or poetry, or railway ties, or shoes, or darning-needles, the thing which gives moral value to his life's work is merely its general usefulness. In spite of all intellectual and æsthetic differences, this most important element of activity is common to all, and the manual labourer, so far as he is industrious, is equal to those who work with their brains. On the other hand, the social parasite, who perhaps has inherited money and uses it only for enjoyment, is generally felt to be on a lower plane than the factory hand who does his duty. For the American this is not an artificial principle, but an instinctive feeling, which may not do away with all the thousand different shadings of social position, but nevertheless consigns them to a secondary place. One may disapprove of such an industrial conception of society, and like better, for example, the æsthetic conception of the Japanese, who teach their youth to despise mercantile business and tastefully to arrange flowers. But it is clear that where such an industrial conception prevails in a nation the working-man will feel a greater self-respect and greater independence of his surroundings, since the millionaire is also then only a fellow-workman.

Undoubtedly just this self-respect of the American labourer makes him the great industrial force which he is. The American manufacturer pays higher wages than any of his competitors in the markets of the world and is not disconcerted at this load, because he knows that the self-respecting working-man equalizes the difference of price by more intense and intelligent labour. It is true that the perfection of labour-saving machinery is a tremendous advantage here, but after all it is the personal quality of the working-man which has brought about that in so many industries ten American workmen do more than fifteen or, as experts often say, twenty Italian workmen. The American manufacturer prefers to hire a hundred heads rather than a thousand hands, even if the wages are equal, and even the greedy capitalist prefers the labourer who is worth thirty dollars a week to one who is worth only twenty. The more the working-man feels himself to be a free co-operator, the more intelligently does he address himself to the work. We hear constantly of improvements which artisans have thought out, and this independent initiative of theirs does not in the least impair the discipline of industry. American discipline does not mean inferiority and the giving up of one's own judgment, but is a free willingness to co-operate and, for the common end, to intrust the leadership to some one else. This other person is exalted to the trustworthy position of leader by the desire of those concerned, so that each man is carrying out his own will in obeying the foreman.

Therefore, everything which in any wise savours of compassion is entirely out of the question for him. In fact, the friendly benevolence, however graciously expressed, intended to remind the workman that he is after all a human creature, perhaps the friendly provision of a house to live in or of some sort of state help for his family, must always be unwelcome to him, since it implies that he is not able, like other fathers of a family, to be forethoughtful and provident. He prefers to do everything which is necessary himself. He insures himself in a life-insurance company and, like anybody else, he looks out for his own interests — tries to improve his conditions by securing good contracts with his employer, by arranging organizations of his fellow-workmen, and by means of his political rights. But whatever he accomplishes, he enjoys it because he has worked in free competition against opposing interests. Any material benefits which he might purchase by enduring the patronizing attitude of capitalists or legislators would be felt to be an actual derogation.

And thus it happens that social democracy, in the technical sense, makes no advance among American workmen. The American labourer does not feel that his position is inferior; he knows that he has an equal opportunity with everybody else, and the idea of entire equality does not attract him, and would even deprive him of what he holds most valuable — namely, his self-initiative, which aims for the highest social reward as a recognition of the highest individual achievement. American society knows no unwritten law whereby the working-man of to-day must be the same to-morrow, and this gives to the whole labour question in America its distinction from the labour question in European aristocratic countries. In most cases the superiors have themselves once been labourers. Millionaires who to-day preside over the destinies of thousands of working-men have often themselves begun with the shovel or hod. The workman knows that he may set his ambition as high as he likes, and to exchange his equal opportunity for an equality of reward would mean for him to sink back into that social condition in which industry is thought to be only a means to something else, and not in itself a valuable activity. Although Bellamy may already dream of the common umbrella, his native country is probably further from social democracy than any country in Europe, because the spirit of self-initiative is here stronger than anywhere else, and because the general public is aware that no class distinctions cut it off from the highest positions in the country. It knows that everything depends on industry, energy, and intelligence.

This does not hinder the working-men, in their fight for better conditions of labour, from adopting many socialistic tenets. The American calls it socialism even to demand that the government own railways, telegraph lines, express companies, or coal-fields, or that the city conduct tramways, or gas or electric-light works. Socialism of this sort is undoubtedly progressing, although the more extravagant ideas find more wordy orators to support them than hearers to give belief. It is also very characteristic that the labour leaders do not make such agitation their life work, but often after a few years go over to one or another civil occupation. The relation between working-man and capitalist, moreover, is always felt to be temporary. A man is on one side of the line to-day and on the other to-morrow. There is no firm boundary between groups of men, but merely a distribution in temporary groups; and this separates the American labour unions from even the English unions, with which otherwise they have much in common.

Many other conditions by which the American working-man's life is separated from the Englishman's are of an economic sort. It is remembered, for instance, how successful the English unions have been in establishing co-operative stores, while in America they have failed in this. The department shops in the large cities have been able to sell cheaper and better goods, and have been in every way more popular. But enough of comparing America with the Old World — we must discuss the actual situation in the New.

The labour movement of the United States really began in the third decade of the last century. Of course, only the North is in question; in the South slavery excluded all alliances and independent movements for improving the condition of the manual labourer. There had been small strikes as early as the eighteenth century, but the real movement began with the factories which were built during the nineteenth.

From the very beginning the demand for shorter hours and higher wages were the main issues. At the same time the American world was filled more or less with fantastic notions of co-operation, and these influenced the course of affairs. Boston and New York were the centres of the new movement. As early as 1825 in New York there appeared the first exclusively labour newspaper, the "Labour Advocate"; it commenced a literature which was to increase like an avalanche. The labourers figured independently in politics in 1830, when they had their own candidate for governor. But all political endeavours of the working people have been mere episodes, and the chief labour movements of the century have taken place outside of politics; the leading unions have generally found that their strength lay in renouncing political agitation. Only when legal measures for or against the interests of labourers have been in question, has there been some mixing in with politics, but the American workmen have never become a political party.

At the beginning of the thirties, working-men of different industries united for the first time in a large organization, such as later became the regular form. But at the outset of the movement there appeared also the opposite movement from the side of the capitalists. For instance, in 1832 merchants and shipholders in Boston met solemnly to declare it their duty to oppose the combinations of working people which were formed for the illegal purpose of preventing the individual workman from making a free choice as regards his hours of labour, and for the purpose of making trouble with their employers, who already paid high wages.

The organization of the working-man and that of the employer have grown steadily, and the nation itself has virtually played the rôle of an attentive but neutral spectator. In the case of direct conflict the sympathy of the country has almost always been on the side of the working-man, since in the concrete case the most impressive point was generally not the opposition between capital and labour, but the personal contrast of the needy day-labourer and the rich employer; and the sentimentality of the American has always favoured the weaker classes. The nation however, has shown an equal amount of sympathy toward capital whenever a general matter of legislation was in question; that is, whenever the problem has seemed more theoretical than personal. In such cases the capitalists have always been felt to be the pioneers of the American nation by putting their enterprise into all sorts of new undertakings, applying their capital and intelligence to economic life; so that they have seemed to a greater extent in need of national protection than the workman, who may always be easily replaced by some one else.

Considering the matter as a whole, it can be said indeed that the nation has preserved a general neutrality, and let both parties virtually alone. A change has very recently taken place. The new conditions of the industrial struggle make it clearer day by day that there are three parties to the conflict, rather than two; that is, not only capitalist and labourer, but also the general public, which is dependent on the industrial output, and therefore so immediately concerned in the settlement of differences as to seem, even in concrete cases, entitled to take active part. The turning-point came perhaps during the coal strike in the winter of 1902–03, when the President himself stood out to represent this third party. But we must follow the development more minutely — must speak of the labour organizations as they exist to-day, of the results of legislation, of the weapons employed by the labourers and those used by the capitalists, of their advantages and disadvantages, and of the latest efforts to solve the problem. Three forms of working-men's organizations can be discriminated to-day — the Knights of Labour, the independent trades-unions, and the federated trades-unions.

The Knights of Labour are by principle different from both of the other groups; and their influence, although once very great, is now waning. Their fundamental idea is a moral one, while that of their rivals is a practical one. This is, of course, not to be taken as meaning that the labour unions pursue immoral ends or the Knights of Labour unpractical ones. The Knights of Labour began very modestly in 1869 as a secret organization, somewhat like the Free Masons, having an elaborate initiation and somewhat unusual procedures. Their constitution began with the motto, "Labour is noble and sacred," and their first endeavours were for the intellectual uplifting of the labourer and opposition to everything which made labour mean or unworthy. The order grew steadily, but at the same time the practical interests of different groups of working-men necessarily came into prominence. In the middle eighties, when they gave up their secret observances, the society had about a million members, and its banner still proclaimed the one sentiment that industry and virtue not wealth are the true measure of individual and national greatness. Their members, they insisted, ought to have a larger share of the things which they produced, so as to have more time for their intellectual, moral, and social development. In this moral spirit, the society worked energetically against strikes and for the peaceful settlement of all disputes.

Its principal weakness was perhaps that, when the membership became large, it began to take part in politics; the Knights demanded a reform in taxation, in the currency, in the credit system, and a number of other matters in line with state socialism. It was also a source of weakness that, even in local meetings, working-men of different trades came together. This was of course quite in accordance with the ethical ideal of the society. As far as the moral problems of the workmen are in question, the baker, tailor, mason, plumber, electrician, and so on, have many nterests which are identical; but practically it turned out that one group had little interest in its neighbour groups, and oftenimes even strongly conflicting interests were discovered. Thus his mixed organization declined in favour of labour societies which comprised members of one and only one trade, so that at the present time the Knights of Labour are said to number only 200,000 and their importance is greatly reduced. It is still undoubted that the idealistic formulation in which they presented he interests of labour to the nation has done much to arouse the public conscience.

At the present time the typical form of organization is the trades-union, and between the independent and the federated trades-unions there is no fundamental difference. There are to-day over two million working-men united in trades-unions; the number increases daily. And this number, which comprises only two-fifths f all wage-earners, is kept down, not because only two-fifths of the members of each trade can agree to unite, but because many trades exist which are not amenable to such organization; the unions include almost all men working in some of the most important trades. The higher the employment and the more it demands of preparation, the stronger is the organization of the employed. Printers, for instance, almost all belong to their union, and in the building and tobacco trades there are very few who are not members. The miners' union includes about 200,000 men, who represent a population of about a million souls. On the other hand, it would be useless and impossible to perfect a close organization where new individuals can be brought in any day and put to work without any experience or training; thus ordinary day-labourers are not organized. The number of two million thus represents the most important trades, and includes the most skilled workers.

The oldest trades-union in America is the International Typographical Union, which began in 1850. It is to be noticed at once that the distinction between national and international trades-unions is a wholly superficial one, for in the hundreds of so-called international unions there has been no effort to stretch out across the ocean. "International" means only that citizens of Canada and, in a few cases, of Mexico are admitted to membership. It has been the experience of other countries, too, that the printing trades were the first to organize. In America the hatmakers followed in 1854, the iron founders in 1859, and the number of organized trades increased rapidly during the sixties and seventies. The special representation of local interests soon demanded, on the one hand, the division of the larger societies into local groups, and, on the other, the affiliation of the larger societies having somewhat similar interests. Thus it has come about that each locality has its local union, and these unions are affiliated in state organizations for purposes of state legislation and completely unified in national or international organizations. On the other hand, the unions belonging to different trades are pledged locally and nationally to mutual support. But here it is no longer a question, as with the Knights of Labour, of the mixing up of diverse interests, but of systematic mutual aid on practical lines.

The largest union of this sort is the American Federation of Labour, which began its existence in Pittsburg in 1881, and has organized a veritable labour republic. The Federation took warning at the outset from the sad fate of previous federations, and resolved to play no part in politics, but to devote itself exclusively to industrial questions. It recognized the industrial autonomy and the special character of each affiliating trades-union, but hoped to gain definite results by co-operation. They first demanded an eight-hour day and aimed to forbid the employment of children under fourteen years of age, to prevent the competition of prison labour and the importation of contract labour; they asked for a change in laws relating to the responsibility of factory owners and for the organization of societies, for the establishment of government bureaus for labour statistics, and much else of a similar sort. At first the Federation had bitter quarrels with the Knights of Labour, and perhaps even as bitter a one with socialistic visionaries in its own ranks. But a firm and healthy basis was soon established, and since the Federation assisted in every way the formation of local, provincial, and state organizations, the parts grew with the help of the whole and the whole with the help of the parts. To-day the Federation includes 111 international trades-unions with 29 state organizations, 542 central organizations for cities, and also 1,850 local unions which are outside of any national or international organizations. The interests of this Federation are represented by 250 weekly and monthly papers. The head office is naturally Washington, where the federal government has its seat. Gompers is its indefatigable president. Outside of this Federation are all the trades-unions of railway employees and several unions of masons and stonecutters. The railway employees have always held aloof; their union dates from 1893, and is said to comprise 200,000 men.

The trades-unions are not open to every one; each member has to pay his initiation fees and make contributions to the local union, and through it to the general organization. Many of the trades-unions even require an examination for entrance; thus the conditions for admission into the union of electrical workers are so difficult that membership is recognized among the employers themselves as the surest evidence of a working-man's competence. Every member is further pledged to attend the regular meetings of the local branch, and in order that these local societies may not be too unwieldy, they are generally divided into districts when the number of members becomes too great to admit of all meeting together. The cigarmakers of the City of New York, for example, have a trades-union of 6,000 members, which is divided into ten smaller bodies. Every single society in the country has its own officials. If the work of the official takes all his time, he receives a salary equal to the regular pay for work in his trade. The small organizations send delegates to the state and national federations; and wherever these provincial or federal affiliations represent different trades, each of these trades has its own representative, and all decisions are made with that technical formality which the American masters so well. In accordance with this paliamentary rigour, every member is absolutely pledged to comply with the decisions of the delegates. Any one who refuses to obey when a strike is ordered thereby loses all his rights.

The rights enjoyed by the members of the trades-unions are in fact considerable. Firstly, the local union is a club and an employment agency, and especially in large cities these two functions are very important for the American working-man. Then there are the arrangements for insurance and aid. Thus the general union of cigarmakers of the country, which combines 414 local unions having a total membership of 34,000 men, has given in the last twenty years $838,000 for the support of strikes, $1,453,000 for aid to ill members, $794,000 for the families of deceased members, $735,000 for travelling expenses, and $917,000 for unemployed members ; and most of the large unions could show similar figures. Yet these are the lesser advantages. The really decisive thing is the concessions which have been won in the economic fight, and which could never have been gotten by the working-men individually. Nevertheless, to-day not a few men hold off from the unions and get rid of paying their dues, because they know that whatever organized labour can achieve, will also help those who stay outside.

The main contention of these trades-unions refers to legislation and wages, and no small part of their work goes in fighting for their own existence — that is, in fighting for the recognition of the union labourer as opposed to the non-union man — a factor which doubtless is becoming more and more important in the industrial disputes. Many a strike has not had wages or short hours of labour or the like in view, but has aimed solely to force the employers officially to recognize the trades-unions, to make contracts with the union delegates rather than with individual men, and to exclude all non-union labourers.

The newly introduced contention for the union label is in the same class. The labels were first used in San Francisco, where it was aimed to exclude the Chinese workmen from competition with Americans. Now the labels are used all over the country. Every box of cigars, every brick, hat, or piano made in factories which employ union labour, bears the copyrighted device which assures the purchasing public that the wares were made under approved social and political conditions. The absence of the label is supposed to be a warning; but for the population of ten millions who are connected with labour unions, it is more than a warning; it is an invitation to boycott, and this is undoubtedly felt as a considerable pressure by manufacturers. The more the factories are thus compelled to concede to the unions, and the more inducements the unions thus offer to prospective members, and the faster therefore these come in, the more power the unions acquire. So the label has become to-day a most effective weapon of the unions.

But this is only the means to an end. We must consider these ends themselves, and first of all labour legislation. Most striking and yet historically necessary is the diversity in the statutes of different states, which was formerly very great but is gradually diminishing. The New England states, and especially Massachusetts, have gone first, and still not so fast as public opinion has often desired. In the thirties there were many lively fights for the legislative regulation of the working hours in factories, and yet even the ten hours a day for women was not established until much later; on the other hand, the employment of children in factories was legislated on at that time, and in this direction the movement progressed more rapidly.

A considerable step was taken in 1869, when Massachusetts established at the expense of the state a bureau for labour statistics, the first in the world; this was required to work up every year a report on all phases of the labour question — economic, industrial, social, hygienic, educational, and political. One state after another imitated this statistical bureau, and especially it led to the establishment of the Department of Labour at Washington, which has already had a world-wide influence. During the seventies there followed strict laws for the supervision of factories, for precautionary measures, and hygienic improvements. Most of the other states came after, but none departed widely from the example of Massachusetts, which was also the first state to make repeated reductions in the working-day. Here it followed the example of the federal government. To be sure, the reduction of the working-day among federal employees was first merely a political catering to the labour vote, but the Federation kept to the point and the separate states followed. Twenty-nine states now prescribe eight hours as the day for all public employees and the federal government does the same.

The legislative changes in the judicial sphere have been also of importance for trades-unions. According to Old English law at the beginning of the nineteenth century, it was conspiracy for workmen to unite for the purposes which the trades-unions to-day hold before themselves. This doctrine of conspiracy, which to be sure from the beginning depended largely on the arbitrary interpretation of the judges, has been weakened from time to time through the century, and has finally given away to legal conceptions which put no obstacles in the way of the peaceful alliance of working-men for the purpose of obtaining better conditions of labour. They especially regard the strike as lawful so long as violence is not resorted to. Nearly all states have now passed laws which so narrow the old conception of criminal conspiracy that it no longer stands in the way of trades-unions. Other legal provisions concern the company stores. In some mining districts far removed from public shops, the company store may still be found, where the company buys the articles needed by its employees and sells these things to them at a high price. But nearly every state has legally done away with this system; it was, indeed, one of the earliest demands of the trades-unions.

There have been great improvements too in legislation relating to the responsibility of employees. The Anglo-Saxon law makes an employer responsible for injury suffered by the workmen by reason of his work, but not responsible if the injuries are due to the carelessness of a fellow-workman. The penalty fell then on the one who had neglected his duty. It was said that the workman on taking up his duties must have known what the dangers were. But the more complicated the conditions of labour have become, the more the security of any individual has depended on a great many fellow-labourers who could not be identified, so that the old law became meaningless. Therefore, the pressure of trades-unions has in the last half century steadily altered and improved the law in this respect. American state law to-day virtually recognizes the responsibility of the employer for every accident, even when due to the carelessness of some other labourer than the one injured.

Thus on the whole a progress has been made all along the line. It is true that some states have still much to do in order to come up with the most advanced states, and the labour unions have still many demands in store which have so far been nowhere complied with — as, for instance, that for the introduction of the Swiss referendum, and so forth. Government insurance is not on this programme — one point in which the American working-man remains individualistic. He prefers to make provision for those dependent on him, against old age, accident and illness, in his own way, by membership in unions or insurance companies. As a fact, more than half the labouring men are insured. Then too the number of industrial concerns is increasing which make a voluntary provision for their employees against illness and old age. This was started by railroad companies, and the largest systems fully realize that it is in their interest to secure steady labour by putting a pension clause in the contract. When a workman takes work under companies which offer such things, he feels it to be a voluntary industrial agreement, while state insurance would offend his sense of independence.

The state has had to deal with the labour question again in the matter of strikes, lockouts, boycotts, and black-lists. During the last two decades of the nineteenth century, there were 22,793 strikes in the country, which involved 117,509 workers; the loss in wages to the workmen was $257,000,000 and in profit to the employers $122,000,000; besides that $16,000,000 were contributed to aid the strikes, so that the total loss made about $400,000,000. The problems here in question are of course much more important than the mere financial loss. About 51 per cent. of these strikes resulted successfully for the workmen, 13 per cent. partially successfully, and in 36 per cent. the employers won.

Since 1741, when the bakers of New York City left work and were immediately condemned for conspiracy, there has been no lack of strikes in the country. The first great strike was among sailors in 1803, but frequent strikes did not occur until about 1830. The first strike of really historical importance was on the railroads in 1877; great irregularities and many street riots accompanied the cessation of work, and the state militia had to be called out to suppress the disturbances in Cincinnati, St. Louis, Chicago, and Pittsburg. The losses were tremendous, the whole land suffered from the tumults, and in the end the working-men won nothing. When in the year 1883 all the telegraphers in the country left their work and demanded additional payment for working on Sunday, most of the country was in sympathy with them; but here too the employers, although they lost millions of dollars, were successful. In 1886 there were great strikes again in the railroad systems of the Southwest.

The bitterness reached its highest point in 1892, when the Carnegie Steel Works at Homestead were the scenes of disorder. Wages were the matter under dispute; the company, which could not come to an agreement with the labour union, proposed to exclude organized labour and introduced non-union workmen. The union sought by the use of violence to prevent the strangers from working; the company called for aid from the state; the union still opposed even the militia, and actual battles took place, which only the declaration of martial law by the governor, after the loss of many lives, was able to suppress.

The Chicago strike in 1894 was more extensive. It began with a strike in the Pullman factories in Chicago, and at its height succeeded in stopping the traffic on a quarter of all American railroads. The interruption of railway connections meant a loss to every person in the country, and the total loss is estimated at $80,000,000. The worst accompaniments of strikes soon appeared — riots, intimidations, assaults, and murders. And again it was necessary to call out troops to restore peace. Great wage disputes followed presently in the iron and steel trades; but these were all surpassed in inner significance by the great coal strike of the winter before last.

The conditions of labour in the anthracite coal mines of Pennsylvania were unfavourable to the labourers. They had bettered themselves in a strike in 1900, but the apparently adequate wages for a day's labour yielded a very small annual income, since there was little employment at some seasons of the year. The working-men felt that the coal trusts refused to raise the wages by juggling with arguments; the capitalists tried to prove to them that the profit on coal did not permit a higher wage. But the labourers knew too well that the apparently low profits were due only to the fact that the trusts had watered their stock, and especially that the coal mines were operated in connection with railroads under the same ownership, so that all profits could be brought on the books to the credit of the railroads instead of the mines. The trades-unions thought the time was ripe for demanding eight hours a day, a ten per cent. increase in wages, and a fundamental recognition of trades-unions, along with a few other technical points. The organized miners, under their leader, Mitchell, offered to wait a month, while the points of difference might be discussed between both parties; Senator Hanna, whose death a short time later took from politics one of the warmest friends of labour, offered his services as mediator, and left no doubt that the workmen would accept some compromise.

In spite of this moderation of the working-men, the representatives of the mine owners refused in any way to treat with them. Their standpoint was that if they recognized the trades-unions in their deliberations, they were beginning on a course which they might not know how to stop; if eight hours were demanded to-day by the trades-unions, seven hours might be demanded in the same way next year. The employers thought it high time once for all to break up the dictatorial power of the trades-unions. President Baer explained that trades-unions are a menace to all American industry. The strike continued. Now the anthracite miners produce five million tons every month, which supply all the homes in the eastern part of the country. A cold winter came on, and the lack of coal throughout the country brought about a condition which resembled the misery and sufferings of a time of siege. In many places it was not even a matter of price, although this was four times what it ordinarily is, but the supply of coal was actually used up. Schools and churches had to be closed in many places. And now the public understood at last perfectly clearly that, if the trades-unions wanted to exert their whole power, the country would be absolutely helpless under their tyranny. Nevertheless, the embitterment turned most strongly against the employers, who still affirmed that there was nothing to arbitrate, but that the workmen simply must give in.

The workmen then put themselves on the wrong side by threatening with violence all men who came to take their places in the mines; indeed, they forced back by barbarous methods the engineers who came to pump out the water which was collecting in the mines. Troops had to be called, but at that moment the President took the first steps toward a solution of the problem by calling representatives of both parties to Washington. A commission was finally appointed, composed of representatives of both parties and well-known men who were neutrally inclined, and after Pierpont Morgan on the side of the capitalists gave the signal to consent to arbitration, the coal miners went back to work. The commission met, and some time later in the year 1903 decided about half of the points under dispute in favour of the miners, the other half against them. This was by no means the last strike; the building trades in many parts of the country, and specially in New York, were thoroughly demoralized during the year 1903, the movement proceeding from the strikes of 5,000 bridge builders: then too, the textile workers of the East and miners of the South have been restless. And at the present time, every day sees some small strike or other inaugurated, and any day may see some very large strike declared. It was the coal strike, however, which set the nation thinking and showed up the dangers which are threatening.

The results of the coal strike had shown the friends of trades-unions more clearly than ever the strength which lies in unity. They had seen that results could be achieved by united efforts such as could never have been gotten by the unorganized workingman. They had seen with satisfaction that the trades-unions had taken a conservative part by putting off the great strike as long as possible; and they had seen that the employers would not have consented for their part to any arbitration. In the end not only many of the union demands had been granted, but, more than that, the policy of the trades-unions had been put in the most favourable light. A whole country had to suffer, human lives were sacrificed and millions lost, and in the end the trades-unions won their point; if the mine owners had been willing in the autumn to do what they had to do in winter, a great deal of injury would have been spared. But the trades-unions could truthfully say that they had been true to their policy and had always preferred peace to war. The majority of votes within the trades-unions was against thoughtless and unnecessary strife, against declaring a strike until all other means had been tried. Many people felt that the interests of that neutral party, the nation at large, were better looked out for by the more thoughtful union leaders than by such capitalisits as were the Pennsylvania coal magnates.

On the other hand, it was felt that the most calmly planned strikes can lead to embitterment and violence, and the tyrannical and murderous suppression of the non-union working-man. And here the American sense of freedom is touched. Every man has the right to decide freely under what conditions he shall work; the strike-breaker was regarded as a hero, and the trusts did their best to convince the world that the interference of the trades-unions in the movements of non-union workmen is a menace to American democracy. The unionists admit that it is unlawful power which they have used, but pretend that they had a moral right; they say that every working-man has a claim on the factory more than his weekly wage: for he has contributed to its success; he has in a way a moral share, which brings him no income, but which ought to assure him of his position. And now, if during a strike an outside person comes in and takes his place, it is like being robbed of something which he owns, and he has the right of asserting his claim with such means as any man would use on being assaulted.

Capitalists turned against the trades-unions with the greater consternation, because these latter put not only the independent working-man, but also the companies, in a powerless position. They showed that their right to manage their own property was gone, and that the capitalist was no longer the owner of his own factory the instant he was not able to treat with the individual working-man, but forced to subject himself to the representatives of trades-unions. It was easy to show that while he, as undertaker of the business, had to take all the risks and be always energetic and industrious, the working-men were simply showing their greed and laziness by wanting shorter days, and that they would never be really satisfied. It was affirmed that the best workman was an unwilling party to the strike, and that he would more gladly attend to his work than to trades-union politics, and that as a fact he let his trades-union be run by irresponsible good-for-nothings, who played the part of demagogues. Every man who had ever saved a cent and laid it up, ought to be on the side of the capitalist.

But the public took a rather different attitude, and felt that the group of capitalists had been revealed in a bad light by the strike, and when their representatives came to instruct the President of the United States, in a brusque way, on the rights of property, the public began to revise its traditional ideas. The public came to see that such large corporations as were here in question were no longer private enterprises in the ordinary sense of the word; that a steel trust or coal trust cannot be such an independent factor in the commonwealth as a grocery shop in a country town. It was felt that the tremendous growth of the business was the product of national forces, and in part dependent on public franchises; wherefore, the business itself, although privately owned, nevertheless had a semi-public character, so that the public should not be refused the right to interfere in its management. Belief in state socialism, in state ownership of railroads and mines, made great progress in those days; and the conviction made still greater progress that the working-man has a moral right to take an active hand in managing the business in which he works.

And so public opinion has come round to think that violence on the part of working-men, and refusal to treat with trades-unions on the part of employers, are equally to be condemned. The community will hardly again permit capital and labour to fight out their battles in public and make the whole nation suffer. It demands that, now that labour is actually organized in unions, disputes shall be brought up for settlement before delegates from both sides, and that where these cannot come to a solution the matter shall be brought before a neutral court of arbitration which both sides agree to recognize.

Of course these disputes will continue to arise, since the price of manufactured articles is always changing; the employer will always try to lower wages in dull times, and the labourers will try to force wages up during busy times. But it may be expected that the leaders of trades-unions will be able to consider the whole situation intelligently and to guide the masses of working-men carefully through their ambitions and disappointments. Although the employers of labour continue to assert that, so soon as they are handed over to the mercies of the trades-unions, the spirit of enterprise will be entirely throttled and capital will decline to offer itself, because all profit is sacrificed to the selfish tyranny of the working people, nevertheless, experience does not show this to be true. Trades-unions are convinced that, in these days of machinery, too small a part of the profit falls to the labouring man; but they know perfectly well that they themselves can prosper only when the industry as a whole is prosperous, and that it cannot prosper if it is burdened by too high wages. Trades-unions know also that after all they will be able to gain their point in courts of arbitration and elsewhere only so long as they have the sympathy of the public on their side, and that every undue encroachment on the profits of capital and every discouragement of the spirit of enterprise will quickly lose them the sympathy of the American nation. If they really attack American industry, public opinion will go against them. That they know, and therefore the confidence is justified that, after all, their demands will never endanger the true interests of capital. Capitalists know to-day that they will always have trades-unions to deal with, and that it will be best to adapt themselves to the situation. Many thoughtful captains of industry admit that the discipline of trades-unions has had some salutary effect, and that some of their propositions, such as the sliding wage-scale, have helped on industry.

Thus both parties are about to recognize each other with a considerable understanding. They instinctively feel that the same condition has developed itself on both sides; on the one side capital is combined in trusts, and on the other labour has organized into unions. Trusts suppress the competition of capital, trades-unions kill the non-union competitor. The trusts use as weapons high dividends, preferential rates, and monopoly of raw material; the unions use the weapons of old-age insurance, free aid during illness, the union label, strikes, and boycotts. Both sides have strengthened their position by the consolidation of many interests;

just as the steel works are allied with large banks, railroads, steamship lines, copper mines, and oil companies, so the leaders of trades-unions take care to spread the disputes of one industry into other industries.

Moreover, both parties fight alike by means of artificially limiting the market; and this is, perhaps, the most dangerous factor of all. While the trusts are continually abandoning factories or temporarily shutting them down in order to curtail production, so the trades-unions restrict the offering of labour. Not every man who wants to learn a trade is admitted to an apprenticeship; the trades-union does not allow young men to come in while old men who have experience are out of work. The regulation of the flow of labour into the trades which require training, and the refusal of union men to work with non-union men, are certainly the most tyrannical features of the situation; but the trades-unions are not embarrassed to find high-sounding arguments for their course, just as the trusts have found for their own similar doings.

Things will continue in this way on both sides, no doubt; and the nation at large can be content, so far at least as, through this concentration and strict discipline on both sides, the outcome of the labour question is considerably simplified. As long as the mass of capitalists is split up and that of working-men chaotically divided, arbitration is difficult, and the results are not binding. But when two well-organized parties oppose each other in a businesslike way, with mutual consideration and respect, the conference will be short, businesslike, and effective.

The next thing necessary is simply an arrangement which shall be so far as possible automatic for appointing an unprejudiced court of arbitration in any case when the two parties are not able to agree. In this matter public opinion has gone energetically to work. In December, 1901, at the instigation of the National Civic League, a conference of leading representatives of capital and labour was called, and this appointed a standing commission to pass on disputes between employers and labourers. All three parties were represented here — capital by the presidents of the largest trusts, railroads, and banks, trades-unions by the leaders of their various organizations, and the public by such men as Grover Cleveland, Charles Francis Adams, Archbishop

Ireland, President Eliot, and others, who enjoy the confidence and esteem of the whole nation.

It has been objected that the millions of unorganized working-men are not represented, but in fact these neutral leading men of the nation are at the same time the representatives of unorganized labour. If these were in any other way to be represented by delegates, they would have to organize in order to choose such delegates. But this is just what unorganized labour does not wish to do. Everything looks as if this permanent commission would have the confidence of the nation and, although created unofficially, would contribute a good deal to prevent the outbreak of real industrial wars. But there can be no doubt that the nation is ready to go further, and that if the two well-organized parties, together with the men in whom both sides put their confidence, are still not able to come to harmonious agreement, nor even to the appointment of a court of arbitration, then the nation will quite likely appoint an official and legally authorized board for compulsory arbitration.

The example of New Zealand is encouraging in this direction, although the experience of a small country may not be immediately applicable to a large one. Nevertheless, there is some wish to imitate that example, and to disregard the outraged feelings of capitalists who predict that American industry will collapse utterly if the country becomes socialistic enough to appoint arbitrators with the power to prescribe to capital what wages it shall pay, and how otherwise it shall carry on business. The nation has learned a good deal in the last two or three years.

A peaceable solution of the problem is promised also from another direction. The dramatic wars have concerned generally very large companies, which employ thousands of workmen. The whole thing has been repeated, however, on a more modest scale, where thousands of working people stood opposed not to large trusts but to hundreds of small employers, who were not separated from the working-men by any social cleft. Here the battles have often been more disastrous for the employers and their helplessness before small unions more patent. Then it became natural for them to imitate the example of the workmen and to form organizations to regulate the situation.

The first employers' union was formed in 1890 by the owners of newspapers, for whom sudden strikes are of course especially disastrous. For ten years very few trades followed this example; but in the last few years trades-unions of employers have been quietly forming in almost all trades, and here the situation has been much more favourable from the outset for bringing employer and labourer to a mutual understanding. While the employers were not organized, an understanding was hard to arrive at; but now both sides are able to make contracts which must be in all respects advantageous, and one of the most important clauses has regularly been that disputes shall be submitted to a court of arbitration.

Whether this solution will be a source of great satisfaction to the public seems doubtful, since, as soon as local employers and working-men close an agreement for offensive and defensive co-operation, the general public is left in the lurch, and an absolute monopoly is created. When, for instance, in a large city, all the proprietors in the electric trades have agreed to employ only union workmen, and all workmen have agreed to work for only such as belong to the employers' union, it is hardly possible for a new employer to step in as competitor and lower prices, since he would have difficulty in getting workmen. The consequence is that every house owner in the city who wants an electric bell must pay such prices as the employers' and workmen's unions have seen fit to agree on. Free competition is killed.

The problem of so-called economic freedom is thus opened up again. Trades-unions are, of course, the product of free and lawful agreement, but one of their most important achievements is to pledge themselves to furnish the employers' union with a certain number of workmen, which is sufficient for all needs. In return for this they receive the promise of the employers to hire only members of the working-men's union. The result is, then, that the workman himself becomes a mere pawn, and is dealt about like a Chinese coolie.

It is clear that these latest movements are able to contribute a great deal, and already have so contributed, to the reconciliation of capital and labour and to an appreciation of their common interests. The right is being more and more conceded to labour unions of controlling certain matters which relate to the discipline and conditions of work, and more assurance is given to the working-men of permanent employment, so that they are able to bring up their families with more confidence and security. And cases of dispute are more and more looked on as differences of opinion between partners of equal rank.

A good deal may still be done on both sides; especially the labour unions must be more strict in their discipline: they must become responsible for seeing that their members refrain from every sort of violence during wage wars, and that every violation of law, particularly with regard to strike-breakers, is avoided. It is true that labour unions have always preached calmness, but have nevertheless looked on willingly when individual members or groups of members, in their anger, have indulged in lawlessness and crime. This must be stopped. It was in the wish to avoid such responsibility that labour unions have hitherto struggled against being forced to become legal corporations; they have not wished to be legally liable for damages committed by their members. But such legal liability will be absolutely necessary if contracts between the unions of employers and those of labourers are to become important. It is perhaps even more necessary for both sides to learn what apparently American public opinion has forgotten, that a court of arbitration must really arbitrate judicially and not merely hit on compromises.

The labour question is still not solved in America; but one must close one's eyes to the events of recent years in order to think that it is unsolvable, or even unlikely to be solved soon. The period of warfare seems in the East nearly over; both sides have found ways of asserting themselves without impairing the progress of the nation's industry. And the nation knows that its progress will be more rapid in proportion as both parties maintain their equilibrium and protect industrial life from the tyranny of monopolies, whether of capital or labour.

PART THREE

INTELLECTUAL LIFE

CHAPTER FOURTEEN

The Spirit of Self-Perfection

THERE are three capital cities in the United States—Washington the political capital, New York the commercial, and Boston the intellectual capital. Everything in Washington is so completely subordinated to the political life that even the outward aspect of the city is markedly different from that of other American cities; buying and selling scarcely exist. In spite of its three hundred thousand inhabitants, one is reminded of Potsdam or Versailles; diplomats, legislators, and officials set the keynote. Washington is unique in the country, and no other large city tries to compete with it; unless, indeed, on a very small scale a few state capitals, like Albany, which are situated away from the commercial centres. Being unique, Washington remains isolated, and its influence is confined to the political sphere. As a result, there is a slight feeling of the unnatural, or even the unreal, about it; any movements emanating from Washington which are not political, hardly come to their full fruition. And although the city aspires to do, and does do, much for art, culture, and especially for science, its general initiative seems always to be lying under the weight of officialdom. It will never become the capital of intellect.

In a like way, New York is really informed by but a single impulse — the struggle for economic greatness. This is the meaning and the moral of its life. In this respect, New York is not, like Washington, unique. Chicago makes terrific strides in emulation of New York; and yet, so far as one now sees, the city of three million dwellers around the mouth of the Hudson will continue to be the economic centre of the New World. The wholesale merchants, the banker potentates, and the corporation attorneys set there the pace, as the senators and diplomats in

Washington, and dominate all the activities of the metropolis. Through their influence New York has become the centre of luxury and fashion, and wealth the most powerful factor in its social life. All this cannot take place, and in such extreme wise, without affecting profoundly the other factors of culture. The commercial spirit can be detected in everything that comes from New York. On the surface it looks as if the metropolis of commerce and luxury might perhaps be usurping for itself a leading place in other matters. And it is true that the politics of New York are important, and that her newspapers have influence throughout the land. But yet a real political centre she will never become; new and great political impulses do not withstand her commercial atmosphere. New York is the chief clearing-house for politics and industry; purely political ideas it transforms into commercial.

This is still more true of strictly intellectual movements. One must not be misled by the fact that there is no other city in the land where so many authors reside, where so many books and magazines are published, or so many works of art of all kinds are sold; or yet where so many apostles of reform lift up their voices. That the millions of inhabitants in New York constitute the greatest theatre for moral and social reforms, does not prove that the true springs of moral energy lie there. And the flourishing state of her literary and artistic activities proceeds, once more, from her economic greatness rather than from any real productive energy or intellectual fruitfulness. The commercial side of the intellectual life of America has very naturally centred itself in New York and there organized; but this outward connection between intellect and the metropolis of trade has very little to do with real intellectual initiative. Such association rather weakens than strengthens the true intellectual life; it subjects art to the influence of fashion, literature to the demands of commerce, and would make science bow to the exigencies of practical life; in short, it makes imminent all the dangers of superficiality. The intellectual life of New York may be outwardly resplendent, but it pays for this in depth; it brings into being no movements of profound significance, and therefore has no standing as a national centre in these respects. As the intellectual life of the political capital bears the stamp of officialdom, so is that of the commercial capital marked with the superficiality characteristic of trade and luxury. Intellectual life will originate new thoughts and spread them through the country only when it is earnest, pure, and deep; and informed, above all, with an ideal.

The capital of the intellectual life is Boston, and just as everything which comes out of Washington is tinged with politics, or out of New York with commerce, so are all the activities of Boston marked by an intellectual striving for ideal excellence. Even its commerce and politics are imbued with its ideals.

It is surprising how this peculiar feature of Boston strikes even the superficial observer. The European, who after the prescribed fashion lands at New York and travels to Philadelphia, Washington, Chicago, and Niagara, and then winds up his journey through the United States in Boston, has in this last place generally the impression that he has already come back from the New World into the Old. The admirable traditions of culture, the thoroughly intellectual character of the society, the predominance of interests which are not commercial — in fact, even the quaint and picturesque look of the city — everything strikes him as being so entirely different from what his fancy had pictured, from its Old World point of view, as being specifically American. And no less is it different from what the rest of his experience of the New World has given him. Not until he knows the country more thoroughly does he begin to understand that really in this Yankee city the true spirit of the purely American life is embodied.

The American himself recognizes this leading position of Boston in the intellectual life of his country, although he often recognizes it with mixed feelings. He is fond, with the light irony of Holmes, to call Boston "the hub of the universe." He likes to poke fun at the Boston woman by calling her a "bluestocking," and the comic papers habitually affirm that in Boston all cabbies speak Latin. But this does not obscure from him the knowledge that almost everything which is intellectually exalted and significant in this country has come from Boston, that Massachusetts, under the leadership of Boston, has become the foremost example in all matters of education and of real culture, and that there, on the ground of the oldest and largest academy of the country — Harvard University — the true home of New World ideals is to be found. And the intellectual pre-eminence of New England is no less recognizable in the representatives of its culture which Boston sends forth through the country; the artistic triumph of the Columbian Exposition may be ascribed to Chicago, but very many of the men who accomplished this work came from Massachusetts; the reform movement against Tammany belongs to the moral annals of New York, but those workers whose moral enthusiasm gained the victory are from New England. This latent impression, that all the best æsthetic and moral and intellectual impulses originate in New England, becomes especially deep the instant one turns one's gaze into the past. The true picture is at the present day somewhat overlaid, because owing to the industrial development of the West the emigration from New England has taken on such large proportions that the essential traits of Massachusetts have been carried through the whole land. In past times, her peculiar pre-eminence was much more marked.

Whoever traces back the origins of American intellectual life must go to the fourth decade of the seventeenth century. Then the colonies in the Southern and Middle States were flourishing as well as the Northern colonies of New England; but only in these last was there any real initiative toward intellectual culture. In the year 1636, only eight years after the foundation of Boston, Harvard College was founded as the first, and for a long while the only, school of higher learning. And among the products of the printing-press which this country gave forth in the whole seventeenth century such an astonishing majority comes from New England that American literary history has no need to consider the other colonies of that time. The most considerable literary figure of the country at that time was Cotton Mather, a Bostonian. The eighteenth century perpetuated these traditions. The greatest thinker of the country, Jonathan Edwards, was developed at Harvard, and Benjamin Franklin was brought up in Boston. The literature of New England was the best which the country had so far produced, and when the time came for breaking away politically from England, then in the same way the moral energy and enthusiasm of Boston took front rank.

Not until these days of political independence did the true

history of the free and independent intellectual life of America begin. Now one name followed close on another, and most of the great ones pertained to New England. Poets like Longfellow, Lowell, and Holmes were Bostonians; Whittier and Hawthorne also sprang from the soil of New England. Here, too, appeared the intellectually leading magazines; in the first half of the century the *North American Review*, in the second half the *Atlantic Monthly*. Here the religious movement of Unitarianism worked itself out, and here was formed that school of philosophers in whose midst stood the shining figure of Ralph Waldo Emerson. Here sounded the most potent words against slavery; here Parker, Garrison, Phillips, and Sumner poured forth their charges against the South into the midst of a public morally aroused. Here, also, first flourished the quiet work of scientific investigation. Since the day when Ticknor and Everett studied in Gôttingen in the year 1815, there sprang up in Massachusetts, more than anywhere else, the custom which caused young American scholars to frequent German schools of higher learning. The historians Prescott, Sparks, Bancroft, Parkman, and Motley were among this number. Here in Boston was the classic ground for the cultivation of serious music, and here was founded the first large public library. And all these movements have continued down to this day. None of the traditions are dead; and any one who is not deceived by superficial impressions knows that the most essential traits of Boston and New England are the ones which, in respect to intellectual life, lead the nation. Quite as the marble Capitol at Washington is the symbol of the political power of America, and the sky-scrapers of lower Broadway are the symbol of America's economic life, so we may say the elm-shaded college yard of Harvard is the symbol of American intellectual capacity and accomplishment.

It may seem astonishing at first that a single vicinity can attain such eminence, and especially that so small a part of the Union is able to impress its character on the whole wide land. The phenomenon, however, becomes almost a matter of course, if we put before ourselves how this world-power slowly grew from the very smallest beginnings, and how this growth did not take place by successive increments of large and compact masses of people who had their own culture and their own independent spirit, but took place by the continual immigration of wanderers who were detached and isolated, and who joined themselves to that which was already here, and so became assimilated. Then, as soon as a beginning had been made, and in a certain place a specific expression had been given to intellectual life, this way of thinking and this general attitude neccessarily became the prevailing ones, and in this way spread abroad farther and farther. If in the seventeenth century, instead of the little New England states, the Southern colonies, say, had developed a characteristic and independent intellectual life, then by the same process of constant assimilation the character and thought of Virginia might have impressed itself on the whole nation as have the character and thought of Massachusetts. Yet it was by no means an accident that the spirit which was destined to be most vital did not proceed from the pleasure-loving Virginians, but rather came from the severely earnest settlers of the North.

The way of thinking of those Northern colonists can be admirably characterized by a single word — they were Puritans. The Puritan spirit influenced the inner life of Boston Bay in the seventeenth century, and consequently the inner life of the whole country down to our time, more deeply and more potently than any other factor. The Puritanical spirit signifies something incomparably precious — it is much more admirable than its detractors dream of; and yet at the same time, it carries with it its decided limitations. For nearly three hundred years the genius of America has nourished itself on these virtues and has suffered by these limitations. That which the Puritans strove for was just what their name signifies — purity; purity in the service of God, purity of character, and, in an evil time, purity of life. Filled with the religious doctrines of Calvinism, that little band of wanderers had crossed the ocean in spite of the severest trials, in order to find free scope for their Puritan ideals; had left that same England where, some time later under Cromwell, they were to achieve a victory, although a short and after all insignificant one. They much more cared for the spotlessness of their faith than for any outward victory, and every impulse of their devout and simple lives was informed by their convictions. Under these circumstances it was no accident that here the intellectual and moral ideals were not obscured by any economic or political preoccupations; but from the very outset were accounted in themselves of prime importance. Harvard College was founded as a school for the Puritan clergy, and almost the entire American literature, which is to say the literature of New England, of the seventeenth century is purely religious, or at any rate is thoroughly permeated with the Calvinistic way of thought.

Of course, externally this is all entirely changed, and it is almost a typical example of this transformation, that Harvard, once a seminary for ministers, to-day prepares not one-fiftieth part of its five thousand students for the clerical calling. Indeed, as early as the year 1700, Yale University was founded in Connecticut, largely in the aim of creating a fortress for the old faith, because Harvard had become too much a place of free thought; and the great scholar of Harvard, the preacher Jonathan Edwards, went away from Boston in anger because it seemed to him, even in the eighteenth century, that the old Calvinistic traditions had been lost. And then finally, in the nineteenth century, appeared Unitarianism — a creed which became the most energetic enemy of Calvinism. These changes and disruptions were, however, rather an internal matter. They were actually nothing but small differences within the Puritan community. From the meagre days of the Pilgrim Fathers down to the time when Emerson in rhapsodic flights preached the ethical idealism of Fichte, and Longfellow wrote his "Psalm of Life," the old Puritan spirit remained predominant.

One fundamental note sounded through the whole. Life was not to be lived for the sake of pleasure, but for the sake of duty. Existence got its sense and value only in ethical endeavour; self-perfection was the great duty which took precedence over all others. Among the particularly dogmatic tenets of the Calvinistic theology this self-searching became, in the last resort, perhaps a somewhat dispiriting searching after inner signs by which God was expected to show somewhat arbitrarily his favour. More broadly taken, however, it signified rather a continual searching of the conscience — a conscious suppression of impure, of worldly, and of selfish impulses; and so in effect it was an untiring moral purification. And if in this theological atmosphere it appeared as if God had led a singularly large number of predestined spirits together into the New England colonies, the reason was obviously this — that in such a community of earncst, self-searching characters a moral purity developed such as was to be found nowhere in the wild turmoil of the Old World. When the entire life is so permeated by ethical ideals, there indeed the nobler part of man's nature cannot be conquered by lower instincts or by the sordid demands of every-day life.

Such a place could not fail to be a favourable environment for any intellectual undertakings. There serious books were more welcome than the merely amusing ones which flourished in the rest of the colonies. In New England more was done for education, the development of law and the service of God, than for any outward show or material prosperity. In short, the life of the intellect throve there from the very outset. And yet of course this spirit of culture necessarily took a turn very different from what it had been in the mother land, different from what it was on the Continent, and different from what it would have been if the Southern colonies had been intellectually dominant.

For the Puritan, absolutely the whole of culture was viewed from the moral point of view. But the moral judgment leads always to the individual; neither in the physical nor in the psychical world can anything be found which has an ethical value except the good will of the individual. No work of culture has any value in itself; it becomes ethically significant only in its relation to the individual will, and all intellectual life has ethically a single aim — to serve the highest development of the individual. From this point of view, therefore, science, poetry, and art have no objective value: for the Puritan, they are nothing to accept and to make himself subordinate to; but they are themselves subordinate means merely toward that one end — the perfection of the man. Life was a moral problem, for which art and science became important only in so far as they nourished the inner growth of every aspirant. In the language of the newer time we might say that a community developed under Puritan influences cared considerably more for the culture of its individual members than for the creation of things intellectual, that the intellectual worker did not set out to perfect art and science, but aimed by means of art and science to perfect himself.

Of course there must be some reciprocal working between the general body of culture and the separate personalities, but the great tendency had to be very different from that which it would have been had the chief emphasis been laid on æsthetic or intellectual productions as such. In Europe during the decisive periods the starting-point has been and to-day is, the objective; and this has only secondarily come to be significant for the subjective individual life. But in Puritan America the soul's welfare stood in the foreground, and only secondarily was the striving for self-perfection, self-searching, and self-culture made to contribute to the advance of objective culture. As a consequence individual characters have had to be markedly fine even at a time in which all creative achievements of enduring significance were very few. Just in the opposite way the history of the culture of non-puritanical Europe has shown the greatest creative achievements at the very times when personal morals were at their lowest ebb.

But the spirit of self-perfection can have still an entirely different source. In ethical idealism the perfection of personality is its own end; but this perfection of the individual may also be a means to an end, an instrument for bringing about the highest possible capacity for achievement in practical life. This is the logic of utilitarianism. For utilitarianism as well as for Puritan idealism the growth of science and art, and the development of moral institutions, are nothing in themselves, but are significant only as they work backward on the minds of the individuals. Idealism demands the intellectual life for the sake of the individual soul's welfare, utilitarianism for the sake of the individual's outward success. A greater antithesis could hardly be thought of; and nevertheless the desire for self-perfection is common to both, and for both the increase of the national products of culture are at the outset indifferent. It is clear that both of these tendencies in their sociological results will always reach out far beyond their initial aims. Puritanism and utilitarianism, although they begin with the individual, nevertheless must bear their fruits in the whole intellectual status of the nation. Ethical idealism aims not only to receive, but also to give. To be sure, it gives especially in order to inspire in others its own spirit of self-perfection, but in order so to inspire and so to work it must give expression to its inner ideals by the creation of objects of art and science. Utilitarianism, on the contrary, must early set such a premium on all achievements which make for prosperity that in the same way again the individual, from purely utilitarian motives, is incited to bring his thought to a creative issue. The intellectual life of the nation which is informed with Puritan and utilitarian impulses, will therefore, after a certain period, advance to a new and national stage of culture; but the highest achievements will be made partly in the service of moral ideals, partly in the service of technical culture. As the result of the first tendency, history, law, literature, philosophy, and religion will come to their flowering; in consequence of the second tendency, science and technique.

In modern Continental Europe, both these tendencies have been rather weakly developed. From the outset idealism has had an intellectual and æsthetic bias. Any great moral earnestness has been merely an episode in the thought of those nations; and in the same way, too, utilitarianism has played really a subordinate rôle in their intellectual life, because the desire for free initiative has never been a striking feature in the intellectual physiognomy. The love of truth, the enjoyment of beauty, and the social premiums for all who minister to this love and pleasure have been in Continental Europe more potent factors in the national intellectual life than either ethical idealism or practical utilitarianism. And it is only because of its steady assimilation of all European immigrants that the Puritan spirit of the New England colonies has become the fundamental trait of the country, and that moral earnestness has not been a mere episode also in the life of America.

There is no further proof necessary that, along with idealism, utilitarianism has in fact been an efficient factor in all intellectual activities of America. Indeed, we have very closely traced out how deeply the desire for self-initiative has worked on the population and been the actual spring of the economic life of all classes. But for the American it has been also a matter of course that the successful results of initiative presuppose, in addition to energy of character, technical training and the best possible liberal education. Here and there, to be sure, there appears a successful self-made man — a man who for his lack of making has only himself to thank — and he comes forward to warn young people to be wary of the higher culture, and to preach to them that the school of practical life is the sole high-road to success. But the exemplary organization of the great commercial corporations is itself a demonstration against any such fallacious paradoxes. Precisely there the person with the best training is always placed at the head, and the actual results of American technique would be still undreamt of if the American had preferred, before the solid intellectual mastery of his problems, really nothing but energy or "dash" or, say, mere audacity. The issues which really seriously interest the American are not between the adherents of culture and the adherents of mere push, undeterred by any culture; the material value of the highest possible intellectual culture has come to be a dogma. The real issues are mainly even to-day those between the Puritanical and utilitarian ideals of self-perfection. Of course those most in the heat of battle are not aware of this; and yet when in the thousandfold discussions the question comes up whether the higher schools and colleges should have fixed courses of instruction for the sake of imparting a uniform and general culture, or whether on the other hand specialization should be allowed to step in and so to advance the time for the technical training, then the Puritans of New England and the utilitarians of the Middle States are ranged against each other.

In fact, it is the Middle, and a little later on the Western, States, where along with the tremendous development of the instinct of individual initiative the pressure for the utilitarian exploitation of the higher intellectual powers has been most lively. Also this side of the American spirit has not sprung up to-day nor yesterday; and its influence is neither an immoral nor a morally indifferent force. Utilitarianism has decidedly its own ethics. It is the robust ethics of the Philistine, with its rather trivial references to the greatest good of the greatest number and citations of the general welfare. Benjamin Franklin, for instance, preached no mean morality, along with his labours for politics and science; but his words, "Honesty is the best policy," put morality on a level with the lightning-rod which he invented. Both are means toward human prosperity. Although born and bred in Boston, Franklin did not feel himself at home there, where for the best people life was thought to be "a trembling walk with God." For him Philadelphia was a more congenial field of activity. To-day there is no single place which is specially noted for its utilitarian turn of mind. It is rather a matter of general dissemination, for the influence of the entire Western population goes in this direction. But no one should for a moment imagine that this utilitarian movement has overcome or destroyed the Puritan spirit. The actual state of the national culture can be understood only as a working together of these two types of the spirit of self-perfection; and even to-day, the Puritan spirit is the stronger — the spirit of New England is in the lead.

All that we have so far spoken of relates to that which is distinctly of national origin; over and above this there is much which the American has adopted from other nations. The most diverse factors work to make this importation from foreign thought more easy. The wealth and the fondness for travel of the American, his craze for collections, and his desire to have in everything the best — this in addition to the uninterrupted stream of immigration and much else — have all brought it about that anything which is foreign is only too quickly adopted in the national culture. Not until very lately has a more or less conscious reaction against this sort of thing stepped in, partly through the increased strengthening of the national consciousness, but more specially through the surprisingly quick rise of native achievement. The time for imitation in architecture has gone by and the prestige of the English romance is at an end. And yet to-day English literature, French art, and German music still exercise here their due and potent influence.

Now, in addition to these influences which spring from the culture of foreign nations, come finally those impulses which are not peculiar to any one nation, but spring up in every country out of the lower instincts and pleasures. Everywhere in the world mere love of diversion tries to step in and to usurp the place of æsthetic pleasure. Everywhere curiosity and sensational abandon are apt to undermine purely logical interests, and everywhere a mere excitability tries to assume the rôle of moral ardour. Everywhere the weak and trivial moral, æsthetic, and intellectual appeals of the variety stage may come to be preferred over the serious appeals of the drama. It is said that this tendency, which was always deeply rooted in man's nature, is felt more noticeably in our nervous and excitable times than it was in the old days. In a similar way one may say that it shows out still stronger in America than it does in other countries. The reason for this is clear. Political democracy is responsible for part of it; for in the name of that equality which it postulates, it instinctively lends more countenance to the æsthetic tastes, the judgment, and the moral inspiration of the butcher, the baker and candlestick-maker than is really desirable if one has at heart the development of absolute culture. Perhaps an even more important factor is the purely economic circumstance that in America the masses possess a greater purchasing power than in any other country, and for this reason are able to exert a more immediate influence on the intellectual life of the land. The great public is not more trivial in the United States than elsewhere; it is rather, as in every democracy, more mature and self-contained; but in America this great public is more than elsewhere in the material position to buy great newspapers, and to support theatres; and is thus able to exert a degrading influence on the intellectual level of both newspaper and theatre.

In this way, then, the tendency of the lower classes toward those things which are trivial may sometimes conceal the fine traits in the picture of the national intellectual life; just as the readiness for imitation may, for a time, bring in many a foreign trait. But nevertheless, there is in fact a clearly recognizable, a free and independent intellectual life, which everywhere reveals the opposition or the balance between Puritanism and utilitarianism, and which is everywhere dominated by that single wish which is common both to Puritans and to utilitarians — the desire for the best possible development of the individual, the desire for self-perfection.

Since, however, it remains a somewhat artificial abstraction to pick out a single trait — even if that is the most typical — from the intellectual make-up of the nation, so of course it is understood from the outset that all the other peculiarities of the American work together with this one to colour and shape his real intellectual life. Everywhere, for instance, one notes the easily kindled enthusiasm of the American and his inexhaustible versatility, his religious temperament and his strongly marked feeling of decorum, his lively sense of justice and his energy, and perhaps most of all his whimsical humour. Each one of these admirable traits involves some corresponding failing. It is natural that impetuous enthusiasm should not make for that dogged persistence which so often has brought victory to various German intellectual movements; so, too, a nice feeling for form grows easily impatient when it is a question of intellectual work requiring a broad and somewhat careless handling. Devotion to the supersensuous is inclined to lead to superstition and mysticism, while a too sensitive feeling for fair play may develop into hysterical sympathy for that which is merely puny; versatility, as is well known, is only too apt to come out in fickle dilettante activities, and the humour that bobs up at every moment destroys easily enough the dignity of the most serious occasion. And yet all this, whether good or bad, is a secondary matter. The spirit of self-perfection remains the central point, and it must be always from this point that we survey the whole field.

A social community which believes its chief duty to be the highest perfection of the individual will direct its main attentions to the church and the school. The church life in America is, for political reasons, almost entirely separated from the influence of the state; but the force with which every person is drawn into some church circle has not for this reason lost, but rather gained, strength. The whole social machine is devised in the interests of religion, and the impatience of the sects and churches against one another is slight indeed as compared with the intolerance of the churches as a whole against irreligion. The boundaries are drawn as widely as possible, so that ethical culture or even Christian Science may be included under the head of religion; but countless purely social influences make strongly toward bringing the spirit of worship in some wise into every man's life, so that an hour of consecration precedes the week of work, and every one in the midst of his earthly turmoil heeds the thought of eternity, in whatever way he will. And these social means are even stronger than any political ones could be.

There is very much which contributes to deepen the religious feeling of the people and to increase the efficiency of the churches. The very numerousness of the different sects is not the least factor in this direction, for it allows every individual conscience to find somewhere its peculiar religious satisfaction. An additional impulse is the high position which woman occupies, for she is more religiously endowed than man. And yet another factor is the many social functions which the churches have taken on themselves. In this last there is much that may seem to the stranger too secular: the church which is at the same time a club, a circulating library, and a place to lounge in, seems at first sight to lose something of its dignity; but just because it has woven itself in by such countless threads to the web of daily life, it has come to pass that no part of the social fabric is quite independent of it. Of course the external appearance of a large city does not strongly indicate this state of things; but the town and country on the other hand give evidence of the strong religious tendency of the population, even to the superficial observer; and he will not understand the Americans if he leaves out of account their religious inwardness. The influence of religion is the only one which is stronger than that of politics itself, and the accomplished professional politicians are sharp to guide their party away from any dangerous competition with that factor.

The church owes its power more or less to the unconscious sentiments in the soul of the people, whereas the high position and support of the public school is the one end toward which the conscious volition of the entire nation is bent with firmest determination. One must picture to one's self the huge extent of the thinly populated country, the incomparable diversity of the population which has come in, bringing many differences of race and language, and finally the outlay of strength which has been necessary to open up the soil to cultivation, in order to have an idea of what huge labours it has taken to plant the land from the Atlantic to the Pacific with a thick sowing of schools. The desire for the best possible school system is for the American actually more than a social duty — it has become a passion; and although here and there it may have gone astray, it has never been afraid of any difficulty.

The European who is accustomed to see the question of education left to the government can hardly realize with what intensity this entire population participates in the solution of theoretical problems and in the overcoming of practical difficulties. No weekly paper or magazine and no lecture programme of any association of thinking men could be found in which questions of nurture and education are not treated. Pedagogical publications are innumerable, and the number of those who are technically informed is nearly identical with the number of those who have brought up children. The discussions in Germany over, we may say, high schools and technical schools, over modern and ancient languages, or the higher education of women, interest a relatively small circle as compared with similar discussions in America. The mere fact that this effort toward the best school instruction has so deeply taken hold of all classes of society, and that it leads all parties and sects and all parts of the country to a united and self-conscious struggle forward is in itself of the highest value for the education of the whole people.

In the broad basis of the public school is built a great system of higher instruction, and the European does not easily find the right point of view from which to take this. The hundreds of colleges, universities, professional schools, and polytechnics seem to the casual observer very often like a merely heterogeneous and disordered collection of separate institutions, because there seems to be no common standard, no general level, no common point of view, and no common end; in short, there seems to be no system. And nevertheless, there is at the bottom of it all an excellent system. It is here that one finds the most elaborate and astonishing achievement of the American spirit, held together in one system by the principle of imperceptible gradations; and no other organization, specially no mere imitation of foreign examples, could so completely bring to expression the American desire for self-perfection.

The topics of school and university would not make up one-half of the history of American popular education. In no other country of the world is the nation so much and so systematically instructed outside of the school as in America, and the thousand forms in which popular education is provided for those who have grown beyond the schools, are once more a lively testimony to the tireless instinct for personal perfection. Evening schools, summer schools, university extension courses, lecture institutes, society classes, and debating clubs, all work together to that end; and to omit these would be to give no true history of American culture. The back-ground of all this, however, is the great national stock of public library books, from which even the poorest person can find the best books and study them amid the most delightful surroundings.

The popular educational libraries, together with the amazingly profuse newspaper and magazine literature, succeed in reaching the whole people; and, in turn, these institutions would not have become so large as they are if the people themselves had not possessed a strong desire for improvement. This thirst for reading is again nothing new; for Hopkinson, who was acquainted with both England and America in the middle of the eighteenth century, reported with surprise the difference in this respect between the two countries. And since that time the development has gone on and on until to-day the magazines are printed by the hundreds of thousands, and historical romances in editions of half a million copies; while public libraries exist not only in every small city, but even in the villages, and those in the large cities are housed in buildings which are truly monuments of architecture. As the influence of books has grown, the native literature has increased and the arts of modelling and sculpture have come forward at an equal pace, as means of popular culture. Museums have arisen, orchestras been established, the theatre developed, and an intellectual life has sprung up which is ready to measure itself against the best that European culture has produced. But the real foundation of this is even to-day not the creative genius, but the average citizen, in his striving after self-perfection and culture.

Once every year the American people go through a period of formal meditation and moral reflection. In the month of June all the schools close. Colleges and universities shut their doors for the long summer vacation; and then, at the end of the year of study, according to an old American custom, some serious message is delivered to those who are about to leave the institutions. To make such a farewell speech is accounted an honour, depending, of course, on the rank of the institution, and the best men in the country are glad to be asked. Thus it happens that, in the few weeks of June, hundreds of the leading men — scholars, statesmen, novelists, reformers, politicians, officials, and philanthropists — vie with one another in impressing on the youth the best, deepest, and most inspiring sentiments; and since these speeches are copied in the newspapers and magazines, they are virtually said to the whole people. The more important utterances generally arouse discussions in the columns of the newspapers, and so the month of June comes to be a time of reflection and meditation, and of a certain refreshment of inspiration and a revival of moral strength. Now, if one looks over these speeches, one sees that they generally are concerned with one of two great themes. Some of them appeal to the youth, saying; Learn and cultivate yourselves, for this is the only way in which you will arrive at becoming useful members of society: while the others urge; Cultivate yourselves, for there is in life nothing more precious than a full and harmonious development of the soul. The latter sentiment is that of the Puritan, while the former is that of the utilitarian. And yet the individualistic tendency is in both cases the same. In both cases youth is urged to find its goal in the perfection of the individual.

CHAPTER FIFTEEN

The Schools and Popular Education

THE Dutch population of New Amsterdam started a school system in the year 1621. The first public Latin school was founded in Boston in the year 1635. The other colonies soon followed. Clearly the English governor of Virginia, Berkeley, had not quite grasped the spirit of the New World, when at about that time he wrote home, that, thank God, no public schools and no printing-press existed here, and when he added his hope that they would not be introduced for a hundred years, since learning brings irreligion and disobedience into the world, and the printing-press disseminates them and fights against the best intentions of the government. For that matter it was precisely Virginia which was the first colony, even before Boston and New York, to consider the question of education. As early as 1619 the treasurer of the Virginia Company had proposed, in the English Parliament, that 15,000 acres of land should be set aside in the interests of a school for higher education. The English churches became interested in the plan, and an abundant supply of money was got together. Ground and buildings had been procured for lower and higher instruction and all was in working order, when in 1622 the fearful Indian war upset everything. The buildings were destroyed, and all thought of public education was for a long time given up. This is how that condition came about which so well pleased Governor Berkeley. But this mishap to the Virginia colony shows at once how the American system of education has not been able to progress in any systematic way, but has suffered frequent reverses through war or political disturbance. And it has developed in the different parts of the country at a very different pace, sometimes even in quite different directions. It was not until after the Civil War — that is, within the last thirty years — that these differences have to a large extent been wiped out. It is only to-day that one can speak of a general American system. The outsider will, therefore, come to a better understanding of the American educational system if he begins his study with conditions as they are to-day, for they are more unified and therefore easier to understand, than if he were to try to understand how the present has historically come from the complicated and rather uninteresting past.

So we shall not ask how the educational system has developed, but rather what it is to-day and what it aims to be. Even the present-day conditions may easily lead a German into some confusion, because he is naturally inclined to compare them with the conditions at home, and such a comparison is not always easy. Therefore, we must picture to ourselves first of all the fundamental points in the system, and describe its principal variations from the conditions in Germany. A few broad strokes will suffice for a first inspection.

The unit of the system in its completest form is a four years' course of instruction. For the easier survey we may think of a boundary drawn at what in Germany would be between the Obersekunda and Prima of a Gymnasium or Realschule. Now, three such units of the system lie before and two after this line of demarcation. The son of a well-to-do family, who is to study medicine in Harvard University, will probably reach this line of demarcation in his eighteenth year. If he is advanced according to the normal scheme he will have entered a primary school at six years of age, the grammar school at ten, and the high school at fourteen. Thus he will complete a twelve years' course in the public schools. Now he crosses our line of demarcation in his eighteenth year and enters college. And as soon as he has finished his four years' course in college he begins his medical studies in the university, and he is twenty-six years old when he has finished. If we count in two years of early preparation in the kindergarten, we shall see that the whole scheme of education involves twenty-two years of study. Now, it is indeed possible that our young medical student will have progressed somewhat more rapidly; perhaps he will have reached the high school after six instead of eight years of study; perhaps he will finish his college course in three years, and it may be that he will never have gone to kindergarten. But we have at first to concern ourselves with the complete plan of education, not with the various changes and abbreviations of it, which are very properly allowed and even favoured.

The line which we call the great boundary is the time when the lad enters college. Now, what is the great significance of this moment? The German, who thinks in terms of Gymnasium and Universität, is almost sure to fall into a misapprehension; for college is neither the one nor the other. So far as the studies themselves go, it coincides rather well with the Prima of the Gymnasium and the first two or three semesters in the philosophical faculty of the German university. And yet even this by no means tells one what a college really is. Above all, it does not explain why the American makes the chief division at the time of entering college, while the German makes it when he enters the medical or law school. This needs to be explained most clearly, because very important factors are here involved, which bear on the future of American civilization. And so we must give especial attention to college and the professional schools. But that discussion is to be reserved for the chapter on the universities. For the present, we have only to deal with the system of instruction in those schools which prepare for college.

And so, leaving the kindergarten out of the question, we shall deal with those three institutions which we have called primary, grammar, and high schools. Usually, the first two of these are classed together as one eight years' course of training. The European will be struck at once that in this system there is only one normal plan of public education. The future merchant, who goes to the high school and ends his studies in the eighteenth year, has to follow the same course of study in the primary and grammar schools as the peasant and labourer who studies only until his fourteenth year, and then leaves school to work in the field or the factory. And this young merchant, although he goes into business when he is eighteen years old, pursues exactly the same studies as the student who is later to go to college and the university. Now in fact, in just this connection the actual conditions are admirably adapted to the most diverse requirements; the public schools find an admirable complement in private schools; and, more than that, certain very complicated differentiations have been brought about within the single school, in order to overcome the most serious defects of this uniformity. Nevertheless, the principle remains; the system is uniform, and the American himself finds therein its chief merit.

The motive for this is clear. Every one, even the most humble, should find his way open; every one must be able to press on as far as his own intelligence permits; in other words — words which the American pedagogue is very fond of uttering — the public school is to make the spirit of caste impossible. It is to wipe out the boundaries between the different classes of society, and it is to see to it, that if the farmer's lad of some remote village feels within himself some higher aspiration, and wants to go beyond the grammar school to the high school and even to college, he shall find no obstacle in his way. His advance must not be impeded by his suddenly finding that his entrance into the high school would need some different sort of previous training.

This general intermingling of the classes of society is thought to be the panacea of democracy. The younger generations are to be removed from all those influences which keep their parents apart, and out of all the classes of society the sturdiest youth are to be free of all prejudice and free to rise to the highest positions. Only in this wise can new sound blood flow through the social organism; only so can the great evils incident to the formation of castes which have hindered old Europe in its mighty progress be from the very outset avoided. The classic myth relates of the hero who gained his strength because he kissed the earth. In this way the American people believe that they will become strong only by returning with every fresh generation to the soil, and if the German Gymnasia were a hundred times better than they are, and if they were able to prepare a boy from early childhood for the highest intellectual accomplishment, America would still find them unsuited to her needs, because from the outset they are designed for only a small portion of the people, and for this reason they make it almost impossible for the great mass of boys to proceed to the universities from the ordinary public schools.

All of this is the traditional confession of belief of the pedagogue of the New World. But now since America, in the most recent times, has nevertheless begun to grow in its social structure considerably more like antiquated Europe, and sees itself less and less able to overcome the tendencies to a spirit of caste, so a sort of mild compromise has been made between the democratic creed and aristocratic tendencies, especially in the large cities of the East. Nevertheless, any one who keeps his eyes open will admit that, so far as the public school goes, intellectual self-perfection is in every way favoured, so that every single child of the people may rise as high as he will. Grammar school leads to the high school, and the high school leads to college.

There is another factor which is closely related to the foregoing. Education is free and obligatory. In olden times there was more the tendency for the parents of the children, rather than for the general taxpayer, to pay for the maintenance of the schools. Indeed, there were times in which the remission of the special school tax was considered almost an act of charity, which only the poorest of the parents would accept. But now it is quite different. The school system knows no difference between rich and poor, and it is a fundamental principle that the support of the schools is a matter for the whole community. The only question is in regard to the high school, since after all only a small percentage of school children comes as far as the high school; and it is unjust, some say, to burden the general taxpayer with the expenses of such school.

Nevertheless, on this point the opinions of those have won who conceive that it is the duty of the community to nurture any effort toward self-culture, even in the poorest child. The chief motive in olden times, wherefore the expenses of the schools were paid by all, was that the school was leading toward religion; to-day the official motive for the application of taxes to the maintenance of schools is the conviction that only an educated and cultivated people can rule itself. The right to vote, it is said, presupposes the right to an education by means of which every citizen becomes able to read the papers of the day and to form his own independent opinion on public matters. But since every public school is open also to the daughters of the citizens who possibly want the right to vote, but do not so far have it, it becomes clear that the above-mentioned political motive is not the whole of the matter. It is enough for technical discussions of taxation, but what the community is really working for is the greatest possible number of the most highly educated individuals. Free instruction is further supplemented in various states — as, for instance, in Massachusetts — by supplying text-books gratis. Some other states go so far as to supply the needy children with clothing. The obligatory character of education goes with the fact that it is free. In this respect, too, the laws of different states are widely divergent. Some require seven, others eight, still others even nine years, of school training. And the school year itself is fixed differently in different states.

These differences between the states point at once to a further fact which has been characteristic of the American school system from the very beginning. Responsibility for the schools rests at the periphery; and in extremely happy fashion the authority is so divided that all variations, wherever they occur, are adaptations to local conditions; and nevertheless unity is preserved. A labile equilibrium of the various administrative factors is brought about by harmonious distribution of the authority, and this is, in all departments of public life, the peculiar faculty of the Americans.

The federal government, as such, has no direct influence on education. The tirelessly active Bureau of Education at Washington, which is under the direction of the admirable pedagogue, Mr. Harris, is essentially a bureau for advice and information and for the taking of statistics. The legal ordinances pertaining to school systems is a matter for the individual state, and the state again leaves it to the individual community, within certain limits of course and under state supervision, to build schools and to organize them, to choose their teachers, their plans of education, and their school-books. And at every point here, exactly as in the striking example of the federal Constitution, the responsibility is divided between the legislative and the executive bodies. The state inspector of schools is co-ordinate with the state legislature, and the school inspector of a city or a country district, who is elected now by the mayor, now by the council, now perhaps directly by the community, is a sort of technical specialist with considerable discretionary power; he is co-ordinated to the school committee, which is elected by the community, and which directs the expenditures and confirms all appointments.

The responsibility for the moral and intellectual standards, for the practical conditions, and for the financial liabilities incurred by every school, rests therefore immediately with the community, which has to pay for their support, and whose children are to derive advantage. And nevertheless, the general oversight of the state sees to it that neither whimsicality nor carelessness abuses this right, nor departs too widely from approved traditions. These authorities are further supplemented in that the state legislature is more or less able to make up for differences between rich and poor districts and between the city and the country, besides directly carrying on certain normal schools in which the teachers for the elementary and grammar schools are trained.

Very great and very diverse advantages are the immediate outcome of this administrative system. Firstly, an interest in the well-being of the schools is developed in every state, city, and town, and the spirit of self-perfection is united with the spirit of self-determination. Secondly, there is a good deal of free play for local differences — differences between states and differences within the state. Nothing would have been more unsuitable than in this whole tremendous territory to institute a rigidly fixed school system, as say by some federal laws or some inter-state agreements. If there were the same educational provisions for the negro states of the South and for the Yankee states of New England, for the thickly settled regions of the East and the prairies of the West, these provisions would be either empty words or else they would tend to drag down the more highly educated parts of the country to the level of the lowest districts. The German who objects to this on the ground of uniformity, does so because he is too apt to think of the great similarity which exists between the different sections of Germany. The only proper basis for a comparison, however, would be his taking Europe as a whole into consideration.

If now the outward unity of this system which we have described is nevertheless to be maintained, it is absolutely necessary that this form shall be filled with very different contents. And this introduction of diversity is intrusted to the state legislatures and local authorities, who are familiar with the special conditions. In this way the so-called school year in the school ordinances of a rich state may be about twice as long as in another state whose poorer population is perhaps not able entirely to do without the economies of child labour. But the differences between the schools take particularly such a form that the attainments of the different schools, corresponding to the culture and prosperity of the state in which they are, and of the community, are consciously designed to be quite different. The remoter rural schools which, on account of the poverty of their patronage perhaps, have to get on with one badly trained teacher and have to carry on four grades of instruction in one school-room, and other schools which employ only university graduates, which bring their scholars together in sumptuous buildings, afford them laboratories and libraries, and have all the wealth of a great city to back them — these schools cannot seriously enter into competition with each other. Two years of study in one place will mean more than four in another; and there is no special danger in this, since this very inequality has brought it about that the completion of one grade in a school by no means carries with it the right to enter the next higher grade of any other school. It is not the case that a scholar who has passed through any grammar school whatsoever will be welcome in every high school. This is regulated by an entrance examination for the higher school, which will not accept merely the certificate of graduation from a lower.

There are still other forms of this differentiation. In the first place, the schools have shown a growing tendency to establish various parallel courses, between which the scholars are allowed to choose. In the simplest case there is, perhaps, on the one hand a very practical plan of education, and a second course which is rather more liberal; or, again, there may be a course for those who are not meaning to study further, and another course for those who are preparing for the entrance examinations to some higher school. The fiction of uniformity is preserved in this way. The child does not, as in Germany, choose between different schools; but he chooses between plans of education in the same school, and every day the tendency deepens to make this elective system more and more labile.

But the most modern pedagogues are not content even with this, and insist, especially in the grade of the high school, that the make-up of the course of study must be more and more, as they say, adapted to the individuality of the scholars; or, as others think, to the whimsies of the parents and the scholars. Since, in accordance with this, the entrance examinations for the colleges leave considerable free play for the choice of specialties, this movement will probably go on developing for some time. It appeals very cleverly to the instincts of both the Puritans and the utilitarians. The Puritan demands the development of all individual gifts, and the utilitarian wants the preparation for an individual career. Nevertheless, there are some indications of an opposite tendency. Even the utilitarian begins to understand that he is best fitted for the fight who bases his profession on the broadest foundation — who begins, therefore, with his specialization as late as possible. And the Puritan, too, cannot wholly forget that nothing is more important for his personal development than the training of the will in the performance of duty, in the overcoming of personal inhibitions, and that therefore for the scholar those studies may well be the most valuable which at the first he seems least inclined to pursue. Further differentiation results from the almost universal opportunity to pass through the schools in a somewhat shorter time. It is also possible for a student to progress more rapidly in one branch of study, and so in different branches to advance at different rates.

We have over and above all these things, and more particularly in the large cities, a factor of differentiation which has so far been quite left out of account. This is the private school. The goal for the student who wants to advance is not the diploma of graduation, but preparation for the entrance examinations which are next higher. This preparation can perhaps be obtained more thoroughly, more quickly, and under more fortunate social conditions, in a private school, which charges a high tuition, but in this way is able to engage the very best teachers, and able perhaps to have smaller classes than the public schools. And such a private school will be able to extend its influence over all education. Large and admirably conducted institutions have grown up, often in some rural vicinity, where several hundred young persons lead a harmonious life together and are educated from their earliest youth, coming home only during vacation. In such ways the private school has taken on the most various forms, corresponding to obvious needs. They find justly the encouragement of the state.

This diversity which we have sketched of public and private educational institutions brings us at once to another principle, which has been and always will be of great significance in American material and intellectual history — the principle that everywhere sharp demarcations between the institutions of different grades are avoided, and that instead, sliding gradations and easy transitions are brought about, by means of which any institution can advance without any hindrance. This is in every case the secret of American success — free play for the creations of private initiative. The slightest aspiration must be allowed to work itself out, and the most modest effort must be helped along. Where anything which is capable of life has sprung up, it should be allowed to grow. Sharp demarcation with official uniformity would make that impossible; for only where such unnoticeably small steps form the transitions, is any continuous inner growth to be expected. We have emphasized the local differences. The grammar school in New York is probably more efficient than the high school in Oklahoma, and the high school in Boston will carry its students probably as far as some little college in Utah.

The thousands of institutions which exist afford a continuous transition between such extremes, and every single institution can set its own goal as high as it wishes to. A school does not, by any act of law, pass into a higher class; but it perfects itself by the fact that the community introduces improvements, makes new changes, appoints better and better teachers, augments the curriculum, and adds to its physical equipment. In such ways, the school year by year imperceptibly raises its standard. And the same is true of the private school. Everything is a matter of growth, and in spite of the outward uniformity of the system every school has its individual standard. If one were to require that only such institutions should exist as had distinctly limited and similar aims, then the American would look on this as he would on an attempt to force all cities to be either of ten thousand, a hundred thousand, or a million inhabitants. Of course, all this would have to be changed, if as in Germany, certain school grades carried with them certain privileges. In America no school diploma carries officially any privilege at all. It is the entrance examination, and not the tests for graduation, which is decisive; and if there is any question of filling a position, the particular schools which the candidates have gone through are the things which are chiefly taken into account.

We must mention one more trait which differentiates the American from the German school system. The American public school is co-educational. Co-education means theoretically that boys and girls are entitled to common education, but practically it means that boys are also tolerated. The idea that the school should not recognize differences of sex is most firmly rooted in the Middle-Western States, where the population is somewhat coldly matter of fact; but it has spread through the entire country. It is said that family life lends the authority for such an intermingling of boys and girls; that, through a constant and mutual influence, the boys are refined and the girls are made hardy; and that, during the years of development, sexual tension is diminished. It is one of the chief attractions that the private school offers to smaller circles that it gives up this hardening of the girls and refining of the boys, and is always either a boys' or a girls' school.

Even more striking than the presence of girls in the boys' schools is, perhaps, the great number of women who figure as teachers. The employment of women teachers began in the Northern States after the Civil War, because as a direct result of the decimation of the population there were not men teachers enough. Since that time this practice has increased throughout the country; and although high schools generally try to get men teachers, the more elementary schools are really wholly in the hands of women. Men do not compete for the lower schools, since the competition of the women has brought down the wages, and more remunerative, not to say more attractive, situations are to be found in plenty. Women, on the other hand, flock in in great numbers, since their whole education has made them look forward to some professional activity, and no other calling seems so peculiarly adapted to the feminine nature. The merits and drawbacks of co-education and of the predominance of women teachers cannot be separated from the general question of woman's rights; and so the due treatment of these conditions must be put off until we come to consider the American woman from all sides.

It is not difficult to criticise rather sharply the school system, and any one living in the midst of American life will feel it a duty to deliver his criticism without parsimony. A system which expects the best it is to have, from the initiative of the periphery, must also expect the ceaseless critical co-operation of the whole nation.

In this way, then, crying and undeniable evils are often pointed out. We hear of political interference in the government of the schools, and of the deficient technical knowledge of local authorities, of the insufficient preparation of the women teachers, the poorness of the methods of instruction, of waste of time, of arbitrary pedagogical experiments, and of much else. In every reproach there is a kernel of truth. The connection of the schools with politics is in a certain sense unavoidable, since all city government is a party government. And the attempts to separate elections for the school committee entirely from politics will probably, for a long time yet, meet with only slight success. Since, however, every party is able to put its hand on discrete and competent men, the only great danger is lest the majority of those concerned misuse their influence for party ends, and perhaps deal out school positions and advancements as a reward for political services.

Such things certainly happen; but they never escape the notice of the opposite party, and are faithfully exploited in the next year's election. In this way any great abuses are quickly checked. The secret doings, which have nothing to do with politics, are a great deal more dangerous. It is certain that the enormous school budgets of the large cities offer the possibility for a deplorable plundering of the public treasury, when it is a question of buying new land for school-houses, of closing building contracts, or of introducing certain text-books. A committee-man who in these ways is willing to abuse his influence is able to derive a considerable profit; and so it may well happen that men come to be on the school boards through political influence or through a professed interest in school matters, who have really no other aim than to get something out of it. It is very hard in such matters to arrive at a really fair judgment, since the rival claimants who are unsuccessful are very apt to frame the opinion that they have been so because the successful man had "connections."

This sharply suspicious tendency and spirit of overwatchfulness on the part of the public are certainly very useful in preserving the complete integrity of the schools, but they occasion such a considerable tumult of rumour that it easily misleads one's judgment as to the real condition of the institutions. In general, the school committees appointed in the local elections perform their work in all conscientiousness. It is, of course, the fact that they are rather frequently ignorant of things which they need to know; but the tendency to leave all technical questions in the hands of pedagogical specialists, and to undertake any innovations only at the advice of the school superintendent and directors, is so general that on the whole things do not go quite so badly as one might expect.

The preparation of the teachers leaves very much to be wished. Those teachers who have been educated in higher seminaries are by no means numerous enough to fill all the public school positions; and even less does the number of college graduates suffice for the needs of the high schools. The fact that the teaching profession is remarkably versed in pedagogics only apparently relieves this defect; for even the very best methods of teaching are of course no substitute for a firm grasp of the subject which is being taught. In the elementary schools the lack of theoretical training in a teacher is, of course, less felt. The instinct of the teacher, her interest in the child, her tact and sympathy, in short the personal element, are what is here most important. And since all this, even in the superficially educated woman, springs purely from her feminity, and since the energetic women are extraordinarily eager and self-sacrificing, so it happens that almost everywhere the elementary schools are better conducted by their women teachers than are the high schools.

So far as method goes, a great deal too much stress is laid on the text-book; too much is taught mechanically out of the book, and too little is directly imparted by the teacher. The teacher submits passively to the text-book; and the American himself is inclined to defend this, since his democratic belief in the power of black and white is unlimited. Before all, he regards it as the chief aim of the public school to prepare the citizen for the independent reading of newspapers and books. Therefore, the scholars are expected to become as much acquainted as possible with the use of books. There is no doubt that the American school children read more newspapers in later life than do the European, and it must also be borne in mind that for the most part the text-books are notably good. Perhaps, in regard to attractiveness, they even go rather too far. In this way not only the books of natural history, but also of history and literature, are crowded with illustrations. The geographies are generally lavishly gotten-up volumes with all sorts of entertaining pictures. The appeals to the eye, both by means of the text-books and even more by the aid of demonstrations and experiments, are carried really to excess. Even the blackboards, which run along all four walls of the school rooms, encourage the teacher to appeal rather more to the eye than to the ear.

Also the much-discussed experimentation with new pedagogical ideas is an unfortunate fact which cannot be denied. A central authority, which was held fully responsible for a large district, would of course be conservative; but where the details of teaching are left entirely to every local school inspector, then of course many shallow reforms and many unnecessary experiments with doubtful methods will be undertaken. The school inspector will feel himself moved to display his modern spirit and to show his pedagogical efficiency in just these ways. And many a private school, in order to make itself attractive to the public, is obliged to introduce the latest pedagogical foibles and to make all sorts of concessions, perhaps against its will. To-day the method of writing will be oblique, to-morrow vertical, and the day after to-morrow "reformed vertical." The pupils to-day are taught to spell, to-morrow to pronounce syllables, the next day to take the whole word as the least unit in language; and a day later they may be taught the meaning of the words by means of appropriate movements.

It is not quite easy for a professional psychologist, who lectures every year to hundreds of students in that subject, to say openly that this irregular and often dilettante craze for reform is encouraged by nothing more than by the interest in psychology which rages throughout the country. The public has been dissatisfied with teachers, and conceived the idea that everything would be better if the pedagogues concerned themselves more with the psychical life of their pupils. And since for this purpose every mother and every teacher has the materials at hand, there has sprung up a pseudo-psychological study of unexampled dimensions. It is only a small step from such a study to very radical reforms. Yet everything here comes back in the end to the independent interests and initiative of the teacher; and although many of these reforms are amateurish and immature, they are nevertheless better than the opposite extreme would be — that is, than a body of indifferent and thoughtless teachers without any initiative at all.

It is also not to be denied that the American school wastes a good deal of time, and accomplishes the same intellectual result with a much greater outlay of time than the German school. There are plenty of reasons for this. Firstly, it is conspicuous throughout the country that Saturday is a day of vacation. This is incidental to the Puritan Sunday. The school day begins at nine o'clock in the morning, and the long summer vacations are everywhere regarded as times for idleness, and are almost never broken in on by any sort of work. Again, the home duties required of the school children are fewer than are required of the German child, and all the instruction is less exacting. The American girls would hardly be able to stand so great a burden if the schools demanded the same as the German boys' schools. Herewith, however, one must not forget that this time which is taken from work is dedicated very specially to the development of the body, to sport and other active exercises, and in this way the perfection of the whole man is by no means neglected. Moreover, America has been able, at least so far, to afford the luxury of this loss of time; the national wealth permits its young men to take up the earning of their daily bread later than European conditions would allow.

When the worst has been said and duly weighed, it remains that the system as a whole is one of which the American may well be proud — a system so thoroughly elastic as to be suited to all parts of the country and to all classes of society. It is a system which indubitably, with its broad foundation in the popular school, embodies all the requirements for the sound development of youth, and one, finally, which is adapted to a nation accustomed to individualism, and which meets the national requirement of perfection of the individual.

And now finally we may give a few figures by way of orientation. In the year 1902 out of the population of over 75,000,000, 17,460,000 pupils attended institutions of learning. This number would be increased by more than half a million if private kindergartens, manual training schools, evening schools, schools for Indians, and so forth were taken into account. The primary and intermediate schools have 16,479,177 scholars, and private schools about 1,240,000. This ratio is changed in favour of the private institutions when we come to the next step above, for the public high schools have 560,000 and the private ones 150,000 students. The remainder is in higher institutions of learning. To consider for the moment only the public schools; instruction is imparted by 127,529 male and 293,759 female teachers. The average salary of a male teacher is more than $46 a month, and of the female teacher $39. The expenditures were something over $213,000,000; and of this about 69 per cent. came from the local taxes, 16 per cent. from the state taxes, and the remainder from fixed endowments. Again, if we consider only the cities of more than 8,000 inhabitants, we find the following figures: in 1902 America had 580 such cities, with 25,000,000 inhabitants, 4,174,812 scholars and 90,744 teachers in the municipal public schools, and 877,210 students in private schools. These municipal systems have 5,025 superintendents, inspectors, etc. The whole outlay for school purposes amounted to about $110,000,000.

The high schools are especially characteristic. The increase of attendance in these schools has been much faster than that of the population. In 1890 there were only 59 pupils for every 10,000 inhabitants; in 1895 there were 79; and in 1900 there were 95. It is noticeable that this increase is entirely in the public schools. Of those 59 scholars in 1890, 36 were in public high schools and 23 in private. By 1900 there were 25 in private, but 70 in the public schools. Of the students in the public high schools 50 per cent. studied Latin, 9 per cent. French, 15 per cent. German. The principal courses of study are English grammar, English literature, history, geography, mathematics, and physics. In the private schools 23 per cent. took French, 18 per cent. German, 10 per cent. Greek. Only 11 per cent. of students in the public high schools go to college, but 32 per cent. of those in private schools. Out of the 1,978 private high schools in the year 1900, 945 were for students of special religious sects; 361 were Roman Catholic, 98 were Episcopalian, 96 Baptist, 93 Presbyterian, 65 Methodist, 55 Quaker, 32 Lutheran, etc. There were more than 1,000 private high schools not under the influence of any church. One real factor of their influence is found in the statistical fact that, in the public high schools, there are 26 scholars for every teacher, while in the private schools only 11.

The following figures will suffice to give an idea of the great differences which exist between the different states: The number of scholars in high schools in the state of Massachusetts is 15 to every 1,000 citizens; in the state of New York, 11; in Illinois, 9; in Texas, 7; in the Carolinas, 5; and in Oklahoma, 3. In the private high schools of the whole country the boys were slightly in the majority; 50.3 per cent. against 49.7 per cent. of girls. In order to give at least a glimpse of this abyss, we may say that in the public high school the boys were only 41.6 per cent., while the girls were 58.4 per cent.

So much for the schools proper. We shall later consider the higher institutions — colleges, universities, and so forth — while the actual expanse of the school system in America, as we have said before, is broader still. In the first place, the kindergarten, a contribution which Germany has made, deserves notice. Very few creations of German thought have won such complete acceptance in the New World as Froebel's system of education; and seldom, indeed, is the German origin of an institution so frankly and freely recognized. Froebel is everywhere praised, and the German word "Kindergarten" has been universally adopted in the English language.

Miss Peabody, of Boston, took the part of pioneer, back in the fifties. Very soon the movement spread to St. Louis and to New York, so that in 1875 there were already about one hundred kindergartens with 3,000 children. To-day there must be about 5,000 kindergartens distributed over the country, with about a quarter of a million children. During this development various tendencies have been noticeable. At first considerable stress was laid on giving some rational sort of occupation to the children of the rich who were not quite old enough for school. Later, however, philanthropic interest in the children of the very poorest part of the population became the leading motive — the children, that is, who, without such careful nurture, would be exposed to dangerous influences. Both of these needs could be satisfied by private initiative. Slowly, however, these two extremes came to meet; not only the richest and poorest, but also the children of the great middle classes from the fourth to the sixth year, were gradually brought under this sort of school training. As soon as the system was recognized to be a need of the entire community, it was naturally adopted into the popular system of instruction. To-day two hundred and fifty cities have kindergartens as a part of their school systems.

Meanwhile there has sprung up still another tendency, which took its origin in Chicago. Chicago probably has the best institution with a four years' course for the preparation of teachers for the kindergarten. In this school not only the professional teachers, but the mothers, are welcomed. And through the means of this institution in Chicago, the endeavour is slowly spreading to educate mothers everywhere how to bring up their children who are still in the nursery so as to be bodily, intellectually, and morally sound. The actual goal of this very reasonable movement may well be the disappearance of the official kindergarten. The child will then find appropriate direction and inspiration in the natural surroundings of its home, and the kindergarten will, as at first, limit itself chiefly to those rich families who wish to purchase their freedom from parental cares, and to such poor families as have to work so hard that they have no time left to look after their children. A slow reaction, moreover, is going on among the public school teachers. The child who comes out of the Froebel school into the primary school is said to be somewhat desultory in his activities, and so perhaps this great popularity of the kindergarten will gradually decrease. Nevertheless, for the moment the kindergarten must be recognized as a passing fashion of very great importance, and, so far as it devotes itself philanthropically to children in the poor districts, its value can hardly be overestimated.

Now, all this instruction of the child before he goes to school is much less significant and less widely disseminated than those thousandfold modes of instruction which are carried on for the development of men and women after they have passed their school days. Any one who knows this country will at once call to mind the innumerable courses of lectures, clubs of study, Chautauqua institutions, university extension courses, women's clubs, summer and correspondence schools, free scientific lectures, and many other such institutions which have developed here more plentifully than in any other country. After having dwelt on the kindergarten, one is somewhat tempted to think also of these as men and women gardens. There is really some resemblance to a sort of intellectual garden, where no painful effort or hard work is laid out for the young men and women who wander there carelessly to pluck the flowers. But it is, perhaps, rather too easy for the trained person to be unjust to such informal means of culture. It is really hard to view the latter in quite the right perspective. Whosoever has once freed himself from all prejudices, and looked carefully into the psychic life of the intellectual middle classes, will feel at once the incomparable value of these peculiar forms of intellectual stimulation, and their great significance for the self-perfection of the great masses.

While the kindergarten was imported from Germany, the university extension movement came from England. This movement, which was very popular about a decade ago, is decidedly now on the wane. Those forms of popular education which are distinctly American have shown themselves to possess the most vigour. There is one name which, above all others, is characteristic of these native institutions. It is Chautauqua. This is the old Indian name for a lake which lies very pleasantly situated in the State of New York, about two hours by train from Buffalo. The name of the lake has gone over to the village on its banks, the name of the village has been carried over to that system of instruction which was first begun there, and now every institution is called Chautauquan which is modelled after that system. Even to-day the school at Chautauqua is the foutain-head of the whole movement. Every summer, and particularly through July and August, when the school-teachers have their vacation, some ten thousand men and women gather together to participate in a few weeks of recreation and intellectual stimulation. The life there is quiet and simple; concerts and lectures are given in the open air in an amphitheatre which seats several thousand, and there are smaller classes of systematic instruction in all departments of learning. The teachers in special courses are mostly professors. The lecturers in the general gatherings are well-known politicians, officials, scholars, ministers, or otherwise distinguished personalities. For the sake of recreation, there are excursions, dramatic performances, and concerts. A few hours of systematic work every day serve as a stimulus for thought and culture, while the mutual influence of the men and women who are so brought together and the whole atmosphere of the place generate a real moral enthusiasm.

The special courses which range from Greek, the study of the Bible, and mathematics to political economy, philosophy, and pedagogics, are supplemented on the one hand by examinations from which the participators get a certificate in black and white which is highly prized among teachers; and on the other side, by suggestions for the further carrying on by private reading of the studies which they have elected. The enthusiastic banner-bearer of Chautauqua is still to-day one of its founders, Bishop Vincent. He has done more than any one else toward bringing harmony into the monotonous and intellectually hungry lives of hundreds of thousands throughout the country, and especially of public school teachers. And in this work the instruction, the religious strengthening, the instillation of personal contentment, patriotic enthusiasm, æsthetic joy in life, and moral inspiration, are not to be separated.

When Theodore Roosevelt, who was then governor of New York, spoke in the Chautauqua amphitheatre to more than ten thousand persons, he turned enthusiastically to Bishop Vincent and said, "I know of nothing in the whole country which is so filled with blessing for the nation." And when he had finished, the whole audience gave him the Chautauqua salute; ten thousand handkerchiefs were waved in the air — an extraordinary sight, which in Chautauqua signifies the greatest appreciation. This custom began years ago, when a deaf scholar had given a lecture, and while the thundering applause was sounding which the speaker himself could not hear, Bishop Vincent brought out this visible token of gratification; and this form of applause not only became a tradition there, but also spread to all other Chautauqua institutions throughout the country. To-day there are more than three hundred of these, many of them in beautifully situated summer resorts, and some equipped with splendid libraries, banquet halls, casinos, and clubs. Some of these concentrate their energies in particular lines of learning, and of course they are very different in scope and merit. And nevertheless the fundamental trait of idealism shows through all these popular academies.

Among other varieties of popular instruction there are the attempts at university extension, which are very familiar. The chief aim is here to utilize the teaching forces and other means of instruction of the higher educational institutions for the benefit of the great masses. Often the thing has been treated as if it were a matter of course, in a political democracy, that colleges and universities ought not to confine themselves to the narrow circles of their actual students, but should go out and down to the artisans and labourers. But it was always asserted that this education should not consist merely in entertaining lectures, but should involve a form of teaching that presupposed a certain participation and serious application on the part of the attendants. And the chief emphasis has been laid on having every subject treated in a series of from six to twelve meetings, on distributing to the hearers a concise outline of the lectures with references to literature, on allowing the audience after the lecture to ask as many questions as it desired, and on holding a written examination at the end of the course. Any one who has passed a certain number of these examinations receives a certificate. In one year, for example, there were 43 places in which the University of Philadelphia gave such courses of lectures. The University of Chicago has arranged as many as 141 courses of six lectures each, in 92 different places. Other higher institutions have done likewise; and if indeed the leading universities of the East have entirely declined to take part, nevertheless the country, and particularly the West, is everywhere scattered with such lecture courses.

These lectures can be divided into two groups; those which are instructive and educate their hearers, and those which are inspiring and awaken enthusiasm. The first are generally illustrated with stereopticon pictures, the last are illustrated with poetical quotations. Here, as everywhere in the world, the educational lectures are often merely tiresome, and the inspiring ones merely bombastic. But the reason for the rapid decline in this whole movement is probably not the bad quality of the lectures, but the great inconvenience which the lecturers feel in going so far from their accustomed haunts. It is not to be doubted that very much good has come after all from this form of instruction. The summer schools have a similar relation to the higher institutions, but a much more thorough-going character; and while the university extension movement is waning, the summer school instruction is on the increase. First of all, even the leading universities take part in it, although it is mostly the second violins who render the music; that is to say, younger instructors rather than the venerable professors are the ones who teach. High school teachers and ministers often return in this way to their alma mater, and the necessity of devoting one's self for six weeks to a single subject gives to the whole enterprise a very much more scholarly character. That interesting summer school which was held a few years ago in Cambridge is still remembered, when Harvard invited at its own expense 1,400 of the most earnest Cuban school teachers, and instilled in them through six long weeks something of American culture.

Again, and this quite independent of the higher institutions and of any formal courses, there are the institutions for free lectures. Indeed, there are so many that one might almost call them lecture factories. The receptive attitude of the American public of all classes toward lectures surpasses the comprehension of the European. In many circles, indeed, this is positively a passion; and the extraordinary plentifulness of opportunity, of course, disciplines and strengthens the demand, which took its origin in the same strong spirit of self-perfection.

A favourable fact is undoubtedly the high perfection to which the lecture has been cultivated in America. As compared with European countries, a larger proportion of lectures may fairly be called works of art as regards both their content and their form. The American is first of all an artist in any sort of enthusiastic and persuasive exposition. For this very reason his lectures are so much more effective than whatever he prints, and for this reason, too, the public flocks to hear him. This state of things has also been favoured by the general custom of going to political meetings and listening to political speeches. In Boston and its suburbs, for example, although it is not larger than Hamburg, no less than five public lectures per day on the average are delivered between September and June. In contrast to German views, it is considered entirely appropriate for lecturers on all public occasions to receive financial compensation; just as any German scholar would accept from a publisher some emolument for his literary productions. This is, of course, not true of lectures at congresses, clubs, or popular gatherings. In a state like Massachusetts, every little town has its woman's club, with regular evenings for lectures by outside speakers; and the condition of the treasury practically decides whether one or two hundred dollars shall be paid for some drawing speaker who will give a distinguished look to the programme; or whether the club will be satisfied with some teacher from the next town who will deliver his last year's lecture on Pericles, or the tubercle bacillus, for twenty dollars. And so it is through the entire country; the quantity decreases as one goes South, and the quality as one goes West.

All this is no new phenomenon in American life. In the year 1639 lectures on religious subjects were so much a matter of course in New England, and Bostonians were so confirmed in the habit of going to lectures, that a law was passed concerning the giving of such lectures. It said that the poor people were tempted by the lecturer to neglect their affairs and to harm their health, as the lectures lasted well into the night. Scientific lectures, however, came into popular appreciation not earlier than the nineteenth century. In the first decade of that century, the famous chemist, Silliman, of Yale University, attained a great success in popular scientific lectures. After the thirties "lyceums" flourished throughout the land, which were educational societies formed for the purpose of establishing public lecture courses.

To be sure, these were generally disconnected lectures, in which political and social topics predominated. Those were the classic days of oratory, when men like Webster, Channing, Everett, Emerson, Parker, Mann, Sumner, Phillips, Beecher, Curtis, and others enthused the nation with their splendid rhetoric, and presented to the masses with pathos that we no longer know those great arguments which led to the Civil War. The activities of later decades emphasized the intellectual side. Splendid institutions have now been organized for popular lectures and lecture courses in all the leading cities. Thus the Peabody Institute in Baltimore, the Pratt Institute in New York, the Armour Institute in Chicago, and the Drexel Institute in Philadelphia have come into existence. The catalogue of the lectures and courses which, for instance, the Pratt Institute announces every winter fills a whole volume; and nevertheless, every one who pays his annual fee of five dollars is entitled to take part in all of them. Every day from morning to night he may listen to lectures by men who are more or less well known throughout the country, and who come specially to New York in order to give their short courses of some six lectures.

The highest undertaking of this sort is the Lowell Institute in Boston. In 1838, after a tour through Egypt, John A. Lowell added a codicil to his will, whereby he gave half of his large income for the free, popular, scientific instruction of his native town. The plan that has been followed for sixty years is of inviting every winter eight or ten of the most distinguished thinkers and investigators in America and England to give cycles of six or twelve connected lectures. The plentiful means of this foundation have made it possible to bring in the really most important men; and on the other hand, for just this reason an invitation to deliver the Lowell Lectures has come to be esteemed a high honour in the English-speaking world. Men like Lyell and Tyndall and many others have come across the ocean; even Agassiz, the well-known geologist, came to the New World first as a Lowell lecturer, and then later settled at Harvard University. Up to this time some five thousand lectures have been held before large audiences by this institute. The great advantage which this has been to the population of Boston can in no wise be estimated, nor can it ever be known how much this influence has done for the spirit of self-perfection in New England.

In a certain sense, however, we have already overstepped the field of popular education. The high standard of the Lowell Institute and the position of its speakers have brought it about that almost every course has been an original exposition of new scientific lines of thought. While the other popular courses have got their material second-hand, or have been at least for the speaker a repetition of his habitual discourses to students, in the Lowell Institute the results of new investigations have been the main thing. And so we have come already to the domain of productive science, of which we shall have later to treat.

One who looks somewhat more deeply will realize that, outside the Lowell Institute, there is no thought in by far the larger part of these lectures and readings, of original scientific endeavour. And the question inevitably comes up, whether the intellectual life of the country does not lose too much of its strength because the members of the community who should be especially devoted to intellectual production are enticed in so many different ways into the paths of mere reproduction. To be sure, it is never a professional duty with these men, but the temptation is so great as to overcome the latent resistance of even the best of them. There are a few, it is true, who see their highest goal in these popular and artistic expositions of their department of science; and a few who feel that their highest call, their most serious life-work, is to bear science philanthropically out to the masses. But it is different with most of them. Many like the rewards; it is such an easy way for the ready speaker, perhaps, of doubling his salary from the university: and especially the younger men whose income is small, find it hard to resist the temptation, although just they are the ones who ought to give all their free energy to becoming proficient in special lines of investigation. Yet even this is not the chief motive. In countless cases where any financial return to the speaker is out of the question, the love of rhetoric exerts a similar temptation. The chief motive, doubtless, is that the American popular opinion is so extraordinarily influenced by the spoken word, and at the same time popular eloquence is spread abroad so widely by the press, that not only a mere passing reputation, but also a strong and lasting influence on the thought of the people, can most readily be gotten in this way.

And so everything works together to bring a large amount of intellectual energy into the service of the people. The individual is hardly able to resist the temptation; and certainly very many thus harm seriously their best energies. Their popularization of knowledge diminishes their own scholarship. They grow adapted to half-educated audiences; their pleasure and capacity for the highest sort of scientific work are weakened by the seductive applause which follows on every pretty turn of thought, and by the deep effect of superficial arguments which avoid and conceal all the real difficulties. This is most especially true of that merely mechanical repetition which is encouraged by the possession of a lecture manuscript. If it is true that Wendell Phillips repeated his speech on the Lost Arts two thousand times, it was doubtless a unique case, and is hardly possible to-day. Nevertheless, to-day we find most regrettably frequent repetitions; and a few competent intellects have entirely abandoned their activities on regular academic lines to travel through the country on lecture tours. For instance, a brilliant historian like John Fiske, would undoubtedly have accomplished much more of permanent importance if he had not written every one of his books, in the first instance, as a set of lectures which he delivered before some dozen mixed audiences.

On the other hand, we must not suppose that these lectures before educational institutions are all hastily and mechanically produced. If the lectures were so trivial their preparation would demand little energy, and their delivery would much less satisfy the ambition of those who write them; and so, on both accounts, they would be much less dangerous for the highest productiveness of their authors. The level is really extremely high. Even the audience of the smallest town is rather pampered; it demands the most finished personal address and a certain tinge of individuality in the exposition. And so even this form of production redounds somewhat to the intellectual life of the nation. The often repeated attempt to depict some phase of reality, uniquely and completely in a one-hour lecture, or to elucidate a problem in such a short time, leads necessarily to a mastery in the art of the essay. Success in this line is made easier by the marked feeling for form which the American possesses. In a surprisingly large number of American books, the chapters read like well-rounded and complete addresses. The book is really a succession of essays, and if one looks more carefully, one will often discover that each one was obviously first thought out as a lecture. Thus the entire system of popular education by means of lectures has worked, beyond doubt, harmfully on creative production, but favourably on the development of artistic form in scientific exposition, on the art of essay, and on the popular dissemination of natural and social sciences and of history and economics most of all.

If one wished to push the inquiry further, and to ask whether these advantages outweigh the disadvantages, the American would decline to discuss the problem within these limits; since the prime factor, which is the effect on the masses who are seeking cultivation, would be left out of account. The work of the scholar is not to be estimated solely with reference to science or to its practical effects, but always with reference to the people's need for self-perfection. And even if pure science in its higher soarings were to suffer thereby, the American would say that in science, as everywhere else, it is not a question of brilliant achievements, but of moral values. For the totality of the nation, he would say, it is morally better to bring serious intellectual awakenings into every quiet corner of the land, than to inscribe a few great achievements on the tablets of fame. Such is the sacrifice which democracy demands. And yet to-day the pendulum begins very slowly to swing back. A certain division of labour is creeping in whereby productive and reproductive activities are more clearly distinguished, and the best intellectual energies are reserved for the highest sort of work, and saved from being wasted on merely trivial tasks.

But even the effect on the masses has not been wholly favourable. We have seen how superficiality has been greatly encouraged. It is, indeed an artificial feeding-ground for that immodesty which we see to spring up so readily in a political democracy, and which gives out its opinion on all questions without being really informed. To be sure, there is no lack of admiration for what is great; on the contrary, such admiration becomes often hysterical. But since it is not based on any sufficient knowledge, it remains after all undiscriminating; the man who admires without understanding, forms a judgment where he should decline to take any attitude at all. It may be, indeed, that the village population under the influence of the last lecture course is talking about Cromwell and Elizabeth instead of about the last village scandal; but if the way in which it talks has not been modified, one cannot say that a change of topic signifies any elevation of standard. And if, indeed, the village is still to gossip, it will seem to many more modest and more amiable if it gossips about some indifferent neighbour, and not about Cromwell.

On the other hand, we must not fail to recognize that, especially in the large institutions, as the Chautauquas, and in the university extension courses and the summer schools, everything possible is done to escape this constant danger. In the first place, the single lectures are very much discouraged, and a course of six to twenty lectures rather is given on a single topic; then the written examinations, with their certificates, and finally, the constant guidance in private reading have their due effect. Indeed, the smallest women's club is particular to put before its members the very best books which relate to the subjects of their lectures; and smaller groups are generally formed to study carefully through together some rather large treatise.

The total amount of actual instruction and intellectual inspiration coming to the people outside of the schools, is, in these ways, immeasurable. And the disadvantages of superficiality are somewhat outweighed by a great increase and enrichment of personality. Of course, one could ask whether this traditional way is really the shortest to its goal. Some may think that the same expenditure of time and energy would give a better result if it were made on a book rather than on a course of lectures. Yet the one does not exclude the other. Hearing the lecture incites to the reading of the book; and nowhere is more reading done than in the United States. There is one other different and quite important factor in the situation. The man who reads is isolated, and any personal influence is suppressed. At a lecture, on the other hand, the peculiarly personal element is brought to the front, both in the speaker and in the hearer — the spoken word touches so much more immediately and vitally than the printed word, and gives to thought an individual colouring. Most of all, the listener is much more personally appealed to than the reader; his very presence in the hall is a public announcement of his participation. He feels himself called, with the other hearers, to a common task. And in this way a moral motive is added to the intellectual. They both work together to fill the life of every man with the desire for culture. Perchance the impersonal book may better satisfy the personal desire for self-perfection, and yet the lecture will be more apt to keep it alive and strengthen it as a force in character and in life.

It is indifferent whether this system of popular education, these lectures before the public, has really brought with it the greatest possible culture and enlightenment. It is at least clear that they have spread everywhere the most profound desire for culture and enlightenment, and for this reason they have been the necessary system for a people so informed with the spirit of individual self-perfection.

CHAPTER SIXTEEN

The Universities

WHEN American industry began, a short time ago, to disturb European circles, people very much exaggerated the danger, because the event was so entirely unexpected. The "American peril" was at the door before any one knew about it, or even supposed that America really possessed an industry which amounted to anything. It will not be long before Europe will experience a like surprise in the intellectual sphere. A great work will certainly appear, as if accomplished in a moment, before any one supposes that America so much as dreams of science and investigation. At the time, people tardily said to themselves that such industry could only have been built on firm rock, and never would have been able to spring up if American economic life had really been founded, as was then supposed, on avarice and corruption. And similarly, in the intellectual sphere, people will have to trace things back, and say in retrospect that such achievements could not be brought forth suddenly, and that serious and competent scientific work throughout the country must really have gone before. It is not here, in this world of intellectual labour, as in the economic world; there is no question of threatening rivalry, there is no scientific competition; there is nothing but co-operation. And yet even here no people can, without danger to its own achievements, afford to ignore what another nation has done. The sooner that Europe, and in particular Germany, acquaints itself with the intellectual life of America, so much more organically and profitably the future labour in common will develop. For any one who knows the real situation can already realize, without the gift of prophecy, that in science more than in other spheres the future will belong to these two countries.

On the part of Germany to-day there prevails an almost discouraging ignorance of everything which pertains to American universities; and we may say, at once, that if we speak of science we shall refer to nothing but the universities. As in Germany, so it is in the United States, in sharp and notable contrast to France and England, that the academic teacher is the real priest of science. In England and France, it is not customary for the great investigator to be at the same time the daily teacher of youth. In America and Germany he is exactly this. America has, to be sure, historians and national economists like Rhodes, Lodge, Roosevelt, Schouler, and others who are outside of academic circles; and very many lawyers, doctors and preachers, who are scientifically productive; and her most conspicuous physicists, so far as reputation goes, like Edison, Bell, Tesla, and so many others, are advancing science indirectly through their discoveries and inventions. Strictly speaking, the officials of the scientific institutions at Washington are likewise outside of the universities, and the greatest intellectual efficiency has always been found among these men. Nevertheless, it remains true that on the whole, the scientific life of the nation goes on in the universities, and that the academic instruction conveyed there is the most powerful source of strength to the entire American people.

The German still has no confidence in American science, is fond of dwelling on the amusing newspaper reports of Western "universities" which are often equivalent to a German Sekunda, or on those extraordinary conditions which prevailed "a short time ago" in the study of medicine. This "short time ago" means, however, in the intellectual life of Germany an entirely different length of time from that which it means in the New World. One is almost tempted to compare the intellectual development of Germany and America by epochs in order to get a proper means of comparing intervals of time in these respective countries. The primitive times of the Germans, from the days of Tacitus down to their conversion to Christianity under Charlemagne in about the year 800, would correspond, then, to the one hundred and fifty years from the discovery of America up to the beginning of the Puritan era in 1630. The next period would embrace in Germany seven hundred years more — up to the time when Germany freed itself from Rome. In America this would be again a century and a half, up to 1776, when the nation freed itself from England. Then follow after the Reformation during a period of three hundred years, the Thirty Years' War, the Renaissance of the eighteenth century, the downfall of the Napoleonic influence, and, finally, the war for freedom. And once again the corresponding intervals on this side of the ocean have been of very much shorter duration; firstly years of war, then the æsthetic rise in the middle of the century, then the sufferings of the Civil War, the period of reconstruction, and, finally, peace. After 1813 a new period commences, which ends in 1870 with the German amalgamation into a nation. Historically incomparable with Germany's great war against the French, America had in 1898 an insignificant war with Spain; but for the national consciousness of the Americans it played, perhaps, no less important a rôle. In fact, there began at that time probably a certain culmination in American intellectual development which in its six years is comparable in effect with what the Germans went through during several decades after the Franco-Prussian War. Indeed, all that happened in America a hundred years ago is felt to lie as far back as the events which took place in Germany three hundred years ago; and, in matters of higher education and scientific research, conditions have probably changed more in the last ten years than they have changed during fifty years in Germany.

The many false ideas, however, depend for credence, so far as they have any foundation, not alone on the reports of the previous condition of things, but also on misleading accounts of the conditions to-day. For even the best-intentioned narrator is very apt to be misled, because he finds it so hard to free himself from ordinary German conceptions. The position of the German schools of higher education is so easily grasped, while that in America is so complicated, that the German is always tempted to bring clearness and order into what he sees as confusion, by forcing it into the simple scheme to which he is accustomed, and thus to misunderstand it.

The German traveller is certain to start from the distinction so familiar to him between the Gymnasium and the university with four faculties, and he always contents himself with making but one inquiry: "Is this institution a university with four faculties?" And when he is told that it is not, he is convinced to his entire satisfaction that it is therefore only a Gymnasium. Indeed, very many of the educated Germans who have lived in America for some decades would still know no better; and, nevertheless, the conditions are really not complicated until one tries to make them fit into this abstract German scheme. The principle of gradations which is manifest in all American institutions is in itself fully as simple as the German principle of sharp demarcations. Most foreigners do not even go so far as to ask whether a given institution is a university. They are quite content to find out whether the word university is a part of its name. If they then ascertain from the catalogue that the studies are about the same as those which are drilled into the pupils of a Sekunda, they can attest the shameful fact: "There are no universities in America to be in any wise compared with the German universities."

In the first place, it should be said that the word "university" is not used in America in the same sense as in Germany, but is almost completely interchangeable with the word "college," as a rather colorless addition to the proper name of any institution whatsoever, so long only as its curriculum goes beyond that of the high school, and so long also as it is not exclusively designed to train ministers of the gospel, doctors, or lawyers. A higher school for medical instruction is called a "medical school," and there are similarly "law schools" and "divinity schools," whereas, in the college or university, as the term is generally used, these three subjects are not taught. College is the older word, and since the institutions in the East are in general the older ones, the name college has been and still is in that region the more common. But in the West, where in general the institutions are on a considerably lower level, the newer name of university is the more usual. No confusion necessarily arises from this, since the institutions which are styled now college and now university represent countless gradations, and the general term is without special significance. No one would think of saying that when he was young he went to a university, any more than he would say that on a journey he visited a city. In order to make the statement entirely clear, he would add the explicit name of the institution. Every specialist knows that a man who has spent four years in Taylor University in Indiana or at Blackburn

University in Illinois, or at Leland University in Louisiana, or at other similar "universities," will not be nearly so well educated as a man who has been to Yale College or Princeton College or Columbia College. The proper name is the only significant designation, and the addition of "college" or "university" tells nothing.

Out of this circumstance there has independently developed, in recent years in pedagogical circles, a second sense for the word "university." By "university" there is coming to be understood an institution which is not only a college or a university in the old sense, but which furthermore has various professional schools. Even in this sense of the word, it is not exactly the same as the German conception, since such an institution includes the college, whereas there is nothing in Germany which would correspond to this collegiate department. Moreover, here belongs also a part of what the Germans have only in the technological institute. Finally, there is one more usage which arises in a way from a confusion of the two that we have mentioned. Some persons are inclined to mean by "university" a first-class college, and by "college" an institution of an inferior standard; and so, finally, the proper name of the institution is the only thing to go by, and the entire higher system of education in the country can be understood only in this way.

Therefore, we shall abstract from the designations of these institutions, and consider only what they really are. We have before us the fact that hundreds of higher institutions of learning exist without any sharp demarcation between them; that is, they form a closely graded scale, commencing with secondary schools and leading up to universities, of which some are in many respects comparable with the best institutions of Germany. In the second place, the groupings of the studies in these institutions are entirely different from those which prevail in Germany, especially owing to the fact that emphasis is laid on the college, which Germany does not have. It could not be different; and this condition is, in fact, the patent of American success. If we try to understand the conditions of to-day from those of yesterday, the real unity of this system comes out sharply. What was, then, we have to ask, the national need for higher instruction at the time when these states organized themselves into one nation?

In the first place, the people had to have preachers, while it was clear, nevertheless, that the state, and therefore the entire political community, was independent of any church, and must never show any favour to one sect over another. And so it became the duty of each separate sect to prepare its own preachers for their religious careers as well or as badly as it was able. The people, again, had to have lawyers and judges. Now the judges, in accordance with the democratic spirit, were elected from the people, and every man had the right to plead his own case in court : — so that if any man proposed to educate and prepare himself to plead other men's cases for them, it was his own business to give himself the proper education and not the business of the community. He had to become an apprentice under experienced attorneys, and the community had not to concern itself in the matter, nor even to see to it that such technical preparation was grounded on real learning. School-teachers were necessary, but in order to satisfy the demands of the times it was hardly necessary for the teacher to go in his own studies very much beyond the members of his classes. A few more years of training than could be had in the public schools was desirable, but there was no thought of scholarship or science. On the lowest level of all, a hundred years ago, stood the science of medicine. It was a purely practical occupation, of which anybody might learn the technique without any special training. He might be an apprentice with some older physician, or he might pick it up in a number of other ways.

As soon as we have understood the early conditions in this way, we can see at once how they would have further to develop. It is obvious that in their own interests the sects would have to found schools for preachers. The administrators of justice would of course consult together and found schools of law, in which every man who paid his tuition might be prepared for the legal career. Doctors would have to come together and found medical schools which, once more, every one with a public school training would be free to attend. Finally, the larger communities would feel the necessity of having schools for training their teachers. In all this the principle of social selection would have to enter in at once. Since there were no formal provisions which might prescribe and fix standards of excellence, so everything would be regulated by the laws of supply and demand. The schools which could furnish successful lawyers, doctors, teachers, and clergymen would become prosperous, while the others would lead a modest existence or perhaps disappear. It would not be, however, merely a question of the good or bad schools, but of schools having entirely different standards, and these adapted to purely local conditions. The older states would, of course, demand better things than the new pioneer states; thickly settled localities would fix higher requirements than rural districts; rich districts higher than poor. In this way some schools would have a longer course of study than others, and some schools demand more previous training as a condition of entrance than others. So it would soon come to mean nothing to say simply that one had taken the legal, or medical, or theological course, as the one school might offer a four years' course and the other a course of two years, and the one, moreover, might demand college training as preparation, and the other merely a grammar-school education. Every school has its own name, and this name is the only thing which characterizes its standard of excellence. In this way there is no harm at all if there are three or four medical schools in one city, and if their several diplomas of graduation are of entirely different value.

What is the result of this? It is a threefold one. In the first place, popular initiative is stimulated to the utmost, and every person and every institution is encouraged to do its best. There are no formal regulations to hamper enterprising impulses, to keep back certain more advanced regions, or to approve mediocrity with an artificial seal of authority. In the second place, technical education is able to adapt itself thoroughly to all the untold local factors, and to give to every region such schools of higher training as it needs, without pulling down any more advanced sections of the country to an artificially mediocre level more adapted to the whole country. In the third place, the free competition between the different institutions insures their ceaseless progress. There are no hard and fixed boundary lines, and whatsoever does not advance surely recedes; that which leads to-day is surpassed to-morrow if it does not adapt itself to the latest requirements. This is true both as regards the quality of the teachers and their means of instruction, as regards the length of the course, and more especially the conditions of entrance. These last have steadily grown throughout the country. Fifty years ago the very best institutions in the most advanced portions of the country demanded no more for entrance than the professional schools of third class situated in more rural regions demand to-day. And this tendency goes steadily onward day by day. If there were any great departures made, the institutions would be disintegrated; the schools which prepare pupils would not be able suddenly to come up to new requirements, and therefore few scholars would be able to prepare for greatly modified entrance examinations. In this way, between the conservative holding to historic traditions and the striving to progress and to exceed other institutions by the highest possible efficiency, a compromise is brought about which results in a gradual but not over-hasty improvement.

We have so far entirely left out of account the state. We can speak here only of the individual state. The country as a whole has as little to do with higher education as with lower. But the single state has, in fact, a significant task — indeed, a double one. Since it aims at no monopoly, but rather gives the freest play to individual initiative, we have recognized the fundamental principle that restrictions are placed nowhere. On the other hand, it becomes the duty of the state to lend a helping hand wherever private activities have been found insufficient. This can happen in two ways: either the state may help to support private institutions which already exist, or it may establish new ones of its own, which in that case offer free tuition to the sons and daughters of all taxpayers. These so-called state universities are, in a way, the crowning feature of the free public school system. Wherever they exist, the sons of farmers have the advantage of free instruction from the kindergarten to the degree of doctor of philosophy.

Now private initiative is weakest where the population is poor or stands on a low level of culture, so that few can be found to contribute sufficient funds to support good institutions, and at the same time the rich citizens of these less advanced states prefer to send their children to the universities of the most advanced states. The result is, and this is what is hardest for the foreigner to understand, that the higher institutions of learning which are subsidized by the state stand for a grade of culture inferior to that of the private institutions, and that not only the leading universities, like Harvard, Columbia, Johns Hopkins, Yale, Chicago, Cornell, and Stanford, carry on their work without the help of the state, but also that the leading Eastern States pay out much less for higher instruction than do the Western. The State of Massachusetts, which stands at the head in matters of education, does not give a cent to its universities, while Ohio entirely supports the Ohio State University and gives aid to six other institutions.

The second task of the states in educational matters is shared alike by all of them; the state supervises all instruction, and, more than that, the state legislature confers on the individual institution the right to award grades, diplomas, and degrees to its students. No institution may change its organization without a civil permit. As culture has advanced the state has found it necessary to make the requirements in the various professional schools rather high. In practice, once more, a continual compromise has been necessary between the need to advance and the desire to stay, by traditions which have been proved and tried and found practical. Here, once again, any universal scheme of organization would have destroyed everything. If a high standard had been fixed it would have hindered private initiative, and given a set-back to Southern and Western states and robbed them of the impulses to development. A lower universal standard, on the other hand, would have impeded the advance of the more progressive portions of the country. Therefore the various state governments have taken a happy middle position in these matters, and their responsibility for the separate institutions has been made even less complete in that the degrees of these institutions carry in themselves no actual rights. Every state has its own laws for the admission of a lawyer to its bar, or to the public practice of medicine, and it is only to a small degree that the diplomas of professional schools are recognized as equivalent to a state examination.

The history of the professional schools for lawyers, ministers, teachers, and physicians in America is by no means the history of the universities. We have so far left out of account the college, which is the nucleus of American education. Let us now go back to it. We saw in the beginning of the development of these states a social community in which preparation for the professions of teaching, preaching, law or medicine implied a technical and specialized training, which every one could obtain for himself without any considerable preparation. There was no thought of a broad, liberal education. Now, to be sure, the level of scholarship required for entrance into the professional schools has steadily risen, the duration and character of the instruction has been steadily improved; but even to-day the impression has not faded from the public consciousness, and is indeed favoured by the great differences in merit between the special schools, that such a practical introduction to the treatment of disease, to court procedure, the mastery of technical problems, or to the art of teaching, does not in itself develop educated men. All this is specialized professional training, which no more broadens the mind than would the professional preparation for the calling of the merchant or manufacturer or captain. Whether a man who is prepared for his special career is also an educated man, depends on the sort of general culture that he has become familiar with. It is thought important for a man to have had a liberal education before entering the commercial house or the medical school, but it is felt to be indifferent whether he has learned his profession at the stock exchange or at the clinic.

The European will find it hard to follow this trend of thought. In Europe the highest institutions of learning are so closely allied to the learned professions, and these themselves have historically developed so completely from the learned studies, that professional erudition and general culture are well-nigh identical. And the general system of distinctions and merits favours in every way the learned professions. How much of this, however, springs out of special conditions may be seen, for instance, from the fact that in Germany an equal social position is given to the officer of the army and to the scholar. Even the American is, in his way, not quite consistent, in so far as he has at all times honoured the profession of the ministry with a degree of esteem that is independent of the previous preparation which the minister had before entering his theological school. This fact has come from the leading position which the clergymen held in the American colonial days, and the close relation which exists between the study of theology and general philosophy.

The fact that by chance one had taken the profession of law, or teaching, or medicine, did not exalt one in the eyes of one's contemporaries above the great mass of average citizens who went about their honest business. The separation of those who were called to social leadership was seen to require, therefore, some principle which should be different from any professional training. At this point we come on yet another historical factor. The nation grew step for step with its commercial activities and undertakings. So long as it was a question of gaining and developing new territory, the highest talent, the best strength and proudest personalities entered the service of this nationally significant work. It was a matter of course that no secondary position in society should be ascribed to these captains of commerce and of industry. The highest degree of culture which they were able to attain necessarily fixed the standard of culture for the whole community; and, therefore, the traditional concept of the gentleman as the man of liberal culture and refinement came to have that great social significance which was reserved in Germany for the learned professions.

In its outer form, the education of such a gentleman was borrowed from England. It was a four years' course coming after the high school, and laying special stress on the classical languages, philosophy, and mathematics — a course which, up to the early twenties, kept a young man in contact with the fine arts and the sciences, with no thought for the practical earning of a livelihood; which, therefore, kept him four years longer from the tumult of the world, and in an ideal community of men who were doing as he was doing; which developed him in work, in sport, in morals and social address. Such was the tradition; the institution was called a college after the English precedent. Any man who went to college belonged to the educated class, and it was indifferent what profession he took up; no studies of the professional school were able to replace a college education. Now, it necessarily happened that the endeavour to have students enter the professional schools with as thorough preparation as possible led eventually to demand of every one who undertook a professional course the complete college education. In fact, this last state of development is already reached in the best institutions of America. For instance, in Harvard and in Johns Hopkins, the diploma of a four years' college course is demanded for entrance into the legal, medical, or theological faculty. But in popular opinion the dividing line between common and superior education is still the line between school and college, and not, as in Germany, between liberal and technical institutions of learning. One who has successfully passed through college becomes a graduate, a gentleman of distinction; he has the degree of bachelor of arts, and those who have this degree are understood to have had a higher education.

This whole complex of relations is reflected within the college itself. It is supposed to be a four years' course which comes after the high school, and we have seen that the high school itself has no fixed standard of instruction. The small prairie college may be no better than the Tertia or Sekunda of a German Realschule, while the large and influential colleges are certainly not at all to be compared simply with German schools, but rather with the German Prima of a Gymnasium, together with the first two or three semesters in the philosophical faculty of a university. Between these extremes there is a long, sliding scale, represented by over six hundred colleges. We must now bear in mind that the college was meant to be the higher school for the general cultivation of gentlemen. Of course, from the outset this idealistic demand was not free from utilitarian considerations; the same instruction could well be utilized as the most appropriate practical training of the school-teacher, and if so, the college becomes secondarily a sort of technical school for pedagogues. But, then, in the same way as the entrance into legal and medical faculties was gradually made more difficult, until now the best of these schools demand collegiate preparation, so also did the training school for teachers necessarily become of more and more professional character, until it gradually quite outgrew the college. The culmination is a philosophical faculty which, from its side, presupposes the college, and which, therefore, takes the student about where a German student enters his fourth semester — a technical school for specialized critical science laying main stress on seminaries, laboratories, and lectures for advanced students. Such a continuation of the college study beyond the time of college — that is, for those who have been graduated from college — is called a graduate school, and its goal is the degree of doctor of philosophy. The graduate school is in this way parallel with the law, medical, or divinity school, which likewise presuppose that their students have been graduated from college.

The utilitarian element inevitably affects the college from another side. A college of the higher type will not be a school with a rigid curriculum, but will adapt itself more or less to the individuality of its students. If it is really to give the most it can, it must, at least during the last years of the college course, be somewhat like a philosophical faculty, and allow some selection among the various studies:— so that every man can best perfect his peculiar talent and can satisfy his inclinations for one or other sort of learning. So soon, now, as such academic freedom has been instituted, it is very liable to be used for utilitarian purposes. The future doctor and the future lawyer in their election of college studies will have the professional school already in mind, and will be preparing themselves for their professional studies. The lawyer will probably study more history, the doctor will study biology, the theologian languages, the future manufacturer may study physics, the banker political economy, and the politician will take up government. And so the ideal training school for gentlemen will not be merely a place for liberal education, but at the same time will provide its own sort of untechnical professional training.

Inasmuch as everything really technical is still excluded, and the majority of college students even to-day come for nothing more than a liberal education, it remains true that the college is first of all a place for the development and refinement of personal character; a place in which the young American spends the richest and happiest years of his life, where he forms his friendships and intellectual preferences which are to last throughout his life, and where the narrow confines of school life are outgrown and the confines of professional education not yet begun; where, in short, everything is broad and free and sunny. For the American the attraction of academic life is wholly centred in the college; the college student is the only one who lives the true student life. Those who study in the four professional faculties are comparable rather to the German medical students of the last clinical semesters — sedate, semi-professional men. The college is the soul of the university. The college is to-day, more than ever, the soul of the whole nation.

We have to mention one more factor, and we shall have brought together all which are of prime importance. We have seen that the professional and the collegiate schools had at the outset different points of view, and were, in fact, entirely independent. It was inevitable that as they developed they should come into closer and closer relations. The name of the college remained during this development the general designation. Special faculties have grouped themselves about the college, while a common administration keeps them together. There are certain local difficulties in this. According to the original idea, a college ought to be in a small, rural, and attractively situated spot. The young man should be removed from ordinary conditions; and as he goes to Jena, Marburg, and Göttingen, so he should go to Princeton or New Haven, or Palo Alto, in order to be away from large cities in a little academic world which is inspired only by the glory of famous teachers and by the youthful happiness of many student generations. A medical or law school, on the other hand, belongs, according to American tradition, in some large city, where there is a plenty of clinical material at hand, and where great attorneys are in contact with the courts. It so happened that the college, as it grew up into a complete university, was especially favoured if it happened to be in the vicinity of a large city, like Harvard College in Cambridge, which had all the attractions of rural quiet and nevertheless was separated from the large city of Boston only by the Charles River bridge. In later times, to be sure, since the idyllic side of college life is everywhere on the wane, and the outward equipment, especially of laboratories, libraries, etc., has everywhere to grow, it is a noticeable advantage for even collegiate prosperity to have the resources of a large city at hand. And, therefore, the institutions in these cities, like New York, Baltimore, Chicago, and San Francisco, develop more rapidly than many colleges which were once famous but which lie in more isolated places.

At the head of the administration there is always a president, a man whose functions are something between those of a Rektor and a Kultus-Minister, most nearly, perhaps, comparable with a Kurator, and yet much more independent, much more dictatorial.

The direction of the university is actually concentrated in his person, and the rise or fall of the institution is in large measure dependent on his official leadership. In olden times the president was almost always a theologian, and at the same time was apt to be professor in moral philosophy. This is true to-day of none but small country colleges, and even there the Puritan tradition disappears as financial and administrative problems come to be important. The large universities have lately come almost always to place a professor of the philosophical faculty at their head. Almost invariably these are men of liberal endowments. Mostly they are men of wide outlook, and only such men are fit for these positions, which belong to the most influential and important in the country. The opinions of men like Eliot of Harvard, Hadley of Yale, Butler of Columbia, Shurman of Cornell, Remsen of Johns Hopkins, Wheeler of California, Harper of Chicago, Jordan of Leland Stanford, Wilson of Princeton, and of many others, are respected and sought on all questions of public life, even in matters extending far beyond education.

The university president is elected for a life term by the administrative council — a deliberative body of men who, without emoluments, serve the destinies of the university, and in a certain sense are the congress of the university as compared with the president. They confirm appointments, regulate expenditures, and theoretically conduct all external business for the university, although practically they follow in large part the recommendations of the faculties. The teaching body is composed everywhere of professors, assistant professors, and instructors. All these receive a fixed stipend. There are no such things as private tuition fees, and unsalaried teachers, like the German Privatdocenten, are virtually unknown. The instruction consists, in general, of courses lasting through a year and not a semester. The academic year begins, in most cases, at the end of September and closes at the end of June.

During his four years' college course the student prefers to remain true to some one college. If this is a small institution, he is very apt, on being graduated, to attend some higher institution. Even the students in professional schools generally come back year after year to the same school till they finish their studies. It is only in the graduate school — that is, the German philosophical faculty — that migration after the German manner has come in fashion; here, in fact, the student frequently studies one year here and one year there, in order to hear the best specialists in his science. Except in the state institutions of the West, the student pays a round sum for the year; in the larger institutions from one hundred to one hundred and fifty dollars. In the smaller colleges the four years' course of study is almost wholly prescribed, and only in the final year is there a certain freedom of choice. The higher the college stands in the matter of scholarship, so much the more its lecture programme approaches that of a university; and in the foremost colleges the student is from the very beginning almost entirely free in his selection of studies.

A freedom in electing between study and laziness is less known. The student may elect his own lectures; he must, however, attend at least a certain number of these, and must generally show in a semi-annual examination that he has spent his time to some purpose. The examinations at the end of the special courses are in the college substituted for a final examination. Any man receives a degree who has passed the written examinations in a certain number of courses. The examinations concern not only what has actually been said in the lectures, but at the same time try to bring out how much the student has learned outside in the way of reading text-books and searching into literature. Originally the students roomed in college buildings, but with the growth of these institutions this factor of college life has declined. In the larger universities the student is, in matters of his daily life, as free as the German; but dwelling in college dormitories still remains the most popular mode of living, since it lends a social attraction to academic life.

To go over from this general plan to a more concrete presentation, we may perhaps sketch briefly a picture of Harvard College, the oldest and largest academy in the country. The colony of Massachusetts established in 1636 a little college in the vicinity of the newly founded city of Boston. The place was called Cambridge in commemoration of the English college in which some of the colonists had received their education. When in 1638 a young English minister, John Harvard, left this little academy half his fortune, it was decided to name the college for its first benefactor. The state had given £400, John Harvard about £800. The school building was one little structure, the number of students was very small, and there were a few clergymen for teachers. On the same spot to-day stands Harvard University, like a little city within a city, with fifty ample buildings, with 550 members of the teaching staff, over five thousand students, with a regular annual budget of a million and a half dollars, and in the enjoyment of bequests which add year by year millions to its regular endowments.

This growth has been constant, outwardly and inwardly; and it has grown in power and in freedom in a way that well befits the spirit of American institutions. Since the colonial régime of the seventeenth century gave to the new institution a deliberative body of seven men — the so-called Corporation — this body has perpetuated itself without interruption down to the present time by its own vote, and without changing any principle of its constitution has developed the home of Puritanism into the theatre of the freest investigation, and the school into a great university of the world.

Now, as then, there stands at the head this body of seven members, each of whom is elected for life. To belong to this is esteemed a high honour. Beside these, there is the board of overseers of thirty members, elected by the graduates from among their own number. Five men are elected every June to hold office for six years in this advisory council. Every Harvard man, five years after he has received his degree of bachelor, has the right to vote. Every appointment and all policies of the university must be confirmed by this board of overseers. Only the best sons of the alma mater are elected to this body. Thus the university administration has an upper and lower house, and it is clear that with such closely knit internal organization the destiny of the university is better guarded than it would be if appointments and expenditures were dependent on the caprice and political intrigues of the party politicians in the state legislature. Just on this account Harvard has declined, for almost a hundred years, all aid from the state; although this was once customary. On the other hand, it would be a mistake to suppose that, say in contrast with Germany, this self-government of the university implies any greater administrative rights for the professors. The German professors have much more administrative influence than their colleagues in America. If, indeed, the advice of the professors in matters of new appointments or promotions is important, nevertheless the administrative bodies are in no wise officially bound to follow the recommendations of the faculty.

The president of the university is Charles W. Eliot, the most distinguished and influential personality in the whole intellectual life of America. Eliot comes from an old Puritan family of New England. He was a professor of chemistry in his thirty-fifth year; and his essays on methods of instruction, together with his talents for organization, had awakened considerable attention, when the overseers, in spite of lively protestations from various sides, were prompted by keen insight in the year 1869 to call him to this high office. It would be an exaggeration to say that the tremendous growth of Harvard in the last three decades is wholly the work of Eliot; for this development is, first of all, the result of that remarkable progress which the intellectual life of the whole land has undergone. But the fact that Harvard during all this time has kept in the very front rank among all academic institutions is certainly due to the efforts of President Eliot; and once again, if the progress at Harvard has resulted in part from the scientific awakening of the whole country, this national movement was itself in no small measure the work of the same man. His influence has extended out beyond the boundaries of New England and far beyond all university circles, and has made itself felt in the whole educational life of the country. He was never a man after the taste of the masses; his quiet and distinguished reserve are too cool and deliberate. And if to-day, on great occasions, he is generally the most important speaker, this is really a triumph for clear and solid thought over the mere tricks of blatancy and rhetoric. Throughout the country he is known as the incomparable master of short and pregnant English.

His life work has contained nothing of the spasmodic; nor have his reforms been in any case sudden ones. To whatever has been necessary he has consecrated his patient energy, going fearlessly toward the goal which he recognized as right, and moving slowly and surely forward. Year by year he has exerted an influence on the immediate circles of his community, and so indirectly on the whole land, to bring up the conditions for entrance into college and professional schools until at the present time all the special faculties of Harvard demand as an entrance requirement a complete college course. He has made Harvard College over into a modern academy, in which every student is entirely free to select the course of studies which he desires, and has introduced through the entire university and for all time, the spirit of impartial investigation. Even the theological faculty has grown under his influence from a sectarian institution of the Unitarian Church into a nonsectarian Christian institution in which future preachers of every sect are able to obtain their preliminary training. And this indefatigable innovator is to-day, as he now has completed his seventieth year, pressing forward with youthful energies to new goals. Just as he has introduced into the college the opportunity of perfectly free specialization, so now he clearly sees that if a college education is necessary for every future student in the special departments of the university, that the college course must be shortened from four to three years, or in other words, must be compressed. There is much opposition to this idea. All traditions and very many apparently weighty arguments seem to speak against it. Nevertheless, any student of average intelligence and energy can now get the Harvard A. B. in three years; before long this will be the rule, and in a short time the entire country will have followed in the steps of this reform.

It is true that Eliot's distinguished position has contributed very much to his outward success — that position which he has filled for thirty-five years, and which in itself guarantees a peculiar influence on academic life. But the decisive thing has been his personality. He is enthusiastic and yet conservative, bold and yet patient, always glad to consider the objections of the youngest teacher; he is religious, and nevertheless a confident exponent of modern science. First of all, he is through and through an aristocrat: his interest is in the single, gifted, and solid personality rather than in the masses; and his conception of the inequality of man is the prime motive of his whole endeavour. But at the same time he is the best of democrats, for he lays the greatest stress on making it possible for the earnest spirit to press on and emerge from the lowest classes of the people. Harvard has set its roots as never before through the whole country, and thereby has drawn on the intellectual and moral energies of the entire nation.

Under the president come the faculties, of which each one is presided over by a dean. The largest faculty is the faculty of arts and sciences, whose members lecture both for the college and for the Graduate School. There is really no sharp distinction, and the announcement of lectures says merely that certain elementary courses are designed for younger students in the college, and that certain others are only for advanced students. Moreover, the seminaries and laboratory courses for scientific research are open only to students of the Graduate School. The rest is common ground.

As always happens, the faculty includes very unlike material, a number of the most distinguished investigators, along with others who are first of all teachers. In general, the older generation of men belongs to that time in which the ability to teach was thought more important than pure scholarship. On the other hand, the middle generation is much devoted to productive investigations. The youngest generation of instructors is somewhat divided. A part holds the ideal of creative research, another part is in a sort of reactionary mood against the modern high estimation of specialized work; and has rather a tendency once more to emphasize the idealistic side of academic activity — the beauty of form and the cultivating value of belles-lettres as opposed to the dry details of scholarship. This last is generally accounted the peculiar work of German influence, and in opposition to this there is a demand for Gallic polish and that scientific connoisseurship of the English gentleman. Since, however, these men are thinking not of the main fact, but rather of certain insignificant excrescences of German work, and since after all nothing but the real work of investigation can lead to new achievements which justify in a real university any advancement to higher academic positions, there is no ground for fearing that this reactionary mood will exert any particularly harmful influence on more serious circles of workers. Such a movement may be even welcomed as a warning against a possible ossification of science. Particularly the college would be untrue to its ideals, if it were to forget the humanities in favour of scientific matters of fact.

The lectures naturally follow the principle of thorough-going specialization, and one who reads the Annual Report will probably be surprised to discover how many students take up Assyrian or Icelandic, Old Bulgarian, or Middle Irish. The same specialization is carried into the seminaries for the advanced students; thus, for instance, in the department of philosophy, there are special seminaries for ethics, psychology, metaphysics, logic, sociology, pedagogy, Greek, and modern philosophy. The theological faculty is the smallest. In spite of an admirable teaching staff there remains something still to do before the spirit of science is brought into perfect harmony with the strongly sectarian character of the American churches. On the other hand, the faculty of law is recognized as the most distinguished in the English-speaking world. The difference between the Anglo-American law and the Romano-German has brought it about that the entire arrangement and method of study here are thoroughly different from the German. From the very beginning law is taught by the study of actual decisions; the introduction of this "case system," in opposition to the usual text-book system, was the most decisive advance of all and fixed the reputation of the law faculty. And this system has been gradually introduced into other leading schools of law. The legal course lasts three years, and each year has its prescribed courses of lectures. In the first year, for instance, students take up contracts, the penal code, property rights, and civil processes. Perhaps the departure from the German method of teaching law is most characteristically shown by the fact that the law students are from the very first day the most industrious students of all. These young men have passed through their rather easy college days, and when now they leave those early years of study in the elm-shaded college yard and withdraw to Austin Hall, the law building of the university, they feel that at last they are beginning their serious life-work. In the upper story of Austin Hall there is a large reading-room for the students, with a legal reference library of over sixty thousand volumes. This hall is filled with students, even late at night, who are quite as busy as if they were young barristers industriously working away on their beginning practice.

The German method is much more followed in the four-year medical course of studies, and still there are here striking differences. The medical faculty of Harvard, which is located in Boston on account of the larger hospitals to be found in the city, is at this moment in the midst of moving. Already work has been commenced on a new medical quadrangle with the most modern and sumptuous edifices. In somewhat the same way, the course of studies is rather under process of reformation. It is in the stage of experimentation, and of course it is true throughout the world that the astonishing advance of medicine has created new problems for the universities. It seems impossible now for a student to master the whole province, since his study time is of course limited. The latest attempt at reform is along the line of the greatest possible concentration. The student is expected for several months morning and night to study only anatomy, to hear anatomical lectures, to dissect and to use the microscope; and then again for several months he devotes himself entirely to physiology, and so on. Much is hoped, secondly, from the intuitive method of instruction. While in Germany the teaching of physiology is chiefly by means of lectures and demonstrations, every Harvard student has in addition during the period of physiological study to work one hundred and eighty hours on prescribed experiments, so that two hours of experimentation follow every one-hour lecture. In certain lines of practical instruction, especially in pathological anatomy, the American is at a disadvantage compared with the German, since the supply of material for autopsy is limited. Popular democratic sentiment is very strong against the idea that a man who dies in a public poor-house must fall a prey to the dissecting knife. The clinical demonstrations are not given in special university clinics, but rather in the large municipal hospitals, where all the chief physicians are pledged to give practical instruction in the form of demonstrations. In the third place, there is an increasing tendency to give to the study of medicine a certain mobility; in other words, to allow a rather early specialization. As to the substance itself which is taught, Harvard's medical school is very much like a German university, and becomes daily more similar. In the American as in the German university, the microscope and the retort have taken precedence over the medicine chest.

Harvard has about five thousand students. Any boy who wishes to enter must pass, at the beginning of the summer, a six-day written examination; and these examinations are conducted in about forty different places of the country under the supervision of officers of the university. Any one coming from other universities is carefully graded according to the standard of scholarship of his particular institution. The amount of study required is not easily determined. Unlike the German plan, every course of lectures is concluded at the end of the year with a three-hour examination, and only the man who passes the examination has the course in question put to his credit. Whoever during the four, or perhaps three, college years has taken eighteen three-hour lecture courses extending through the year receives the bachelor's degree. In practice, indeed, the matter becomes enormously complicated, yet extensive administrative machinery regulates every case with due justice. In the legal and medical faculties, everything is dependent on the final examinations of the year. In the philosophical two, or more often three, years of study after the bachelor's degree lead to the doctorate of philosophy.

The graduate student always works industriously through the year, but the college student may be one of various types. Part of these men work no less industriously than the advanced students; while another part, and by no means the worst, would not for anything be guilty of such misbehaviour. These men are not in Harvard to learn facts, but they have come to college for a certain atmosphere — in order to assimilate by reflection, as they say. Of course, the lectures of enthusiastic professors and a good book or two belong to this atmosphere; and yet, who can say that the hours spent at the club, on the foot-ball field, at the theatre, in the Boston hotel, on the river or on horse-back do not contribute quite as much — not to mention the informal discussions about God and the world, especially the literary and athletic worlds, as they sit together at their window seats on the crimson cushions and smoke their cigarettes? Harvard has the reputation through the country of being the rich man's university, and it is true that many live here in a degree of luxury of which few German students would ever think. And yet there are as many who go through college on the most modest means, who perhaps earn their own livelihood or receive financial aid from the college. A systematic evasion of lectures or excessive drinking or card-playing plays no role at all. The distinctly youthful exuberance of the students is discharged most especially in the field of sport, which gets an incomparable influence on the students' minds by means of the friendly rivalry between different colleges. The foot-ball game between Harvard and Yale in November, or the base-ball game in June, or the New London races, are national events, for which special trains transport thousands of visitors. Next to the historical traditions it is indeed sport, which holds the body of Harvard students most firmly together, and those who belong to the same class most firmly of all — that is, those who are to receive their A. B. in the same year. Year after year the Harvard graduates come back to Boston in order to see their old class-mates again. They know that to be a Harvard man means for their whole life to be the body-guard of the nation. They will stand for Harvard, their sons will go to Harvard, and to Harvard they will contribute with generous hands out of their material prosperity.

Harvard reflects all the interests of the nation, and all its social contrasts. It has its political, religious, literary and musical clubs, its scientific and social organizations, its daily paper for the discussion of Harvard's interests, edited by students, and three monthly magazines; it has its public and serious parliamentary debates, and most popular of all, operatic performances in the burlesque vein given by students. Thousands of most diverse personalities work out their life problems in this little city of lecture halls, laboratories, museums, libraries, banquet halls, and club buildings, which are scattered about the ancient elm-shaded yard. Each student has come, in the ardour and ambition of youth, to these halls where so many intellectual leaders have taught and so many great men of the outside world have spent their student years; and each one goes away once more into the world a better and stronger man.

One thing that a European visitor particularly expects to find in the lecture room of an American university is not found in Harvard. There are no women students in the school. Women graduates who are well advanced are admitted to the seminaries and to scientific research in the laboratories, but they are excluded from the college; and the same is true of Yale, Columbia, Princeton, and Johns Hopkins. Of course, Harvard has no prejudice against the higher education of women; but Harvard is itself an institution for men. In an indirect way, the teaching staff of Harvard University is utilized for the benefit of women, since only a stone's throw from the Harvard College gate is Radcliffe

College, which is for women, and in which only Harvard instructors give lectures.

This picture of the largest university will stand as typical for the others, although of course each one of the great academies has its own peculiarities. While Harvard seeks to unite humanitarian and specialized work, Johns Hopkins aims to give only the latter, while Yale and Princeton aim more particularly at the former. Johns Hopkins in Baltimore is a workshop of productive investigation, and in the province of natural sciences and medicine Johns Hopkins has been a brilliant example to the whole country. Yale University, in New Haven, stands first of all for culture and personal development, although many a shining name in scholarship is graven on the tablets of Yale. Columbia University, in New York, gets its peculiar character from that great city which is its background; and this to a much greater extent than the University of Chicago, which has created its own environment and atmosphere on the farthest outskirts of that great city. Chicago, and Cornell University at Ithaca, the University of Pennsylvania, Ann Arbor in Michigan, Berkeley and Stanford in California are the principal institutions which admit women, and therein are outwardly distinguished from the large institutions of the East.

The male students from the West have somewhat less polish, but are certainly not less industrious. The Western students come generally out of more modest conditions, and are therefore less indifferent with regard to their own future. The student from Ann Arbor, Minnesota, or Nebraska would compare with the student at Yale or Princeton about as a student at Königsberg or Breslau would compare with one at Heidelberg or Bonn. Along with that he comes from a lower level of public school education. The Western institutions are forced to content themselves with less exacting conditions for entrance, and the South has at the present time no academies at all which are to be compared seriously with the great universities of the country.

Next to Harvard the oldest university is Yale, which a short time ago celebrated its two-hundredth anniversary. After Yale comes Princeton, whose foundation took place in the middle of the eighteenth century. Yale was founded as a protest against the liberal tendencies of Harvard. Puritan orthodoxy had been rather overridden at Harvard, and so created for itself a more secure fortress in the colony of Connecticut. In this the mass of the population was strictly in sympathy with the church; the free spirit of Harvard was too advanced for the people, and remained so in a certain way for nearly two centuries. Therein has lain the strength of Yale. Until a short time ago Yale had the more popular place in the nation; it was the democratic rallying-ground in contrast with Harvard, which was too haughtily aristocratic. Yale was the religious and the conservative stronghold as contrasted with the free thought and progress of Harvard. For some time it seemed as if the opposition of Yale against the modern spirit would really prejudice its higher interests, and it slowly fell somewhat from its great historic position. But recently, under its young, widely known president, Hadley, the political economist, it has been making energetic and very successful endeavours to recover its lost position.

The history of Columbia University, in New York, began as early as 1754. At that time it was King's College, which after the War for Independence was rechristened Columbia College. But the real greatness of Columbia began only in the last few decades, with a development which is unparalleled. Under its president, Seth Low, the famous medical, legal, and political economical faculties were brought into closer relations with the college, the Graduate School was organized, Teachers' College was developed, the general entrance conditions were brought up, and on Morningside Heights a magnificent new university quadrangle was erected. When Seth Low left the university, after ten years of irreproachable and masterly administration, in order to become Mayor of New York in the service of the Reform party, he was succeeded in the presidency by Butler, a young man who since his earliest years had shown extraordinary talents for administration, and who for many years as editor of the best pedagogical magazine had become thoroughly familiar with the needs of academic instruction. Columbia is favoured by every circumstance. If signs are not deceptive, Columbia will soon stand nearest to Harvard at the head of American universities. While Harvard and Yale, Princeton, Pennsylvania, and Columbia are the most successful creations of the Colonial days, Johns Hopkins and Chicago, Cornell and Leland Stanford are the chief representatives of those institutions which have recently been founded by private munificence. The state universities of Wisconsin, Michigan, Nebraska, Kansas, Minnesota, Missouri, and California may be mentioned, finally, as the most notable state universities.

Johns Hopkins was an able railroad president, who died after a long life, in 1873, and bequeathed seven million dollars for a university and academy to be founded in his native city of Baltimore. The administrative council elected Gilman as its president, and it is Gilman's memorable service to have accomplished that of which America was most in need in that moment of transition — an academy which should concentrate its entire strength on the furtherance of serious scientific investigation quite without concessions to the English college idea, without any attempt to reach a great circle of students, or without any effort to annex a legal or theological faculty. Its sole aim was to attract really eminent specialists as teachers in its philosophical faculties, to equip laboratories and seminaries in the most approved manner, to fill these with advanced students, and to inspire these students with a zeal for scientific productiveness. This experiment has succeeded remarkably. It is clear to-day that the further development of the American university will not consist in developing the special professional school, but will rather combine the ideals of the college with the ideals of original research. But at that time when the new spirit which had been imported from Germany began to ferment, it was of the first importance that some such institution should avowedly, without being hampered by any traditions, take up the cause of that method which seeks to initiate the future school-teacher into the secrets of the laboratory. Since Gilman retired, a short time ago, the famous chemist, Ira Remsen, has taken his place. A brilliant professor of Johns Hopkins, Stanley Hall, has undertaken a similar experiment on a much more modest scale, in the city of Worcester, with the millions which were given by the philanthropist Clark. His Clark University has remained something of a torso, but has likewise succeeded in advancing the impulse for productive science in many directions, especially in psychology and education.

In the year 1868, Cornell University was founded in the town of Ithaca, from the gifts of Ezra Cornell; and this university had almost exactly opposite aims. It has aimed to create a university for the people, where every man could find what he needed for his own education; it has become a stronghold for the utilitarian spirit. The truly American spirit of restless initiative has perhaps nowhere in the academic world found more characteristic expression than in this energetic dwelling-place of science. The first president was the eminent historian, Andrew D. White, who was appointed later to his happy mission as Ambassador to Berlin. At the present day the philosopher Shurman stands at the helm, whose efforts in colonial politics are widely known. Senator Stanford, of California, aimed to accomplish for the extreme West the same thing that Cornell had done for the East, when in memory of his deceased son he applied his entire property to the foundation of an academy in the vicinity of San Francisco. Leland Stanford is, so far as its financial endowment goes, probably the richest university in the country. As far as its internal efficiency has gone, the thirty million dollars have not meant so much, since the West has to depend on its own students and it has to take them as it finds them. In spite of this, the university accomplishes an excellent work in many directions under the leadership of the zoölogist Jordan, its possibly too energetic president. While its rival, the State University of California, near the Golden Gate of San Francisco, is perhaps the most superbly situated university in the world, Leland Stanford can lay claim to being the more picturesque. It is a dream in stone conjured up under the Californian palms. Finally, quite different, more strenuous than all others, some say more Chicagoan, is the University of Chicago, to which the petroleum prince, Rockefeller, has deflected some twelve million dollars. The University of Chicago has everything and offers everything. It pays the highest salaries, it is open the whole year through, it has accommodations for women, and welcomes summer guests who come to stay only a couple of months. It has the richest programme of collateral lectures, of university publications and of its own periodicals, has an organic alliance with no end of smaller colleges in the country, has observatories on the hill-tops and laboratories by the sea; and, whatever it lacks to-day, it is bound to have to-morrow. It is almost uncanny how busily and energetically this university has developed itself in a few years under the distinguished and brilliant presidential policy of Harper.

One must admire the great work. It is possible that this place is still not equal to the older Eastern universities as the home of quiet maturity and reflection; but for hard, scholarly work it has few rivals in the world.

Johns Hopkins and Cornell, Stanford and Chicago, have been carefully designed and built according to one consistent plan, while the state universities have developed slowly out of small colleges more like the old institutions of Colonial days. Their history is for the most part uneventful; it is a steady and toilsome working to the top, which has been limited not so much by the finances of the states, but rather by the conditions of the schools in the regions about them. The largest state university is that of Michigan, at Ann Arbor, not far from Detroit. In number of students it is next to Harvard. One of its specialties is a homœopathic medical faculty in addition to the allopathic.

It would be a great mistake to suppose that, with the blossoming out of the large and middle-sized universities, all of which have colleges as one of their departments, the small colleges have ceased to play their part. Quite on the contrary; in a certain sense the small college situated in rural seclusion has found a new task to work out in contrast to the great universities. It is only in the small college that the young student is able to come into personal contact with the professor, and only there can his special individuality be taken into account by his alma mater. One scheme does not fit all the students, and not only in those regions where the homely college represents the highest attainable instruction of its kind, but also in many districts of the maturest culture, the college is for many youths the most favourable place for development. Thus the New England States would feel a great loss to the cause of culture if such old colleges as Williams, Brown, Amherst, and Dartmouth should simply deliver over its students to Harvard.

These smaller colleges fulfil a special mission, therefore, and they do their best when they do not try to seem more than they really are. There was the danger that the colleges would think themselves improved by introducing some fragments of research work into their curriculum, and so spoiling a good humanitarian college by offering a bad imitation of a university. Of course, there can be no talk of a sharp separation between college and university, for the reasons which we have emphasized many times before. It is necessary, as we have seen, that there should be a long continuous scale from the smallest college up to the largest university. It is true that many of the small institutions are entirely superfluous, and not capable of any great development, and so from year to year some are bound to disappear or to be absorbed by others. Many are really business enterprises, and many more are sectarian institutions. But in general there exists among these institutions a healthy struggle for existence which prospers the strongest of them and makes them do their best. The right of existence of many of the small and isolated professional schools is much more questionable. Almost all the best medical, legal, and theological schools of this order have already been assimilated to this or that college, and the growing together of the academies which started separately and from small beginnings into organic universities is in conformity with the centralizing tendency everywhere in progress in our time.

Many of the smaller colleges are, like all the state institutions, open to both sexes. Besides these, however, there thrive certain colleges which are exclusively for women. The best known of these are Bryn Mawr, Vassar, Wellesley, Smith, Radcliffe, and Barnard. Barnard College, in New York, stands in the same relation to Columbia University as Radcliffe College does to Harvard. Every one of these leading women's colleges has its own physiognomy, and appeals rather to its special type of young woman. Vassar, Wellesley, Smith, and Bryn Mawr lie in quiet, retired little towns or villages: and the four years of college life spent together by something like a thousand blooming, happy young women between the years of eighteen and twenty-two, in college halls which are surrounded by attractive parks, are four years of extraordinary charm. Only Bryn Mawr and Radcliffe lay any special stress on the advanced critical work of the graduates. In Smith, Vassar, and Wellesley it is mostly a matter of assimilation, and the standard of scholarship is not much higher than that of the German Arbiturientenexamen, together with possibly one or two semesters of the philosophical faculty. In Wellesley, women are almost the only teachers; while in Bryn Mawr almost all are men, and in Smith the teachers are both men and women.

In statistical language, the following conditions are found to hold. If for the moment we put college and graduate schools together as the "philosophical faculty," there studied in the year 1900 in the philosophical faculties, 1,308 students for every million inhabitants; in the legal faculties 166, in the medical 333, and in the theological faculties 106. Ten years previously the corresponding figures were 877, 72, 266, 112, respectively, and twenty-five years ago they were 744, 61, 196, and 120, respectively. Thus the increase in the last ten years has been a remarkable one; theology alone shows some diminution in its numbers. If we consider now the philosophical faculties more closely, we discover the surprising fact that in the last decade the male students have increased 61 per cent., while the female have increased 149 per cent. The degrees conferred in the year 1900 were as follows: college degrees of bachelor of arts — to men 5,129, to women 2,140. The degree of bachelor of science, which is somewhat lower in its standard, and requires no classical preparation, was given to 2,473 men and 591 women. The degree of doctor of philosophy to 322 men and 20 women. The private endowment of all colleges together amounts to 360 million dollars, of which 160 million consist in income-bearing securities. The annual income amounted to 28 millions, not counting donations of that year, of which 11 millions came from the fees of students, about 7 millions were the interest on endowments, and 7.5 millions were contributed by the government. Thus the student pays about 39 per cent. of what his tuition costs. The larger donations for the year amounted to about 12 millions more. The number of colleges for men or for both sexes was 480, for women alone 141. This figure says very little; since, in the case of many women's institutions, the name college is more monstrously abused than in any other, and in the West and South is assumed by every upstart girls' school. There are only 13 women's colleges which come up to a high standard, and it may at once be added that the number of polytechnic and agricultural schools whose conditions for entrance correspond on the average to those of the colleges amounts to 43. Also these stand on many different levels, and at the head of them all is the Massachusetts Institute of Technology, in Boston, which is now under the brilliant leadership of President Pritchett. Almost all the technical schools are state institutions.

There were, in the year 1900, 151 medical faculties having

25,213 students: all except three provide a four years' course of study. Besides these, there were 7,928 dental students studying in 54 dental schools, and 4,042 students of pharmacy in 53 separate institutions. There were 12,516 law students, and 8,009 theological students. Out of the law students 151, and of the theological 181, were women.

CHAPTER SEVENTEEN

Science

ONE who surveys, without prejudice, the academic life of the country in reference to scientific work will receive a deep impression of the energy and carefulness with which this enormous national machinery of education furthers the higher intellectual life. And the continuous gradation of institutions by which the higher academy is able to adapt itself to every local need, so that no least remnant of free initiative can be lost and unlimited development is made possible at every point, must be recognized by every one as the best conceivable system for the country.

It is not to be denied that it brings with it certain difficulties and disadvantages. The administrative difficulties which proceed from the apparent incomparability of the institutions are really not serious, although the foreigner who is accustomed to uniformity in his universities, Gymnasia, certificates and doctorial diplomas, is inclined to overemphasize these difficulties in America. The real disadvantages of the system of continuous gradations is found, not in the outer administration, but in its inner methods. The German undergraduate takes the attitude of one who learns; his teacher must be thoroughly well informed, but no one expects a school-teacher himself to advance science. The graduate student, on the other hand, is supposed to take a critical attitude, and therefore his teacher has to be a teacher of methods — that is, he must be a productive investigator. Wherever, as in Germany, there lies a sharp distinction between these two provinces, it is easy to keep the spirit of investigation pure; but where, as in America, one merges into the other, the principles at stake are far too likely to be confused. Men who fundamentally are nothing but able school-teachers are then able to work up and stand beside the best investigators in the university faculties, because the principle of promotion on the ground of scientific production solely cannot be so clearly separated from the methods of selection which are adapted to the lower grades of instruction. To be sure, this has its advantages in other directions; because, in so far as there is no sharp demarcation, the spirit of investigation can also grow from above down, and therefore in many a smaller college there will be more productive scientists teaching than would be found, perhaps, in a German school; but yet the influences of the lower on the higher departments of instruction are the predominant ones. Investigation thrives best when the young scholar knows that his advancement depends ultimately on strictly scientific achievements, and not on work of a popular sort, nor on success in the teaching of second-hand knowledge. This fact has often been brought home to the public mind in recent years, and the leading universities have already more and more recognized the principle of considering scientific achievements to be the main ground for preferment.

But productive scholarship is interfered with in still other ways. Professors are often too much busied with administrative concerns; and although this sort of administrative influence may be attractive for many professors, its exercise requires much sacrifice of time. More particularly, the professors of most institutions, although there are many exceptions among the leading universities, are overloaded with lectures, and herein the graded transition from low to high works unfavourably. Especially in Western institutions, the administrative bodies do not see why the university professor should not lecture as many hours in the week as a school teacher; and most dangerous of all, as we have already mentioned in speaking of popular education, is the fact that the scholar is tempted, by high social and financial rewards, to give scientifically unproductive popular lectures and to write popular essays.

And the list of factors which have worked against scientific productiveness can be still further increased. To be sure, it would be false here to repeat the old tale that the American professor is threatened in his freedom by the whimsical demands of rich patrons, who have founded or handsomely endowed many of the universities. That is merely newspaper gossip; and the three or four cases which have busied public opinion in the last ten years and have been ridiculously overestimated, are found, on closer inspection, to have been cases which could have come up as well in any non-partisan institution in the world. There may have been mistakes on both sides; perhaps the university councils have acted with unnecessary rigour or lack of tact, but it has yet to be proved that there has been actual injustice anywhere. Even in small colleges purely scientific activity never interferes with the welfare of a professor. A blatant disrespect for religion would hurt his further prospects there, to be sure, just as in the Western state institutions the committees appointed by the legislature would dislike a hostile political attitude. Yet not even in the smallest college has any professor ever suffered the least prejudice by reason of his scientific labours. Science in America is not hampered by any lack of academic freedom.

On the other hand, the American university lacks one of the most important forces of German universities — the Privatdocent, who lives only for science, and without compensation places his teaching abilities in the service of his own scientific development. The young American scholar is welcome only where a paid position is vacant; but if he finds no empty instructorship in a large university, he is obliged to be content with a position in a small college, where the entire intellectual atmosphere, as regards the studies, apparatus, and amount of work exacted, all work against his desire to be scientifically productive, and finally perhaps kill it entirely. The large universities are just beginning to institute the system of voluntary docents — which, to be sure, encounters administrative difficulties. There is also a dangerous tendency toward academic in-breeding. The former students of an institution are always noticeably preferred for any vacant position, and the claims of capable scholars are often disregarded for the sake of quite insignificant men. Scientific productiveness meets further with the material obstacle of the high cost of printing in America, which makes it often more difficult for the young student here than in Germany to find a publisher for his works.

Against all this there are some external advantages: first, the lavishness of the accessories of investigation. The equipment of laboratories, libraries, museums, observatories, special institutes, and the fitting out of expeditions yield their due benefits. Then there are various sorts of free assistance — fellowships, travelling scholarships, and other foundations — which make every year many young scholars free for scientific work. There is also the admirable "sabbatical year." The large universities give every professor leave of absence every seventh year, with the express purpose of allowing him time for his own scholarly labours. Another favourable circumstance is the excellent habit of work which every American acquires during his student years; and here it is not to be doubted that the American is on the average, and in consequence of his system has to be, more industrious than the German average student. From the beginning of his course, he is credited with only such lecture courses as he has passed examinations on, and these are so arranged as to necessitate not only presence at the lectures, but also the study of prescribed treatises; the student is obliged to apply himself with considerable diligence. A student who should give himself entirely to idling, as may happen in Germany, would not finish his first college year. If the local foot-ball gossip is no more sensible than the talk at duelling clubs, at least the practice of drinking beer in the morning and playing skat have no evil counterpart of comparable importance in America. The American student recreates himself on the athletic field rather than in the ale-house. Germany is exceedingly sparing of time and strength during school years, but lets both be wasted in the universities to the great advantage of a strong personality here and there, but to the injury of the average man. America wastes a good deal of time during school years, but is more sparing during the college and university courses, and there accustoms each student to good, hard work.

And most of all, the intellectual make-up of the American is especially adapted to scientific achievements. This temperament, owing to the historical development of the nation, has so far addressed itself to political, industrial, and judicial problems, but a return to theoretical science has set in; and there, most of all, the happy combination of inventiveness, enthusiasm, and persistence in pursuit of a goal, of intellectual freedom and elasticity, of feeling for form and of idealistic instinct for self-perfection will yield, perhaps soon, remarkable triumphs.

We have hitherto spoken only of the furtherance of science by the higher institutions of learning, but we must look at least hastily on what is being done outside of academic circles. We see, then, first of all, the magnificent government institutions at Washington which, without doing any teaching, are in the sole service of science. The cultivation of the sciences by twenty-eight special institutions and an army of 6,000 persons, conducted at an annual expense of more than $8,000,000, is certainly a unique feature of American government. There is no other government in the world which is organized for such a many-sided scientific work; and nevertheless, everything which is done there is closely related to the true interests of government — that is, not to the interests of the dominant political party, but to those of the great self-governing nation. All the institutes, as different as they are in their special work, have this in common — that they work on problems which relate to the country, population, products, and the general conditions of America, so that they meet first of all the national needs of an economical, social, intellectual, political, and hygienic sort, and only in a secondary way contribute to abstract science.

The work of these government institutes is peculiar, moreover, in that the results are published in many handsomely gotten-up volumes, and sent free of cost to hundreds of thousands of applicants. The institutions are devoted partly to science and partly to political economy. Among the scientific institutes are the admirable Bureau of Geological Survey, which has six hundred officials, and undertakes not only geological but also palæontological and hydrographic investigations, and carries on mineralogical and lithological laboratories; then the Geodetic Survey, which studies the coasts, rivers, lakes, and mountains of the country; the Marine Observatory, for taking astronomical observations; the Weather Bureau, which conducts more than one hundred and fifty meteorological stations; the Bureau of Biology, which makes a special study of the geographical distribution of plants and animals; the Bureau of Botany, which studies especially all problems connected with seeds; the Bureau of Forestry, which scientifically works on questions of the national timber supply; the important Bureau of Entomology, which has studied with great success the relations of insects to agriculture; the Bureau of Agriculture, which statistically works out experiments on planting, and which directs government experiment stations situated throughout the country; the Department of Fisheries, which conducts stations for marine biology; and many others. Among the political economic institutes in the broad sense of the word are the Bureau of Labour, which undertakes purely sociological investigations into labour conditions; the Corporation Bureau, which studies the conditions of organized business; the Bureau of General Statistics; the Census Bureau, which every ten years takes a census more complete than that of any other country. The Census of 1890 consisted of 39 large folio volumes, and the collecting of information alone cost $10,000,000. The Census of 1900 is still in course of publication. The Bureau of Education also belongs here, which studies purely theoretically the statistics of education. Then there are the Bureau of Immigration and several others. All these bureaus are really designed to impart instruction and advice; they have no authority to enforce any measures. But the extraordinary publicity which is given to their printed reports gives them a very considerable influence; and the thoroughness with which the investigations are carried on, thanks to the liberal appropriations of Congress, makes of these bureaus scientific and economic institutions of the highest order.

We have still to speak of the most famous of the government bureaus, the Smithsonian Institution. In 1836 the government came into the possession, by bequest, of the whole property of the Englishman Smithson, as a principal with which an institution should be founded bearing his name, and serving the advance and dissemination of science. It was never known just why this Oxonian and mineralogist left his large property to the city of Washington, which then numbered only 5,000 inhabitants. Although he had never visited America, he wrote to a friend: "The best blood of England flows in my veins; my father's family is from Northumberland, my mother's is related to kings. But I desire to have my name remembered when the titles of the Northumberlands and the Percys shall have been forgotten." His instinct guided him aright, and the Smithsonian Institution is to-day an intellectual centre in Washington — that city which is the political centre of the New World. It should be mentioned, in passing, that Congress accepted the bequest only after lively opposition; it was objected that to receive the gift of a foreigner was beneath the dignity of the government. As a fact, however, the success of the institution is not due so much to this foreign endowment as to the able labours of its three presidents: the physicist Henry, who served from 1846 to 1878, the zoölogist Baird from 1878 to 1887, and the physicist Langley, who has been at the head since 1887. All three have been successful in finding ways by which the institute could serve the growth and dissemination of science.

It was agreed from the outset not to found a university which would compete with others already existing, but an institute to complement all existing institutions, and to be a sort of centre among them. The great institution was divided into the following divisions: first, the National Museum, in which the visible results of all the national expeditions and excavations are gathered and arranged. The American idea is that a scientific museum should not be a series of articles with their labels, but rather a series of instructive labels, illustrated by typical specimens. Only in this way, it is thought, does a museum really help to educate the masses. The collection, which is visited every year by more than 300,000 persons, includes 750,000 ethnological and anthropological objects; almost 2,000,000 zoölogical, 400,000 botanical, and almost 300,000 palæontological specimens. Then there is the National Zoölogical Park, which contains animal species that are dying out; the Astrophysical Observatory, in which Langley carries on his famous experiments on the invisible portion of the solar spectrum; the Ethnological Bureau, which specially studies the Indian; and much else. The department of exchanges of this institute is a unique affair; it negotiates exchanges between scientists, libraries, and other American institutions, and also between these and European institutions. As external as this service may seem, it has become indispensable to the work of American science. Moreover, the library of the institution is among the most important in the country; and its zoölogical, ethnological, physical, and geological publications, which are distributed free to 4,000 libraries, already fill hundreds of volumes.

Any one examining the many-sided and happily circumstanced

scientific work of these twenty-eight institutes at Washington will come to feel that the equipment could be used to better advantage if actual teaching were to be undertaken, and that the organization of the institutes into a national university attracting students from all parts of the country would tend to stimulate their achievements. In fact, the thought of a national university as the crowning point of the educational system of the country has always been entertained in Washington; and those who favour this idea are able to point to George Washington as the one who first conceived such a plan. In spite of vigorous agitation, this plan is still not realized, chiefly because the traditions of the country make education the concern of the separate states, and reserve it for such institutions as are independent of politics.

It is a different question, whether the time will not come when the nation will desire an institution of a higher sort — one which will not rival the other large universities of the country, but will stand above them all and assume new duties. A purely scientific institution might exist, admitting students only after they have passed their doctorial examination, and of which the professors should be elected by the vote of their colleagues through the country. There is much need of such a university; but the time may not be ripe for it now, and it may be a matter of the far future. And yet at the present rate at which science is developing in the country, the far future means only ten or fifteen years hence. When the time is ripe, the needed hundreds of millions of dollars will be forthcoming.

For the present, a sort of half-way station to a national university at Washington has been reached. This is the Carnegie Institute, whose efficiency can so far not be wholly estimated. With a provisional capital of $10,000,000 given by Andrew Carnegie, it is proposed to aid scientific investigations throughout the country, and on the recommendation of competent men to advance to young scientists the necessary means for productive investigations. There is, unfortunately, a danger here that in this way the other universities and foundations of the country may feel relieved of their responsibility, and so relax their efforts. It may be that people will look to the centre for that which formerly came from the periphery, and that in this way the general industry will become less intense. Most of all, the Carnegie Institute has, up to this point, lacked broad fruitful ideas and a real programme of what it proposes to do. If the institute cannot do better than it has so far done, it is to be feared that its arbitrary and unsystematic aid will do, in the long run, more harm than good to the scientific life of the country.

The same general conditions, on a smaller scale and with many variations, are found outside of Washington in a hundred different scientific museums and collections — biological, hygienic, medical, historical, economic, and experimental institutions; zoölogical and botanical gardens; astronomical observatories; biological stations, which are found sometimes under state or city administration, sometimes under private or corporate management. Thus the Marine Laboratory at Woods Hole is a meeting-place every summer for the best biologists. Sometimes important collections can be found in the most unlikely places — as, for instance, in the historic museum of the city of Salem, which, although it has gone to sleep to-day, is still proud of its history. The large cities, however, like New York, Philadelphia, Boston, Chicago, and Baltimore, have established admirable institutions, on which scientific work everywhere depends. Then there are the political capitals, such as Albany, with their institutions. That German who is most thoroughly acquainted with conditions of scientific collections, Professor Meyer, the director of the scientific museums at Dresden, has given his opinion in his admirable work on the museums of the Eastern United States as follows: "I have received a profound impression of American capabilities in this direction, and can even say that the museums of natural history of that country are generally on a higher plane than those of Europe. We have, so far as buildings and administrative machinery go, very few good and many moderate or downright poor museums, while the Americans have many more good and many fewer bad ones; and those which are poor are improving at the rapid American pace, while with us improvement is hopelessly slow."

There is still another important factor in the scientific societies, whose membership, to be sure, is chiefly composed of the personnel of the higher educational institutions, but which nevertheless exert an independent influence on scientific life. The National Academy of Science is officially at the head. It was founded in 1863, having a hundred members and electing five new members each year. While its annual meetings in Washington observe only the ordinary scientific programme, the society has as a special function the advising of Congress and the government on scientific matters. Thus, this academy drew up the plans for organizing the Geological Survey and for replanting the national forests. The political atmosphere of Washington, however, has not been too favourable to the success of the Academy, and it has never attained the national significance of the Paris and London academies.

The American Historical Association has a similar character; and its transactions are published at the expense of the government. The popular associations, of course, reach much larger circles; thus, for instance, the American Society for the Advancement of Science, which has existed for fifty years, has about the same functions as the German Naturforscherversammlung. It brings together at its annual meetings, which are always held in different places, a thousand or so scientists, and holds in different sections a great many lectures. Still more popular are the meetings of the similarly organized National Educational Association, which brings together more than ten thousand members at its summer meetings, which are often held in pleasant and retired spots. In these and similar sessions, scientific work is popularized, while in the specialized societies it is stimulated toward greater profundity. In fact, there is no medical, natural-historical, legal, theological, historical, economic, philological, or philosophical specialty which has not its special national societies with annual congresses. It is increasingly the custom to hold these popular sessions during the summer holidays, but the strictly scientific congresses during the first week in January. The physicians, by exception, meet at Easter. In order that the business-like separation of subjects may not exclude a certain contact of scientific neighbours, it is increasingly the plan to organize groups of congresses; thus, the seven societies of anatomy, physiology, morphology, plant physiology, psychology, anthropology, and folk-lore always meet at the same time in the same city.

Besides these wandering meetings, finally, there are the local societies. Of these, the veteran is the Academy in Philadelphia. It was founded by Franklin in 1743, and so far as its membership goes, may claim to have a national character. In a similar way the American Academy, founded in 1780, has its home in Boston. Then there are the New York Academy, the Washington Academy, which has recently enlarged so as to include members from the whole country, and which ultimately will probably merge into the National Academy; the academies of Baltimore, Chicago, New Haven, and a hundred smaller associations, which for the most part are not merely interested in spreading scientific information, but in helping on the results of science.

We cannot hope to call the complete roll here of scientific production. Our purpose was merely to relate some of the favourable and unfavourable influences under which the American has to make his contribution to the science of the day. Merely for a first orientation, we may give some more detailed accounts in a few departments. At first sight, one might be tempted to give a sketch of present-day production by directly depicting the production with reference to the special higher institutions. Much more than in Germany, the results of scientific research are brought before the public eye with the official seal of some university. Every large educational institution publishes its own contributions to many different sciences; thus, the University of Chicago, which perhaps goes furthest in this respect, publishes journals of sociology, pedagogy, biblical studies, geology, astronomy, botany, etc.; and, besides these, regular series of studies in science, government, classical philology, Germanic and Romance languages, English philology, anthropology, and physiology. Johns Hopkins University publishes mathematical, chemical, and biological magazines; a journal for experimental medicine, one for psychiatry, for modern philology, for history, and Assyriology. Among the periodical publications of Harvard University, the astronomical, zoölogical, cryptogamic, ethnological, Oriental, classical philological, modern philological, historical, and economic journals are the best known. Columbia, Pennsylvania, and several other universities publish equally many journals. There are also a great many books published under the auspices of institutions of learning, which relate to expeditions or other special matters. Thus, for instance, Yale University, on the occasion of its two-hundredth anniversary in 1901, published commemorative scientific papers by its professors in twenty-five large volumes; the papers themselves ranging from such subjects as the Hindu epic and Greek metre to thermo-dymamics and physiological chemistry.

The various universities have always been known to have their scientific specialties. That of Johns Hopkins is natural science; of Columbia, the science of government; of Harvard, literature and philosophy. But the universities are, of course, not confined to their specialties; for instance, Johns Hopkins has done very much in philology, Columbia in biology, and while Harvard has been famous for its literary men, like Longfellow, Holmes, Norton and Child, it has also had such distinguished men on its faculty as the zoölogist Agassiz, the botanist Gray, and the astronomer Pickering.

It may be more natural to classify scientific production according to the separate sciences. The list is too long to be given entire. The venerable subject of philosophy is generally placed first in the university catalogues of lectures. This subject shows at once how much and how little is being done. A German, to be sure, is apt to have false standards in this matter; for if he thinks of German philosophy, he recalls the names of Kant, Schopenhauer, Fichte, and Hegel; and he asks what America has produced to compare with these. But we have seen that the work of productive science was commenced in the New World only a few decades ago, and for this reason we must compare the present day in America with the present day in Germany; and to be just, we should compare the American scholar only with the younger and middle-aged Germans who have developed under the scientific conditions of the last thirty years — that is, with men not over sixty years old. Young geniuses are not plentiful, even in Germany to-day; and not only are men like Kant and Hegel lacking in philosophy, but also in other departments of science; men like Ranke and Helmholtz seem not to belong to our day of specialization. A new wave of idealistic and broadly generalizing thought is advancing. The time of great thinkers will come again; but a young country is not to be blamed for the spirit of the times, nor ought its present accomplishment to be measured after the standards of happier days. If we make a perfectly fair comparison, we shall find that American philosophy is at present up to that of any other country.

Externally, in the first place, America makes a massive showing, even if we leave out of account philosophical literature of the more popular sort. While, for example, England has only two really important philosophical magazines, America has at least five which are as good as the English; and if philosophy is taken in the customary wider sense, sociological and pedagogical journals must be included, which are nowhere surpassed. The emphasis is laid differently in America and Germany; and this difference, which may be seen in almost all sciences, generally, though not always, has deeper grounds than merely personal ones, and is in every case apt to distort the judgment of a foreigner. America, for instance, is astonishingly unproductive in the history of philosophy. Every need seems to be satisfied by translations from the German or by very perfunctory text-book compilations. On the other hand, the theory of knowledge, ethics, and above all psychology, are very prosperous. Disputes in epistemology have always been carried on in America, and the Calvinistic theology, more especially, arrived at important conclusions. At the beginning of the eighteenth century lived Jonathan Edwards, who was perhaps the greatest metaphysical mind in the history of America. The transcendental way of thought, which is profoundly planted in the American soul, was nurtured by German idealism, and found expression through the genius of Emerson. Then, in more systematic and academic ways, there have been philosophers like Porter and McCosh, who stood under Scotch influence and fought against positivism; others, like Harris and Everett, who have represented German tendencies; while Draper, Fiske, Cope, Leconte, and others have preached the philosophy of science. In the front ranks today of philosophers are Ladd, Dewey, Fullerton, Bowne, Ormond, Howison, Santayana, Palmer, Strong, Hibben, Creighton, Lloyd, and most influential of all, Royce, whose latest work, "The World and the Individual," is perhaps the most significant epistemological system of our day.

Psychology is the most favoured of all the philosophical disciplines in America at the present time. This is shown outwardly in the growth of laboratories for experimental psychology, which in size and equipment far exceed those of Europe. America has more than forty laboratories. Foremost in this psychological movement is William James, who is, next to Wundt, the most distinguished psychologist living, and whose remarkable analysis of conscious phenomena has been set down with a freshness and liveliness, an energy and discrimination, which are highly characteristic of American intellect. Then there are other well-known investigators like Stanley Hall, Cattell, Baldwin, Ladd, Sanford, Titchener, Angell, Miss Calkins, Scripture, and many others. In pedagogy, which is now disporting itself in a great display of paper and ink, the names of Harris, Eliot, Butler, Hall, Da Garmo, and Hanus are the most respected.

Just as theological and metaphysical speculations, ever since the early Colonial days, have preceded present-day scientific philosophy, so in the science of history systematic investigators were preceded in early days by the Colonial historians, beginning with Bradford and Winthrop. A people which are so restless to make history, so proud of their doings, so grateful to their heroes, and which more than any other people base their law and public policy avowedly on precedent, will necessarily have enjoyed the recounting of their own past. America has had a systematic history, however, only since the thirties, and two periods of work are generally distinguished; an earlier one, in which historians undertook to cover the whole subject of American history, or at least very large portions of it, and a later period embracing the last decade, in which historical interest has been devoted to minuter studies. Bancroft and Parkman stand for the first movement. George Bancroft began to write his history in 1830, and worked patiently thereon for half a century. By 1883 the development of the country, from its discovery up to the adoption of the American Constitution, had been completed in a thorough-going fashion. Parkman was the greater genius, and one who opened an entirely new perspective in American history by his investigations and fascinating descriptions of the wars between the English and the French colonists. The great works of Hildreth and Tucker should also be mentioned here.

The period of specialized work, of course, covers less ground. The large monographs of Henry Adams, John Fiske, Rhodes, Schouler, McMaster, Eggleston, Roosevelt, and of Von Holst, if an adoptive son of America may be included, are accounted the best pieces of work. They have described American history partly by geographical regions and partly by periods; and they show great diversity of style, as may be seen by comparing the martial tone of Holst and the majestic calmness of Rhodes. To these must be added the biographies, of which the best known form the series of "American Statesmen." Americans are particularly fond of studying a portion of national history from the life of some especially active personality. Then too, for twenty years, there has been a considerable and indispensable fabrication of historical research. Large general works and reference books, like those of Winsor, Hart, and others; the biographies, archive studies, correspondences, local histories, often published by learned societies; series of monographs, journals, the chief of which is the *American Historical Review* — in short, everything necessary to the modern cultivation of historical science are to be found abundantly. The Revolution, the beginnings of the Federation, the Civil War, and Congress are specially favoured topics. It is almost a matter of course that the independent investigation into European history is very little attempted; although very good things have been done, such as Prescott's work on Spanish history, Motley's Rise of the Dutch Republic; and in recent times, for instance, Taylor has made important studies in English history, Perkins in French, Henderson in German, Thayer in Italian, Lea and Emerton in ecclesiastical history, Mahan in the history of naval warfare, and similarly others.

This lively interest in philosophy and history is itself enough to disprove the old fable that American science is directed only toward material ends. Perhaps, to be sure, some one might say that philosophy is practiced to better mankind and history to teach politicians some practical lessons, while both statements are in point of fact false. No such charge, however, can be made against classical philology; and yet no one can read the transactions, which constitute many volumes, of the five hundred members of the Philological Association, or read the numbers of the *American Journal of Philology*, or the classical studies published by Harvard, Cornell, and Chicago, without feeling distinctly that here is scientific work of the strictest sort, and that the methods of investigations are steadily improving. The movement is younger in this department than in the others. To be sure, the classical authors have been well known in America for two centuries; but in no province has the dilettanteism of the English gentleman so thoroughly prevailed. It was not until the young philologians commenced to visit German universities, and especially Göttingen, that a thorough-going philology was introduced. And such a work as the forty-four students of the great classicist, Gildersleeve, published on the occasion of his seventieth birthday, would have been impossible twenty years ago. The greatest interest is devoted to syntactical investigation, in which the best-known works are those of Goodwin, Gildersleeve, and Hale; while there are some works on lexicography and comparative languages, and fewer still on textual criticism. Every classical philologian knows the names of Hadley, Beck, Allen, Lane, Warren, Smyth, White, Wheeler, Shorey, Dressler, and many others.

There is an unusual interest in Oriental philology, which is slightly influenced indeed by practical motives. For instance, the great religious interest taken in the Bible — not by scientists, but by the general public — has sent out special expeditions and done much to advance the study of cuneiform inscriptions. The Assyrian collections of the University of Pennsylvania are accounted, in many respects, the most complete in existence. Its curator, Hilprecht, is well known, and Lyon, Haupt, and others almost as well. Whitney, of Yale, was undoubtedly the leader in Sanskrit. Lanman, of Harvard, is his most famous successor, and besides him are Jackson, Buck, Bloomfield, and others. Toy is the great authority on Semitic languages.

It would lead us too far away if we were to follow philological science into modern languages. As a matter of course, the English language and literature are the most studied; in fact, English philology has had its real home in the New World since the days of Child. Francis James Child, one of the most winning personalities in the history of American scholarship, has contributed much on Chaucer and ancient English dramas; and as his great work, has gathered together English and Scottish ballads into a collection of ten volumes. This work has often been esteemed as America's greatest contribution to philology. Kittredge, who has succeeded Child at Harvard, works on much the same lines. Lounsbury is known especially for his brilliant works on Chaucer; Manley has also studied Chaucer and the pre-Shakesperian drama; Gummere the early ballads, while Wendell and Furness are the great Shakesperian scholars. The Arthurian legends have been especially studied by Schofield, Mead, Bruce, and others; the Anglo-Saxon language by Bright, Cook, Brown, and Callaway. Lowell was the first great critic of literature, and he has been followed by Gates and many others. The belles-lettres themselves have given rise to a large historical and critical literature, such as the admirable general works of Steadman, Richardson, and Tyler, and the monographs by Woodberry, Cabot, Norton, Warner, and Higginson. The very best work, however, on American literature, in spite of all aspersions cast on the extreme aristocrat, is Barrett Wendell's "Literary History of America." We might mention a long list of works on Romance and Germanic languages and literature. At least emphasis must be laid on one, Kuno Francke's extraordinary book on "Social Influences in German Literature," the work of the most gifted herald of German culture in America. We may also mention the works of Thomas and Hempl in Germanic, and Todd, Elliot, and Cohn in romance languages.

Political economy is the favourite study of the American, since the history of this country has been determined by economic factors more directly than that of any other nation, and since all the different economic periods have been lived through in the still surveyable past. In a sense, the country looks like a tremendous experimental laboratory of political economy. The country is so unevenly developed that the most diverse economic stages are to be found in regions which are geographically near each other, and everything goes on, as it were, under the scientific magnifying glass of the statistical student. Remarkably enough, the actual history of economics has been rather neglected in American studies, in spite of many beginnings made in Germany on the history of American economics. The chief attention of the nation has been given rather to the systematic analysis and deductive investigation of special conditions. In political economy there are, of course, first the well-known agitators like Henry Carey, the great protectionist of the first half of the century; Henry George, the single-tax theorist, whose book, "Progress and Poverty," found in 1879 extraordinary circulation; and Bellamy, whose "Utopia" was in much the same style: and the political tracts on economic subjects are far too numerous to think of mentioning. The really scientific works form another group. At first we find the pioneer efforts of the seventies and eighties — Wells's work on tariff and commerce, Charles Francis Adams's work on railways, Sumner's on the history of American finance, Atkinson's on production and distribution, Wright's on wages, Knox's on banking, and the general treatises of Walker, who conducted the censuses of 1870 and 1880. In recent times the chief works are those of Hadley on railroads, of Clark on capital, of James on political finance and municipal administration, of Ely on taxation, of Taussig on tariff, silver and wages, of Jenks on trusts, of Brooks on labour movements, of Seligman on the politics of taxation, of H. C. Adams on scientific finance, of Gross on the history of English economics, of Patten on economic theory, and of Lowell on the science of government. Moreover, the political economists and students of government have an unusually large number of journals at their disposal. In sociology there are Giddings, Small, and Ward, known everywhere, and after them Willcox, Ripley, and others.

We have spent too much time over the historical disciplines. Let us look at the opposite pole of the scientific globe from the mental sciences to the natural sciences, and at first to mathematics. Mathematicians were especially late in waking up to really scientific achievements; and this was scarcely ten years ago, so that all the productive mathematicians are the younger professors. Of the older period, there are but three mathematicians of great importance — Benjamin Peirce, perhaps the most brilliant of American mathematicians, and his pupils, Hill and Newcomb. Their chief interest has been mathematical astronomy. Of their generation are also Willard Gibbs in mathematical physics, McClintock in algebra, and Charles Peirce in mathematical logic. In the last ten years, it is no longer a question of a few great names. The younger generation has taken its inspiration from Germany and France, and is busily at work in pure mathematics; there are Moore and Dixon, of Chicago; Storey and Taber, of Clark; Böcher and Osgood, of Harvard; White at Evanston; Van Vleck at Wesleyan, and many others.

We find again, in the natural sciences, that the American by no means favours only practical studies. There is no less practical a science than astronomy, and yet we find a series of great successes.

This is externally noticeable in a general interest in astronomy; no other country in the world has so many well-equipped observatories as the United States, and no other country manufactures such perfect astronomical lenses. America has perfected the technique of astronomy. Roland, for instance, has improved the astronomical spectroscope, and Pickering has made brilliant contributions to photometry. The catalogue of stars by Gould and Langley is an indispensable work, and America has contributed its full share to the observation of asteroids and comets. Newcomb, however, who is the leader since forty years, has done the most brilliant work, in his thorough computations of stellar paths and masses. We should also not forget Chandler's determination of magnitudes, Young's work on the sun, Newton's on meteorites, and Barnard's on comets.

Surprisingly enough, the development of scientific physics has been less brilliant so far. Only in optics has really anything of high importance been done; but in this field there have been such accomplishments as Michelson's measurements of lightwaves, Rowland's studies of concave gratings, Newcomb's measurements on the speed of light, and Langley's studies of the ultrared rays. In all other fields the work is somewhat disconnected; although, to be sure, in the branches of electricity, acoustics, and heat, important discoveries have been made by Trowbridge, Woodward, Barus, Wood, Cross, Nichols, Hall, B. O. Pierce, Sabine, and many others. In purely technical subjects, especially those related to electricity, much has been done of serious scientific importance ; and these triumphs in technical branches are, of course, famous throughout the world. From the hand tool of the workman to locomotives and bridges, American mechanics have been victorious. Applied physics has yielded the modern bicycle, the sewing-machine, the printing-press, tool-making machinery, and a thousand other substitutes for muscular labour; has also perfected the telegraph, the incandescent lamp, the telephone and the phonograph, and every day brings some new laurel to the American inventor. But it is not to be supposed that Edison, Tesla, and Bell are the sole representatives of American physics. Quiet scientific work of the highest order is carried on in a dozen laboratories. Meteorology ought to be mentioned as a branch of physics; it has been favoured by the large field of observation which America offers and has developed brilliantly under Ferrel, Hazen, Greely, Harrington, Mendenhall, Rotch, and others.

It is still more true of chemistry than of physics that advance has been independent of the industrial application of science. The leading chemists have all worked in the interests of pure science; and this work started at the beginning of the last century, when Benjamin Silliman, of Yale, the editor of the first magazine for natural science, laid the foundations for his scientific school. He was followed in succeeding generations by Hare, Smith, Hunt, and most notably Cooke, whose studies on the periodic law and the atomic weight of oxygen are specially valuable. Of later men there are Willard Gibbs, the Nestor of chemical thermo-dynamics, who became famous by his theory of the phase rule, and Wolcott Gibbs through his studies on complex acids. Crafts is known for his researches into organic compounds, and Mallet by classical investigations into the atomic weight of aluminum. Other valuable contributions have been Hillebrand's analysis of minerals, Stieglitz's organic syntheses, Noyes's studies on ions, the work of Clark and Richards on atomic weights, Gooch's technical discoveries, Hill's synthetic production of benzol compounds, Warren's work with mineral oils, Baskerville's study of thorium, not to mention the highly prized text-books of Ira Remsen, the discoverer of saccharin. Among the physiological and agricultural chemists, the best known are Chittenden, Pfaff, Atwater, and Hilgard. The pioneer of physical chemistry is Richards, of Harvard, probably the only American professor so far who has been called to the position of a full professor at a German university. He remained in America, although invited to Göttingen. Bancroft and Noyes are at work on the same branch of chemistry.

The work in chemistry is allied in many ways to mineralogy, petrography, and geology. Oddly enough, mineralogy has centred distinctly at one place — Yale University. The elder Dana used to work there, whose "System of Mineralogy" first appeared in 1837, and while frequently revised has remained for half a century the standard book in any language; Dana's chemical classification of minerals has also found general acceptance. His son, the crystallographer, worked here, as also Brush and Penfield, who has investigated more kinds of stone than any other living man. Beside these well-known leaders, there are such men as

Lawrence Smith, Cooke, Gerth, Shepard, and Wolff. The advances in geology have been still more brilliant, since nature made America an incomparable field of study. Hall had already made an early beginning here, and Dana and Whitney, Hayden and King, Powell and Gilbert, Davis, Shaler, and Branner have continued the work. Remains of the Glacial Epoch and mountain formation have been the favourite topics. And the investigation which has frequently been connected with practical mining interests is among the most important, and in Europe the most highly regarded of American scientific achievements.

Closely related to the geological are the geographical studies. The Government Bureau of Survey figures prominently here, by reason of its magnificent equipment. Most famous are the coast surveys of Pache and Mendenhall, and the land surveys of Rogers, Whitney, and Gannet. The hydrographic investigations of Maury have perhaps had more influence on geography, and his physical geography of the ocean has opened up new lines of inquiry; Guyot has done most to spread the interests of geography. Americans have always been greatly interested in expeditions to dangerous lands, wherefore many Americans have been pioneers, missionaries, and scientific travellers. In this spirit Lewis and Clark explored the Northwest, Wilkes crossed the Pacific Ocean, Perry went to Japan, and Stanley to Africa; others have travelled to South America, and many expeditions have been started for the North Pole since the first expedition of Kane in 1853. Palæontology has been well represented in America, and has contributed a good deal to the advance in geology. Hall commenced the work with studies on invertebrate fossils; then came Hyatt, who studied fossil cephalopods, Scudder fossil insects, Beecher brachiopods; and then Leidy, Cope, Osborne, and above all, the great scientist, Marsh — all of whom have studied fossil vertebrates.

Almost every one of these men was at the same time a systematic zoölogist. Especially in former days, many young men devoted themselves to systematic zoölogy under the leadership of Audubon, whose pioneer work on "The Birds of America" appeared in 1827; then later of Say, the first investigator of butterflies and mussels; and still later of Louis Agassiz, the great student of jelly-fish, hydroids and polyps, whose son, Alexander Agassiz, has carried on the famous studies of coral islands. Besides these men have laboured LeConte, Gill, Packard, and Verrill in the province of invertebrates; Baird, Ridgeway, Huntington, Allen, Meriam, and Jordan in the field of vertebrates. At the present time interest in America as well as in Europe is turning toward histology and embryology. Here, too, the two Agassizes have taken the lead, the senior Agassiz with his studies on turtles, the younger Agassiz in studies on starfishes. Next to theirs come the admirable works of Wyman, Whitman, Brooks, Minot, Mark, and Wilson, and the investigations of Davenport on the subject of variation. The phenomenon of life has been studied now by zoölogists and again by biologists and physiologists. Here belong the researches into the conscious life of lower animals carried on by Lee and Parker, and the excellent investigations of the German-American Jacques Loeb, of California, who has placed the tropisms of animals and the processes of fertilization in a wholly new light. Of his colleagues in physiology, the best known are Bowditch, Howell, Porter, and Meltzer.

The highest organism which the natural scientist can study is man, taken not historically, but anthropologically. The American has been forced to turn to anthropology and to ethnology, since circumstances have put at his hand some hundred types of Indians, with the most diverse languages and customs, and since, moreover, peoples have streamed from every part of the world to this country; millions of African negroes are here, the ground is covered with the remains of former Indian life, and the strange civilizations of Central America have left their remains near by. The Ethnological Bureau at Washington and the Peabody Museum at Harvard have instituted many expeditions and investigations. In recent times the works of Morgan, Hale, Brinton, Powell, Dall, Putnam, McGee, and Boas have opened new perspectives, especially on the subject of the American Indian.

The American flora has contributed no less new material to science than the American fauna. European botanists had commenced the work with tours of observation, when in the middle of the last century Asa Gray began his admirable life-work. He was in the closest sympathy with European botanists, and published in all more than four hundred papers on the classification and systematic study of the profuse material. Gray died in 1888, undoubtedly the greatest botanist that America has produced. His labours have been supplemented by his teacher, Torrey; by Chapman, who worked up the southeastern part of the country; by scientific travellers, such as Wright and Watson; by Engelmann, who studied cacti; Bebb, who studied the fields; by Coulter, the expert on the plants of the Rocky Mountains; by Bailey and many others. This great work is more or less pervaded by the ideas of Gray; but in the last twenty years it has branched off in several directions under a number of leaders. Farlow has reached out into cryptogamic botany, Goodale into plant physiology, and Sargent into dendrology. There has been, moreover, considerable specialization and subdivision of labour in the botanical gardens of New York, Boston, and St. Louis, and the herbaria and botanical institutes of various universities and of the agricultural experiment stations. These institutions put forth publications under the editorship of such able botanists as Robinson, Trelease, Fernald, Smith, and True; and these works are not excelled by those of any other country.

We have had, perhaps, too much of mere names; and yet these have been only examples, calculated to show the strength and the weakness of the scientific development of America. We have sought specially to keep within the limits of the "philosophical faculties." It would be interesting to go into the subjects of theology, law and medicine, and of technology in a similar way; but it would lead too far. Yet whether the unprejudiced observer considers such disciplines as we have described, or whether he looks out into neighbouring academic fields, he will find the same flourishing condition of things — a bold, healthy, and intelligent progress, with a complete understanding of the true aim of science, with tireless industry, able organization, and optimistic energy.

Of course, the actual achievements are very uneven; they are, in some directions, superior to those of England and France — in a few directions even to those of Germany, but in others far inferior to German attainments. We have seen that the conditions a short time ago were unfortunate for science, and that only recently have they given way to more favourable factors. Most people see such favourable factors first of all in the financial support offered to the investigator; but the chief aid for such work does not lie in the providing of appliances. Endowments can do no more than supply books, apparatus, laboratories, and collections for those who wish to study, but all that never makes a great scientist; the average level of study may be improved by material support, but it will never be brought above a certain level of mediocrity. For, after all, science depends chiefly on the personal factor; and good men can do everything, even on narrow means.

The more important factor in the opulence which science now enjoys is an indirect one; it improves the social status of scientific workers, so that better human material is now attracted to the scientific career. As long as scientific life meant poverty and dependence, the only people attracted to it were men of the school-teaching stamp; the better men have craved something fuller and greater, and have wished to expend their strength in the more thoroughly living province of industrial and commercial life, where alone the great social premiums were to be found. But now the case is different. Science has been recognized by the nation; scientific and university life has become rich in significance, the professor is no longer a school-teacher, and the right kind of young scholar is stepping into the arena. Another factor is working in the same direction. Substantial families are coming to the third generation, when they go over from trade to art and science. The sons of the best people with great vitality and great personality prefer now to work in the laboratory rather than in the bank. Each one brings Yankee intelligence and Yankee energy with him. This social reappraisement of science, and its effect on the quality of men who become productive scholars, are the best indication of the coming greatness of American science.

CHAPTER EIGHTEEN

Literature

WHAT does the American read? In "Jōrn Uhl," the apprentice in the Hamburg bookshop says to his friend: "If I am to tell you how to be wise and cunning, then go where there are no books. Do you know, if I had not had my father, I should have gone to America — for a fact! And it would have gone hard with anybody who poked a book at me." In that way many a man in Europe, who is long past his apprenticeship, still pictures to himself America: Over in America nobody bothers about books. And he would not credit the statement that nowhere else are so many books read as in America. The American's fondness for reading finds clearest expression in the growth of libraries, and in few matters of civilization is America so well fitted to teach the Old World a lesson. Europe has many large and ancient collections of books, and Germany more than all the rest; but they serve only one single purpose — that of scientific investigation; they are the laboratories of research. They are chiefly lodged with the great universities, and even the large municipal libraries are mostly used by those who need material for productive labours, or wish to become conversant with special topics.

Exactly the same type of large library has grown up in America; and here, too, it is chiefly the universities whose stock of books is at the service of the scientific world. Besides these, there are special libraries belonging to learned societies, state law libraries, special libraries of government bureaus and of museums, and largest of all the Library of Congress. The collection of such scientific books began at the earliest colonial period, and at first under theological auspices. The Calvinist Church, more than any other, inclined to the study of books. As early as 1790 the catalogue of Harvard

College contained 350 pages, of which 150 were taken up by theological works. Harvard has to-day almost a million books, mostly in the department of literature, philology, history, philosophy, and jurisprudence. There are, moreover, in Boston the state library of law, with over a hundred thousand volumes; the Athenæum, with more than two hundred thousand books; the large scientific library of the Institute of Technology, and many others. Similarly, in other large cities, the university libraries are the nucleus for scientific labours, and are surrounded by admirable special libraries, particularly in New York, Chicago, and Philadelphia. Then, too, the small academic towns, like Princeton, Ithaca, New Haven, and others, have valuable collections of books, which in special subjects are often unique. For many years the American university libraries have been the chief purchasers of the special collections left by deceased European professors. And it often happens, especially through the gift of grateful alumni, that collections of the greatest scientific value, which could not be duplicated, come into the possession even of lesser institutions.

In many departments of investigation, Washington takes the lead with the large collection of the various scientific, economic, and technical bureaus of the government. The best known of these is the unique medical library of the War Department. Then there is the Library of Congress, with many more than a million volumes, which to-day has an official right to one copy of every book published in the United States, and so may claim to be a national library. It is still not comparable to the many-sided and complete collection of the British Museum; the national library is one-sided, or at least shows striking gaps. Having started as the Library of Congress, it has, aside from its one copy of every American book and the books on natural science belonging to the Smithsonian Institution, few books except those on politics, history, political economy, and law. The lack of space for books, which existed until a few years ago, made it seem inexpedient to spend money for purposes other than the convenience of Congressmen. But the American people, in its love for books, has now erected such a building as the world had never before seen devoted to the storing of books. The new Congressional Library was opened in 1897, and since the stacks have still room for several million volumes, the library will soon grow to an all-round completeness like that at London. This library has a specially valuable collection of manuscripts and correspondences.

All the collections of books which we have so far mentioned are virtually like those of Germany. But since they mostly date from the nineteenth century, the American libraries are more modern, and contain less dead weight in the way of unused folios. Much more important is their greatly superior accessibility. Their reading-rooms are more comfortable and better lighted, their catalogues more convenient, library hours longer, and, above all, books are much more easily and quickly delivered. Brooks Adams said recently, about the library at Washington as a place for work, that this building is well-nigh perfect; it is large, light, convenient, and well provided with attendants. In Paris and London, one works in dusty, forbidding, and overcrowded rooms, while here the reading-rooms are numerous, attractive, and comfortable. In the National Library at Paris, one has to wait an hour for a book; in the British Museum, half an hour; and in Washington, five minutes. This rapid service, which makes such a great difference to the student, is found everywhere in America; and everywhere the books are housed in buildings which are palatial, although perhaps not so beautiful as the Washington Library.

Still, all these differences are unessential; in principle the academic libraries are alike in the New and Old Worlds. The great difference between Europe and America begins with the libraries which are not learned, but which are designed to serve popular education. The American public library which is not for science, but for education, is to the European counterpart as the Pullman express train to the village post-chaise.

The scientific libraries of Boston, including that of Harvard University, contain nearly two million printed works; but the largest library of all is distinct from these. It is housed on Copley Square, in a renaissance palace by the side of the Art Museum, and opposite the most beautiful church in America. The staircase of yellow marble, the wonderful wall-paintings, the fascinating arcade on the inner court, and the sunlit halls are indeed beautiful. And in and out, from early morning till late evening, weekday and Sunday, move the people of Boston. The stream of men divides in the lower vestibule. Some go to the newspaper room, where several hundred daily newspapers, a dozen of them German, hang on racks. Others wander to the magazine rooms, where the weekly and monthly papers of the world are waiting to be read. Others ascend to the upper stories, where Sargent's famous pictures of the Prophets allure the lover of art, in order to look over more valuable special editions and the art magazines, geographical charts, and musical works. The largest stream of all goes to the second floor, partly into the huge quiet reading-room, partly into the rotunda, which contains the catalogue, partly into the hall containing the famous frescoes of the Holy Grail, where the books are given out. Here a million and a half books are delivered every year to be taken home and read. And no one has to wait; an apparatus carries the applicant's card with wonderful speed to the stacks, and the desired book is sent back in automatic cars. Little children meanwhile wander into the juvenile room, where they find the best books for children. And everything invites even the least patient reader to sit down quietly with some sort of a volume — everything is so tempting, so convenient and comfortable, and so surpassingly beautiful. And all this is free to the humblest working-man.

And still, if the citizen of Massachusetts were to be asked of what feature of the public libraries he is most proud, he would probably not mention this magnificent palace in Boston, the capital of the state, but rather the 350 free public libraries scattered through the smaller cities and towns of this state, which is after all only one-third as large as Bavaria. It is these many libraries which do the broadest work for the people. Each little collection, wherever it is, is the centre of intellectual and moral enlightenment, and plants and nourishes the desire for self-perfection. Of course, Massachusetts has done more in this respect than any other part of the country — especially more than the South, which is backward in this respect. But there is no longer any city of moderate size which has not a large public library, and there is no state which does not encourage in every possible way the establishment of public libraries in every small community, giving financial aid if it is necessary.

Public libraries have become the favourite Christmas present of philanthropists, and while the hospitals, universities, and museums have still no reason for complaint, the churches now find that superfluous millions are less apt to go to gay church windows than to well-chosen book collections. In the year 1900 there existed more than 5,383 public libraries having over a thousand volumes; of these 144 had more than fifty thousand, and 54 had more than a hundred thousand volumes. All together contained, according to the statistics of 1900, more than forty-four million volumes and more than seven million pamphlets; and the average growth was over 8 per cent. There are probably to-day, therefore, fifteen million volumes more on the shelves. The many thousand libraries which have fewer than 999 books are over and above all this.

The make-up of such public libraries may be seen from the sample catalogue gotten out by the Library Association a few years since, as a typical collection of five thousand books. This catalogue which, with the exception of the most important foreign classics, contains only books in English, including, however, many translations, contains 227 general reference books, 756 books on history, 635 on biography, 413 on travel, 355 on natural science, 694 in belles-lettres, 809 novels, 225 on art, 220 on religion, 424 on social science, 268 on technical subjects, etc. The cost of this sample collection is $12,000. The proportions between the several divisions are about the same in larger collections. In smaller collections, belles-lettres have a somewhat greater share. The general interest taken by the nation in this matter is shown by the fact that the first edition of twenty thousand copies of this sample catalogue, of six hundred pages, was soon exhausted.

The many-sidedness of this catalogue points also to the manifold functions of the public library. It is meant to raise the educational level of the people, and this can be done in three ways: first, interest may be stimulated along new lines; second, those who wish to perfect themselves in their own subjects or in whatsoever special topics, may be provided with technical literature; and third, the general desire for literary entertainment may be satisfied by books of the best or at least not of the worst sort. The directors of libraries see their duties to lie in all three directions. The libraries guide the tastes and interests of the general public, and try to replace the ordinary servant-girl's novel with the best romances of the day and shallow literature with works which are truly instructive. And no community is quite content until its public library has become a sort of general meeting-place and substitute for the saloon and the club. America is the working-man's paradise, and attractive enough to the rich man; but the ordinary man of the middle classes, who in Germany finds his chief comfort in the Bierhalle, would find little comfort in America if it were not for the public library, which offers him a home. Thus the public library has come to be a recognized instrument of culture along with the public school; and in all American outposts the school teacher and librarian are among the pioneers.

The learned library cannot do this. To be sure, the university library can help to spread information, and conversely the public library makes room for thousands of volumes on all sorts of scientific topics. But the emphasis is laid very differently in the two cases, and if it were not so neither library would best fulfil its purpose. The extreme quiet of the reference library and the bustle and stir of the public library do not go together. In the one direction America has followed the dignified traditions of Europe; in the other, it has opened new paths and travelled on at a rapid pace. Every year discovers new ideas and plans, new schemes for equipment and the selection of books, for cataloguing, and for otherwise gaining in utility. When, for instance, the library in Providence commenced to post a complete list of books and writings pertaining to the subject of every lecture which was given in the city, it was the initiation of a great movement. The juvenile departments are the product of recent years, and are constantly increasing in popularity. There are even, in some cases, departments for blind readers. The state commissions are new, and so also the travelling libraries, which are carried from one village to another.

The great schools for librarians are also new. The German librarian is mostly a scholar; but the American believes that he has improved on the European library systems, not so much by his ample financial resources as by having broken with the academic custom, and having secured librarians with a special library training. And since there are such officials in many thousand libraries, and the great institutions create a constant demand for such persons, the library schools, which offer generally a three years' course, have been found very successful.

Admittedly, all this technical apparatus is expensive; the Boston library expends every year a quarter of a million dollars for administrative expenses. But the American taxpayer supports this more gladly than any other burden, knowing that the public library is the best weapon against alcoholism and crime, against corruption and discontent, and that the democratic country can flourish only when the instinct of self-perfection as it exists in every American is thoroughly satisfied.

The reading of the American nation is not to be estimated wholly by the books in public libraries, since it also includes a tremendous quantity of printed material that goes to the home of every citizen. Three hundred and forty American publishers place their wares every year on the market, and the part bought by the public libraries is a very small proportion. A successful novel generally reaches its third hundred thousand; of course, such gigantic editions are limited to novels and school-books. The number of annual book publications is much smaller than in Germany; but it must be considered that, first, the American electrotype process does not lend itself to new and revised editions; and that small brochures are replaced in America by the magazine articles. On the other hand, the number of copies published is perhaps larger than in Germany. And then, too, among the upper classes, a great many German, French, and Italian books are purchased from Europe.

The great feature for all classes of the population is the tremendous production of periodical literature. Statistics show that in the United States in the year 1903, there were published 2,300 daily papers, more than 15,000 weeklies, 2,800 monthlies, and 200 quarterlies — in all, 21,000 periodicals. These are more periodicals than are published in all Europe; in Germany alone there are 7,500. The tremendous significance of these figures, particularly as compared with the European, becomes clear only when one considers the number of copies which these periodicals circulate. Not merely the newspapers of the three cities having over a million inhabitants, but also those of the larger provincial towns, reach a circulation of hundreds of thousands; and more surprising still is the unparalleled circulation of the weekly and monthly papers. Huge piles of magazines, containing the most serious sort of essays, are sold from every news-stand in a few hours. And anybody who knows New England is not surprised at the statement which T. W. Higginson makes in his recollections, that he came once to a small Massachusetts village of only twenty-four homes, nineteen of which subscribed to the *Atlantic Monthly*, a publication which is most nearly comparable to the *Deutsche Rundschau*.

The surprisingly large sales of expensive books among rich families is quite as gratifying as the huge consumption of magazines among the middle classes. Editions de luxe are often sold entire at fabulous prices before the edition is out, and illustrated scientific works costing hundreds of dollars always find a ready sale. These are merely the symptoms of the fact that every American home has its book-cases proportionate to its resources, and large private libraries are found not merely in the homes of scholars and specialists. In the palaces of merchant princes, the library is often the handsomest room, although it is sometimes so papered with books that it looks as if the architect had supplied them along with the rugs and chandeliers. One more commonly finds that the library is the real living-room of the house. If one looks about in such treasure apartments, one soon loses the sense of wonder completely; rare editions and valuable curiosities are there brought together with the greatest care and intelligence into an appropriate home. There are probably very few German private houses with collections of books and paintings comparable, for instance, to that of J. Montgomery Sears in Boston. The whole interior is so wonderfully harmonious that even the autograph poems and letters of Goethe and Schiller seem a matter of course. But from the book-shelves of the millionaire to the carefully selected little shelf of the poor school-ma'am, from the monumental home of the national library to the modest little library building of every small village, from the nervous and rapid perusal of the scholar to the slow making-out of the working-man who pores over his newspaper on the street corner, or of the shopgirl with the latest novel in the elevated train, there is everywhere life and activity centring around the world of print, and this popularity of books is growing day by day.

By far the most of what the American reads is written by Americans. This does not mean that any important book which appears in other parts of the world escapes him; on the contrary just as the American everywhere wants only the best, uses the latest machines and listens to the most famous musicians, so in the matter of literature he is observant of every new tendency in poetry, whether from Norway or Italy, and the great works of the world's literature have their thoughtful readers. There are probably more persons who read Dante in Boston than in Berlin. Of German intellectual productions, the scientific books are most read, and if strictly scientific they are read in the original by the best educated Americans; the popular books are mostly read in translation. Of the belles-lettres, Schiller and Lessing are generally put aside with the school-books, while Goethe and Heine remain welcome; and beside them are translations of modern story-writers from Freytag and Spielhagen down to Sudermann. French literature is more apt to be read in the original than German, but with increasing distaste. The moral feeling of the American is separated by such a chasm from the atmosphere of the Parisian romance that modern French literature has never become so popular in America as it has in Germany.

As a matter of course, English literature of every sort has by far the greatest influence; English magazines are little read or appreciated, while English poetry, novels, dramas, and works of general interest are as much read in America as in England. Books so unlike as the novels of Mrs. Ward, of Du Maurier, and of Kipling have about the same very large circulation; and all the standard literature of England, from Chaucer to Browning, forms the educational background of every American, especially of every American woman. In spite of all this, it remains true that the most of that which is read in the United States is written by Americans.

How and what does the American write?

Europe has a ready answer, and pieces together a mental picture of "echt amerikanische" literature out of its unfriendly prejudices, mostly reminiscent of Buffalo Bill and Barnum's circus. It is still not forgotten how England suddenly celebrated Joaquin Miller's freakish and inartistic poems of the Western prairie as the great American achievement, and called this tasteless versifier, who was wholly unrecognized in his own country, the American

Byron. He was not only unimportant, but he was not typically American. And of American humour the European observer has about as just an opinion. Nothing but ridiculous caricatures are considered. Mark Twain's first writings, whose sole secret was their wild exaggeration, were more popular in Germany than in America; while the truly American humour of Lowell or Holmes has lain unnoticed. The American is supposed to be quite destitute of any sense for form or measure, and to be in every way inartistic; and if any true poet were to be granted to the New World, he would be expected to be noisy like Niagara. In this sense the real literature of America has hitherto remained un-American, perhaps too un-American. For the main thing which it has lacked has been force. There have been men like Uhland, Geibel, and Heyse, but there has so far been no one like Hebbel.

There is no absolutely new note in American literature, and especially no one trait which is common to all American writings and which is not found in any European. If there is anything unique in American literature, it is perhaps the peculiar combination of elements long familiar. An enthusiastic American has said that to be American means to be both fresh and mature, and this is in fact a combination which is new, and which well characterizes the literary temperament of the country. To be fresh and young generally means to be immature, and to be mature and seasoned means to have lost the enthusiasm and freshness of youth. Of course, this is not a contradiction realized. It would be impossible, for instance, to be both naïve and mature; but the American is not and never has been naïve. Just as this nation has never had a childhood, has never originated ballads, epics, and popular songs, like other peoples during their naïve beginnings, because this nation brought with it from Europe a finished culture; so the vigorous youthfulness in the national literary temperament has in it nothing of naïve simplicity. It is the enthusiasm of youth, but not the innocence of boyhood. It would also be impossible to be both fresh and decadent; the American is mature but not over-ripe, not weakened by the sceptical ennui of senility.

To be fresh means to be confident, optimistic and eager, lively, unspoiled, and courageous; it means to strive toward one's best ideals with the ardour of youth; while to be mature means to understand things in their historic connection, in their true proportions, and with a due feeling for form; to be mature means to be simple, and reposeful, and not breathlessly anxious over the outcome of things. To be sure, this optimistic feeling of strength, this enthusiastic self-confidence, is hardly able to seize the things which are finest and most subtle. It looks only into the full sunlight, never into the shadows with their less obvious beauties. There are no half-tones, no sentimental and uncertain moods; wonder and meditation come into the soul only with pessimism. And most of all, the enthusiasm of youth not only looks on but wants to work, to change and to make over; and so the American is less an artist than an insistent herald. Behind the observer stands always the reformer, enthusiastic to improve the world. On the other hand, the disillusionment of maturity should have cooled the passions, soothed hot inspiration, and put the breathless tragic muse to sleep. It avoids dramatic excitement, holds aloof, and looks on with quiet friendliness and sober understanding of mankind. So it happens that finished art is incompatible with such an enthusiastic eagerness to press onward, and sensuous emotion is incompatible with such an idealism. And so we find in the American temperament a finished feeling for form, but a more ethical than artistic content, and we find humour without its favourite attendant of sentiment. Of course, the exceptions crowd quickly to mind to contradict the formula: had not Poe the demoniac inspiration; was not Hawthorne a thorough artist; did not Whitman violate all rules of form; and does not Henry James see the half-tones? And still such variations from the usual are due to exceptional circumstances, and every formula can apply only in a general way.

Still, in these general traits, one can see the workings of great forces. This enthusiastic self-confidence and youthful optimism in literature are only another expression of American initiative, which has developed so powerfully in the fight with nature during the colonial and pioneer days, and which has made the industrial power of America. And, as Barrett Wendell has shown, not a little of this enthusiastic and spontaneous character is inherited from the old English stock of three hundred years ago. In England itself, the industrial development changed the people; the subjects of Queen Victoria were very little like those of

Queen Elizabeth; the spontaneity of Shakespeare's time no longer suits the smug and insular John Bull. But that same English stock found in America conditions that were well calculated to arouse its spontaneity and enthusiasm.

Then, on the other hand, the clear, composed, and formal maturity which distinguish the literary work of the new nation is traceable principally to the excellent influence of English literature. The ancient culture of England spared this nation a period of immaturity. Then, too, there has been the intellectual domination of the New England States, whose Puritan spirit has given to literature its ethical quality, and at the same time contributed a certain quiet superiority to the common turmoil. Throughout the century, and even to-day, almost all of the best literature originates with those who are consciously reacting against the vulgar taste. Just because the number of sellers and readers of books is so much greater than in Europe, the unliterary circles of readers who, as everywhere, enjoy the broadly vulgar, must by their numbers excite the disgust of the real friend of literature; and this conscious duty of opposition, which becomes a sort of mission, sharpens the artistic consciousness, fortifies the feeling of form, and struggles against all that is immature.

Undoubtedly these external conditions are as responsible for many of the failings of American literature as for its excellences; most of all for the lack of shading and twilight tones, of all that is dreamy, pessimistic, sentimental, and "decadent." This is a lack in the American life which in other important connections is doubtless a great advantage. There are no old castles, no crumbling ruins, no picturesque customs, no church mysticism, nor wonderful symbols; there are no striking contrasts between social groups, no romantic vagabondage, and none of the fascinating pomp of monarchy. Everywhere is solid and healthy contentment, thrifty and well clothed, on broad streets, and under a bright sun. It is no accident that true poets have not described their own surroundings, but have taken their material so far as it has been American, as did Hawthorne, from the colonial times which were already a part of the romantic past, or out of the Indian legends, or later from the remote adventurous life of the West, or from the negro life in far Southern plantations; the daily life surrounding the poet was not yet suitable for poetry. And by being so cruelly clear and without atmosphere as not to invite poetic treatment, it has left the whole literature somewhat glaringly sharp, sane, and homely.

Fiction stands in the centre of the characteristic literary productions; but also literature in the broader sense, including everything which interprets human destinies, as history and philosophy, or even more broadly including all the written products of the nation, everything reflects the essential traits of the literary temperament. In fact, the practical literature, especially the newspaper, reveals the American physiognomy most clearly. In better circles in America, it is proper to deplore the newspaper as a literary product, and to look on it as a necessary evil; and doubtless most newspapers serve up a great deal that is trivial and vulgar, and treat it in a trivial and vulgar way. But no one is forced, except by his own love for the sensational, to choose his daily reading out of this majority. Everybody knows that there is a minority of earnest and admirable papers at his disposal. Apart from newspaper politics and apart from the admirable industrial organization of the newspaper — both of which we have previously spoken of — the newspapers of the country are a literary product whose high merit is too often under-estimated. The American newspapers, and of these not merely the largest, are an intellectual product of well-maintained uniformity of standard.

To be sure, the style is often light, the logic unsound, the information superficial; but, taken as a whole, the newspaper has unity and character. Thousands of loose-jointed intellects crowd into journalism every year — more than in any other country; but American journalism, like the nation as a whole, has an amazing power of assimilation. Just as thousands of Russians and Italians land every year in the rags of their wretchedness, and in a few years become earnest American citizens, so many land on the shores of American journalism who were not intended to be the teachers or entertainers of humanity, and who nevertheless in a few years are quite assimilated. The American newspapers, from Boston to San Francisco, are alike in style and thought; and it must be said, in spite of all prejudices, that the American newspaper is certainly literature. The American knows no difference between unpolitical chatter written with a literary ambition and unliterary comment written with a political ambition. In one sense the whole newspaper is political, while at the same time it is nothing but feuilleton, from the editorials, of which every large newspaper has three or four each day, to the small paragraphs, notes, and announcements with which the editorial page generally closes. From the Washington letter to the sporting gossip, everything tries in a way to have artistic merit, and everything bears the stamp of American literature. Nothing is pedantic. There is often a great lack of information and of perspective — perhaps, even, of conscientiousness in the examination of complaints — but everything is fresh, optimistic, clear and forcible, and always humorous between the lines.

In the weekly papers, America achieves still more. The light, fresh, and direct American style there finds its most congenial field. The same is true of the monthly papers in a somewhat more ambitious and permanent way. The leading social and political monthlies, like the venerable *North American Review*, which errs merely in laying too much emphasis on the names of its well-known contributors, and others are quite up to the best English reviews. The more purely literary *Atlantic Monthly*, which was founded in 1857 by a small circle of Boston friends, Lowell, Longfellow, Emerson, Holmes, Whittier, and Motley, and which has always attracted the best talent of the country, is most nearly comparable to the *Revue des Deux Mondes*. Every monthly paper specially cultivates that literary form for which America has shown the most pronounced talent — the essay. The magazine essay entirely takes the place of the German brochure, a form which is almost unknown in America. The brochure, depending as it does wholly on its own merits to attract the attention of the public, must be in some way sensational to make up for its diminutive size; while an essay which is brought before the reader on the responsibility of a magazine needs no such motive power. It is one among many, and takes its due place, being only one of the items of interest that make up the magazine.

While in German literary circles the problems of the day are mostly argued in brochures, and the essay is a miniature book really written for the easy instruction of a public which would not read long books, the American essay is half-way between. It is living and satirical like the German brochure, but conservative and instructive like the German "Abhandlung." Only when a number of essays on related topics come from the same pen are they put together and published as a separate book. We have already mentioned that America is oversupplied with such volumes of essays, which have almost all the same history — they were first lectures, then magazine articles, and now they are revised and published in book form. Their value is, of course, very diverse; but in general, they are interesting and important, often epoch-making, and the form is admirable. A distinguished treatment, pointed humour, a rich and clear diction, uncommonly happy metaphors, and a careful polish are united so as to make one forget the undeniable haste with which the material is gathered and the superficiality of the conclusions arrived at. So it happens that the essayists who appear in book form are much more appreciated by the reading public than their German colleagues, and that every year sees several hundred such volumes put on the market. The motto, "fresh and mature," is nowhere more appropriate.

But the American remains an American, even in the apparently international realm of science. It is a matter of course for an historian to write in the personal style. Parkman, Motley, Prescott, and Fiske are very different types of historians; and nevertheless, they have in common the same way of approaching the subject and of giving to it form and life. But even in so purely a scientific work as William James's two-volume "Principles of Psychology," one finds such forcible and convincing turns of thought, so personal a form given to abstract facts, and such freshness together with such ripe mastery, as could come only from an American.

Oratory may be accounted an off-shoot of actual literature. A nation of politicians must reserve an honourable place for the orator, and for many years thousands of factors in public life have contributed to develop oratory, to encourage the slightest talent for speaking, and to reward able speakers well. Every great movement in American history has been initiated by eloquent speakers. Before the Revolution, Adams and Otis, Quincy and Henry, precipitated the Revolution by their burning words. And no one can discuss the great movement leading up to the Civil War without considering the oratory of Choate, Clay, Calhoun, Hayne, Garrison, and Sumner; of Wendell Phillips, the great popular leader, and Edward Everett, the great academician, and of Daniel Webster, the greatest statesman of them all.

In the present times of peace, the orator is less important than the essayist, and most of the party speeches to-day have not even a modest place in literature. But if one follows a Presidential campaign, listens to the leading lawyers of the courts, or follows the parliamentary debates of university students, one knows that the rhetorical talent of the American has not died since those days of quickening, and would spring up again strong and vigorous if any great subject, greater than were silver coinage or the Philippine policy, should excite again the nation. Keenness of understanding, admirable sense of form in the single sentence as in the structure of the whole, startling comparisons, telling ridicule, careful management of the climax, and the tone of conviction seem to be everybody's gift. Here and there the phrase is hollow and thought is sacrificed to sound, but the general tendency goes toward brevity and simplicity. A most delightful variation of oratory is found in table eloquence; the true American after-dinner speech is a finished work of art. Often, of course, there are ordinary speeches which simply go from one story to another, quite content merely to relate them well. In the best speeches the pointed anecdote is not lacking either, but it merely decorates the introduction; the speaker then approaches his real subject half playfully and half in earnest, very sympathetically, and seeming always to let his thoughts choose words for themselves. The speeches at the Capitol are sometimes better than those in the Reichstag; but those at American banquets are not only better than the speeches at Festessen and Kommersen, but they are also qualitatively different — true literary works of art, for which the American is especially fitted by the freshness, humour, enthusiasm, and sense of symmetry which are naturally his.

Whoever looks about among journalists, essayists, historians, and orators will return more than once to the subject of belles-lettres; and this is truer in America than elsewhere. As we have already seen, pure literature is strongly biased toward the practical; it is glad to serve great ideas, whether moral or social. Poetry itself is sometimes an essay or sermon. We need not think here of romances which merely sermonize, and are therefore artistically second-rate, such as "Uncle Tom's Cabin," or of such literary rubbish as Bellamy's "Utopia"; even true poets like Whittier must, in the history of emancipation, be classed with the political writers. And although the problem novel in the three-volume English form is not favoured in America because of its poor literary form, the short satirical and clean-cut society novel, which may break away at any moment into the essay or journalistic manner, has become all the more popular. Further, this being the time of America's industrial struggle, society has not become so intellectually aristocratic that being a poet is a life profession. The leading novelists have had to be active in almost all fields of literature; they have frequently begun as journalists, and have generally been essayists, editors, or professors at the same time.

The eighteenth century was unfruitful for the New World, in lyric as in epic literature. The literary history discovers many names, but they are of men who created nothing original, and who cannot be compared with the great English geniuses. America was internally as well as externally dependent on England; and if one compares the utter intellectual unfruitfulness of Canada to-day with the feverish activity of her southern neighbour, one will inevitably ask whether political colonies can ever create literature. When freedom was first obtained by the colonies, a condition of new equilibrium was reached after a couple of decades of uncertainty and unrest, and then American literature woke up. Even then it was not free, and did not care to be free, from English precedents; and yet there were original personalities which came to the front. Washington Irving was, as Thackeray said, the first ambassador which the New World of literature sent to the Old. English influences are unmistakable in the tales of Irving, although he was a strong and original writer. His "Sketch-Book," published in 1819, has remained the most popular of his books, and the poetic muse has never been hunted away from the shores of the Hudson where Rip Van Winkle passed his long slumbers.

The American novel had still not appeared. The romances of Brown, laid in Pennsylvania, were highly inartistic in spite of their forcible presentation. Then James Fenimore Cooper discovered the untouched treasures of the infinite wilderness. His "Spy" appeared in 1821, and he was at once hailed as the American Scott. In the next year appeared "The Pioneers," the first of his Leather-stocking Tales of wild Indian life. And after Cooper's thirty-two romances there followed many tales by lesser writers. Miss Sedgwick was the first woman to attain literary popularity, and her romances were the first which depicted the life of New England. At the same time a New England youth began to write verses which, by their serene beauty, were incomparably above all earlier lyric attempts of his native land. Bryant's first volume of poems appeared in 1821, and therewith America had a literature, and England's sarcastic question, "Who ever reads an American book?" was not asked again.

The movement quickly grew to its first culmination. A brilliant period commenced in the thirties, when Hawthorne, Holmes, Emerson, Longfellow, Thoreau, Curtis, and Margaret Fuller, all of New England, became the luminaries of the literary New World. And like the prelude to a great epoch rings the song of the one incomparable Edgar Allan Poe, who did not fight for ideas like a moral New Englander, but sang simply in the love of song. Poe's melancholy, demoniacal, and melodious poetry was a marvellous fountain in the country of hard and sober work. And Poe was the first whose fantasy transformed the short story into a thing of the highest poetical form. In New England no one was so profoundly a poet as Nathaniel Hawthorne, the author of "The Scarlet Letter." His "Marble Faun," of which the scene is laid in Italy, may show him in his fullest maturity, but his greatest strength lay in the romances of Massachusetts, which in their emotional impressiveness and artistic finish are as beautiful as an autumn day in New England. Ralph Waldo Emerson, the rhapsodical philosopher, wrote poems teeming over with thought, and yet true poems, while Whittier was the inspired bard of freedom; and besides these there was the trio of friends, Longfellow, Lowell, and Holmes. Harvard professors they were, and men of distinguished ability, whose literary culture made them the proper educators of the nation. Thomas Wentworth Higginson is the only one of this circle now living, remaining over, as it were, from that golden age. He fought at first to free the slaves, and then he became the stout defender of the emancipation of women, and is to-day, as then, the master of the reflective essay. His life is full of "cheerful yesterdays"; his fame is sure of "confident to-morrows."

Longfellow is, to the German, mainly the sensitive transposer of German poetry; his sketch-book, "Hyperion," opened up the German world of myth, and brought the German romance across the ocean. His ballads and his delightful idyll of "Evangeline" clothed New England life, as it were, in German sentiment; and even his Indian edda, "Hiawatha," sounds as if from a German troubadour wandering through the Indian country. Longfellow became the favourite poet of the American home, and American youth still makes its pilgrimage to the house in Cambridge where he once lived. Lowell was perhaps more gifted than Longfellow, and certainly he was the more many-sided. His art ranged from the profoundest pathos by which American patriotism was aroused in those days of danger, to the broadest and most whimsical humour freely expressed in dialect verses; and he also wrote the most finished idyllic poetry and keenly satirical and critical essays. It is common to exalt his humorous verses, "The Biglow Papers," to the highest place of typical literary productions of America; nevertheless, his essential quality was fine and academic. Real American humour undoubtedly finds its truer expression in Holmes. Holmes was also a lyric poet, but his greatest work was the set of books by the "Autocrat." His "Autocrat of the Breakfast Table" has that serious smile which makes world literature. It was the first of a long series, and at the writing he was a professor of anatomy, sixty-four years old.

Then there were many lesser lights around these great ones. At the middle of the century Harriet Beecher Stowe wrote her "Uncle Tom's Cabin," of which ten thousand copies were sold every day for many months. And romance literature in general began to increase. At the same time appeared the beautiful songs of Bayard Taylor, whose later translation of Faust has never been surpassed, and the scarcely less admirable lyrics of Stedman and Stoddard. So it happened that at the time when the Civil War broke out, America, although deficient in every sort of productive science except history, had a brilliant literature. Science needed, first of all, solid academic institutions, which could only be built patiently, stone on stone — a work which has been witnessed by the last three decades of the century. Poetry, however, needed only the inner voice which speaks to the susceptible heart, and the encouragement of the people. For science there has been a steady, quiet growth, parallel with the growth of the institutions; for letters there have been changing fortunes, times of prosperity and times of stagnation. When the powder and smoke of the Civil War had blown away the happy days of literature were over; it began to languish, and only at the present day is it commencing to thrive once more.

This does not mean that there has been no talent for three decades, or that the general interest in literature has flagged. Ambitious writers of romance like Howells, James, Crawford, and Cable; novelists like Aldrich, Bret Harte, and Hale, Mary Wilkins, and Sarah Orne Jewett; poets like Lanier and Whitman, and humourists like Stockton and Mark Twain, have done much excellent work, and work that is partly great, and have shown the way to large provinces of literary endeavour. Nevertheless, compared with the great achievements which had gone before, theirs is rather a time of intermission. And yet many persons are quite prepared to say that Howells is the greatest of all American authors, and his realistic analyses among the very best modern romances. And Howells himself pays the same tribute to Mark Twain's later and maturer writings.

But there is one poet about whom only the future can really decide; this is Walt Whitman. His "Leaves of Grass," with their apparently formless verse, were greatly praised by some; by others felt to be barbarous and tasteless. There has been a dispute similar to that over Zarathustra of Nietzsche. And even as regards content, Whitman may be compared with Nietzsche, the radical democrat with the extreme aristocrat, for the exaggerated democratic exaltation of the ego leads finally to a point in which every single man is an absolute dictator in his own world, and therefore comes to feel himself unique, and proudly demands the right of the Uebermensch. "When they fight, I keep silent, go bathing, or sit marvelling at myself," says this prophet of democracy. "In order to learn, I sat at the feet of great masters. Oh, that these great masters might return once more to learn of me." The similarity between American and German intellects could readily be traced further, and was, perhaps, not wholly unfitted to reveal a certain broad literary perspective. As we have compared Whitman and Nietzsche, so we might compare Bryant with Platen, Poe with Heine, Hawthorne with Freytag, Lowell with Uhland,

Whittier with Rückert, Holmes with Keller, Howells with Fontane, Crawford with Heyse, and so on, and we should compare thus contemporaries of rather equal rank. But such a parallelism, of course, could not be drawn too far, since it would be easy to show in any such pair important traits to belie the comparison.

In the positively bewildering literature of to-day, the novel and the short story strongly predominate. The Americans have always shown a special aptitude and fondness for the short story. Poe was the true master of that form, and the grace with which Aldrich has told the story of Marjorie Daw, and Davis of Van Bibber, the energy with which Hale has cogently depicted the Man Without a Country, or Bret Harte the American pioneer, and the intimacy with which Miss Wilkins and Miss Jewett have perpetuated the quieter aspects of human existence, show a true instinct for art. A profound appreciation, fresh vigour, and fine feeling for form, graceful humour and all the good qualities of American literature, combine to make the short story a perfect thing. It is not the German *Novelle*, but is, rather, comparable to the French *conte*. The short stories are not all of the single type; some are masculine and others feminine in manner. The finely cut story, which is short because the charm of the incidents would vanish if narrated in greater detail, is of the feminine type. And, of the masculine, is the story told in cold, sharp relief, which is short because it is energetic and impatient of any protracted waits. In both cases, everything unessential is left out. Perhaps the American is nowhere more himself than here; and short stories are produced in great numbers and are specially fostered by the monthly magazines.

Of humourists there are fewer to-day than formerly. Neither the refined humour of Irving, Lowell, and Holmes, nor the broader humour of Bret Harte and Mark Twain, finds many representatives of real literary importance. There are several, it is true, who are delighted with Dooley's contemporary comment in the Irish dialect, but there is a much truer wit in the delicately satirical society novels of Henry James, and to a less degree in those of Grant, Herrick, Bates, and a hundred others, or in the romances of common life, such as Westcott's "David Harum."

The historical romance has flourished greatly. At first the fantasy went to far regions, and the traditional old figures of romance were tricked out in the gayest foreign costumes. The most popular of all has been Wallace's "Ben Hur." The Americans have long since followed the road which German writers have taken from Ebers to Dahn and Wildenbruch, and have revived their own national past. To be sure, the tremendous editions of these books are due rather to the desire for information than the love of poetry. The public likes to learn its national history while being entertained, since the national consciousness has developed so noticeably in the last decade and the social life of America in the seventeenth and eighteenth centuries has doubtless become thus living and real for millions of Americans. Aesthetic motives predominate, nevertheless, and although books like Churchill's "The Crisis," Bacheller's "D'ri and I," Miss Johnston's "Audrey," Ford's "Janice Meredith," and others similar are merely books of the day, and will be replaced by others on the next Christmas-trees, nevertheless they are works of considerable artistic merit. They are forcibly constructed, dramatic, full of invention and delightful diction. It is undeniable that the general level of the American romance is to-day not inferior to that of Germany.

Historical romance aims, first of all, to awaken the national consciousness. So, for instance, the romances of the versatile physician, Weir Mitchell, are first of all histories of the Revolutionary period of the whole nation, and, secondarily, histories of early Pennsylvania. But the story which depends on local colour flourishes too. Here shows itself strongly that trait which is distinguishable in American writing through the whole century, from Irving, Cooper, and Bryant to the present day — the love of nature. Almost every part of the country has found some writer to celebrate its landscape and customs, not merely the curious inhabitants of the prairie and gold-fields, but the outwardly unromantic characters of the New England village and the Tennessee mountains, of the Southern plantations and the Western States. And new stories of this sort appear every day. Especially the new West figures prominently in literature; and the tireless ambition on which the city of Chicago is founded is often depicted with much talent. The novels of Fuller, Norris, and others are all extraordinarily forceful descriptions of Western life and civilization. The South of to-day, which shows symptoms of awaking to new life, is described more from the Northern than from the Southern point of view. It is surprising that the mental life of the American negro has attracted so little attention, since the short stories of Chestnut point to unexplored treasures.

The longer efforts are always in prose, and since the time of Evangeline epic verse has found almost no representative. Verse is almost wholly lyrical. The history of American lyric is contained in the large and admirable collections of Stedman, Onderdonk, and others; and it is the history of, perhaps, the most complete achievement of American literature. One who knows the American only in the usual caricature, and does not know what an idealist the Yankee is, would be surprised to learn that the lyric poem has become his favourite field. The romantic novel, which appeals to the masses, may have, perhaps, a commercial motive, while the book of verse is an entirely disinterested production. The lyric, in its fresh, intense, and finished way, reveals the inner being of American literature, and surprisingly much lyric verse is being written to-day. Even political newspapers, like the *Boston Transcript*, publish every day some lyric poem; and although here as everywhere many volumes of indifferent verse see the light of day, still the feeling for form is so general that one finds very seldom anything wholly bad and very often bits of deep significance and beauty. Here, too, the best-known things are not the most admirable. We hear too much of Markham's "The Man With the Hoe," and too little of Santayana's sonnets or of Josephine Preston Peabody. Here, too, local colour is happily in evidence — as, for instance, in the well-known verses of Riley. The Western poet goes a different road from the Eastern. The South has never again sent a messenger so full of melodies as Sidney Lanier.

There is a strong lyric tendency also in the dramatic compositions of the day. The true drama has always been more neglected than any other branch of art, and if it is true that the Americans have preserved the temperament and point of view of Elizabethan England, it is high time for some American Shakespeare to step forth. Until now, extremely few plays of real literary worth have been written between the Atlantic and the Pacific Oceans. Dramatists there have been always, and the stage is now more than ever supplied by native talent; but literature is too little considered here. The rural dramas having the local colour of Virginia and New England are generally better than the society pieces: and the very popular dramatizations of novels are stirring, but utterly cheap. On the other hand, the American has often applied the lyric gift in dramatic verse, and in dramas of philosophic significance such as Santayana's admirable "Lucifer" or Moody's "Masque of Judgment." The stunted growth of American dramatic writing is closely connected with the history of the American stage, a subject which may lead us from literature to the sister arts.

CHAPTER NINETEEN

Art

THE history of the theatre leads us once more back to Puritan New England. Every one knows that the Puritan regarded the theatre as the very temple of vice, and the former association of the theatre and the bar-room — a tradition that came from England — naturally failed to make public opinion more favourable. In the year 1750 theatrical productions were entirely forbidden in Boston. One theatre was built in 1794, and a few others later, but the public feeling against demoralizing influences of the stage so grew that one theatre after another was turned from its profane uses and made over into a lecture hall or something of the sort. In 1839 it was publicly declared that Boston should never again have a theatre. Nevertheless by 1870, it had five theatres, and to-day it has fifteen. Other cities have always been more liberal toward the theatre, and in the city of New York, since 1733, ninety-five theatres have been built, of which more than thirty are still standing to-day and in active operation. Thus the Puritan spirit seems long since to have disappeared, and the backwardness of the drama seems not to be connected with the religious past of the country. But this is not the case.

Let us survey the situation. There is certainly no lack of theatres, for almost every town has its "opera house," and the large cities have really too many. Nor is there any lack of histrionic talent; for, although the great Shakespearian actor, Edwin Booth, has no worthy successor, we have still actors who are greatly applauded and loved — Mansfield, Sothern, Jefferson, Drew, and Gillette; Maude Adams, Mrs. Fiske, Blanche Bates, Henrietta Crosman, Julia Arthur, Julia Marlowe, Ada Rehan, Nance O'Neill, and many others who are certainly sincere artists; and the most brilliant actors of Europe, Irving and Tree, Dusé, Bernhardt, Sorma, and Campbell come almost every year to play in this country. The American's natural versatility gives him a great advantage for the theatrical career; and so it is no accident that amateur theatricals are nowhere else so popular, especially among student men and women. The equipments of the stage, moreover, leave very little to be desired, and the settings sometimes surpass anything which can be seen in Europe; one often sees marvellous effects and most convincing illusions. And these, with the American good humour, verve, and self-assurance, and the beauty of American women, bring many a graceful comedy and light opera to a really artistic performance. The great public, too, is quite content, and fills the theatres to overflowing. It seems almost unjust to criticise unfavourably the country's theatres.

But the general public is not the only nor even the most important factor; the discriminating public is not satisfied. Artistic productions of the more serious sort are drowned out by a great tide of worthless entertainments; and however amusing or diverting the comedies, farces, rural pieces, operettas, melodramas, and dramatized novels may be, they are thoroughly unworthy of a people that is so ceaselessly striving for cultivation and self-perfection. Such pieces should not have the assurance to invade the territory of true art. And, although the lack of good plays is less noticeable, if one looks at the announcements of what is to be given in New York on any single evening, it is tremendously borne home on one by the bad practice of repeating the plays night after night for many weeks, so that a person who wants to see real art has soon seen every production which is worth while. In this respect New York is distinctly behind Paris, Berlin, or Vienna, although about on a level with London; and in the other large cities of America the situation is rather worse. Everywhere the stage caters to the vulgar taste, and for one Hamlet there are ten Geishas.

It cannot be otherwise, since the theatre is entirely a business matter with the managers. Sometimes there is an artist like the late Daly, who is ready to conduct a theatre from the truly artistic point of view, and who offers admirable performances; but this is an expensive luxury, and there are few who will afford it. It is a question of making money, and therefore of offering humorous or sentimental pieces which fill the theatre. There is another fact of which the European hardly knows; it is cheaper to engage a company to play a single piece for a whole year with mechanical regularity than to hire actors to give the study necessary to a diversified repertoire. After many repetitions, even mediocre actors can attain a certain skill, while in repertoire only good actors are found at all satisfactory, and the average will not be tolerated by the pampered public. Then, too, the accessories are much cheaper for a single piece.

Now, in a town of moderate size, one piece cannot be repeated many nights, so that the companies have to travel about. The best companies stay not less than a week, and if the town is large enough, they stay from four to six weeks. These companies are known by the name of the piece which they are presenting, or by the name of the leading actor, the "star." The theatre in itself is a mere tenantless shell. In early fall the whole list of companies which are to people its stage through the next thirty weeks is arranged. In this way, it is true that the small city is able to see the best actors and the newest pieces. Yet one sees how sterile this principle is by considering some of the extreme cases. Jefferson has played his Rip Van Winkle and almost nothing else for thirty years; and the young people of Chicago, Philadelphia, and Boston would be very unhappy if he were not to come in this rôle for a couple of weeks every winter. And he has thus become several times a millionaire.

But the business spirit has not stopped with this. The hundreds of companies compete with one another, so that very naturally a theatrical trust has been formed. The syndicate of Klaw, Erlanger & Frohman was organized in 1896 with thirty-seven leading theatres in large cities, all pledged to present none but companies belonging to the syndicate, while, in return, the syndicate agreed to keep the theatres busy every week in the season. The favourite actors and the favourite companies were secured, and the independent actors who resisted the tyranny found that in most of the large cities only second-rate theatres were open to them. One after another had to give in, and now the great trust under the command of Frohman has virtually the whole theatrical business of the country in its hands. The trust operates shrewdly and squarely; it knows its public, offers variety, follows the fashions, gives the great mimes their favourite rôles, pays them and the theatre owners well, relieves the actors from the struggle for promotion, and vastly amuses the public. It is impossible to resist this situation, which is so adverse to art.

All are agreed that there is only one way to better matters. Permanent companies must be organized, in the large cities at first, to play in repertoire. And these must be subsidized, so as not to be dependent for their support on the taste of the general public. Then and then only will the dramatic art be able to thrive, or the theatre become an educational institution, and so slowly cultivate a better demand, which in the end will come to make even the most eclectic theatre self-supporting. So it has always been on the European Continent; princes and municipalities have rivalled with one another to raise the level of dramatic art above what it would have to be if financially dependent solely on the box-office. In the United States there is certainly no lack of means or good will to encourage such an educational institution. Untold millions go to libraries, museums, and universities, and we may well ask why the slightest attempt has not been made to provide, by gift or from the public treasury, for a temple to the drama.

It is just here that the old Puritan prejudice is still felt to-day. The theatre is no longer under the ban of the law, but no step can be taken toward a subvention of the theatre. Most taxpayers in America would look with disfavour on any project to support a theatre from public funds. Why a theatre more than a hotel or restaurant? The theatre remains a place of frivolous amusement, and for that reason no millionaires have so far endowed a theatre. Men like Carnegie know too well that the general mass of people would blame them if they were to give their millions to the theatre, as long as a single town was still wishing for its library or its college.

The history of music in America has shown what can be attained by endowment — how the public demand can be educated so that even the very best art will finally be self-supporting. The development of the Boston Symphony Orchestra, which is still the best musical organization in the country, is thoroughly typical. It was realized that symphony concerts, like the best given in Germany, would not be self-supporting, in view of the deficient musical education of the country. In 1880 Boston had two symphony orchestras, but both were of little account. They were composed of over-busied musicians, who could not spare the time needed for study and rehearsals. Then one of the most liberal and appreciative men of the country, Henry Lee Higginson, came forward and engaged the best musicians whom he could find, to give all their time and energy to an orchestra; and he himself guaranteed the expenses. During the first few years he paid out a fortune annually, but year by year the sum grew less, and to-day Boston so thoroughly enjoys its twenty-four symphony concerts, which are not surpassed by those of any European orchestra, that the large music-hall is too small to hold those who wish to attend. This example has been imitated, and now New York, Chicago, Philadelphia, and other cities have excellent and permanent orchestras.

Likewise various cities, but especially New York, enjoy a few weeks of German, French, and Italian opera which is equal to the best opera in Europe, by a company that brings together the best singers of Europe and America. In the case of opera the love of music has prevailed over the prejudice against the theatre. Extraordinarily high subscriptions for the boxes, and a reduced rental of the Metropolitan Opera House, which was erected by patrons of art, have given brilliant support to the undertaking. Without going into questions of principle, an impartial friend of music must admit that even the performances of Parsifal were artistically not inferior to those of Bayreuth, and the audience was quite as much in sympathy with the great masterpiece as are the assemblages of tourists at Bayreuth. The artistic education proceeding from these larger centres is felt through the entire country, and there is a growing desire for less ambitious but permanent opera companies.

The symphony and the opera are not the only evidences of the serious love of music in America. Every large city has its conservatory and its surplus of trained music teachers, and almost every city has societies which give oratorios, and innumerable singing clubs, chamber concerts, and regular musical festivals. Even the concerts by other soloists than that fashionable favourite of American ladies, Paderewski, are well attended. And these are not new movements; opera was given in New York as early as 1750, and the English opera of the eighteenth century was followed in 1825 by Italian opera. Also Baltimore, Philadelphia, and New Orleans early developed a love for music.

Boston has been the great centre for oratorio. The Händel and Haydn Society dates from 1810, and in 1820 a great many concerts were given all through the East, even in small towns. And the influence of the musical Germans was strongly felt by the middle of the century. The Germania Orchestra of Boston was founded in 1848, and now all the Western cities where German influences are strong, such as Milwaukee, Cincinnati, Chicago, and St. Louis, are centres of music, with many male choruses and much private cultivation of music in the home.

The churches, moreover, are a considerable support to music. The Puritan spirit disliked secular music no less than the theatre; but the popular hymns were always associated with the service of God, and so the love for music grew and its cultivation spread. Progress was made from the simplest melodies to fugue arrangements; organs and stringed instruments were introduced; the youth was educated in music, and finally in the last century church worship was made more attractive by having the best music obtainable. And thus, through the whole country, chorus and solo singing and instrumental skill have been everywhere favoured by the popular religious instinct.

So much for the performance of music. Musical composition has not reached nearly such a high point. It is sufficient to look over the programmes of recent years. Wagner leads among operatic composers, then follow Verdi, Gounod, and Mozart; Beethoven is the sovereign of the concert-hall, and The Messiah and The Creation are the most popular oratorios. Sometimes a suspicion has been expressed that American composers must have been systematically suppressed by the leading German conductors like Damrosch, Seidl, Gericke, Thomas, and Paur. But this is not remotely true. The American public is much more to be blamed; for, although so patriotic in every other matter, it looks on every native musical composition with distrust, and will hardly accept even the American singer or player until he has first won his laurels in Europe.

Still, there has been some composition in America. There were religious composers in the eighteenth century, and when everything English was put away at the time of the Revolution, the colonists replaced the psalm-tunes which they had brought over with original airs. Billings and his school were especially popular, although there was an early reaction against what he was pleased to call fugues. The nineteenth century brought forth little more than band-master music, with no sign of inspiration in real orchestral or operatic music. Only lately there have stepped into the field such eminent composers as MacDowell, Paine, Chadwick, Strong, Beech, Buck, Parker, and Foot. Paine's opera of "Azara," Chadwick's overtures, and MacDowell's interesting compositions show how American music will develop.

More popular was a modest branch of musical composition, the song in the style of folk-songs. America has no actual folk-songs. The average European imagines "Yankee Doodle" to be the real American song, anonymous and dreadful as it is, and in diplomatic circles the antiquated and bombastic "Hail Columbia" is conceived to be the official hymn of America. The Americans themselves recognize neither of these airs. The "Star Spangled Banner" is the only song which can be called national; it was written in 1814 to an old and probably English melody. The Civil War left certain other songs which stir the breast of every patriotic American.

On the other hand, folk-songs have developed in only one part of the country — on the Southern plantations — and with a very local colouring. The negro slaves sang these songs first, although it is unlikely that they are really African songs. They seem to be Irish and Scotch ballads, which the negroes heard on the Mississippi steamboats. Baptist and Methodist psalm-tunes and French melodies were also caught up by the musical negroes and modified to their peculiar melody and rhythm. A remarkable sadness pervades all these Southern airs.

Many song composers have imitated this most unique musical product of the country. In the middle of the century Stephen Foster rose to rapid popularity with his "Old Folks at Home," which became the popular song, rivalled only by "Home Sweet Home," which was taken from the text of an American opera, but of which the melody is said to have originated in Sicily. There are to-day all sorts of composers, some in the sentimental style and others in the light opera vein, whose street tunes are instantly sung, whistled and played on hurdy-gurdies from the Atlantic to the Pacific, and, worst of all, stridently rendered by the graphophones, with megaphone attachments, on verandahs in summer. There are composers of church hymns, of marches *à la* Sousa, and writers of piano pieces by the wholesale. All serious musicians agree that the American, unlike the Englishman, is decidedly musically inclined, but he is the incontestable master of only a very modest musical art — he can whistle as nobody else.

Unlike American music, American paintings are no longer strange to Europe. In the art division of the last Paris Exposition Americans took their share of the honours, and they are highly appreciated at most of the Berlin and Munich picture shows. Sargent and Whistler are the best known. Sargent, as the painter of elegant ladies, prosperous men, and interesting children, has undoubtedly the surest and most refined gift with his brush of any son of the New World. When, a few years ago, a large exhibition of his works was brought together in Boston, one felt on standing before that gathering of ultra-polite and almost living humanity, that in him the elegant world has found its most brilliant, though perhaps not its most flattering, transcriber. Whistler is doubtless the greater, the real sovereign. This most nervous of all artists has reproduced his human victims with positively uncanny perspicacity. Like Henry James, the novelist, he fathoms each human riddle, and expresses it intangibly, mysteriously. Everything is mood and suggestion, the dull and heavy is volatilized, the whole is a sceptical rendering in rich twilight tones.

America is proud of both artists, and still one may doubt whether the art of the New World would be justly represented if it sent across the ocean only these two pampered and somewhat whimsical artists. Firstly, in spite of much brilliant other work, they are both best known as portraitists, while it becomes plainer every day that landscape painting is the most typical American means of expression. The profound feeling for nature, which pervades American poetry and reflects the national life and struggle therewith, brings the American to study landscape. Many persons think even that if American artists were to send ever so many easel pictures across the ocean, the artistic public of Europe would still have no adequate judgment of American painting, because the best talent is busied with the larger pieces intended for wall decoration. The great number of monumental buildings, with their large wall surfaces and the desire for ambitious creations, attract the American to-day to wall-painting. And they try to strengthen the national character of this tendency by a democratic argument. The easel picture, it is said, is a luxury designed for the house of the wealthy and is, therefore, decadent, while the art of a nation which is working out a democracy must pertain to the people; and therefore just as early art adorned the temples and churches, this art must adorn the walls of public buildings, libraries, judicial chambers, legislatures, theatres, railway stations and city halls. And the more this comes to be the case, the less correct it is to judge the pinctile efforts of the time by the framed pictures that come into the exhibitions. Moreover, many of the more successful painters do not take the trouble to send any of their works across the ocean.

Sargent and Whistler also — and this is more important — speak a language which is not American, while the country has now developed its own grammar of painting, and the most representative artists are seldom seen in Europe. In painting, as in so many other branches, the United States has developed from the provincial to the cosmopolitan and from the cosmopolitan to the national, and is just now taking this last step. It is very characteristic that the untutored provincial has grown into the national only by passing through a cosmopolitan stage. The faltering powers of the beginner do not achieve a self-conscious expression of national individuality until they have first industriously and systematically imitated foreign methods, and so attained a complete mastery of the medium of expression.

At first the country, whose poor population was not able to pay much attention to pictures, turned entirely to England. West and Copley are the only pre-Revolutionary Americans whose pictures possess any value. The portraits of their predecessors — as, for instance, those in Memorial Hall at Harvard — are stiff, hard, and expressionless. Then came Gilbert Stuart at the end of the eighteenth century, whose portraits of George and Martha Washington are famous, and who showed himself an artistic genius and quite the equal of the great English portraitists. John

Trumbull, an officer in the Revolutionary Army, who lived at the same time, was still more important for the national history by his war pictures, the best of which were considerably above contemporary productions. The historical wall-paintings which he made in 1817, for the Capitol at Washington, are in his later and inferior manner. They seem to-day, like everything which was done in the early part of the century to decorate the Capitol, hackneyed and tiresome. And if one goes from the Capitol to the Congressional Library, which shows the condition of art at the end of the nineteenth century, one feels how far the public taste of Trumbull's time was from appreciating true art. Portraiture was the only art which attained tolerable excellence, where, besides Stuart, there were Peale, Wright, and Savage. Then came the day of the "American Titian," Allston, whose Biblical pictures were greatly praised for their brilliant colouring.

Hitherto artists had gone to England to study or, indeed, sometimes to Italy. In the second third of the century they went to Düsseldorf; they painted American landscapes, American popular life, and historical pictures of American heroes, all in German fashion. They delighted in genre studies in the Dusseldorf manner, and painted the Hudson River all bathed in German moonlight. While the popular school was still painting the world in blackish brown, the artistic secession began at about the time of the Civil War. Then artists began to go to Paris and Munich, and American painting developed more freely. It was a time of earnest, profound, and independent study such as had so far never been. The artist learned to draw, learned to see values, and, in the end, to be natural. The number of artists now began to increase, and to-day Americans produce thousands of pictures each year, and one who sees the European exhibitions in summer and the American in winter does not feel that the latter are on a much lower level.

Since Allston's time the leaders in landscape have been Cole, Bierstadt, Kensett, and Gifford; in genre, Leslie, Woodville, and particularly Mount; in historical painting, Lentze and White; and in portraiture, Inman and Elliott. The first who preached the new doctrine of individuality and colour was Hunt, and in the early seventies the new school just graduated from Paris and Munich was bravely at work. There are many well-known names in the last thirty years, and it is a matter rather of individual choice what pictures one prefers of all the large number. Yet no one would omit George Inness from the list, since he has seen American landscapes more individually than any one else. Besides his pictures every one knows the marines of Winslow Homer, the street scenes of Childe Hassam, the heads of Eaton, the autumn forests of Enneking, the apple trees in spring-time of Appleton Brown, the delicate landscapes of Weir and Tryon, the wall pictures of Abbey, Cox, and Low, Gaugengigl's little figure paintings, Vedder's ambitious symbolism, the brilliant portraits of Cecilia Beaux and Chase, the women's heads of Tarbell, the ideal figures of Abbot Thayer, and the works of a hundred other American artists, not to mention those who are really more familiar in London, Paris, and Munich than in America itself.

Besides the oil pictures, there are excellent water-colours, pastelles, and etchings; and, perhaps most characteristic of all, there is the stained glass of La Farge, Lathrop, the late Mrs. Whitman, Goodhue, and others. The workers in pen-and-ink are highly accomplished, of whom the best known is Gibson, whose American women are not only artistic, but have been socially influential on American ideals and manners. His sketches for Life have been themselves models for real life. Nor should we forget Pennell, the master of atmosphere in pen-and-ink.

Sculpture has developed more slowly. It presupposes a higher understanding of art than does painting; and, besides that, the prudishness of the Puritan has affected it adversely. When John Brazee, the first American amateur sculptor, in the early part of the nineteenth century, asked advice of the president of the New York Academy of Arts, he was told that he would better wait a hundred years before practicing sculpture in America. The speech admirably showed the general lack of interest in plastic art. But the impetuous pressure toward self-perfection existing in the nation shortened the century into decades; people began to journey through Italy. The pioneers of sculpture were Greenough, Powers, Crawford, and Palmer, and their statues are still valued for their historical interest. The theatrical genre groups of John Rogers became very popular; and Randolph Rogers, who created the Columbus bronze doors of the Capitol, was really an artist. Then came Storey, Ball, Rinehart, Hosmer, Mead, and many others with works of greater maturity. Squares and public buildings were filled with monuments and busts which, to be sure, were generally more interesting politically than artistically, and which to-day wait patiently for a charitable earthquake. And yet they show how the taste for plastic art has slowly worked upward.

More recent movements, which are connected with the names of Ward, Warner, Partridge, French, MacMonnies, and St. Gaudens, have already left many beautiful examples of sculpture. Cities are jealously watchful now that only real works of art shall be erected, and that monuments which are to be seen by millions of people shall be really characteristic examples of good art. More than anything else, sculpture has at length come into a closer sympathy with architecture than perhaps it has in any other country. The admirable sculptural decorations of the Chicago World's Fair, the effective Dewey Triumphal Arch and the permanent plastic decorations of the Congressional Library, the more restrained and distinguished decorations of the Court of Appeals in New York City, and of many similar buildings show clearly that American sculpture has ended its period of immaturity. Such a work as St. Gaudens's Shaw Memorial in Boston is among the most beautiful examples of modern sculpture; and it is thoroughly American, not only because the negro regiment marches behind the mounted colonel, but because the American subject is handled in the American spirit. These men are depicted with striking vigour, and the young hero riding to his death is conceived with Puritan sobriety. Vigorous and mature is the American, in plastic art as well as in poetry.

The development of architecture has been a very different one. A people must be housed, and cannot stay out of doors until it has learned what is beautiful in architecture People could wait for poetry, music, and painting while they were busy in keeping off the Indians and felling the forests; but they had to have houses at once. And since at that time they had no independent interests in art, they imitated forms with which they had been familiar, and everywhere perpetuated the architectural ideas of their mother country. But the builder is at a disadvantage beside the painter, the singer, and the poet, in that when he imitates he cannot even do that as he will, but is bound down by climate, by social requirements, and especially by his building material. And when he is placed in new surroundings, he is forced to strike out for himself.

Although the American colonist remained under the influence of English architecture, his environment forced him in the first place to build his house of wood instead of stone as in England, and in wood he could not so easily copy the pattern. It had to be a new variation of the older art. And so architecture, although it more slavishly followed the mother country than any other art, was the earliest to strike out in some respects on an independent course. It borrowed its forms, but originated their applications; and while it slowly adopted new ideas of style and became gradually free of European styles, it became free even earlier in their technical application, owing to the new American conditions. More than any other feature of her civilization, American architecture reveals the entire history of the people from the days when the Puritans lived in little wooden villages to the present era of the sky-scraper of the large cities; and in this growth more than in that of any other art the whole country participates, and specially the West, with its tremendous energy, which is awkward with the violin-bow and the crayon but is well versed in piling stone on stone.

In colonial days, English renaissance architecture was imitated in wood, a material which necessitated slender columns and called for finer detail and more graceful lines than were possible in stone. One sees to-day, especially in the New England States, many such buildings quite unaltered; and the better of these in Salem, Cambridge, and Newport are, in spite of their lightness, substantial and distinguished as no European would think possible in so ordinary a material as wood. Large, beautiful halls, with broad, open staircases and broad balusters, greet the visitor; large fireplaces, with handsomely carved chimney-pieces, high wainscotings on the walls and beautiful beams across the ceilings. The more modest houses show the same thing on a smaller scale. There was this one style through the whole town, and its rules were regarded as canonical. In certain parts of the country there were inconspicuous traces of Spanish, French, and Dutch influence, which survive to-day in many places, especially in the South, and contribute to the picturesqueness of the architectural whole.

After the Revolutionary period, people wished to break with English traditions, and the immigration from many different countries brought a great variety of architectural stimulation. A time of general imitation had arrived, for in architecture also the country was to grow from the provincial to the national through a cosmopolitan stage. At the end of the eighteenth century, architecture was chiefly influenced by the classic Greek. Farmhouses masqueraded as big temples, and the thoughtless application of this form became so monotonous that it was not continued very long in private houses. Then the Capitol at Washington was begun by Latrobe and finished by the more competent Bulfinch, and it became the model for almost all state capitols of the Union. Bulfinch himself designed the famous State House of Massachusetts, but it was the Puritan spirit of Boston which selected the austere Greek temple to typify the public spirit. The entire century, in spite of many variations, stood under this influence, and until recently nobody has ventured to put up a civil structure in a freer, more picturesque style.

Many of these single state capitols built during the century, such as the old one at Albany, are admirable; while the post-offices, custom-houses, and other buildings dedicated to federal uses have been put up until recently cheaply and without thought. Lately, however, the architect has been given freer play. Meanwhile taste had wandered from the classic era to the Middle Ages, and the English Gothic had come to be popular. The romantic took the place of the classic, and the buildings were made picturesque. The effect of this was most happy on church edifices, and about the middle of the century Richard Upjohn, "the father of American architecture," built a number of famous churches in the Gothic style.

But in secular edifices this spirit went wholly to architectural lawlessness. People were too little trained to preserve a discipline of style along with the freedom of the picturesque. And even more unfortunate than the lack of training of the architect, who committed improprieties because uncertain in his judgment, there was the tastelessness of the parvenu patron, and this particularly in the West. Then came the time of unrest and vulgar splurge, when in a single residential street palaces from all parts of the world were cheaply copied, and just as in Europe forgotten styles were superficially reproduced. The Queen Anne style became fashionable; and then native colonial and Dutch motives were revived.

This period is now long past. The last twenty-five years in the East and the last ten years in the West have seen this tasteless, hap-hazard, and ignorant experimenting with different styles give place to building which is thoughtful, independent, and generally beautiful; though, of course, much that is ugly has continued to be built. Architecture itself has developed a careful school, and the public has been trained by the architects. Of course, many regrettable buildings survive from former periods, so that the general impression to-day is often very confused; but the newer streets in the residential, as well as the business, portions of cities and towns display the fitting homes and office buildings of a wealthy, independent, and art-loving people. In comparison with Europe, a negative feature may be remarked; namely, the notable absence of rococo tendencies. It is sometimes found in interior decorations, but never on exteriors.

The positive features which especially strike the European are the prevalence of Romanesque and of the sky-scrapers. The round arch of the Romans comes more immediately from southern France; but since its introduction to America, notably by the architectural genius Richardson, the round arch has become far more popular than in Europe, and has given rise to a characteristic American style, which is represented to-day in hundreds of substantial buildings all over the country. There is something heavy, rigid, and at the same time energetic, in these great arches resting on short massive columns, in the great, pointed, round towers, in the heavy balconies and the low arcades. The primitive force of America has found its artistic expression here, and the ease with which the new style has adapted itself to castle-like residences, banks, museums, and business houses, and the quickness with which it has been adopted, in the old streets of Boston as in the newer ones of Chicago and Minneapolis, all show clearly that it is a really living style, and not merely an architectural whim.

The Romanesque style grew from an artistic idea, while the

sky-scraper has developed through economic exigencies. New York is an island, wherefore the stage of her great business life cannot be extended, and every inch has had to be most advantageously employed. It was necessary to build higher than commercial structures have ever been carried in Europe. At first these buildings were twenty stories high, but now they are even thirty. To rest such colossal structures on stone walls would have necessitated making the walls of the lower stories so thick as to take up all the most desirable room, and stone was therefore replaced by steel. The entire structure is simply a steel framework, lightly cased in stone. Herewith arose quite new architectural problems. The sub-division of the twenty-story façade was a much simpler problem than the disposal of the interior space, where perhaps twenty elevators have to be speeding up and down, and ten thousand men going in and out each day. The problem has been admirably solved. The absolute adaptation of the building to its requirements, and its execution in the most appropriate material — namely, steel and marble — the shaping of the rooms to the required ends, and the carrying out of every detail in a thoroughly artistic spirit make a visit to the best office buildings of New York an æsthetic delight. And since very many of these are now built side of one another, they give the sky-line of the city a strength and significance which strike every one who is mature enough to find beauty in that to which he is not accustomed. When the problem had once been solved, it was natural for other industrial cities to imitate New York, and the sky-scraper is now planted all over the West.

American architecture of to-day is happily situated, because the population is rapidly growing, is extraordinarily wealthy, and seriously fond of art. An architect who has to be economical, must make beauty secondary to utility. In the western part of the country, considerable economy is often exercised and mostly in the very worst way. The pretentious appearance of the building is preserved, but the construction is made cheap; the exterior is made of stucco instead of stone, and the interior finish is not carved, but pressed. This may not, after all, be so much for the sake of economy, as by reason of a deficient æsthetic sense. People who would not think of preferring a chromo-lithograph to an oil-painting do not as yet feel a similar distinction between architectural materials. For the most part, however, the buildings now erected are rich and substantial. The large public and semi-public buildings, court-houses and universities, state capitols and city halls, libraries and museums are generally brilliant examples of architecture. The same is true of the buildings for industrial corporation, offices, banks, hotels, life-insurance companies, stock-exchanges, counting-houses, railway stations, theatres and clubs, all of which, by their restrained beauty, inspire confidence and attract the eye. These are companies with such large capital that they never think of exercising economy on their buildings. The architect can do quite as he likes. New York has a dozen large hotels, each one of which is, perhaps, more splendid in marble and other stones than any hotel in Europe; and while Chicago, Boston, and other cities have fewer such hotels, they have equally handsome ones.

The fabulously rapid and still relatively late growth of handsome public buildings in the last decade is interesting from still another point of view. It reveals a trait in the American public mind which we have repeatedly contrasted with the thought of Europe. American ambitions have grown out of the desire for self-perfection. The American's own person must be scrupulously, neatly, and carefully dressed, his own house must be beautiful; and only when the whole nation, as it were, has satisfied the needs of the individual can æsthetic feeling go out to the community as a whole — from the individual persons to the city, from the private house to the public building. It has been exactly the opposite on the European Continent. The ideal individual was later than the ideal community. Splendid public buildings were first put up in Europe, while people resided in ugly and uninviting houses.

There was a period in which the American did not mind stepping from his daily bath, and going from his sumptuous home immaculately attired to a railway station or court-house which was screamingly hideous and reeking with dirt. And similarly there was a time in which the Germans and the French moved in and out of the wonderful architectural monuments of their past in dirty clothing, and perhaps without having bathed for many days. In Germany the public building has influenced the individual, and eventually worked toward beautifying his house. In America the individual and the private house have only very slowly spread their æsthetic ideals through the public buildings. The final results in both countries must be the same. There is exactly the same contrast in the ethical field; whereas in Germany and France public morals have spread into private life, in America individual morals have spread into public life. As soon as the transition has commenced it proceeds rapidly.

In Germany few private houses are now built without a bathroom, and in America few public buildings without consideration for what is beautiful. The great change in railway stations indicates the rapidity of the movement. Even ten years ago there were huge car-sheds in the cities, and little huts in country districts, which so completely lacked any pretensions to beauty that æsthetic criticism was simply out of place. Now, on the contrary, most of the large cities have palatial stations, of which some are among the most beautiful in the world, and many railway companies have built attractive little stations all along their lines. As soon as such a state of things has come about, a reciprocal influence takes place between the individual and the communal desire for perfection, and the æsthetic level of the nation rises daily. So, too, the different arts stimulate one another. The architect plans his work from year to year more with the painter and sculptor in mind, so that the erection of new buildings and the growth and wealth of the people benefit not merely architecture, but the other arts as well.

Still other factors are doing their part to elevate the artistic life of the United States. And here particularly works the improved organization of the artistic professions. In former times, the true artist had to prefer Europe to his native home, because in his home he found no congenial spirits; this is now wholly changed. There is still the complaint that the American cities are even now no Kunststädte; and, compared with Munich or with Paris, this is still true. But New York is no more and no less a Kunststädte than is Berlin. In all the large cities of America the connoisseurs and patrons of art have organized themselves in clubs, and the national organizations of architects, painters, and sculptors, have become influential factors in public life; and the large art schools with well-known teachers and the studios of private masters have become great centres for artistic endeavour. A general historical study of architecture has even been introduced in universities, and already the erection of a national academy of art is so actively discussed that it will probably be very soon realized. Certainly every American artist will continue to visit Europe, as every German artist visits Italy; but all the conditions are now ripe in America for developing native talent on native soil.

The artistic education of the public is not less important nor far behind the professional education of the artist. We have discussed the general appreciation of architecture, and the same public education is quietly going on in the art museums. Of course, the public art galleries of America are necessarily far behind those of Europe, since the art treasures of the world were for the most part distributed when America began to collect. And yet it is surprising what treasures have been secured, and in some branches of modern painting and industrial art the American collections are not to be surpassed. Thus the Japanese collection of pottery in Boston has nowhere its equal, and the Metropolitan Museum in New York leads the world in several respects. Modern German art is unfortunately ill represented, but modern French admirably. Here is a large field open for a proper German ambition; German art needs to be recognized much more throughout the country. It must show that American distrust is absolutely unjustified, that it has made greater artistic advances than any other nation, and that German pictures are quite worthy of a large place in the collections.

There are many extraordinary private collections which were gathered during the cosmopolitan period that the nation has gone through. Just as foreign architecture was imitated, so the treasures of foreign countries in art and decoration were secured at any price; and owing to the great wealth, the most valuable things were bought, often without intelligent appreciation, but never without a stimulating effect. One is often surprised to find famous European paintings in private houses, often in remote Western cities; and the fact that for many years Americans have been the best patrons of art in the markets of the world, could not have been without its results. At the height of this collecting period American art itself probably suffered: a moderately good French picture was preferred to a better American picture; but all these treasures have indirectly benefited native art, and still do benefit it, so much that the better artists of the country are much opposed to the absurd protective tariff that is laid on foreign works of art. The Italian palace of Mrs. Gardner in Boston contains the most superb private collection; but just here one sees that the cosmopolitan period of collection and imitation is, after all, merely an episode in the history of American art. An Italian palace has no organic place in New England, although the artistic merits of the Gardner collection are perhaps nowhere surpassed.

The temporary exhibitions which are just now much in fashion have, perhaps, more influence than the permanent museums. Every large city has its annual exhibitions, and in the artistic centres, one special collection comes after another. And the strongest general stimulation has emanated from the great expositions. When the nation visited Philadelphia in 1876, the American artistic sense was just waking up, and the impetus there started was of decisive significance. It is said that the taste for colour in household decoration and fittings, for handsome carpets and draperies, came into the country at that time. When Chicago built its Court of Honour in 1893, which was more beautiful than what Paris could do seven years later, the country became for the first time aware that American art could stand on its own feet, and this æsthetic self-consciousness has stimulated endeavour through the entire nation. In Chicago, for the first time, the connection between architecture and sculpture came properly to be appreciated; and, more than all else, the art of the whole world was then brought into the American West, and that which previously had been familiar only to the artistic section between Boston and Washington was offered to the masses in Illinois, Michigan, Ohio, and Missouri. Chicago has remained since that time one of the centres of American architecture, and the æsthetic level of the entire West was raised, although it is still below that of the Eastern States. And once more, after a very short pause, St. Louis is ambitious enough to try the bold experiment which New York and Boston, like Berlin and Munich, have always avoided. The World's Fair at St. Louis will surely give new impetus to American art, and especially to the artistic endeavour of the Western States.

If a feeling for art is really to pervade the people, the influence must not begin when persons are old enough to visit a world's fair, but rather in childhood. The instruction in drawing, or rather in art, since drawing is only one of the branches, must undertake the æsthetic education of the youth in school. It cannot be denied that America has more need of such æsthetic training of children than Germany. The Anglo-Saxon love of sport leads the youth almost solely to the bodily games which stimulate the fancy much less than the German games of children, and other influences are also lacking to direct the children's emotional life in the road of æsthetic pleasure. On the other hand, it must be admitted that the problem has been well solved in America. The American art training in school, say on the Prang system, which more than 20,000 teachers are using in class instruction, is a true development of the natural sense of beauty. The child learns to observe, learns technique, learns the value of lines and colours, and learns, more than all, to create beauty. In place of merely copying he divides and fills a given space harmoniously, and so little by little goes on to make small works of art. Generations which have enjoyed such influences must look on their environment with new eyes, and even in the poorest surroundings instinctively transform what they have, in the interests of beauty.

Corresponding to these popular stimulations of the sense of beauty is the wish to decorate the surroundings of daily life, most of all the interior; even in more modest circles to make them bright, pleasing, and livable, whereas they have too long been bare and meaningless. The arts and crafts have taken great steps forward, have gotten the services of true artists, and accomplished wonderful results. The glittering glasses of Tiffany and many other things from his world-famous studios are unsurpassed. There are also the wonderfully attractive silver objects of Gorham, the clay vases of the Rockwood Pottery, objects in cut-glass and pearl, furniture in Old English and Colonial designs, and much else of a similar nature. And for the artistic sense it is more significant and important that at last even the cheap fabrics manufactured for the large masses reveal more and more an appreciation of beauty. Even the cheap furniture and ornaments have to-day considerable character; and no less characteristic is the general demand, which is much greater than that of Europe, for Oriental rugs. The extravagant display of flowers in the large cities, the splendid parks and park-ways such as surround Boston, the beautification of landscapes which Charles Eliot has so admirably effected, and in social life the increasing fondness for coloured and æsthetic symbols, such as the gay academic costumes, the beautiful typography and book-bindings, and a thousand other things of the same sort, indicate a fresh, vigorous, and intense appreciation of beauty.

While such a sense for visible beauty has been developed by the wealth and the artistic instruction of the country, one special condition more has affected not only the fine arts but also poetry and literature. This is the development of the national feeling, which more than anything else has stimulated literary and artistic life. The American feels that he has entered the exclusive circle of world powers, and must like the best of them realize and express his own nature. He is conscious of a mission, and the national feeling is unified much less by a common past than by a common ideal for the future. His national feeling is not sentimental, but aggressive; the American knows that his goal is to become typically American. All this gives him the courage to be individual, to have his own points of view, and since he has now studied history and mastered technique, this means no longer to be odd and freakish, but to be truly original and creative. He is now for the first time thoroughly aware what a wealth of artistic problems is offered by his own continent, by his history, by his surroundings, and by his social conditions. And just as American science has been most successful in developing the history, geography, geology, zoölogy, and anthropology of the American Continent, so now his new art and literature are looking about for American material.

His hopes are high; he sees indications of a new art approaching which will excite the admiration of the world. He feels that the great writer is not far off who will express the New World in the great American novel. Who shall say that these hopes may not be realized to-morrow? For it is certain that he enjoys an unusual combination of favourable conditions for developing a world force. Here are a people thoroughly educated in the appreciation of literature and art — a people in the hey-day of success, with their national feeling growing, and having, by reason of their economic prosperity, the amplest means for encouraging art; a people who find in their own country untold treasures of artistic and literary problems, and who in the structure of their government and customs favour talent wherever it is found; a people who have learned much in cosmopolitan studies and to-day have mastered every technique, who have absorbed the temperament and ambitions of the most diverse races and yet developed their own consistent, national consciousness, in which indomitable will, fertile invention, Puritan morals, and irrepressible humour form a combination that has never before been known. The times seem ripe for something great

CHAPTER TWENTY

Religion

THE individualistic conception of life and the religious conceptions of the world favour each other. The more that an individual's religious temperament sees this earthly life merely as a preparation for the heavenly, the more he puts all his efforts into the development of his individual personality. General concepts, civilizations, and political powers cannot, as such, enter the gates of heaven; and the perfection of the individual soul is the only thing which makes for eternal salvation. On the other hand, the more deeply individualism and the desire for self-perfection have taken hold on a person, so much the deeper is his conviction that the short shrift before death is not the whole meaning of human existence, and that his craving for personal development hints at an existence beyond this world. Through such individualism, it is true, religion is in a sense narrowed; the idea of immortality is unduly emphasized. Yet the whole life of an individualistic nation is necessarily religious. The entire American people are in fact profoundly religious, and have been from the day when the Pilgrim Fathers landed, down to the present moment.

On the other hand, individualism cannot decide whether we ought to look on God with fear or with joy, to conceive Him as revengeful or benevolent, to think human nature sinful or good. The two most independent American thinkers of the eighteenth century, Jonathan Edwards and Benjamin Franklin, represent here the two extremes. The men who have made American history and culture took in early times the point of view of Edwards, but take to-day rather that of Franklin.

Can it be said that America is really religious to-day? From first impressions, a European may judge the opposite; first and most of all, he observes that the government does not concern itself with the church. Article VI of the Constitution expressly forbids the filling of any office or any political position of honour in the United States being made dependent on religion, and the first amendment adds that Congress may never pass a law aiming to establish any official religion or to hinder religious freedom. This provision of the Constitution is closely followed in the Constitutions of the several states. The government has nothing to do with the church; that is, the church lacks the powerful support of the state which it receives in all monarchical countries; and in fact the state interprets this neutrality prescribed by the Constitution so rigorously that, for example, statistics of religious adherence for the last great census were obtained from the church organizations, because the state has not the right to inquire into the religious faith of citizens. Ecclesiastics pass no state examinations to show their fitness to preach; millions of people belong to no church organization; the lower masses are not reached by any church, and the public schools have no religious instruction. It might thus appear as if the whole country were as indifferent to religion as European humourists have declared it to be, in saying that the Almighty Dollar is the American's only god.

On looking more closely, one finds very soon that the opposite is the case. Although it is true that the state is not concerned with religion, yet this provision of the Constitution in no wise signifies any wish to encourage religious indifference. The states which united to form the Federation were profoundly religious; both Protestants and Catholics had come to the New World to find religious freedom, had made great renunciations to live in their faith untroubled by the persecutions of the Old World, and every sect of Europe had adherents on this side of the ocean. Not a few of the states were, in their general temperament, actually theocratic. Not only in Puritan New England had the church all the power in her hands, but in the colony of Virginia, the seat of the English High-Churchmen, it was originally the law that one who remained twice away from church was flogged, and on the third time punished with death. When America broke away from England, almost every state had its special and pronounced religious complexion. The majority of the population in the separate colonies had generally forced their religion on the whole community, and religious interests were everywhere in the foreground.

Although, finally, Jefferson's proposition constitutionally to separate church and state was accepted, this move is not to be interpreted as indifference, but rather as a wish to avoid religious conflicts. In view of such pronounced differences as those between Puritans, Quakers, High-Churchmen, Catholics, etc., the establishment of any church as a state institution would have required a subordination of the other sects which would have been felt as suppression. The separation of the church from the state simply meant freedom for every sect. Then, too, not all the separate states followed the federal precedent; the New England States especially favoured, by their taxation laws, the Calvinistic faith until the beginning of the nineteenth century; and Massachusetts was the last to introduce complete religious neutrality, as lately as 1833. In the Southern States, the relations between church and state were more easily severed; and in the Middle States, even during colonial times, there was general religious freedom.

Whether or not the separation was rapid or slow, or whether it took place under the passive submission, or through the active efforts of the clergy, the churches everywhere soon became the warmest supporter of this new condition of things. All the clergy found that in this way the interests of religion were best preserved. The state does nothing to-day for the churches except by way of laws in single states against blasphemy and the disturbance of religious worship, and by the recognition, but not the requirement, of church marriage. There are also remnants of the connection in the recognized duty of the President to appoint the annual day of Thanksgiving, and in cases of signal danger to appoint days of fasting and prayer, and one more remnant in the fact that the legislatures are opened by daily prayer. Otherwise, the state and church move in separate dimensions of space, as it were, and there is no attempt to change this condition.

It was, therefore, no case of an orthodox minority being forced to content itself with an unchurchly state; but neither party nor sect nor state had the slightest wish to see church and state united. The appreciation of this mutual independence is so great that public opinion turns at once against any church which tries to exert a political influence, whether by supporting a certain political body in local elections or by trying to obtain public moneys for its educational institutions and hospitals. When, for instance, the principal anti-Catholic organization, the so-called American Protective Association, became regrettably wide-spread, it got its strength, not from any Protestant ecclesiastical opposition, but only from the political antipathy against that church which seemed the most inclined to introduce such un-American side influences in party politics. Every one felt that a great American principle was there at stake.

Thus the legal status of the churches is that of a large private corporation, and nobody is required to connect himself with any church. Special ecclesiastical legislation is, therefore, superfluous; every church may organize, appoint officers, and regulate its property matters and disciplinary questions as it likes, and any disputed points are settled by civil law, as in the case of all corporations. Just as with business companies, a certain sort of collective responsibility is required; but the competition between churches, as between industrial corporations, is unhampered, and the relation of the individual to his church is that of ordinary contract. One hundred and forty-eight different sects appeal to-day for public favour. To the European this sounds at first like secularization, like a lowering of the church to the level of a stock company — like profanation. And still no Catholic bishop nor Orthodox minister would wish it different. Now how does this come about?

In the first place individualism has even here victoriously carried through its desire for self-determination. Nobody is bound to belong to any congregation, and one who belongs is therefore willing to submit himself to its organization, to subscribe to its by-laws, and to support its expenditures. Nobody pays public taxes for any church, nor is under ecclesiastical authority which he does not freely recognize. The church is, therefore, essentially relieved of any suspicion of interfering with individual freedom. The individual himself is for the same reason not only free to adopt or to reject religion, but also to express his personal views in any form or creed whatsoever. Only where the church exercises no authority on thought or conscience can it be supported by the spirit of self-determination. Thus, the Mennonite Church has already developed twelve sects, the Baptist thirteen, the

Methodist seventeen, and all of these are equally countenanced. At the same time the reproach can never be made that the church owes its success to the assistance of the state: what it does is by its own might; and so its success is thoroughly intrinsic and genuine, its zeal is quickened, and its whole activities kept apart from the world of political strife and directed toward ideals.

The church which is not supported by any written laws of the state is not, for that reason, dependent alone on the religious ideals of its adherents, but also on the unwritten law of the social community. The less the authority of the state, the more the society as a whole realizes its duties; and while society remains indifferent as long as religion is enforced by external means, it becomes energetic as soon as it feels itself responsible for the general religious situation. The church has had no greater fortune than in having religion made independent of the state and made the affair of society at large. Here an obligation could be developed, which is perhaps more firm and energetic than that of the state, but which is nevertheless not felt as an interference, firstly, because the political individual is untouched, and secondly, because the allegiance to a certain social class is not predetermined, but becomes the goal and the honourable achievement of the individual. Of course, even the social obligation would not have developed had there not been a deep religious consciousness living in the people; but such individual piety has been able to take much deeper root in a soil socially so favourable. A religiously inclined population, which has made churchliness a social and not a political obligation, affords the American church the most favourable condition for its success that could be imagined.

One may see even from the grouping of sects, how much the church is supported by society. If anywhere democracy seems natural, it should be in the eyes of God; and yet, if Americans show anywhere social demarcations, it is in the province of religion. This is true, not only of different churches where the expense of membership is so unequal that in large cities rich and poor are farther apart on Sundays than on week-days, but it is true of the sects themselves. Methodists and Episcopalians or Baptists and Unitarians form in general utterly different social groups, and one of these sects is socially predominant in one section of the country, another in another. But just because religious differences are so closely related to the differences existing in the social world, the relations between the sects are thoroughly friendly. Each has its natural sphere.

It is certain that the large number of sects are helpful in this direction, since they make the distinction between related faiths extremely small, sometimes even unintelligible to all except the theological epicure; and, indeed, they often rest on purely local or ancestral distinctions. Thus the German Reformed and the Dutch Reformed churches are called two sects, and even the African Methodist Episcopalians and the Coloured Methodist Episcopalians wish to be distinguished from each other as from the other negro sects. Where large parties oppose each other, a war for principles can break out; but where the religions merge into one another through many small gradations, the consciousness of difference is less likely to be joined to any feeling of opposition. The real opponent of churches is the common enemy, the atheist, although the more straitlaced congregations are not quite sure that the Unitarians, who are most nearly comparable to members of the German Protestantenverein, are not best classed with the atheists. And, lastly, envy and jealousy do not belong to the American optimistic temperament, which does not grudge another his success. Thus everything works together to make the churches get on peacefully with one another. The religion of the country stretches from one end to the other, like a brilliant and many-hued rainbow.

The commingling of church and society is shown everywhere. The church is popular, religious worship is observed in the home, the minister is esteemed, divine worship is well attended, the work of the church is generously supported, and the cause of religion is favoured by the social community. These outlines may now be filled in by a few details. The American grows up with a knowledge of the Bible. The church, Sabbath-school, and the home influences work together; a true piety rules in every farmhouse, and whosoever supposes this to be in any-wise hypocrisy has no notion of the actual conditions. In many city homes of artisans the occupants do not know the Bible and do not wish to know it; but they are in no-wise hypocritical, and in the country at large religion is so firmly rooted that people are much more likely to make sham pretences of general enlightenment than of religious belief. Thus, it is mostly a matter of course that festivals, banquets, and other meetings which in Germany would not call for any religious demonstration whatsoever, are opened and closed by prayer. Religious discussions are carried on with animation in every class of society, and one who travels about through the country finds that business and religion are the two great topics of conversation, while after them come politics. It is only among individuals who are so religiously disposed, that such vagaries of the supernatural consciousness, as spiritualism, healing by prayer, etc., could excite so much interest. But also normal religious questions interest an incomparably large circle of people; nine hundred ecclesiastical newspapers and magazines are regularly published and circulated by the millions.

We have said, furthermore, that divine service is well attended, and that clergymen are highly esteemed. In the non-political life, especially in the East, the great preachers are among the most influential people of the day. The most brilliant ecclesiastic of recent decades was, by common consent, Phillips Brooks, by whose speech and personality every one was attracted and ennobled; and it has often been said that at his death, a few years ago, the country mourned as never before since the death of Lincoln. No one equal to him has appeared since, but there are many ministers whose ethical influence must be accounted among the great factors of public life; and this is true, not only of the Protestant ministers, but also of several Catholic ecclesiastics.

The same is true in the more modest communities. The influence of the preacher is more profound in small communities of America than it is in Germany. But it is weakened at once if the representative of the church descends to politics. He is welcomed as an appropriate fellow-worker only in questions that border both on politics and on morals — as, for instance, the temperance question. The high position of the clergy is interestingly shown from the fact that the profession is very often recruited from the best classes of society. Owing to the American effort to obliterate social differentiation as much as possible, it is difficult to make sure of the facts of the situation; but it seems pretty certain that the men who study for the ministry, especially in the Episcopalian, Presbyterian, Congregational, and Unitarian churches, are better born than the men who become school teachers and physicians.

The preacher steps into the pulpit and faces his hearers in a way which is typically American. Of course, it is impossible to reduce the ministerial bearing in the 194,000 churches of the country to a single formula; but one thing may always be noted, by the European, in contrast to what he has seen at home — the obvious reference of the sermon to the worldly interests of the congregation. Its outer form already shows this; the similes and metaphors are borrowed from ordinary and even vulgar life, the applications are often trivial, but forcible and striking, and even anecdotes are introduced and given in colloquial form. More than that, the topic itself is chosen so as to concern personally nearly every one sitting in the pews; the latest vexation or disappointment, the cherished hope, or the duty lying nearest to the individual forms the starting-point of the sermon, and the words of the Bible are brought home to the needs of the hearers like an expected guest. The preacher does not try to lure the soul away from daily life, but he tries to bring something higher into that life and there to make it living; and if he is the right sort of a preacher, this never works as a cheapening of what is divine, but as an exaltation of what is human.

Doubtless it is just on this account that the church is so popular and the services so well attended. To be sure, frequently the minister is a sensational pulpit elocutionist, who exploits the latest scandal or the newest question of the day in order to interest the public and attract the curious to church. Often the worldly quality of the sermon tends to another form of depreciation. The sermon becomes a lecture in general culture, a scientific dissertation, or an educational exercise. Of course, the abandonment of the strictly religious form of sermon brings many temptations to all except the best preachers; yet, in general, the American sermon is unusually powerful.

The popularity of the church does not depend only on the applicability of the sermon, but in part on social factors which are not nearly so strong in any part of Europe. If the congregation desires to bring the general public to church, it will gain its end most surely by offering attractions of a religiously indifferent nature. These attractions may indirectly assist the moral work of the church, although their immediate motive is to stimulate church-going. The man who goes to church merely in order to hear the excellent music has necessarily to listen to the sermon; and one who joins the church for the sake of its secular advantages is at least in that way detained from the frivolous enjoyments of irreligious circles. Thus, the church has gradually become a social centre with functions which are as unknown in Germany as the "parlours" which belong to every church in America. The means of social attraction must naturally be adapted to the character of the congregation; the picnics which are popular in the small towns, with their raffles and social games, their lemonade and cake, would not be appropriate to the wealthy churches on Fifth Avenue. In the large cities, æsthetic attractions must be substituted — splendid windows, soft carpets, fine music, elegant costumes, and fashionable bazars for charity's sake.

But the social enjoyment consists not solely in what goes on within the walls of the church, but specially in the small cities and rural districts the church is the mediator of almost all social intercourse. A person who moves to a new part of the town or to an entirely new village, allies himself to some congregation if he is of the middle classes, in order to form social connections; and this is the more natural since, in the religious as in the social life of America, the women are the most active part of the family. Even the Young Men's Christian Associations and similar social organizations under church auspices play an important rôle utterly unlike anything in Europe. In Germany such organizations are popularly accounted flabby, and their very name has a stale flavour. In America they are the centres of social activity, even in large cities, and have an extraordinary influence on the hundreds of thousands of members who meet together in the splendid club buildings, and who are as much interested in sport and education as in religion.

How fully the church dominates social life may be seen in the prevalent custom of church weddings. The state does not make a civil wedding obligatory. As soon as the local civil board has officially licensed the married couple, the wedding may legally be performed either by a civil officer or by a minister; yet it is a matter of course with the great majority of the population that the rings shall be exchanged before the altar. An avowed atheist is not received in any social circles above that of the ordinary saloon, and while a politician need not fear that his particular religion will prevent his being supported by the members of other churches, he has no prospects for election to any office if he should be found an actual materialist. When Ingersoll, who was the great confessed atheist of the country, travelled from city to city for many years preaching somewhat grotesquely and with the looseness of a political agitator, the arguments of David Friedrich Strauss, in return for an admission price, he found everywhere large audiences for his striking oratory, but very few believers among all the curious listeners.

The man who is convinced that this mechanical interaction of material forces is the whole reality of the world, and who therefore in his soul recognizes no connection between his will and a moral or spiritual power — in short, the man who does not believe something, no matter whether he has learned it from the church or from philosophy — is regarded by the typical American as a curious sort of person and of an inferior type; the American does not quite understand what such a man means by his life. By picturing to one's self the history of America as the history of a people descended from those who have been religiously persecuted, and who have made a home for such as are persecuted, ever since the days when the "Mayflower" landed with the Puritans down to these days when the Jews are flocking over the ocean from Russia and the Armenians from Turkey, and by picturing how this people have had to open up and master the country by hard fighting and hard work, and how they were therefore constrained to a rigid sense of duty, a serious conception of life, and an existence almost devoid of pleasure, and how now all historical and social traditions and all educational influences strengthen the belief in God and the striving for the soul's salvation — one sees that it cannot be otherwise, and that the moral certainty of the nation cannot be shaken by so-called arguments.

It is true, of course, that one hears on all sides complaints against the increasing ungodliness; and it is not to be denied that the proletariat of the large cities is for the most part outside of the church. The population which owns no church allegiance is estimated at five millions, but among these there is a relatively large fraction of indifferent persons, who are too lazy to go to church; a freethinking animosity to religion is uncommon. The American who feels that his church no longer corresponds to his own belief has an ample opportunity to choose among all the many sects one which is just adapted to himself. He will leave his own church in order to join some other straightway; but even if he leaves church attendance in future to his wife and daughters, or if he with his whole family leaves the congregation, this generally means that he can serve God without a minister. Real irreligion does not fit his character; and any doubt which science may perhaps occasion in him ends, not by shaking his religion, but by making it more liberal. This process of increasing freedom from dogma and of intellectualization of the church goes on steadily in the upper classes of society. The development of the Unitarian Church out of Orthodox Calvinism has been most influential on the intellectual life of the nation, but its fundamental religious tone has not been lessened thereby.

To be churchly means not only to comply with the ordinances of the church, but to contribute to the funds of the church and to give one's labour. And since the state does not impose any taxes in the interests of the church, material support is wholly dependent on the good will of the community. In fact, lay activity is everywhere helpful. Of this the Sunday-schools are typical, which are visited by eight million children, and supported everywhere by the willing labour of unpaid teachers. The known property belonging to churches is estimated at seven hundred million dollars, and the rental of seats brings them handsome incomes. More than this, all church property is exempt from taxation.

Nevertheless, so many ecclesiastical needs remain unsatisfied that a great deal of money has to be raised by mite-boxes, official subscriptions, and bequests, in order for the churches to meet their expenses; and they seldom beg in vain. Members of the congregations carry on their shoulders the missions among the irreligious population in large cities and the heathen of foreign lands, the expense of church buildings, and of schools and hospitals belonging to the sect, and the salaries of ministers. The theological faculties are likewise church institutions, whether they are formally connected with universities or not. There are to-day 154 such seminaries, and this number has for some time remained almost unchanged. In 1870 there were only 80, but there were 142 in 1880, and 145 in 1890. It appears from the statistics that, of the present 154, only 21 have more than a hundred students, while twelve have less than ten students. The total number of students was

8,009, and of teachers 994. The property of these theological seminaries amounts to thirty-four million dollars, and more than a million was given them during the last year.

The pedagogical function of the church is not limited to the Sunday-school for children and the seminaries for ministers; but in these two branches it has a monopoly, while in all other fields, from the elementary school to the university, it competes with secular institutions, or more exactly, it complements their work. We have already shown how important a rôle private initiative plays in the educational life of the United States, and it is only natural that such private institutions should be welcomed by a part of the public when they bear the sanction of one or another religious faith. There are grammar schools, high schools, colleges, and universities of the most diverse sects to meet this need; and their relation to religion itself is equally diverse, and ranges from a very close to a very loose one. Boston College, for instance, is an excellent Catholic institution consisting of a high school and college under the instruction of Jesuits, in which the education is at every moment strongly sectarian. The university of Chicago, on the other hand, is nominally a Baptist institution: yet nobody asks whether a professor who is to be appointed is a Baptist; no student is conscious of its Baptist character, and no lectures give any indication thereof. Its Baptist quality is limited to the statute that the president of the university and two-thirds of the board of overseers must be Baptists, as was the founder of the institution.

While among the larger universities, Harvard, Columbia, Johns Hopkins, Princeton, Cornell, and all state universities, are officially independent of any sect, Yale is, for instance, said to be Congregational, although neither teachers nor students trouble themselves with the question. The smaller colleges have a much more truly sectarian character; and there is no doubt that this is approved by large circles, especially in the Middle and Western States. The sectarian colleges outnumber the non-sectarian; and, to take a random example, we may note that in the state of Michigan the State University at Ann Arbor is independent of sect, while Adrian College is Methodist, Albion College Episcopalian, Alma College Presbyterian, Detroit College Catholic, Hilledale College Baptist, Hope College Reformed, and

Olivet College is Congregational. This inclination, especially noticeable in country districts, to a religious education however so slightly coloured, shows how deeply religion pervades the whole people.

To follow the separate religions and their diverse religious off-shoots cannot be our purpose; we must be content with a few superficial outlines. There is no really new religious thought to record; an American religion has, so far, not appeared. The history of the church in the New World has only to report how European religions have grown under new conditions. The apparently new associations are only unimportant variations. Some enthusiasts have appeared from time to time to preach a new religion with original distortions of the moral or social sense, but they have expressed no moral yearning of the time, and have remained without any deep influence. This rests in good part on the conservative nature of Americans. They snatch enthusiastically at the newest improvements and the most modern reform, but it must be a reform and not a revolution. The historical continuity must be preserved. The Mormons, the Spiritualists, and the adherents of Christian Science might, with some propriety, be called pure American sects; but although all three of these excite much public curiosity, they have no importance among those religions which are making the civilization of the present moment.

The religions of the United States which have the most communicants are the Methodist, Baptist, and Roman Catholic. The religions, however, which have had the most important influence on culture are the Congregational, Episcopalian, Presbyterian, and Unitarian. Besides these, there are the Lutheran, the Reformed, and the Jewish churches; all the other denominations are small and uninfluential. The churches which we have named can be more or less distinguished by their locality, although they are represented in almost every state. The Congregationalists and Unitarians are specially numerous in the New England States, the Episcopalians and Presbyterians in New York and Pennsylvania, while the Methodists are specially strong in the South, the Baptists in the Middle West, and the Catholics all through the East. Such special demarcation rests firstly on the relation of the churches to different races which have settled in different places; the Episcopalians and Congregationalists are mainly English, the Presbyterians are Scotch, the Catholics are Irish and South German, the Lutherans are North German and Scandinavian, the Reformed Church is German and Dutch, and Methodism has spread widely among the negroes.

In close connection herewith are the social distinctions. The Methodist, Baptist, and Catholic religions are specially religions of the masses; the others are more exclusive. It is especially those religions of the lower classes which yield to every tendency toward breaking up into sects; only Catholicism maintains a firm unity in the New as in the Old World.

The old Calvinistic faith which was brought over by the Puritans to the New England colonies still lives in the Congregational Church. This church has played a greater political part than any other from the colonial days, when no one could vote who was not a communicant, down to the time when it took an active stand against slavery. Its expansion was limited by an agreement with the Presbyterian Church; only since this was given up, has it entered all the states of the Union. And yet to-day there are in Massachusetts almost 700 Congregational church buildings, and 400 in the small State of Connecticut; but only 300 in the State of New York, 100 in Pennsylvania, a few in the West, and still fewer in the South.

As in the case of all churches, the proportion of the population belonging to this church can only be approximately given. Since the official census may ask no questions concerning religion, we have to rely on the figures of the church itself, which regularly refer to the actual members in the congregations. Now in these Evangelical, Catholic, and Jewish congregations, the conditions for membership are so unlike that the figures are not directly comparable; and even among the Evangelical churches, it is clearly false to find the total number of souls allied to that church, as this is usually found, by multiplying the number of communicants by some average figure, like 3.5. In view of the social and ethnical differences between these churches, the percentage of children, for instance, is very different. It may be said then, although with caution, that the Congregational population embraces about two million souls; but their importance in the shaping of American civilization has greatly exceeded their numerical representation. The spirit of this church has lent ethical seriousness and a vigorous sense of duty to the whole nation. It has founded the first schools, and is responsible for the independence of the country.

It is even more necessary to weigh the votes and not to count them, when we speak of the optimistic daughter church of austere Calvinism, the Unitarian. Probably not more than one quarter of a million persons belong to the Unitarian Church; but the influence of these people on literature and life, science and philosophy, has been incomparable. The church has existed officially since 1815, although the new faith began to spread much earlier within the Calvinistic Church itself. There is nothing theologically new here, since the main teachings, that the Trinity is only a dogma, that God is One, and that Christ was an exemplary man but not God, go back, of course, to the fourth century. These are the Arian ideas, which have also been held in Europe in times past. The significance of the American Trinitarian controversy does not lie in the province of theology. In a sense, the Unitarian Church has no binding belief, but aims only to be an influence of ever-increasing faith in God, which welcomes investigation, advance, and difference of individual thought, within the unity of a moral and ideal view of the universe.

Thus it has been an entirely natural development, for example, for the theological faculty of Harvard University to go over from the Congregational to the Unitarian faith as early as the second decade of the last century, and in recent times to become non-sectarian and broadly Christian, filling its professional chairs with theologians of the most diverse denominations. The significance for civilization does not lie in the Unitarian view of God, but in its anti-Calvinistic conception of man. This church says that man is not naturally sinful, but, being the image of God, is naturally good, and that the salvation of his soul is not determined by a predestination of divine grace, but by his own right-willing. Channing was the Unitarian leader, and the thinkers and writers in the middle of the century followed in his footsteps. Their work was a source of moral optimism. This confession has necessarily remained small by reason of its radical theology, which too little satisfies the imagination of the profoundly pious; but the Unitarian ideas have come everywhere into the worship of aristocratic churches.

The Episcopalian faith, which is English Protestantism, came to the shores of the New World even earlier than the faith of Calvin.

The English faith was organized in Virginia as early as 1607, and for a long time no other faith was even tolerated; and in the middle colonies the English High Church spread rapidly under the influence of many missionaries from England. The secession of the colonies from the mother country was destined to bring a check, but soon after the war the Episcopalian Church of America organized itself independently, and grew steadily through the East. It has to-day seventy-five bishops. It is governed by a council which meets every three years in two divisions—an upper, which consists of bishops, and a lower, composed of delegates sent from the various dioceses. The diocese elects its own bishop. Their creed is, to all intents and purposes, identical with that of the Church of England, and some two million souls are affiliated with this church.

Also the Presbyterian Church of the New World goes back to the seventeenth century; it was first definitely organized in the beginning of the eighteenth, under Scotch and Irish influences. It stands on a Calvinistic foundation, but the church government is the distinguishing feature; at its head are the elders, the Presbyters. Twelve different sects have grown out of this church—as, for instance, the Cumberland Presbyterians, who broke away in a popular religious movement in 1810; other sects had started already on European soil—as, for instance, the Presbyterian Church of Wales, which is perpetuated in America. The Presbyterian population amounts to about four million souls.

The Methodist and Baptist congregations are much larger. Methodism comes from that great movement, at the University of Oxford in 1729, of John and Charles Wesley, whose Sacred Club, with its Biblical bigotry, was, on account of its methodical precision, ridiculed as the Methodist Club; and the nickname was accepted and held to. It was a question of bringing the English church closer to the heart, of profoundly moving every individual and instilling a deeper piety in the people. In order to preach the word of God, it needed neither professional theologians nor church buildings; laymen were to be the preachers, and the canopy of heaven their church. The movement began to spread in America in 1766, and while in England it remained for a longer time nominally within the established church, American Methodism took very early a different course from Episcopalianism.

The peculiar organization of the congregation is a prominent feature. Candidates for membership are accepted after a six months' probation, popular prayer-meetings are held at any chosen spot, the lay preachers are permitted to deliver religious talks without giving up their secular occupations, and no pastor may remain longer than five years over any congregation. These and other provisions are rather in the nature of concessions to the religious needs of ordinary people; the special items of faith differ slightly from those of the mother church, and are of comparatively little significance. The number of communicants has grown rapidly, especially among the negroes of the South, owing to the large camp-meetings, where many persons sing and pray together, and work themselves up to a more or less hysterical point of excitement under the open sky. As is usual among less cultivated classes, the tendency to form sects has been very great; small groups are continually breaking away, because they cannot believe in this or that feature of the main church. Seventeen principal groups may be distinguished, and some of these only by the colour of the communicants. The Methodist Episcopalians are by far the most numerous, and all the Methodist churches together must embrace more than sixteen million people.

The twelve or thirteen sects of Baptists are in some cases widely different in the matter of faith, although the main body of regular Baptists are Calvinistic, and the church is organized like the Calvinistic Congregational Church. Each congregation governs itself, and the one point which all have in common is that they renounce infant baptism; he only may be baptized who is formally able to acknowledge Christ, and he must be baptized not by sprinkling, but by immersion. This cult originated in Switzerland at the time of the Reformation, and gradually gained adherents all through Europe, but it first became widely spread in America, where it embraces about twelve million people. Just as Methodism is a sort of popular form of the Episcopalian Church, the Baptist faith is a popularization of the Congregational Church. The main division of the regular Baptists is made between the Northern and Southern churches, a division which originated in the middle of the century, owing to the diversity of opinion about slavery; and the third main group of Baptists is made up of negroes.

The first Lutherans to come to the New World were Dutchmen, who landed on Manhattan Island in 1623. But the Dutch authorities there suppressed all churches except the Reformed Church, and it was not until New York came into the hands of the English that the Lutheran Church got its freedom. Lutherans from the Palatinate settled in Pennsylvania in 1710, and in the middle of the eighteenth century began their definite organization into synods under the influence of their pastor, Mühlenberg. The church grew in consequence of German, and later of Scandinavian, immigration. Most of its communicants still speak German, Swedish, Norwegian, Finnish, and Icelandic, and those who speak English are mostly of German descent. All together they make a population of four million persons, of whom one-fifth live in Pennsylvania. The Lutherans have formed sixteen sects.

There is another small Protestant sect, which likewise originated in Germany; this is the sect of Mennonites. As is well known, they combine the Baptist refusal of infant baptism with the principle of non-resistance. They came from Germany to Pennsylvania at the end of the seventeenth century in order to escape persecution, and were there known as the German Friends. Their little band has the honour of having registered, in 1688, the first protest against American slavery. Their numbers have since been augmented from Holland, Switzerland, Germany, and Russia, and to-day the largest part of the Mennonites is said to be in America — in spite of which they number hardly more than 150,000 persons.

In many respects the Quakers may be compared with the Mennonites. The Quaker Church was founded in the middle of the seventeenth century by an Englishman, John Fox, and spread to America as early as 1656, where it now numbers, perhaps, 400,000 persons, living chiefly in Indiana, Ohio, and Pennsylvania. The Quakers lay great emphasis on silence, and even in their meetings they observe long pauses, in which each member communes with the Holy Spirit. The sins for which a Quaker may be excommunicated from his church are the denial of the divinity of Christ or of the divine origin of the Bible, enlistment in the army, encouragement of war, trading in alcohol, drunkenness, blasphemy, making wagers, participation in lotteries, giving an oath in court, and requiring an oath. They dress in black or grey, and are known for their mild, gentle, and yielding characters.

The Roman Catholic Church in America is little different from the Church in Europe. It has grown rapidly in the nineteenth century, owing to the tremendous numbers of Irish, South German, Polish, Hungarian, Italian, and Spanish immigrants. Catholic missionaries, it is true, were the first Christian ministers in the New World. They accompanied the Spanish expeditions, and their first bishop landed in 1528. Maryland was the chief English colony of Catholics, while most of the other colonies were very intolerant of the Romish Church. In 1700 New York, which has to-day a half million Catholics, is said to have had only seven Catholic families; and even in 1800 the Catholic population of the whole United States was estimated at less than 150,000. In 1840 they had increased tenfold, and number to-day probably ten millions, with sixteen archbishops and a cardinal. The Catholic centres, in the order of the size of congregations, are, New York, Boston, Chicago, Philadelphia, St. Paul, New Orleans, Baltimore, Cleveland, Buffalo, Newark, Providence, Pittsburg, Cincinnati, and Milwaukee.

The Jews, who are said to have first come from Brazil in 1654, have likewise increased rapidly in recent years, owing to the extraordinary immigration from the East of Europe. They must number to-day about a million people, and if the latest estimates are correct, nearly one-half of these have not gone farther than New York City, which would therefore have a larger Jewish population than any other city in the world. The larger part of these people are Russian Jews, who live together in great poverty and are very little Americanized. The division made by the census into Orthodox and Reformed Jews does not represent two sects, but merely a manner of grouping, since the congregations present a very gradual transition from rigid Asiatic orthodoxy to a reform so complete as to be hardly Jewish at all, and in which the rabbis are merely lecturers on "ethical culture."

Many other churches might be mentioned, such as the widely spread sect of Disciples of Christ, which originated in America, or the Moravians, Dunkards, and others which have come from Europe. But it will be enough here to speak of only a few specially typical sects that have been manufactured in America. The profane expression is in place, since they are all artificially devised organizations, whose founders have often been thought dishonest; such are the Adventists, the Mormons, the Spiritualists, and the Christian Scientists. The Adventists were gathered in by William Miller, of Massachusetts, who in the year 1831 calculated from figures which he found in the Bible that Christ would appear again on earth in the year 1843. This prophecy caused a great many small congregations to spring up, and when the momentous year came and brought disillusionment, and even after a second similar disappointment at a later year, these congregations did not break up, but contented themselves with the less risky prediction that Christ would make His appearance soon. There are Adventists in all the states, and especially in Michigan. They have broken up into smaller sects, of which a few are always making new computations for the coming of Christ. In all, they amount to about two hundred thousand people.

More famous, or perhaps more notorious, are the Mormons. Their first prophet, Joseph Smith, began in 1823, when he was eighteen years of age, to have dreams in which he was intrusted with a religious mission. Four years later, with the help of certain persons of his dreams, he "discovered" the Book of Mormon — a set of metal tablets on which the history of America was written in "reformed Egyptian" characters. The first American colony had been organized, according to the Book of Mormon, by a race of people which had helped to build the Tower of Babel, and which in 600 B.C. had settled in South America. The American Indians, the book says, descend from this race; and Christ also, it says, was for a time in America. Finally, an angel came who appointed Smith and a friend of his as priests, and they then began the regular formation of a church. Miracles were rumoured; missionaries were sent out and congregations formed in several states, even before polygamy was ordained. In 1843 Smith received the inspired message which proclaimed the new ordinance of "heavenly marriage." In the following year Smith was murdered, and his successor, Brigham Young, when hostile demonstrations became frequent, led the group of believers on a bold expedition into what was at that time the almost impassable West — to Utah, on the Great Salt Lake.

The settlement grew, and under its rigorously theocratic government made remarkable economic progress. A large garden was planted in the wilderness, and Salt Lake City is to-day a large, modern town on the railroad line to California, and the Mormons compose only half its population. But they alone and under terrific difficulties carried civilization across the prairies, and as a token of their industry the largest church in America stands there, the Mormon Temple, which they built by forty years of labour, exactly according to the plans which Young saw in a vision. While people are readily admitted to the curious hall of prayer, no strangers are allowed to enter the Temple. Polygamy was introduced, undoubtedly, from no immoral motives, but from the religious belief that an unmarried woman will not go to heaven. Economic motives may have helped the matter along, since the priests permitted new marriages only when the contracting parties had sufficient means to support several families, and so used the satisfaction of polygamous instincts as a reward for unusual economic industry.

The stern morality of the American people has always looked on the Mormon tribe as a thorn in the flesh, and yet it was difficult for a long time for the federal government to suppress the abuse. Serious opposition began in the early eighties with the passing of special laws; thousands of Mormons were put in prison, and millions of dollars were paid in fines. The Mormons fought with every legal means, but were repudiated by the Supreme Court, and finally gave in. In the year 1890 their president, Woodruff, published an ordinance forbidding new polygamous marriages. This has not prevented the Mormons from holding polygamy sacred, and they have abandoned it only on compulsion. The marriages which were solemnized before 1890 are still in force. Such polygamous families do not impress a stranger unfavourably, since, in spite of its complexity, their family life appears to be a happy one. From Utah the sect has spread to Idaho and other Western States, and embraces now perhaps half a million people.

There have been some other curious religious congregations with unusual marriage ordinances. For instance, the Oneida Community has had an apparently most immoral form of cohabitation. It is here a question not so much of religion as of a communistic and economic experiment. Such experiments are, for the most part, short-lived and flourish secretly. Celibacy is practised by fifteen communities of Shakers, who live in a communistic way. They broke away from the Quakers at the end of the eighteenth century, and have unique religious ideas. God, and, therefore, every human soul, is thought to be a double principle, both male and female. The male principle was revealed in Christ, the female in an English woman, Anne Lee, a Quakeress whose visions during imprisonment occasioned the formation of this sect.

The Shakers were so called because they are "shaken" by religious fervour; and the lower classes of the American populace are uncommonly predisposed to this ecstatic and hysterical religious excitement. General revivals, great camp-meetings, and hysterical and tumultuous meetings of prayer, with theatrical conversions and divine illuminations, have always played a prominent rôle in America. Thus at the end of the fifties, after a time of declining piety, a wave of religious conversion swept over the country, having all the appearance of a nervous epidemic. The doings of the rapidly growing Salvation Army also often have a somewhat neurotic character.

It is difficult to say why this is so. As in every form of hysteria, suggestion is, of course, an important factor; but the manifestations are so marked that there must be some special disposition thereto. It almost seems as if a lack of other stimulants produced a pathological demand for religious excitement. Certainly in those portions of the country which are most affected, the life of the great masses, at least until recently, has been colourless and dull. There has been no stimulation of the fancy, such as is afforded by the Catholic Church, or in former days was provided by the romantic events of monarchical history. People have lacked the stimulation of amusements, festivals, the theatre and music; daily life has been hard, morality rigorous, and alcohol was thought sinful. Where religion has been the single intellectual stimulus, it has become an intoxicant for the pining soul: and persons drank until they obtained a sort of hysterical relief from deadly reality.

The seeds of mysticism easily take root on such a soil, and it is no accident that the chief mystical movements of our times have gone on in America, the country which so many suppose to be the theatre of purely material interests. Here we find, first of all, the Spiritualistic movement which began in 1848, when mysterious knockings were heard by the Fox family in a village of New York State. The sounds were interpreted as messages from dead friends, and as soon as these spirits commenced their material manifestations it was only a short step for them to appear in person. The leading card of Spiritualism is its supposed proof of life after death, and all its other features are secondary.

On the other hand, it is natural for a teaching which depends on such mysterious phenomena to turn its interest to other supposably unexplained phenomena, and therewith to become a general rallying-ground for mysticism. Although the Spiritualistic Church has about fifty thousand members, these are by no means all of the actual Spiritualists in America. Indeed, if Spiritualism were to be taken in a broader sense, including a belief in telepathic influences, mysterious communications, etc., the number of believers would mount into the millions, with some adherents in the most highly educated circles. Even in enlightened Boston a Spiritualistic church stands in the best section of the town. Its services have been grievously exposed from time to time, but the deceptions have been quickly forgotten, and this successful "religious" enterprise is once more given credence. A short time ago, in Philadelphia, the spirit of Darwin was constrained to write a pious final contribution to his works for the benefit of a well-paying audience, on a typewriter which stood in the middle of the room, and which, of course, could be easily operated electrically from some other room.

To be sure, it would be unfair to say that all spiritualism is based on deception, although the lively wish to see dead relatives, or receive communications from them, puts a high premium on the pious fraud. Indeed, it would be over-hasty to say that all the spiritualistic conceptions go against the laws of nature; for, since the philosophy of Spiritualism has conceived of an ether organism which pervades the molecular body and survives death, it has fairly cleverly met the demands of casual explanation. And it may well be thought probable that in the world of mental influences there is much remaining to be found out, just as a hundred years ago there were hypnotism and Röntgen rays; so that the zeal of very many people to assist in the solving of these mysteries is, perhaps, easily understood.

But just where these most serious motives prevail and all idea of conscious deception is excluded, one sees the profound affiliation of intellectual interests with the mystical tendency. Even the Society for Psychical Research, which aims to investigate mysterious phenomena in a thoroughly scientific way, has, after all, mostly held the interest of men who are more inclined to mysticism than to science. Mrs. Piper, of Arlington, may be called the most important spiritualistic medium, and Hodgson her most interesting prophet. The whole movement is, after all, religious. Spiritualism has a near neighbour in Theosophy, which is specially strong in California. The great literary charm of Hindu philosophy makes this form of mysticism more attractive to minds that are repelled by its vulgar forms. Hindu mysticism has, undoubtedly, a future in America.

There is a still larger circle of people who believe in Christian Science, the discovery of Mary Baker G. Eddy. When Mrs. Eddy suffered a severe illness at Lynn in 1867, she was seized by the idea that all illness might be only an illusion or hallucination of the soul, since God alone is real, and in Him there can be naught but good. It was therefore necessary only to realize this deceptive unreality, in order to relieve the soul of its error and so to regain health. She herself became well and proceeded to read her principle of mental healing into the Bible, and so to develop a metaphysical system. She commenced her work of healing without medicine, and in 1875 published her book, "Science and Health, With a Key to the Holy Scriptures." The book is a medium-sized work, has a system not unskilfully constructed, although unskilfully expressed, and one who is familiar with the history of philosophy will find in it not one original thought. In spite of this, the book must be called one of the most successful of modern times. It is a rather expensive book, but has been bought by the hundreds of thousands. Congregations have formed all over the country, and built some magnificent churches; and, finally, the infectious bacillus of this social malady has been wafted across the ocean. The great feature of this new sect is its practice of healing; there are to-day some thirty institutions giving instruction in the art of metaphysical healing, and the public supports thousands of spiritual healers.

The movement is benefited by the general mistrust of academic medicine which pervades the lower classes of America, as may be seen from the ridiculous popularity of patent medicines. The cult is also undoubtedly helped by actual and often surprising cures. The healing power of faith is no new discovery; the effects of auto-suggestion are always important in nervous disorders, and there are indeed few pathological conditions in which nervous disorders do not play a part. Mrs. Eddy's disciples, in their consultation offices, do with the help of the inner consistency of their metaphysical system, which the logic of the average patient cannot break down, what Catholicism does at Lourdes by stimulating the imagination. The main support of Christian Science is, after all, the general mystical and religious disposition. Where religion plays such a mighty rôle in the popular mind, religious vagaries and perversions must be the order of the day; but even the perversions show how thoroughly the whole American people is pervaded by the religious spirit.

Not only would it be unfair to estimate the religion of America by its perversions, but even if the religious life of the country were amply described in the many forms of its conservative congregations and confessions, the most important thing would be still unmentioned: the spirit of moral self-perfection common to all the religions of the country. To be sure, it is not to be supposed that all the morality in this nation is of religious origin. One sees clearly that this is not the case if one looks at American social ethics, which are independent of religious ethics, and if one notices how often motives from the two spheres unite in bringing about certain actions. The Americans would have developed a marked morality if they had not been brought up in church; but the church has co-operated, specially when the nation was young and when far-reaching impulses were being developed. And while the forms of faith have changed, the moral ideas have remained much the same.

Benjamin Wadsworth was president of Harvard College in the beginning of the eighteenth century, and no greater religious contrast could be found than that between him and his present successor in office; between the orthodox Calvinist who said that it is by God's unmerited grace that we are not all burning in the flames of hell, as our sins so richly deserve, and the liberal Unitarian of to-day. And yet President Eliot could rightly say that, even after these two hundred years, he gladly subscribes to all the moral tenets of his early predecessor. Wadsworth exhorted parents to teach their sons to live soberly, virtuously, and in the fear of God; to keep them from idleness, pride, envy, and malice; to teach them simple, kindly, and courteous behaviour; to see that they learn to be useful in the world, and so marry and carry on their daily business as to avoid temptation and to grow in grace and in the fear of God.

Benjamin Franklin's catalogue of virtues which he desired to realize in himself, was: temperance, silence, order, simplicity, industry, honesty, justice, self-restraint, purity, peacefulness, continence, and modesty. In this he was not thinking of the church, but his worldly morals came to much the same thing as the Puritan's ethics. The goal is everywhere moral self-perfection — to learn, first of all, to govern one's natural desires, not for the sake of the effect on others, but for the effect on one's self. To put it extremely, the religious admonition might have read: Give, not that your neighbour may have more, but that you may have less; not in order to give your neighbour pleasure, but to discipline yourself in overcoming greed. The social morality developed the opposite motives; and even to-day the joining of both tendencies may be followed everywhere, and especially in many philanthropic deeds. The two extremes go together: social enthusiasm for being helpful, and the fundamentally religious instinct to give alms.

Within the circle of ecclesiastical influences, moral concern for the self is everywhere in great evidence — the desire to be sober, temperate, industrious, modest, and God-fearing. It has been said that these centuries of self-mastery are the cause of America's final triumph. Too many other factors are there left out of account, but undoubtedly the theocratic discipline which held back all immoderation and indulgence, and often intolerantly extinguished the lower instincts, has profoundly influenced national life. And to this all churches have contributed alike. It seems as if the Calvinistic God of severity had been complemented by a God of love; but practically all churches have worked as if it was necessary, first of all, to improve radically evil men, to convert evildoers, and to uproot natural instincts. The American church is to-day what it has always been, whether in or outside of Calvinism, a church militant, strong in its battle against unrighteous desires. To be churchly means to be in the battle-camp of a party; in the camp itself they make merry, but every one is armed against the enemy.

The final result in the great masses of people is an uncommonly high degree of personal purity as compared with the masses of

Europe. Here one is not to think of the slums of large cities nor of the masses of still un-Americanized immigrants from Southern Europe, nor of those people who are under the influence of temporary abnormal conditions, such as the adventurers who flock together wherever gold and silver are discovered. One must look at the people in the fields and the work-shops, in the country and the small city, or at the average citizen of the large city, and one will get from these bustling millions an impression of moral earnestness, simplicity, and purity. These people are poor in imagination and vulgar; and yet one feels that, in the humble home where the average man has probably grown up, the family Bible lay on the table. It is not accidental that the zealous Puritans of Colonial times believed not only that man is preserved from hell-fire by the special grace of God, but also that the colonists were a chosen people and favoured by God with a remarkably large proportion who enjoyed His grace. They saw a moral rigour everywhere around them, and could not suppose that such Puritan living was the path to everlasting torment. Since then life has become endlessly complicated, the pressure of circumstances has increased, temptations are a thousandfold more numerous, and consequently the general level of morality has shifted. Much is to-day called harmless which was then called sinful; but to-day, as then, the number of those who live above the general level of moral requirements is astonishingly large.

As everywhere in the world, so in America; temptation and distress fill the prisons with unfortunate and mistaken human beings. But this fact belongs in a wholly different social connection. We are thinking here of the life of those who are not amenable to law; for intemperance, envy, incontinence, coarseness, servility, brutality, lack of character and kindness, and vulgarity are, in themselves, not punishable. If we speak of those who are thus within the law, we find that life in America is purer, simpler, and more moral than in Europe. And the average American who lives for some time on the Continent of Europe comes home dismayed at the exaggerated and specious politeness of Europe and rejoiced at the greater humanity of the Americans. The incontinence of France, the intemperance of Germany, the business dishonesty of Southern Europe, are favourite examples in America of European lack of virtue; and aside from all local differences, the Americans believe that they find everywhere in Europe the symptoms of moral decadence and laxity, and on finding the same things in large American cities, they put the blame on Europe.

At first sight it looks as if one who lives in a glass house were throwing stones. The foreigner, on hearing of American Sabbath observance, piety, temperance, continence, benevolence, and honesty, is at once inclined to call up the other side of the situation: he has seen cases of hypocrisy, he knows how many divorces and bank robberies there are; he has heard about benevolence from purely selfish motives, and about corruption.

All this is true, and, nevertheless, false. On examining the situation more closely, the foreigner will see that however many sins there are, the life of the people is intrinsically pure and moral and devout. It is true that there are many divorces, and that these are made extremely easy in some states; but infidelity is seldom the motive. The cause lies in the democratic spirit of self-determination, which wants to loosen bonds that individuals no longer freely recognize. It might be said that this is a higher individual morality which ends marriage when it has lost its inner sanctity. The American divorce does not indicate any lack of marriage fidelity; married life is, throughout the nation, distinctly purer than it is in Europe, and this is still more true of the life of young men. To be sure, it is easy to get material for piquant booklets, as "From Darkest America," and there is very much vice in Chicago, New Orleans, and San Francisco. The American is no saint, and a large city is a large city the world over. But undoubtedly the sexual tension is incomparably less in American life than in European, as may be seen by comparing the life of American students with that of German students of the same age. This is not due to deficient romantic feeling, for there is nowhere more flirting going on than in America; but a genuine respect of womanhood, without regard to social class, lends purity to the life of the men.

It is true that American temperance does not prevent some men from drinking too much, and the regular prohibition laws of many of the states have not succeeded in suppressing a desire for physiological stimulation; and it may be even affirmed that the legal interdiction of the sale of alcohol in states or communities, unless an overwhelming majority of the population believes in abstinence, has done more harm than good. But it is clear that the fight against alcohol which has been carried on for a hundred years, and notably by the church, has done an infinite amount of good. The whole nation is strongly set against tippling, and only the dregs of society gather in the saloons. And much more has been done by moral than by legislative influence to suppress the unhappy licentious and criminal consequences of drink among the lower classes; and among higher classes the deadening intellectual influence of sitting in beer-houses and so wasting strength, time, and moral vigour, is almost unknown. In good society one does not drink in the presence of ladies except at dinner, and the total abstainer becomes thereby no more conspicuous than the man in Germany who will not smoke ; and those who drink at table are content with very little. Evening table gatherings, such as the German Kommerse, are accounted incorrect, and drunkenness is dishonourable. These ideas are making their way among the lower classes; railway companies and other corporations have not the least difficulty in employing only temperance men. The temperance movement, in spite of its mistakes and exaggerations, and aside from its great benefit to the health of the social organism, represents a splendid advance in moral self-control. A nation which accounts as immoral all indulgence in alcohol that interferes with self-control has made thereby a tremendous ethical advance.

It would be still easier to expose the caricatures which are published relative to Sabbath observance. One may say it is hypocritical for the law to forbid theatrical performances on Sunday for which the scenes are changed and the curtain dropped, but to allow several New York theatres to perform the cheapest vaudeville without curtain and without a change of scenes. But the fact is merely that the heavy immigration from Europe has brought about conditions in the metropolis which do not accord with the ideas of the rural majority in the state. In Boston no one would think of evading such a law, because the theatres would remain empty; where the attempt has been made to keep large exhibitions open on Sunday, it has been unsuccessful.

The American people still cling to a quiet Sabbath observance, and the day of rest and meditation is a national institution. No law and no scruples forbid the railway companies to run more trains on Sunday than on other days, as they do in Germany; but instead of this there are fewer railway trains, and these are poorly patronized. People do not travel on Sunday, even if they no longer visit the grave-yard, which was the Puritan idea of a permissible Sunday stroll. Concessions are more and more made to Sunday amusements, it is true; golf is played on Sunday in many places, and in contrast to England the Sunday newspapers have become so voluminous that if one read their fifty or sixty pages through, one would not have time to go to church. But in the main the entire American-born population, without constraint and therefore without hypocrisy, observes Sunday as a day of self-abnegation; and even many men who are not abstainers during the week drink no wine on Sunday.

The masses of the people are to a high degree truthful and honourable. It has been well said that the American has no talent for lying, and mistrust of a man's word strikes the Yankee as specifically European. From the street urchin to the minister of state, frankness is the predominant trait; and all institutions are arranged for a thorough-going and often exaggerated confidence. We have shown before that in the means of conveyance, such as street cars, the honesty of the public is not watched, that in the country the farm-house door is hardly locked, and that the most important mercantile agreements are concluded by a word of mouth or nod of the head. There are scoundrels who abuse all this, who swindle the street-car companies and circulate false checks; but the present customs could never have arisen if the general public had not justified this blind confidence. It is true that many a bank cashier robs the treasury; but it is much more characteristic to see a newspaper boy, when one gives him five cents by mistake, run after one in order to return the right amount. It is true that many an Irish politician has entered politics in order to steal from the public funds, but it is a more characteristic fact that everywhere letters too large to go in the letter-box are laid on top of it in the confidence that they will not be stolen. A school-boy who lies to the teacher often has, in Europe, the sympathy of the whole class, but not in America; children despise a lie, and in this sense the true American remains a child through life.

As the American education makes for honesty, so it does for self-sacrifice, which is the finest result of the Puritan idea of self-perfection. The ascetic sacrifice for the mere sake of sacrifice goes against the American love of activity, although if the many

New England popular tales are really taken from life, even this way of pleasing God is not uncommon in the North-Eastern States. But all classes of the population are willing to make sacrifices for an end, however abstract and impersonal. The spirit of sacrifice is not genuine when it parades itself before the public; it works in secret. But anybody who watches what goes on quietly, who notes the life of the teacher, the minister, and the physician in all country districts, who sees how parents sometimes suffer in order to give their children a better education than they themselves had, will be surprised at the infinite and patient sacrifices which are daily made by hard-working people. The spirit of quiet forbearance, so little noticeable on the surface, is clear to every one who looks somewhat deeply into American life.

Thus the more dangerous forms of missionary activity have always attracted Americans; and nowhere else has the nurse's profession, which requires so much patience, attracted so many women. All the world knows the sacrificing spirit which was shown during the war against slavery, and there is no less of that spirit in times of peace. Every day one observes the readiness of men to risk their own lives in order to save those of others; and one is surprised to see that the public understands this as a matter of course. The more modest and naturally more frequent form of self-sacrifice consists in giving of one's own possessions, whether a small sum to the contribution-box of the Salvation Army, or a present of millions to benevolent institutions. It is true that private benefactions are open to interpretation; sometimes they are made for the sake of social recognition, more often they are merely superficial, inconsiderate, or ill-timed, and therefore they are often detrimental to the community. But after all allowances, the volume of contributions to all benevolent purposes is simply astonishing; and here, too, the historical development shows that of all motives the religious has been the strongest.

Yet in all these movements the religious motive, the soul's salvation, has been only one among other influences that are rather social. American philanthropy is perhaps more often religiously coloured than it is in Germany; but the more benefaction comes to be in the hands of organizations with a trained administration, the more the social and economic factors appear. In the same way, Sunday observance and temperance have come to be social problems which are almost distinct from ecclesiastical considerations; and if the American is honest, upright, and pure, he himself scarcely knows to-day whether he is so as a Christian or as a gentleman. Questions of morality point everywhere from religious to social considerations.

PART FOUR

SOCIAL LIFE

CHAPTER TWENTY-ONE

The Spirit of Self-Assertion

ON landing in New York, the European expects new impressions and surprises — most of all, from the evidences of general equality in this New World. Some have heard, with misgivings, of the horrors of upstart equality; but more look with glad expectancy on the country where no traditions of caste impose distinctions between human beings, and where the Declararation of Independence has solemnly recognized as a fundamental truth that all men are born free and equal. Those who fear the equality are generally soon put at ease. They find that social classes, even in New York, are nicely distinguished; no work-stained overalls are found where a frock coat is in order. The other travellers are just as quickly disillusioned in their hopes of equality. It is a short distance from the luxury of Fifth Avenue to miserable tenement districts; — an abrupt social contrast, in all its Old World sharpness and hardness.

If the newcomer, then, in his surprise turns to those who know the country, his questions will be differently answered by different persons. The average citizen will try to save the reputation of equality. No doubt, he says, equality rules in America — equality before the law, and equality of political rights. And such average patriot would be surprised to hear that this sort of equality is found in Europe also. But perhaps our new-comer chances on a mind of less typical habit. This one may reply, with the incomparably sly wink of the thoughtful American, that there is no more equality in America than in Europe. We indulge in such glittering generalities in our Declaration of Independence, to give our good local politicians a congenial theme on public holidays, and so that badly paid shop clerks may solace themselves with such brave assertions as a compensation for their small pay. But we are not so foolish as to run amuck of nature, which after all has very wisely made men unlike one another.

But both replies are in a way false, or, at least, do not touch the root of the matter. It is undeniable that one can no longer speak of an equality of wealth or means of enjoyment, or even, in spite of occasional modest claims to the contrary, of an equal opportunity for education and development. In spite of this, it is a mistake to suppose that on this account the spirit of equality is found only in judicial and political spheres. There is another, a social equality, of which most Americans are not conscious, because they do not know and can hardly imagine what life would be without such equality; they do not meditate on social equality, because, unlike political or legal equality, it is not abstractly formulative. The American is first aware of it after living some time in Europe, and the European grasps the idea only after a serious study of American life.

The social sentiment of equality, although variously tinged yet virtually the same throughout the United States, in nowise militates against social distinctions which result from difference of education, wealth, occupation, and achievement. But it does demand that all these different distinctions shall be considered external to the real personality. Fundamentally, all Americans are equal. The statement must not be misunderstood. It by no means coincides with the religious distinction that men are equal in the eyes of God, and it is not to be associated with any ethical ideas of life. Equality before God, and the equal worth of a moral act, whether done by the greatest or the humblest of God's children, are not social conceptions; they are significant only in religious, and not in social, life. And these two spheres can everywhere be separated. It can even be said that, as profoundly as religion pervades every-day life in America, the characteristic principle of equality in the social community is wholly independent of the ethics of the New Testament.

It is still less a metaphysical conception. The American popular mind does not at all sympathize with the philosophical idea that individuality is only an appearance, and that we are all fundamentally one being. The American thinks pluralistically, and brings to his metaphysics a firm belief in the absolute significance of the individual. And finally, the American principle of equality which we wish to grasp is not rationally humanitarian; whether all human beings are really equal is left out of account. It is a question actually of this one social community living together in the United States and having to regulate its social affairs.

Let us suppose that a group of similarly employed good friends were on an excursion, and that the young people for the sake of diversion were agreed to represent for a while various sorts of human occupation — one is to play millionaire, another beggar, still others judge, teacher, artisan, labourer, high official, and valet. Each one plays his part with the greatest abandon; one commands and the other obeys, one dictates and the other trembles. And yet behind it all there is a pleasant feeling that at bottom they are all just alike, and that the whole game is worth while merely because they know that one is in fact as good as another. If a real beggar or servant were to come into the circle, there would be no more fun, and the game would be wholly meaningless. Strange as it may sound, this feeling is at the bottom of social life in America. Every one says to himself: All of us who inhabit this incomparable country are at bottom comrades; one bakes bread and the other eats it, one sits on the coachman's box and the other rides inside; but this is all because we have agreed so to assign the rôles. One commands and the other obeys, but with a mutual understanding that this merely happens to be the most appropriate distribution of functions under the circumstances in which we happen to be placed.

The real man, it is felt, is not affected by this differentiation, and it would not be worth while either to command or to obey if all men did not tacitly understand that each esteems the other as an equal. A division of labour is necessary, but as long as any one does the work apportioned to him he belongs of course to the fraternal circle, quite as well as the one who by reason of industrial conditions or natural talents comes to take a more distinguished or agreeable position. Whoever makes this claim honestly for himself assumes that every one else does likewise. On the other hand, whosoever thinks himself equal to those above him, but superior to those beneath him, conceives external differences to be intrinsic, and makes thus a presumptuous demand for himself. The man who truly sees social equality as a real part of the social contract, will feel toward those above as toward those below him.

He will make his own claims good by the very act of recognizing the claims of others. The spirit of social self-assertion requires the intrinsic equality of all one's neighbours who belong to the social community in question.

So long as one seeks equality by trying to imitate one's more wealthy, more educated, or more powerful neighbours and trying to gloze over the differences, or by consciously lowering one's self to the level of the poor, the uninfluential, and the uneducated, and either by spiritual or by material aid obliterating the distinction, one is not really believing in equality, but is considering the outer distinctions as something actual. Indeed, the zeal to wipe out distinctions is the most obvious admission that one feels actual differences to exist in the social fabric. Where the spirit of self-assertion, with the recognition of one's neighbour as an equal social being, prevails, there will be no lack of striving for outward similarity, of trying to help one's self along, and of helping others up to one's own position; but this is looked on as a technical matter and not as referring intrinsically to the participants in the social game.

It is doubtful whether a European can fully appreciate this social point of view, because he is too apt to distort the idea into an ethical one. He is ready to abstract artificially from all social differences, and to put the ethical idea of moral equality in the stead of social differentiation. The social system is secondary then to the moral system, as in fact religion actually teaches. The American, however, goes in just the opposite direction. He presupposes, as a matter of course, that the citizens of the United States are socially equal, whether they live in the White House or work in the coal mine; and this point of view is not dependent on any ethical theory, but is itself the basis of such a theory. When we were speaking of the influence of religion on morality, we especially emphasized the fact that religious ethics are everywhere complemented by a purely social ethic, and now we meet this new form of ethics. Religion requires a morality of which the principle is clearly, though somewhat derogatorily, designated in philosophical discussions as the morality of submission, and which finds its counterpart in the ethical theories of moral lordship — the forcible and conscious suppression of the weak. Now the American constructs a morality of comradeship which is as far from the morality of submission as from that of lordship; which is unlike either the morality of the pietist based on the religious idea of immortality, or the morality of Nietzsche, based on biological exigencies. This morality of comradeship is based entirely on the idea of society.

This does not mean that it is a question of fulfilling moral requirements in order to escape social difficulties, or to gain social advantages, but of recognizing this morality simply as a social requirement. Such actions may be called moral because they are unselfish and arise from no other motive than that of the inner desire; and still they are not, in the ordinary sense, moral because they are not universally valid, and refer no further than the circle of the special social community. They may be compared to the requirements which arise in some communities out of a peculiar conception of honour; but the society here is a whole nation, without caste and without distinction. And, moreover, an idea of honour gets its force from the self-assertion of a personality, while the social morality of the American arises in a demand for the recognition of another. The fundamental feeling is that the whole social interplay would have no meaning, and social ambition and success would yield no pleasure, if it were not clearly understood that every other member of the social community is equal to one's self, and that he has the absolute right to make such a claim.

The criminal and the man without honour have forfeited that right; they are excluded from the community and cut off from the social game. But distinctions of position, of education, of heredity, and of property, have nothing to do with this right. If we are to strive for social success, we must be perfectly sure at the outset that we are all comrades, participating in the various labours of the great gay world with mutual approval and mutual esteem; and we must show that we believe this, by our actions. And because here it is not a question of rigorous morality, but rather of the moral consequences of social ideals, the ethical goes by inappreciable steps into the ethically indifferent, into purely social customs and habits; and in many cases into evils and abuses that follow from the same social ideals. We may picture to ourselves the salient traits which are essential to this spirit of social self-assertion.

A stranger first notices, perhaps, the perfect confidence with which everybody goes about his business, without feeling oppressed by those above nor exalted by those beneath him. He feels himself an equal among equals. There is no condescension to those beneath nor servility to those above. The typical American feels himself in every social situation self-assured and equal; he is simply master of himself, polite but frank, reserved but always kind. He detests patronage and condescension as much as servility and obsequiousness. For condescension emphasizes the difference in the rank, and presumes to challenge a possible forgetting of this difference by suggesting that both the persons do recognize the distinction as intrinsic. A man who asserts his true equality and expects in every other honourable man the same self-assertion, scarcely understands how purely technical differences of social position can affect the inner relations of man to man.

One who grows up in such a social atmosphere does not lose his feeling of assurance on coming into quite a different society. Archibald Forbes, the Englishman, describes somewhere the American war correspondent, MacGahan, who was the son of an Ohio farmer, as he appeared in a Russian camp. "Never before," writes Forbes, "have I seen a young man appear so confident among high officers and officials. There was no trace in his manner of impudence or presumption. It was as if he had conceived the matter on a single principle: I am a man — a man who, in an honourable way and for a specific purpose, which you know or which I will gladly tell you, needs something which you are best able to give me — information, a pass, or something of the sort; therefore I ask it of you. It is indifferent to the logic of the situation whether you are a small lieutenant or a general in command, a messenger boy, or an imperial chancellor." And some one else has added, "MacGahan could do anything with Ignatieff; he calmly paid court to Mme. Ignatieff, patronized Prince Gortschakoff, and gave a friendly nod to the Grand Duke Nicholas."

It is not surprising that Englishmen are the ones who feel this trait of the Americans most markedly. England, which is most similar to America politically, is, in this respect of real belief in social equality, most dissimilar; and in curious contrast to Russia, which is politically the very furthest removed from America, but which in its common life has developed most of all a feeling of social equality. And still the American feeling is very different from the Russian. In the Russian man, all the deeper sensibilities are coloured by a religious conception; he accounts himself at bottom, neither better nor worse than the most miserable: whereas the American feels, on the contrary, that he is at bottom not inferior to the very best. The Russian sense of equality pulls down and the American exalts.

As for the Englishman, Muirhead relates as follows in his book, "The Land of Contrasts": "There is something wonderfully rare and delicate in the finest blossoms of American civilization — something that can hardly be paralleled in Europe. The mind that has been brought up in an atmosphere theoretically free from all false standards and conventional distinctions acquires a singularly unbiased, detached, absolute, purely human way of viewing life. In Matthew Arnold's phrase, 'it sees life steadily and sees it whole'; just this attitude seems unattainable in England; neither in my reading nor my personal experience have I encountered what I mean elsewhere than in America. . . . The true-born American is absolutely incapable of comprehending the sense of difference between a lord and a plebeian that is forced on the most philosophical among ourselves by the mere pressure of the social atmosphere. It is for him a fourth dimension of space; it may be talked about, but practically it has no existence. . . . The British radical philosopher may attain the height of saying, 'With a great sum obtained I this freedom'; the American may honestly reply, 'But I was free-born.'"

But what Muirhead thus says of the colour of the finest flowers is true, if we look more closely, of the entire flora; it may not be so delicate and exquisite as in these flowers; it is often mixed with cruder colours, but every plant on American soil, if it is not just an ordinary weed, has a little of that dye.

It is not correct to suppose that inequalities of wealth work directly against this feeling. In spite of all efforts and ambitions toward wealth and the tendencies to ostentation, the American lacks just that which makes the possession of property a distinction of personal worth — the offensive lack of consideration toward inferiors and the envy of superiors. As gladly as the American gets the best and dearest that his purse can buy, he feels no desire to impress the difference on those who are less prosperous. He does not care to outdo the poorer man; his luxury signifies his personal pleasure in expenditure as an indication of his success in the world. But so far as he thinks of those who are looking on, it is of those richer persons whom he would like to imitate, and not of those who can afford less than himself.

Envy was not planted in the American soul. Envy is not directed at the possession, but at the possessor; and therefore, it recognizes that the possessor is made better by what he owns. A person who asserts himself strains every nerve to improve his own condition, but never envies those who are more favoured. And envy would be to him as great a degradation as pure servility. Undoubtedly here is one of the most effective checks to socialism. Socialism may not spring directly from envy, but a people given to envy are very ready to listen to socialism; and in America socialism remains a foreign cult, which is preached to deaf ears. A man who feels himself inferior, and who envies his wealthier fellows, would be glad to bring about an artificial equality by equalizing ownership: whereas the man who accounts himself equal to every one else is ready to concede the external inequality which lends fresh impetus and courageous endeavour to his existence; and this the more as the accumulation of capital becomes an obviously technical matter, not immediately contributory to the enjoyment of life. The billionaire enjoys no more than the millionaire, but merely works with a more complicated and powerful apparatus. Even direct economic dependence does not depress the spirit of self-assertion. We shall have later to speak, indeed, of strong opposite tendencies, and to speak of social differentiation; but this trait remains everywhere. It is much more strongly in evidence in town and country than in the large city, and much more in the West than in the East.

The tokens of greeting are thoroughly characteristic. An American doffs his hat to ladies out of respect to the sex; but men meet one another without that formality, and the finer differences in the nod of the head, expression of the eyes, and movements of the hat indicate the degree of personal familiarity and liking, but not of social position. Position is something technical, professional, and external, which is not in question when two men meet on the street. They greet because they know each other, and in this mutual relation of personal acquaintance they are merely equal human beings, and not the representatives of professional grades. The careful German adjustment of the arc through which the hat is carried and of the angle to which the body bends, in deference to social position, strikes the American as nonsensical. The fundamental disregard of titles and orders is, of course, closely connected with such a feeling. This has two sides, and has particularly its exceptions, which we shall not fail to speak of; but, on the whole, titles and orders are under the ban. The American feels too clearly that every form of exaltation is at the same time a degradation, for it is only when all are equal that no one is inferior, and so soon as some one is distinguished, the principle of the inequality is admitted and he in turn subordinates himself to others.

It would be unfair to draw the conclusion from this that Americans hate every sort of subordination. On the contrary, one who watches American workmen at their labour, or studies the organization of great business houses, or the playing of games under the direction of a captain, knows that for a specific purpose American subordination can become absolute. The much-boasted American talent for organization could not have been so brilliantly confirmed if it had not found everywhere an absolute willingness for conscious subordination. But the foot-ball player does not feel himself inferior to the captain whose directions he follows. The profound objection to subordination comes out only where it is not a question of dividing up labour, but of the real classification and grading of men. It is naturally strongest, therefore, in regard to hereditary titles where the distinction clearly cannot be based on the personal merits of the inheritor.

One of the most interesting consequences of this feeling is very noticeable to a stranger. The American thinks that any kind of work which is honourable is in principle suitable for everybody. To be sure, this looks differently in theory and in practice; the banker does not care to be a commercial traveller, nor the commercial traveller a bar-tender, nor the bar-tender a street-cleaner; and this not merely because he regards his own work as pleasanter, but as more respectable. Nevertheless, it is at once conspicuous with what readiness every useful sort of labour is recognized as honourable; and while the European of the better classes is vexed by the query how one can work and nevertheless remain respectable, the American finds it much harder to understand how one can remain respectable without working. The way in which thousands of young students, both men and women, support themselves during their years of study is typical. The German student would feel that some sort of teaching or writing was the only work suitable to him; at the utmost he would undertake type-writing. But we have seen in connection with the universities that the American student in narrow circumstances is not afraid during the summer vacations to work as porter in a hotel, or as horse-car driver, in order to stay a year longer at the university. Or perhaps, during the student year, he will earn a part of his board by taking care of a furnace. And none of the sons of millionaires who sit beside him in the lecture rooms will look down on him on that account. The thoughtless fellow who heaps up debts is despised, but not the day-labourer's son, who delivers milk in the early morning in order to devote his day to science.

This is everywhere the background of social conceptions. No honourable work is a discredit, because the real social personality is not touched by the casual rôle which may be assumed in the economic fabric. Therefore it is quite characteristic that the only labour which is really disliked is such as involves immediate personal dependence, such as that of servants. The chamber-maid has generally much easier work than the shop girl; yet all women flock to the shops and factories, and few care to go into household service. Almost all servants are immigrants from Ireland, Scotland, Sweden, and Germany, except the negroes and the Chinese of the West. Even the first generation of children born in the country decline to become servants. With the single individual, it is of course a matter of imitating his comrades and following general prejudices; but these prejudices have grown logically out of the social ideals. The working-man professionally serves industry and civilization, while the servant appears to have no other end than complying with the will of another person. The working-man adjusts himself to an abstract task, quite as his employer; while the servant sells a part of his free-will and therefore his social equality, to another man.

Most notorious is the fixed idea that blacking shoes is the lowest of all menial services; and this is an hallucination which afflicts not only those born in the country, but even the immigrant from Northern Europe, as soon as he passes the Statue of Liberty in

New York harbour. The problem of getting shoes blacked would be serious were it not for the several million negroes in the country and the heavy immigration from Southern Europe which does not get the instant prejudice against shoe-polish. But the theoretical problem of why servants will gladly work very hard, but strike when it comes to blacking shoes, is still not solved. There is possibly some vague idea that blacking shoes is a symbol of grovelling at some one's feet, and therefore involves the utmost sacrifice of one's self-respect.

Closely connected with this is the American aversion against giving or accepting fees. Any one giving a fee in a street-car would not be understood, and there are few things so unsympathetic to the American who travels in Europe as the way in which the lower classes look for an obolus in return for every trivial service or attention. A small boy who accompanies a stranger for some distance through a village street in order to point out the way, would feel insulted if he were offered a coin for his kindness. The waiters in the large hotels are less offended by tips, for they have adopted the custom brought over by European waiters; but this custom has not spread much beyond the large cities. It is, in general, still true that the real American will accept pay only in so far as he can justly demand it for his labour. Everything above that makes him dependent on the kindness of some one else, and is therefore not a professional, but a personal matter, and for the moment obliterates social equality.

Just as any sort of work which does not involve the sacrifice of the worker's free-will is suitable for every one, so the individual is very much less identified with his occupation than he is in Europe. He very often changes his occupation. A clergyman who is tired of the pulpit goes into a mercantile employment, and a merchant who has acquired some new interests proceeds to study until he is proficient in that field; a lawyer enters the industrial field, a manufacturer enters politics, a book dealer undertakes a retail furniture business, and a letter-carrier becomes a restaurant keeper. The American does not feel that a man is made by the accidents of his industrial position, but that the real man puts his professional clothes on or lays them off without being internally affected. The belief in social equality minimizes to the utmost the significance of a change of occupation; and it may be that the well-known versatility and adaptability of the American are mainly due to this fact. For he is so much more conscious than any European that a change of environment in nowise alters his personality, and therefore requires no really new internal adjustment, which would be difficult always, but only an outward change — the mastery of a new technique.

A foreigner is most astonished at these changes of occupation when they come after a sudden reverse of fortune. The readiness and quietness with which an American takes such a thing would be absolutely impossible, if the spirit of self-assertion had not taught him through his whole life that outward circumstances do not make the man. If a millionaire loses his property to-day, his wife is ready to-morrow to open a boarding-house; circumstances have changed, and as it has been her lot in the past to conduct her salon in a palace, it is now her business to provide a good noon-day meal for young clerks. She enjoyed the first a great deal more, and yet it too brought its burdens. The change is one of occupation, and does not change her personality. The onlooker is again and again reminded of actors who play their part; they appear to live in every rôle for the moment that they are playing it, but it is really indifferent to them at bottom whether they are called on to play in a cloak of ermine or in blue-jeans. One is as good as the other, even when the parts require one to swagger about and the other to sweat.

If the members of the community feel themselves really equal, they will lay special importance, in their social intercourse, on all such factors as likewise do not accentuate external differences, but bind man to man without regard to position, wealth, or culture. This is the reason of the remarkable hold which sport has on American life. The American likes sport of every sort, especially such games as foot-ball and base-ball, rowing, wrestling, tennis and golf and polo, in all of which bodily exercise is used in competition. After these in favour come hunting, fishing, yachting, riding, swimming, and gymnastic exercises. The sport of mountain-climbing is less popular, and in general the American is not a great walker.

American sport is, indeed, combined with many unsportsmanlike elements. In the first place, betting has taken on such proportions that financial considerations are unduly influential, and the identification of opposing teams with special clubs, universities, or cities too often brings it about, that the sportsmanlike desire to see the best side win is often made secondary to the unsportsmanlike desire to see one's own side win at any cost. And yet even the fervour with which the spectators on the grand-stand manifest their partisanship is only another expression of the fact that the average American is intensely moved by sport; and this interest is so great as to overcome all social distinctions and create, for the time being, an absolutely equal fellow-feeling.

Base-ball is the most popular game, and is played during the spring and summer. The autumn game of foot-ball is too complicated, and has become too much of a "science" to be a thoroughly popular game. In the huge crowds which flock to see a university foot-ball game, the larger part is not always aware of what is happening at every moment, and can appreciate only the more brilliant plays. Tennis and golf are too expensive to be popular; and in golf, moreover, the success of a player is too independent of the skill of his antagonist. Water sports are out of the question in many localities. But every lad in city or country plays base-ball. It can be played everywhere, can be easily followed by spectators, and combines the interest of team work with the more naïve interest in the brilliant single play. It is said that on every warm Saturday afternoon, base-ball matches are played in more than thirty thousand places, before audiences of some five million amateurs in sport. Around the grounds sit labouring men, clergymen, shop-boys, professors, muckers, and millionaires, all participating with a community of interest and feeling of equality as if they were worlds removed from the petty business where social differences are considered.

There is only one more sovereign power than the spirit of sport in breaking down all social distinctions; it is American humour. We could not speak of political or intellectual life without emphasizing this irrepressible humour; but we must not forget it for a moment in speaking of social life, for its influence pervades every social situation. The only question is whether it is the humour which overcomes every disturbance of the social equilibrium and so restores the consciousness of free and equal self-assertion, or whether it is this consciousness which fosters humour and seeks expression in a good-natured lack of respect. No immoderation, no improper presumption, and no pomposity can survive the first humorous comment, and the American does not wait long for this. The soap-bubble is pricked amid general laughter, and equality is restored. Whether it is in a small matter or whether in a question of national importance, a latent humour pervades all social life.

Not a single American newspaper appears in the morning without some political joke or whimsical comment, a humorous story, or a satirical article; and those who are familiar with American papers and then look into the European newspaper, find the greatest contrast to be in the absence of humour. And the same is true of daily life; the American is always ready for a joke and has one always on his lips, however dry the subject of discussion may be, and however diverse the social "position" of those present. A happy humorous turn will remind them all that they are equal fellow-citizens, and that they are not to take their different functions in life too solemnly, nor to suppose that their varied outward circumstances introduce any real inequality. As soon as Americans hear a good story, they come at once to an understanding, and it is well-known that many political personalities have succeeded because of their wit, even if its quantity was more than its quality.

American humour is most typically uttered with great seriousness; the most biting jest or the most extravagant nonsense is brought out so demurely as not at all to suggest the real intent. The American is a master at this, and often remarks the Englishman's incapacity to follow him. The familiar American criticism of their English cousins is, in spite of *Punch*, certainly exaggerated — as if there were no humour at all in the country which produced Dickens. But it cannot be denied that American humour to-day is fresher and more spontaneous. And this may be in large part due to the irrepressible feeling of equality which so carries humour into every social sphere. The assurance of this feeling also makes the American ready to caricature himself or his very best friend. But it is necessary especially to observe the masses, the participants in a festival, citizens on voting day, popular crowds on the streets or in halls, in order to feel how all-powerful their humour is. A good word thrown in makes all of them forget their political differences, and an amusing occurrence repays them for every disappointment. They say, Let's forget the foolish quarrel about trivial differences; we would rather be good-natured, now that we are reminded, in spite of all differences, of our social equality.

Now, out of this feeling of equality there spring far-reaching duties. Especially there are those which concern one's self, and these are the same as proceeded from the Puritan spirit of self-perfection. They are the same requirements, although they are expressed in different ethical language and somewhat differently accentuated. The fundamental impulse in this group of feelings is wholly un-Puritan and entirely social. I assert myself to be equal to all others who are worthy of esteem, and therefore I must recognize for myself all the duties which those who are richer, more educated, and more influential impose on themselves; in short, I must behave like a gentleman. The motto, which certainly has nothing to do with religion, is *noblesse oblige;* but the nobility consists in being a citizen of America, and as such subordinate to no man. The duties which accrue are, however, quite similar to religious obligations. The gentleman requires of himself firstly self-control and social discipline. Also in this connection we find a sexual purity which is not known on the Continent; one may sit in jovial men's society after dinner with cigars around the fireplace a hundred times without ever hearing an unclean story : and if a young fellow tried to boast to his friends of his amorous adventures, in the European manner, he would be snubbed. Nowhere in the world is a young girl so safe in the protection of a young man.

The gentleman is marked, first of all, by his character; everything which is low, unworthy, malicious, or even petty is fundamentally disagreeable to him. The true American is not to be judged by certain scandal-mongering papers, nor by city politics. As known in private life, he is admirable in all his social attitudes. He has a real distaste, often in part æsthetic, for what is vulgar or impure; and this is true in wider as in more exclusive circles. In business he may look sharply to his own advantage; but even there he is not stingy or trivial, and he will seldom make use of a petty advantage, of doubtful actions, or dishonourable flattery and obsequiousness in order to gain his end, nor be brutal toward a weak competitor. That is opposed to the American national character.

It is less opposed, however, to the assimilated immigrant population, especially the Irish.

The relation of one man to his neighbour is correspondingly upright. The spirit of self-assertion educates to politeness, helpfulness, good-nature, and magnanimity. European books on America are fond of saying that the fundamental principle of American life is, "Help yourself." If that is understood to mean that the individual person is not expected to keep quiet and wait for some higher power to help him, and is expected, instead of waiting for the government, to go ahead and accomplish things for himself, it is true. We have already everywhere discovered the principle of individual and private initiative to be the great strength of the American state; the community is to act only when the strength of the individual is not sufficient. And the American believes in self-help in still another sense. He teaches his children to think early of economic independence; the sons even of the wealthy man are to begin with a small income and work up for themselves. Here the traditions of the pioneers are in a way perpetuated, for they had to conquer the soil by their own hard work. This training in self-help has contributed very much to make the American strong, and will doubtless continue to be regarded as the proper plan of education, however much the increasing prosperity may tend in the opposite direction.

On the other hand, the motto "Help yourself" is thoroughly misleading, if it is taken to mean that every one must help himself because his neighbour will not help him. A readiness to help in every way is one of the most marked traits of the American, from the superficial courtesy to the noblest self-sacrifice. The American's unlimited hospitality is well known. Where it is a question of mutual social intercourse, hospitality is no special virtue, and the lavish extravagance of present-day hospitality is rather a mistake. But it is different when the guest is a stranger, who has brought, perhaps, merely a short note of introduction. The heartiness with which such an one is promptly taken into the house and provided with every sort of convenience, arises from a much deeper impulse than mere delight in well-to-do sociability. In the large cities, the American affords his guests such lodging and entertainment as a European is accustomed to bestow only in the country.

More or less remotely, all hospitality involves an idea of exchange; the entirely one-sided devotion begins first in philanthropy. When men feel themselves essentially equal, they may welcome external dissimilarities which incite them to redoubled efforts; but they will not like to see this unlikeness go beyond a certain point. Differences of power, education, and wealth are necessary to keep the social machinery moving; but there is a certain lower boundary where helplessness, illiteracy, and poverty do really threaten the true personality. And then the whole significance of social community is lost. One's neighbour must not be debased nor deprived by outward circumstances of his inner self; he must have at once the means of working for culture and striving for power and possessions. Otherwise, an inner unlikeness would arise which would have to be recognized, and which would then contradict the presuppositions of democratic society. The feeling of justice is aroused at the sight of helplessness, the desire for reform at the sight of illiteracy; and poverty inspires eager assistance.

In its outward effects social helpfulness amounts to the same as religious benevolence, although they are at bottom far removed, and their difference may be recognized, however much they work into one another. In the world of self-perfection there is pity for the needy, and benevolence is offered as a religious sacrifice. In the world of self-assertion, the consciousness of right is uppermost, which will not suffer the debasing influence of poverty; and here benevolence is felt as a social duty by the performance of which social equality is preserved. It is a natural consequence of pity and sacrifice to encourage beggary and unsystematic alms-giving; and the fact that in America everything is directed against beggary and against letting anybody feel that he is receiving alms, speaks for the predominance of the social over the religious motive in America. The one who receives alms lowers himself, while the true social purpose is not in the charitable intent to help up the fallen, but to protect the social organism from the pathological symptom of such debasement; the belief in equality and the right of self-assertion must not be taken from any individual in America. The other extreme, state aid, legal enactments, or illness and accident insurance, or insurance against old age or lack of employment, would be politically impossible. They would be an attempt on the individual's right of self-determination, which would be opposed for the sake of principle. The American social system demands, rather, development along a line somewhere between individual alms-giving and government insurance. It is a question of creating permanent social organizations to do away with poverty, illness, depravity, crime, and distress in a systematic, intelligent fashion.

The connection with the state would thus be preserved, since the state poor-laws supervise and regulate such organizations; on the other hand, the connection with individuals would be preserved, since they derive most of their means from private gifts and enlist a great deal of personal service, particularly that of women. Besides these private and semi-public organizations, there is the co-operation of certain state institutions on the one hand, and on the other of quiet individual benevolence, for which any amount of organization always leaves plenty of scope. Care of the poor and of children, social settlements and educational funds, whatever the forms of helpfulness, the same spirit of almost exaggerated benevolence inspires the gift of unlimited money, advice, time, and strength. Philanthropy could be improved in its outward technique in many states. Too often politics have a disturbing influence; inexperience and religious narrowness are in evidence; efforts are sometimes directed partly against one another; and many conditions of distress arising from the mixed population of the great thinly settled tracts of land, present problems which are still unsolved. But this has nothing to do with the recognition of the benevolent traits of American character.

The readiness of the American to give to good purposes is the more impressive the closer one looks. From a distance, one sees gifts of millions of dollars which less impress one; everybody knows that men like Carnegie, Rockefeller, and Vanderbilt make no sacrifices in contributing sums even in seven figures. But the person who is nearer the scene observes that there is also the widow's mite, and that the well-to-do middle class often gives away a proportion of its income that seems almost too large, according to European ideas. And this giving is never a thoughtless throwing away; the giver always investigates. Almost everybody has a special interest, where he fulfils his benevolent duties thoughtfully and intelligently. Vanity hardly figures at all; the largest gifts are often anonymous and unheard of by the newspapers. Those who are often in the position of appealing to American public spirit for good purposes, soon lose the feeling that they are reminding the public of a duty or asking for an offering. The American gives in a way which suggests that he is delighted to be called on for so worthy a cause; he often adds a word of thanks to a contribution which is larger than was expected, for having his attention called to the cause in hand.

And his benevolence is not all a matter of the check-book. Whether the wind has blown some one's hat off in the street, or some greater mischance has brought unhappiness, the American feels that he lives in the midst of a kindly disposed community. A feeling of comradeship is always more or less in evidence. In any case of sudden accident or misfortune, the way in which the American unselfishly lends a hand, or the crowd instinctively organizes itself to give aid, always astonishes a newcomer.

This fundamental motive shows itself in many ways; magnanimity is one of the most characteristic variations. The American takes no advantage of the weakness or misfortune of another; he likes competition, but that presupposes that the competitors have equal advantages. An opponent's disadvantage takes away the pleasure of victory. During the Spanish War, the ovations accorded to the Spanish "heroes" were often decidedly beyond the limits of good taste; and even during the Civil War, when the embitterment was extreme, people outdid themselves in their kind treatment of the prisoners. And leading men of the North have lately proposed, in spirited public addresses, to erect a national monument to General Lee, the great leader of the Southern States. As in war so it is in peace. The presidential candidates of the two parties arranged some years ago to speak in the same places during the same week; but one of them was detained by illness in his family, and the other cancelled his speeches in order not to profit by the misfortune of his opponent. In the case of a difference of opinion which is settled by vote, say in a small club or committee meeting, the cheerful submission of the minority is generally surpassed by the magnanimity of the majority.

This same magnanimity is shown in helping the weak; there are no better-natured, more considerate, and patient people than the American, so long as the social side of life is in question. Their temperamental coolness and humour stand them in good stead. At bottom it is the feeling that they are all equal, and that if one has made a miss-step to-day and needs help, one needed it one's self yesterday, and may need it again to-morrow. The accident that one is doing one's duty at the moment while another is careless, indiscreet, or foolish is not to be magnified nor taken to mean that one's self is a better sort of a man. Such kindliness greatly makes for general informality.

Among the current complaints of Europeans is, that the American life lacks just this serene cordiality, the German Gemütlichkeit. It is true, indeed, that the rhythm of American life is quicker and more energetic; so that the stranger, until he has become accustomed to the more strenuous pace, remains at first oppressed by a disagreeable sense of haste; just as the American who visits Germany has at first a disagreeable feeling of hide-bound pedantry and careless indifference. Such a first impression is superficial. As soon as the American is adapted to the adagio of German life, he feels that the slowness is not carelessness; and the German, when he has learned the smarter marching time of American life, knows in the same way that the quick, strong accent by no means excludes serenity and comfort. It is true that in the two countries these feelings are differently distributed. The German Christmastide is certainly more fervent and serene than the American, but it is a question whether German popular life has any holiday more warmly solemnized than the Thanksgiving Day of New England. The American nature favours a purely social comfort which has less to do with sentiment and feeling than with the sense of affiliation.

German informality develops itself always among social equals, because in Germany social differences seem to extend to the deepest traits of personality; but social distinctions do not stand in the way of the sympathetic intercourse of Americans, because they hardly ever forget that such differences are external. In this sense the South German enjoys more Gemütlichkeit than the North German, and the American more than any European. The most indiscriminately chosen group can be brought to a unity of feeling by the merest comical or pathetic accident, so that all social distinctions fall away like dead leaves. In the most dignified assembly, as at the busiest office, a single word or jest creates unconsciously a sympathetic mood, in which the youngest messenger and the most important director come at once into equality. A feeling runs through the whole social life, as if one would like to say, with a jovial wink, that no one believes really in all the social distinctions, but is looking for what is good in the inner personality.

The most energetic expression of this inner striving for equality lies in the feeling of justice. There is no province in which American and German feelings are so different. This is especially true in the matter of penal law. A crime is naturally a crime here as there, and the differences in penalty are mainly due to different political, social, and industrial institutions. The American is perhaps astonished at the rigour of German law regarding the press or *lèse majesté*, and at the mild punishment for duelling, or certain social delinquencies; while the German is amazed at the severe American laws relating to temperance and at the mild punishment for slander of officials, etc. But all this does not show the least difference in the sense of justice, but only in the institution. The real difference is deeper. The German, we might say, lays the chief emphasis in seeing to it that on no account a criminal shall evade the law, while the American will on no account let an innocent man be punished. It is a matter of course that every social community includes delinquents, and that for the protection of society a penal code must do its best to suppress, to intimidate, or to improve the lawless will. But in view of such necessary machinery, the American feels that every effort should be made that his guiltless neighbour shall not be molested, since the neighbour is one like himself. It is better for a hundred guilty persons to escape the punishment they deserve than for a single innocent person to be in the least aggrieved.

The real distinctions, therefore, do not lie in the penal code, but in the way it is administered; to put it extremely, the German who is accused is guilty until he proves his innocence, while the American is innocent until he is proved guilty. A single example will make the matter clear. Any one in the United States who has been charged with murder or any other misdeed and on trial found not guilty, can never again during his whole life be tried for the same crime; not even if entirely new and convincing evidence comes up later, nor even if he should himself confess the crime. The American jurist says that the state has been given sufficient opportunity to prove the defendant's guilt. If the counsel of the state as plaintiff has not been able to convince the jury, the accused man is legally innocent, and is protected as a matter of principle from the dread of any renewal of the accusation. In American legal opinion the German method of procedure involves a certain arbitrariness, which according to the opinion of many lawyers, is tolerated in Germany only because of the admirable quality of the judges. American jurists say that about half of the testimony admitted in the German court-room, and two-thirds admitted in the French, are entirely incompatible with the legal supposition that every man is innocent until proved guilty.

The different use of the oath is also characteristic of these two countries. The sworn testimony on the basis of "information and belief" is admitted without more ado, and so two contradictory pieces of evidence under oath are not only admissible, but are very common; and the German acceptance of the oath of one party and exclusion of that of the other seems a downright impossibility from the point of view of American law. In the same category is the requirement that the verdict of the jury shall be unanimous. The twelve jurymen may not leave the court except under surveillance until they have pronounced the verdict; and thus it happens that they often have to sleep and eat for days in the court house in order to be guarded from outside influences. If after all they can come to no agreement, the case is dropped and the situation remains exactly as it was before the trial; and the state attorney is free to bring a new accusation. Only an unanimous "guilty" or "not guilty" can be accepted. In this connection, too, is found the unusual significance of the judicial injunctions, and especially of the writ of habeas corpus, derived from Magna Charta, which says that no free man is to be deprived of life, liberty, or property, except according to the law of the land and by the verdict of his peers.

On looking over the judicial practice of the country as a whole, one will feel, quite as in Germany, that this great machinery succeeds in punishing crime and protecting society; but in America the instinctive fear of the law is accompanied by a profounder feeling that any innocent man is perfectly safe. Every trial shows, in a way, most clearly the negative side of the process, that the rights of the defendant are to be carefully protected. And if a newcomer in the country recalls certain exaggerated reports in German newspapers of corruption in American courts, he should bear in mind the words of Choate. Shortly before going as ambassador to England, he made a speech before a society of jurists, of which he was president, on the advantages and disadvantages of trial by jury. As to the theoretical possibility of bribery in such cases, he said that he could pass the matter over, since, during his experience of forty years in law, he had not seen a single case in which even one member of any jury had been accused of having been bribed. Unreliability in the administration of justice would do away at once with the fundamental principle of American social life. When men believe sincerely in their equality, they naturally develop a strong sense of justice, and regard the protection of the innocent man against every sort of prejudice, hostility, dislike, or disregard as the very highest function of the law.

We have depicted the brighter side of the American sense of equality, and may now, with a few strokes, put in the shadows. No one has denied that there are unfortunate features, although some assert that they must be accepted or else more important advantages sacrificed. A stranger is at once struck by the tendency to uniformity which arises from the belief in general equality. The spirit of comradeship is unfavourable to individual differentiation, no matter whether it is a question of a man's hat and necktie or his religion and his theory of the universe. He is expected to demonstrate his uniformity by seeming no different from every one else. In outward matters this monotony is considerably favoured by industrial conditions, which produce staple articles in great quantities and distribute them from one end of the country to another. Exactly the same designs in fashion, arts and crafts, furniture and machinery are put on exhibition at the same time in the show-windows from New York to San Francisco. On the other hand, it is the economic custom of the American to replace everything which he uses very frequently. This is due to the cheapness of all manufactured articles and the high price of the manual labour which is necessary to make repairs. It is actually cheaper to buy new shoes and underclothing at frequent intervals than to have the old ones mended, and this also provides every man with the latest styles. If a new style of collar is brought out to-day, there will, say among the thousands of Harvard students, be hardly a hundred to-morrow wearing the old style. This tendency is, of course, aided by the general prosperity, which enables an unusually large proportion of persons to have considerably more than they need, and to indulge, perhaps imitatively, in the fashionable luxuries of the day.

As much as the general prosperity favours this rapid adoption of new fashions, it is still clear that wealth might, in itself, also help its possessors to distinguish themselves in outward ways; but this does not happen in the United States by reason of these prevalent social ideals. Now, the desire to do as others do affects even the inner life; one must play the same game and must read the same novel, not because one thinks it is better, but because others do it, and because one feels in inner accord with the social community only by loving and hating the same things as it. Those who do not like what others like, find themselves extremists at once; they are instinctively held off by society as bizarre or over-intense, and relegated to the social periphery. There are too few intermediate stages between the many who follow one another and the few who follow no one, and the finer shadings of personality are too much lost in this way. Americans ape one another as the officers of an army, and not merely in uniform, but in the adjustment of all their habits and desires, until comradeship becomes sterile uniformity.

In many ways the American inventive talent tends to relieve the general monotony. But this effort all the time to discover new solutions of this or that social problem, new surprises, new entertainments, is itself only a sort of game which is played at by all uniformly. The small city imitates the large one, the rural population imitates the metropolitan; no profession cares to keep its own social individuality; and the press and politics of the entire country tend to obliterate all professional and local differences in social life, and to make of the whole nation a huge assembly of gentlemen and ladies who, whether high or low, desire to be just gentlemen and ladies at large. It is still not difficult to-day to distinguish a gentleman of Omaha from a New Yorker; but this is in spite of the former, who, as a matter of principle, aims to present the same appearance. East and West, and recently in both North and South, one sees the same countenance, and it is seldom that one hears something of an intelligent effort to kindle local sentiment in contrast to national uniformity. There is an appeal to provincialism to free itself from the system of empty mutual imitation, and yet everybody must see that the profoundest instincts of this country are unfavourable to the development of individual peculiarities.

The dangers of this uniformity are chiefly æsthetic, although it is not to be forgotten that uniformity very easily grows into intellectual mediocrity, and under some circumstances may bring about a certain ethical listlessness. On the other hand, the unfavourable effects of that good-nature which dominates American life are all of them ethical. Their amiable good-nature is, in a certain sense, the great virtue of the Americans; in another sense, their great failing. It is actually at bottom his good-nature which permits him everywhere to overlook carelessness and crookedness, and so opposes with a latent resistance all efforts at reform. The individual, like the nation, has no gift for being cross; men avoid for their own, but more especially for others' sake, the disagreeable excitement. Since the country is prosperous and the world wags pretty well, no one ought to grumble if he is now and then imposed on, or if some one gets an advantage over him, or makes misuse of power. Among comrades nobody ought to play the stern pontiff.

An earnest observer of the country said, not long since, that the hope of the country does not lie in those amiable people who never drop the smile from their lips, but in those who, on due provocation, get thoroughly excited. Dust is settling on the country, and there is no great excitement to shake it off. The cobwebs of economic interests are being spun from point to point, and will finally hide the nation's ideals. Good-nature produces a great deal of self-content in the United States, and those are not the worst friends of the country who wish it might have "bad times" once more, so that this pleasant smile might disappear, and the general indifference give place to a real agitation of spirit. The affair with Spain brought nothing of the sort; there was only enough anger to produce a pleasant prickling sensation, and the easy victory strengthened in every way the national feeling of contentment. There have been a few large disasters, due to somebody's neglect of duty, such as the burning of a Chicago theatre, which have done something to stimulate the public conscience and to impress on people how dangerous it is to let things go just as they will; but even the disastrous accidents which result from this carelessness are quickly forgotten.

The shadows are darkest where the spirit of social equality attempts artificially to do away with those differences which properly exist in school and family life. It may be partly a reaction against the over-strict bringing up of former generations; but everywhere pedagogical maxims seem senselessly aiming to carry over the idea of equality from the great social world into the nursery. It has become a dogma to avoid all constraint and, if possible, all punishment of children, and to make every correction and rebuke by appealing to their insight and good-will. Thus the whole education and schooling goes along the line of least resistance; the child must follow all his own inclinations. And this idea is nothing at bottom but a final consequence of the recognition of social equality between all persons. To constrain another person, even if he is a mere child, means to infringe his personal liberty, to offer him an ethical affront, and so to accustom him to a sort of dependence that appears to be at variance with the American idea. Of course, the best people know that lack of discipline is not freedom, and that no strength is cultivated in the child that has always followed the line of least resistance and never experienced any friction. But the mass of people thoughtlessly overlooks this, and is content to see even in the family the respect of children for their parents and elders sacrificed to this favourite dogma.

Nature happily corrects many of these evils. It may be sport, most of all, which early in the child's life introduces a severe discipline; and here the American principle is saved, since the outwardly rigid discipline which is enforced on every participant in the game is, nevertheless, at every moment felt to be his own will. The boy has himself sought out his comrades. If he had also chosen his parents there would be nothing against their giving him a good, sound punishment occasionally, instead of yielding indulgently to all his moods. If sport and the severe competition of public life were not here to save, it would be incomprehensible that such spoiled children should grow up into a population which keeps itself so strictly organized. Lack of discipline remains, however, in evidence wherever the constraint appears to be artificial and not self-chosen. Where, for instance, the discipline of the army sometimes leads to situations which apparently contradict "sound common sense," the free American will never forget that the uniform is nothing but an external detail apart from his inner self. And even the commanding general will resort to the publicity of the press. In intellectual matters, all this is repeated in the lack of respect shown in forming judgment; every one thinks himself competent to decide all questions, and the most competent judgments of others are often discounted, because every one thinks himself quite as good and desires to assert himself, and feels in nowise called on to listen with respect to the profounder knowledge, reasoning, or experience of another.

We have so far said nothing of those whose self-assertion and claims to equality are the most characteristic expression of American life — the American women. We must not merely add a word about them at the end of the chapter; they are, at least, a chapter by themselves. And many who have studied American life would say that they are the entire story.

CHAPTER TWENTY-TWO

The Self-Assertion of Women

IT is said that the United States is the only country in which parents are disappointed on the appearance of a boy baby, but will greet the arrival of a girl with undisguised pleasure. Who will blame them? What, after all, will a boy baby come to be? He will go to work early in life, while his sisters are left to go on and on with their education. He may work for a position in society, but it will be mainly in order to let his wife play a rôle; he may amass property, but most of all in order to provide bountifully for his daughter. He will have to stand all his life that she may sit; will have to work early and late, in order that she may shine. Is it really worth while to bring up a boy? But the little princess in the cradle has, indeed, a right to look out on the world with laughing eyes. She will enjoy all the privileges which nature specially ordained for woman, and will reach out confidently, moreover, for those things which nature designed peculiarly for man. No road is closed to her; she can follow every inclination of her soul, and go through life pampered and imperious. Will she marry? She may not care to, but nobody will think if she does not that it is because she is not able to realize any cherished desire. Will she be happy? Human destiny is, after all, destiny; but so far as nature and society, material blessings, and intellectual considerations can contribute toward a happy life, then surely the young American woman is more favoured by fortune than either man or woman in any other part of the world can hope to be. Is this advantage of hers also a gain to the family, to society, and the nation?

It is not perfectly correct to speak of the American woman as a type — the Southern girl is so different from the daughter of New England, the women of California so different from those of

Chicago, and the different elements of population are so much more traceable in women than in men. And yet one does get a characteristic picture of the average woman. It may be too much influenced by the feminine figures which move in the better circles to be a faithful average likeness. Perhaps the young girl student has been too often the model, perhaps there is a reminiscence of the Gibson girl; and nevertheless, one discovers some general features of such youth in the fair women whose hair has turned grey, and there is something common to the daughters of distinguished families and the young women of the less favoured classes.

The American woman is a tall, trim figure, with erect and firm carriage; she is a bit like the English girl, and yet very different. This latter is a trifle stiff, while the American girl is decidedly graceful; the lines of her figure are well moulded, and her appearance is always aided by the perfect taste of her raiment. In the expression of her face there is resolution and self-control, and with the resolution a subtle mischievous expression which is both tactful and amiable. And with her evident self-control there is a certain winsome mobility and seemingly unreserved graciousness. The strength appears not to contradict the grace, the determination not to be at variance with the playfulness; her eyes and play of expression reveal the versatile spirit, fresh enthusiasm, and easy wit; yet her forehead shows how earnestly she may think and desire to be helpful in society, and how little contented simply to flirt and to please men.

And then her expression may change so suddenly that one asks in vain whether this energy was, perhaps, merely put on; was perhaps a whimsical caprice; perhaps her intellectual versatility was merely an elegant superficiality. Is she at bottom only in search of enjoyment? Is this show of independence real moral self-assertion, and this decision real courage, or does she emancipate herself merely out of ennui; is it a search for excitement? And is her eagerness to reach out for everything merely an effect of her environment which is ready to give everything? But could this slim figure really be so wonderfully seductive, if her eyes and features did not awaken doubt and unsolved questions; if everything were clear, simple, and obvious? Woman is everywhere full of contradictions; and if the American woman is different from all her sisters, it is because the contradictions in her face and mien seem more modern, more complex and unfathomable.

But it is vain to speak of the American woman without considering her relations to her environment—the background, as it were, of her existence, the customs and institutions under which she has grown up and continues to live. We must speak of the education and schooling, the studies and occupations of women, of their social and domestic position, their influence, and their organized efforts; and then we shall be better able critically to evaluate that in the American woman which is good, and that which is perhaps ominous.

The life of the American girl is different from that of her European sisters from the moment when she enters school. Public school instruction is co-educational, without exception in the lower grades, and usually in the upper. Of the six hundred and twenty-eight cities of the country, five hundred and eighty-seven have public schools for boys and girls together, from the primary to the most advanced classes; and of those cities that remain, only thirteen, and all of them are in the East, separate the boys and girls in every grade. In the country, boys and girls are always together at school. In private schools in cities, the instruction is more apt to be apart; but the public schools educate 91 per cent. of the youth—that is, about 7,700,000 boys and 7,600,000 girls.

Co-education has been adopted to a different extent in the different states, and even in the different grades of school has not developed equally. The instruction of boys and girls together has spread from the elementary classes, and while the idea took the West by storm, it was less immediately adopted by the conservative East. Practical exigencies, and especially the matter of economy, have greatly affected this development; and yet, on the whole, it has been favoured by principle. There is no doubt that, quite apart from the expense, a return to separate instruction for boys and girls would be regarded by the majority of the people today as an unallowable step backward: there has been considerable theoretical discussion of the matter; but the fact remains that the nation regards the great experiment as successful. This does not mean that the American thoughtlessly ignores sex differences in education; he is aware that the bodily, moral, and intellectual strength of the two sexes is different, and that their development proceeds along different lines. But firstly, the American school system, as we have seen, leaves in general great freedom in the selection of studies. The girls may take more French, while the boys in the same class more often study Latin; and many subjects are introduced in the curriculum expressly for one or the other sex — such as sewing, cooking, and type-writing for the girls, and carpentry for the boys.

It is said, moreover, that just as boys and girls eat the same food at the family table, although it goes to make very different sorts of bodies, so too the same intellectual nourishment will be digested in a different way, and not work against the normal intellectual differences. It is important only for the instruction like the nourishment to be of the best sort, and it is feared that the girls' school would drop below the level of the boys' school if the two were to be made distinct. Equal thoroughness is assured only by having one school. Opponents of the idea affirm that this one school is virtually nothing but a boys' school after all, with girls merely in attendance, and that the school is not sufficiently adapted to the make-up of the young girls.

The main point, however, lies not in the similarity of instruction, but in the bringing together of boys and girls. It is true that the success of expensive private schools in large cities proves that there is considerable desire among parents to have their sons go to school with boys and their daughters only with girls; but the nation, as a whole, does not take this point of view, but believes that boys and girls, growing up as they do together in the home and destined to live together as adults, should become accustomed to one another during the formative period of school instruction. The girls, it is said, are made stronger by actually working with the boys; their seriousness is emphasized and their energy developed, while the boys are refined by contact with the gentler sex — induced to be courteous, and influenced toward æsthetic things. And if theorists were actually to fear the opposite result — that is, that the boys should be made weak and hysterical and the girls rough and coarse — they would need only to look to practical experience, which speaks unanimously to the contrary.

A still less well-grounded fear is that of those who wish to separate the sexes especially during the adolescent period. So far as this exceedingly complicated question admits of a brief summing up, the nation finds that the sexual tension is decreased by the contact in the school; the common intellectual labour, common ambitions, and the common anxieties awaken comradeship and diminish all ideas of difference. Boys and girls who daily and hourly hear one another recite their lessons, and who write together at the black-board, are for one another no objects of romantic longing or seductive mystery. Such a result may be deplored from another point of view — namely, that for reasons not connected with the school, such romanticism is desirable; but one must admit that the discouragement of unripe passion in the years of development means purer and healthier relations between the sexes, both physically and mentally. All regrettable one-sidedness is done away with. Just as in the stereoscope a normal perception of depth is brought out by the combination of two flat pictures, so here the constant combination of the masculine and feminine points of view results in a normal feeling of reality.

Then, too, the school in this wise prepares the way for later social intercourse. Boys and girls are brought together without special supervision, innocently and as a matter of course, from the nursery to early manhood and womanhood. It is only the artificial separation of the two sexes, the American says, which produces that unsound condition of the fancy that makes the relation of the sexes on the European Continent so frivolous and dubious. The moral atmosphere of the United States is undoubtedly much freer from unhealthful miasms. A cooler and less sensual temperament contributes much to this, but the comradely intercourse of boys and girls from the early school days to the time of marriage is undoubtedly an equally purifying force. The small boy very early feels himself the natural protector of his weaker playmate, and the girl can always, whether in the nursery or as a young lady in her mother's parlour, receive her friends alone, even when her parents are not at home. A little coquetry keeps alive a certain sense of difference, always, but any least transgression is entirely precluded on both sides. The boy profoundly respects his girl friend as he does his own sister, and she could not be safer than in his protection. The gallantry of the European is at bottom egotistic. It is kind in order to win, and flatters in order to please; while the gallantry of the American is not aimed to seduce, but to serve; it does not play with the idea of male submission, but sincerely and truly gives the woman first place.

The only logical consequence, when boys and girls enjoy not only equivalent but absolutely equal school training, is that their further education shall go on parallel. We have seen the peculiar position of the American college; how it is almost incomparable with any German institution, being a sort of intermediate member between the high school and true university — the scene of a four-year intellectual activity, resembling in some respects the German school, and in others the German university. We have seen how the college removes the young man from the parental influences from his eighteenth to twenty-second years, and places him in a new, small, and academic world of special ideals which is centred around some beautiful college yard. We have seen how two things happen in these years; on the one hand, he is prepared for his future occupation, especially if he is to enter a professional faculty of the university, and on the other he receives a broad, humanitarian training. We have seen also that these hundreds of colleges form a scale of very small gradations, whose different steps are adapted to the different social needs of various sections of the country; that the better colleges are like a German Prima, with three or four semesters in the philosophical faculty of a university, and that the inferior colleges hardly reach the level of the Unterprima. In such an institution, we have found the source of the best that is in American intellectual life. Now this institution opens wide its doors to women.

Here, in truth, co-education is less prominent. The conservative tendency of Eastern colleges has worked against the admission of women into the better of them, and the advantages of colleges for none but women are so well attested that the East at least will hardly make a change, although the Middle and Western States look on it virtually as a sin against inborn human rights, to establish colleges for anything but the education of both sexes alike. It was easier to oppose mixed education in the college sphere than in the school, because the common elementary training was needed at the outset for both sexes, while the demand for college training for women came up much later, when the tradition of colleges for men was already well established. Harvard College was already two hundred years old when, for the first time, an American college as an experiment admitted women; this was Oberlin College in Ohio, which began the movement in 1833. The first women's college was established, three years later, in Georgia — a pioneer institution in the South.

But progress was slow. It was not until 1862 that the government gave ten million acres of land for educational institutions; and then higher institutions became much more numerous, especially in the West, and from that time it was agreed that women should have equal privileges with men in these new colleges. Since then co-education in college and university has grown to be more and more the rule, except in the East. All state colleges and universities are open to women, and also the endowed universities — Brown, Chicago, Cornell, Leland Stanford, and the University of Pennsylvania; some few others, as Yale, Columbia, and Johns Hopkins, allow women to attend the graduate schools or the professional faculties, but not the college. Statistics for all the colleges in the country show that, in the year 1880, only 51 per cent. were co-educational; in 1890 there were 65 per cent., and in 1900, 72 per cent. Practically, however, the most significant form of female college education is not the co-educational, but one which creates a special college paradise for young women, where there are no male beguilements and distractions.

There are six principal institutions which have taken the lead in making the college life of women the significant thing that it now is. Vassar College was the first, established on the Hudson River in 1861; then came Wellesley College, near Boston; Bryn Mawr, near Philadelphia; Smith College, in Northampton; Radcliffe College, in Cambridge; Barnard, in New York. There is a large number of similar institutions, as Holyoke, Baltimore, and others in ever-diminishing series down to institutions which are hardly distinguishable from girls' high schools. The number of girls attending strictly women's colleges in the whole country, in 1900, was 23,900; while in mixed colleges and in the collegiate departments of universities there were 19,200 women students — just a quarter of the total number of college students. It is notable here that the students in women's colleges since 1890 have increased by 700, and in mixed colleges by 9,000. It may be mentioned, in passing, that there are 35,000 women students in normal schools.

The instruction in women's colleges is mostly by women, who number 1,744 — that is, about 71 per cent. of the instructors — while in mixed colleges the 857 women are only 10 per cent. of the teaching staff. In the leading co-educational universities, like Chicago, Ann Arbor, Leland Stanford, Berkeley, and others, the women are almost wholly taught by men. The leading women's colleges pursue different policies. Wellesley has almost exclusively women; Bryn Mawr, Vassar, and Smith have both; Radcliffe and Barnard are peculiar, in that by their by-laws Radcliffe is taught only by Harvard instructors, and Barnard only by instructors in Columbia University. This identification with the teaching staffs of Harvard and Columbia assures these two women's colleges an especially high intellectual level. And the same thing is accomplished, of course, for women by their being admitted to full privileges in Chicago, Stanford, and in the large state universities, such as Ann Arbor. But one can realize the whole charm and poetry of women's colleges only on a visit to the quiet groves of Wellesley, Bryn Mawr, Vassar, or Smith.

In broad, handsomely kept parks there lie scattered about attractive villas, monumental halls of instruction, club-houses and laboratories; and here some thousand girls, seldom younger than eighteen nor older than twenty-five, spend four happy years at work and play, apart from all worldly cares. They row, play tennis and basket-ball, and go through gymnastic exercises; and, as a result, every girl leaves college fresher, healthier, and stronger than when she entered it. And the type of pale, over-worked neurasthenic is unknown. These girls have their own ambitions in this miniature world — their positions of honour, their meetings, their clubs and social sets; in which, however, only personality, talent, and temperament count, while wealth or parental influence does not come in question. The life is happy; there are dancing, theatrical performances, and innumerable other diversions from the opening celebration in the fall to the festivities in June, when the academic year closes. And the life is also earnest. There is no day without its hours of conscientious labour in the lecture hall, the library or study, whether this is in preparation for later teaching, for professional life or, as is more often the case, solely for the harmonious development of all the student's faculties. One who looks on these fresh young girls in their light costumes, the venerable English mitre-caps on their heads, sitting in the alcoves of the library or playing in the open air, or in their formal debates, in the seminary or in the festive procession on class-day, — sees that here is a source of the purest and subtlest idealism going out into American life.

On such a foundation rests the professional training of the real university. Since the girl students in all the colleges of the country outdo the men in their studies, win the highest prizes, and attend the most difficult lectures, the old slander about deficient brain substance and mental incapacity can no longer serve as a pretext for closing the university to competing womanhood. In fact, the graduate schools, which correspond to the advanced portion of a German philosophical faculty, and the legal and medical faculties of all state universities and of a few private universities are open to women. But one is not to suppose that the number of women who are thus preparing for the learned professions, as that of medicine, law, or the ministry, is very large. There are to-day 44,000 women college students, but only 1,253 women graduate students; and in 1890 there were only 369. There are hardly more than a thousand in the purely professional faculties, and these form only 3 per cent. of the total number of students. The American women study mostly in colleges, therefore, and their aim is generally to get a well-grounded, liberal education, corresponding to a Gymnasium training, together with a few semesters in the philosophical faculty. But there are no limitations by principle; woman as such is denied no "rights," and the verdict is unanimous that this national experiment is technically successful. There is no indication of moral deterioration, of a lowered level of instruction, or of a mutual hindrance between men and women in the matter of study. The university, in short, opens the way to the learned professions.

When a European hears of the independent careers of American women, he is apt to imagine something which is unknown to him — a woman in the judicial wig or the minister's robe; a woman doctor or university professor. Thus he represents to himself the self-supporting women, and he easily forgets that their number is vanishingly small beside the masses of those who earn their living with very much less preparation. The professional life of the American woman, her instinct to support herself, and so to make herself equal to the man in the social and economic worlds, cannot be understood merely from figures; for statistics would show a much larger percentage of women in other countries who earn their living, where the instinct for independence is very much less. The motive is the main point. One might say that the European woman works because the land is too poor to support the family by the labour of the man alone. The American woman works because she wants her own career. In travelling through Europe, one notices women toiling painfully in the fields; this is not necessary in America, unless among the negroes. Passing through New England, one sees a hammock in front of every farm-house, and often catches the sound of a piano; the wives and daughters have never thought of working in the fields. But women crowd into all occupations in the cities, in order to have an independent existence and to make themselves useful. They would rather work in a factory or teach than to stay on the farm and spend their time at house-work or embroidery.

As a matter of course, very many families are actually in need, and innumerable motives may lead a woman to the earning of a living. But if one compares the changes in the statistics of different employments, and looks into the psychology of the different kinds of occupation, one sees clearly that the spirit of self-determination is the decisive factor, and that women compete most strongly in the professions which involve some rational interest, and that they know where it pays to crowd the men out. There is no male profession. outside of the soldiery and the fire department, into which women have not felt themselves called. Between the Atlantic and Pacific oceans there are 45 female locomotive engineers, 31 elevator attendants, 167 masons, 5 pilots, 196 blacksmiths, 625 coal miners, 3 auctioneers, and 1,320 professional huntresses.

Apart from such curiosities, and looking at only the large groups, we shall discover the following professional activity of women: In 1900, when the last census was made, there were 23,754,000 men and 5,319,000 women at paid employment — that is, only 18 per cent. of the bread-winners were women. Of these, only 971,000 were engaged in agriculture as against 9,404,000 men, while in the so-called professions, the intellectual occupations, there were 430,000 women against 828,000 men. In domestic positions, there were

2,095,000 women against 3,485,000 men; in trade there were 503,-000 against 4,263,000, and in manufactures 1,313,000 against 5,772,000. The total number of wage-earning women has steadily increased. In 1890 it amounted to only 17 per cent., and in 1880 to only 15 per cent. The proportions in different parts of the country are different, and not only according to the local forms of industry, but also to the different stages of civilization; the more advanced the civilization, the more the women go into intellectual employments. Among a hundred wage-earning women, for instance, in the North Atlantic States, there are only 1.9 per cent. engaged in agriculture, but 7.6 per cent. in intellectual occupations, 37.5 per cent. engaged in domestic service, 12.9 per cent. in trade, and 40.1 per cent. in manufactures. In the Southern Middle States, on the other hand, out of a hundred women only 7.2 per cent. are in manufactures, 2.6 per cent. in trade, and 4.4 per cent in intellectual professions.

Of these occupations, the most interesting are the intellectual, domestic, and trading activities of women. The great majority in intellectual employments are teachers; the whole story of American culture is told by the fact that there are 327,000 women pedagogues — an increase of 80,000 in ten years — and only 111,-000 male teachers. The number of physicians has increased from 4,557 in 1890 to 7,399 in 1900; but this is not ominous in comparison with their 124,000 male colleagues. There are 52,000 musicians and music teachers, 11,000 teachers in drawing, 5,984 authors — a figure which has doubled since 1890; and in the newspaper world the troup of women reporters and journalists has grown in ten years from 888 to 2,193. There are 8,000 women officials employed by the state, over 1,000 architects produce feminine architecture, and 3,405 ministers preach the gospel.

Turning to domestic activity, we find of course the international corps of house-servants to include the greater part; they number 1,283,000, and the statistics do not say whether, perhaps, one or two of these who have a white skin were born in the country. This number was 1,216,000 in 1890, so that it has increased only 5.5 per cent.; while during the same time population has increased 20.7 per cent., and the increasing wealth has greatly raised the demand for service. Let us compare with this the increased number of trained nurses, whose occupation is an arduous but independent and in itself useful career. The number of trained nurses has increased from 41,000 to 108,000 — that is, by 163 per cent. The figures for all such domestic employments as admit of social independence have also increased. The female restaurant keepers have increased from 86,000 to 147,000; the boarding-house proprietresses number 59,455, double the figure of ten years ago. The independent profession of washer-woman attracts 325,-000, while there are only 124,000 independent domestic labourers as compared with 2,454,000 men in the same occupations. The increase in the figures for such free professions as are classed under trade and commerce is in part even more striking. The number of female insurance agents, which in 1890 was less than 5,000, is now more than 10,000; book-keepers have increased from 27,000 to 74,000; sales-women, from 58,000 to 149,000; typists and stenographers from 21,000 to 86,000 — that is, fourfold — and there are now 22,000 telephone and telegraph operators. The number of shop-keepers at 34,000 has not increased much, and is relatively small beside the 756,000 men. There are only 261 women wholesale merchants against 42,000 men, 946 women commercial travellers against 91,000 men; the profession of lady banker has decreased shamefully from 510 to 293, although this is no ground for despairing of the future of American banking, since the number of bankers other than women has increased in the same time from 35,000 to 72,000.

Finally, let us look at industry and manufactures. The number of seamstresses has been the same for ten years with mathematical exactitude; that is, 146,000. Since the population has increased by one-fifth, it is clear that this form of work has been unpopular, doubtless because it involves personal abasement and exposure to the arbitrariness of customers, and is therefore unfavourable to self-assertion. At the same time the workers in woollen and cotton factories have increased from 92,000 to 120,-000, in silk factories from 20,000 to 32,000, and in cigar factories from 27,000 to 43,000. There are 344,000 garment-workers, 86,000 milliners, 15,000 book-binders, 16,000 printers, 17,000 box-makers, and 39,000 in the shoe industry. The whole picture shows a body of women whose labour is hardly necessary to support the families of the nation, but who are firmly resolved to assert themselves in economic and intellectual competition, who press their way into all sorts of occupations, but avoid as far as possible anything which restricts their personal independence, and seek out any occupation which augments their personality and their consciousness of independence. If all women who were not born on American soil, or if so were born of coloured parentage, were omitted from these statistics, then the self-asserting quality of American women who earn their living would come out incomparably more clearly.

The bread-winning activity of women is, however, only a fraction of their activity outside of the home. If of the 39,000,000 men in the country, 23,754,000 have an occupation, and of the 37,000,000 women only 5,319,000 work for a living, it is clear that the great majority of grown-up women earn nothing. But nobody who knows American life would take these women who earn no wages from the list of those who exert a great influence outside of the family circle, and assert themselves in the social organization. Between the two broad oceans there is hardly any significant movement outside of trade and politics which is not aided by unpaid women, who work purely out of ideal motives. Vanity, ambition, self-importance, love of diversion, and social aspirations of all kinds, of course, play a part; but the actual labour which women perform in the interests of the church or school, of public welfare, social reform, music, art, popular education, care of the sick, beautification and sanitation of cities, every day and everywhere, represents incontestably a powerful in-born idealism.

Only one motive more, which is by no means unidealistic, dictates this purely practical devotion; it is the motive of helping on this very self-assertion of women. Work is done for the sake of work, but more or less in the consciousness that one is a woman and that whatever good one does, raises the position of the sex. Thus, in women's clubs and organizations, through noisy agitation or quieter feminine influences, the American woman's spirit of self-assertion impresses itself in a hundred thousand ways. Women are the majority in every public lecture and in every broadly benevolent undertaking; schools and churches, the care of the poor and the ill are enlivened by their zeal, and in this respect the East and the West feel quite alike. Certainly this influence beyond the home does not end with direct self-conscious labour; it goes on where there are no women presidents, secretaries, treasurers, and committee members, but wherever women go for enjoyment and relaxation. Women form a large majority in art exhibitions, concerts, theatres, and in church services; women decide the fate of every new novel; and everywhere women stand in the foreground, wide awake and self-assertive.

It is incredible to the European how very much the unselfish and high-minded women of America are able to accomplish, and how so many of them can combine a vast deal of practical work with living in the midst of bustling social affairs, and themselves entertaining perhaps in a brilliant way. Such a woman will go early in the morning to the committee meeting of her club, inspect a school or poor-house on the way, then help to draw up by-laws for a society, deliver an address, preside at some other meeting, and meet high officials in the interests of some public work. She expends her energy for every new movement, keeps in touch with every new tendency in art and literature, and is yet a pleasant and comfortable mother in her own home. This youthful freshness never succumbs to age. In Boston, the widow of the zoölogist Agassiz, although now eighty years of age, is still tirelessly active as honourary president of Radcliffe College; and Julia Ward Howe, the well-known poetess, in spite of her eighty-four years, presides at every meeting of the Boston Authors' Club, still with her quiet but fresh and delightful humour.

The leadership of women which is a problem to be discussed, as far as public life is concerned, is an absolute dogma which it would be sacrilege to call in question, so far as social and domestic life go. Just as Lincoln said that the American government is a government "of the people, by the people, and for the people," so certainly American society is a government of the women, by the women, and for the women. The part which the wife plays determines so unconditionally the social status of every home, that even a man who has his own social ambitions can accomplish his end in no better way than by doing everything to further the plans and even the whims of his wife. And the luxury in which she is maintained is so entirely a symbol of social position that the man comes instinctively to believe that he is himself enjoying society when he worries and over-works in order to provide jewelry and funds for the elaborate entertainments of his wife.

Just as the wife of the millionaire has her place arranged to suit herself, so the modest townswoman does in her small home, and so also the wife of the day labourer, in her still narrower surroundings. The man pushes the baby carriage, builds the kitchen fire, and takes care of the furnace, so that his wife can attend to getting fashionable clothing; he denies himself cigars in order to send her into the country for the summer. And she takes this as a matter of course. She has seen this done from her childhood by all men, and she would be offended if her husband were to do anything less. The American woman's spirit of self-assertion would be aroused directly if social equality were to be interpreted in such a ridiculous way as to make the man anything but the social inferior.

The outward noise would make one believe that the self-assertion of the feminine soul were most energetically concerned with political rights; woman's suffrage is the great watchword. But the general noise is deceptive; the demands for equal school and college education for young women, for admission to industrial positions on the same footing with men, for an independent existence and life career for every woman who wants it, and for social domination — all these are impulses which really pervade the national consciousness. But the demand for equal suffrage is not nearly so universal. In the nature of things, it is often put forth by radical lecturers on woman's rights; and it is natural that some large societies support the efforts, and that even masculine logic should offer no objections in many cases. The familiar arguments known to all the world have hardly been augmented by a single new reason on the woman's side. But the old arguments appear on the surface to be such sound deductions from all the fundamental political, social, and economic principles of America that they come here to have new force. If in spite of this their practical success is still exceedingly small, and the most energetic opposition is not from the stronger sex but from the women themselves, it shows clearly that there is some strong opposing impulse in the American public mind. The social self-assertion of women, in which every American believes with all his heart, is just as little likely ever to lead to universal political suffrage for women as American industrial self-assertion will ever lead to socialism.

But the irony of world history has brought it about that women began with just those rights which to-day some of them are demanding. When English law was brought across the ocean by the colonists in the seventeenth century, the women had the constitutional right to vote, and in exceptional cases made use of it; not one of the constitutions of the thirteen states limited the suffrage to men. The State of New York was the first to improve or to injure its constitution by adding the qualification "male," in the year 1778. One state followed after another, and New Jersey was the last, in 1844. But just as the last door was closed, the hue and cry was raised that they all ought to be opened. The first woman's convention to make an urgent appeal for the restoring of these rights was held in New York in 1848. There was a violent opposition; but the movement extended to a great many states, and finally, in 1866, a national organization was formed which asked for a national law. This was just after the Civil War, when the amendment giving the suffrage to the negroes was the chief subject of political discussion. A petition with eighty thousand signatures was gotten up urging that the Constitution should be interpreted so as to give women the right to vote. Two women brought legal action, which went up through all the courts to the Supreme Court, but was there decided against the women, and therefore the sex has not the suffrage.

No national movements have, therefore, to-day any practical significance unless three-quarters of all state legislatures can be induced to vote for an amendment to the Constitution in favour of woman's suffrage — that is, to vote that no state be allowed to exclude women from the ballot. This is hardly more likely to happen than a Constitutional amendment to introduce hereditary monarchy. Meanwhile, the agitation in the various states has by no means entirely stopped. Time after time attempts have been made to alter the constitution of a single state, but unsuccessfully. The only states to introduce complete woman's suffrage have been Wyoming in 1869, Colorado in 1893, and Utah in 1895. Kansas allows women to vote in municipal elections. The agitation has been really successful in only one direction; it has succeeded in getting from a majority of the states the right to vote for the local school committees.

Such experience as the country has had with woman's suffrage has not been specially favourable to the movement. A good deal goes to show that, even if full privileges were granted, they would remain a dead letter for the overwhelming majority of women. The average woman does not wish to go into politics. It has been affirmed that in the modern way of living, with servants to do all the house-work, factories to do the spinning and weaving and every sort of economic convenience, the married woman has too little to do, and needs the political field in which to give her energies free play. But so long as statistics show that four-fifths of the married women in the country do all their house-work, and so long as such a great variety of ethical, intellectual, æsthetic and social duties lie before every woman, it is no wonder that very few are eager to take on new responsibilities at the ballot-box. Those, however, who would make most use of the suffrage would be, as the women who oppose the movement say, the worst female element of the large cities, and they would bring in all the worst evils of a low class of voters led by demagogues. Political corruption at the ballot would receive a new and specially dangerous impetus; the political machines would win new and disgusting strength from the feebleness of these women to resist political pressure, and instead of women's ennobling and refining political ethics, as their partisans hope, they would be more apt to drag politics down to the very depths. Those who oppose the movement see a decided prejudice to political soundness even in the mere numerical doubling of the voting class.

Most of all, the conservative element can assert, with an excellent array of facts, that the healthy progress of woman's self-assertion best proceeds by keeping away from politics and turning directly toward the improvement of the conditions of living and of instruction, toward the opening up of professions, the framing of industrial laws, and other reforms. The radical political demands of women in all other fields, and most especially in the socialistic direction, inclining as they naturally do to be extreme, have worked rather to hinder than to aid the social progress of women. Even where the social independence of women is properly contested, there works the deterring consideration that politics might bring about differences between husband and wife. Taken all in all, the self-assertion of women in political matters is hardly a practical question. One who looks into their tracts and propaganda feels for a long while that the last one he has read, on which ever side it is, is wrong; but when he has come to a point where he meets only the old arguments revamped, he feels that on the whole the radical side has still less justice than the other. And the nation has come to the same conclusion. We may thus leave politics quite out of account in turning finally to the main question which relates to women; this is, How has this remarkable self-assertion of woman affected the life of the nation, both on the whole and in special spheres?

Let us look first at the sphere of the family. The situation here is often decidedly misinterpreted; the frequent divorces in America are cited very often in order to put American family life in an unfavourable light. According to the census report of 1900, the ratio of divorced to married men was 0.6 per cent., and of women 0.8 per cent.; while in 1890 the respective figures were only 0.4 per cent. and 0.6 per cent. Nevertheless, the total number of divorced persons is only 0.3 per cent. of the whole population, as compared with 5.1 per cent. who are widows, 36.5 per cent. who are married, and 57.9 per cent. of bachelors — with a small remainder unaccounted for. It is true that divorced persons who have re-married are here included among the married persons; but even if the number of dissolved marriages is somewhat greater than it appears in the statistics, that fact shows nothing as to the moral status of marriage in America.

Anybody familiar with the country knows that, much more often than in Europe, the real grounds which lead to divorce — not the mere legal pretexts given — are highly ethical ones. We have hinted at this when we analyzed the religious life; the main reason is the ethical objection to continuing externally in a marriage which has ceased to be spiritually congenial. It is the women especially, and generally the very best women, who prefer to take the step, with all the hardships which it involves, to prolonging a marriage which is spiritually hypocritical and immoral. Infidelity of the woman is the ground of divorce in only a vanishingly small number of cases, and the sexual purity of marriage is on a high plane throughout the people. The pure atmosphere of this somewhat unemotional people, which makes it possible for any woman to wend her way without escort through the streets of a large city in the evening and to travel alone across the Continent, and which protects the girl on the street from being stared at or rudely accosted, protects even more the married woman. Although French society dramas are presented on the American stage, one feels from the general attitude of the public that it really fails to understand the psychology of what is being performed, because all the ethical presuppositions are so entirely different. What the Parisian finds piquant, the New Englander finds shameless; and the woman over whom the Frenchman smiles disgusts the American.

And in still another sense American marriage is purer than the European; it lacks the commercial element. As characteristic as this fact is in economic life, it is even more significant in social life. This does not mean that the man who pays court to the daughter of a millionaire is entirely unconscious of the economic advantages which such a marriage would bring. But the systematic searching around for a dowry, with some woman attached to it, is unknown in the New World, and is thoroughly un-American. This may be seen in American plays; the familiar German comediès, in which the search for a rich bride is a favourite motive, strike the American public as entirely vapid and humourless. Americans either do not understand or else look down with pity on the marital depravity of the Old World, and such stage scenes are as intrinsically foreign as those others, so familiar to Europe, in which the rich young nobleman who after all marries the poor governess, is held up as a remarkable example of magnanimity.

The purely human elements are the only ones which count in marriage. It is a congenial affiliation of two persons, without regard to social advantage or disadvantage, if only the persons care for each other. And this idea is common to the whole nation, and gives marriage a high moral status. Moreover, the surpassing education of the young American woman, her college life, works in one way to exalt marriage. If she has learned anything in her college atmosphere, it is moral seriousness. She has gone there to face duties squarely and energetically, to account small things small, and large things large; and so, when she approaches the new duty of making a home, she overcomes all obstacles there with profound moral determination.

In spite of this, one may ask, Is her development in the right direction for subsequent events? While so much has contributed to the exaltation and purity of her marriage, has she not learned a great deal else which tends rather indirectly and perhaps unnoticeably to disorganize marriage, the home, the family, and the people? Is the increasing social self-assertion of woman really in the interests of culture? Let us picture to ourselves the contrast, say with Germany. There too the interests in the social advance of women is lively on all sides; but the situation is wholly different. Four main tendencies may be easily picked out. One relates to a very small number of exceptional women who have shown great talent or perhaps real genius. Such women are to be emancipated and to have their own life career. But the few who are called to do great things in art or science or otherwise, are not very apt to wait for others to emancipate them, and the number of these women is so small that this movement has hardly any social or economic importance in comparison with the other three which concern large numbers of women.

Of these other three, the first concerns the women of the lower classes, who throughout Germany are so poor that they have to earn a livelihood, and are in danger of sacrificing their family life. The lever is applied to improve their social condition, to put legal limits to the labour of women, and to protect them, so that the poor man's wife shall have more opportunities in the family. Another movement is to benefit the daughters of more well-to-do people, to give them when they marry, a more intellectual career, to elevate the wife through a broader education above the pettiness of purely domestic interests and the superficiality of ordinary social life, and so to make her the true comrade of her husband. And the last movement concerns those millions of women who cannot marry because women are not only the more numerous, but also because one-tenth of German men will not marry. They are urged to replace the advantages which they would have in marriage by a life occupation; and although women of the lower classes have had enough opportunity to work, those of the upper classes have until recently been excluded from any such blessing. A great deal has been done here to improve the situation and partly in direct imitation of the American example.

But the real background of all these movements in Germany has been the conviction that marriage is the natural destiny of woman. The aim has been to improve marriage in the lower classes by relieving the woman of degrading labour, in upper classes by giving the woman a superior education; and the other two movements are merely expedients to supply some sort of substitute for life's profoundest blessing, which is found only in marriage. There is no such background in America; there is a desire to protect American marriage, but it is not presupposed that marriage is, in and of itself, the highest good for woman. The completion of woman's destiny lies rather in giving to her as to the man an intrinsically high life content whether she is married or not married; it is a question of her individual existence, as of his. Marriage is thus not the centre, and an independent career is in no sense a compensation or a makeshift; even the betterment of marriage is only intended as a means of bettering the individual. Woman is on exactly the same footing as man. The fundamental German principle that woman's destiny is found in marriage, while the man is married only incidentally, involves at once the inequality of the sexes; and this fundamental inequality is only slightly lessened by these four new German movements. It is a secondary consequence that the woman is growing to be more nearly like the man. But according to the American point of view, her fundamental equality is the foundation principle; both alike aim to expand their individual personalities, to have their own valuable life content, and by marriage to benefit each other. And only secondarily, after marriage is accomplished, does the consequence appear that necessarily the woman has her special duties and her corresponding special rights; and then the principle of equality between the two finds its limitations. Now when this takes place, the self-assertion of the American woman is found to be not wholly favourable to the institution of marriage; it gives the married woman a more interesting life content, but it inclines the unmarried woman much less toward marriage; it robs society of that great support of marriage — the feeling that it is woman's destiny.

Here, again, the most diverse factors work together. The social freedom of communication between men and women, the secure propriety of associating with men, and the independent freedom to go about which is peculiar to the American girl's education give to the unmarried girl all those rights and advantages which in Europe she does not have until she is married. The American girl has really nothing but duties to face, domestic cares and perhaps quite unaccustomed burdens, in case she marries a man in limited circumstances; externally she has nothing to gain, and internally she is little disturbed by any great passion. She flirts from her youth up, and is the incomparable mistress of this little social art; but the moving passion is apt to be neglected, and one may question whether all her mischievous roguery and graceful coquetry are anything more than a social accomplishment, like dancing or skating or playing golf — whether it in any way touches the heart. It is a diversion, and not a true life content.

Then, too, the girl has a feeling of intellectual superiority which for the most part is entirely justified. The European girl has been brought up to believe in the superiority of the man, accustomed to feel that her own gifts are incomplete, that they come to have real value only in conjunction with a man, and her inferior scientific training suggests to her unconsciously that she will be intellectually exalted when she allies herself to some man. That will fill out her intellectual personality. The American girl has hardly ever such an idea; she has learned in the school-room how foolish boys are, how lazy and careless, and then, too, she has continued her own education it may be years after the men of her acquaintance have gone into practical life. Many high schools have one-third of their pupils boys and two-thirds girls, and the ratio grows in favour of the girls. Moreover, everything tends to give the girl her own aspirations and plans independent of any man — aspirations which are not essentially furthered or completed by her marriage alliance. American women often laugh at the way in which German women introduce abstract questions at the Kaffeeklatsch: "Now my husband says—." The intellectual personality of the American girl must develop so much the more independently of male influence as the distinction which commences in school years is even more actual in the years of maturity. The older the American man grows the more he concentrates himself on business or politics, while his wife in a certain way continues her schooling, devotes her entire time to every sort of intellectual stimulation; the wife reads books, while the husband reads newspapers. It is undeniable that in the average American home the woman makes the profounder intellectual impression on every visitor, and the number of women is continually growing who instinctively feel that there is no advantage in marrying a man who is intellectually an inferior; they would rather remain single than contract a marriage in which they have to be the intellectual head.

While, therefore, there are neither novel social advantages nor any emotional urgency, nor yet intellectual inducements, to persuade women to marry, there are other circumstances which urge her strongly not to do so. In the first place, marriage may interfere directly with the life career which she has planned for herself. A woman who has taken an occupation to save herself from misery looks on marriage with a man who earns enough to support a family as a sort of salvation; while the woman who has chosen some calling because her life means so much more if it is useful to the world, who is earnestly devoted to her work, truly ambitious and thoroughly competent, ponders a long time before she goes into a marriage which necessarily puts an end to all this. She may well prefer to sacrifice some sentimental inclination to the profound interest she feels in her work.

The American girl is, moreover, not fond of domestic cares. It would not be fair to say that she is a bad house-keeper, for the number of wives who have to get along without servants is much greater than in Germany. And even in spite of the various economic advantages which she enjoys, it is undeniable that the American woman takes her home duties seriously, looks after every detail, and keeps the whole matter well in hand. But nevertheless, she feels very differently toward her capacities along this line. The German woman feels that her household is a source of joy; the American woman, that it is a necessary evil. The American woman loves to adorn her home and tries to express in it her own personality, not less than her German sister; but everything beyond this — the mere technique of house-keeping, cleaning, purchasing, repairing, and hiring servants — she feels to be, after all, somewhat degrading. The young woman who has been to college attacks her household duties seriously and conscientiously, but with the feeling that she would rather sacrifice herself by nursing the suffering patients in a hospital. The perfect economic appliances for American house-keeping save a great deal of labour which the German wife has to perform, and perhaps just on that account the American woman feels that the rest of it is vexatious work which women have to do until some new machines can be devised to take their places. This disinclination to household drudgery pervades the whole nation, and it is only the older generations in country districts that take a pride in their immaculate house-keeping, while the younger generations even there have the tendency to shirk household work. The daughters of farmers would rather work in a factory, because it is so much more stimulating and lively, than ironing or washing dishes or tending baby brother and sister at home; for the same reason, they will not become domestic servants for any one else. And so, for the upper and the lower classes, the disinclination to house-work stands very much in the way of marriage.

This disinclination affects marriage in still another way. Families are tending more and more to give up separate houses and live in family hotels, or, if more modestly circumstanced, in boarding-houses. The expense of servants has something to do with this, but the more important factor is the saving of work for the wife. The necessary consequence is the dissolution of intimate family life. When a dozen families eat year in and year out in the same dining-room, the close relations which should prevail in the family take on a very different shading. And thus it is that the intellectual self-assertion of women works, in the most diverse ways, against the formation of marriages and against family life. There is one argument, however, which is always urged by the opponents of woman's emancipation which is not valid—at least, not for America. It is the blue-stocking bugbear. This unattractive type of woman is not produced by higher education in America. Many a young American girl, who has arrived at years of personal independence during her college life, may have lost her interest in the average sort of marriage; but she has by no means lost the attraction she exerts on men.

The tendency of woman's self-assertion against marriage appears to go even further; the exaggerated expression, "race suicide," has sometimes been used. It is true that the increase of native population, especially in the more civilized parts of the country, is ominously small; this is probably the result of diverse factors. There are physicians, for instance, who claim that the intellectual training of women and the nervous excitement incident to their independent, self-reliant attitude are among the main causes; but more important, others say, are the voluntary precautions which are dictated by the desire of ease and comfort. This last is a serious factor, and there lies behind it again the spirit of self-assertion; the woman wants to live out her own life, and her individualistic instinct works against the large family. But there is nothing here which threatens the whole nation; since, even aside from the very large immigration which introduces healthy, prolific, and sturdy elements, the births of the whole country exceed those of almost any of the European nations. In Germany, between 1890 and 1900, for every thousand inhabitants the births numbered annually 36.2 and the deaths 22.5 — so that there were 13.7 more births; in England the births were 30.1 and deaths 18.4, with a difference of 11.7; in the United States the births were 35.1 and deaths 17.4, with a difference of 17.7 more births.

Of course, these figures would make all anxiety seem ridiculous, if the proportions were equally distributed over the country, and through all the elements of the population. As a matter of fact, however, there are the greatest differences. In Massachusetts, for instance, we may distinguish three classes of population; those white persons whose parents were born in the country, and those whose parents were foreigners, and the blacks. This negro population of Massachusetts has the same birth and death rate as the negro elsewhere; for every thousand persons there are 17.4 more births than deaths. For the second class — that is, the families of foreign parentage – there are actually 45.6 more births than deaths; while in the white families of native parentage there are only 3.8. In some other North Atlantic States, the condition is still worse; in New Hampshire, for instance, the excess of births in families of foreign parentage is 58.5, while in those of native parentage the situation is actually reversed, and there are 10.4 more deaths than births. So it happens that for all the New England States, the native white population, in the narrower sense, has a death preponderance of 1.5 for every thousand inhabitants; so that, in the intellectually superior part of the country, the strictly native population is not maintaining itself.

Interesting statistics recently gathered at Harvard University show that its graduates are also not holding their own. Out of 881 students who were graduated more than twenty-five years ago, 634 are married, and they have 1,262 children. On the probable assumption that they will have no more children, and that these are half males, we find that 881 student graduates in 1877 leave in 1902 only 631 sons. The climatic conditions cannot be blamed for this, since the surplus of births in families born of foreign parents is not only very great, but is far greater than in any of the European countries from which these immigrant parents came. Of European countries, Hungary has the greatest excess of births — namely, 40.5, as compared with 13.7 in Germany. That population of America which comes from German, Irish, Swedish, French, and Italian parentage has, even in New England, a birth surplus of 44.5. The general conditions of the country seem, therefore, favourable to fecundity, and this casts a greater suspicion on social conditions and ideals. And the circumstance must not be overlooked, that the increased pressure of women into wage-earning occupations lessens the opportunities of the men, and so contributes indirectly to prevent the man from starting his home early in life. In short, from whatever side we look at it, the self-assertion of woman exalts her at the expense of the family — perfects the individual, but injures society; makes the American woman perhaps the finest flower of civilization, but awakens at the same time serious fears for the propagation of the American race.

There are threatening clouds in other quarters of the horizon. The much-discussed retroactive effect of feminine emancipation on the family should not distract attention from its effect on culture as a whole. Here the dissimilarity to the German conditions is obvious. The German woman's movement aims to give the woman a most significant rôle in general matters of culture, but still does not doubt, as a matter of course, that the general trend of culture will be determined by the men. Just as it is a dogmatic presupposition in Germany that marriage is the most desirable occupation for women, so it is tacitly presupposed that intellectual culture will take its actual stamp from the men. In America not only this view of marriage, but even this view of culture, has been opposed for a long time; and the people behave as if both were antiquated and superstitious notions, devised by the stronger sex for its own convenience, and as if their reversal would benefit the entire race.

Anybody who looks the matter squarely in the face is not left to doubt that everything in America is tending not only to sacrifice the superiority of man and to give the woman an equal position, but to reverse the old situation and make her very much the superior. In business, law, and politics, the American man is still sovereign, and in spite of the many women who press into the mercantile professions he is still in a position where he serves rather than directs. And it is very characteristic of the moral purity of the people that, in spite of the incomparable social power of women, they have not a trace of personal influence on important political events. On the other hand, they dictate in matters of education, religion, literature and art, social problems, and public morals. Painting, music, and the theatre cater to woman, and for her the city is beautified and purified; although she does not do it herself, it is her taste and feeling which decide everything; she determines public opinion, and distributes all the rewards at her good pleasure. If the family problem is shown in a lurid light by the decrease of births in the native New England population, the problem of culture comes out into broad daylight only in those figures which we have seen before; the 327,614 women teachers and the 111,710 men.

Thus three-quarters of American education is administered by women; and even in the high school where the boys go till they are eighteen or nineteen years old, 57.7 per cent. of the teachers are women; and in those normal schools where both men and women go to fit themselves for teaching, 71.3 per cent. of the instructors are women. It appears, then, that the young men of the country, even in the years when boyhood ripens to youth, receive the larger part of their intellectual impetus from women teachers, and that all of those who are going to be school teachers and shape the young souls of the nation are in their turn predominantly under the influence of women. In colleges and universities this is still not the case, but soon will be if things are not changed; the great number of young women who pass their doctorial examinations and become specialists in science will have more and more to seek university professorships, or else they will have studied in vain. And here, as in the school, the economic conditions strongly favour the woman; since she has no family to support, she can accept a position on a salary so much smaller that the man is more and more crowded from the field. And it may be clearly foreseen that, if other social factors do not change, women will enter as competitors in every field where the labour does not require specifically masculine strength. So it has been in the factories; so it is in the schools; and so, in a few decades, it may be in the universities and in the churches.

Even although the professorial chairs still belong for the most part to men, the presence of numerous women in the auditorium cannot be wholly without influence on the routine of work. The lecturer is forced to notice, as is the speaker in any public gathering, that at least two-thirds of his hearers present the cheerful aspect of gay millinery and lace collar, so that intellectual culture and public opinion on non-political questions come more and more to be dominated by women—as many persons are beginning to see. Most of them greet this unique turn in human history as the peculiar advantage of this nation; the man looks after the industry and politics, and the woman after moral, religious, artistic, and intellectual matters. If there is any doubt that she is competent to do this, most Americans are satisfied to observe the earnestness and conscientiousness with which the American woman attends to her duties, at the zeal and success with which she applies herself to her studies, and at her victory over men wherever she competes.

Here and there, however, and their number is increasing every day, men are feeling that earnestness is not necessarily power, zeal is not mastery, and that success means little if the judgment is pronounced by those who are partial to the winners. The triumph in industrial competition is no honour if it consists in bidding under the market price. In fact, it is not merely a question of the division of labour, but a fundamental change in the character of the labour. An impartial observer of the achievements of American women as teachers or as university students, in professional life or social reform or any other public capacity, is forced to admire the performance, and even to recognize certain unique merits; but he has to admit that it is a special sort of work, and different from the achievements of men. The emancipation of the American woman and her higher education, although carried almost to the last extreme, give not the slightest indication even yet that woman is able to accomplish in the intellectual field the same that man accomplishes. What she does is not inferior, but it is entirely different; and the work which, in all other civilized countries, is done by men cannot in the United States be slipped into the hands of women without being profoundly altered in character.

The feminine mind has the tendency to unify all ideas, while a man rather separates independent classes. Each of these positions has advantages and drawbacks. The immediate products of the feminine temperament are tactfulness and æsthetic insight, sure instincts, enthusiasm, and purity; and, on the other hand, a lack of logical consecutiveness, a tendency to over-hasty generalization, under-estimation of the abstract and the deep, and an inclination to be governed by feeling and emotion. Even these weaknesses may be beautiful in domestic life and attractive in the social sphere; they soften the hard and bitter life of men. But women have not the force to perform those public duties of civilization which need the harder logic of man. If the entire culture of the nation is womanized, it will be in the end weak and without decisive influence on the progress of the world.

The intellectual high life in colleges and universities, which seems to speak more clearly for the intellectual equality of women, brings out exactly this difference. That which is accomplished by the best women's colleges is exemplary and admirable; but it is in a world which is, after all, a small artificial world, with all rough places smoothed over and illumined with a soft light instead of the hard daylight. Although in the mixed universities women often do better than men, it is not to be forgotten that the American lecture system, with its many examinations, puts a higher value on industry, attention, and good-will than on critical acumen or logical creativeness. It cannot be denied that, even a short time since, the American university cultivated in every department the spirit of learning rather than of investigation — was reproductive rather than productive — and that the more recent development which has laid the emphasis on productive investigation has gone on for the most part in the leading Eastern universities, such as Harvard, Johns Hopkins, Columbia, Yale, and Princeton, where women are still not admitted, while the Western universities, and most of all the state universities, which are found only in the West, where women are in a majority, belong in many respects to the old type. To be sure, there are several American women whose scientific work is admirable, and to be classed with the best professional achievements of the country; but they are still rare exceptions. The tendency to learn rather than to produce pervades all the great masses of women; they study with extraordinary zeal up to the point where critical production should begin, and there they are all too apt to stop. And unless one persistently looks at the very few exceptions, one would hardly assert that the true spirit of science could unfold and grow if American women were to be its only guardians.

This distinction is much plainer in the lower walks of life. The half-educated American man refrains from judging what is beyond his scope; but an American woman who has scarcely a shred of education looks in vain for any subject on which she has not firm convictions already at hand, and her influence upon public opinion — politics always apart — spins a web of triviality and misconception over the whole culture. Cobwebs are not ropes, and a good broom can sweep them down; but the arrogance of this feminine lack of knowledge is the symptom of a profound trait in the feminine soul, and points to dangers springing from the domination of women in intellectual life. In no other civilized land is scientific medicine so systematically hindered by quack doctors, patent medicines, and mental healing; the armies of uneducated women protect them. And in no other civilized land are ethical conceptions so worm-eaten by superstitions and spiritualistic hocus-pocus; hysterical women carry the day. In no other country is the steady and sound advance of social and pedagogical reform so checked by whimsies and short-lived innovations, and good sound work held back by the partisans of confused ideas; here the women work havoc with their social and pedagogical alarms.

This does not mean, however, that a good deal of the work of American women is not better done by them than it would be by the men. In the first place, there is no doubt that the assistance of women in teaching has had very happy results on American culture. When it was necessary to tame the wild West of its pioneer roughness and to introduce good manners, the milder influence of women in the school-room was far more useful than that of men could have been; and so far as it is a question of making over the immigrant children of the large cities into young Americans, the patient woman teacher is invaluable. And the drama of the school-room is played in other more public places; in a thousand ways the participation of women in public life has refined and toned down American culture and enriched and beautified it, but not made it profounder or stronger. Woman's inborn dilettanteism works too often for superficiality rather than profundity.

And it is indubitable that this undertaking of the burdens of intellectual culture by woman has been necessary to the nation's progress—a kind of division of labour imperatively indicated by the tremendous economic and political duties which have precocupied the men. No European country has ever had to accomplish economically, technically, and politically, in so short a time, that which the United States has accomplished in the last fifty years in perfecting its civilization. The strength of the men has been so thoroughly enlisted that intellectual culture could not have been developed or even maintained if the zeal and earnestness of women had not for a time taken up the work. But is this to be only for a time? Will the man bethink himself that his political and economic one-sidedness will in the end hurt the nation? This is one of the greatest questions for the future of this country. It is not a question of woman's retrograding or losing any of her splendid acquirements; no one could wish that this fine intellectuality, this womanly seriousness, this desire for a meaning in her life should be thoughtlessly sacrificed, nor that the sisters and the mothers of the nation should ever become mere dolls or domestic machines. Nothing of this should be lost or needs to be lost. But a compensatory movement must be undertaken by the men of the country in order to make up for amateurish superficiality and an inconsequential logic of the emotions.

In itself, the intellectual domination of the women will have the tendency to strengthen itself, the more the higher life bears the feminine stamp. For by so much, men are less attracted to it. Thus the number of male school teachers becomes smaller all the time, because the majority of women teachers makes the school more and more a place where a man does not feel at home. But other factors in public opinion work strongly in the opposite direction; industrial life has made its great strides, the land is opened up, the devastations of the Civil War are repaired, internal disturbances have yielded to internal unity, recognition among the world powers has been won, and within a short time the wealth of the country has increased many fold. It will be a natural reaction if the energies of men are somewhat withdrawn from industry and agriculture, from politics and war, and once more bestowed on things intellectual. The strength of this reaction will decide whether the self-assertion of the American women will, in the end, have been an unalloyed blessing to the country or an affliction. Woman will never contribute momentously to the culture of the world by remaining intellectually celibate.

CHAPTER TWENTY-THREE

Aristocratic Tendencies

IN the caricatures of the American which are so gladly drawn by the European, and so innocently believed in, there is generally, beside the shirt-sleeved clown who bawls "equality" and the barbarian who chases the dollar, the rich heiress bent on swapping her millions for a coronet. The longing for bankrupt suitors of undoubted pedigree is supposed to be the one symptom of any social aspiration, which the Yankee exhibits. The American begs leave to differ. He is not surprised that the young American woman of good family, with her fine intellectual freshness and her faculty of adaptation, should be sought out by men of all nations; nor is he filled with awe if there are some suitors of historic lineage among the rest. But the day is long gone in which such marriages are looked on as an enviable piece of good fortune for the daughter of any American citizen. Even the newspapers lightly smile at such marriages to a title, and they are becoming less and less frequent in the really best circles of American society. Besides, no such cheap and superficial aspirations are really indicative of aristocratic tendencies. The American is, by principle, very far from making his way into the international aristocracy of Europe, and he neither does nor will he ever attempt any artificial imitation of aristocratic institutions.

It is a capital mistake to suppose that the American, put face to face with European princedom, forgets or tries to hide his democracy. Aristocratic institutions, particularly those of England, interest him as a bit out of history; he seeks such social contact just as he wanders through quaint castles, without wishing thereby to transfer his own country house on the Hudson into a decaying group of walls and turrets. He takes an æsthetic pleasure in the brilliancy of courts, the pomp of military life, the wealth and colour of symbols; and, quite independently of that, he feels indeed a lively interest in certain fascinating figures of European politics — most of all, perhaps, in the German Kaiser. But whether his interest is historical, æsthetic, or personal, it is never accompanied by any feeling of inferiority to the persons who represent these aristocratic institutions. When Prince Henry, on his visit to the New World, quickly won the hearts of Americans as a man, there was nothing in the tone or accent of the greetings addressed to him which was out of accord with the fundamental key of democracy. The dinner speakers commenced their speeches in the democratic fashion, which is always first to address the presiding host: "Mr. Mayor, your Royal Highness."

At the same time the peculiarly democratic contempt for things monarchical is disappearing, too; the cultivated American feels increasingly that every form of state has arisen from historic conditions, and that one is not in and for itself better than another. He feels that he is not untrue to his republican fatherland in attesting his respect for crowned heads. He shows most of all his respect, because it is just the friendly, neighbourly intercourse which makes possible a relation of mutual recognition. Democracy is itself the gainer by giving up the absurd pose of looking down on aristocracy. Thus it happens that, of recent years, even native-born Americans have sometimes received European orders. They know well enough that it will not do to wear the button-hole decoration on American soil, but they feel it to be ungracious to decline what is offered in a friendly spirit; unless, indeed, it is a politician who wishes to accentuate and propagate a certain principle. Democracy feels sure enough of itself to be able to accept a courtesy which is offered, with equal courtesy; but nobody supposes, for a moment, that European monarchical decorations have any magic to exalt a man above his democratic equality. Indeed, the feeling of entire equality, and the belief in a mutual recognition of such equality, are almost the presupposition of modern times, and only in Irish mass-meetings do we still hear protests against European tyranny. This much is sure: America shows not the slightest tendency to become aristocratic by imitating the historic aristocracies of Europe.

There are many who seem to believe that, therefore, the only aristocracy of America consists in the clique of multi-millionaires which holds its court in Newport and Fifth Avenue. The whole country observes their follies and eccentricities; their family gatherings are described at length by the press, quite as any court ceremonies are described in European papers; and to be taken into this sacred circle is supposed to be the life ambition of industrious millionaires. Many Americans who are under the influence of the sensational press would probably agree with this; and, judging by outward symptoms, one might in fact suppose that these Crœsuses along the Cliff-walk at Newport were really the responsible social leaders of America. This must seem very contemptible to all who look on from a distance, for everything which the papers tell to the four winds of heaven about these people is an insult to real and sound American feeling. The fountains of perfumery, the dinners on horseback, the cotillons where the favours are sun-bursts of real gems — in short, the senseless throwing away of wealth in the mere interests of rivalry and without even any æsthetic compensations, cannot profoundly impress a nation of pioneers.

On looking more closely, one sees that the facts are not so bad, and that the penny-a-liners rather than the multi-millionaires are responsible for such sensational versions. In fact, in spite of many extravagances, there is a great deal of taste and refinement in those very circles; much good sense, an appreciation of true art, honest pleasure in sport, especially if it is on a grand scale; polished address, accomplished elegance in costume, and at table a hospitality which proudly represents a rich country. In the matter of style and address, these people are in fact leaders, and deserve to be. Their society, it is true, is less interesting than that of many very much more modest circles; but the same is true throughout the world of those people who make pleasure their sole duty in life. Their ostentatious enjoyments display much less individuality, and are more along prescribed lines, than those of European circles which live in a comparable luxury — a fact which is due largely to the universal uniformity of fashion that prevails in every class of Americans, and that is too little tolerant of individual picturesqueness. In spite of all this, neither diplomatic Washington, nor intellectual Boston, nor hospitable Baltimore, nor conservative Philadelphia, nor indomitable Chicago, nor cosmopolitan San Francisco, can point to any collection of persons which, in that world where one is to be amused expensively at any cost, is better qualified to take the lead than just the Four Hundred of New York and Newport.

And yet there is a fundamental error in the whole calculation. It is simply not true that these circles exercise any sort of leadership for the nation, or have become the starting-point of a New World aristocracy. The average American, if he is still the true Puritan, is outraged on reading of a wedding ceremony where more money is spent on decorating the church than the combined yearly salaries of thirty school teachers, or of the sons of great industrial leaders wasting their days in drinking cocktails and racing their automobiles. If, on the other hand, he is a true city-bred man, he takes a considerable pleasure in reading in the newspaper about the design and equipment of the latest yacht, the decorations in the ball-room of the recently built palace, or about the latest divorce doings in those elect circles. The two sorts of readers — that is, the vexed and the amused — agree only in one thing; — neither of them takes all this seriously from the national point of view. The one is outraged that in his large, healthy, and hard-working country, such folderol and licentiousness are gaped at or tolerated. And the other is pleased that his country has become so rich and strong as to be able to afford such luxuriousness and extravagance; he looks on quizzically as at a vaudeville theatre, but even he does not take the actors in this social vaudeville the least bit seriously. The one accounts this clique a sort of moral slum, and the other a quickly passing and interesting froth; and both parties overestimate the eccentric whimsies and underestimate the actual constant influence of these circles in improving the taste for art and in really refining manners. But this clique is accounted a real aristocracy merely by itself and by the tradesmen who purvey to it.

In spite of this, American society is beginning to show important differentiations. It is not a mere sentimental and fanciful aristocracy, trying to imitate European monarchicalism, and it is not the pseudo-aristocracy dancing around the golden dinner-set; it is an aristocracy of leading groups of people, which has risen slowly in the social life of the nation, and now affords the starting-point of a steadily increasing individuation of social layers. The influence of wealth is not absent here, but it is not mere wealth as such which exalts these people to the nobility; nor is the historical principle of family inheritance left out of account, although it is not merely the number of one's identifiable ancestors that counts. It is, most of all, the profounder marks of education and of personal talent. And out of the combination of all these factors and their interpenetration proceed a New World group of leaders, which has in fact a national significance.

If one were to name a single person who should typically represent this new aristocracy, it would be Theodore Roosevelt. In the year 1649, Claes Roosevelt settled in New Netherlands, which is now New York, and from generation to generation his sturdy descendants have worked for the public good. James Roosevelt, the great-grandfather of the President, gave his services without remuneration to the Continental Army in the war for independence; the grandfather left the largest part of his fortune to charitable purposes; and the father was tirelessly active in furthering patriotic undertakings during the Civil War. And as this family inherited its public spirit, so also it inherited substance and a taste for sport and social life.

Now this product of old family traditions has been greatly influenced by the best intellectual culture of New England. Theodore Roosevelt is distinctly a Harvard graduate; all the elements of his nature got new strength from the classic world of Harvard. The history of his nation has been his favourite study, and he has written historical treatises of great breadth of view. Therewith he possesses a strong talent for administration, and has advanced rapidly by reason of his actual achievements. And thus education, public service, wealth, and family traditions have combined to make a character which exalts this man socially much higher than the Presidential office alone could do. McKinley was in some ways greater, perhaps — but in McKinley's world there was no third dimension of aristocratic differentiation; it was a flat picture, where one might not ask nor expect any diversification in the other dimension. Roosevelt is the first aristocrat since many years, to come into the White House.

Aristocratic shadings can occur in a country that is so firmly grounded in democracy only when the movement goes in both directions, upward and downward, and when it evolves on both sides. If it were a question on the one side of demanding rights and forcing credence in pretentious display, and on the other side of demanding any sort of submission from less favoured persons or assigning them an inferior position, the whole effort would be hopeless. The claim to prerogative which is supported by an ostentation calculated to hypnotize the vulgar and a corresponding obsequiousness of the weak, can do nothing more than perhaps to preserve aristocracy after it has taken deep historic root. But such a degenerate form cannot be the first stage of aristocracy in a new country. When a new aristocracy is formed, it must boast not of prerogatives, but of duties, and the feeling of those not included cannot be one of inferiority, but of confidence. And this is the mood which is growing in America.

Such duties are most clearly recognized by wealth, and wealth has perhaps contributed most to begin the aristocratic differentiation in American society; but it has not been the wealth which goes into extravagant display or other arrogant demonstration, but the wealth which works toward the civilized advance of the nation. However much it may contradict the prejudices of the Old World, wealth alone does not confer a social status in America. Of course, property everywhere makes independence; but so long as it remains merely the power to hire things done, it creates no social differentiation. The American does not regard a man with awe because he stands well with trades-people and stock-brokers, but discriminates sharply between the possessions and the possessor. In his business life he is so accustomed to dealing with impersonal corporations, that the power to dispense large sums of money gives a man no personal dignity in his eyes. Just in the Western cities, where society centres about questions of money much more than in the East, the notion of property differentiation between men is developed least of all so far as it concerns social station. The mere circumstance that one man has speculated fortunately and the other unfortunately, that the real estate of one has appreciated and of the other deteriorated in value, occasions no belief in the inner difference of the two men; the changes are purely economic, and suggest nothing of a social difference.

At most there is a certain curiosity, since property opens up a world of possibilities to a man; and he is considerably scrutinized by his neighbours to see what he will do. In this sense especially in the small and middle-sized cities, the local magnates are the centre of public interest, just as the billionaires are in large cities. But to be the object of such newspaper curiosity does not mean to be elevated in the general respect. The millionaire is in this respect very much like the operatic tenor; or, to put it less graciously, the hero of the last poisoning case. It is the more a question of a mere stimulation to the public fancy, since in reality the differences are surprisingly small.

If one looks away from the extravagant eccentricities of small circles, the difference in general mode of life is on the whole very little in evidence. The many citizens in the large American city who have a property of five to ten million dollars seem to live hardly differently from the unfortunate many who have to get on with only a simple million. On the other hand, the average man with a modest income exerts all his strength to appear in clothing and social habits as rich as possible. He does not take care to store up a dowry for his children, and he lays by little because he does not care to become a bond-holder; he would rather work to his dying day, and teach his children while they are young to stand on their own feet. So it happens that the differences which actually exist are very little in evidence; the banker has his palace and his coach, and his wife wears sealskin; but his shoe-maker has also his own house, his horse and buggy, and his wife wears a very good imitation of seal — which one has to rub against in order to recognize.

But the situation becomes very different when it is a question of wealth, not as a means of actual enjoyment, but as a measure of the personal capacities that have earned it. Then the whole importance of the possession is indeed transferred to the possessor. We must again emphasize the fact that this is the real impulse underlying American economic life — wealth is the criterion of individual achievements, of self-initiative; and since the whole nation stretches every nerve in a restless demonstration of this self-initiative, the person who is more successful than his neighbours gains necessarily their instinctive admiration. The wealth won by lucky gambles in stocks, or inherited, or derived from a merely accidental appreciation of values or by a chance monopoly, is not respected; but the wealth amassed by caution and brilliant fore-sight, by indomitable energy and tireless initiative, or by fasci-nating originality and courage, meets with full recognition. The

American sees in such a creator of material wealth the model of his pioneer virtues, the born leader of economic progress, and he looks up to him in sincere admiration, and respects him far higher than his neighbour in the next palace who has accidentally fallen heir to a tenfold larger sum. It is not the power which wealth confers, but the power which has conferred wealth, that is respected.

And then there is a more important factor — the respect for that force of mind which puts wealth, even if it is only a modest amount, in the service of higher ends. Men have different tastes; one who builds hospitals may not understand the importance of patronizing the fine arts; one who supports universities may do very little for the church; or another who collects sculptures may have no interest in the education of the negro. But the fundamental dogma of American society is that wealth confers distinction only on a man who works for ideal ends; and perhaps the deepest impulse toward the accumulation of wealth, after the economic power which it confers, is the desire for just this sort of dignity. And this desire is deeper undoubtedly than the wish for pleasure, which anyhow is somewhat limited by the outward uniformity of American life. How far social recognition is gotten by public-spirited activities and how far social recognition incites men to such activity, is in any particular case hard to decide. But as a matter of fact, a social condition has come about in which the *noblesse oblige* of property is recognized on all sides, and in which public opinion is more discriminating as to the social respect which should be meted out to this or that public deed, than it could be if it were a question of conferring with the greatest nicety orders and titles of different values.

The right of the individual to specialize in various directions, to focus his benefactions on Catholic deaf-mutes or on students of insects, on church windows, or clay cylinders with cuneiform inscriptions, is recognized fully. Confident of the good-will of men of property, so many diverse claims have arisen, that it would be quite impossible for a single man out of mere general sympathy with civilization to lend a helping hand in all directions. The Americans esteem just that carefulness with which the rich man sees to it that his property is applied according to his personal ideas and knowledge. It is only thereby that his gifts have a profound personal significance, and are fundamentally distinguished from sentimental sacrifice or from ostentatious patronage. Giving is a serious matter, to which wealthy men daily and hourly devote conscientious labour. A man like Carnegie, whose useful bequests already amount to more than a hundred million dollars, could dispose at once of his entire property if he were in a single week to respond favourably to all the calls which are made on him. He receives every day hundreds of such letters of request, and gives almost his entire strength to carrying out his benevolent plans.

And the same is true on a smaller scale of all classes. Every true American feels that his wealth puts him in a position of public confidence, and the intensity with which he manifests this conviction decides the social esteem in which his property is held. The real aristocrats of wealth in this part of the world are those men whom public opinion respects both for the gaining and the using of their property; both factors, in a way, have to be united. The admirable personal talents which accumulate large properties, and the lofty ideals which put them to the best uses, may appear to be quite independent matters, and indeed they sometimes do exclude each other, but the aristocratic ideal demands the two together. And the Americans notice when either one is absent; they notice when wealth is amassed in imposing quantities, but then employed trivially or selfishly; or, on the other hand, when it is employed for the very highest ends, but in the opinion of competent men has been accumulated improperly. The public feels more and more inclined to look into the business methods of men who make large gifts. The American does not recognize the *non olet*, and there have often been lively discussions when ill-gotten wealth has been offered in public benefaction.

Wealth gotten by distinguished enterprise and integrity, and employed conscientiously and thoughtfully, confers in fact high social distinction. But it is only one factor among others. A second factor is family tradition, the dignity of a name long respected for civil high-mindedness and refinement. A European has only the barest impression of the great social significance of American genealogies, and would be surprised to see in the large libraries whole walls of book-shelves that contain nothing but works on the lineage of American families. The family tree of the single family of Whitney, of Connecticut, takes up three thick volumes amounting to 2,700 pages; and there even exists a thick and handsome volume with the genealogies of American families of royal extraction. There are not only special papers devoted to the scientific study of genealogies, but even some of the large daily papers have a section devoted to this subject. Much of this is mere curiosity and sport — a fashionable whim, which collects ancestors much like coins or postage stamps. Although the preserving of family traditions and an expansive pride in historic lineage do not contradict democratic principles, yet the interest in pedigree, if it takes real hold on the public mind, very soon leads to a genuine social differentiation.

Such differentiation will be superficial at first. If none but descendants of Puritans who came over in the "Mayflower" are invited to a set of dances, a spirit of exclusiveness is shown which is indeed undemocratic; but this sort of thing is in fact only a playful matter in American society. The large organizations that choose their membership on the ground of peculiar ancestry make no pretence to special privileges, and many of them are nothing but philanthropic societies. On the other hand, if the aristocracy of family were to assume special rights, it would be no innovation on American soil, because in the earliest colonial days many of the social differences of English society were brought over, and the English class spirit did not dispppear until after the Revolution, when the younger sons of English gentlemen no longer came over to this country. In the South, a considerable spirit of aristocracy persisted until after the Civil War.

Such superficial differentiation has virtually disappeared to-day. The mere tinsel of family aristocracy has been torn off, but for this reason the real importance and achievements of certain families come out all the more clearly. The representatives of venerable family names are looked on with peculiar public confidence; and the more the American nation becomes acquainted with the history of these families, which have been active on American soil for eight or ten generations, the more it respects their descendants of the present day.

It is true that conditions are still provincial, and that almost no family has a national significance. The names of the first families of Virginia, which are universally revered in the South, are almost unknown in the North; the descendants of Knickerbocker families, whose very name must not be mentioned in New York without a certain air of solemnity, are very much less considered in Baltimore or Philadelphia; and the western part of the country is naturally still too young to have established such traditions at all until recently. But the following is a typical example for the East:

Harvard University is governed by seven men who are chosen to fill this responsible position, solely because the academic community has profound confidence both in their integrity and in their breadth of view. And yet it is no accident that among these seven men, there is not one whose family has not been of service to the State of Massachusetts for seven generations. So that, even in such a model democratic community as Puritan New England, the names of families that have played an important public part in the middle of the seventeenth century are as much respected as the old "märkische Adel" in Prussia. And although they are without the privileges of nobility, the whole dignity of the past is felt by every educated person to be preserved in such family names.

But the most important factor in the aristocratic differentiation of America is higher education and culture, and this becomes more important every day. In speaking of universities, we have carefully explained why higher culture is less closely connected with the learned professions in America than in the European countries. We have seen that the learned professions are fed by professional and very practical schools, which turn out a doctor, lawyer, or preacher without requiring a broad and liberal previous training; and how, on the other hand, the college has been the independent institution for higher culture, and how these two institutions have slowly grown together in the course of time, so that the college course has come at length to be the regular preparation for those who attend professional schools. Now, in considering the social importance of higher individual culture, we have not to consider the learned professions, but rather the general college training; and in this respect we find undoubtedly that common opinion has slowly shifted toward an aristocratic point of view. The social importance ascribed to a college graduate is all the time growing.

It was kept back for a long time by unfortunate prejudices. Because other than intellectual forces had made the nation strong, and everywhere in the foreground of public activity there were vigorous and influential men who had not continued their education beyond the public grammar school, so the masses instinctively believed that insight, real energy, and enterprise were better developed in the school of life than in the world of books. The college student was thought of as a weakling, in a way, who might have many fine theories about things, but who would never take hold to help solve the great national problems — a sort of academic "mugwump," but not a leader. The banking-house, factory, farm, the mine, the law office, and the political position were all thought better places for the young American man than the college lecture halls. And perhaps the unpractical character of college studies was no more feared than the artificial social atmosphere. It was felt that an ideal atmosphere was created in the college to which the mind in its best period of development too readily adapted itself, so that it came out virtually unprepared for the crude reality of practical life. This has been a dogma in political life ever since the Presidency of Andrew Jackson, and almost equally so in economic life.

This has profoundly changed now, and changes more with every year. It is not a question of identifying the higher culture with the learned professions, as in Germany— there is no reason for this; and such a point of view has developed in Germany only by an accident of history. In America it is still thought that a graduate of one of these colleges — that is, a man who has gone about as far as the German student of philosophy in the third or fourth semester — is equal to anybody in culture, no matter whether he afterward becomes a manufacturer, or banker, or lawyer, or a philologian. The change has taken place in regard to what is expected of the college student; distrust has vanished, and people realize that the intellectual discipline which he has had until his twenty-second year in the artificial and ideal world is after all the best training for the great duties of public life, and that academic training, less by its subject-matter than by its methods, is the best possible preparation for practical activity.

The man of academic training is the only one who sees things in their right perspective, and gives them the right values. Even the large merchant knows to-day that the young man who left college at twenty-two will be, when he is twenty-seven years of age, generally ahead of his contemporaries who left school at seventeen and "went to work." The great self-made men do indeed say a good deal to comfort those who have had only a school training, but it may be noted that they send their own sons to college. As a matter of fact, the leading positions in the disposal of the nation are almost entirely in the hands of men of academic training, and the mistrust of the theorizing college spirit has given place to a situation in which university presidents and professors have much to say on all practical questions of public life, and the college graduates are the real supporters of every movement toward reform and civilization.

All in all, it can no longer be denied that a class of national leaders has risen above the social life of the masses, and not wholly, as democracy would really require, by reason of their personal talents. A wealthy man has a certain advantage by his wealth, the man of family by his lineage, the man of academic training by the fact that his parents were able to send him to the university. This is neither plutocracy nor hereditary aristocracy, nor intellectual snobbery. We have seen that wealth wins consideration only when well expended, that ancestry brings no privileges or prerogatives with it, and that an academic education is not equivalent to merely technical erudition. The personal factor is not lacking, since we have seen that the rich man must plan his benefactions, the man of family must play his public part, and that academic training is in the reach of every young man who will try for it. The fundamental principles of democracy are therefore not destroyed, but they are modified. The spirit of self-assertion which calls for absolute equality is everywhere brought face to face with men who are superior, whose claims cannot be discounted, and who are tacitly admitted to belong rightfully to an upper class.

Differentiation, once more, works not merely upward, but also downward; the public leader pushes himself ahead, and at the same time the great masses are looking for some one whom they may follow. It is not a matter of subjection, but of confidence — confidence in men who are recognizedly better than many others. There can be no doubt that a reaction is going on throughout America to-day, not against democracy, but against those opinions which have prevailed in the democracy ever since the days of the pioneers. A great many people feel instinctively that the time is ripe to oppose the one-sidedness of domination by the masses; people are forcibly impressed by the fact that in politics, government, literature and art, the great achievements are thwarted by vulgar influences, that the original individual is impressed into the ordinary mould, and that dilettanteism and mediocrity rule triumphant and keep out the best talents from public life. People see the tyranny of greed, the reproach of municipal corruption, the unwholesome influence of a sensational press and of unscrupulous capital. They see how public life becomes blatant, irresponsible, and vulgar; how all authority and respect must disappear if democracy is not to be curbed at any point.

The time has come, a great many feel, in which the moral influence of authority is needed, and the educational influence of those more cultivated persons who will not yield to the æsthetic tastes of the vulgar must be infused into the democracy. The trained man must speak where the masses would otherwise act from mere caprice; the disciplined mind must lead where incompetence is heading for blind alleys; the best minds must have some say and people must be forced to listen, so that other voices and opinions shall have weight than those that make the babel of the streets. The eclectic must prevail over the vulgar taste, and the profound over the superficial, since it is clear that only in that way will America advance beyond her present stage of development. America has created a new political world, and must now turn to æsthetics and culture. Such a reaction has not happened to-day or yesterday, but has been going on steadily in the last few decades, and to-day it is so strong as to overcome all resistance. The desire for the beauty and dignity of culture, for authority and thoroughness, is creeping into every corner of American life.

The time is already passing which would do away with all discipline and submission in school and family life; public life brings the trained expert everywhere into prominence. The disgust at the vulgarity of daily life, as in the visible appearance of city streets, increases rapidly. The sense of beauty is everywhere at work; and men of taste, education, and traditions, rather than the city fathers who are elected by the rabble, are finally being called to positions of leadership. The democratic spirit is not crumbling, and certainly the rights of the masses are not to be displaced by the rights of the better educated and more æsthetic; but democracy is in a way to be perfected, to be brought as high as it can be brought by giving a representation to really all the forces that are in the social organism, and by not permitting the more refined ones to be suppressed by the weight of the masses. The nation has come to that maturity where the public is ready to let itself be led by the best men.

It is true that the public taste still prevails too widely in many branches of social life; there is too much triviality; too many institutions are built on the false principles that everybody knows best what is good for him, and too many undertakings flatter the taste which they should educate. But opposite tendencies are present everywhere. The more the economic development of the country is rounded off, the greater is its demand for social differentiation, for the recognition of certain influences as superior, for subordination, and for finer organization. Just as economic life has long since given up free competition, and the great corporations show admirably that subordination is necessary to great purposes, and the world of labour has become an army with strictest discipline and blind allegiance, so in the non-economic world a tendency toward subordination, individuation, and aristocracy becomes every moment more evident.

To this tendency there is added the new conception of the state. Democracy is, from the outset, individualistic. We have seen everywhere that the fundamental force in this community is the belief of every man in his own personality and that of others. The state has been the sum total of individuals, and the state as something more than the individual has appeared as a bare abstraction. The individual alone has asserted itself, perfected and guided itself, and taken all the initiative. And this belief in the person is no less firm to-day; but another belief has come up. This is a belief in the ethical reality of the state. Public opinion is still afraid that if this belief increases, the old confidence in the value of the individual, and therewith of all the fundamental virtues of American democracy, may be shaken. But the belief spreads from day to day, and produces its change in public opinion. Politics are trending as are so many other branches of life; the emphasis is passing from the individual to the totality. As we have seen that the Americans adorned their houses before their public buildings, quite the opposite of what Europeans have done, so they have given political value to the millions of individuals long before they laid weight on the one collective will of the state. The men who would have sacrificed everything rather than cheat their neighbours have had no conscientious scruples in plundering the state.

It is different to-day. The feeling grows that honour toward the state, sacrifice for it, and confidence in it are even more important than the respect for the totality of individuals. These opinions cannot be spread abroad without having their far-reaching consequences; the state is visible only in symbols, and its representatives get their significance by symbolizing not the population, but the abstract state. The individual representative of government is thus exalted personally above the democratic level. To fill an office means not merely to do work, but to experience a broadening of personality, much as that which the priest feels in his office; it is an enlargement which demands on the other side respect and subordination. This tendency is still in its beginnings, and will never be so strong as in Europe, because the self-assertion of the individual is too lively. Nevertheless, these new notes in the harmony are much louder and more persistent than they were ten years ago.

Thus there are many forces which work to check the spirit of self-assertion; in spite of the liveliest feeling of equality, a social differentiation is practically working itself out in all American life. Differences of occupation are, perhaps, the least significant; a profession which has such a great claim to superiority as, for instance, that of the army officer in Germany, does not exist in the United States. Perhaps the legal profession would be looked on as the most important, and certainly it absorbs a very large proportion of the best strength of the nation. The high position given the jurist is probably in good part because, unlike his Continental colleague, as we have explained at length, he actually takes part in shaping the law. In a different way the preacher is very greatly respected, but his profession decreases slowly in attractiveness for the best talents of the country. The academic professions, on the other hand, have drawn such talent more and more, and will continue to do so as the distinction grows sharper between the college teacher and the real university professor. The pre-eminently reproductive activities are naturally less enticing than those which are creative, and wherever talent is attracted it quickly accomplishes great things, and these work to improve the social status of the profession. The political profession, as such, is far down in the scale; only governors, senators, and the highest ministerial officials play an important social part. Of course, one cannot speak of the especial recognition of mercantile or industrial professions, because these offer too great a variety of attainment; but certainly their most influential representatives are socially inferior to none in the community.

Social differentiation does not rest on a sharp discrimination of profession, and yet it is realized from the highest to the lowest circles of society, and to a degree which fifty years ago would have greatly antagonized at least the entire northern part of the country. In Washington, the exclusive hostess invites only the wives of senators, but not those of representatives, to her table; and in the Bowery, according to the accounts, the children of the peanut vendor do not deign to play with the children of the hurdy-gurdy man, who are vastly more humble. The Four Hundred in the large city quietly but resolutely decline to invite newly made millionaires to dinner; and the seamstress, who comes to the house to sew or mend, refuses to sit down at table with the servants. Already, in the large cities, the children of better families are not sent to public, but to private schools. The railroads have only one class of passenger coach; but the best society declines that, and rides in the Pullman cars. The same distinctions hold everywhere, and not merely as a matter of greater luxury for the rich, but as a real social distinction. At the theatre, the person who socially belongs in the parquet prefers to sit in one of the worst seats there to going into the balcony, where he does not belong, even though he might hear and see better.

The increasing sympathy with badges, costumes, and uniforms — in short, with the symbols of differentiation — is very typical. There was a time in which a free American would have refused to wear a special livery; but to-day nobody objects, from the elevator boy to the judge, to wear the marks of office. The holiday processions of working-men and veterans become gayer and gayer. Those who have seen the recent inaugurations of the presidents of Yale and Columbia have witnessed parades of hundreds of gay and, it seemed, partly fantastic costumes, such as are now worn at every university celebration in America — symbolic emblems which would have seemed impossible in this monotonous democracy twenty years ago.

The inner life of universities gives also lively indication of social cleavage. In Harvard and Yale, there are exclusive clubs of the social leaders among the students. It is true that hundreds of students go through the university without paying any attention to such things; but there are almost as many more whose chief ambition is to be elected into an exclusive circle, and who would feel compensated by no sort of scientific success if they were disappointed in their aspirations for club life. In the same way many families which have become wealthy in the West move to New York or Boston, in the vain hope of breaking into society. The social difference between near-lying residential sections is, indeed, much greater than in Europe; and real estate on a street which comes to be occupied by socially inferior elements rapidly depreciates, because the inhabitants of any residential section must stand on the same plane.

The transformations which the place of the President in public consciousness has gone through are very characteristic. A newly elected President is to-day inaugurated with almost monarchical pomp, and he reviews the Navy, as he never would have thought of doing some years ago. He sits down first at the table and is served first. An invitation to the White House is felt as a command which takes precedence over any other engagement. All this has happened recently. It was not long ago that persons refused an invitation to the White House, because of previous engagements. In social life all men were merely "gentlemen," regardless of the capacities which they had during business hours, and in matters of invitation one visited the host who was first to invite one. All this is different now.

There is even some indication of the use of titles. Twenty years ago students addressed their professors with a mister, but to-day more often with the title of professor; and the abuse of military titles which goes on in the West amuses the whole country. In the army itself aristocratic tendencies are strongly manifest, but only here and there come to general notice. Contrary to the spirit of official appointments, men are not advanced so rapidly who work up from a socially inferior level, but the social élite is favoured.

Etiquette in social life is becoming more complicated; there is more formality, more symbolism in social intercourse. A nation which pays every year more than six million dollars for cut roses and four millions for carnations has certainly learned to decorate social life. There is even more etiquette in professional life. The professional behaviour of lawyers, physicians, and scholars is in some respects, at least in the East, more narrowly prescribed than it is even in Europe.

Looking at the situation as a whole, one sees the power of this new spirit, not so much in these petty symptoms as in the great movements of which we have spoken at length in other connections. There is the spirit of imperialism in foreign politics, and it cannot expand in its pride without working against the old democratic tendencies. There is the spirit of militarism, triumphantly proud of the victorious army and navy, demanding strict discipline and blind obedience to the commander. There is the spirit of racial pride, which persecutes the negro and the Chinese, and hinders the immigration of Eastern and Southern Europeans. There is the spirit of centralization, exalting the power of the state above the conflicting desires of the individual, and in economic matters hoping more from the intelligent initiative of the state as a whole than from the free competition of individuals, and assigning to the Federation tremendous undertakings, such as the irrigation of the West and the cutting of the Panama Canal. There is the spirit of aristocracy, tempting more and more the academically cultured and the wealthy into the political arena. There is the spirit of social differentiation coming into art and science, and bringing to the life of the nation ideals of beauty and of knowledge which are far above the vulgar comprehension. Eclectic taste is winning a victory over popular taste. The judgment of the most learned, the refinement of the most educated, and the wisdom of the most mature are being made prominent before the public mind. We have already seen how this new spirit grows and unfolds, and how the one-sidedness and eccentricities of political, economic, intellectual, and artistic democracy are being outgrown day by day, and how the America of Roosevelt's time is shaping itself in accordance with the civilizations of Western Europe.

There are some who behold this development with profound concern. That which has made America's greatness, which seemed to be her mission in the world, was the belief in the ethical worth of the individual. The doctrines of self-determination, self-initiative, and self-assertion, and the civilization which rested on such a foundation, have nothing to hope and much to fear from social differentiation and imperialism. Aristocratic tendencies appear to undermine this ethical democracy, and the imperialistic symbols of our day mock the traditions of the past. There will certainly be many reactions against these aristocratic tendencies; perhaps they will be only small movements working through the press and at the ballot-box against the encroachments on the spirit of the past and against the expansion of office, and hindering those aristocratic tendencies which depart too far from the traditions of the masses. Perhaps, some day, there will be a great reaction. Perhaps the tremendous power possessed by the labouring classes in the country will lead to battles for ethical principles, in which the modern æsthetic development will be reversed; it would not be the first time on American soil that ethical reform has produced social deterioration, for "reform" means always the victory of naked, equalizing logic over the conservative forces which represent historic differentiation. So the Revolution abolished the patrician society of New England, whose aristocratic members survive in the portraits of Copley; and the day may come when trades-unions will be victorious over that aristocracy which Sargent is now painting. Even the reform which emancipated the slaves destroyed a true and chivalrous aristocracy in the South.

But it is more likely that the steady development will go on, and that there will be a harmonious co-operation between the fundamental democratic forces and the lesser aristocratic ones. It cannot be doubted that that democracy of which we have aimed to describe the real intent, will remain the fundamental force under the American Constitution; and however strict military discipline may become, however aristocratic the social differentiations, however imperialistic the politics, however esoteric art and science, undoubtedly the greatest question put by every American to his brother will be: "What do you, purely as an individual, amount to?" The ethical rights and the ethical duties of the individual will be the ultimate standard, and aristocratic pomp will always be suppressed in America whenever it commences to restrain the passion for justice and for self-determination.

The most serious Americans are in the position of Tantalus; they see, in a thousand ways and at a thousand places, that a certain advance could be made if somehow the vulgar masses could be got out of the way; they see how civic and national ends could be attained almost without trouble by the ample means of the country, if as in Europe, the most intelligent minds could be put in control. They want all this most seriously; and yet they cannot have it, because in the bottom of their hearts they really do not wish it. They feel too profoundly that the gain would be only apparent, that the moral force of the nation would be sacrificed if a single citizen should lose the confidence that he himself is responsible for the nation which he helps to guide and to make. The easy attainment of success is only a secondary matter; the purity of the individual will is the main consideration. With this stands or falls American culture. Development is first of all an ethical problem; just because the world is incomplete, is hard, and unbeautiful, and everywhere needs to be transformed by human labour, just on that account human life is inexhaustibly valuable. This is the fundamental thought, and will remain so as long as the New World remains true to its ideals. The finer notes are only an overtone in the great chord; it is only faintly discerned that the world is valuable when it is beautiful — after it has been mastered and completed.

In this opposition between the ethical and the æsthetic, between the democratic and the aristocratic, America will never sacrifice her fundamental conviction, will never follow aristocratic tendencies further than where they are needed to correct the dangerous one-sidedness and the excrescences of democratic individualism; at least, never so far that any danger will threaten the democracy. The pride of the true American is, once and for all, not the American country, nor yet American achievements, but the American personality.

One who seeks the profoundest reality that history has to offer, not in the temporal unfolding of events, but in the interplay of human wills, will agree with the American's judgment of himself. Looking at the people of the New World even from afar, one will find the fascination, novelty, and greatness of the American world mission, not in what the American has accomplished, but in what he desires and will desire.

Nevertheless, this will not seem strange or foreign to any German. In the depths of his soul, he has himself a similar play of desires. In the course of history, reverence and faithfulness developed in the German soul more strongly than the individualistic craving for self-determination and self-assertion; aristocratic love of beauty and truth developed before the democratic spirit of self-initiative. But to-day, in modern Germany, these very instincts are being aroused, just as in modern America those forces are growing which have long dominated the German soul.

The American still puts the higher value on the personal, the German on the over-personal; the American on the intrinsic value of the creating will, the German on the intrinsic value of the absolute ideal. But every day sees the difference reduced, and brings the two nations nearer to a similar attitude of mind. Moreover, both of these fundamental tendencies are equally idealistic, and both of these nations are therefore destined to understand and to esteem each other, mutually to extend their friendship, to emulate each other, and to work together, so that in the confused play of temporal forces the intrinsically valuable shall be victorious over the temporary and fleeting, the ideal over the accidental. For both nations feel together, in the depths of their being, that in order to give meaning to life man must believe in timeless ideals.

THE END

THE McCLURE PRESS, NEW YORK

INDEX

INDEX

D

E

F

G

H

I

J